Implementing CRM

Wiley Series in Information Systems

CURRENT VOLUMES IN THE SERIES

Currie: *The Global Information Society*
Elliot: *Electronic Commerce-B2C Strategies and Models*
Galliers & Baets: *Information Technology & Organizational Transformation-Innovation for the 21st Century Organization*
Groth: *Future Organizational Design-The Scope for the IT-Based Enterprise*
Knights & Murray: *Managers Divided: Organizational Politics & Information Technology Management*
Krcmar, Bjorn-Anderson & O'Callaghan: *EDI in Europe: How It Works in Practice*
McKeen & Smith: *Making IT Happen - Critical Issues in IT Management*
McKeen & Smith: *Management Challenges in IS – Successful Strategies and Appropriate Action*
Mingers & Willcocks: *Social Theory and Philosophy for Information Systems*
Remeny, Sherwood-Smith & White: *Achieving Maximum Value from Information Systems – A Process Approach*
Renkema: *The IT Value Quest – How to Capture the Business Value of IT-Based Infrastructure*
Silver: *Systems that Support Decision Makers – Description and Analysis*
Timmers: *Electronic Commerce – Strategies and Models for Business-to-Business Trading*
Walsham: *Making a World of Difference – IT in a Global Context*
Ward & Daniel: *Benefits Management: Delivering Value from IS & IT Investment*
Ward & Peppard: *Strategic Planning for Information Systems, 3rd Edition*
Wigand, Picot & Reichwald: *Information, Organization & Management – Expanding Markets and Corporate Boundaries*
Willcocks & Lacity: *Strategic Sourcing of Information Systems – Perspectives and Practices*
Willcocks & Lester: *Beyond the IT Productivity Paradox*
King & Lyytinen: *The State of the Field*

Implementing CRM: From Technology to Knowledge

David Jesse Finnegan
Leslie P. Willcocks

BICENTENNIAL 1807 WILEY 2007 BICENTENNIAL

John Wiley & Sons, Ltd

Telephone +44 (0) 1243 779777

Email (for orders and customer service enquiries): cs-books@wiley.co.uk
Visit our Home Page on www.wiley.com

Other Wiley Editorial Offices

John Wiley & Sons Inc., 111 River Street, Hoboken, NJ 07030, USA

Jossey-Bass, 989 Market Street, San Francisco, CA 94103-1741, USA

Wiley-VCH Verlag GmbH, Boschstr. 12, D-69469 Weinheim, Germany

John Wiley & Sons Australia Ltd, 42 McDougall Street, Milton, Queensland 4064, Australia

John Wiley & Sons (Asia) Pte Ltd, 2 Clementi Loop #02-01, Jin Xing Distripark, Singapore 129809

John Wiley & Sons Canada Ltd, 6045 Freemont Blvd, Mississauga, ONT, L5R 4J3

Wiley also publishes its books in a variety of electronic formats. Some content that appears in print may not be available in electronic books.

Anniversary Logo Design: Richard J. Pacifico

Library of Congress Cataloging in Publication Data

Finnegan, David.
Implementing CRM: from technology to knowledge/David Finnegan, Leslie P. Willcocks.
p. cm. — (John Wiley series in information systems)
Includes bibliographical references and index.
ISBN-13: 978-0-470-06526-6 (pbk.: alk. paper)
ISBN-10: 0-470-06526-5 (pbk.: alk. paper)
1. Customer relations—Management. 2. Customer services. I. Willcocks, Leslie.
II. Title.

HF5415.5.F563 2007
658.8′12—dc22

2006100398

British Library Cataloguing in Publication Data

A catalogue record for this book is available from the British Library

ISBN 978-0-470-06526-6 (pbk)

Typeset in 11/12.5pt Palatino by Integra Software Services Pvt. Ltd, Pondicherry, India
Printed and bound in Great Britain by TJ International Ltd, Padstow, Cornwall.
This book is printed on acid-free paper responsibly manufactured from sustainable forestry in which at least two trees are planted for each one used for paper production.

To my family

– David Jesse Finnegan

To my beloved brother Rodger, departed this year

– Leslie P. Willcocks

Contents

About the Authors

Dr David Jesse Finnegan MBA (Aston) PhD (Warwick) David has twelve years senior management experience and is a CRM and Systems Integration Specialist. He works internationally as an integration consultant and trainer, while developing postgraduate academic programmes for several universities in the UK and USA. He is also presently working as an assistant Professor at Warwick Business School—The University of Warwick UK. He has worked in a range of roles, including with the Swedish Home Office. He has over ten years experience in Leadership Training, System integration, Business Analyses and Business Process Re-engineering in B2B and B2C environments. His PhD at Warwick University was sponsored by ESRC (Economic and Social Research Council). He has an MBA with a specialism in E-business from Aston Business School.

Dr Leslie P. Willcocks BA (Cantab), MA (Cantab, Oxon, London), PGCE, DLS, PHD (Cantab), FBCS Leslie has an international reputation for his work on outsourcing, information systems, IT strategies, evaluation and organizational change. He is Professor in Technology Work and Globalization at the London School of Economics and Political Science, and for the last 16 years has been editor/co-editor of the *Journal of Information Technology*. He has co-authored 28 books, and has published over 150 refereed papers in journals such as *Harvard Business Review, Sloan Management Review, California Management Review, MIS Quarterly, Public Administration, Journal of Strategic Information Systems, EJIS, ISJ, MISQ Executive, CACM,* and *Journal of Management Studies.* Recent titles include (with Mary Lacity) **Global Sourcing of Business and IT Services** (Palgrave, 2006) and (edited with Allen Lee) **Major Currents in The Information Systems Field** (Sage, 2007).

Preface

Theories on relationship marketing were developed at the end of the 1980s, under the motto "from transaction to relation" (Hakansson & Snehota, 1995). Researchers showed that companies have both economic and social relationships. In addition to economic transactions there is, sometimes, a development of trust. These relationships may give benefits to both sides; among them are a higher degree of customer loyalty, lower marketing costs, mutual learning and other forms of strategic cooperation. Developing long-term customer relationships is a part of the company's strategy development, and should involve every level of the company (Hakansson & Snehota, 1995).

Since relationship marketing is heavily dependent on the richness of customer information, and also on frequent communications with the customers, the pioneers were aware at an early stage of the potential benefits to be derived from IT. Today, CRM systems represent a large and growing part of the software industry (Tafti, 2002).

Ciborra and Failla (2002) describe CRM as an information infrastructure, consisting of processes, people and technology. CRM is linked to the BPR thinking, in the way that CRM is also process oriented, and focused on dramatic and fundamental change. CRM structures and supports all activities in a business transaction lifecycle, from the first lead to fulfillment. CRM is a long-term business strategy, where the CRM system is an important component. The reason for the high expectations is that the CRM systems seem to connect the two central resources of the modern, "flat" and decentralized company: namely, the core competence of the knowledge workers, and the company relationships to its most important customers (Kay, 1993).

For our purposes, a CRM system would seem to hold three promises for the knowledge based organization. First, it gives each worker a tool to manage her personal contacts, activities, documents etc. As Drucker has stated, "managing oneself" has become the management challenge for the knowledge worker (Drucker, 1999). Secondly, it provides a tool for dialogue marketing, allowing the company to individualize marketing activities, whereby the customer gets only the information he/she wants and needs (Hakansson & Snehota, 1995).

And finally, it represents a synergic potential for the company. If all this information could be utilised in market analysis and product concept development, it might be a basis for new products and markets, transcending the barriers of business functions and locations. This is not trivial. If successfully implemented this implies that the CRM systems could be an important technology for the non-hierarchical, knowledge-based organization of the 21st century. A good CRM system focuses and supports all marketing activities, will promote good customer relations, higher ROI over time, and better organized and targeted marketing.

However, as this book shows, implementing CRM is hard. As Ciborra states, "CRM seems to have no built in mechanisms by which it acquires its own momentum and the diffusion becomes a self-feeding process" (Ciborra, 2000). This seems to leave us with two alternatives. The first is to accept an upward struggle of organizational interventions and in particular use the managerial tools of change management. As our own work here, and others, (Schwartz *et al.*, 2002; Tafti, 2002) show, the challenge is a large one, and not necessarily successful.

The second option is to accept the technological drift, that the system will be used in other ways than intended. The mechanisms at work at micro level are only partly controllable by management techniques, and often so interwoven with local culture and routines that in practice it is impossible to predict the outcome. In the view of CRM's close ties to strategic management and BPR this becomes a paradox that needs to be worked through in organizational change efforts. This book focuses on the actuality of implementing CRM. It uncovers the micropolitical, behavioural, pyschological and knowledge issues that are all too often neglected in CRM implementations, and provides frameworks and ideas for how implementing CRM can be better handled.

The first two chapters provide overviews of the developments in CRM since 1998. The second chapter details the relationship between trying to implement CRM in a much broader setting requiring systems integration not just of technical systems but also in a business process reengineering sense. The third chapter provides an original in-depth analysis of important neglected concepts in CRM implementation relating to culture, knowledge and pyschological contracts—uncovered by our detailed research in the major case work for this book. From this we develop a comprehensive conceptual framework for understanding and analyzing CRM implementation. The next two chapters (5 and 6) provide in-depth rich descriptions of private sector and public sector CRM implementations, using multiple practitioner quotes about their opinions, experiences and learnings. Chapter 7 brings together the book using the analytical framework to provide detailed lessons and prescriptions for undertaking CRM implementation. The final chapter covers implications for practitioners and how future CRM developments can be better managed. We conclude with References, a Note on Research Methodology and Index.

OBJECTIVES

Our objectives in this book are:

- to provide a detailed overview of the state-of-play with CRM and its implementation;
- to link CRM with the key area and issue of systems integration;
- to analyze critically existing implementation theories;
- to identify and define the role of sub-cultures in the implementation process;
- to assess the role of non-codified knowledge and its significance in the implementation process of an IT system;
- to assess knowledge sharing aids/barriers across sub-cultures and their impact upon implementation;
- to assess the role of psychological contracts and its linkages with knowledge sharing and subculture interactions;
- to analyze critically the implementation of CRM systems from a knowledge sharing perspective;
- to provide detailed lessons and prescriptions from what we have learned about the neglected areas that explain why CRM implementation still underperform in practical business contexts.

Series Preface

The information systems community has grown considerably in the twenty years that we have been publishing the Wiley Series in Information Systems. We are pleased to be a part of the growth of the field, and believe that this series has played and continues to play an important role in the intellectual development of the discipline. The primary objective of the series is to publish scholarly works which reflect the best of the research in the information systems community. These works should help guide the IS practitioner community regarding what strategies it ought to adopt to be successful in the future. Books in the Series should also help advanced students—particularly those at the graduate level—understand the myriad issues surrounding the broad area of management of IS.

To this end, the current volume—*Implementing CRM: From Technology to Knowledge* by David Finnegan and Leslie Willcocks—provides a welcomed addition. Customer relationship management, or CRM, is a very important topic for many in the field as they have to come to grips with managing relationships, both internal and external to the firm. In this book, Finnegan and Willcocks offer an impressive analysis of the broad CRM arena, noting that its implementation is not the straightforward process that many of the trade publications would have us believe. They state that the failure rate of large CRM projects may be as high at 70%. Through the lens of two detailed case studies, the authors investigate why CRM is not necessarily the panacea that many believe. Their insightful analysis explores the political, behavioural, psychological and knowledge issues that are often neglected in CRM implementations. Their framework will allow organizations to better implement CRM solutions.

Overall, this is an impressive book and advances the state of the field markedly. It should be on the bookshelf of every serious IS academic and practitioner. We are delighted to have it as part of our Wiley Series in Information Systems.

Rudy Hirschheim

1
Introduction and CRM Overview

INTRODUCTION

Firms are continually seeking new ways to forge close relationships with their most valuable customers. They know these loyal customers are the source of most of their profits and that any slowing of the rate of defections helps to grow the customer base. With recent advances in networking and database management technologies, firms have both the motivation and the means for moving closer to their valuable customers. Under the umbrella of customer relationship management, firms are being urged to integrate customer data from different departments and channels, use the information to learn which customers have the greatest profit potential, and then tailor their communications and offerings to accommodate and serve these customers.

Yet firms are finding that customer relationship management (CRM) is no panacea. First, a strategy of building close customer relationships is neither appropriate nor feasible for every market or customer. Customers only enter willingly into relationships that are perceived as beneficial, and only a few such relationships are likely to be of a close and committed nature. Second, efforts to forge relationships are continually being undercut by pervasive countervailing forces. The loyal and valuable customers of one firm are attractive prospects to be pursued by their rivals, and vice versa. This leads to unremitting efforts to neutralize or leap-frog the advantages that engender loyalty, a process aided by the rapid diffusion of the practices that created the advantages in the first place. Third, the organizational capability needed to provide a seamless and personalized experience to each customer is much harder to master than a transactional or product-focused approach where the future of the relationship is not an over-riding consideration. The obvious steps of copying best practices, deploying the latest CRM software, assembling a customer database, and proclaiming good intentions are not enough to overcome a weak capability. This raises the question of what accounts for differences in the ability of competitors to manage customer relationships? Why are some firms more closely connected to their customers, and rewarded with higher rates of loyalty and lower rates of defection? What factors distinguish firms that are more capable than their rivals? How do they achieve the alignment in their organization that enables them to better execute the core CRM process? What actions are most effective at strengthening the customer relating capability?

GAINING CRM ADVANTAGE

For some preliminary answers, we draw on a survey of 352 senior managers and in-depth interviews with managers in another fifteen firms carried out by the Wharton School, University of Pennsylvania in October 2002. Relationship leaders consistently outperformed followers by drawing on a superior customer-relating capability to implement a customer responsive strategy. This strategy put the emphasis on offering superior customer value through complete solutions and a willingness to cater to individual requirements, even to the extent of entering into close partnerships. Customers valued the resulting benefits of time savings, trustworthiness, superior responsiveness to service requests and a closer fit to their needs because of personalized solutions.

According to Christensen and Overdorf (2000), superior performance would seem to come from orchestrating all three components of the customer relating capability: (1) an organizational *orientation* that makes customer retention a priority, and gives employees wide latitude to satisfy customers, as part of an overall willingness to treat different customers differently, (2) *information* about relationships, reflecting the availability, quality and depth of relevant customer information and the systems for sharing this information across the firm, and (3) a *configuration* that includes the structure of the organization, processes for personalizing the offering and the incentives for building relationships. Because these three components have to mesh together like gears in a transmission, any initiative that concentrates on one at the expense of the others is bound to disappoint.

But this formulation misses out how problematic it can be to introduce new technologies across the functions of an organization. Increasingly, organizational ability to implement new IT solutions is of crucial importance for the company's ability to change (Willcocks *et al.*, 2003). In practice, in portraying IT as essentially a commodity, and an infrastructure, Carr (2003) greatly underestimated both the importance and complexity of IT implementation, but also the degree to which implementation capability could itself be a differentiator in terms of IT performance, and in the marketplace. Both strategically and economically, it is therefore vital that a company has the skills to implement information systems fast. As documented in the Information Systems (IS) research literature we will look at in the next two chapters, implementing information systems into an organization is hard, and often unsuccessful (Markus 2004; Willcocks *et al.*, 2003). This is also the case with CRM systems, and perhaps even more so.

While there are well-known and impressive success stories (GMAC 2002, Sprint 2002), failure rates of CRM projects may be as high as 70% (Tafti 2002). Comparing the large expectations regarding CRM with the actual results in companies, a sobering picture, and sometimes one of downright disappointment, emerges. Why is it so difficult? It is documented that most problems in CRM implementation are not technical. Instead, common problems include organizational change and fluctuation, different views on customer information and changes in the business, for example mergers (Schwartz *et al.*, 2002).

Argyris and Schön (1996) describe the gap between intent and realization—between what strategists have recommended the organization to do and what it is actually capable of doing—as a major challenge for strategic management theory. The core of the challenge is not related to the strategic analysis itself, but at the level of real-time micro-processes including all the small decisions managers and employees take during the implementation of change and creation of knowledge. Examples may include problem solving, communication with employees, inter-departmental conflicts and single customer relationships; situations where the battles of change and learning really happens.

The gap between intent and outcome may also be described as technological drift (Ciborra *et al.*, 2000). Arguing that the modern knowledge-based organization cannot be as planned and controlled as an industrial enterprise was considered to be, Ciborra suggests that the alignment between technology and organization is a process of conflict and negotiation between different actors, including the technology itself. This process is only partly controllable in a modern organization with empowered employees. On the level of micro-actions there will often be choices and options of behaviour. There may be several ways of reaching a goal or solving a problem. The actual behaviour may be influenced as much by practical considerations using technology as by managerial goal-setting, and the accumulated result of these small decisions may gradually alter the course of how information systems are used.

We think these aspects are underrated in the change management literature, and will illustrate this point in the actual cases. We suggest in this book, and find plenty of evidence for the claim, that studying micro processes, and the defensive routines at work in an organization, is highly relevant for understanding the implementation puzzle of CRM. This book, at its core, tells the story of two CRM projects and describes in some detail how a knowledge-based organization can address the challenges.

THE PROMISE OF CRM SYSTEMS

The development of CRM systems followed chronologically that of Enterprise Resource Planning (ERP) systems (Chalmeta, 2006). With relationship marketing proposing that keeping existing customers is cheaper than acquiring new ones, a need for better understanding existing customers was developed, making relationship marketing dependant on up-to-date and rich information about customers and IT having a great potential (Bygstad, 2003), and setting this way the ground for the development of Customer Relationship Management (CRM) systems. Several theories on relationship marketing were developed at the end of the 1980s, under the motto "from transaction to relation" (see for example Hakansson & Snehota 1995, Piercy, 2001). The increased interest in "one to one" marketing (Peppers & Rogers, 1993) raised the potential for shifting from a mass to individualized or "one-to-one" marketing. Relationship-based approaches have been increasingly advocated over the last fifteen years (e.g., Grönroos, 1994; Gummesson, 2002b; Vargo & Lusch, 2004). Researchers showed that companies have both economic and social relationships. In addition to economic transactions there is, sometimes, a development of trust. These relationships may give benefits to both sides. Among these can be a higher degree of customer loyalty, lower marketing costs, mutual learning and other forms of strategic cooperation. Developing long-term customer relationships is a part of an organization's strategy development, and should involve every level of the company (Hakansson & Snehota, 1995).

Since relationship marketing is heavily dependent on the richness of customer information, and also on frequent communications with customers, pioneers in this area were aware at an early stage of the potential benefits to be derived from IT. Today, CRM systems represent a large and growing part of the software industry (Tafti 2002). Ciborra and Failla (2000) describe CRM as an information infrastructure, consisting of processes, people and technology. CRM is linked to the business process reengineering (BPR) thinking, in the way that CRM can also be process oriented, and focused on dramatic and fundamental change. CRM can structure and support all activities in a business transaction lifecycle, from the first lead to fulfillment. By the new century CRM was being seen as a long-term business strategy, where the IT-enabled CRM system must be an important component. The reason for such high expectations is that the CRM systems seem to connect the two central resources of the much discussed modern, "flat", decentralized company: namely, the core competence of its knowledge workers, and company relationships with its most important customers (Kay 1993; Rigby *et al.*, 2002).

A CRM system would seem to hold three promises for a knowledge based organization. First, it gives each worker a tool to manage his/her personal contacts, activities, documents, etc. According to Drucker, "managing oneself" has become the management challenge for the knowledge worker (Drucker 1999). Secondly, it provides a tool for dialogue marketing, allowing the company to individualize marketing activities, whereby the customer gets only the information he/she wants and needs (Hakansson & Snehota 1995). Finally, it represents a synergic potential for the company. If all this information could be utilized in market analysis and product concept development, it might be the basis for new products and markets, transcending the barriers of business functions and locations. This is not trivial. If CRM systems can be successfully implemented, with all the complexity that involves, they could represent a key technology for the much mooted non-hierarchical, knowledge-based organization of the 21st century.

According to those working in this field, good CRM system should focus and support all marketing activities, build good customer relations, provide higher ROI over time through well organized and targeted marketing (see for example Goodhue *et al.*, 2002; Yu, 2001). But implementing CRM is hard. Commenting their own case research findings, Ciborra *et al.* (2000) found CRM having no built in mechanisms by which it acquired its own momentum and by which diffusion became a self-feeding process. This may just have been immaturity in implementation process management at the organizations studied, but, if not, it seems to leave us with two alternatives. The first is to accept an upward struggle of organizational interventions and in particular use of the managerial tools of change management. As our work will show, along with others (Schwartz *et al.*,

2002; Tafti 2002), the challenge is a large one, and not necessarily successful.

The second option is to accept technological drift, that the system will be used in other ways than intended. The mechanisms at work at micro level are only partly controllable by management techniques, and often so interwoven with local culture and routines that in practice it is impossible to predict the outcome. In the view of CRM's close ties to strategic management and BPR this means implementation becomes complex, unpredictable and fuzzy and somewhat paradoxical. Leonard-Barton (1985) caught further elements of this paradox that needs to be managed in major systems implementation:

> The higher the organizational level at which managers define a problem or need, the greater the probability of successful implementation. At the same time, however, the closer the definition and solution of problems or needs are to end-users, the greater the probability of success. Implementation managers must draw up their . . . plans [for IT systems] in light of this apparent paradox.

In this book we embark on further research to look into this paradox and in particular study the micro level actions in successful CRM projects.

THE EVOLUTION OF CRM

It is difficult to define precisely what customer relationship management (CRM) means to everyone. The term has been applied to almost every element of business that even remotely interacts with a customer. In its infancy, CRM systems were a series of mainframe or server-based applications specific to sales, marketing and support business functions. The applications were lightweight by today's standards and did little more than capture and file critical data. But as cultural boundaries within organizations weakened, individual fiefdoms of information gave way to sophisticated applications that could span business functions. By doing so, these applications made possible the vision of a single view of the customer. For the first time, organizations could track and analyze shifting customer needs, link marketing campaigns to sales results, and monitor sales activities for improved forecasting accuracy and manufacturing demand.

The arrival of CRM (Customer Relationship Management) systems has reinforced the importance of knowledge management and its linkages with IT implementation. The ultimate goal of CRM is to recognize and treat each customer as an individual. CRM intends to integrate people, process, and technology to maximize relationships with the customers. According to Goldenberg (2002) CRM is a comprehensive approach that provides seamless coordination between al customer-facing functions and increasingly leverages the Internet. The higher the level of IT the higher is the integration of the CRM into the organization's IT/IS architecture and more effective/efficient is the management of customer relationships leading to customers expanded profiles and personalization (Stefanou *et al*, 2003).

However, CRM requires a "customer centric" business philosophy and culture to support effective marketing, sales and service processes. The main goal is to optimize the customer value within the customer lifecycle. According to Parvatiyar and Sheth (2001), Reinartz *et al.* (2004) and Payne and Frow (2005) CRM is defined as a comprehensive strategy and adequate cross-functional processes facilitated by information and communication technologies leveraging customer knowledge to enhance customer value and, as a result, shareholder value.

Some authors emphasize the implementation of a single technological solution, others the implementation of a series of customer-oriented technology solutions and the final group stresses the holistic approach. CRM software does not operate independently but serves to integrate disparate enterprise systems aiming to provide a single view of the organization to the customer and vice versa. So care has to be taken for systems integration to succeed (Lam, 2005). CRM demands an integration of marketing, sales and service activities to establish a consistent and versatile interface to the customer (Meyer & Kolbe, 2005).

Rigby and Ledingham (2004) argue, managers should not be distracted by the capabilities of the CRM software but concentrate instead on what it should do—both for their companies and for their customers. CRM has evolved since its earliest incarnations, driven originally by an inside-out focus, through three phases of evolution: technology, integration and process. Recently we have also seen a major leap forward to a fourth phase: customer-driven CRM—an outside-in approach that for its proponents is presented as having immense financial promise (Watson *et al.*, 2005):

1. *Technology*: In its earliest incarnation, CRM meant applying automation to existing sales, marketing, support and channel processes as organizations attempted to improve communications, planning, opportunity and campaign management, forecasting, problem solving, and to share best practices. To some degree, it worked. However, automating poorly performing activities or

processes rarely improves the quality of the outcome. So, for the most part, the quality of the return on investment (ROI) was meagre—if measurable at all. The promise of the technology was there, but few organizations were realizing the pinnacle of performance. The metric of success was increased efficiency in sales, marketing, support and channel processes.

2. *Integration*: By developing cross-functional integration, supported by data warehousing and shared roles and responsibilities, organizations began to create a customized view of the customer. Support issues, Web hits, sales calls and marketing inquiries started building a deeper understanding of each customer and allowed aggressive organizations to adapt their tactics to fit individual needs. Integration focused around two primary components:

   - *Make it easier to do business with the seller*: Instead of operational silos that inhibited superior customer relationships, the organization as a whole took ownership and responsibility for customer satisfaction. With a single view of the customer, it was much easier for anyone to respond to sales opportunities or impending support issues and take appropriate steps. Expected benefits were improved retention and lower support costs.
   - *Predictive modelling*: Data mining of an aggregate of corporate knowledge and the customer contact experience was used to improve operational and sales performance. By applying complex algorithms to a history of purchasing or inquiry characteristics, it became practical to predict the demands of individual customers. Up-selling, cross-selling, even the ability to pre-empt potential problems, was now possible for all customer-facing representatives. Expected benefits are to have better cross-selling/up-selling and improved product offerings or delivery.

3. *Process*: By rethinking the quality and effectiveness of customer-related processes, many organizations began to eliminate unnecessary activities, improve outdated processes, and redesign activities that had failed to deliver the desired outcomes. Then, by re-creating the process through an understanding of the capabilities of the technology, the outcomes were more predictable and the promises for a meaningful ROI more substantial and realistic. The metrics for success became the improved effectiveness in serving the customer.

Thus far, almost everything about CRM has focused on improving the effectiveness and efficiency of the seller's organization. Organizations have evolved from sales representatives working from paper notebooks, or a card system, to a tightly integrated network that sees movement in sales activity, predicts product demand on manufacturing, and manages the logistics of complex teams to serve the buyer and seller. Marketing, support services, channel management, revenue management, resource allocation/management, forecasting, manufacturing, logistics and even research and development have all seen the benefits of a well-designed CRM strategy.

However, the past decade of CRM and its associated improvements have been based on three assumptions:

1. The past would be a logical foundation to predict future customer needs and profitability.
2. Demand for traditional value propositions would remain constant.
3. Better customer relationships would deter attrition.

All three of these assumptions were not necessarily good ones to start with but failed—or at least became unstable—in a post-September 11 environment. Historical purchases or inquiries are not a clear indication of future needs as buyers are rapidly redefining requirements to satisfy their current business, market or shareholder demands. Value propositions are changing in highly competitive markets as sellers are working aggressively to re-establish structural bonds. And, driven by sensitive financial markets, buyers move to whichever supplier can provide the best aligned, most cost effective solution that promises to stabilize, or improve, their business performance. These factors are driving CRM into a fourth phase.

CUSTOMER-DRIVEN CRM—THE FOURTH PHASE

These days, revenue performance has become the central theme for CRM as organizations seek to achieve and maintain expected financial results. Senior executives have been asking:

- Which of my customers have the potential for a high-profit, sustainable relationship?
- What defines profitable and unprofitable customer segments?
- What must change to realize that optimal potential?
- Where's my opportunity for growth?
- Where's my risk for loss?
- Am I making the right decisions related to balancing acquisition, cross-selling and up-selling—and for the right customer groups?

The epiphany is not in the questions themselves, but in the fact that they are being asked after a decade of CRM investments. It is important to understand that a disruptive change has occurred causing large segments of customer organizations to reassess many of their basic needs, values and assumptions. This has been triggered by the rising power of the technologies becoming available, the uncertain complexities of the post-September 11 world, and the deepening competition felt in the 2001–2005 semi-recession experienced in the developed economies. Organizations are now challenging everything from how they create value, to how they serve their markets, to how they meet shareholder expectations. It is the answers to these questions that create the framework for phase four CRM. And without a deep understanding of what's going on in the customer's head—specifically what will influence buying behaviour—it is difficult to establish customer strategies that mutually serve the needs and expectations of the buyer and seller communities. Let us look at this proposition in a little more detail.

Understanding the Difference

In the past, CRM has followed a basic balanced scorecard technique involving four categories: customer, financial, operations, and people. From an inside-out perspective, organizations first analyzed the needs and capabilities of *operations* and their *people* to determine what could be delivered to the *customer*. From that, they drew conclusions and predictions to determine the impact on the *financial* category.

As this has changed, so have the priorities. More recently, the focus is first on the customers:

- What will they buy, when, why and for how much?
- What creates value for them, and does this create a structural bond?
- What services can we perform that merit premium margins?
- Can we establish a new market segmentation strategy focused on potential profitability and willingness to purchase?
- Do we understand their business drivers, financial metrics, buying process and decision criteria?

Customer driven CRM means that organizations first understand the *customer*, then move inward to *operations*. Within the context of the customer, the systems and infrastructure capabilities needed to serve those customers and segmentation-based requirements must be reassessed. Next, it is imperative to explore the skills and competency requirements for the *people* component of the CRM design. A decade of CRM has taught organizations that nothing happens until their people interact with the customer in a manner consistent with new CRM customer strategies and systems. And, finally, it is suggested, an organization should be well positioned to apply predictive modelling algorithms to establish a *financial* model with exceptional accuracy. Not an easy task, but case studies are showing financial predictions that can demonstrate account-level forecasting with over 80 % accuracy.

If this fourth phase sounds long overdue, then it is useful to point to the long-term habit of organizations not to be that customer-focused, as opposed to internally, operationally and product-focused and organised. In turn this leads to the tricky area of how one can implement fully fledged fourth phase CRM systems that, by their nature need to be cross-organizational in design, and involve multiple stakeholders with varying interests, in their implementation and use.

IT-ENABLED CRM: REVISITING THE ISSUE OF IMPLEMENTATION

Information Technology (IT) implementation has been discussed and critically analyzed over four decades. But while research into the phenomena has been regular and rewarding it has also focused on certain issues rather than others. Moreover new technologies and applications—like CRM have frequently come along, raising questions about new impacts, new management problems to solve, and whether the research findings still hold. Here we will alert ourselves to the major issues in the literature so as to give context to why we have undertaken this work on CRM implementation, and why it takes the direction it does. In particular we highlight macro rather than micro-focus, neglect of knowledge and systems integration issues, perennial and much needed foci on culture, strategy and business process re-engineering, the neglect of power and stakeholder involvement, and also of the distinctive characteristics of the technology being implemented. At the same time we point out the many areas where there is an abiding literature and studies, but comment that this work has not as yet been applied to specific cases of CRM implementation.

On revisiting the academic and practitioner literatures, one can see that they tend to focus on the more macro issues faced in the big picture of the implementation lifecycle of a new technology. Yet, as we shall see, identifying the micro elements in the small picture is also vital for a successful implementation of a new technology. Chapter 3 reveals what we mean by micro here. A further issue is key and was neglected in the 1990s but has been more frequently addressed in recent years. Since the 1990s the issue of knowledge management and its linkage with Information Systems (IS) strategy has become more recognized. A further issue that has received belated attention is that of systems integration. The arrival of enterprise systems such as Enterprise Resource Planning (ERP) pushed organizations towards system integration and made them rethink their knowledge management strategies in order effectively to transfer information across their various business units (Shanks *et al.*, 2003). As a result organizations have been moving away from a "part technology" (mainly focused on independent systems without any considerations of holistic system integration) strategy towards a greater focus on system integration strategy. Research on systems integration and its implementation has not, at the time of writing, kept up with these developments, though we do offer such a focus in our own research.

Information technology is pervasive in many industries and is clearly reshaping some. It has a very strong impact on organizational culture (Alvesson, 2002; Claver *et al.*, 2001). It affects the whole cultural web of an organization, reshaping and transforming it accordingly, or alternatively, in conditions of organizational conservatism, the IT can have an augmentative effect, reasserting or indeed amplifying existing power structures and following the lines of existing functions and cultures (Willcocks & Mason, 1987; see also Chapter 2).

Unquestionably, information systems (IS), along with their supporting information technology (IT), continue to increase in importance in nearly all organizations. As organizations work hard to develop and apply IT in new ways, the need to identify and implement an IS strategic plan becomes increasingly critical. To date, however, implementations of IS strategies have not had high success rates. This has been true for years, and much continues to be published on how to develop an IS strategy. In the next chapter we provide a framework for what we know so far about positioning IS strategy work, and our case studies detail the practical issues involved in trying to develop and apply such strategy.

Business process reengineering had its heyday as a 1990s fad and is now becoming a routinised part of how organizations envisage changing themselves (Davenport, 1993). Organizations continue to update their technical systems rapidly. IT is becoming the core of the business process content setting. But despite recommendations and rhetoric, this technical innovation in the business process is often implemented with little or no regard to the end-users/internal customers (internal customers are the in-house end-users of the system interacting with external customers using the system), the impact on job roles, job satisfaction and subsequent ability to serve the external customer. A lack of interaction between the decision makers, the IT experts and the customers (internal as well as external) during the implementation process of IT systems, results in systems being less efficient and user friendly. While implementing the business process using IT as a tool has gained greater attention in the last few years, the human, cultural, and political aspects of implementation continue to be downplayed, to the point, in some implementations, of being dealt with only when crisis point is reached (Willcocks *et al.*, 2003; Markus, 2004). Of course, CRM implementation also involves business process re-engineering, so much of this can pass into how CRM itself is implemented.

When we turn to the links between stakeholders' perceptions (based on the differential interests, expectations and power, this too has a long history of being researched in most type of IT implementations (Long & Fahey, 2000) but has rarely been examined in detail in the context of the implementation process of a CRM system. Our own research in this book attempts to rectify many of these omissions by attempting to investigate the "R" of CRM implementation from a knowledge management perspective. While broader contexts are given due weight, the focus is also narrowed down to knowledge sharing enablers and inhibitors in connection with the roll out of new CRM systems. This research also treats technologies and organizations as mutually dependent and dynamically emergent.

There is still much opportunity for the IS field to act on Markus and Robey's (1988) quite early suggestion to move beyond a relatively simple black-boxed view of technology towards a more powerful conceptualization of the role of IT artefacts in organizations. Furthermore, Orlikowski and Iacono (2001) after reviewing numerous (N = 188) articles, argue the need to put technology back into the study of information systems.

While we address many of these areas in our own study, we have also taken into account that there is much to draw upon in previous studies. For example, Davidson (2002) argues how frames and shifts in frame salience (frames are cognitive structures or mental models that are held by individuals) influence sense-making during requirement determination. Our own study helps to understand how interpretive power is exercised in an IS project. Moving on from frames to shared frames, Orlikowski and Gash (1994) show shared frames as closely related to the concept of sub-cultures. Individuals—drawing on their shared frames—engage in symbolic action and thereby construct a social reality that reflects their common assumptions, beliefs and understandings and that includes particular rules, rituals and customary practice. According to Geertz (1973) and Van Maanen and Barley (1985), sub-cultures rely heavily on cognitive elements such as common frames of reference. Drawing on such work, or its spirit, our research looks at the perceptions of different stakeholders and their linkages with knowledge sharing across sub-cultural boundaries in the implementation process of the CRM system as important factors, needing to be critically analyzed.

We also draw upon those scholars that can be used to make a case for the importance of culture during the implementation of an IT system (for example Agar, 1994; Alvesson, 2002; Burns and Stalker, 1961; Claver *et al.*, 2001). Indeed there has been a wide consensus over the culture gap that exists between IT experts and the users/business experts and a lot of research findings to show that this can impact on implementation in many ways (Bloomfield & Vurdubaki, 1994; Fincham, 1994; Grindley, 1992; Hinton, 1994; Kumar & Bjorn-Andersen, 1990). Here we research the relevance of these findings in attempts to implement CRM. We also find very little mentioned regarding knowledge sharing across different hierarchical sub-cultures and its impact on the adaptation of a CRM system. An investigation initially identifying the key sub-cultures in a CRM environment and then mapping the knowledge sharing process across them would produce a rich picture of knowledge sharing phenomena, and that again is something we attempt in this book.

We go further in looking at scholars such as Van Maanen (1986) who states that informal settings can aid/facilitate the sharing of knowledge across sub-cultures, but we find in CRM implementation that much still needs to be investigated about how to attain Boland and Tenkasi's (1996) "mutual perspective taking". Some scholars argue that psychological contracts play an important role in the outcome of an interaction between individuals, though no link has been established between knowledge sharing and psychological contracts—something we again attempt here in our CRM research.

The current system integration trends investigated by Ross (2003) neglect to address fully the micro-level socio-cognitive issues related to knowledge sharing mechanisms across the sub-cultural boundaries of an organization. Cognitive issues such as unwritten expectations—the outcome of a tacit agreement between individuals—can play important role in the sharing of non-codified/tacit knowledge across the sub-cultures in an organization. Scholars (Boland & Tenkasi, 1996; Iansiti, 1993; Lawrence & Lorsch, 1967; Newell *et al.*, 2002) talk about "knowing of what others know", "mutual perspective taking", "shared mental space" and "T-shaped skills", as aids to tacit knowledge/non-codified sharing. However they do not address the micro processes that lead to a "mutual perspective taking" and the rest. According to Rousseau (1995), a psychological contract is an unwritten set of expectations between everyone in an organization and, unlike the written contract, is constantly changing. Many scholars (Anderson & René, 1998; Rousseau, 1995; Shore & Barksdale, 1998; Thibaut & Kelley, 1959) argue that psychological contracts play an important role in the outcome of interaction between individuals.

Bringing all these issues together, our contribution in this book is to investigate fully how organizations embark on the implementation process for CRM systems, with due weight given to external and internal contexts, history, process, technologies and substance of change. But we add further depth to the analysis by providing a distinctive focus also on the linkages between sub-cultural interactions, psychological contracts and non-codified knowledge sharing in the implementation process of CRM systems.

CONCLUSION: THIS BOOK

In this chapter we have outlined the reasons why CRM systems have figured increasingly in organizational debates about internal informational efficiency and customer-facing competitive advantage. We spelt out the promise of CRM and provided a brief overview of the evolution of CRM capabilities into a fourth phase. We also indicated that, even if Carr (2003) was correct in his assumption that IT was now essentially a commodity and only of importance as infrastructure—(in fact he was only selectively correct), then he still greatly downplayed the importance and complexity of IT implementation, but also the degree to which implementation capability could itself be a differentiator in terms of IT performance, and in the marketplace. And CRM as an IT application is a prime example of the potential for such differentiation available from technology, information and implementation capability.

Tracking this issue into the IT implementation literature, we found some major omissions but also much that could be drawn upon. We also identified many previous studies that have not been used in IT implementation research, but offer a rich vein of promise, as we will detail in Chapter 3.

The rest of the book proceeds as follows. Chapter 2 provides a distinctive, holistic overview of what has been found so far about how IT projects that are organizational and business change projects can be managed. As such the chapter draws upon a range of IT and CRM implementation studies, including the authors' own. Because the research findings from these studies cover more traditional ground and are fairly robust, the chapter takes a more prescriptive tone than later chapters. Its purpose it to give a larger but consistent context for the more exploratory review and detailed micro studies that follow in Chapters 3–6.

In Chapter 3 we provide a detailed review of five literatures that we identified as needing to inform our studies of CRM implementation. These are IT implementation, organizational cultures and sub-cultures, knowledge and knowledge sharing, psychological contracts, and Customer Relationship Management (CRM) systems. This critical review leads to two preliminary frameworks and the development of an initial research question with which to carry out and analyse the results of a pilot study. Chapter 4 documents the tools for investigation, in particular the use of a qualitative, processual research approach. It also describes the pilot studies we conducted at our two research sites, provides a preliminary analysis of the findings, and details how we refined our research questions and analytical frameworks for the main research.

Chapters 5 and 6 provide detailed accounts of and insights into two case studies of CRM implementation drawn form the private and public sectors. Chapter 7 then presents a cross-case and cross-sector analysis using our improvised version of Pettigrew's (1985, 1990) frame work. In the first part we critically analyze and compare the process of implementation of CRM systems from our contemporary situations, comparing issues such as staff stability, user commitment, user training and management support. We then compare the knowledge sharing issues using our framework of interdependencies between subculture interaction, psychological contracts and knowledge sharing. In the second part of Chapter 7 we use Willcocks and Harrow's (1992) contextual analysis framework in order to compare the similarities and deviations in the CRM implementation processes from our two research sites. Chapter 8 discusses the contributions our research makes to theory, research approach, and practice. It also discusses several limitations of our work and provides reflections on the possible directions for further research.

2
Positioning CRM as IT-Enabled Business Change

INTRODUCTION

For any IT strategy, the implementation stage will reveal where prior analysis, design and planning have been inadequate. Frequently what have been termed "implementation problems" are in fact the results of failures in these earlier activities. Implementation will bring its own unpredictabilities that need to be handled. Not least of these are human factors. In fact, in the usual implementation scenario it is only at this stage, when changes become manifest and real, that people seriously begin to question what is going to happen.

People become even more important for other reasons also. As information-based technologies enter the core of organizational functioning, IT implementations increasingly also represent major business change projects. People's responses, adjustments and learning become crucial areas of managerial concern. Moreover, the value of IT is only as high as its business utilization. This means that it is not enough to merely install a system. A system has to be institutionalized, so that there is a leveraging fit between technology, skills and processes. Nowhere is this more true than for a modern customer relationship management system. Typically this will not only cross an organization's many functions; it will also be by definition inter-organizational.

In such IT-enabled organizational change projects as ERP and CRM, to take only two examples, we regularly find that these human and organizational costs of technical change and innovation are now typically three to four times the technical costs of implementation.

This suggests that the behavioural and organizational change dimensions deserve sustained senior management attention to getting them right. The message is clear. It is in the interests of all organizations, even, indeed especially, the most commercially driven, to assign much more importance to people factors rather than technical issues when implementing computer-based information systems.

This is not the accepted view, and indeed at the root of many implementation problems is the overriding influence of traditional systems analysis and design practices and traditional managerial attitudes to IT. In particular, human and organizational issues are reduced merely to limiting resistance to change, the need to organize training, and the need to have enough staff of the right type available in the right place at the right time. In this way an over-concentration on the technical can result in failure to deal with non-technical emerging issues. In turn, problems in these areas can begin to interfere with technical issues. Here the crux of the problem lies in the manner in which implementation is defined and conceptualized.

This chapter examines the proposition that CRM implementation is organizational change, and points to the uses and limitations of Organization Development (OD) approaches to handling technological change. Various implementation strategies are examined. The key role of culture is examined, at a high level, with a more micro-view being pursued in later chapters. Participation and its uses are discussed and various guidelines proposed for minimising implementation problems. Finally, the chapter develops a political-cultural contingencies approach to systems implementation. This places at centre stage the **organizational context** in which CRM implementation occurs. All this will act as a high level view of holistic CRM implementation, as a prelude to the in-depth micro-studies provided in Chapters 3 through to 6. The objective of this chapter is to provide a distinctive holistic overview of what has been found out so far about how IT projects that are organizational and business change projects can be managed. As such the chapter draws upon a range of IT and CRM implementation studies, including the authors' own (Chung *et al.*, 2004; Geib *et al.*, 2005; Goodhue *et al.*, 2002; Marchand & Meadows, 2006; Markus, 2004; Shanks *et al.*, 2003; Watson *et al.*, 2005; Willcocks & Mason, 1987; Willcocks *et al.*, 2003; Willcocks & Sauer, 2001). Because the research findings from these studies cover more traditional ground and are fairly robust, the chapter takes a more prescriptive tone than later chapters. Its purpose it to give a larger context for the more exploratory review and micro studies that follow in Chapters 3 to 6.

THE DIMENSIONS OF CHANGE: E-BUSINESS, CHARLES SCHWAB AND CRM AS EXAMPLE

To get a fix on the dimensions of change involved in major IT projects, it is useful to revisit the e-business bubble for examples. As "pure play" dot.coms and those moving "from bricks to clicks" faltered throughout 2001 and into 2002, it became evident that there were few quick fixes to be had in moving to e-business. In an MIT Sloan Management Review article "Pathways To E-Business Leadership" Willcocks and Plant (2001) reported findings from a study of 78 corporations from 1999–2001. They showed the management success factors that distinguished the winners from the laggards. They found evolutionary, but no overnight, successes. The technical issues were large enough here, involving the building of an e-business infrastructure that embraced legacy and ERP systems, together with web-based technologies, new technologies and software as they became relevant to the business. But the real killer was attempting to integrate the technology platform with new processes and skills while working through legacy organizational structures, culture, and management processes. This links back to the point made in the previous chapter about the critical importance of linking IT strategy with re-engineering.

In fact, well into the first decade of this new century, very few organizations had matched Dell, Cisco Systems, Fidelity Investments and Charles Schwab in making it through to being able to leverage significant profitability from their e-business investments. On our estimates this can take from two to four years to achieve. The size of the changes needed, and a way of decomposing the challenge of e-transformation into its interconnected components, is suggested in Figure 2.1.

At the top of the framework are **stakeholders**, whose changing expectations and requirements need to be monitored in the light of the outcomes from the organization's business activities. The expected result of a moves to e-business should be an improved outcome for stakeholders. The firm is then viewed as having a **strategic intent**, including a competitive strategy and related customer value propositions. Specific **organizational capabilities** and enabling **infrastructure** are required to deliver on this intent. A strategic view of transformation can be described as the alignment over time between strategic intent and organizational capabilities, grounded in competitive advantage and responding to particular external forces, to achieve a superior outcome for stakeholders.

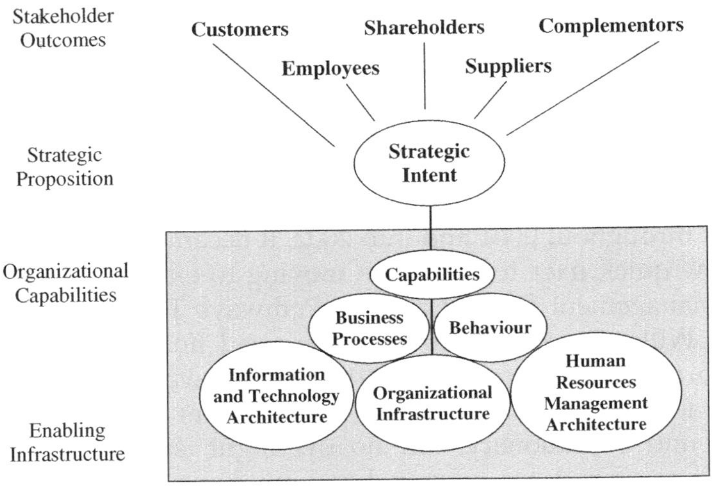

Figure 2.1 *Framework For Targeting IT-Enabled Change (Adapted from Keith Ruddle, in Willcocks and Sauer (eds), 2001)*

Clearly such dynamic alignment is very difficult to achieve, and brings on-going change headaches. Firstly, capabilities have to be delivered through the execution of **business processes** by people adopting distinctive, culturally determined **behaviours**, the latter built on certain values and belief systems (see below). Secondly, this delivery has to be enabled by various interrelated elements of **architectural infrastructure**. These are: **information and technology infrastructure** (management information systems, IT systems, information strategy); **organizational infrastructure** (structures, management control systems, communication and coordination mechanisms); and **human resource management architecture** (skills, people development, processes, reward and motivation systems). Let us illustrate an effective journey of targeted change by describing the successful transformation of Charles Schwab into an e-business.

Case Study: How Charles Schwab Moved from Bricks to Clicks (and CRM)

US-based broker Charles Schwab had no exposure on the Internet before 1996. By mid-2000, it had about 7 million customers (Active On-line accounted for 3.7 million), and $US800 billion worth of funds under management. In 2000 it handled some 1.7 million trades a week, with over 70 % made on-line on its schwab.com site. It also operated in several countries outside the USA and throughout

2001/2, despite adverse trading conditions, continued to be the largest single Internet-based broker.

Schwab's move to the web was driven from the top, though the company had a history of innovation. In October 1995, its stand-alone e.Schwab web site was launched to provide investors with account and research information. In March 1996 it was the first major brokerage firm to offer discount and limited trading via the Internet. In 1998 electronic brokerage was integrated into the main body of the company. Pricing and availability were reorganized so that every Schwab customer could deal with Schwab through any channel, and experience consistency in Internet pricing and service. This move cost the company some $125 million, but paid off in terms of subsequent revenues.

By the end of 1998, 58 % of transactions were on-line, representing $4billion worth of trades each week. The site offered trading of stocks, mutual funds, US treasuries, listed corporate bonds and options. It also supplied a range of tools to give access to an investor's account holding and to information providers. Available also were interactive investment guides, calculators for retirement and college planning, and real-time quotes. Internet trading has allowed reductions in commission throughout the industry. In 1999 Schwab charged $29.95 per trade; the equivalent via phone was $80. However the company's growth strategy is not explained by being the cheapest. For example at that time, E-Trade was charging $15 per trade, and subsequently there have been several price wars in USA and elsewhere. Rather for CEO Charles Schwab: "the transforming event is the ability to deliver personalized information to the customer at virtually no cost... this is possible because the Net is totally imbedded in the centre of our business." Note here the CRM dimensions of this implementation.

By 2000 Charles Schwab was offering an array of financial services and products, investment guidance and trading and brokerage services through a network of over 300 branches, offices, telephone service centres, automated phone services and the Internet. For Schwab, technology and customer service would seem to be two sides of the same coin. According to its CIO: "technology allows us to deliver on a twin commitment: offering customers convenient access to a wealth of services, and delivering exceptional service at reasonable prices". Throughout 2000 it continued to expand its services on-line, for example in April establishing an alliance with E-LOAN to offer customers a complete mortgage solution, including the ability to research, compare and apply for a mortgage loan on-line. By March 2000 Schwab.com was averaging 40 million hits a day. Customers could screen thousands of mutual funds, track investment performance', get real-time stock quotes, enter trade orders, view asset allocation models, participate in on-line forums with investment experts, and conduct research. Additionally, using MySchwab.com—a free link with Internet portal Excite, customers could create customized investment information like Watch lists of stocks, and receive current news and content. By late 2001 on-line trading generally was down some 47% at some times compared to 2000. Nevertheless Schwab remained the leading on-line broker.

Here one can see a process of migration over a five year period. Schwab started with a reputation and strong brand in retail stockbroking and investing. Innovation was valued by top management and the nature of the **strategic intent** was heavily determined by learning about what customers valued and used, and by realization that the Internet needed to be integrated into the core of the business. As a result Schwab developed on the Web a range of differentiated services as well as offering competitive pricing. New **behaviours** were developed based on customer orientation, new services and experimentation. Within three years **business processes** were reassembled to fit with the Web-based business. On the information and technology front, the web-site "front office" was developed with high functionality and easy-to-use facilities. It also featured such aspects as personalized pages for research and account management, and customized services and information. Meanwhile the **information and technology infrastructure** eventually included effective use of database management, XML and related technologies, management information systems and effective collection, analysis and uses of information. Schwab became very certain in the 1990s of the opportunity to differentiate itself by the use of leading edge technology and by 2000 had done so.

On **organization infrastructure,** Schwab greatly restructured itself for the virtual world in terms of roles, responsibilities and by moving from budgets to dynamic management measurement tools. It had already decentralized the company into "customer enterprises" in 1994. It further flattened its structure in the late 1990s when it reinvented itself as a into what it called the "new model for full-service investing". On **human resources management architecture** Schwab established strong values through the co-CEOs' style of leadership. It also looked to provide individual incentives for risk and growth, moved to 360-degree appraisals, and separated out personal development from any fixation with quantified performance measures. It also sought to cultivate commitment through gender parity and diversity.

Such a case reveals that there can be no quick technology, or any other, fix when moving to e-business, or CRM. It is indeed a long haul, even for those moving quickly, but especially for large "bricks and mortar" companies. The framework allows the organization undertaking large-scale technical change to isolate the many factors that need to be focused on. It also stresses that it is the **integration** of supporting infrastructure with processes, behaviours, and strategic intent that will serve to determine ultimately the degrees of success experienced. A similar conclusion can be made from other CRM studies (see for example Chung *et al.*, 2004; Geib *et al.*, 2005; Marchand & Meadows, 2006).

MANAGING THE CRM CHANGE PROCESS: BEYOND THE QUICK FIX

From these considerations it becomes necessary to reconceptualize CRM implementation as a process involving the introduction of changes connected with computer-based systems into social and political organizational areas where the acceptance and the very definition of the success of those changes tend to be continually renegotiated. This is a point Markus (2004) makes in her studies of technochange management. The issue is neatly captured by Peter Keen:

> Implementation is not just the installation of a technical system in an organization but the institutionalization of its use in the ongoing context of jobs, formal and informal structures, and personal and group processes. Installation does not guarantee institutionalization. Implementation includes the technical process of installation and the behavioural process of managing change. (Keen, 1981)

Organizational members are often unwilling to change long-established attitudes and patterns of behaviour. Furthermore, given the introduction of a computer system, people's behaviour and attitudes may not change at all, or may change for a short time before reverting back to older patterns. The ways of working that result influence the extent to which the new system is utilized as was originally designed, if at all. Lewin (1980) (and later Schein) addressed such problems by developing a model for intervening at the individual, group or organizational levels. Figure 2.2 shows this useful model and its development by Kolb and Frohman (1970).

From these models a crucial point emerges. As discussed, physical systems implementation may be treated as a late stage, but the implementation of the necessary *behaviour* change to support the emerging system must occur right from the beginning of the project

Lewin/Schein life approach	**Kolb/Frphman approach**	**Systems development cycle approach**
1. *Unfreezing*	(a) *Scouting* Organization and change agent jointly explore mutual needs and abilities Entry point selected (b) *Entry* Problems, goals stated, Development of mutual contract and expectations Establish trust, commitment and felt need for change (c) *Diagnosis* Collect data to define problems Detailed assessment of organization's and change agent's resources for change Establish feasible goals	1. *Definition* Proposal defined Feasibility assessment Information requirements analysis Conceptual design 2. *Development* Physical systems & database design Program development Procedure development
2. *Changing*	(d) *Planning* Define operational objectives Identify alternative solutions, action steps and possible resistance to change Develop action plan (e) *Action* Putting into practice 'best' solution Keeping practice flexible in the face of unanticapted consequences (f) *Stabilization and evaluation* Assess 'success' of change and need for further action or termination	3. *Installation and operation* Conversion 4. *Maintenance*
3. *Refreezing*	(g) *Termination* Confirm new behaviour patterns Ensure handover of responsibility and ownership of system to client is complete Cease work on project	5. *Post-audit*

***Figure* 2.2** *Addressing Behavioural Change in Strategic CRM Projects*

(Marchand & Meadows, 2006). Failure to grasp the significance of this point for systems development can lead to the so-called "people problems" frequently experienced at the implementation and subsequent operating stages—and, as we shall see, were experienced in our two CRM cases to varying degrees.

Advantages of the models include the emphases on change as process rather than a "one off", and the need for careful planning. The overall approach suggests the need in CRM projects for:

(a) establishing a felt need for CRM;
(b) establishing the support required to see the project through to satisfactory systems operation;
(c) monitoring the progress of the project, and responding to resistance to the change process and the emerging system;
(d) developing user commitment to the system.

Under item (b), establishing support may mean not only securing top management support but also making that visible to the organization. Establishing change-agent credibility is crucial. User understanding and active acceptance of objectives and methods is also needed. A project champion who can make available required organizational resources is important throughout the project. Such methods are aimed at creating a "critical mass" in favour of and actively supporting the CRM inplementation process. At the end of the project, commitment (item (d) should be expressed as the users "owning" the system, willing to use it and able to do so without the change agent's presence. In Lewin's terms, this means refreezing—locking the new behaviours into place so that they become the norm.

These models emphasize the much-neglected need to focus on behavioural change when implementing any CRM system. When an IT system is linked strongly to strategy delivery—as we saw in the Charles Schwab case—a more all-encompassing integrated approach to change and delivery is needed (Chung *et al.*, 2004; Markus, 2004). Kilmann's (1989) well researched work provides the basis for such an approach. In Figure 2.3 we update and develop his framework to take into account our own experiences with strategic projects, including the CRM projects researched in this book.

Kilmann rightly points out that there will be barriers to change. He also rightly points out that few organizations take an holistic

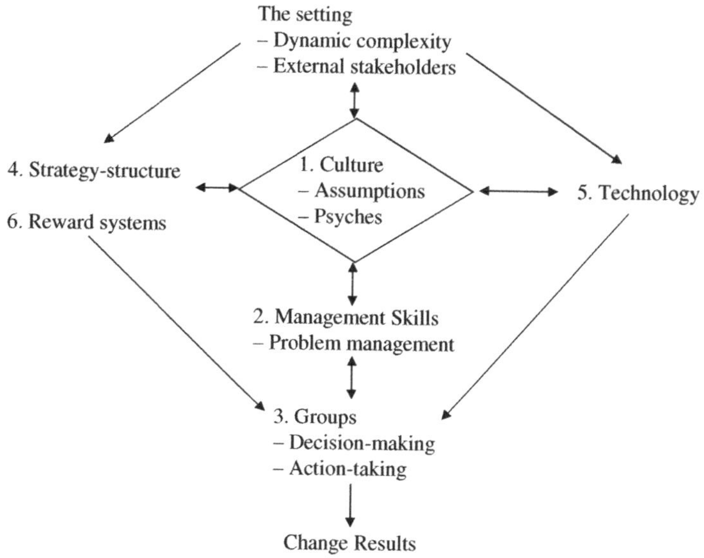

Figure 2.3 *Managing Barriers To Success In CRM Implementation: An Integrated Approach (adapted from Kilmann, 1989)*

enough approach to dealing with these barriers, and mobilizing the organization for change. Kilmann argues convincingly that there are two types of barrier that managers can do little about. One is **the setting**—the external environment with its dynamic complexity, and external stakeholders. The other is **the psyche** of people—the innermost qualities of the human mind and spirit which translate into what people want, fear, resist and defend—that cannot be changed in a short period of time, if at all. However, an accurate understanding of organizational members' psyches is essential to managing organizations and solving problems. The setting and human psyche are the relatively unchangeable givens which any planned change must understand and work with.

The good news, however, is that all the other likely barriers shown in Figure 2.3—strategy, structure, reward systems, culture, people's assumptions, technology, management skills, how groups are organized and perform—**are** manageable and changeable, provided that an integrated, planned approach to change is adopted (Chung *et al.*, 2004; Goodhue *et al.*, 2002; Markus, 2004; Shanks *et al.*, 2003). So what does this consist of? Our own version gives much more detail to the technology issues than does Kilmann, but is consistent with his findings. The first three tracks that need attention are culture, management skills and team-building. These adjust the behavioural infrastructure of the organization. Without first developing an adaptive inner organization, any adjustments to the outer organization—strategy, structure, rewards, systems and technologies—would be cosmetic and short-lived. However, there must also be from the start a strong sense of how all these factors fit together. For example, it is not enough to have a strategy without also at the same time establishing how technology can leverage, or even change that strategy, and whether a supportive culture is feasible. This means adaptation becomes a vital component of the implementation process in order to achieve politically feasible "fit" between the factors.

If this is not achieved, then action on a single factor, however powerful, will be negated by the barriers posed by the other factors. For example, if the strategy is based on false assumptions, then all technology can do is provide an efficient underpinning for what might be tantamount to "disaster faster". How groups are rewarded influences the decisions and actions they take. As we have seen in the Charles Schwab case, implementing and institutionalizing the changes may well take several years. However, Kilmann suggests the following sequence as the most effective approach. He also suggests starting with a single, primary business unit first. In this case, the integrated change may well take up to a year, and the figures below reflect this example.

1. The Culture Track. At the centre of the barriers to success framework in Figure 2.3 is **culture**, defined as shared values, beliefs, expectations, norms, the unwritten rules of the game, "the way things are done round here". Connected to culture are **assumptions,** that is, beliefs taken for granted to be true but that may turn out to be false under closer analysis, for example the technology is not important to the future of our industry, the consumer will buy what the firm produces. The key diagnostic questions here are: does this culture support the behaviour needed for organizational success? Are the critical assumptions that affect all major business decisions up-to-date, based on reality, explicit and understood?

Kilmann found many cultures to be dysfunctional and negative, embodying norms such as "don't argue with the boss, don't share information with other groups, don't be bearer of bad news, laugh at those who suggest new ways of doing things. We can add that many senior managements and organizational members may also have a negative view on IT, seeing it as a cash sink, a cost to be minimized, irrelevant to this business, with a poor track record, and the CIO positioned as a specialist functional manager (Feeny, 2001). Kilmann also found that organizational members typically preferred to work in more positive cultures. He suggests a six month culture track focusing on enhancing trust, communication, information sharing and willingness to change, and identifying the culture and norms the organizational members wish to commit to—for Kilmann, the conditions that must exist before any other improvement effort can succeed. All organizational members need to participate in this, and the team-building track.

2. Management-Skills Track. Managerial styles and skills must be diagnosed to see how well these fit with strategy, and dynamic complexity of the environment. In settings of dynamic complexity the problems may not be clear, and managers may need to handle change constantly. The question here is: do managers throughout the organization apply the right skills for addressing complex problems. Typically this management skills track will start three months into the culture track and may well run for some eight months. The purpose here is to provide all management personnel with new ways of coping with complex problems and the hidden managerial assumptions that may prove misleading.

3. Team-Building Track. In modern organizations, complex problems need multiple contributions from members of one or more groups. Kilmann found a close link between group decision making, action and organizational results. The **team building** track infuses the new culture and updated management skills into each work-unit—thereby instilling cooperation organization-wide so that complex problems can be addressed with all the expertise and information available. Team building should start some six months into the planned change, as the culture track ends, with managers being brought back into their organizational units to ensure the newly internalized culture and management skills are transferred directly into the job.

4. Strategy-Structure Track. After some nine months, and half-way through the team building track, the originally formulated strategy and structure will need revisiting. **Strategy** refers to all the documents that indicate direction: statements of mission, purpose, goals and objectives. **Structure** refers to the way resources are organized into action: charts, policy statements, job descriptions, formal rules, regulations and work procedures. Is there clarity and agreement about objectives? Does the way of working and developing culture support strategy or require adjustments? Does the structure actually enable or inhibit direction and productive ways of working? These questions will be addressed by small groups of leaders from every part of the organization and their conclusions acted upon by senior change managers. Thus this track develops either a completely new or a revised strategic plan for the firm, then aligns divisions, departments, work groups, jobs and all resources, with the new strategic direction.

5. Technology Track. Our experience is that information-based systems and technologies need to be "first-order thinking" done at the time of, and included in, first formulation of strategy, and that a robust feasibility analysis of organizational readiness to accept and deliver the technological changes is also carried out then, and an implementation plan drawn up (Willcocks *et al.*, 2003). Half-way through track 4, it will become obvious what organizational culture, managerial skills, and readiness are in place, and changes in strategy and structure will also need to be adjusted to. The groups in track 4 will need to regularly consult with those responsible for technology delivery, and driving out business benefits from the CRM project(s).

6. Reward System Track. The reward system includes all documented methods to attract and retain employees, and, in particular, to motivate them to high levels of performance. The **reward system track** sees a small group of leaders establishing a performance-based reward system that sustains all improvements by officially sanctioning the new culture, use of updated management skills, cooperative team efforts, working within the new strategy and delivering the requisite technologies. The new reward system will start to be developed half way through the strategy-structure track when it begins to become clearer what the objective measures will be for success at individual employee and group levels.

It is important to evaluate the results from each track, not least so that, in a large organization, planned changes can be implemented flexibly, and more effectively, in other business units. However, for Kilmann, evaluation is not merely a reality check at the end of the process but something that needs to be performed throughout. It also needs to be part of a further "shadow" or "politics" track that runs parallel to all the other tracks from the very start, and right through to the completion of the change process. We focus below particularly on the implications for delivering the technological aspects of business strategy.

MANAGING THE SHADOW TRACK: A POLITICAL APPROACH TO IT-ENABLED CRM IMPLEMENTATION

This section outlines the basics of a political approach to IT-based change implementation, which is developed from Kilmann's idea of a "shadow track". Bringing a CRM system into effective operation in an organization is not solely about getting the politics right. However, getting the politics wrong has turned many an IT project into a long-term damage limitation exercise. How can this be avoided?

IT people commonly see the planning, designing, organizing and controlling of IT-based projects as rational behaviours. However, these activities are also essentially political. One must ask-whose plans, whose designs and whose objectives? Furthermore, organizations are inevitably political arenas with individuals, groups and coalitions attempting to influence others and events to protect and meet their own needs, interests and goals. An organization where members' goals, perceptions or interests do not conflict is a rare one indeed. "Playing politics" may not always be the primary activity, but it is an ever-present one to some degree. Two important considerations arise from this.

Firstly, the design and development of CRM systems inevitably implies the ability to bring them into successful operation. However, while IT professionals may rarely be questioned in technical matters like analysis and design or hardware and software selection, such expertise and associated technical qualifications may form an insufficient power base these days for fulfilling the responsibility for seeing a project implemented. Unfortunately, IT professionals too often ascribe a rationality and a common sense to their projects that is not shared by those directly affected by implementation outcomes. As a result, they fail to acquire and mobilize power and develop strategies to achieve objectives, and the system flounders at the implementation stage. Of course, faced with gathering signs of organizational hostility toward what they themselves regard as a technically high-quality product, IT professionals may well have fled from responsibility for project acceptance long before implementation.

Secondly, organizational politics breed in times of technological change. The extent of political activity during CRM implementation will depend on the extent to which power has been mobilized behind the project, and other options and paths of resistance are closed off before implementation. Political activity will become more obvious where there persist unclear goals and outcomes, different goals, the need to allocate limited resources, differing definitions of organizational problems and differences in information made available. Mangham's (1979) finding is that:

> In circumstances in which people share power, differ about what must be done, and where these differences are of some consequence, decisions and actions will be the result of a political process.

Just looking at the implications of CRM systems for an organization, the introduction of new technology will release political energy because of its anticipated and actual organizational and social impacts, and the manner in which it is designed and implemented. A political approach may be more appropriate where the technological change impinges on core activities, will be pervasive and cut across departmental boundaries and will have numerous users. However, even in minor applications, the existing power structure will be disturbed in some way by new technology. It also represents a new organizational resource around which ownership' struggles will cluster. In this way, the implementation process will reproduce, but also amplify, existing strains in the organization's political system.

In practice, political activity may well reach its highest throughout implementation as people's fears become realized. This can be a function of people avoiding facing up to the implications of computerization at earlier stages. Also, failure to participate in change will be rational behaviour as Kilmann points out, where the rewards for doing so do not seem commensurate with the efforts necessary, where there is a good chance of feeling manipulated and where the cultural norms of the organization do not encourage trust and openness in interpersonal relations. It also may be a function of the approach to implementation. Historically, IT has been implemented with the minimum of participation, the output of selective and reassuring information, and little regard for the workplace relations implications. Such an approach is marked by highly political activity during implementation and subsequently.

Thus it is crucial to understand a particular organization's political structure and how different types and levels of IT and digitisation relate to political activity. Such understanding is the first step in planning and implementing CRM systems. A political perspective implies the possibility of resistance and the need to gain organizational acceptance for CRM technology. This is where contingency comes in; that is, being prepared to adapt the system to the political circumstances prevailing, while also being willing and able to operate in and change those circumstances. As Markus (1983) put it:

> If the implementor can divorce the need to see a system up and working from the need to achieve a particular result, several degrees of freedom exist.

The Concept of Power

A central concept that needs to be understood when managing change is that of power. Power is inherent in organizational relations. Its exercise both creates and arises from societal and organizational context. Matters such as how labour is divided, how the organization is departmentalized, and how different categories of worker are rewarded are all the products of political activity. In turn, these results give for different people various degrees of control over information, decision-making, resources, punishments and the access of others to these. Power may also arise on an individual basis; for example, in terms of expertise, personal qualities and ability to be liked and persuade others. As a social relation within an organization, power becomes expressed as people pursue aspirations through action to try to achieve outcomes. It is an interdependence relating to how skilfully people mobilize or deploy resources (power bases) and how important and scarce those resources are perceived or experienced to be by the parties in the relationship.

Power implies influence, control over resources and sanction. However, there is power in the threat of sanctions, in the potential of power. As Pettigrew (1985) puts it:

> Control... may not be enough; there is also the issue of skilful use of resources. The most effective strategy may not always be to pull the trigger.

Power is exercised not only by those who are in the dominant coalition but also by, as well as through, lower-level stakeholders in an organization. Participants in a power relationship are rarely on equal terms but always have some influence over each other, because power relationships imply some degree of mutual dependence for all parties. As far as computers are concerned, even low-level operators in computer systems can corrupt data, modify software in unrecognizable ways and damage the system in serious and costly ways.

But as IT has become strategically important to organizations, so they hand over an important power resource to certain individuals and groups, not least IT professionals. This highlights the importance of gaining the acceptance and support of key personnel once IT is up and running. It may also be wise to gain acceptance by those involved at and affected by the introduction stage of a computer project. How can these two objectives be achieved? An important power resource lies in the establishment of the legitimacy of change and subsequent operation. Establishing legitimacy is tied in with politics as the management of meaning. This involves developing amongst employees shared norms and internalized values and beliefs that elicit their co-operation and commitment in system introduction and operation (see the Culture Track above). Given the vulnerability of computer systems to low-level participant activity, it is not surprising to have found hi-tech companies like Microsoft, IBM and Hewlett-Packard developing cultures based on high rewards, attractive personnel policies, encouragement of initiative and pleasant work conditions. In some hi-tech companies, computer technology for home-working and teleworking has developed further this marriage between enhanced business performance through cost reductions, labour flexibility and "putting people first" personnel policies. The development not just of power bases but also of an organizational culture that will support and sustain technological change lies at the heart of a political-cultural contingencies approach to introducing IT-based systems into organizations.

Change Agents

An argument can be made that IT professionals should not be involved where political problems are likely to result; they lack the political skills needed to handle these. A counter argument is that such skills have become an important part of an IT professional's job if a computer application is to be successful. Additionally, IT professionals' interventions into an organization are necessarily political for reasons already advanced. But further, political problems will inevitably develop, given the trepidation and ambivalence generated historically by the IT professionals' specialist culture, the trade language and the mystery of an expertise needed but inaccessible to many organizational members.

In fact, it is a mistake to assume that IT professionals have not had enough power in the past. The problem has more often been too much power applied in ways that distorted and harmed the very implementation they were promoting. The culture of expertise and the identification of IT with "improvement" and "progress" are in fact hard to argue against in organizations. We have found over the years a number of instances where otherwise unpalatable changes in work practices, reward systems and structures were accepted because the otherwise bitter pill of change was often coated in the sugar of "IT progress and investment".

IT professionals and CRM implementors may well exploit this mystique of technology; managers will accept their legitimate claims and hand over responsibility for computerization to IT specialists; the latter can then make policy decisions in management's absence almost without being aware of doing so. The difficult problem over the last decade has been for IT professionals to come to accept how dangerous such a narrow "political" approach can be for the successful implementation of IT-based business projects. At implementation, what becomes a crucial determinant of system success becomes system compatibility with, and its use and acceptance by, the emergent political and cultural structure. IT professionals need to develop wider political skills and sensitivity to promote this outcome. As we shall see in the case studies in Chapters 5 and 6, it is also important than business managers also accept their own responsibilities for effective delivery. All need to ensure that a shadow track is managed so that politics do not become a barrier but a support for IT-based change. How can this be achieved? Figure 2.4 shows the process.

The Power Audit

A first step is analyzing the existing political and cultural system of the organization. This means establishing membership of the dominant coalition and the sources of their influence. It also requires close analysis of lower-level participants, their power bases and the manner in which they, as well as the dominant coalition, are likely to support or resist any level of IT adoption, and how crucial such responses might be to system development and implementation.

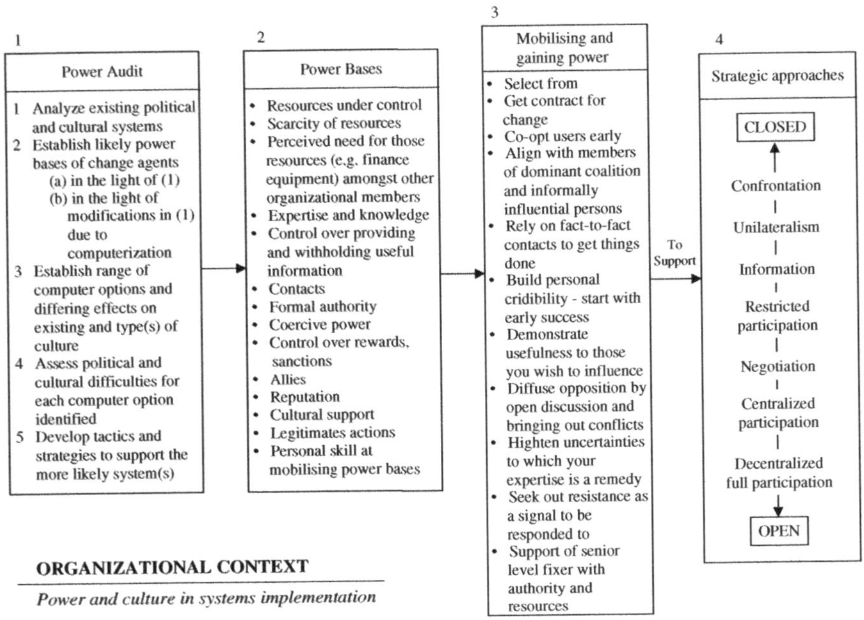

Figure 2.4 *Strategy for Managing the Politics of CRM Systems Implementation*

A second step is establishing the likely power bases of the change agents in the context of the existing political and cultural systems; also, how these power bases can be modified in the course of IT implementation (see Figure 2.4 "Power Bases").

The third step is to establish a range of possible CRM options and their differing effects on the existing distribution of power. More radical shifts in power distribution will require different strategies and alliances, and a much more careful political approach.

The fourth step requires an assessment of the political and cultural problems likely to be engendered in the course of developing and implementing each of the CRM options identified. A preliminary assessment of the political feasibility of each proposed system can then be made.

The fifth step is to develop strategies and tactics to support the more likely systems and make an assessment of how successful differing combinations of systems, tactics and strategies are likely to be.

The power audit assists the change agents in understanding the existing power structure and culture, who is influential, who will resist different types of system, who will be affected in what ways by different proposals, and how different change strategies will be affected when different individuals and groups mobilize their power. It will end with an understanding of the political complexity of computerization but also a clearer idea of the political feasibility of different types of system, design methodology and change approaches.

Mobilizing/Gaining Power

How can influence be managed? Political goals need to be formulated, and an ends-means analysis carried out (i.e. what do we wish to achieve, and how do we go about achieving it?). Targets to be influenced are then identified, and incentives desired by the targets determined. Implementation involves mobilizing these incentives and monitoring the results.

The management of politics and culture must continue throughout the technology project. In organizational settings, a political approach is rarely just a matter of accumulating enough power at the beginning of a project to do what you like thereafter. Various approaches to influencing the process of IT implementation are possible. Keen (1981) suggests that the IT function be headed by a senior-level fixer with resources and authority to negotiate with those affected by any new system. A steering committee including senior-level managers will become actively involved in highly political aspects of the computer project. Under this umbrella, systems staff can establish credibility and influence events tactically:

— Make sure you have a contract for change.
— Seek out resistance and treat it as a signal to be responded to.
— Rely on face-to-face contracts.
— Become an insider and work hard to build personal credibility.
— Co-opt users early.

Other tactics might include presenting a non-threatening image, aligning with powerful others, developing liaisons, developing stature and credibility by attending to a client's immediate needs before gaining approval for a less well understood project, and diffusing opposition by open discussion and bringing out conflicts. In research on internal consultancy by systems analysts, programmers and operations researchers, Pettigrew (1985) found at least five power resources that can be mobilized. A crucial one is expertise. The change agent can increase client dependence by heightening uncertainties to which the application of their expertise would be a remedy. Internal consultant activities across departmental boundaries also gives privileged access to, and so control over, organizational information. Political sensitivity and establishing relations with those with power is also important, as is the gaining of "assessed stature" by identifying and serving the interests of relevant others. Group support by departmental colleagues and related consultant groups is a further power source that could be developed.

Implementation Problems

There are three problem areas in implementation to which this political approach needs to be addressed specifically. One is resistance to change, another is the danger of the change process running out of control, and the third, and related, problem is how to maintain influence over the political dynamics of change. We need to reiterate that CRM systems implementation must be seen in the context of wider objectives than the limited goal of gaining acceptance for a specific system. This implies that system modifications may be necessary in the face of politico-cultural problems. But, anyway, implementation should serve as an important period for learning about system design imperfections at the technical level as well.

Techniques for reducing resistance to change include:

- the need to make visible any organizational dissatisfaction with present systems;
- addressing people's attention to the consequences of not computerizing;
- building in rewards and reasons for people to support the transition and the future system;
- developing an appropriate degree, level and type of participation for different affected parties;
- giving people the opportunity and time to disengage from the present state;
- setting up temporary structures to maintain control over the project in the transition period.

Keen's (1981) recommendations above are relevant here. Also, adequate planning and resources are needed to see the transition through. There is also the need to develop and communicate clear images of the future to organizational members, and establish multiple and consistent leverage points, aimed not just at individuals but also at social relations, task and structural changes. It is also important, as Kilmann suggests above, to build in feedback mechanisms to monitor developments as early as possible.

Keeping power on the side of the CRM project and handling the power dynamics of change is crucial. Here one needs to ensure that leaders and key groups maintain active support for change, that a culture and climate of success is created, but also that enough stability remains, and the pace of change is judged, so that the changes remain acceptable to involved parties. The selection and implementation of a strategic approach is also a crucial aspect.

Strategic Approach

"Contingency" implies retaining a flexible approach to CRM implementation and building in opportunities to modify design where it is seen to be deficient. A contingency approach also means adopting a **change strategy** appropriate to the organizational circumstances in which those responsible for implementation find themselves. As Kilmann suggests, such a strategy involves intervening in the technical, political and cultural systems of the organization at one and the same time.

Change strategies range from being **closed** to **open** (see Figure 2.4). Closed strategies are marked by a minimum of communications and consultation, negligible participation in design and implementation by the vast majority of interested parties, and the development of systems by IT specialists to achieve managerial objectives which tend to be control- and finance-focussed. Closed strategies are linked closely with the introduction of centralized computer systems. Closed strategies are often linked with confrontational industrial relations at implementation, though this is not a necessary relationship, and depends on the power realities pertaining. Often these mean that little confrontation is necessary and the system is introduced unilaterally by systems professionals and management. This may be a sensible approach where the system is technically sound, and designed to minimize dependence on user skills and co-operation, or where organizational culture supports authoritarian management styles. Kilmann points out that in these circumstances, the approach he advocates is inappropriate; it just would not work. Most organizational members would not support the proposed changes voluntarily.

By 2006 such closed strategies would be less appropriate for many IT-based business projects, including CRM projects such as the ones we studied stretching from 1999 to 2005. More open strategies stress participative design, communications, consultation, and willingness to modify technical systems, job design and work organization in the face of user feedback. Open strategies tend to be associated with negotiated change by agreement and consultative machinery in the formal industrial relations sphere. Clearly, one best change strategy for all circumstances cannot be advocated. Open strategies are more relevant where there is underlying support for the aims of the project, where there is a large number of affected parties, where there are differing views on how computerization can be achieved, where power to resist introduction is widely distributed, and where user involvement will provide vital information for system development. Closed strategies will tend to be preferred where the benefits of participation are low, where there is widespread agreement and support for computerization, where the promoters of the system are all powerful, or where the level of disagreement and hostility about the system is so high that participation is perceived to serve little purpose.

CONCLUSION

Where dependent on traditional systems design methodologies, IT project management has been technically oriented, with human issues perceived as mainly arising at the implementation stage. Furthermore, implementation itself has often been viewed as a discrete "one-off", late event in a systems project. The failure to consider many human issues as significant until late in the project means that when they emerge there is often a reluctance amongst implementors to adapt, let alone abandon, the computer-based system in which so much time, money and labour has already been invested. People-management as an essential and primary implementation task can then become a self-fulfilling prophecy with a vengeance, with human issues and problems, and lack of user acceptance, persisting throughout the system's subsequent use.

A key task, then is to manage behaviour and politics as intrinsic parts of IT-enabled change from the beginning. Particularly crucial is the management of the politics of computerization. From a project and change management viewpoint, this means ensuring that the system becomes politically acceptable enough to be used effectively, and that a culture exists to sustain its continued use. However, technology will only form part of the overall change process. In this chapter we have located delivery of business and IT strategies in a holistic approach to managing programmed change. However, we need to stress that the principles outlined here would seem to apply to all change projects in contemporary organizations. Politics do breed in times of change. The politics or "shadow" track is planned for and followed, or managers find their way there by chance, unexpectedly, and invariably under less favourable circumstances.

In this chapter we have brought together the learnings from previous studies, including our own, to put forward a prescriptive, holistic view of how CRM systems can be implemented. The objective here has been to lay out what is already known, to provide a heuristic consistent with what follows, but also to set the context for the more in-depth exploratory, new work that needs to be done in this area, which is represented in Chapters 3 through to 6. We begin this work in the next chapter by providing a detailed review of the literatures that can be drawn upon for studying CRM implementation in a more in-depth, more organizationally, socially, personally and knowledge orientated manner than previously attempted.

3
CRM Implementation: The Neglected Roles of Culture, Knowledge and Psychological Contracts

INTRODUCTION

This chapter aims to discuss and analyze critically the existing academic understanding of IT systems implementation processes and their role and impact in organizational cultures. There are five research themes that can usefully be brought together to provide a lens for analyzing our CRM case histories, and indeed CRM generally. These themes are: IT implementation, organizational cultures and sub-cultures, knowledge and knowledge sharing, psychological contracts, and Customer Relationship Management (CRM) systems. This chapter will consider and critique each in turn.

Our review will use Pettigrew's (1985, 1990) framework as the basis for analyzing existing implementation theories, and linking them with organizational culture, knowledge management and psychological contracts as key, neglected ingredients in an organization's internal context (Pettigrew, 1985, 1990, 1997). We identify key sub-cultures and will discuss subculture gaps from a knowledge management perspective. We also assess the roles of knowledge, and knowledge transfer across key sub-cultures. This involves also pinpointing knowledge sharing aids/barriers across key sub-cultures and the impact of these aids/barriers upon implementation. Also the impact of psychological contracts and subculture interactions on knowledge sharing in the implementation. A CRM environment maps well on to the investigation of knowledge sharing issues. This is because it is so dependent on the transfer of knowledge from the back to the front-office, which is essential in giving a good service to the external customers and achieving successful resolutions of customer queries. An investigation of psychological contracts and their interdependencies with subculture interaction and knowledge sharing will enhance our understanding of the successes and failures of customer queries, as just one example.

In referring to Figure 3.1 readers will note the absence of the work of Hofstede, amongst others. We felt that using scholars such as Geert Hofstede with their linkages with cultural studies will expand the culture part of our literature in less fruitful directions, and do injustice to the knowledge part. Sometimes Hofstede claims to have identified differences between national cultures and sometimes claims that he has identified those cultures. The focus of his analysis of the IBM questionnaire data is on differences. But relying on that analysis he often refers to absolute and not comparative characteristics of specific national cultures. We also think that the cultural dimensions as suggested by Hofstede deliver a rather ambiguous message regarding culture, and may not suit our study which intends to place its emphasis on knowledge sharing issues. We have used Schein, however, who has elaborated on Hofstede's work and suits this study with its linkages with knowledge sharing.

Knowledge sharing phenomena across the subcultural boundaries in a CRM system are highly dependent on understanding previous implementation theories and their linkages with culture and knowledge. We are reviewing the five areas as mentioned earlier in our literature in order to probe more deeply into the knowledge sharing issues by using Pettigrew's framework. These areas allow us to make the linkage between subculture interaction and knowledge sharing in a CRM environment. By choosing the specific literature areas we also attempt to show that CRM is just another IS system. Previous IS literature can be highly important in understanding knowledge issues in the implementation of a CRM. We also attempt to integrate the psychological contracts literature with that of IS implementation in providing a multidisciplinary lens to probe the knowledge sharing phenomena at a micro level.

The themes emerging as a result of the review will be used to construct an analytic framework. The analytical framework was used to guide the data collection and analysis in a pilot study as part of our processual analysis (Pettigrew, 1997), as will emerge in Chapter 4. The results of this analysis were then used to revise and expand the framework to better reflect the pilot results. The revised framework and the refined research questions were then used as the basis for further empirical work as detailed in Chapters 5 and 6.

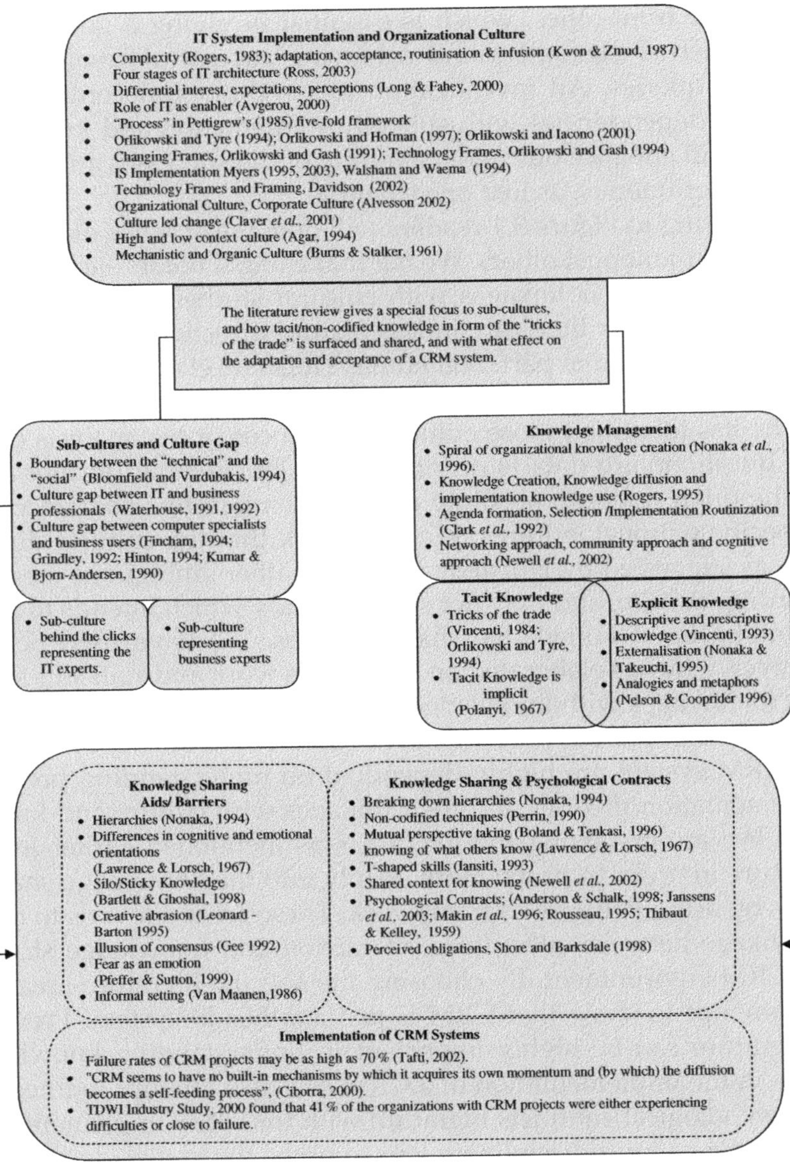

Figure 3.1 Summary of the literature review

IT SYSTEMS IMPLEMENTATION AND ORGANIZATIONAL CULTURE

In Figure 3.1 we provide a summary of the literature reviewed in this Chapter, and highlight the five areas studied. At the top is IS implementation and its linkages with culture. Further down on the left-hand side we place the literature on subcultures and subculture gaps. Moving across right is the knowledge management section. This is also where we make the link between knowledge sharing, subcultures and psychological contracts. Finally we make the linkage between knowledge sharing, subcultures and psychological contracts within CRM systems. In this section we begin the discussion and critique of the five literatures.

IS Implementation

The introduction of information and communication technologies clearly impacts on organizational behaviour, and consequently culture. It affects the whole cultural web of an organization, reshaping, reinforcing and transforming it accordingly (Claver *et al.*, 2001). Information systems (IS—business applications), along with supporting information technology (IT—supply of technologies), continue to have large and rising operational impacts in all organizations. As organizations work to develop and apply IT in new ways, the need to identify and implement an IS strategic plan becomes increasingly critical. To date, however, implementations of IT systems have had mixed success rates, our own end-of-millenium study for example finding 26 % of projects producing very disappointing results, while 5 % were complete failures. (Willcocks & Graeser, 2001; Willcocks *et al.*, 2003).

Rogers (1995) has synthesized over 1,500 studies into a theory of innovation diffusion. According to him, diffusion is a process by which an innovation is communicated through certain channels over time among the members of a social system. He further identified five conceptual characteristics of innovations that help explain differences in adoption rates: relative advantage, compatibility, complexity, trialability and observability. Rogers recognizes that diffusion is strongly related to time. The research literature supports strongly the first three conceptual characteristics as major determinants of success or failure of IS (information systems) defined typically in terms of IS usage and/or user satisfaction with the system (Cooper & Zmud, 1990; Kwon & Zmud, 1987; Tornatzky & Klein, 1982). A stage model is developed by Kwon and Zmud (1987) into six stages: initiation, decision, adaptation, acceptance, routinization and infusion, thus recognizing that diffusion is a process that will evolve and materialize gradually. The focus of this research is more on adaptation and acceptance and knowledge sharing issues during these two phases in the implementation of a CRM system. A close understanding of the process of adaptation is critical for several reasons. First, users' adaptation to technologies in use often help to shape further development and research activities (Dutton & Thomas, 1985). Second, the operating efficiency ultimately achieved with a new technology depends heavily on users' modifications (Dutton & Thomas, 1984; Markus, 2004). Third, modifications affect the technology in use and its physical and organizational context (Leonard-Barton, 1988). Davis (1989) argues that perceived usefulness is a strong correlate of user acceptance. Thus an adaptation and acceptance phase provides an interesting opportunity to investigate not only how a CRM system has been adapted by its stakeholders, but also how the system is being evolved over time as the users find new ways and uses of working with the system after the closure of the "window of opportunity" (Orlikowski and Iacono, 2001; Orlikowski & Tyre, 1994). Cross communication concerning new uses and ways of working may improve the evolving dynamics of the system. This research attempts to investigate the "complexity" from an implementation perspective that is the degree to which a CRM system implementation is perceived as difficult to understand. Different sub-cultures may not be able to communicate with each other if the implementation is not communicated and understood. Examining this communication from a knowledge management perspective can potentially help to assess the knowledge sharing barriers that inhibit the sharing of knowledge across the sub-cultures and thus delay a successful implementation of a technical innovation.

Davidson (2002) argues how frames (frames are cognitive structures or mental models that are held by individuals) and shifts in frame salience influence sense-making during requirement determination. Their study helps to understand how interpretive power is exercised in an IS project. Moving on from frames to shared frames, Orlikowski and Gash (1994), state that concept of shared frames is closely related to that of sub-cultures. Individuals—drawing on their shared frames—engage in symbolic action and thereby construct a social reality that reflects their common assumptions, beliefs and understandings and that includes particular rules, rituals and customary practice. According to Geertz (1973) and Van Maanen and Barley (1985) sub-cultures rely heavily on cognitive elements such as common frames of reference. Innovation diffusion theory recognises that while the technical attributes of innovation per se may not be significant, perceptions of technology do matter and are important factors influencing technology adoption.

Pre-existing structures and cultures (internal context) may shape differing stakeholder perceptions regarding the new systems and its implementation and performance ("Process" and "Outcome", Pettigrew, 1997). The perception of different stakeholders and its linkages with knowledge sharing in the implementation process is an important factor, and needs to be analyzed critically. This analysis will be in terms of differential interests, expectations and power (Long and Fahey, 2000). This will give a clearer picture of IT—Human interaction. According to Orlikowski and Gash (1994) to interact with technology, people have to make sense of it; and in this sense-making process, they develop particular assumptions, expectations, and knowledge of the technology, which then serve to shape subsequent actions toward it. While these interpretations become taken-for-granted and are rarely brought to the surface and reflected on, they nevertheless remain significant in influencing how actors in organizations think about and act toward technology. Furthermore, Walsham (1993) confirms that contextual conditions of history and different stakeholder perspectives create the conditions for conflict at the level of process in Pettigrew's (1985) five-fold framework.

This research attempts to investigate the "how" of CRM development, implementation and usage focussing on the "Process" in Pettigrew's (1985) five-fold framework from a knowledge management perspective. The focus is narrowed down to the implementation process and the factors that enable and inhibit a successful rollout of a CRM system. According to Willcocks and Margetts (1994) the "Process" in Pettigrew's framework adopted for risk analysis for IS contains the following:

- User commitment;
- User training and experience;
- Project time;
- Project team experience;
- Staff stability;
- Project management;
- Management support.

What they do not discuss in particular is the knowledge possessed by individuals involved in the process. Furthermore the backgrounds of such individuals are worth investigating. The individuals for example in a project team may come from diverse sub-cultures. Understanding the aids/barriers to knowledge sharing across these sub-cultures may improve the communication and enable process stability. These ideas are represented in Figure 3.1.

Organizational Cultures

Claver *et al.* (2001) argue that organizational culture works as a "glue" in the organization and cannot be ignored while formulating a strategy. They also identify a relationship between information systems and organizational culture. The authors analyze the information system and organizational culture as two closely related issues in any firm. The organizations with a mechanistic culture (Burns & Stalker, 1961) tend to standardize the system implementation compared with the organizations with an organic culture, where the implementation process for an IT system is more culture led. Claver *et al.* (2001) also underline the cultural consistency which the implementation of an IS requires. They conclude by claiming what many others have frequently found—that IT systems are implemented following technical analysis and considerations, with little if any regard for business needs. However, if the corporate culture of a company is dominated by business experts with limited knowledge regarding IT the reverse can happen. The business experts may implement a new system without understanding the implications of the implementation process. El Sawy (1985) argues that if IT specialists are members of a corporation or are directly related to it, they are part of an organizational culture and none of them should be excluded from an analysis of organizational behaviour in the face of IT.

Avison and Myers (1995) emphasize the potential role of anthropology as a source discipline for information systems. Although anthropology has been largely neglected in the IS research literature, it is argued that important insights can be gained by adopting an anthropological perspective on information systems phenomena. They illustrate the value of an anthropological perspective by looking at the relationship between information technology and organizational culture. Avison and Myers (1995) stress the fact that the concept of culture has generally been used rather narrowly in the IS literature, and argue that a more critical, anthropological view of the relationship between IT and organizational culture is required. The importance of a relationship between the organizational culture and IT is recognized and the facts regarding culture being a complex issue are argued. However, Avison and Myers (1995) do not explore the area of how the IT implementation affects the complexity of subculture interactions in an organization from a knowledge management perspective.

Claver *et al.* (2001) puts emphasis on organizational culture laying down the guidelines for the acquisition of IT and its later development into an information system. Pliskin *et al.* (1993) point out that the same information system may have a different meaning for different people, such as system analysts and users, who may not have the same points of view concerning the system. The question is, how does IT implementation relate to the complexity of a culture in an organization? Do the sub-cultures at different stages of the implementation process inhibit or enable the process of implementation? Examining the implementation process from a different angle that is from an IT perspective, the view of Boland *et al.* (1994) is justified due to the specific weight IT/IS is progressively gaining in all business areas. Due to its dynamic speedy impact, IT/IS will create a shared, common vision, which will become a cultural value. There are, however, no clear guidelines other than that the organizational culture needs to be considered before implementing an IT system. Although there is a link made between the IT and organizational culture in the research, the proposition driving the research represented in this book is that it would be necessary to explore the impact of IT systems on the organizational culture, and in particular from a knowledge management perspective.

Mintzberg (1987), and Orlikowski and Hofman (1997), suggest that people talk about strategies in one way, that is as a plan with fixed steps to achieve a known goal, while implementing them in another, more ad hoc way, to accommodate unforeseen circumstances. The question raised is "What makes the process of implementation change its course and move away from the original plan" Avgerou (2000) challenges the tendency of the Information Systems literature to subsume IT innovation in processes of organizational change, either with the role of "enabler" of organizational objectives, or as an instrument appropriated by situated organizational actors. Avgerou (2000) further argues that Information system development is incremental and cumulative, gradually transforming the landscape of the workplace and the nature of the work itself. This means that potentially the IT development and implementation process has cultural effects that can enable or inhibit IT effectiveness.

SUB-CULTURES AND SUB-CULTURE GAPS

Organizational sub-cultures may be defined as distinct clusters of understandings, behaviours, and cultural forms that identify groups of people on different levels of hierarchies in the organization. They can be occupational and differ noticeably from the common organizational culture in which they are embedded, either intensifying its understandings and practices or deviating from them (Trice & Morand, 1991). Louis (1985) argues that the sub-cultures are the set of understandings or meanings shared by a group of people. The meanings are largely tacit among members, are clearly relevant to a particular group, and are distinctive to the group. Sub-cultures can be loosely coupled with each other, sometimes cooperating and sometimes acting on basis of conflicting interests.

Bloomfield and Vurdubaki (1994) highlight the problematic nature of the boundary between the "technical" and the "social" and its consequences in respect of understanding the relationship between technological and organizational change. The power shown by the technical experts needs to be balanced by bringing in the social part of the organization. The authors pick a very sensitive area of research to explore; they have highlighted the need for participation. However, they do not explore in depth the perceptions of the actors (social and technical) regarding implementation of an IT system. The boundary itself can act as a gap between the different sub-cultures during the implementation process. The surveys done by Price Waterhouse (1991, 1992) stated that 47% of the IT directors in UK see that their main problem is the culture gap existing between IT and business professionals. Furthermore, 56% of IT directors believed that the culture gap is losing or seriously delaying IT opportunities for their company to gain competitive advantage.

In addition, several authors have discussed the culture gap between systems analysts and computer specialists charged with information systems implementation and business users (Fincham, 1994; Grindley, 1992; Hinton, 1994; Kumar & Bjorn-Andersen, 1990). In an overview of the literature Willcocks *et al.*, (2003) corroborate the persistence of these types of culture gaps into the new century (see also Figure 3.1, for an overview). Boland and Tenkasi (1996) argue that, in order to develop new products, the separate domains must interact and learn from each other in ways that will yield new insights into a problem and new ideas for the successful production of improved products. There have been various attempts made to improve the communication and participation between the sub-cultures to enable a successful implementation of an IT system. Among these are: Systems Development Life Cycles (SDLC) in which well defined phases of development provide bases for management control (Davis & Olson, 1985); Mumford *et al.* (1978) with their concept of user participation; Social Technical System (STS) by Bostrom and Heinen (1997); Soft System Methodology (SSM) (Checkland, 1981); and Joint Application Design (JAD) by IBM (1977). These studies show that the need for improving the communication between the sub-cultures is vital. These attempts so far, however, have not investigated in depth the subculture interactions at a micro level and the resulting distinctive perspective on knowledge sharing in the implementation process that might result.

The knowledge pervading sub-cultures can be vital for a successful implementation of a CRM (Customer Relationship Management) system. Knowledge sharing is a key factor in the implementation process. To understand the impact of knowledge sharing upon the implementation process of a CRM system, we need to examine the modes of interaction between sub-cultures. Strong hierarchical enterprises prevent smooth cross-functional communication and consequently inhibit cross-functional cooperation or knowledge sharing. Breaking down hierarchies can enable knowledge sharing (Nonaka, 1994). Organizations that maintain hierarchical levels and silos will not encourage it. Knowledge in such organizations frequently becomes "sticky" that is, residing in one area or silo and not easily moved to the other parts of the organization (Bartlett & Ghoshal, 1998). The non-codified techniques play an important role in industrial production and in technical and technological innovation (Perrin, 1990).

KNOWLEDGE MANAGEMENT/KNOWLEDGE SHARING

Having identified the importance of understanding knowledge, its sharing and the degree to which knowledge can be managed, it is useful to look at the literature on types of knowledge. It is also important to identify the elements that facilitate/inhibit the sharing of knowledge across various sub-cultures in an organization. But first of all let us attempt to define what knowledge actually is, and how it is different from data, information, knowledge, understanding and, an even less clear concept, wisdom. Ackoff (1989) states that the first four categories relate to the past; they deal with what has been or what is known. According to Ackoff, only the fifth category, wisdom, deals with the future because it incorporates vision and design. With wisdom, people can create the future rather than just grasp the present and past. But achieving wisdom is not easy, it is suggested; people must move successively through the other categories.

Data according to Ackoff (1989) is raw. It simply exists and has no significance beyond its existence (in and of itself). It can exist in any form, usable or not. It does not have meaning of itself. In computer parlance, a spreadsheet generally starts out by holding data. Information is data that has been given meaning by way of relational connection. This "meaning" can be useful, but does not have to be. In computer parlance, a relational database makes information from the data stored within it. A shorthand description for present purposes would be that data is a record, while information uses data to give a message.

Knowledge according to Ackoff (1989) is the appropriate collection of information, such that its intent is to be useful. Knowledge is a deterministic process. When someone "memorizes" information (as less-aspiring test-bound students often do), then they have amassed knowledge. This knowledge has useful meaning to them, but it does not provide for, in and of itself, integration such as would infer further knowledge. For example, elementary school children memorize, or amass knowledge of, the "times table". They can tell you that "$2 \times 2 = 4$" because they have amassed that knowledge (it being included in the times table). But when asked what is "1267×300", they can not respond correctly because that entry is not in their times table. To answer correctly such a question requires a true cognitive and analytical ability that is only encompassed in the next level... understanding. In computer parlance, most of the applications we use (modelling, simulation, etc.) exercise some type of stored knowledge. Our shorthand for knowledge is that it is a more, or less, useful model of how the world works. Following Polanyi (1966), knowledge invariably has a non-reducible, personal tacit element.

Understanding is an interpolative and probabilistic process. It is cognitive and analytical. It is the process by which I can take knowledge and synthesize new knowledge from the previously held knowledge. The difference between understanding and knowledge is the difference between "learning" and "memorizing". People who have understanding can undertake useful actions because they can synthesize new knowledge, or in some cases, at least new information, from what is previously known (and understood). That is, understanding can build upon currently held information, knowledge and understanding itself. In computer parlance, integration systems possess understanding in the sense that they are able to synthesize new knowledge from previously stored information and knowledge.

Wisdom according to Ackoff (1989) is an extrapolative and non-deterministic, non-probabilistic process. It calls upon all the previous levels of consciousness, and specifically upon special types of human programming (moral, ethical codes, etc.). It beckons us towards gaining understanding about that of which there has previously been no understanding, and in doing so, goes far beyond understanding itself. It is the essence of philosophical probing. Unlike the previous four levels, it asks questions to which there is no (easily-achievable) answer, and in some cases, to which there can be no humanly-known answers. Wisdom is therefore, the process by which we also discern, or judge, between right and wrong, good and bad. Computers do not have, and may never have the ability to possess wisdom. Wisdom is a uniquely human state. Wisdom has also been characterized as the result of learning and using knowledge for a strategic advantage. (To some extent one can see linkages here with the concepts, as we use them, of "tricks of the trade", special know how and personal knowledge). After gaining knowledge, wisdom is used to meet new situations. Wisdom is tacit and resides in the minds of the users ("embrained" as put by Thompson and Walsham, 2004). As Churchman (1982) put it in "Thought and Wisdom", "Wisdom is thought combined with a concern for ethics". These ideas are particularly difficult to ground let alone study, and in this research we tend not to use the category wisdom, finding the vocabulary around concepts like personal knowledge, tacit knowledge, tricks of the trade and know-how sufficient for our needs.

Technological Knowledge

Technology knowledge is specific knowledge needed to produce a product for a market (Vincenti, 1984, 1993). Vincenti (1993) further divides technological knowledge into three categories; descriptive, prescriptive, and tacit/non-codified. Both descriptive and prescriptive knowledge are explicit/codified knowledge. Descriptive knowledge describes things as they are in reality, whereas prescriptive knowledge prescribes what is to be done in order to reach a desired result. Tacit/non-codified knowledge is implicit in human activity.

Descriptive Knowledge

Descriptive knowledge implies factual statements about such matters as material properties, technical information, and tool characteristics. Descriptive knowledge is in close proximity to explicit/codified knowledge since it describes things as they are; it can be in the form of rules, abstract concepts and general principles, and it often has a consistent and generalizable structure (Herschbach, 1995; Nonaka *et al.*, 1996; Vincenti, 1993).

Prescriptive Knowledge

Prescriptive knowledge is based on efforts to gain a greater effectiveness, such as improved operations (Vincenti, 1993). The basis of prescriptive knowledge is often the experience obtained through trial and error. Because the basis of prescriptive knowledge consists of less scientific principles, and because it is an outgrowth of specific application, it is not easily codified in a general form. "The easier knowledge is codified, the easier it can be transmitted", argues Perrin (1990).

Tacit/Non-codified Knowledge

Tacit/non-codified or what Polanyi calls personal, knowledge is implicit and is largely the outcome of exercising individual judgment, skill and practice (Polanyi, 1966). A large part of tacit/non-codified knowledge cannot be transmitted through written or oral form. It is personal knowledge, it is subjective knowledge, and it is immediate and specific knowledge. Tacit/non-codified knowledge often constitutes the "tricks of the trade" experienced workers learn, and it is often protected or restricted knowledge (Orlikowski and Tyre, 1994; Vincenti, 1984). Specialists simply do not, and often cannot, reveal all they know. Tacit/non-codified knowledge and prescriptive knowledge are closely related in practice since both deal with procedures.

Scarbrough and Corbett (1992) note that many of the crucial, incremental improvements in process technology, for instance, occur on the shop-floor. Specialists, however, simply do not reveal all that they know. Tacit/non-codified knowledge is primarily transmitted and learned by working side by side with the experienced technician or craftsman (Herschbach, 1995). Tacit/non-codified knowledge consists of the hands-on skills, best practices, special know-how, heuristic intuitions, and so on. Tacit/non-codified knowledge is personal knowledge that is hard to formalize or articulate (Polanyi, 1958, 1973).

Tacit/non-codified knowledge cannot easily be expressed formally. Descriptions, diagrams, and metaphors help to explain tacit knowledge. Tacit knowledge results largely from an individual's experiences. Tacit knowledge is embedded in technological activity to a greater extent than is normally recognized (Herschbach, 1995). In addition, tacit/non-codified knowledge has not disappeared with the use of more sophisticated ways of manufacturing based on the application of science and descriptive knowledge. "On the contrary, new forms of know-how have appeared and all these non-codified techniques play an important role both in industrial production and in technical and technological innovation" (Perrin, 1990). Polanyi (1966) has demonstrated that all human action involves some form of tacit/non-codified knowledge (Nonaka and Takeuchi, 1995).

The distinction between tacit/non-codified knowledge and explicit/codified knowledge is not, however, clear but problematic. Polanyi (1966) has pointed out that, "These two are not sharply divided. While tacit/non-codified knowledge can be possessed by itself, explicit/codified knowledge must rely on being tacit/non-codifiedly understood and applied. Hence all knowledge is either tacit/non-codified or rooted in tacit/non-codified knowledge." The knowledge management literature often postulates that tacit/non-codified knowledge is the opposite of explicit/codified knowledge (Choi & Lee, 1997). Nonaka and Takeuchi (1995) define explicit/codified knowledge or codified knowledge as knowledge that can be articulated and in formal language including grammatical statements, mathematical expressions, specifications, and manuals. Such explicit/codified knowledge, they conclude, can be transmitted easily and formally between individuals. Choo (1998) suggests that explicit/codified knowledge is knowledge that is made manifest through language, symbols, objects, and artefacts. According to Choo, tacit knowledge can also be shared through analogies, metaphors, models, and stories (Choo, 1998). However, in line with Polanyi's (1966) work, we assume that all kind of knowledge includes a tacit/non-codified dimension. Between the two poles, knowledge is partly explicit, or articulated, and partly tacit/non-codified. Hence, applying explicit/codified knowledge requires mastery of the associated tacit/non-codified knowledge.

Knowledge Sharing Aids/Barriers

The research on social information processing (Salancik & Pfeffer, 1978), power (Pettigrew, 1973; Pfeffer, 1980), specialization (Burns & Stalker, 1961; Daft & Lengel 1986; Lawrence & Lorsch, 1967), and organizational cultures (Gregory, 1983; Pettigrew, 1979, Riley, 1983; Schein, 1985; Strauss, 1978) further suggests that people tend to share assumptions, knowledge and expectations with others with whom they have close working relationships. Similarly, social interaction and negotiation over time create opportunities for the development and exchange of similar points of view (Brown and Diguid, 1998; Gray *et al.*, 1985; Isabella, 1990).

According to Nonaka (1994) knowledge intensive firms, competitive advantage and product success are a result of collaborative, ongoing learning. Success depends not only on how effective the diverse individuals are able to organize and develop their unique knowledge competencies but also how they can integrate and utilize their distinctive knowledge both effectively and synergistically (Nonaka, 1994). The synergy can be obtained if the aids/barriers to the knowledge sharing across the sub-cultures are understood. According to Boland and Tenkasi (1996) it requires a process of "mutual perspective taking" where distinctive individual knowledge is exchanged, evaluated and integrated with that of the others in the organization. In essence, developing a comprehensive knowledge base amongst a community of highly differentiated yet reciprocally dependent individual specialists requires an ongoing process of "mutual perspective taking" where individual knowledge and theories of meaning are surfaced, reflected on, exchanged, evaluated and integrated with others in the organization. Much of social behaviour is predicated on assumptions an actor makes about the knowledge, beliefs and motives of others. This is the beginning of the process of perspective taking, and is fundamental to communication. The mechanisms of a perspective taking process are quite complex. The existing theories do not explore fully the mechanisms at a micro level.

In any communication, the "knowing of what others know" is a necessary component for co-ordinated action to take place (Bakhtin, 1981; Krauss & Fussell, 1991; Mead, 1934). The mechanisms proposed by Lawrence and Lorsch (1967) to enable the "knowing of what others know" were predominantly structural in nature (liaisons, project teams, matrices, etc). They were rational devices for enriching the interdepartmental communication of the organization through better management of the channels of communication, and that generally glossed over the problem of human meaning and interpretation. According to Lawrence and Lorsch (1967) the particularities of the environment, task and technologies faced by an organization's sub-cultures are associated with differences in cognitive and emotional orientations among individuals in these sub-cultures.

Meyer and Rowan (1977) argue that sub-cultures at the periphery of an organization may not share information fully with sub-cultures at its technical core. Barriers to knowledge sharing can make the implementation process for a CRM (Customer Relationship Management) system time consuming and eventually unsuccessful. The four stages of Nonaka and Takeuchi (1995)—socialization, externalization, combination and internalization—would take a long time and at times will never happen. If tacit/non-codified knowledge is viewed, as Polanyi (1958) proposes, as highly individual and achievable only through personal experience, diffusion seems to be impossible. Other researchers propose a more positive attitude to diffusion of tacit/non-codified knowledge. Irrespective of the opinion of means of knowledge diffusion researchers consent in that there are difficulties in sharing tacit/non-codified knowledge (Nonaka & Kono, 1998). Here again a case is made for further investigation regarding the tacit/non-codified knowledge, how it is surfaced and shared across sub-cultures and with what effect. The sub-cultures interacting face to face will tend to generate a conflict of ideas. According to Leonard-Barton (1995) this creative abrasion can positively influence the performance. Interaction between the sub-cultures must happen over a prolonged period (Newell *et al.*, 2002). This interaction over a prolonged period may help to develop cross cultural knowledge, which Iansiti (1993) calls T-shaped skills. This is to say that individuals possess a depth in their own skills combined with a breadth of understanding of other sub-cultures. Wathne *et al.* (1996) argues that factors such as accuracy, timeliness, adequacy and credibility of interactions influence perceptions of honesty and openness, and are essential to achieving more frequent and relevant knowledge sharing between the partners.

Krogh *et al.* (2000) describe how effective knowledge creation depends on the physical, virtual and emotional context of an organization. They discuss the importance of the notion of reciprocity of relationships. When a relationship is felt to be reciprocal then a trust develops which can work to overcome power-based relationships. It can be that the inability of an individual to deal with a new situation, new event, new context or new information is an obstacle to knowledge creation. The authors conclude that an organization must actively pursue the work context as a learning organization where the individuals of that organization are attuned to learning new things. Learning implies encountering and assimilating new facts.

Differing cultures within an organization also affect the efficient sharing of knowledge. These cultures can arise from different educational backgrounds, differential interests, perceptions, expectations and power (Long & Fahey, 2000). The investigation of differential interests, expectations, perceptions and power in a CRM setting from a knowledge sharing perspective thus becomes vital. Newell *et al.* (2002) further argue that attempts to manage knowledge work, especially where the objective is knowledge sharing, need to focus not just on transferring knowledge about facts and things but also creating a "shared context for knowing". A mutual understanding in form of shared mental space, shared experiences, emotions and ideas will be the ultimate outcome of such a prolonged interaction between the sub-cultures. However prolonged interaction in a formal setting may not result in a free sharing of knowledge across the sub-cultures (Kunda, 1991). Also unless they are questioned critically and their individual theories of meaning are exposed, people from different backgrounds subject to normal discourse agree unproblematically at the level of words and truly believe that they are indicating the same referent domain of meaning giving rise to an illusion of consensus (Gee, 1992).

People can participate in an illusion of consensus over mutual contradictory theories of meaning unless they are engaged in an experience that requires them to reveal their unique theories of meaning. This false consensus effect, in which people assume that others are more similar to themselves than is actually the case, is a form of bias (Ross *et al.*, 1977). This can happen especially in situations where job security is low, knowledge as a power becomes vital for the individuals and knowledge might be seen as a kind of insurance against losing the job (Davenport *et al.*, 1998). People, who are able to control relevant resources, and thereby increase others' dependence on them, are able to achieve the outcomes they desire (Salancik & Pfeffer, 1978). This requires that an actor seeking power must decrease his or her dependence on others. Pfeffer and Sutton (1999) discuss fear as an emotion that prevents organizations acting on knowledge. This fear can inhibit the sharing of tacit/non-codified knowledge, which exists in the form of the "tricks of the trade", short-cuts, heuristic intuition and special know how across the sub-cultures of the implementation process of a CRM system.

KNOWLEDGE SHARING AND PSYCHOLOGICAL CONTRACTS

Some scholars (Anderson & Schalk, 1998; Makin *et al.*, 1996; Rousseau, 1995; Shore & Barksdale, 1998; Thibaut & Kelley, 1959) argue that psychological contracts play an important role in the outcome of interaction between individuals. According to Rousseau (1995), a psychological contract is an unwritten set of expectations between everyone in an organization and, unlike the written contract, is constantly changing. Shore and Barksdale (1998) consider psychological contracts to be balanced if the perceived obligations of the employee and the employer are at the same level. They define the level of obligation as the extent to which the employee and employer feel obligated to fulfil a particular term of contract. The extent to which an employee and employer feel obligated to one another takes place as follows: mutual high-obligations, mutual low-obligations, employee over-obligation, and employee under-obligation (Shore & Barksdale, 1998).

In the case of "mutual high-obligations", the psychological contract is balanced as both parties have high obligations to each other. According to Shore and Barksdale (1998), this type of psychological contract obtains the best results in terms of the employees' affective involvement. It also obtains the best results in terms of their intention to stay or leave their perception of their future within the organization and the perceived support that they receive from the organization. In contrast, a psychological contract of mutual low obligations is again characterized by balance but with both parties having low obligations. As a result of the low perceived employee obligations, Shore and Barksdale (1998) argue that this type of psychological contract secures poorer results for the organization than the previous type. On the other hand employee over-obligation and employee under-obligation are not balanced. In the case of the last type of psychological contract, the lack of balance and low employee obligations is expected to attain the poorest results.

Whilst studying a variety of psychological contracts, Janssens *et al.* (2003) used a feature-oriented approach across a large, representative sample that covered different hierarchical layers and relevant professional categories. Six different clusters were found: loyal, instrumental, weak, unattached, investing and strong. These were discovered to have different patterns of employer and employee obligations, a different profile and different levels of affective commitment and employability. According to Janssens *et al.* (2003), when investigating the employer obligation of long-term involvement and the employee obligations of personal investment, it was found that flexibility and loyalty are related to high affective commitment. Affective commitment was mainly found in the clusters of strong, investing and loyal psychological contracts. This study, however, does not explore a relationship between the types of psychological contracts and the knowledge sharing.

There are individual and group dimensions to the psychological contract. Rousseau (1995) identifies four types of contract an individual may engage in: two are focused on the individual (psychological and implied) and two are group-related (normative and social). Group-related contracts may be seen as manifestations of the organizational culture (normative contract) and the wider environmental culture (social contract) or context in which the employee was brought up and currently lives. An Individual contract is based on beliefs relating to promises made and accepted, and relies on third party interpretation, for example perception of a potential employee. A Shared contract is dependent on a group's shared culture that has evolved from common beliefs (Rousseau, 1995). To date few links have been established between non-codified knowledge sharing and psychological contracts. Investigation of tacit knowledge sharing across the subculture and their linkages with psychological contracts thus becomes important.

Different scholars talk about "knowing of what others know" (Lawrence & Lorsch, 1967), "mutual perspective taking" (Boland & Tenkasi, 1996), "shared mental space" (Newell *et al.* (2002), and "T-shaped skills" (Iansiti, 1993) as aids to tacit/non-codified knowledge sharing. However they do not address the micro processes that lead to the above. This research aims to fill this knowledge gap by investigating the micro elements for example different types of psychological contracts and their linkage with knowledge sharing across the key sub-cultures with resulting affects on the adaptation of CRM systems and their acceptance.

Fear as an emotion is closely linked with the kind of psychological contract that exists between the two sub-cultures. Rousseau (1995) asserts that mutuality is the key for a psychological contract to provide acceptable outcomes—she argues that it is only when both parties have something to gain that they will work to ensure a successful result. However at least part of such a psychological contract will be implicit (Makin *et al.*, 1996), resulting in a lack of clarity for both parties (Anderson & Schalk, 1998). Although each party has a clear and conscious view about the key elements of the exchange they expect (such as reward for achieving goals or the sense of obligation to work late to meet a deadline), other elements will be subconscious and therefore much harder to define (Makin *et al.*, 1996). There are other elements that can be present in a psychological contract, such as selfish motives. In social psychology this phenomenon has been studied in the prisoner's dilemma game, in which the highest outcomes for both participants can be achieved if both cooperate, but a high proportion of participants tend to make selfish choices that lead to lower outcomes for both (Thibaut & Kelley, 1959).

There are further considerations to explore attitudes of conflict avoidance and some conservative habits may also prevent the transfer of knowledge, if this knowledge contains some new thoughts or innovative ideas. If most leading members of an organization are not comfortable with change and not willing to take risks, new ideas may be covered very easily, different views and perspectives would be hidden, and therefore knowledge not culturally legitimated may be suppressed ("don't rock the boat" attitude) (Fahey & Prusak, 1998). This can happen during the implementation process of a CRM system and can inhibit the development of an individual opinion or ideas. Fahey and Prusak (1998) call it one of the eleven deadliest sins of Knowledge Management not to establish, challenge and align a shared context for the members of an organization. This shared context requires engagement in open, honest, supportive, and critical dialogue to develop different and new views. A process of surfacing and examining interpretations can allow the shaking of the background of consensus and open the possibility of mutual interpretation. This can enable the achievement of a new definition of the situation in which all participants can share (Habermas, 1979). An informal setting according to Van Maanen (1986) can help to voice the differences and face the conflicts in a constructive manner.

There is a need for employees to have some self-motivated creativity and some sense of "care-why" (Quinn *et al.*, 1996) in order to foster knowledge sharing. Part of the problem is that typically the benefits of the contribution to a knowledge database are received by a different stakeholder at a later point in time, and not usually by the provider but by his or her colleagues.

Perception and language are considered one of the main difficulties in sharing tacit/non-codified knowledge. Perceptually the characteristic of unconsciousness entails a problem of people not being aware of the full range of their knowledge (Polanyi, 1958). Explicit/codified knowledge is easy to recognize in oneself but the feeling of a missing link or the elements of intuition are harder to pinpoint. This kind of knowledge is so internalized that it has often become a natural part of our behaviour or way of thinking. Just as we do not have to be conscious of our heart beating we do not exert ourselves in reflecting on our tacit/non-codified knowledge.

According to Nelson and Cooprider (1996), difficulties with language lie in the fact that tacit/non-codified knowledge is held in a non-verbal form. To articulate something that seems natural and obvious is hard for most people. More experience and deeper knowledge leads to higher tacit/non-codified knowledge and that leads to greater difficulties in articulating the knowledge. In some companies a certain lack of a legitimate language is perceptible, which is known and acceptable for all involved people and can carry personal knowledge. This covers the need for a common language to communicate knowledge and special language features like analogies and metaphors to externalize tacit/non-codified knowledge hidden in individual mental models, viewpoints, working models, schemata, paradigms and beliefs (Nelson & Cooprider, 1996).

Distance can also raise difficulties in today's work-life. The need for face-to-face interaction is often perceived as a prerequisite for diffusion of tacit/non-codified knowledge. Polanyi (1958) shows other possibilities in an example of learning tacit/non-codified knowledge of chess by studying earlier chess-masters games. In this case the tacit/non-codified knowledge is communicated with the help of an intermediary in material form. But still the most common way of sharing tacit/non-codified knowledge takes place in face-to-face interaction. In these days when organizations tend to disperse into more distant, virtual or global forms, face-to-face interaction becomes more the exception than the rule (Bennett & Gabriel, 1999). The situation can become worse if the staff turnover is high. The rapid changing of stakeholders especially during the implementation process of a CRM system can cause difficulties in the sharing of tacit/non-codified knowledge. Again refer to Figure 3.1 for an overview.

CUSTOMER RELATIONSHIP MANAGEMENT AND INTEGRATION

Finally, we research a specific type of systems implementation, namely Customer Relationship Management, also known as "CRM". Though often presented as a recent phenomenon, in fact CRM systems have evolved gradually over the last decade, though they have only recently received market and research attention as information systems applications. In earlier times one can posit the more frequent situation where merchants knew their customers, including even the members of their households. They knew their daily, even monthly and yearly needs and planned the stock accordingly to meet the demands or more correctly "needs" of their customers. The knowledge of knowing customers and a close interaction with them gave the result of a good relationship and a good relationship resulted in a better understanding of the customers' needs.

Presently, many companies are trying to go back to the basics of such arrangements, in theory at least, believing that IT can facilitate through technology what was previously provided largely by human memory, manual recording and human relationships. However, in reality when people in the industry talk about CRM, they really mean keeping an eye on their customers, extracting their time, information and last but not the least the money from their wallets. This could hardly be called relationship building. According to Bose (2002), CRM requires a certain "leap of faith" by a firm. A survey done by "The Data Warehousing Institute" (TDWI Industry Study, 2000) of more than 1,500 companies found that 41 % of the organizations with CRM projects were either experiencing difficulties or close to failure. The survey further revealed that 91 % either have or plan to deploy a CRM solution in the near future. The survey also reveals that only 22 % of companies have appointed a chief customer officer to facilitate change. Failure rates of CRM projects may be as high as 70 % (Tafti, 2002). Therefore, as we pointed out in the first chapter, implementing CRM effectively can be hard to do.

CRM software attempts to integrate business processes of managing customers onto a single enterprise-wide information system. The major benefits of CRM are improved customer satisfactions and increased efficiencies in customer support. Organizations face many challenges in the overall related ERP (Enterprise Resource Planning) integration—the challenges of integration of various functional CRM modules from the same vendors, the challenge of integration with other e-business software applications, and the challenge of integration with legacy systems. The primary measure of success for ERP/CRM implementation is ERP integration.

Integration of E-Business Applications

E-business is the combination of strategies, technologies and processes to coordinate electronically both internal and external business processes, and manage enterprise-wide resources. For our purposes, the relevant e-business software systems generally fall into four categories: Enterprise Resource Planning (ERP), Customer Relationship Management (CRM), Supply Chain Management (SCM) and Sales Force Automation (SFA). To get the most out of CRM systems, CRM should be tightly integrated with other e-business software—Supply Chain Management, ERP, Sales Force Automation, Business to Business (B2B) exchange and the e-commerce storefront on the Internet.

Integration of CRM Modules

Packaged CRM software consists of many functional modules—pre-sales module, post-sales module, contact module and service module. Organizations tend to install modules from the same CRM vendors in the initial CRM implementation. Not all companies will purchase all CRM modules from a CRM vendor (Siebel, Lagan, SAP, Oracle, PeopleSoft, etc.). The implementation of a CRM project takes a few months to years, depending on size, complexity of organization, the IT inheritance. In the latter phases of CRM implementation, organizations may have to choose modules from different vendors, or a new version of the module from the same vendor.

Integration with Legacy Systems

Legacy systems at many organizations, have accumulated huge amount of data vital to the survival, operations, and expansion of their businesses. Integration of CRM systems with legacy systems is more complex than integration of CRM modules and Integration of E-Business Applications. It routinely requires the installation of third-party interface software for the communication between CRM software systems and legacy systems. Second generation CRM systems use Relational Database Management Systems (RDBMS) to store customer data. Conversion from data in legacy systems to RDBMS is a time-consuming process. Different EAI (Enterprise Application Integration) tools are used to overcome this hurdle. While most interface software provide API (Application Programming Interface) for CRM to access legacy systems, some vendors offer an integration module that automates or accelerates the transformation of legacy application logic and data into reusable components with XML, SOAP, J2EE and .NET interfaces.

A study done by Goodhue *et al.* (2002) found three important CRM targets:

- Applications—Individual applications that deliver business value;
- Infrastructure—A data, software, and hardware infrastructure that supports CRM applications and will also support future applications;
- Transformation—An organization transformation made possible through comprehensive CRM efforts.

In summary, CRM as organizational change, as opposed to a technical implementation, is noticeably understudied, and this presents an overwhelming case for the present research. This research attempts to investigate the implementation process of CRM with a special focus on the "transformation" part. By using the existing theories of IT implementation it attempts to investigate the adaptation and acceptance of the system by its stakeholders. That is, how the stakeholders of the system and the system itself are evolving through finding new uses, workarounds, upgrades, patches, cookies, viruses, and failures in so called societal and organizational transformation processes (Orlikowski & Iacono, 2001). The research will investigate the stakeholder involvement from a B2C perspective. Both the companies chosen for gathering empirical data have a differential customer base. As a result, interaction between the internal customers and external customers will also be different. Investigating the modes of these interactions will give an insight to how tacit/non-codified knowledge is surfaced and shared and with what effect on the implementation of a CRM system.

Both internal and external customers need to be kept in the focus of this study. Most post-mortems of CRM failures trace the problems back to the alignment of incentives and metrics, and the absence of a customer-facing organization. Another pitfall is to concentrate on the customer contact processes without making corresponding changes in internal structures and systems (Digby *et al.*, 2002). This study aims to focus on the process of "adaptation and acceptance" of the system, covering both the internal and external customers as part of the stakeholder analysis. The research in particular, will study the knowledge sharing loop between the front and back-office to identify and investigate the knowledge silos. Sponsorship of CRM, according to Goodhue *et al.* (2002), is initiated by senior management. This research will investigate the involvement of senior management and the grassroots including the external customer from a knowledge sharing perspective.

CONCLUSION: TOWARD A PRELIMINARY FRAMEWORK

This review has focussed on aspects of culture and knowledge in order to analyze critically and more fully than previously attempted the implementation process of CRM systems within a organizations. Themes of stakeholder perception, knowledge sharing, psychological contracts and subculture interactions have emerged, and flagged the importance of stakeholder perceptions.

There is a consensus over the importance of understanding the implementation process. Over the years, several attempts to explore different elements of the implementation process have been made. However, the links between stakeholders' perceptions (based on the differential interests, expectations and power) and knowledge sharing in the implementation process of a CRM system have not really been explored. This research attempts to investigate the "how" of knowledge sharing in CRM implementations.

The studies investigating the implementation process of an IT system are outdated or give only a one sided view at a macro level. This research treats technologies and organizations as mutually dependent and dynamically emergent. There is still much opportunity for the IS (Information Systems) field to move beyond a relatively simple black-boxed view of technology towards more powerful conceptualization of the role of IT artefacts in organizations (Markus & Robey, 1988). Furthermore, Orlikowski and Iacono (2001) after reviewing numerous (N = 188) articles, argue the need to put technology back into the study of information systems. The literature gap regarding the linkage between the existing implementation theories and Customer Relationship Management (CRM) systems from a knowledge management perspective is identified. This research aims to fill the gap by testing the extant knowledge regarding IT implementation, but in a CRM environment.

Different scholars make a case for the importance of culture during the implementation of an IT system. However, not much is said about the culture "behind the clicks" (IT culture). There is a consensus over the culture gap that exists between the IT experts and the users/business experts and is delaying the implementation. Yet there is very little mentioned regarding the knowledge sharing across different sub-cultures and its impact on the adaptation and acceptance of a CRM system. Why the knowledge silos/stickiness exists needs to be investigated further. Some scholars seem to agree over the difficulties of tacit/non-codified knowledge sharing. Despite this, there is a lack of consensus over the methods needed to overcome the inhibitors of tacit/non-codified knowledge sharing.

There is some consensus that informal settings can aid/facilitate the transfer of knowledge across sub-cultures, but much still needs to be investigated over how to attain Boland and Tenkasi's (1996) "mutual perspective taking". As recorded above, some scholars argue that psychological contracts play an important role in the outcome of an interaction between individuals, though no link has been established between knowledge sharing and psychological contracts. Similarly, scholars argue that people can participate in an illusion of consensus where they assume that others are more similar to themselves than usually is the case. Forces of power and fear with their linkages with knowledge sharing were discussed. Existing research revealed that factors aiding/inhibiting knowledge sharing vary depending on the situations and surroundings.

Scholars talk about "knowing of what others know", "mutual perspective taking", "shared mental space" and "T-shaped skills", as aids to tacit/non-codified knowledge sharing. However they do not address the micro processes for example different types of psychological contracts and their linkage with knowledge sharing that lead to a "mutual perspective taking" and the rest. This research aims to fill this knowledge gap by investigating the micro elements (psychological contracts) that lead to a shared mental space to enable tacit/non-codified knowledge sharing to an explicit form across the key sub-cultures and its affect on the adaptation and acceptance of a CRM system. The linkage of non-codified knowledge sharing and its effect on the "adaptation and acceptance" of a CRM system remains yet to be explored. The analyses of issues regarding knowledge sharing across the sub-cultures of the implementation process of an IT system have elucidated the discussion of knowledge sharing aids/barriers across them.

This review has generated the following preliminary research question:

In an organizational context over time, how is tacit/non-codified knowledge surfaced and shared across key sub-cultures and with what effect on the adaptation and acceptance of a CRM system?

To address the above, stakeholders of the system, key sub-cultures of stakeholders and their interactions need to be identified. This will

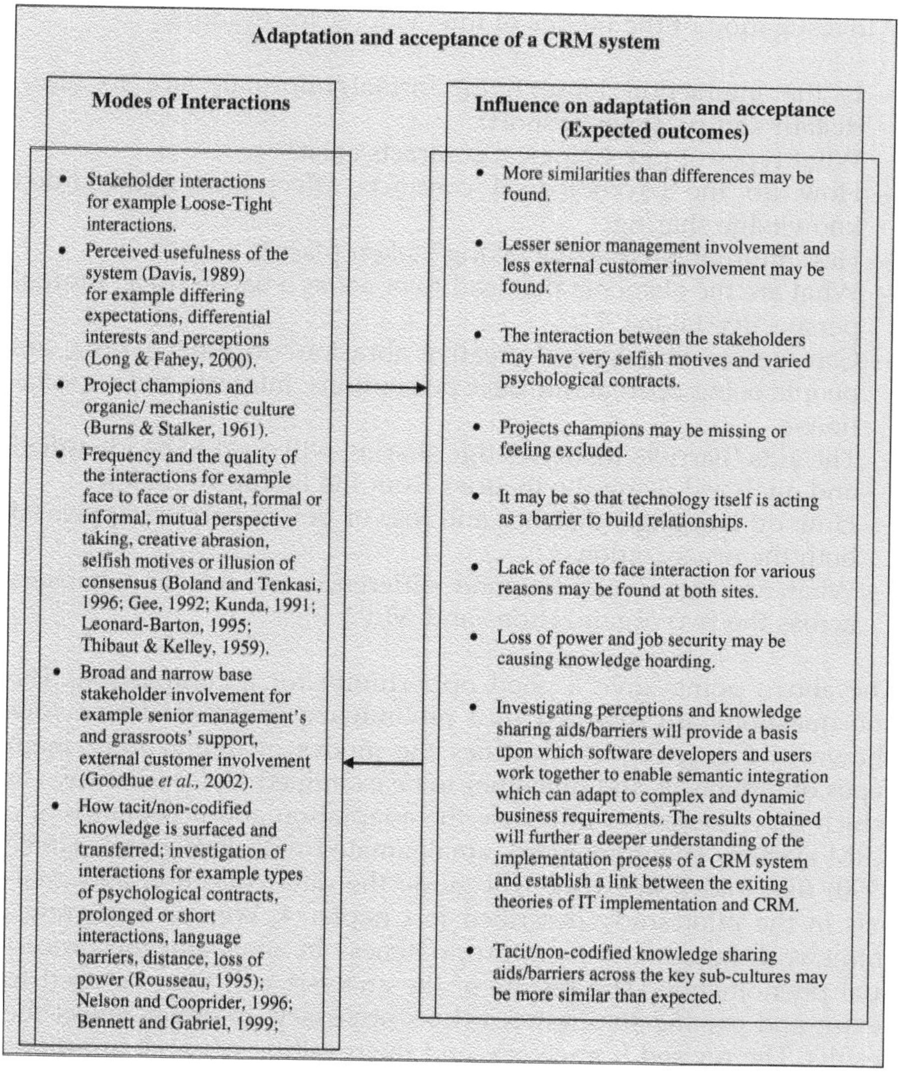

Figure 3.2 *Analytic Framework*

be carried out in terms of whether the interaction had a broad or a narrow base. Senior management and grass root involvement will be investigated. This will include the external customers. The benefits of such an involvement will also be discussed. Stakeholders' perceptions, interests and expectations would need to be identified. Differing stakeholders' perceptions regarding the effectiveness of CRM system from both the sites will be compared and their causes discussed.

Investigation of the modes of interactions, for example:

- Is the interaction loose/tight, formal/informal, face to face/distant and prolonged/short?
- What types of psychological contracts exist?
- How do the psychological contracts affect tacit/non-codified knowledge sharing?
- Has "mutual perspective taking" taken place?
- What are the elements that lead to or act as a barrier to a "mutual perspective taking"?
- Can we see the signs of creative abrasion? In other words, are people being open about their perceptions, interests and expectations?
- The aids/barriers to knowledge sharing will need to be identified and analyzed using the theories from the literature review.
- How do language, distance and loss of power barriers appear at both the organizations?
- What are the similarities and differences of aids and barriers across the two organizations and why?

The above points give a good opportunity for a comparison. The sub questions are reflected in a preliminary analytical framework shown in Figure 3.2. It identifies the modes of interactions, main types of influences and outcomes to be examined and posits ways in which they interact to influence the adaptation and acceptance of a CRM system. This framework amalgamated with Pettigrew's (1985, 1990) five fold framework will guide the data collection and analysis in the pilot study described in Chapter 4. We use Pettigrew's framework because of its appropriateness in analysing the processual phenomenon. The results of the analysis will then be used to revise and expand the framework as necessary, to better reflect the results. The revised framework, and the resulting research questions about influences on adaptation and acceptance and modes of interaction, can then form the basis for the detailed empirical work in Chapters 5 and 6.

4
Tools for Investigation: Methods, Pilot Study and Frameworks

INTRODUCTION

In research work, it is important to show how findings were arrived at, so that readers can make their own judgements about the robustness and reliability of what is claimed, and can make their own assessments about how the research contribution may be used. One of our objectives in this chapter is to show the research process in detail so that such judgements can be made. But a further objective in presenting this chapter is more proselytizing. That is to underline how painstaking rigorous research needs to be, and to suggest that the processual, qualitative approach adopted here leads to a much richer understanding of IT implementation processes than all too often appears in Information Systems studies, and indeed Management Studies. And a richer understanding has consequences, not least of which is that it can lead to better explanations of why things turn out as they do, thus empowering remedial action, and also greater clarity about possible better ways of CRM implementation in the future. A final objective in showing the detailed research process is to provide enough detail to encourage future researchers, if they adjudge it rewarding, to adopt this type of approach.

The pilot work detailed in this chapter was carried out to create an enhanced understanding of the contemporary situation at two organizations, namely a UK City Council (UKCC) and an International Enterprise (IE). It also provided the basis for a refined research question, refined the reviewed literature and tested the preliminary research methodology. In these respects this pilot chapter is essentially exploratory and refining, as part of our processual analysis.

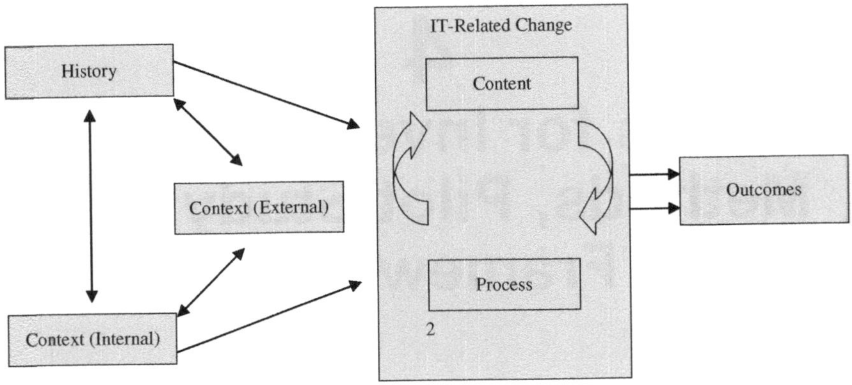

Figure 4.1 Framework employed for preliminary data analysis (Pettigrew, 1985)

Thus the pilot was carried out as part of a Pettigrew (1997) type analysis, to understand the micro elements (in our research, the role of psychological contracts) in the process of implementation of a CRM (Customer Relationship System) system from a knowledge management perspective. The pilot intended to secure an improved understanding of the micro mechanisms and patterns of the implementation processes of CRM systems at both sites, in order to develop sense-making before the main study, and avoid the "death-by-data" typical of more grounded theory type research approaches.

The summary of the reviewed literature appearing in Figure 3.1 used Pettigrew's (1985, 1990) framework to cover the history and internal context of IT implementation (see Figure 4.1). However, this pilot research gives a special focus to the "Process" part of the implementation of a CRM system. Theories discussed in the literature review are used to complement Pettigrew's (1985, 1990) framework. The same framework, because of its suitability, is then used to carry out an initial analysis of the evolving situation at both research sites. In a preliminary analysis we compare the "Process" component of the two cases in a cross-case analysis. This pilot work then leads to the building of more refined versions of our research methods together with a detailed analytical framework to be used for the main studies detailed in Chapters 5 and 6.

METHODS: LOOKING AT PROCESS

The pilot used Pettigrew's (1985) five-fold framework, because of its suitability to a processual study, to analyze the internal and external context linking it with history (Pettigrew, 1997). Theories from the literature review and outside the review were used to analyse "why" and "how" issues in relation to the internal and external context at both sites. Time and history are central to processual analysis and act as building blocks enhancing the understanding of the contemporary situation at both research sites (Pettigrew, 1997). The pilot attempted (by amalgamating the analytic framework in Figure 3.1. with Pettigrew's (1985) framework) to reveal the patterns embedded in these building blocks. These patterns emerged in the form of themes during the analysis of empirical data and helped in comparing the characteristics across the two research sites. The themes also related to theories regarding IT implementation, culture and knowledge, already discussed in Chapter 3.

This pilot used a comparative longitudinal case study approach to collect and critically analyze empirical data from both sites. The techniques for collecting data from both sites included historical analyses, comprising the consideration of data from project reports and minutes of project team meetings; attending informal staff meetings and conducting interviews with stakeholders during both of which observations were made and notes were taken (Bell, 1992). The variety of methods chosen to gather data (historical analyses, interviews and taking of field notes) created a useful form of triangulation (Yin, 1994).

Interviews with stakeholders in the pilot were conducted in the form of semi-structured in-depth interviews. According to King (1994) an in-depth interview is a direct personal interview in which a single respondent is probed by an interviewer to uncover underlying motivations, beliefs, attitudes and feelings on a topic. It has a low degree of structure, a high proportion of open questions and a focus on specific situations and action sequences in the interview process (King, 1994).

Ten semi-structured interviews were conducted with the stakeholders of CRM systems at each site. The interviews were loosely structured consisting of open-ended questions mapping the area to be explored, at least initially, whilst allowing the interviewer or interviewee to diverge in order to pursue an idea or response in more detail. Interviewees included people from senior management, middle management and end-users of the CRM system at each site. Appointments for in-depth interviews were made over the phone and most of the interviews were conducted face to face. An interview guide was used to help to keep the focus on the key aspects of the literature review. The interview guide included a number of topics: introduction regarding the personal background and role of the respondent, implementation process, stakeholder perceptions regarding knowledge management, sharing and retention, and stakeholder evaluation to understand to what extent the system has been successful (see Appendix A for interview guideline details).

The interviewees were informed about the subject over the phone. Interviews were conducted in an informal manner to put the respondent at ease, which developed a good atmosphere for a relaxed conversation. All the interviews started with informal discussions regarding their learning experience of the CRM system. Although the interviews in this research were semi-structured with a broad set of themes, they were kept rather open in order to allow the respondents to develop their perspectives rather than constrained by the perceptions of the researcher. Probing was used as a means of stimulating the flow of discussion where necessary. Interviews were audio taped by the interviewer for which informed consent had been obtained. Notes taken during the interviews helped to gather information on what happened during the interviews. These also served to clarify the researcher's concept of what was being said. Having transcribed the recorded interviews, colour coding was used to help in analyzing the data. Colour coding helped to increase the consistency of the analysis. It also facilitated searching, marking up, linking and reorganizing data in a short period of time (Denzin & Lincoln, 2000). The data from key stakeholders from both sites was compared to find the similarities and dissimilarities across the cases using cross-case analysis.

Non-disclosure agreements with IE.COM and UKCC were signed. The analysis conducted mostly employed non-sensitive information. Any sensitive information gathered from both sites was treated with care and mutual agreement to use such data was gained from respective departments. It should be stressed that the accounts that follow are partial and exploratory, but rich enough to allow us to formulate a more refined research approach, more usable frameworks for analysis, and a clearer understanding of what to focus on in later more detailed work. That said, the fundamentals of qualitative research described in this section were utilised in the main studies because, as we shall see, they proved resilient and rewarding in the pilot phase. In what follows we endeavour to create an account highly informed by respondents' views and perspectives, while making connections with the academic literature where relevant, and providing our own construction, through the structuring and highlighting of events and comments.

CASE 1: A UK CITY COUNCIL (UKCC)

City Council's IT History: Linking External and Internal Contexts

Origins and implications of outsourcing

During 1994 UKCC made a decision to move from a centralized IT structure to increased autonomy over buying in and outsourcing IT services by departments. As a result, the role of central IT became more of a support function. According to a CRM Project Manager, "Vanilla" or off the shelf applications seemed to be popular in UKCC as they required less in-house expertise.

According to a former head of IT, in-house implementation and development expertise during that period was limited. In particular it lacked programmers. IT expertise was in the form of business or system analysts. UKCC did not have any programmers or any really technical people on-site. When they chose new packages they really had to be good, and not require a lot of technical skill to make them work (Former Head of IT). As a result the role of the central IT centre was diverted into supporting departments which would go out to buy solutions to meet their individual needs (CRM Project Manager). UKCC were keen on setting up an integration strategy.

IT solutions at UKCC were bought in by different departments with little regard for cross departmental integration, resulting in technology bottlenecks (Holland & Ben, 1999). According to a Former Head of IT and a CRM Project Manager, the pattern of outsourcing the programming to a third part vendor and the buying of hundreds of solutions continued for many years. The CRM Project Manager further stated that UKCC had realized over the last few years (1999 and subsequently) that it was not efficient as an organization and a lot of things that it was doing with the re-organization of IT were about trying to re-establish standards. The sub-cultures formed as a result of this IT autonomy may have different interests, expectations and needed further investigation.

External context

According to the Office of the Deputy Prime Minister (2000), City Council (UKCC) was given the task of ensuring that all the services were available to the citizens through electronic means by 2005. This put some pressure on the UKCC public services. UKCC needed to exploit new technology to meet rising customer expectations successfully in the same way as the private sector if they were not to be accused of delivering poor quality services. The above illustrates the government deadlines and speed of new legislation that Willcocks and Margetts (1994) talk about as pressure factors exposing the organizations towards consultant and supplier markets.

Internal context at UKCC

Under this section the culture of the UKCC, in particular the subcultures and subculture-gap using the theories from the literature review are discussed (Fincham, 1994; Grindley, 1992; Hinton, 1994; Kumar & Bjorn-Andersen, 1990; Louis, 1985).

Several sub-cultures were identified during this pilot at UKCC. The CRM project was originally perceived to have an IT-led approach. The revised approach after Former Head of IT left was perceived as business led. According to the Contract Manager (in Corporate Customer Relations), one group of people (led by the Former Head of IT) had a positive attitude towards CRM implementation with an integrative approach, while the other group (led by the Strategic Director of Resources) had a "call-answering" focus. The group of people with the "call-answering" or non-integrative approach were more concerned with answering the calls as the main priority.

The above indicates a cultural gap between the social and technical (Bloomfield & Vurdubaki, 1994), that is, in this context, between the human resource department, service agents, end users, and some managers on the one hand, and the programmers, IT technicians, developers and systems analysts on the other.

The public was not getting through over the phone, and that had caused great concern within UKCC. This triggered politicians to look for ways forward. The IT-led group which included the Former Head of IT, CRM Programme Manager and the CRM consultant UKCC Consultant, were concerned about establishing a strong link between the front-office and back-offices using a middleware to integrate the system (Holland & Ben, 1999; Louis, 1985). The designed middleware was not being sufficiently effective to start with. This was slowing down the progress of implementation. Hence, a non-integrative approach, under the Strategic Director of Resources supported by the CRM Business Manager and other like-minded people, was taken on board as a better alternative. The problematic nature of the differing cultures, one stemming from an IT background and the other from a financial background created a hurdle with some serious consequences in the form of people leaving the project thus slowing down the progress (Bloomfield & Vurdubaki, 1994; Price Waterhouse, 1991, 1992).

A decision within the organization to give departments more IT freedom took away central control and weakened the influence and further development of a homogeneous IT culture. Each department developed different solutions as it was always cheaper to go and buy off-the-shelf proprietary systems. Problems arose when different departments wanted to communicate with each other through a degree of system integration (CRM Project Manager). The departments had gathered knowledge over the years that they may find hard to release without seeing any clear benefits. Individuals sitting with certain knowledge may have fear of losing their power or position by releasing their knowledge completely (Davenport *et al.*, 1998).

If one follows Leonard-Barton and Kraus (1985), making the knowledge, residing in the above mentioned vertical silos, mobile across the departments at UKCC was important. The knowledge possessed by the departments can be in explicit or implicit state, both codified and non-codified (Perrin, 1990). In other words, it can be in descriptive, prescriptive or tacit form (Herschbach, 1995; Nonaka and Takeuchi, 1995; Vincenti, 1993). It becomes vital to investigate the elements that facilitated the sharing of knowledge residing in various forms across the departmental sub-cultures at UKCC.

The "Content" of IT Related Change

UKCC was concerned about their public call-answering capacity. According to its CRM Programme Manager, an internal evaluation done by the City Council (UKCC) showed that less than 10% of people could get through on their first call to UKCC. UKCC had been looking at establishing a corporate contact centre for a number of years.

UKCC started looking at establishing a corporate contact centre. As explained by the Former Head of IT, one of the key requirements identified was the need to set up some form of corporate access database. By doing so, they could record and monitor the contacts and: "that would be an important component of any contact centre that was established—and that's when we started looking at CRM as an issue" (Former Head of IT). The above statement describes the UKCC rationale for a CRM solution. They intended to use a CRM system to improve the call-answering service to their customers.

The CRM project did not seem to have a project champion. However, the idea of a CRM system was endorsed enthusiastically and sponsored by the chief executive, CEO. The CRM Programme Manager suggested that the chief executive was most keen to improve the communications with the public and felt that everything was too diverse and too spread over the Authority. There needed to be a greater focus on receiving communication from the public:

> The Chief Executive saw a very good working call centre in Brisbane and suggested having one in once he got back (CRM Programme Manager).

The above indicates that the project had a project sponsor in the form of the Chief Executive (Goodhue *et al.*, 2002; Willcocks & Sykes, 2000).

From thereon the CRM project started to take shape and develop. Several key events took place before the system went live. A description of key events during the implementation may help to enhance the understanding regarding the implementation process of CRM system at UKCC.

The CRM idea is born

The Former Head of IT started to work with the idea of a CRM system as a solution to UKCC call answering problem. He adds:

> There's another key character, who is still working here called Danny McNair (not his real name). Danny is brilliant. He sees things, brings them all together and if you ask the right questions, out it all comes into a strategic whole. It was Danny that told me, 'This is what's it's really about, not just answering the phone but connecting the agents to the back-office systems and logging everything in the middle'. That was critical and Danny and I talked about it all the time. Danny got it spot on and it was really really important. So immediately we started developing the idea for a government computing conference. (Former Head of IT)

According to the Former Head of IT, the first big presentation on CRM was in 1999 to a government computing conference and on that occasion the former Head of IT had expressed the idea of every authority in the country having its own CRM but all linked together through the Internet, so any citizen anywhere could actually link into the CRM. His idea was received positively. The Deputy Leader of the UKCC was interested in promoting modern techniques. He got the Former Head of IT and Strategic Director of Resources together and gave them the go-ahead regarding a CRM project. At this stage the Strategic Director was more concerned about answering the calls more effectively than anything else (Former Head of IT). Significantly, the Strategic Director and Head of IT held different and potentially conflicting underlying views which did not surface until a later stage of the CRM project (Pliskin *et al.*, 1993).

Wathne *et al.* (1996) argue that factors such as accuracy, timeliness, adequacy and credibility of interactions influence perceptions of honesty and openness, and are essential to achieving more frequent and relevant knowledge sharing between the partners. A creative abrasion between the Strategic Director of Resources and Former Head of IT at an early stage of the CRM X project could have helped to create a "shared context for knowing", leading to a mutual perspective and thus could have facilitated knowledge sharing between the two and even across the sub-cultures (Boland &Tenkasi, 1996; Newell *et al.*, 2002).

According to Krogh. *et al.* 2000) effective knowledge creation depends on the physical, virtual and emotional context of an organization. They discuss the importance of the notion of reciprocity of relationships. When a relationship is felt to be reciprocal then a trust develops which can work to overcome power-based relationships. The relationship between the Former Head of IT and Strategic Director of Resources was not felt to be reciprocal. This resulted in lack of trust on both sides. The psychological contracts as a result of conflicting ideas may have been based upon differing motives. A mutual perspective towards CRM X was absent (Boland & Tenkasi, 1996).

The outsourcing of implementation

According to the Former Head of IT, UKCC wanted to outsource the implementation. The UKCC Consultant, who had a good track record, was employed during May 2000 (Former Head of IT). However, much of his experience was from the private sector which differs from the public sector (Willcocks & Harrow, 1992). Together with the UKCC Consultant, three more consultants were hired (Former Head of IT).

The Former Head of IT pointed out that one of these consultants was James Haddon (not his real name), who had a background in work study for over 20 years in the public sector. He also had experience in call centres and script design. He was hired to do business process re-engineering in terms of process analysis in relation to the targeted areas for a contact centre. The consultants' initial role was to investigate neighbourhood offices and council tax. The UKCC Consultant's role was to manage the consultants and also to act as an advisor to the Former Head of IT. However, the consultants hired lacked specific knowledge of UKCC culture and its operations.

Selection of supplier

The CRM Project Manager stated that from May 2000 onwards UKCC were going through a process of putting requirements together with a view to going out to tender. There were also some presentations from suppliers. Fourteen were invited, of whom five replied. CRM X Provider was chosen.

The criterion against which CRM X Provider was selected was best value, expressed as a 70/30 split—70 % functional, 30 % cost for the procurement. CRM X Provider won on all counts and the Strategic Director of Resources agreed to put in a contract with CRM X Provider even though they were a small company. UKCC took CRM X Provider on board with their partner, called Cavendish, and that was part of the strategy had 39 people facing systems, so the idea was: "We'd better get in bed with somebody who's very good at doing integration, because we aren't" (Former Head of IT).

UKCC entered into contract negotiations with CRM X Provider, provider of software called CRM X. UKCC also went on a site visit to Sussex Police in Brighton during October/November to observe their gazetteer using a CRM application. In December 2000, the decision to take on board CRM X Provider was made. The contract was signed with CRM X Provider during March 2001. Keeping in view the limited programming expertise in UKCC, an off-the-shelf package was chosen. It could be configured and implemented fairly quickly. There were also possibilities for back-office integration through inbuilt XML facility in the package.

The "Process" of CRM Implementation

This section covers the "how" of the implementation—how things were done and how they were perceived by different stakeholders. It discusses the staff retention issues, user/stakeholder commitment, project team experience, and user training (Pettigrew, 1985, 1990, 1997).

Staff retention issues

During January 2001, the CRM Business Manager was appointed. According to the Temporary Head of IT:

> It was felt that the project was over-weighted with IT and light on business need. The business need, according to the Strategic Director of Resources, was to bring back the focus towards call answering issues.

The number of people who could actually get through to UKCC was as low as 10 % on first call. This business issue was identified in the Citizen Mori survey (Temporary Head of IT).

CRM project manager (CRM Programme Manager) resigns from the CRM project

The CRM Programme Manager was also the CRM Project Manager at the point when the new CRM Business Manager arrived. The CRM Business Manager and Programme Manager got off to a bad start (CRM Project Manager). The CRM Programme Manager got on very well with the UKCC Consultant; the Business Manager did not. This could have perhaps caused some of the problems:

> It was a delicate issue but perhaps it did come down a lot to personalities at the end of the day. (CRM Project Manager)

According to the CRM Project Manager, shortly after that, when the new CRM Business Manager arrived with different views about how the project should be run, it was felt that perhaps the CRM Programme Manager should leave the project. The project then changed direction towards a call answering focus and away from the integrated approach focus. At that point a new CRM Project Manager was also appointed. According to the CRM Business Manager the team needed to be refreshed:

> My management style is different from his (former programme manager)... I had clear views about where I wanted it to go and they didn't quite fit with his views and those of the UKCC Consultant. I didn't feel there was enough business ownership so I decided that we needed to refresh the team.

The CRM Programme Manager was quite upset about the whole situation and felt let down by the senior management, as he was there before the CRM Business Manager had been appointed:

> It got very personal—he was very personal—he made personal comments towards me—I was very upset because he'd been on a commission a long time for the Council—not a lot of output, and I saw him for what he was really.

The non-reciprocal psychological contracts present between the Strategic Director of Resources and Former Head of IT can also be seen between the CRM Business Manager and CRM Programme Manager. A process of "mutual perspective taking" where distinctive individual knowledge is exchanged, evaluated and integrated with that of the others in the organization, was missing in the above case too (Boland & Tenkasi, 1996).

Head of IT (Former Head of IT) leaves UKCC

The Strategic Director of Resources wanted to outsource the call centre management to Independent Company, partnering with CRM X Provider. The Former Head of IT, on the other hand, had a view that it might slow things down. He was keen on back-office integration in the system. His view was shared by both the CRM Programme Manager and UKCC Consultant. The Strategic Director took a different view, "Her view was 'To hell with boys playing', but much more important is—Get the telephones answered!' " (Former Head of IT). The Former Head of IT gave six months, notice before leaving during October 2001. Time for "Toys for boys" (Former Head of IT) was over and contract with Independent Company was signed.

Change of direction in the "Process"

The Strategic Director of Resources decided to outsource to Independent Company as Former Head of IT left during October 2001. Outsourcing to Independent Company was more of a political decision as there were issues with regard to the performance of officers providing service. The Deputy Leader appeared to be the person pushing this idea forward. In April 2001 the UKCC Consultant presented a report to the Strategic Director of Resources, in which he promoted the idea of integration between front and back-office using CRM X. That idea was never acted upon and the UKCC Consultant was relieved of his services. The rest of the consultants were assigned the role of designing scripts for the contact centre (CRM Programme Manager).

The Temporary Head of IT stated that the management of the contact centre was given to Independent Company. In normal circumstances the City Council would have moved all the call centre staff over to the contact centre, which would have necessitated transfer of undertakings legally. The politicians were not prepared to do that. According to the Temporary Head of IT they seconded people from UKCC to Independent Company. In this arrangement, the management of the staff was done by Independent Company. However, all the staff's terms and conditions were managed by the City Council (Temporary Head of IT).

Stakeholder commitment

UKCC CRM had senior management sponsorship in form of the CEO, who saw a CRM system in action on his trip to Brisbane:

> Our Deputy Leader saw this as a good opportunity to kill two birds with one stone. One, this would eliminate the call answering

> issues that the city was having. The second, that implementation of a CRM system will be in line with the government directive. (CRM Programme Manager)

Both the Former Head of IT and Strategic Director of Resources bought the CRM idea initially. However, as they started to work on the implementation plan, their differing opinions became more explicit and their psychological contracts became more individual than mutual. The Former Head of IT was perceived to be IT-led, whereas the Strategic Director of Resources wanted to focus on resolving the issue of public calls not getting through to UKCC. They may have started with a mutual understanding on the surface (Anderson & Schalk, 1998). As they interacted more closely and creative abrasion took place, the implicit part of their psychological contract become more explicit (Makin *et al.*, 1996). It could be that at least part of such a psychological contract was implicit, resulting in a lack of clarity for both parties (Makin *et al.*, 1996).

Creative abrasion can influence performance positively (Leonard-Barton, 1995). In the above case, however, it created a divide and slowed down the CRM project. This also resulted in the Former Head of IT resigning and subsequent suspension of the original "CRM X" development in favour of the revised "Contact CRM X" solution.

The arrival of the new CRM Business Manager changed the direction of the project towards a call-answering focus and away from the integrated approach focus. The CRM Programme Manager did not share that view either and left the project. This narrowed down the stakeholder base. There were also hopes to keep the customer contact centre internal. As Business Manager, Environmental Services stated:

> we'd been working on the assumption, all the way through, that the call centre would be set up but it would probably be internally run and managed and it was a bit of a shock to some people on the group that hang on, because I think some people had sort of seen roles for themselves within the subsequent development of the organisation and I'm going to run this and I'm going to be doing that as we were sort of bought into it, and that was suddenly taken away and it was going to be a managed service. So I think at that point a lot of people probably lost a little bit of interest.

Other changes at the senior management level influenced subsequent developments. According to the CRM Programme Manager, the Deputy Leader remained in the picture for a while providing support to the Former Head of IT and Strategic Director of Resources. The CEO left with 12 months' notice.

User training issues in the "Process" of IT related change

The training provided by Independent Company to the contact centre agents was more in the form of descriptive knowledge, which included what the system can do and how the written scripts can be used to answer the incoming calls (Herschbach, 1995; Nonaka and Takeuchi, 1995; Vincenti, 1993). However, there were some issues regarding the training.

> I felt it was inadequate, I felt it was poorly managed, I didn't feel that the trainers were aware of how to utilise the system any better than the people they were training. (Contact Duty Manager)
>
> They hadn't for instance, (they didn't deliver) very high quality training materials to go with the training so the staff were, having been trained, walking away and not having anything they could refer to. (CRM Project Manager)
>
> I think we neglected, I think we could have spent more time on helping Independent Company employees understand how the Council works. (CRM Business Manager)

Training provided by Independent Company did not impress the UKCC staff and management. However, this could be due to the fact that Independent Company did not have enough knowledge about UKCC departmental culture. Their interactions with UKCC were not on a prolonged basis, and may not have allowed any creative abrasion to take place (Newell *et al.*, 2002). This resulted in a training which perhaps was not based on "mutual perspective taking" (Boland & Tenkasi, 1996). A reason, behind a lack of "mutual perspective taking", could have been that there was an agreement on senior management level which may have had a mutual psychological contract. However, it was not shared by the people on the floor. According to Leonard-Barton and Kraus (1985) it is important to plan for the transfer of knowledge from the old operations, in which people knew the materials and the product very well, to the new processes. They further argue that the developers of the new process often know their tools well, but rarely do they understand the materials and processes to which their software is applied or the people on the floor who have been working with both for years. In the above situation secondees from the back-offices were put in the contact centre environment, however their knowledge was not exploited to complement and enhance the quality of the end-user training.

The UKCC senior management, when signing the contract with Independent Company, may have had an illusion of consensus that did not expose the innermost feelings of individuals involved

(Gee, 1992). Hence it resulted in inadequate training material and lack of communication between the parties. The UKCC staff were more trained and experienced with considerable codified knowledge regarding UKCC and its culture. More than half of the contact centre staff were existing UKCC staff as secondees. Their training needs may have been different from those of any new-comer (non-secondee).

Observations on the way in which the system went live

> To start with, five UKCC services were supposed to go on board with CRM X. This got reduced to three. It was very much a political directive as to which went in and which did not. UKCC did an awful lot of work with Leisure, and then all of a sudden they dropped Leisure because Revenues became more important, so they just had to dump all the Leisure work. (CRM Project Manager)

Furthermore, the pilot testing did not involve a collective testing. Each department did their own tests with the system. This did not enable any close interaction between the different departments. Hence, the opportunity for any prolonged creative abrasion to take place, as recommended by Newell *et al.* (2002), was not there. Different departments may also have had different psychological contracts. These differing psychological contracts may have inhibited the free flow of knowledge from one department to another. The sense of shared benefits which could have helped in the mobility of knowledge silos and hoarding has been missing at the departmental level.

There was no external customer involvement in the process of implementation of CRM X. UKCC had tried it before and it did not work. According to the Temporary Head of IT:

> It was much better to take something to the citizens, get it changed and validated, rather than giving them a blank piece of paper and saying, 'This is what we are going to do. How do you want to do it?'

The system went live in March 2002. This included the contact centre using the CRM X solution/software, providing services for Environmental Waste, Neighbourhood Advice and Council Tax. Prior to that, from about July/August 2001, a pilot of the CRM system with Environmental Services was done, which was one of the first service areas that went live. However, the system went live without physically having a contact centre in place. It was done in the existing office. The product was used to see how it interacted with

UKCC's back-end system and what values it generated and problems it caused. There were some major issues with that pilot, around the technical side in getting it to talk correctly with the back-end system. Another issue was that Environmental Services at that point were in the process of renewing their back-end system. Difficulties with the pilot indicate that a clear purpose, well defined and communicated, could have been missing (Leonard-Barton & Kraus, 1985).

"Outcomes" (Pettigrew, 1985, 1990) in the CRM implementation at UKCC

Outcomes in this case are discussed in terms of how the system process was shaped by the internal and external contexts and how the process affected the performance of the users of the system (Pettigrew, 1997).

The window of opportunity for adoption started to close (Orlikowski & Tyre, 1994)

As the users of the system became more familiar with the systems and its strengths and weaknesses, the workarounds, the shortcuts and the tricks of the trade started to surface (Orlikowski, 1993; Orlikowski & Iacono, 2001; Vincenti, 1984).

According to our respondents (a non-secondee end-user, Contact Centre, Birmingham), initially the call centre agents tried to use the CRM X CRM system as much as they could. But as time passed they started to realize that answering the calls was taking too long. So they started to make notes while answering the calls using the system as little as possible.

Interviews with the agents showed that they learned to take notes manually while on call and then after the call put the logs on the system. This was the case especially with agents from the revenue and benefits section. A brief interview with the recruitment section showed that they used CRM X CRM for salutation purposes only. They then had to log into the back-office system separately. This was the case with both benefits and revenues departments, according to our respondents. This shows that, as the system adaptation time passed people were finding new ways of working with the CRM X system. One way was using it as little as possible. The system was getting adapted by the users rather than users adopting the system (Orlikowski & Tyre, 1994). The "tricks of the trade" and shortcuts that were being discovered as the system got adapted by its users, would be worth investigating further.

Differing perceptions, interests and expectations (Long & Fahey, 2000)

A senior manager from Neighbourhood Office wanted his department to play a leading role in the CRM X implementation. He suggested that the contact centre should have been under their responsibility. The contact centre (Independent Company) management at UKCC has differing perceptions regarding the CRM X. Some seemed to have an opinion that CRM X was doing what it was supposed to do. In other words, providing help as a tool to answer the incoming calls.

The benefit of the externally managed contact centre was that there were, within the contract, clear quantifiable performance indicators that said, "Yes, X number of calls have got to be answered to hit a certain percentage call rate". However , according to a Business Manager, Environmental Services, there were quality issues that needed addressing. The eventual aim was for CRM X CRM to be a fully integrated solution and then UKCC would start to get benefits. Training had improved, according to the Contact Duty Manager. Some feedback from the staff had been picked up by the trainers and resulted in some improvements in training the new comers (Vincenti, 1993). However, according to some reports, some of the contact centre advisors still did not see CRM X system as a facilitating tool and were quite sceptical about it.

The contact centre managed by Independent Company went live in March 2003. It was divided into three sections. Section one had advisors handling calls regarding Environmental Services and Neighbourhood Advice. Section two dealt with Benefits and Revenue. Section three (which went live in January 2004) dealt with Recruitment Services. Advisors in all the sections used CRM X CRM system to read scripts, in order correctly to use the salutations.

According to an IT programmer, in handling the calls related to the environmental services the CRM X system used a middleware called "Connect" supplied by a company called MVM, to interact with the back-office system. The call centre agents were able to provide help to the callers on information requests and specific issues such as programming the disposal of bulky waste items or missed bin collections. However, not all the call centre agents had access to the full version of the back-office system. Only the UKCC secondees were given full access (Business Manager, Environmental Services Department). This meant that non-secondees with a customer query passed on the information manually to the secondees in order to achieve a resolution.

Secondees from UKCC were trained separately from non-secondees in the CRM X CRM system. A collective training of call centre staff could have provided an opportunity for the staff to interact with each other on an informal basis. Such interaction on an informal level might perhaps have helped to start the process of "mutual perspective taking" (Boland & Tenkasi, 1996) and a shared ownership, potentially leading to "mutual high-obligations" psychological contracts thus facilitating knowledge sharing (Shore & Barksdale 1998).

According to the Contact Duty Manager, secondees carried with them the UKCC culture, whereas the non-secondees hired by Independent Company to handle the incoming calls did not. Secondees were more aware of the process loop in handling incoming calls because of their UKCC background. This knowledge possessed by the secondees has not been exploited fully. The training was short, only three to four weeks according to the Contact Duty Manager and was different for secondees as compared to non-secondees (Wathne *et al.*, 1996). "T-shaped skills" and "knowing of what others know" could not be fully developed due to the shortage of time and lack of prolonged cross-cultural interaction between secondees and non-secondees (Bakhtin, 1981; Iansiti, 1993; Krauss & Fussell, 1991; Lawrence & Lorsch, 1967). According to the Contact Duty Manager, there was very little interaction between the three sections based at the contact centre. The chances of creative abrasion taking place were limited. The common coffee or lunch room was mainly used by the recruitment services. The limited interaction taking place was in more formal types of setting. Lack of informal settings at the contact centre worked as an inhibitor to the transfer of various forms of knowledge. This combined with lack of "mutual high-obligations" psychological contracts due to the departmental subculture (Shore & Barksdale, 1998) and vertical knowledge silos may have inhibited knowledge sharing across the departments and between the front-office and back-office in a CRM environment. The above knowledge sharing phenomenon needs to be investigated further to understand the impact of psychological contracts and subculture interactions on non-codified knowledge sharing. For an overview of the initial analysis of the contemporary situation at UKCC see Figure 4.2.

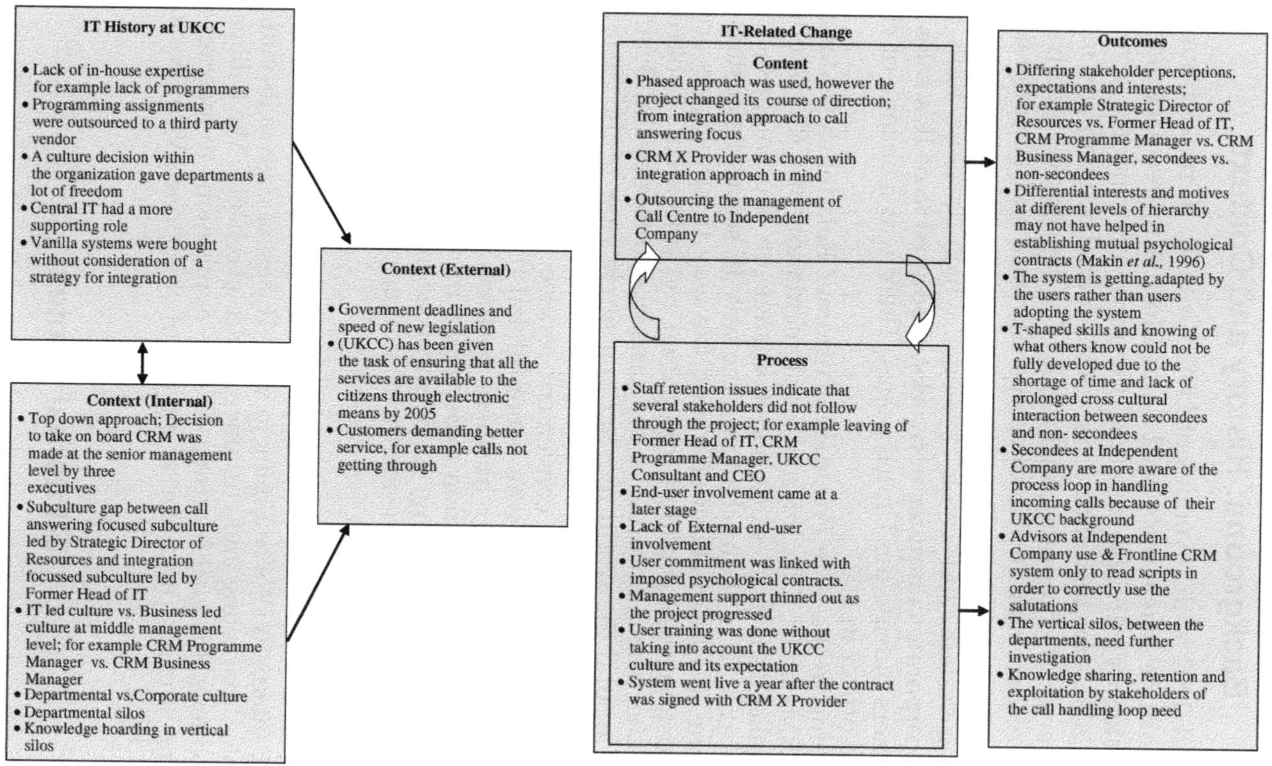

Figure 4.2 *A summary of analysis using Pettigrew (1985, 1990)*

CASE STUDY 2: IE AND CRM Y IMPLEMENTATION

Background: History and Context

IE finished 2002 with revenues of US$81 billion. IE ranked number one on Fortune magazine's 2002 "Ten Most Admired Companies" list (IT category). IE also received the most US patents—a record 22,257 in 2002—for the tenth consecutive year. The company makes a broad range of computers, including PCs, notebooks, mainframes and network servers. It also develops software and peripherals. In addition, IE owns Lotus® Development, maker of the Lotus Notes® messaging system, and Tivoli® Systems, which develops tools that manage corporate computer networks. About 60 % of IE's sales are to customers outside the United States. There was a change of chief executive officer in 2001.

According to the Vice President, Customer Relationship Management (CRM) at IE, IE's internal implementation of CRM Y eBusiness Applications is a story about change on the smallest, most personal scale. It is about changing the way IE serves its customers, one by one. It is also about changing the way IE employees access timely customer information, individual by individual. Looked at from another angle, however, it concerns IE employees and Business Partners around the world moving to a single view of the customer and accessing that customer information anywhere, in real-time. It is about enabling fast, convenient service for customers worldwide, and improving the way major, global IE divisions collaborate with each other and their business partners. In short, it is about one company's determination to become a more globally integrated, customer-focused company, with unprecedented speed and scale, responding to whatever means the customer chooses to do business with IE:

> Our goal is to be viewed as one IE by our customers and to work as one IE internally. We're aiming to make IE best of class in its industry for sales, marketing and customer service excellence. We believe we can achieve this goal by using CRM Y applications to leverage our existing strengths as a market-intelligent enterprise. (Vice President, CRM, IE)

IE Internal Context

Focusing on sub-cultures, these were observed at three levels: senior management level, Pre-Deployment Team (PDT) level and within the PDTs (end-user sub cultures). CRM legacy data was in a poor state. However, this was not discovered until the data migration began. Hence stakeholders from the senior management may have had differing perceptions regarding the contemporary situations in the various business units. The differing perceptions of stakeholders were influenced by their different interests, expectations and power (Long & Fahey, 2000; Willcocks *et al.*, 2003). Senior management under-estimated the amount of post-implementation training needed for end-users. Consequently after the initial user experience, they had to set up workshops to assist with user queries regarding the new system. The learning-on-the-job method did not seem to work particularly well:

> We needed a better transition plan—30 to 45 days out—as to 'what do I do now' as opposed to just assume that they would have everything - that they would learn "kind of" on the job. (Vice Chairman, World CRM Deployment)

There were also team hierarchies at different levels:

> There was one team but it had lots of different dimensions, so we had one team at the world wide level and then we had three individual geography based teams, one for the Americas, one for Europe and one for Asia Pacific. (CRM Operations Manager)

The decision to take on board CRM Y was made at the top level in December 1999 by three executives.

Content and Process of Implementation

This section covers proposed changes, including their substance, and how things were done and issues perceived (Pettigrew, 1985, 1990). This is discussed in terms of the rationale for CRM Y, the type of approach employed to implement the CRM Y (big bang or phased). It will also discuss how the project was managed and what support was made available during the implementation process of CRM Y. Issues regarding user training and user commitment are also discussed.

IE had already implemented hundreds of customer-focused applications internally. However, each was dedicated to a separate business division. Previous initiatives were unable to provide a global customer overview. Enterprise-wide CRM technologies like CRM Y *e*Business Applications had, in 1998, just arrived on the market. These packages were geared to help companies like IE achieve a higher level of consistency and responsiveness, and eliminate building CRM functionality internally from scratch, thus enabling rapid execution. They are also designed to eliminate the headaches of inconsistency across multiple divisions or business units. IE wanted the business to have a consolidated view each time it interacted with its customers. For a company as big and as complex as IE, this was no easy feat. They decided to replace most existing CRM applications with a single system called CRM Y. This posed a great challenge regarding the implementation of CRM Y in 160 countries with 11 lines of business.

The initial rollout was to 26 IE.COM call centres. The CRM-driven change included everything—from acclimatizing call centre agents to a new user interface to shifting voluminous, disparate customer data onto a common database, re-engineering sales processes and, eventually, creating a global helpdesk:

> This deployment demonstrates again that we can do it all from design, implementation and processes to hardware, software and middleware. The only other way to accomplish this would be to form partnerships, but that would require integration since components would be less likely to work together. (IE CRM Project Executive)

The contract with CRM Y was signed in January 2000 and negotiated during that period. According to Vice Chairman, World CRM Deployment, IE had agreed to a plan of phased deployment both geographic and potentially functional in its design in the second quarter of year 2000. Implementation started with additional functionality to the IE.COM call centre community in North America, firstly in Smyrna Georgia. Then it expanded horizontally, meaning into other call centre organizations in North America and then into EMEA (Europe, Middle East and Africa) and to Asia Pacific through 2001. Additional functions rolled out to North America and subsequently in the European geographies, East Africa and Asia Pacific. The second set of functionality (launched January 2002) was originally agreed to, in its basic form, as activity management where the users of the CRM Y environment of CRM system could make requests to others on their team within and across their organizations. After that second wave of function, IE started to add functions simultaneously across all three geographies (the Americas, EMEA and Asia Pacific) because they knew now that they could do that based on the success of the first two waves.

During May 2002, the third release concerned the ability to share customer leads with IE's external channels, their business partners. IE simultaneously deployed "lead management" across all three geographies. This was done within a three week span over all the geographies, excluding Japan, Korea, Taiwan and China. The fourth release IE delivered was field sales support. This concluded the three major elements of the sales process, including opportunity management, activity management and account management. Opportunity management was critical to IE's sales process, activity management was a function deployed as their second functional wave, while contact and account management represented the new area of managing customer contact information.

During 2003, IE were in their fifth wave of marketing capability to be deployed in North America and EMEA. During the period of review (2003–4) deployment was on hold in Asia, with a number of issues being worked through. Thus, in summary, functional waves with horizontal expansion were implemented, following what Vice Chairman, World CRM Deployment called a called "broad not deep" approach.

CRM Y implementation in the UK

As an illustration, we look at the implementation at IE.COM located in UK. At IE.COM, five business units came on board. PDT teams to action the implementation process and to train the users were formed. The first to come on board was IE.COM, also called the PDT1.

According to the CRM Deployment Leader, IE worked to a strict deadline of 29 January 2001 to go live, employing the "broad but not deep" approach. The next European country to come on board was linked via parallel meetings. Process definition, mapping and transition across all processes was carried out. Appropriate team function workshops and documents to be actioned were created. Data migration work was a critical success factor to meet the project deadline. Data migration was important as the data needed to be moved from the existing legacy systems and over to the new system. A shadow database was created to map the data from the legacy systems before putting it on the new system.

In December 2000, territory assignment activities commenced to ensure that, on migration, all "Tele Coverage" agents had the correct accounts and the opportunities on which they were working. Helpdesk training was set up, in-house experienced agents utilized and live helpdesk function set up to go live on cut-over date. During December-January 2000/2001, data testing activities across the transfer from old to new system were carried out. The data stored in the shadow data base was tested prior to moving it to the new system. IE.COM (also known as PDT1) went live on 29 January 2001.

Project management of CRM implementation

Prior to making the decision to acquire the system, IE invested in excess of three years in coming to a common set of well defined processes. These processes comprise the inputs, the outputs and the workflows of all of their key sales and support activities. They also include opportunity management, customer satisfaction, relationship management, and offering information.

In 1997 a support group had been developed to focus on five audiences: call centres.com; field sales, face-to-face sales, marketing and business partners:

> their task was to understand the job that each one of those audience groups did, how it was evolving and how CRM Y would be deployed to them and in effect they were the source of the guidance on how we would configure CRM Y to meet the needs of those users. (CRM Operations Manager)

IE also formed a CRM Y development group. These were the people who actually knew the CRM Y product inside out, took the input from the audience leads, and translated that into specific configuration of CRM Y to respond to individual user needs. However, according to a pilot user/end-user at IE.COM, she would have liked to see more end-user involvement. Relatedly, according to the Vice Chairman, World CRM Deployment, IE underestimated the quality and the state of the legacy data. This complicated the data migration process.

A deployment team was made responsible for taking output from the Development Group and planning and executing deployment of CRM Y releases/upgrades to their end users:

> They had the technical preparation, they had the end user communication and education and they had the actual physical cut-over management. That group really had two major sub-groups to it, one was the deployment planners and leaders, and these were the people that really focused on the planning, the development of the education, and development of communication. (CRM Operations Manager)

This was the stage, according to our respondents (end-users), where end-users got involved in the implementation process in terms of getting a two and half day training

The CRM Executive reported to a group called the Investment Review Board:

> The two key players who remained constant throughout the life of the project was the Senior Executive responsible for sales and distribution in IE and the Corporation CIO. (CRM Operations Manager)

Over the three geographies IE tried to replicate the above. At the geography level, in each one of the three IE geographies, the America's, Europe and Asia Pacific, there was a mirror image of two of the three legs. They tried to replicate the audience focus and the deployment focus at the geography level. However, they did not duplicate the Development Group. The development was done once at a world wide level and the release/upgrade was then implemented commonly to all three geographies.

User/stakeholder commitment

There was initial senior management support to spread an integrative culture through using CRM Y. Executive leadership was involved in this project full-time starting at a Vice Presidential level:

> This was a team charged with end-to-end responsibility . . . they were full time people with inclusion of all the geography teams and all the business units, dedicated full time for multi-year commitment to make this happen. (Vice Chairman, World CRM Deployment)

This showed commitment at senior level. However, implementation was done through a relatively imposed approach. According to several respondents, "broad but not deep" did not penetrate enough to expose local discrepancies and issues. Implementation teams did gather information to benchmark good working practice at IE. Local stakeholder perceptions at senior and middle management level were taken into consideration. However, according to staff at IE.COM for example, stakeholder involvement at the ground level came at a later stage. Moreover no external customer involvement was considered at any stage, which challenges the "broad but not deep" approach:

> We did not use customers for any validation or walk-throughs or anything like that. (Vice Chairman, World CRM Deployment)

Furthermore, the implementation was somewhat rushed. The issues with data migration were not taken into consideration:

> What we probably would have done in retrospect, if we were given a chance to re-do this, is extend our timetables a little bit. We had very aggressive plans. (Vice Chairman, World CRM Deployment)

Moreover, the quality of data was in a bad shape, but this was not realized until the time of data migration. This data misfit created quality issues regarding the legacy data.

Stakeholder involvement at the floor level came at a later stage, according to one a "super-user". Super users at IE.COM UK were selected by IE.COM managers at the point when a Manager from IE USA came down to facilitate the implementation, six months after the signing of the CRM Y contract.

In conclusion, user commitment may also have been affected by the lack of involvement in the decision making process in buying the systems. End-users were involved in the implementation process at a later stage. No external customer involvement was taken into consideration.

User training and experience

Super-users were trained first, and then used as trainers for the rest of the end-users before the release date. The duration of the training programme was three to four weeks, with two and a half days per user effectively. Training duration seems to have been rushed and once more the focus was on the "broad but not deep" methodology. The short training duration led to an illusion of consensus between the parties (Gee, 1992). In our analysis, a false consensus existed between the trainers/super-users at IE.COM, in which trainers assumed that end-users were more similar to themselves than actually was the case (Ross *et al.*, 1977). A "shared context for knowing" could not take place due to the lack of shared and "mutual high-obligations" psychological contracts (Newell *et al.*, 2002; Shore & Barksdale, 1998).

Training duration was very short, and did not give enough time for users to understand and feel comfortable with the system (Bingi *et al.* 1999). The trainer from Atlanta spent too short a time at IE.COM. Time constraints prevented full transfer of perceived benefits of the system from the trainer to super-users and from these to end-users (Pliskin *et al.*, 1993). End-users were put on a two and a half day course prior to the system going live. Moreover they had to learn the system to be able to retain their job security (Davenport *et al.*, 1998).

Knowledge sharing issues in the CRM implementation

At the vertical level of hierarchy there was a management system called Signature Sales Leadership, which facilitated some knowledge sharing as it was used to gather data. Corrective action was taken during the weekly review whenever an out-of-bounds condition was identified. If there were pervasive issues that IE found consistently occurring across all the geographies, or all the brands, those were brought up to a sales operations review at a world wide level and they reviewed the process/design, or the tool capability and function, and at a global level. However, there was no system that captured, retained and exploited the tacit knowledge owned by the end-users:

> Within CRM Y are some data points and reference capabilities and analytical functionality etc but quite honestly there is no vehicle within CRM Y or CRM itself to capture tacit knowledge and then share that across other sales organizations. (Vice Chairman, World CRM Deployment)

According to the CRM Process Manager for IE.COM, at a lower level of hierarchy CRM smart website was used. From this website the end-users and their managers could take part in the latest development of the CRM tool. This allowed the end-users to take advantage of the prescriptive knowledge available in order to improve their work (Vincenti, 1993).

The adoption phase was rushed through. End-users did not get enough time to get to know the system well and were still locked in the old mindset with a familiar looking green screen (Deployment Leader). This led to the window of opportunity for adoption of the system starting to close and the system being adapted by the end-users (Orlikowski & Tyre, 1994). This was accompanied by negative talk in the toilets—people not being able to log on to the system which inhibited their performance—annoyance being expressed openly as well, for example "CRM Y's down, I can't log on, I've got three customers screaming at me, you've got to sort it out" (CRM Deployment Leader).

Following from the above, some free transfer of knowledge took place in informal settings (Kunda, 1991). However, this transfer of knowledge was in the form of a negative spiral which may not have helped in motivating adoption of the new system.

Some people however, were faster than others in picking up the system. They were more IT literate and had a "can do" attitude. The tricks of the trade, the short cuts, were getting born in the heads of the end-users. However, due to the competitive nature of the job, those work-arounds or short cuts may rarely get transferred (Vincenti, 1984). "So it could be—but in an ideal world it shouldn't be like that—we're all fighting them, the competitors. We're trying to win customers—we shouldn't be fighting each other—it happens though" (end-user). Élites possessing the knowledge find it hard to let it go and to share it openly with their colleagues (Davenport *et al.*, 1998):

> Everyone is protecting their sheep, because they are their opportunities, and they are numbers so they will be counted. (Andrew Nunes)

This exposes a subculture gap, where élites were on one side of the gap and may share the knowledge only among themselves. This can result in knowledge silos containing knowledge in the form of work-arounds and local knowledge which may remain embedded in certain groups or sub-cultures (Orlikowski & Tyre, 1994; Vincenti, 1984). This increases the dependence of non-elites on the elites (also called "gurus" by the CRM Deployment Leader at IE.COM) and "gurus" not only create job security for themselves but also increase the dependence of others on them (Salancik & Pfeffer, 1978). Some tacit knowledge may have got transformed into an explicit form through the reciprocity of relationships by way of informal interaction (Krogh *et al.*, 2000):

> Once a month we have a core and we talk mainly about the process side of things. But if one person is having something happen, then we'll always check to see if it's applicable in other countries. And I think it's something that's automatically happening—it's just something that you're not really aware of (CRM Process Manager).

The above was done in a formal setting which may have inhibited a free transfer of knowledge across sub-cultures (Kunda, 1991). Furthermore, CRM Y was implemented in five PDTs (Pre Deployment Teams) at IE.COM UK, but not concurrently. Consequently systems did not interlock with each other over a period of time. PDT5 (Database Marketing) came on board at a later stage. PDT1 (IE.COM) had the new system up and running, whereas the PDT5 was still using the old system and this continued for about eighteen months. All the PDTs had their own set up and did not interact with each other on a regular basis. They did, however, have a vertical reporting system and a help-desk that they shared with other PDTs. The latter was linked further with a business unit called the Service Management and that in turn is linked with the Project Team EMEA (Europe, Middle East and Africa) and World Wide Factory. There was no horizontal interaction structure that would facilitate the transfer of any "prescriptive knowledge" (Vincenti, 1993) across the PDTs (Service Manager). However, the vertical reporting system may have enabled some knowledge sharing. Knowledge, in particular tacit knowledge, may still have resided in vertical silos within the PDTs. Knowledge in such silos could become "sticky" that is, residing in one area or silo and not easily moved to the other parts of the organization (Bartlett & Ghoshal, 1998).

PDT1, had further six subsections that went live at the same time. They were: GSMB (Global Small and Medium Businesses), Sectors, Software specialist, Business Partners, Tele sales (based in Dublin) and Web team. Problems within these subunits were reported via the help-desk to the Service Management. Service Management then worked with the query and tried to resolve it. However end-users from IE.COM atIE.COM when talking to someone at helpdesk could end up explaining a local issue to an IT technician in a far away country. Alternatively, they could contact the Operation Team or Focal Point, based locally, to facilitate a face-to-face interaction in which case the local support would still have had to contact the help-desk (Bennett & Gabriel, 1999). So there was no way of by passing a vertical reporting system. While end-users could seek help from the super-users via their team leaders, there was no guarantee they would get help because "gurus" could be reluctant to pass on their personally held knowledge. The "gurus" may have developed their own "guru" subculture— which needs further investigation.

Furthermore, CRM Y was implemented in five Pre Deployment Teams (PDTs). PDT5 (Database Marketing) came on board at a later stage. PDT1 had the new system up and running, whereas the PDT5 was still using the old system and this continued for about 18 months without systems interlocking with each other. All the PDTs had their own set up and did not interact with each other on a regular basis. They did, however, have a vertical reporting system and a help-desk that they shared with other PDTs. The help-desk was linked further with a business unit called the Service Management. Service Management was linked further with the Project Team EMEA (Europe, Middle East and Africa) and World Wide Factory. There was no horizontal interaction structure that would facilitate the transfer of any prescriptive knowledge across the PDTs (Manager, Service Management). However, the vertical reporting system may have enabled some knowledge sharing. Knowledge, in particular the tacit/non-codified knowledge, may have resided in vertical silos within the PDTs. This needs to be investigated further.

The knowledge creation, retention and exploitation within the above six sub-units at IE.COM is worth investigating further. This would help to identify and understand the process of non-codified knowledge sharing across the various subsections within IE.COM. For an overview of the initial analysis of the contemporary situation at IE, see Figure 4.3

IMPLEMENTATION PROCESS: A PRELIMINARY ANALYSIS

This chapter set out to investigate the CRM implementation at both research sites, namely UKCC and IE. The chapter focused on CRM X implementation at UKCC and CRM Y implementation at IE. Special focus was given to IE.CM in UK atIE.COM. Case research methods were applied as both the CRM applications were in a formative

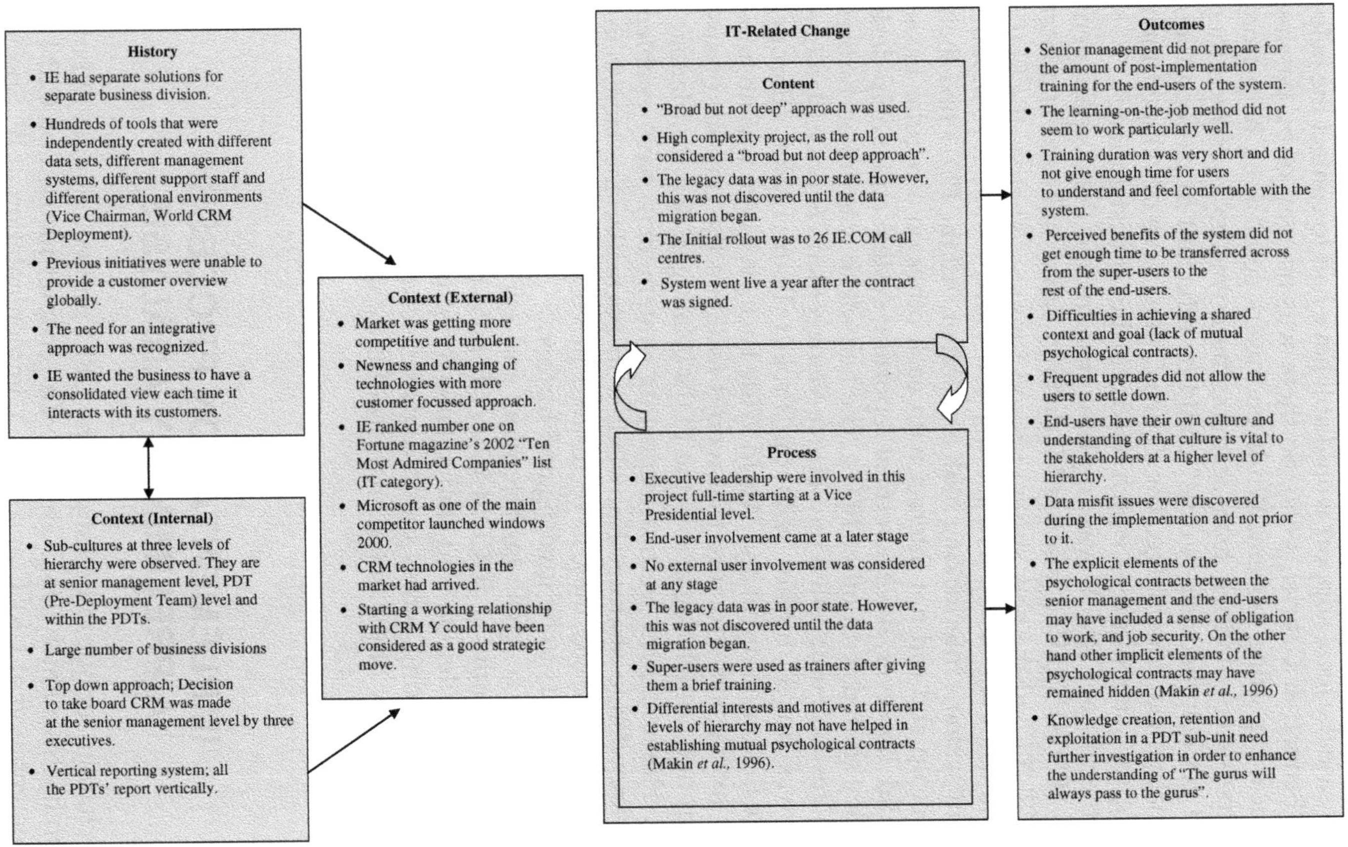

Figure 4.3 *A summary of analysis using Pettigrew (1985, 1990)*

stage and experience of the subjects and their perceptions was vital (Benbasat *et al.*, 1987).

The chapter was structured to describe the key events and then discuss the "how" and "why" questions regarding those events in terms of an initial analysis. Theories, both from within the literature review and outside it, were applied to enhance the understanding of CRM systems and their implementation at both the sites. The framework adopted to explain the "Process" by Willcocks and Margetts (1994) was used to highlight the key points raised in the initial analysis regarding the CRM systems at both sites. Here we make a preliminary cross-case analysis of findings, with a particular focus on the "Process" component of our analytical framework.

Management Support

Management support at senior management level was provided for both the projects. The support thinned out as people at UKCC started to leave. At IE they had employed full-time teams and committed resources to facilitate the implementation of CRM Y. However, they did not legislate for the poor state of the legacy data. Also the training seems to have been rushed at both sites. The initial motive behind bringing in the CRM system at UKCC was to get the calls answered. At IE they wanted to integrate the different business units. "Broad but not deep" methodology deployed by IE did not consider the expectations and the training needs of the end-users (Long & Fahey, 2000).

User Commitment

User commitment was linked very much with imposed psychological contracts at both sites (Rousseau, 1995). At UKCC users clearly found work-arounds in terms of using the manual methods to answer a call rather than using the CRM system itself. However, they ended up using the system to ensure the job requirement. At IE the end-users had to use the system as there were no other options. At both sites users had not been able to see the shared benefits fully yet and hence the psychological contracts were not completely of a "mutual high-obligations" type (Shore & Barksdale, 1998). At both sites user commitment had potential links with job security (Davenport *et al.*, 1998).

A "mutual perspective taking" had not happened fully due to the competitive nature of the job at IE and the secondee/non-secondee relationship situation at UKCC (Boland & Tenkasi, 1996). Furthermore, the content of an apparently mutual perspective may not have been allowed to surface, or be challenged, thus avoiding any interpretations which could shake up the illusion of consensus between stakeholders of the system (Fahey and Prusak, 1998). This was the case at UKCC. As the project progressed and the innermost feelings were exposed, people started to leave the project. The achievement of a new definition of the situation in which all participants could share had not yet taken place (Habermas, 1979).

User commitment may also have been affected by the lack of involvement in the decision making process in buying the systems. Decisions to buy the systems were taken at senior management level. End-users were involved in the implementation process at a later stage in both (UKCC and IE.COM) cases. No external user involvement was taken into consideration by either site.

User Training and Experience

Training at both the sites was an issue. At UKCC it was done without taking into account the UKCC culture and its expectations. At IE.COM user training was very short and also lacked the understanding of the end-user culture. Super-users at IE.COM trained the end-users without personally having sufficient experience to share the benefits to the end-users of CRM Y (CRM Deployment Leader). Trainers may have experienced an illusion of consensus with the users of the system at IE.COM. A false consensus effect may have existed between the trainers/super-users at IE.COM, in which trainers assumed that end-users were more similar to themselves than actually was the case (Ross *et al.*, 1977).

Project Time

Both the systems went live a year after the contract was signed with the respective vendors. In UKCC's case CRM X Provider (manufacturer of CRM X) also brought in Cavendish to help with the integration of the back-office systems. Subsequently UKCC also outsourced their call centre management to Independent Company. Consequences of outsourcing included some people resigning from the project and secondee/non-secondee relationship issues.

At IE.COM data migration and training suffered due to the lack of time. Training time per user at IE.COM was less compared to the training time at UKCC. At IE.COM only two and a half day's training was given before putting the end-users on the new system. Also, the IE system got updated with various releases all the time, compared to UKCC, where the only updates done were in the form of updated transcripts. The system at UKCC had not undergone such changes as it had at IE.COM.

Project Team Experience

The project team at UKCC went through its ups and downs. The CRM programme manager resigned soon after the new business manager's arrival. More people left, including the chief executive and the head of IT services as a result of a power struggle and conflicts (Jehn, 1995). Frequent changes of personnel may not have allowed the group to attain cohesiveness contributing to a less productive output (Kirkman & Shapiro, 1997). UKCC re-aligned their strategy and moved back from a complete integration approach to having a call answering system with limited integration.

IE had also committed full-time teams to working with the implementation. However, they underestimated the end-user training needs and consequently devoted insufficient time to training and education. They also struggled with data migration and did not take into consideration the poor state of legacy data in different business units.

Staff Stability

Staff turnover at the floor level at both the sites was very high. This did not allow staff interactions to come to a state of mutual perspective-taking where shared learning can take place (Boland & Tenkasi, 1996). The competitive nature of the work at IE.COM made it even more difficult for any creative abrasion to take place and may not have enabled people to share their innermost feelings to improve the cohesiveness of the groups (Leonard-Barton, 1995). The staff at floor level may not have got the opportunity or have the time to get engaged in what other members are involved in. At IE different PDTs rarely got the opportunity to sit down and share ideas on a regular basis to develop their common knowledge (Iansiti, 1993).

At UKCC people from the contact centre did not have many interactions with the back-office. The secondees felt left out at the contact centre. Furthermore their contract with UKCC did not allow them to be upgraded to a team leader position (Contact Centre Duty Manager). Non-secondees on the other hand could get promoted. Relationships at the contact centre between the secondees and the outsourced management were more power-based in style. This resulted in a scenario where UKCC secondees with a lot of experience and UKCC cultural knowledge felt inferior to their non-seconded colleagues.

There was also a high turnover of staff at senior level at UKCC. This did not help the project to get stabilized or the new staff to settle either. The resulting psychological contracts were more of an imposed than a "mutual high-obligations" type (Shore & Barksdale, 1998). Creative abrasion that could facilitate the development of "T-shaped skills" and sharing of "tricks of the trade" rarely took place. Stakeholders at different level of hierarchy interacted with each other from within their silos and the transfer of knowledge could remain limited to the silos.

Knowledge Sharing

Knowledge silos found at UKCC were at different hierarchical levels. At senior management level the sub-cultural gap between the Strategic Director of Resources's team and that of the Former Head of IT created a divide. The divide continued with the CRM Programme Manager getting replaced with a new business manager. Due to a lack of "mutual perspective taking" and "shared understanding" the psychological contracts were more imposed than "mutual high-obligations" in type (Shore & Barksdale, 1998). This inhibited the process of developing positive creative abrasion, thus resulting in knowledge hoarding in the silos.

Due to a strong vertical reporting structure, which resulted in power based relationships at IE.COM, knowledge hoarding occurred in vertical silos. In addition to this, knowledge was not being transferred freely along horizontal axes (across the end-user business units) due to the competitive nature of the job.

This chapter suggests that psychological contracts play an important role in knowledge sharing. It also suggests that imposed psychological contracts (employee under obligation) tend to promote power based relationships (Shore & Barksdale, 1998). Explicit elements of psychological contracts between senior management and end-users include a sense of obligation to work, and job security. Importantly implicit elements of psychological contracts remain hidden (Makin *et al.*, 1996) producing illusions of consensus, which influence and inhibit adoption and acceptance of the CRM system.

The micro mechanisms, for example psychological contracts, underlying the development of "mutual perspective","shared mental space", "T-shaped skills" and "knowing of what others know" need further investigation in order to fully understand the elements that inhibit or facilitate the sharing of "tricks of the trade" and work-arounds across the sub-cultures of a post CRM implementation environment. A further investigation of interdependencies between psychological contracts, sub-culture interactions and non-codified knowledge sharing can enhance our understanding regarding the knowledge sharing phenomenon in a CRM environment.

Both sites were at adaptation and acceptance stage where they were trying to develop the systems to promote the integration, and streamline the processes as much as possible. The impact of knowledge creation, retention and exploitation on the ongoing process of implementation is of high importance to both the organizations.

How knowledge, in particular tacit knowledge, is created, retained and exploited has not been fully addressed in this chapter. However, this chapter has potentially helped to expose areas that are worth exploring further: the tricks of the trade, the short cuts and work-arounds that are carried in the heads of the end-users of the system, their hands-on skills, including best practices and special know-how (Orlikowski & Iacono, 2001; Polanyi, 1973; Vincenti, 1984). In order to understand the above, one needs to understand the micro-elements (psychological contracts in our project) in the process of mutual perspective formation (Boland & Tenkasi, 1996) which facilitate tacit knowledge sharing. Scholars argue that tacit knowledge sharing is dependent on a creative abrasion type of environment where inner-most feelings are revealed (Leonard-Barton, 1995). Furthermore, it also depends on the types of psychological contracts in that creative abrasion environment (Rousseau, 1995). On the whole, the micro-elements that lead to "mutual perspective taking" would need to be investigated further at both sites. This will help to understand how the "tricks of the trade", the shortcuts, special know how, work-arounds, surface and transfer across the sub-cultures, individuals and groups.

REFINING METHODS, RESEARCH QUESTIONS AND FRAMEWORKS

Reviewing Methods

The methods of gathering data included historical analysis, face-to-face semi-structured in-depth interviews, telephone interviews and observations. The recurring themes in the gathered data raised many "how" and "why" types of questions (Hyde, 2000). These were used as constructs in the initial analysis of the implementation processes at both sites. The pilot helped to test the methodology and its appropriateness regarding the continuation of this research.

The comparative longitudinal case study approach used fitted well with this type of research as the focus of research is concerned with the effects and impact of the CRM system within the organization rather than the technical aspects of the CRM system alone (Myers, 1997). Comparison of similarities and differences regarding the adaptation and acceptance at both sites enriched the analysis and created more depth in drawing theoretical conclusions (Darke *et al.*, 1998; Pettigrew, 1997; Yin, 1994).

The "managing in" of CRM systems, and indeed their subsequent management has thrown up some common problems for UKCC and IE (Willcocks, 1991; Willcocks *et al.*, 2003; see also Chapter 2). This means that the expected outcome of this study may reveal more similarities and fewer differences in CRM implementation in both organizations.

Data in this pilot was also collected through observations at both sites (UKCC and IE.COM). The use of observation as a method of data collection is well documented (Bell, 1992). This was achieved through attending the staff meetings both at IE.COM and UKCC. Furthermore, workshops were carried out at both sites to involve key stakeholders of the CRM systems. This helped to refine not only the literature review but also the research questions and the guidelines for the final set (fifteen at each site) of interviews (see Appendix B).

Semi-structured in-depth interviews were constructed at both sites. The strengths of this method were that it was flexible and could be used to address quite focussed questions about aspects of organizational processes such as a specific decision making process (King, 1994). Interviews helped to probe the stakeholders of the system at both sites and were a useful tool with which to gather differing perceptions. The majority of the interviews were carried out on a face to face basis using an interview guideline. The face-to-face method gave an opportunity to gather the information through observing the characteristics of the interviewees during the interviews. The interview guide (Appendix A) helped to keep the focus on the key aspects of the literature review. It included a number of topics: introduction regarding the role of the respondent, implementation process, key events with dates, stakeholder perceptions regarding the key events, knowledge creation, retention and its exploitation.

The interview questions were open in order to allow the respondents to develop their perspectives rather than constrained by the perceptions of the researcher. Probing was used as a means of stimulating the flow of discussion where necessary. Interviews were audio taped and notes were taken by the interviewer. The note taking helped to gather information on what happened during the interview and clarified the researcher's understanding of what was being said.

Having transcribed the recorded interviews, manual colour coding was done and data was organized under recurring themes. This facilitated searching, marking up, linking and reorganising of data in a short period of time (Denzin & Lincoln, 2000). The recurring themes were used as constructs in the initial analysis of the implementation at both sites.

The variety of methods chosen created a useful form of triangulation (Yin, 1994). The data from key stake holders was then compared to find the similarities and dissimilarities between the cases using cross-case analysis. However, at this stage special attention was given to within-case analysis to enhance understanding of the implementation process of the CRM systems at both sites. The initial analysis provided a good base to probe further, with a special focus on non-codified knowledge sharing across the various sub-cultures at both sites. Continuous contacts with both companies were made to establish a good working relationship. Relationships at different levels of hierarchies at both the sites helped the researcher to gain further insight into the contemporary situation at both sites.

Refining the Literature Review Framework

The initial literature review was revised and developed in parallel with the initial data analysis carried out in this chapter. The initial literature review included a focus on how aspects of culture, psychological contracts and knowledge management can critically affect the implementation process of an IT system within an organization. Themes of stakeholder perceptions, psychological contracts knowledge sharing and subculture interactions have emerged strongly from the pilot study. Our refined review aims to integrate disparate literatures in order to provide a set of lenses and concepts to further study the introduction of CRM systems. Our new overview of this integration is shown in Figure 4.4. Some comment on this framework, and where it leads to, is useful.

In the general literature, there is a consensus over the importance of understanding the implementation process. Over the years, many attempts to explore different elements of the implementation process have been made. However, the links between stakeholders' perceptions (based on the differential interests, expectations and power) and non-codified knowledge sharing in the implementation process of a new technology have not been explored in depth. This research attempts to investigate the above mentioned knowledge sharing process by linking it with the "R" of the CRM implementation. The focus is narrowed down to the enablers and inhibitors to non-codified knowledge sharing in connection with a roll out of a new CRM system. There is a gap in the literature regarding the linkage between the existing implementation theories at micro level and CRM systems.

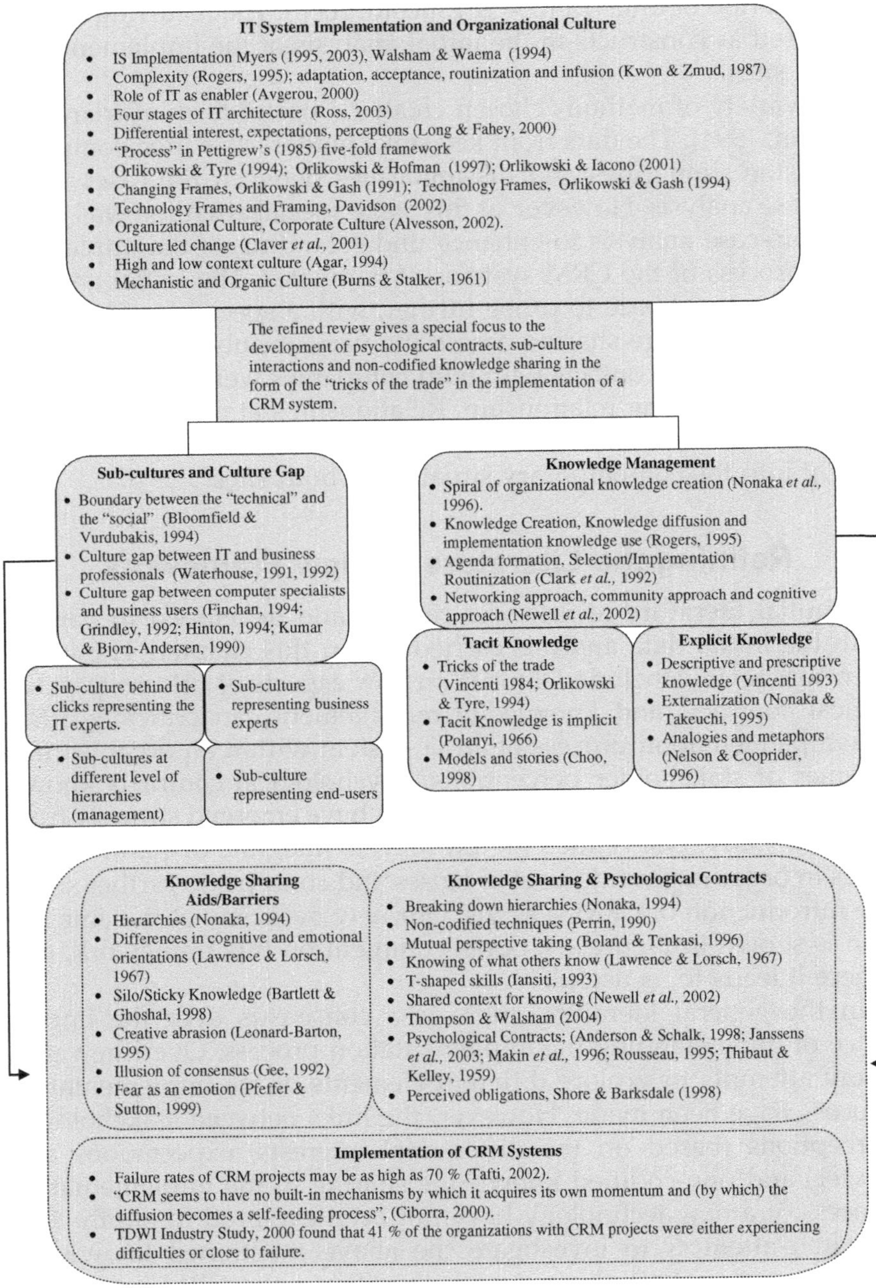

Figure 4.4 *Summary of refined literature review showing identified sub-cultures*

Moreover our pilot reveals that the literature gap—in studying the micro elements such as psychological contracts and their impact on knowledge sharing across the key sub-cultures in a CRM environment—is a serious omission. And while our review also revealed a consensus that informal settings can aid/facilitate the sharing of knowledge across sub-cultures, much still needs to be investigated over how to attain the "knowing of what others know", "shared context for knowing", and "mutual perspective taking". As recorded earlier, some scholars argue that psychological contracts play an important role in the outcome of an interaction between individuals, though no link has been established between non-codified knowledge sharing and psychological contracts. While different scholars talk about "knowing of what others know", "mutual perspective taking", "shared mental space" and "T-shaped skills", as aids to tacit knowledge sharing, they do not address the micro-elements that lead to these tacit/ non-codified knowledge sharing aids. And they certainly do not do this when studying CRM implementation. Our research, then, aims to fill this knowledge gap by investigating the micro-elements, in this case the types of psychological contracts. In particular the study will investigate psychological contracts that lead to a "mutual perspective taking" and "shared mental space", enabling tacit knowledge to be shared in an explicit form across key sub-cultures. It will also investigate the resulting affects on the adoption and acceptance of a CRM system.

Refined Research Questions

At the time of pilot study both research sites were at adaptation and acceptance stage where they were trying to develop the systems to promote the system integration, and streamline the processes as much as possible. The impact of knowledge creation, retention and exploitation on the ongoing process of implementation was of high importance to both the organizations.

How knowledge, in particular tacit knowledge, is created, retained and exploited has not been fully addressed in this chapter. However, this chapter has potentially helped to expose areas that are worth exploring further: the "tricks of the trade", the short cuts and work-arounds that are born in the heads of the end-users of the system, their hands-on skills, including best practices and special know-how (Orlikowski & Iacono, 2001; Polanyi, 1973; Vincenti, 1984). In order to understand the above, one needs to understand the micro-elements (psychological contracts in our project) in the process of "mutual perspective" formation (Boland & Tenkasi, 1996) which facilitate tacit knowledge sharing. On the whole the micro-elements that lead to "mutual perspective taking" would need to be investigated further at both sites. This will help to understand how the "tricks of the trade", the shortcuts, work-arounds surface and get shared across the sub-cultures, individuals and groups.

As a result of the pilot we refined our research questions to:

(a) How do the tricks of trade, special know how, the shortcuts, the work-arounds surface and get shared across the various sub-cultures during the adaptation phase of a CRM system, and with what effect?
(b) How are the psychological contracts linked with various types of knowledge sharings and sub-cultures and why?

These refined research questions have some research consequences. Certain salient features identified in Figure 4.4 need more emphasis in the research process. In particular, for our final case-work we made sure we carried out research across the following key sub-cultures identified in the pilot:

- sub-cultures at senior management level;
- sub-cultures at middle management level;
- sub-cultures at the floor level that are end-users;
- subculture represented by the IT experts here referred to as "the culture behind the clicks";
- subculture represented by the business expert.

We also ensured that we asked ourselves and respondents salient questions to elicit types of Psychological Contracts and how these linked with interactions across and within identified sub-cultures:

- What types of interactions, prolonged/limited, are taking place?
- What types of Psychological Contracts are linked with respective knowledge sharings and why?

Stakeholders from each subculture were interviewed again as part of our processual analysis throughout 2004 to see if their perceptions regarding the system had changed over time (Pettigrew, 1997). The information regarding their interaction was gathered through observations during team meetings, staff meetings and in-depth interviews. The types of psychological contracts identified, were matched with their respective interaction across and within the key sub-cultures. A rich picture eventually emerged showing the details of linkages, of psychological contracts with stakeholder interactions, and their impact on knowledge sharing. As we shall see, this helped us to understand which types of psychological contracts were linked with their respective knowledge sharings and why.

CONCLUSION: RESEARCHING CRM IMPLEMENTATION

This chapter has been a testing ground for methods, research enactment, and for developing further our understanding of what is worth researching, and also frameworks for analyzing research outcomes. The research methods proved resilient, while the pilot also confirmed, but also extended our view of the importance of neglected issues in the study of CRM implementations. This led to refinements in our research methods, literature review framework and research questions. Building on these we now develop further how we will go about describing and analyzing further the two CRM implementation cases.

Each case in Chapters 5 and 6 is divided into two parts, namely Part I and Part II. Part I goes through the interpretive narrative describing the course of events during a certain period of time at each research site. Part II is the analytic part and discusses the course of events, linking them to relevant theories from the refined literature review. A "within-case analysis" is carried out using the refined framework as a result of the pilot chapter and the theories discussed in the literature review. In Chapter 7, a cross-case analysis is carried out to compare the similarities and dissimilarities across the two cases in order to obtain an improved understanding of the rich picture.

The framework adopted from Pettigrew's (1985, 1990) six categories model contributed to developing a deeper insight into the contemporary situations and understanding the phenomena at both research sites. This framework in its improvised form as shown in Figure 4.5 is used further in the final analysis due to its proven appropriateness for this research (for more detail on this approach see Appendix C). The resulting salient features from the pilot study are used as a lens to focus on knowledge sharing issues linked with psychological contracts for final data analysis. These features have their links with the literature review (Davidson, 2002; Orlikowski and Gash, 1991, 1994; Pettigrew, 1985; Willcocks & Margetts, 1994). Some of the salient features were also picked up during the initial analysis and, in order to answer our research questions, their significance cannot be denied. We discuss these salient features in detail below.

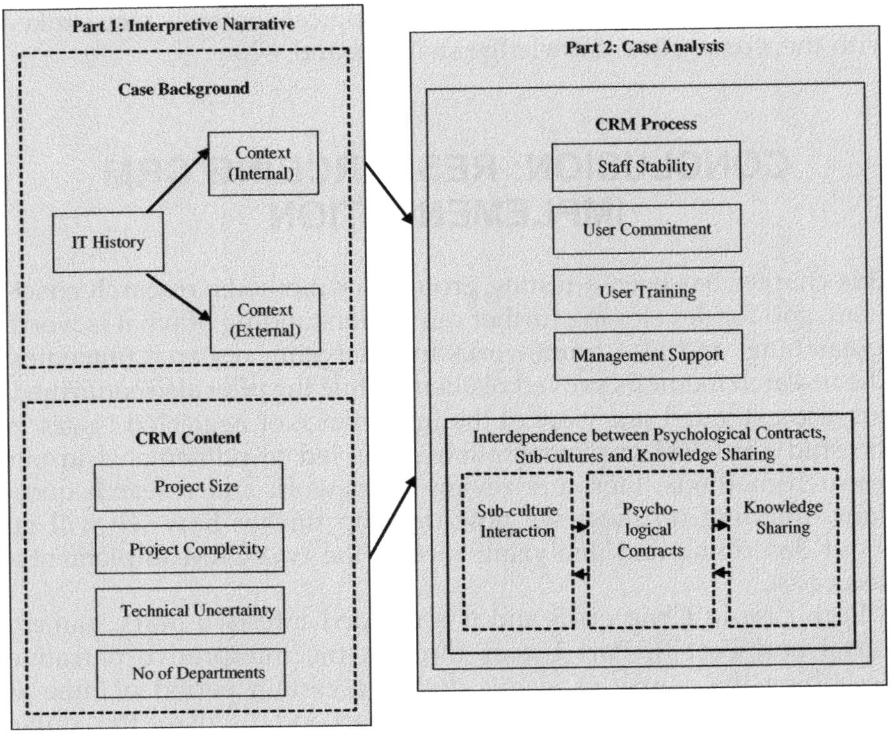

Figure 4.5 *Framework for final data collection and analysis*

Chapters 5 and 6 are organized according to the following schema:

Part 1—Interpretive Narrative

Company background

- IT History: IT history/background of the research sites.
- Internal Context: IS infrastructure and management; how much is outsourced and why?
- External Context: Market competition, government policies and supplier availability.

Content of the CRM project:

- Project Size: Whether it was a Big Bang (radical) approach or a step by step expansion (incremental).
- Project Complexity: Scale and complexity of project tasks, for example data migration.

- Technical Uncertainty: Understanding of business processes by the technical team. To what extent was the system integrated with existing business process.
- Number of Departments: Whether the user involvement had a narrow or broad base.

Part 2—Case Analyses

Process:

- Staff stability: staff retention issues; rewarding systems in place.
- User/Stakeholder commitment: how the user/stakeholder commitment has changed over time.
- User training: how is current user training being managed and have any training issues arisen from training?
- Management support: whether the support has increased after the implementation or decreased and with what effect.
- Knowledge sharing: what type of knowledge and how is it being shared, what is inhibiting/facilitating knowledge sharing?
- Sub-culture interaction: interaction between the end-users and management, between IT experts and business experts, and between the subgroups within the end-user groups.

In Chapters 5 and 6 that follow we present the second cycle of our longitudinal study. After having described history and context in an interpretive narrative we discuss and analyze critically processual and content issues from a knowledge perspective. We also present our analyses regarding psychological contracts and their interdependencies on subculture interactions and non-codified knowledge sharing.

5
CRM Implementation Case: A UK City Council Case Study (UKCC)

INTRODUCTION

This chapter presents the chronological description for the period 1999–2004, with a thematic account of a UK City Council's (UKCC's) initiative to deploy a CRM Solution to promote system integration. It uses the framework in Figure 4.5 to go into detail, and initially discusses the history, context and content (first part) as represented in Figures 5.1 and 5.2. It also uses the "Process" component of the framework to carry out a within-case analysis of the UKCC implementation and post implementation environment at (second part—see Figure 5.4.). After the case analysis, the section closes with a summary.

THE UKCC CASE PART 1—HISTORY CONTEXT AND CONTENT OF CRM

Case Background (IT History, Internal and External Contexts)

In this section, we describe briefly the history and internal context for IT at the UKCC. According to Pettigrew (1997), "The past is alive in the present and may shape the emerging future."

The UKCC analyzed in this case is one of the largest local authority in the UK. It has evolved from being one of the UK's cultural capitals to one of Europe's premiere conference and public events cities. It

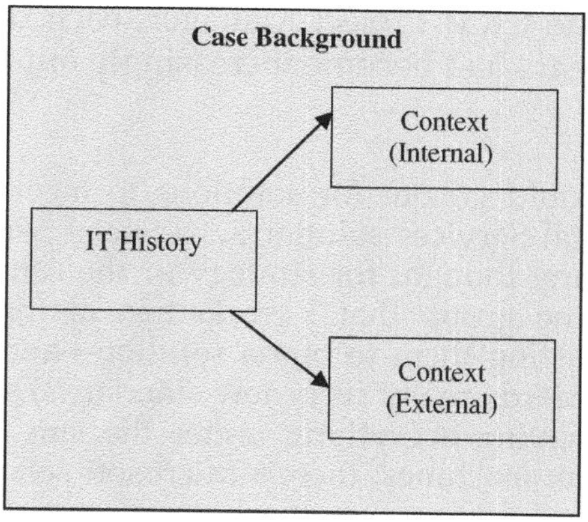

Figure 5.1 IT Background at the UKCC, including internal and external context

is a lively, prosperous and cosmopolitan city, offering a rich mix of culture, history, shopping, community life and the arts, comprising 11 parliamentary constituencies, 40 electoral wards and more than one million people.

Outsourcing of IT

In 1994 senior management at the UKCC made a decision to move away from a centralized IT structure, increasing autonomy over buying and outsourcing of IT services by departments. As a result, the role of central IT became more of a support function:

> If you think about the timing of that—that was at the time that PCs were really taking off and departments realized that they could afford to go out and just buy PCs. They didn't have to come to the centre and have a mainframe solution, or whatever, so over a number of years PCs started to proliferate—little IT groups grew in departments—and then there was very much a decision, a culture decision within the organisation, to allow departments a lot of freedom so that central control went. (CRM Project Manager).

According to Willcocks and Margetts (1994), the newness and attractiveness (convenience/pricing) of technology, as well as internal dissatisfaction with centralized control and government pressure, also led many public sector organizations, including our case example, to expose themselves to the consultancy and supplier markets. The following enlarges on the impact of the external context on the internal context, affecting the UKCC's IT strategic planning (Pettigrew, 1997).

According to the CRM Project Manager, each department at the UKCC over the years had become increasingly autonomous in terms of its IT:

> Departments would go out for solutions to meet their needs... so an Environmental Services solution... a Social Services solution... without really any thought for strategy or the centre—and certainly my group, or the group that I worked in at that point, was just focussed on assisting them to buy a solution—and it didn't have to fit into any standards really (very few standards) so we are left with this legacy of having everything under the sun out there—there's Unix, there's Vax machines, there's Microsoft servers, anything you can think of is out there, Sun machine, all sorts of things are out there.

Our respondent went on to express her frustration:

> We've got very few truly corporate solutions. We've got a finance system and we've got an HR system, beyond that, because we've got lots of different businesses and we've tried to look at SAP for example. But it always needs so much tweaking when it gets out into the departments that it's always cheaper to go and buy an off-the-shelf Propriety Leisure System /Propriety Environmental Services system / Propriety Museum System.

According to this respondent, "vanilla" applications seemed to be popular in the UKCC as they required less in-house expertise, a general trend also found elsewhere (Parr & Shanks, 2000; Willcocks & Sykes, 2000). The Head of the UKCC IT (up to October 2001) justified outsourcing in this way:

> When I was here I was the Head of IT and I had a staff of about 70 or 80 IT staff, but the IT staff were business analysts and system analysts and they weren't programmers. There were one or two people who were experts in Lotus Notes, but we didn't have programmers like COBOL programmers or anything like that. The programming assignments had all been outsourced to a vendor in 1989.

In-house implementation and development expertise during that period was limited. In particular, it lacked programmers. IT expertise was in the form of business or system analysts. The UKCC had no programmers or any really technical people on-site. According to the Former Head of IT, when they chose new packages they really had to be good, and not require a lot of technical skill to make them work. Thus the UKCC lacked a balanced mix of technical and business expertise, something seen as an inhibitor in previous implementation studies (see for example, Parr & Shanks, 2000). As a result, the role of the IT centre was diverted into supporting departments which would go out to buy solutions to meet their individual needs.

Various applications developed without consideration of a strategy for integration:

> This resulted in separate solutions for environmental services and social services respectively, without any thought for strategy. (CRM Project Manager)

System integration was a particularly difficult task:

> Everything's a balancing act, isn't it? But that's the situation we've inherited and that's why today (2004) when you say, 'Try to join things up.' Why are we so keen on trying to get an integration strategy together that enables us to do that? Because it isn't simply a case of saying! Well we've got four or five core systems, we've got hundreds of systems out there, hundreds and hundreds that do all sorts of different things in different ways. (CRM Project Manager).

Thus it would seem that IT solutions were bought in by different departments with little regard for cross departmental integration resulting in similar technology bottlenecks as recorded by Holland and Ben (1999) in their study of ERP systems implementation. According to our respondents, the pattern of outsourcing the programming to A VENDOR and buying of hundreds of solutions continued for many years.

The UKCC had realized over the last few years that it was not efficient as an organization and a lot of things that had been done on the re-organization of IT since 1999 were about trying to re-establish standards, though not without difficulties:

> But you can only go so far, with our re-organization. I'd have loved to have said, 'Right! All IT staff are now centralized'. But that's going too far because the departments have (are used to) their autonomy and won't release. (CRM Project Manager)

The literature suggests that sub-cultures formed as a result of the above IT autonomy may have different interests, expectations and power (Long & Fahey, 2000). As the departments acquired their own systems, the knowledge created did not get shared across the departmental sub-cultures due to the lack of system integration. A further investigation (later in this chapter) of these sub-cultures in different departments will assist in understanding knowledge sharing mechanisms.

Impact of political directives in the "Outer Context"

It is important to understand the larger political context and its impact for a UK the UKCC like our research site. According to the Office of the Deputy Prime Minister (2000), the UKCC was given the task of ensuring that all the services were available to the citizens through electronic means by 2005. This government directive was intended to promote continuous improvement of local government services to the public. The government had stated its commitment to promoting continuous improvement in local government services through Electronic Service Delivery (ESD), to achieve the target of 100 % ESD capability by 2005 (Office of the Deputy Prime Minister, 2002). Furthermore, this vision intended to modernize the way public sector delivers policies, programmes and services to its customers/citizens. The above illustrates the government deadlines and speed of new legislation that Willcocks and Margetts (1994) talk about as pressure factors, pushing the organizations towards consultant and supplier markets.

The purpose of IEG (Interactive Electronic Government) was to build local government services around the needs of customer/citizens rather than the organizational structures of service providers, giving its customers a "one-stop-service". All levels of government were encouraged to make full use of the potential for electronic service delivery to improve the responsiveness and quality of services. This potentially would result in different parts of the public sector working together seamlessly to deliver services more effectively and efficiently. This is where the IEG directive links with the idea of a CRM system, as proponents of CRM systems claim to facilitate a one-stop-shop for customers. New technology should not replace personal contact but it should make it better supported (Office of the Deputy Prime Minister, 2002). The government's agenda, according to the office of the Deputy Prime Minister, has been driven by social expectations—such as people's expectations to be able to deal with organizations by many different means, not just traditional face-to-face contact. The Hewson Group (2002) concluded from their research that society has become 24 × 7, non-stop, faster paced and full of opportunities to travel or experience a wider range of pursuits, and an essential part of this turn-of-the-century culture in western democracies has been an expectation of higher standards of customer service. As a result of these raised expectations, and explicit in central and local government exhortations, is the demand that public services need to exploit new technology to meet rising customer expectations successfully in the same way as the private sector if they are to avoid being accused of delivering poor quality services.

The CRM Business Manager at the UKCC commented:

> The UKCC is committed to improving services and fostering closer relationships between the Council and the Public. Evidence from recent annual customer opinion surveys conducted by MORI and customer feedback suggested that the Council has significant problems in responding to telephone calls. For a number of reasons, an unacceptably large number of calls (30 %) fail, either because the caller can't get through or doesn't get to the right person who could act on it. This leads to confusion as to whom customers should contact, difficulty in finding numbers, being passed from department to department and the provision of inaccurate and out-of-date information.

The above indicates a main reason for the implementation of a CRM system and a Corporate Contact Centre. However, various stakeholders had differing views and motives, resulting in sub-cultures which we will discuss in detail below.

The internal context at the UKCC

In this section the sub-cultures and subculture-gaps at the UKCC are discussed, using theories from the literature review (Fincham, 1994; Grindley, 1992; Hinton 1994; Kumar & Bjorn-Andersen, 1990; Louis, 1985).

Several sub-cultures were identified during the initial analyses at the UKCC:

1. Sub-cultures at senior management level.
2. Sub-cultures at middle management level.
3. Sub-cultures at the floor level that are end-users (these will be discussed at a later stage while analyzing the "Process" part of our analytic framework in this chapter).
4. Subculture represented by IT experts here referred to as "the culture behind the clicks".
5. Subculture represented by business experts.

The CRM project was originally perceived to have an IT-led approach. The revised approach after the Former Head of IT left in October 2001 was perceived as business led. According to the Contract Manager, Corporate Customer Relations, one group of people (led by Former Head of IT) had a positive attitude towards CRM implementation with an integrative approach, while the other group (led by the Strategic Director of Resources) had a less integrative, more "call-answering" focus.

This gave rise to two sub-cultures at the senior management level:

> As a result of that, the priority has gone into that area rather than developing CRM, collecting a lot of data about customers, using that data to shape services in the future. That's the area that's still weak at the moment (mid 2004). (Contract Manager, Corporate Customer Relations)

This points to a cultural gap between the social and technical (Bloomfield & Vurdubaki, 1994), that is, in this context, between the human resource department, service agents, end users, and some managers on the one hand, and on the other the programmers, IT technicians, developers and systems analysts. The public was not getting through unproblematically over the phone, causing considerable concern within the UKCC. This triggered politicians to look for ways forward. The IT-led group which included the Former Head of IT, CRM Programme Manager and the UKCC Consultant were concerned about establishing a strong link between the front- and back-offices using middleware to integrate the system, as we have seen in other systems implementations (Holland & Ben, 1999; Louis, 1985). Initially, the middleware design proved insufficiently effective, and this slowed down the process of implementation. Hence, a non-integrative approach, under the Strategic Director of Resources, supported by the Business Manager and other like-minded people, was taken on board as a better alternative. The problematic nature of the differing cultures, one stemming from an IT background and the other from a financial background created a further hurdle with some serious consequences in the form of people leaving the project, thus slowing down implementation progress—an issue with parallels in other implementations (Bloomfield & Vurdubaki, 1994; Price Waterhouse, 1991, 1992).

Each IT unit in the UKCC had developed increasing autonomy during the 1990s and into 2004. Furthermore, a culture decision within the organization to give departments more IT freedom took away the central control and weakened the influence of corporate culture on the departments. This strengthened the departmental sub-cultures (sub-cultures at middle management level). By 2004 every department had different solutions, as it always seemed cheaper to go and buy off-the-shelf systems for self-use. But problems arose when different departments wanted to communicate with each other without the necessary system integration. This situation was not helped by the fact that departments had gathered knowledge over the years that some found hard to release without seeing any clear benefits. As Davenport *et al.* (1998) argue, individuals sitting with certain knowledge may have fear of losing their power or position by releasing their knowledge completely. At our UKCC knowledge hoarding gave rise to vertical silos:

> This type of knowledge hoarding has given rise to vertical silos in the UKCC at a departmental level. (CRM Programme Manager)

According to Leonard-Barton and Kraus (1985), making the knowledge residing in such vertical silos mobile across departments is an important facilitator of implementation. Such knowledge possessed by the departments can be in explicit or implicit state, both codified and non-codified (Perrin, 1990). In other words, it can be in descriptive, prescriptive or tacit form (Herschbach, 1995; Nonaka and Takeuchi, 1995; Vincenti, 1993). It becomes vital to investigate the elements that facilitate the sharing of knowledge residing in various forms across the departmental sub-cultures in our case example.

Moving towards CRM

Central government in the UK had legislated that 100 % of all public interactions with local government bodies must be made available by electronic means by April 2005 (Office of the Deputy Prime Minister, 2002). The British public had, despite assertions to the contrary, enjoyed two decades of rising standards of service in virtually every walk of commercial life (Hewson Group, 2002). In order to meet these expectations public services were increasingly looking towards implementing Customer Relationship Management (CRM) systems.

By late 1998 the UKCC was concerned about their public call-answering capacity. An internal evaluation showed that less than 10 % of people could get through on their first call to the UKCC. The Council had been looking at establishing a corporate contact centre for a number of years:

> Various consultants were brought in for short periods about the idea, but it had never really got off the ground. It was being looked after by the Transportation Department. They were looking at an initiative called 'Street Scene' where they would have contact from the public regarding all issues affecting the streets, and they felt that that would form the basis from which other contacts from the public could be established. (CRM Programme Manager)

Moreover:

> 70,000 phone calls were received in a day; I think we answered about 1,000 (some fantastically bad figure). There's all sorts of reasons for

> it, not bad people, but very bad organization, management, things like that. It was the CRM Programme Manager that really got things going well. (Former Head of IT)

According to the CRM Programme Manager:

> The IT Director, was keen to get something off the ground and felt that no other department could really pursue the initiative because they had gone as far as they could. Former Head of IT suggested that central IT pick up the baton and try and run with it as a corporate initiative, not just based on 'Street Scene' but generally, in other wider areas in relation to corporate issues involving contact with the public.

As a result, the UKCC started looking at establishing a corporate contact centre. According to several respondents, one of the key requirements identified was the need to set up some form of corporate access database. By doing so, they could record and monitor the contacts and "that would be an important component of any contact centre that was established—and that's when we started looking at CRM as an issue" (Former Head of IT). The above statement describes the UKCC rationale for a CRM solution. They intended to use a CRM system to improve the call-answering service to their customers.

According to the CRM Programme Manager, the CEO at the time was well aware of the protracted dialogue that had taken place: "It was one of these initiatives that had just been kicked around." He further argued that it had never really had a project champion, so when the Former Head of IT suggested that Central IT take up the initiative his suggestion was enthusiastically endorsed by the chief executive. The CRM Programme Manager also indicated that the chief executive was very keen to improve the communications with the public and felt that everything was too diverse and too spread over the Authority.

CRM vision starts to move towards reality

There needed to be a greater focus on receiving communication from the public:

> The Chief Executive saw a very good working call centre in Brisbane and suggested having one in the UKCC once he got back. (CRM Programme Manager)

The above indicates that the project had a project sponsor in the form of the Chief Executive, one of the strong recommendations coming out of parallel research on IT project implementation (see for example Goodhue *et al.*, 2002, Willcocks & Sykes, 2000). From thereon the CRM project started to take shape and develop. Several key events took place before the system went live. A description of key events during the implementation may help to enhance the understanding regarding the implementation process of CRM system at our research site.

The Former Head of IT started to work with the idea of a CRM system as a solution to the UKCC call answering problem:

> There's another key character, who is still working here, the Contract Manager, Corporate Customer Relations. He is brilliant. He sees things, brings them all together and if you ask the right questions, out it all comes into a strategic whole. It was him that told me, 'This is what's it's really about, Former Head of IT, not just answering the phone but connecting the agents to the back-office systems and logging everything in the middle.' That was critical and he [Contract Manager] and I talked about it all the time. He got it spot on and it was really important. So immediately we started developing the idea for a government computing conference.

The first big presentation on CRM was in 1999 to a government computing conference and on that occasion the Former Head of IT had expressed the idea of every authority in the country having its own CRM but all linked together through the Internet, so any citizen anywhere could actually link into the CRM. Former Head of IT's idea was received positively. The Deputy Leader of the UKCC was interested in promoting modern techniques. He got the Former Head of IT and the Strategic Director of Resources together and gave them the go-ahead regarding a CRM project. At this stage, according to several respondents, the Strategic Director of Resources was more concerned about answering the calls more effectively than anything else. Significantly the Former Head of IT and Strategic Director held different and potentially conflicting underlying views that did not surface until a later stage of the CRM project, an issue that appeared also in research by Pliskin *et al.* (1993).

Wathne *et al.* (1996) argue that factors such as accuracy, timelines, adequacy and credibility of interactions influence perceptions of honesty and openness, and are essential to achieving more frequent and relevant knowledge sharing between the partners. According to several studies, a creative abrasion—here between the Strategic Director of Resources and Former Head of IT—at an early stage of a project, in this instance the CRM X project, could have helped to create a "shared context for knowing", leading to a mutual perspective. This could have facilitated knowledge sharing between the two and even across the sub-cultures (Boland & Tenkasi, 1996; Newell *et al.*, 2002).

According to Krogh *et al.*, (2000), effective knowledge creation depends on the physical, virtual and emotional context of an organization. They discuss the importance of the notion of reciprocity of relationships. When a relationship is felt to be reciprocal then a trust develops which can work to overcome power-based relationships. Relationships between the Former Head of IT and Strategic Director of Resources were not felt to be reciprocal. This resulted in lack of trust from both sides. Their psychological contracts were low on trust and loyalty, resulting from conflicting ideas, motives and interests. A mutual perspective towards CRM X was absent (Boland & Tenkasi, 1996).

Preparation for a CRM solution

According to the "Managed Service Business Case Draft" prepared by the CRM Programme Manager and the Contract Manager in 1999, CRM would be at the core in enabling the management of the citizens' relationship and ensuring a consistency of approach across the customer facing operations within the Authority. The delivery of the CRM solution would underpin all these initiatives and provide a single view of the citizen shared across all access points. The draft further states that the fundamental requirement within the Customer Service environment would be the ability of the Service Provision to integrate seamlessly with the back-office systems and facilitate a single presentation of customer data to the operators. This would ensure both improved efficiency as well as end-to-end accountability for the customer transaction. This requirement is regarded in the Business Case Draft as one of the principal criteria for the selection of the CRM solution.

The Report from the Former Head of IT to Chief Officers' Group was delivered on 1 December 1999. According to this, as shown in Figure 5.2, the provision of a CRM system would provide a common view of the customer shared across the distribution channels, utilizing a common database. There would be a requirement for the operators of the one-stop-shops and Contact Centre to utilize the CRM system. The creation of the CRM solution needed to embrace the changing communication methods that would emerge over the next three years—for example, according to the document, e-mail handling capability was set to form 15% of total transactions, Interactive TV would play a key role, as well as the traditional channels (Source: Managed Service Business Case Draft).

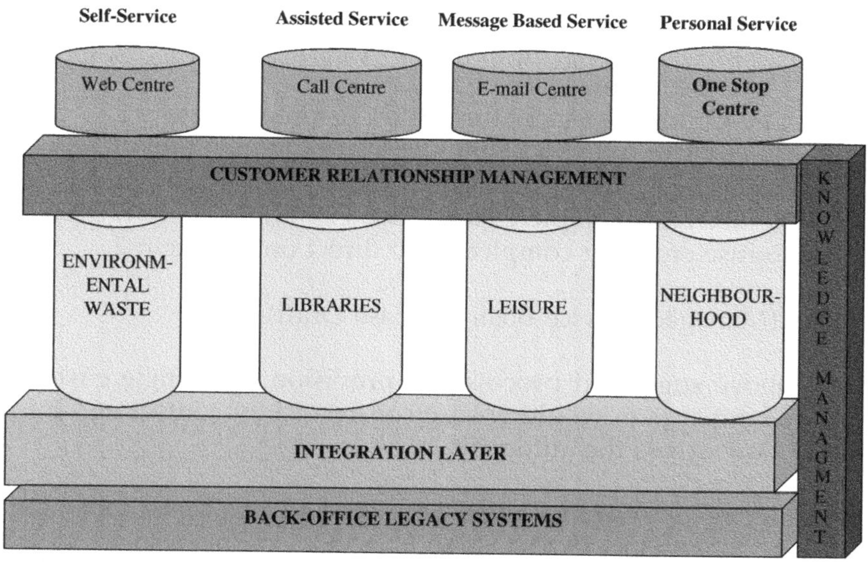

Figure 5.2 *Proposed Technical Infrastructure regarding CRM at the UKCC (1999)*

Furthermore, according to the Former Head of IT, key drivers for the new initiative needed to establish corporate standards for:

— Common Database
— Common Telephony architecture
— Common Customer Management system
— Common Working Processes
— Common Working Practices
— Multi Channel Accessibility

For example:

Current End to End process for Refuse collection

1. The Customer Contacts the Call Centre
2. The Call Centre Agent captures the Customer's; data
3. The Call Centre Agent transmits a Request to the DSO
4. The DSO produces a Job Request Form
5. The Job Request Form is issued to the Refuse crew to complete the work
6. The Refuse crew completes the work
7. The completed Job Request Form is returned to the DSO
8. The DSO log the completed Job Request Form details back onto the System

Suggested revised End to End process for Refuse collection

1. The Customer Contacts the Call Centre
2. The Call Centre Agent captures the Customer's data
3. The Call Centre Agent transmits a Request to the Refuse Crew (via System 2)
4. The Refuse crew completes the work
5. The Refuse crew log completed job direct onto System 2

Source: (Managed Service Business Case Draft)

In the above suggested process, the provision of a single customer management system would ensure consistency of contact and information flow across the authority.

Outsourcing of implementation—the out sourcing trend continues

According to the Former Head of IT, primarily the UKCC felt that it needed someone who had the right implementation experience. The UKCC Consultant, who had a good track record, was employed from May 2000. However, much of his experience was from the private sector which differs from the public sector in several distinctive ways (Willcocks & Harrow, 1992). Together with the UKCC Consultant, three more consultants were hired.

One of these consultants had a background in work study for over 20 years in the public sector. He also had experience in call centres and script design. He was hired to do business process re-engineering in terms of process analysis in relation to the targeted areas for a contact centre. Their initial role was to investigate neighbourhood offices and council tax. The UKCC Consultant's role was to manage the consultants and also to act as an advisor to the Former Head of IT. The hired consultants lacked specific knowledge of the UKCC culture and its operations. This necessitated their working closely with the UKCC if they were to acquire that type of knowledge and share their own knowledge in order to facilitate knowledge sharing in both directions.

From May 2000 onwards the UKCC went through a process of putting requirements together with a view to going out to tender. There were also some presentations from suppliers. Fourteen were invited, of whom five replied. A CRM vendor was chosen. The criterion against which A CRM vendor was selected was best value, expressed as a 70/30 split, 70 % functional, 30 % cost for the procurement. A CRM vendor won on all counts and Strategic Director of Resources agreed to contract with A CRM vendor, even though they were a small company. The UKCC took a CRM vendor on board together with their partner, as part of the strategy. The council had only 39 systems-facing people, so the idea was, in the Former Head of IT's words, that:

> We'd better get in bed with somebody who's very good at doing integration, because we aren't.

The council entered into contract negotiations with a CRM vendor, the provider of software called X. The council also went on a site visit to Sussex Police in Brighton during October/November 2000 to observe their gazetteer using a CRM application. In December 2000, the decision to sign with the CRM vendor was made, the contract being finalized in March 2001. Keeping in view the limited programming expertise in the City Council, an off-the-shelf package was chosen. It could be configured and implemented fairly quickly. There were also possibilities for back-office integration through an in-built XML facility in the package. However, these capabilities were not exploited due to the lack of in house IT expertise. Outsourcing was carried out without any prolonged discussion with the departments. This led to creating of under-obligation types of psychological contracts between the partners (Shore & Barksdale, 1998). The impact of these weak psychological contracts on knowledge sharing is discussed under the "Process" part of our framework at a later stage in this chapter.

CRM Project Content

Project size

The system goes live: developments from March 2002

The system went live in March 2002. This included the Corporate Contact Centre managed by yet another outsourced vendor, using the X solution/software, providing services for Environmental Waste, Neighbourhood Advice and Council Tax. Prior to that, from about July/August 2001, a pilot of the CRM system with Environmental Services was done, which was one of the first service areas that went live. However, the system tested without physically having a contact centre in place. It was done in the existing office. The product was used to see how it interacted with the council's back-end system and what values it generated and problems it caused. There were some major issues with that pilot, centred on the technical side in getting it to talk correctly with the back-end system. One issue was that Environmental Services at that point were in the process of renewing their back-end system. Difficulties with the pilot indicate that, against

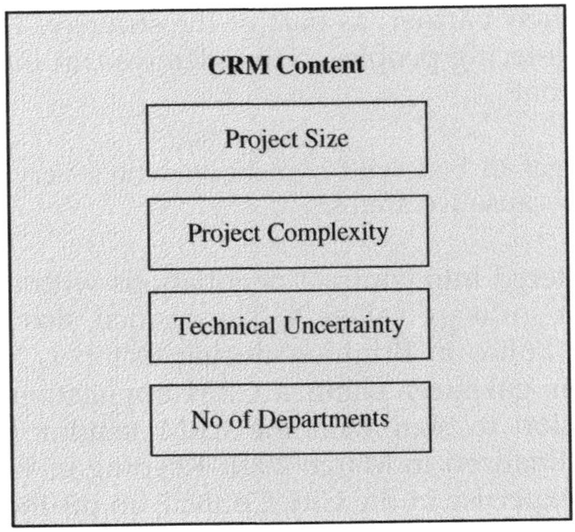

Figure 5.3 *Content of the CRM Project at the UKCC*

Leonard-Barton and Kraus (1985) a clear purpose, well defined and communicated, was missing.

The pilot test did not involve collective testing. Each department did its own tests with the system independently. This did not enable any close interaction between the different departments. Hence, the opportunity for any prolonged creative abrasion to take place, as recommended by Newell *et al.* (2002), was not there. Different departments also had weak, under-obligation types of psychological contracts with Corporate Customer Relations, who were the driving force for CRM X. This was a result of limited stakeholder involvement in the CRM Project. Departments felt left out. As many respondents reported to us, these weak psychological contracts—as a result of limited interactions in both horizontal and vertical directions—undoubtedly inhibited the free flow of knowledge from one department to another and from departments to Corporate Customer Relations. A sense of shared benefits which could have helped in the mobility of knowledge silos and hoarding was missing at the departmental level.

Just as seriously, there was no external customer involvement in the process of implementation of X. In fact the UKCC had tried it before and it had not worked. According to the Temporary Head of IT:

> It was much better to take something to the citizens, get it changed and validated, rather than giving them a blank piece of paper and saying, 'This is what we are going to do. How do you want to do it?'

The UKCC using a prudent approach started small and involved only three departments to start with. They were:

— Environmental Services
— Neighbourhood Advice
— Council Tax

According to the CRM Project Manager:

> To start with, five UKCC services were supposed to go on board with CRM X. This got reduced to three. It was very much a political directive as to which went in and which did not. The Council did an awful lot of work with Leisure, and then all of a sudden they dropped Leisure because Revenues became more important, so they just had to dump all the Leisure work.

The UKCC Contact Centre first went live March 2002. Three main services, Revenues (which included Council Tax), Neighbourhood Advice (which are general enquiries) and Environmental Waste for domestic customers (which also includes abandoned car vehicles) were included from the start. During the year 2003 the Benefits Service front-end also went in, so telephone enquiries for Benefits then went into the Contact Centre. At the very end of 2003 in December, two relatively small services, Recruitment and Home Works went on board. Later in April 2004 Anti Social Behaviour and finally in July 2004 the Leadership Line also came on board.

Department of benefits

When benefit enquiries came in, the agents accessed two or three main UKCC systems. There was a script flow process, but the script flow would only take them through certain types of enquiry, to actually answer the detail on the enquiry they needed to access the mainframe systems that held the key information. According to Corporate Customer Relations:

> It's either guidance, 'Can I claim? How would I claim? What are the rules about claiming?'—or it's detailed enquiries about existing claims, or it might be—'I applied two weeks ago, what's happened to my claim? Where is it in the process? How close am I to getting it sorted or what is holding it up?' And within the mainframe system are certain codes and information about where it is in that process and the agent would then use that information and explain to the customer, "Right at the moment we're awaiting a reply from your Landlord about your proof of rent'—or whatever it may be.

Benefits advisors tended not to use X CRM system as they had two back-office systems called Multi Benefit Assessment System (MBAS) and Document Management System (DMS). Both were 14 year old mainframe systems also called "Green Screens" by the users.

Department of recruitment

If a member of the public wanted to apply for a job within the UKCC then they phoned the Contact Centre. It only dealt with the initial information regarding a job advert. It could send a job application upon the caller's request or clarify any simple detail surrounding the advert. The Contact Centre, having taken the initial call, furnished the application and then informed the UKCC's Human Resources system that the form had gone out. Moreover, if that form then came back in, it would come back in at the Central Department, the back-office, not the Contact Centre.

Home works

Home works involved members of the property owning public being able to get information from the UKCC regarding assistance in funding the upgrading/repairing of their own property. They were given advice on borrowing money to carry out repairs and maintenance. The service was predominantly a referral service.

A Corporate Customer Relations manager commented:

> Home Works/House Proud will advertise on buses throughout the City. Please get in touch if you want to do up your house and you may qualify, because there's some qualification criteria for these services.

The advisor at the Contact Centre only dealt with the initial qualification involving asking questions regarding the caller's personal information after which the advisor referred the case to the back-office. Corporate Customer Relations admitted that it was mainly a one-directional process. Information travelled only from front-office to back-office. No knowledge sharing occurred in the opposite direction. The back-office, after receiving the initial assessment, then got in touch with the customer, or potential customer, and furnished them with guidance on how to proceed. It dealt with the case from there on.

Anti-Social behaviour line

According to a Corporate Customer Relations manager:

> The position with Anti-Social Behaviour is there's a Central Government initiative for Authorities to be more reactive to anti-social problems.

The Anti-Social Behaviour Line basically received complaints and offers guidance. A member of the public would phone in with a particular anti-social problem and the agents would guide them in terms of their rights and possible procedures.

One respondent explained the above with the following example:

> For example, they might not be happy with some activities going on and it might be that under the current legislation there's not a lot else that can be done. So kids playing football somewhere, they might deem it anti-social but legally it's not so anti-social. So they will be given what information they can.

Leadership line

The leadership line according to the Corporate Customer Relations manager was:

> a telephonic line that has its own unique number that the Deputy Leader, or the Leader for that matter, of the UKCC, if they want to go on a radio station and publish or promote a certain campaign and they say, I want to know the public's feeling about it, then that's the number they'll probably give out. And what happens with those enquiries is, those enquires are then fed back to the Deputy Leader's office, via e-mail, so it might be a particular campaign that the Deputy Leader or the Leader wants to promote and says to the . . . might go on the radio, for example, and say, I want to know people's concerns about, I don't know, illegal car clamping, that was one of the issues.

The call centre then took the calls and fed the data into the Deputy Leader's office via e-mail. X CRM System was used scarcely, if at all. Moreover the whole process, of taking calls and referrals to the back-office, was a one way reporting system, with no two way communication between the Front and the back-office apart from in the case of Environmental Services. However, the back-office at the Environmental Services was not satisfied with the service provided by the front-office customer service advisors, also known as agents. According to the Business Manager, Environmental Services:

> X System at the moment I've seen absolutely no benefit from. It's not really been of that much interest to me. My focus has been on trying to get the businesses used right, so we're not spending money unnecessarily. My understanding is that there is a mass of data sat in X in relation to who's been contacting the City and details of callers are recorded, but I've no idea still what use that information is being

> put to, or even how I can access it. So to all intents and purposes CRM X itself is being of very little use to me as a business representative. In terms of the Contact Centre running itself—big advantage—and the big advantage we've had is that calls are answered, whereas before it wasn't resourced to handle all the enquiries that were coming in, so we've solved that problem. What I'm not sure about, and will take some convincing, is the quality of what is said when the person (caller) gets through to them, or the quality of the data that is recorded to enable the business to do its job.

The above statement shows that knowledge sharing was in one direction only. The information loop was kept open and did not get a chance to be completed. Lack of trust regarding the quality of Front-Office service using X CRM appeared to be an issue between the Environmental Department and the front-office. Reciprocity in the relationships was missing. This gives rise to a "mutual low-obligation" type of psychological contract with a lack of shared mental space or shared understanding (Krogh *et al.*, 2000; Newell *et al.*, 2002; Shore & Barksdale, 1998). The lack of shared understanding may have resulted from a lack of prolonged social interaction between the groups (Gray *et al.*, 1985; Isabella 1990; Newell *et al.*, 2002) as creative abrasion did not take place due to a lack of prolonged interaction between the Environmental Department and the front-office (Contact Centre managed by An Independent Company). Knowledge sharing in the above case was limited due to the lack of prolonged social interaction which could have provided opportunities for creative abrasion resulting in "mutual high-obligations" types of psychological contracts. This is also argued by Gregory (1983), Pettigrew (1979), Riley (1983), Schein (1985) and Strauss (1978) who further suggest that people tend to share assumptions, knowledge, and expectations with others with whom they have close working relationships.

Although the size of the project initially was fairly small, the geographic separation between front-office and back-office increased the distance between the two. This resulted in limited face to face interaction. The lack of in-house IT expertise at the UKCC further added to the difficulties in aligning business processes with system integration. Not only was there an unbalanced mix between IT and business expertise but also a lack of prolonged in-depth interaction and creative abrasion between the Front and back-offices (Leonard-Barton, 1995; Newell *et al.*, 2002; Parr and Shanks, 2000). Such abrasion as took place was of a predominantly negative form resulting in mistrust. Poor communication not only created problems between Front and back-offices but also in other areas such as between secondees and non-secondees.

Project complexity

The CRM project at the UKCC became more complex due to differing individual interpretations of the objectives. The Strategic Director of Resources did not want to waste time in discussing the complexities of system integration and was pressurized by the fact that customers were not getting through to the Council. The Former Head of IT and CRM Programme Manager were in favour of a robust solution that would have taken more time.

The Strategic Director of Resources was primarily concerned about the high costs and time constraints and wanted the project to be launched as quickly as possible. Delay in understanding the system requirements was caused by a lack of marriage between business processes and IT capabilities.

The Business and IT sub-cultures in the above did not share a mutual perspective (Boland & Tenkasi, 1996). Success depends not only on how effectively diverse individuals are able to organize and develop their unique knowledge competencies, but also how they can integrate and utilize their distinctive knowledge synergistically (Nonaka, 1994). Such synergy can be obtained if barriers to knowledge sharing across the key sub-cultures are understood. It requires a process of mutual "perspective taking" where distinctive individual knowledge is exchanged, evaluated and integrated with that of the others in the organization (Boland & Tenkasi, 1996).

The fact that each department had outsourced their system to different vendors did not help matters. A complete system integration was clearly going to be time consuming and time was something the Strategic Director of Resources was running short of.

In social psychology the above discussed phenomenon has been studied in the prisoner's dilemma game, in which the highest outcomes for both participants can be achieved if both co-operate, but a high proportion of participants tend to make selfish choices that lead to lower outcomes for both (Thibaut & Kelley, 1959). Due to time constraints and lack of a mutual perspective between the Strategic Director of Resources and Former Head of IT, a decision made by the Strategic Director did not take into account the system integration argument put forward by the Former Head of IT and CRM Programme Manager. This resulted in increased project complexity and technical uncertainty which we will now discuss further.

Technical uncertainty

Lack of a good mix between IT and Business expertise increased technical uncertainty (Parr & Shanks, 2000). According to the Business Manager, Environmental Services:

> The IT Section at, on the Client side, Corporate Customer Relations and IT Programmer and whatever, haven't really got a grasp of business, yet they are responsible for specifying changes to a system.

Due to departmental outsourcing, a vast amount of data got stored in several different systems without any communication links across them. Integration of these legacy based systems to CRM X turned out to be a difficult task. Data migration suffered as the data remained stored in the mainframe legacy systems in the back-offices. As the Corporate Head of Programme Management put it:

> We have quite a few different back-end systems, because effectively for an organisation as vast as the council and with . . . the business diversity, because that's one of the big differences between Local Authorities and the private sector—is that if you go into one of our Departments and you'll find five, six, seven different, completely different diverse business functions that are all multi-million pound businesses in their own right, which means that we don't have any ERP solution that will meet all our requirements, there isn't one. So what you get is you get a series of departmental solutions and what Local Government has been bad at over the years and we're now trying to resurrect, is you do get silos, so you get silos of information and departmental solutions. So none of our solutions are customer based, they're all of Unix servers, different Unix servers, with different package solutions because there isn't one that you can go off and buy and say, we'll have that for the enterprise. So it is a big difficult integration problem to get into the back-end systems.

Although there was an inbuilt integration capability (XML) in the X system, according to the IT Programmer the manufacturer of CRM X did not have enough knowledge to exploit XML integration, to establish a link between CRM X and existing main frame systems in the back-offices. As a result, their EAI (Enterprise Applications Integration) remained incomplete. This resulted in end-users logging in separately into their legacy/main frame systems and using CRM X only for salutation purposes. This also caused some delay in the service. Further delay was caused by mandatory duplication:

> Actually, the amount of time we spend advising somebody can be a lot less that the time its takes, particularly if the call is something for

> a different Department, but once you've gone through all the data protection stuff to open up the plane you have to put loads on it because you've looked into it. So the amount of time you can spend logging, pass to a different Department, you have to do it three times on three different systems. (an end-user).

Technicality as an issue was also evident from the comments made by end users of the CRM X system:

> No, I just feel technically its ineffective; I just feel there are too many technical problems with it. It doesn't want to perform, if I was to list all the technical issues I have with that PC and all the technical issues that I've had to log through it to other providers we would seriously have reams and reams of paper. (an end-user)

The UKCC dealt with its IT skills shortage by outsourcing most of the IT infrastructure. As the departments grew larger and more independent, so did the IT systems. However, the systems grew bigger without any overall integration between the departments. The above reports indicate that the Council's outsourcing strategy of IT functions did not pay off in the case of CRM system integration. This was due to the lack of advanced system integration knowledge by the service provider (manufacturer of CRM X). End-users, especially secondees were moved from the back-offices to sit in a call centre managed by The Independent Company but still used their old systems to resolve the customer queries, using CRM X mainly for salutation purposes.

The above scenario resembles the study by Willcocks and Margetts (1994) on risks in large projects. The separation of IT management from policy making and business process alignment created a divide between IT Management and Business Process Owners at the UKCC. The e-government directive as discussed previously wanted to ensure a "one-stop-service" for local authority customers. To be able to provide an integrative service it was important to have the various systems in different departments communicating with each other. System integration, according to Strategic Director of Resources, seemed a time consuming task. However, without thorough system integration in alignment with the business processes this could not have been achieved.

Total number of departments on board the CRM X project

As per December 2004 seven departments had come on board. However, there was no integration between the front and back-offices. This may have been due to a limited understanding of XML integration by the service provider. Majority of the customer queries continued to be resolved without using the CRM X. There was also dissatisfaction among the stakeholders from back-offices because of their exclusion from the decision making process:

> As a business we were very unhappy, very unhappy, we weren't involved in the decision. (Business Manager, Environmental Services)

According to the Principal Benefits Manager responsible for the Benefits Service, he was not involved in any way during the planning, tendering or steering group meetings of CRM X that took place prior to implementation. Moreover, there was no end-user involvement in the planning or decision making process to take on board CRM X. Others expected the Contact Centre to be under the management of their own department:

> It was late on into the process, it was decided it wouldn't come to Neighbourhood Offices because for most of the year we had assumed that it would be part of it though nobody ever said it was, but it was, I'd anticipated, and my Line Manager had anticipated, that the place for the telephonic version of the Neighbourhood Office would be in with the same service that was delivering face-to-face contact. (Neighbourhood Advice Officer)

Differing perceptions, interests and expectations (Long & Fahey, 2000)

Our respondent from Neighbourhood Office claimed that his department was going to play a leading role in the CRM X implementation. He argued:

> My role then was Constituency Manager for some Neighbourhood Offices but also leading on IT issues generally. So I had always had a direct link into central IT over our use of new technology, and at that time it was anticipated that the corporate call centre would become part of the network of Neighbourhood Offices. So it was anticipated that my organization would be the responsible organisation for the use of Front Line, so I was part of the initial set-up of that organization, and in fact a lot of the tender documentation was based upon work we did two or three years previously, on what we wanted CRM to look like.

Our respondent further argued that the Contact Centre should have been under their responsibility:

> We didn't have the money to buy in the solution that we wanted at that time, but very shortly after that discussions began about having

> a telephone corporate call centre, and as we are the front end of the Council, on face-to-face contacts, the natural place for the call centre to belong is in our organisation.

The contact centre management at the UKCC has had differing perceptions regarding the CRM X. Some seemed to have an opinion that by 2004 CRM X was now doing what it was supposed to do, in other words, providing help as a tool to answer the incoming calls. Others thought that it could do better than that:

> I manage the voice network at the UKCC and we receive 40 million calls per annum from the public. A miniscule percentage of that is handled by the call centre, a miniscule percentage. The potential for further cascading the CRM solution has not been tapped yet. (CRM Programme Manager)

Lack of a broad stakeholder base in the decision making process also took away an opportunity for prolonged interactions between the departments. According to Orlikowski and Gash (1994) to interact with technology, people have to make sense of it; and in this sense-making process, they develop particular assumptions, expectations and knowledge of the technology, which then serve to shape subsequent actions toward it. While these interpretations become taken-for-granted and are rarely brought to the surface and reflected on, they nevertheless remain significant in influencing how actors in organizations think about and act toward technology. In the case of our research site the lack of a broad base and stakeholder involvement resulted in a system (CRM X) which was far from integrated with the back-offices (departments). A broad stakeholder base including the end-users and external customers could have led to creative abrasion regarding the new technology. This could have produced a shared understanding and a mutual perspective with respect to stakeholder expectations and differential interests.

Furthermore, Walsham (1993) confirms that contextual conditions of history and different stakeholder perspectives create the conditions for conflict at the level of process in Pettigrew's (1985) five-fold framework. Conflict between interests was evident at senior management level between the Strategic Director of Resources and Former Head of IT. This conflict also trickled down at middle management level between the CRM Programme Manager and Business Manager resulting in CRM Programme Manager's resignation. The conflict continued in the form of differing expectations expressed by our respondents from different departments and the end-users at the Independent Company managed Contact Centre. We will discuss the impact of this conflict on various business processes under the following heading.

THE UKCC CASE PART 2: ANALYSIS OF THE "PROCESS" OF CRM X

The "Process" of CRM Implementation January 2001–Dec 2004

The process was closely monitored through observations, interviews and attending several staff meetings during the period of January 2001–December 2004. A participative research method allowed a deeper insight into softer issues as they happened.

In this section we will discuss various business processes and the impact that CRM X had on them. Process in this case is discussed in terms of how the system implementation process was shaped by the "history", internal and external contexts, and how the "content" and "process" have affected the performance of the users of the system (Pettigrew, 1997). This chapter discusses staff retention issues, user/stakeholder commitment, and user training (Pettigrew, 1985, 1990, 1997). Finally we discuss the microelements, namely psychological contracts and their linkages with subculture interaction and knowledge sharing. We also analyze how our findings resonate with the extant research literature.

Staff Stability at the UK CC

The CRM project at the UKCC had difficulties in retaining staff throughout the project life cycle. This was due to the lack of a shared understanding and a shared mental space (Newell *et al.*, 2002). A main underlying factor to the above could have been a lack of mutuality, and, as Boland and Tenkasi (1996) put it, the lack of "mutual perspective taking" resulting in a "mutual low-obligation" type of psychological contract between the Strategic Director of Resources and Former Head of IT and the people around them (Rousseau, 1995). As a result the staff turnover was high. Below we critically analyze staff retention issues stemming from the lack of a mutual perspective towards CRM X at our research site.

The project began to change focus (from a system integration approach towards a call answering one) early on during its design and development stage. During January 2001, a new Business Manager was appointed for the CRM project:

> It was felt that the project was over-weighted with IT and light on business need. The business need according to Strategic Director of

> Resources, was to bring back the focus towards call answering issues. (Former head of IT)

The number of people who could actually get through to the UKCC was as low as 10% on first call. This business issue, according to the Former Head of IT and Temporary Head of IT, was identified in the 2001 Citizen Mori survey.

CRM project manager resigns from the CRM project

The CRM Programme Manager was also CRM project manager when a new Business Manager arrived during May 2001. The Business Manager and CRM Programme Manager got off to a bad start. The CRM Programme Manager got on very well with the UKCC Consultant, but the Business Manager did not. This perhaps caused some of the subsequent problems:

> It was a delicate issue but perhaps it did come down a lot to personalities at the end of the day. (CRM Project Manager)

With the arrival of the new Business Manager, the project changed direction towards a call answering focus and away from the integrated approach focus. The CRM Programme Manager did not share that view, and duly left the project. The interaction between the Business Manager and CRM Programme Manager lacked a mutual perspective and was based on a "mutual low-obligation" type of psychological contract between them due to the lack of a mutual perspective and shared understanding (Boland & Tenkasi, 1996; Rousseau, 1995). It was at this time that the CRM Project Manager was appointed. The team needed to be refreshed:

> My management style is different from the Programme Managers's management style, I had clear views about where I wanted it to go and they didn't quite fit with the views of both Programme Managers and the UKCC consultant. I didn't feel there was enough business ownership so I decided that we needed to refresh the team. (Business Manager)

The non-reciprocal type of psychological contract present between the Strategic Director of Resources and Former Head of IT can also be seen between the Business Manager and CRM Programme Manager:

> There was quite a bit of tension obviously, between CRM Programme Manager and Business Manager, there was tension between the two of them. (IT programmer)

A process of "mutual perspective taking" where distinctive individual knowledge is exchanged, evaluated and integrated with that of the others in the organization, was missing, and, following Boland and Tenkasi (1996), with equally deleterious consequences.

Yet another outsourcing and its impact on staff stability

An Independent Company was chosen to manage the CRM call centre (also called the Corporate Contact Centre) and the Former Head of IT left the UKCC (October 2001). The Strategic Director of Resources wanted to outsource the call centre management to an Independent Company, who were partners with a CRM vendor. According to the Business Manager this was because the Council already had four call centres prior to establishing the Corporate Contact Centre, but, according to the feedback, the majority of those call centres were performing poorly:

> Prior to setting up the Corporate Contact Centre the feed back that we'd had from customers was that 30 % of people couldn't even get through, never mind get the problem resolved—so we'd got a huge issue about just access in the first instance.

The Business Manager pointed further towards a case for outsourcing:

> So we'd had that direct feed back from customers. We'd certainly had it from Members, as well from Councillors, telling us the feed back from their Constituents, and so we felt we needed to improve the access. Now we'd got four (centres) in the Council already. They weren't performing very well—what the Council didn't want to do was create the same thing but in a different location. They really wanted to say, "This is a new service with a different culture, customer focus culture, the people on that phone will own the problem etc etc,"—so they didn't want it to be perceived as the same thing but somewhere in a different place.

According to the Business Manager and Strategic Director of Resources, the UKCC felt that it was an opportunity to look at other people to deliver it. However, within the tender they did invite an in-house bid:

> There was a guy who at the time was Head of Revenues and having been given the Lead Officer for the Council, looked at it and decided that he felt there was insufficient experience in-house in order to deliver that service to the requirements, so he actually partnered with the Independent Company so the bid was a joint bid from the UKCC and the Independent Company and when we went through the evaluation process that was the bid that actually went through. So it wasn't a solely private sector bid it was actually done in partnership with the in-house team. (Business Manager)

The Former Head of IT, on the other hand, believed this might slow things down. He was keen on back-office integration in the system. His view was shared by both the CRM Programme Manager and the UKCC Consultant. But the Strategic Director took a different view:

> Her view was 'To hell with boys playing . . . much more important is—Get the telephones answered!' (Former Director of IT)

The Strategic Director of Resources decided to outsource to the Independent Company as the Former Head of IT left during October 2001. Though he gave six months notice before leaving, his views were not taken on board. During December 2001, the decision was made to outsource the management of the CRM call centre the earlier mentioned Independent Company. The contract was signed during March 2002, thus beginning the transition programme.

According to the Temporary Head of IT, outsourcing to the Independent Company was more of a political decision as there were issues with regard to the performance of officers providing service. The Deputy Leader appeared to be the person pushing this idea forward.

In April 2001, the UKCC Consultant presented a report to the Strategic Director of Resources, in which he promoted the idea of integration between front and back-office using CRM X. That idea was never acted upon, but the consultant was relieved of his services. The rest of the consultants were assigned the role of designing scripts for the CRM Contact Centre.

The management of the Contact Centre was given to the Independent Company. In normal circumstances the UKCC would have moved all the call centre staff over to the contact centre, necessitating sharing of undertakings legally. The politicians were not prepared to do that. According to the Temporary Head of IT, they seconded people from the Council to the Independent Company. In this arrangement, the management of the staff was done by the

Independent Company. However, all the staff's terms and conditions were managed by the UKCC.

The Staff Stability Issues Continue Over 2003 and Throughout 2004

The Business Manager moved back to her old job to a different Council on 24 November 2003, While the Business Manager and Temporary Head of IT were replaced.

Secondees start to move back to the UKCC

Furthermore, the secondees under the Independent Company management as per September 2004 were applying for jobs to go back to the UKCC and their back-offices. As per August 2004, according to a non-secondee Team Manager at the Independent Company Corporate Contact Centre, the secondees were going through a phase of redeployment back to the UKCC. They had been at the Contact Centre over two years:

> Originally a lot of the secondees did raise a lot of issues internally with the UKCC regarding the whole outsourcing process. After two years the initial review by the Council was, 'Re-deploy them all back into the Council'. They're all getting re-deployed back into different areas of the Council. So they're not going back to their own specialised fields, but wherever they can actually find them a job.

Secondees carried with them considerable codified and non-codified knowledge and experience from back-offices. In returning to the Council they took with them their expertise and experience thus depriving the Independent Company of an important asset, namely non-codified/tacit knowledge:

> Secondees are definitely a great asset to any contract, because the knowledge and experience that they have is something that they need to download and pass on to any other outsourcing organisation. (Team Manager).

During their stay under the Independent Company Management, secondee expertise was not exploited to its full potential. Secondees were used in training non-secondees in a very limited form:

> It was very limited because the Independent Company have their own trainers. (Non-secondee Team Manager—the Independent Company)

Moreover training:

> Wasn't exploited to the full extent. We're probably looking at outsourcing or looking at an organisation like this—it probably would be better to have the UKCC (or having secondees) actually doing the training, or playing a big role in training, because obviously the knowledge and experience would then be shared.

According to a Senior Accounting Assistant in Council Tax, the outsourcing had not worked:

> I'd said that basically because it's gone to private industry. So, I mean, the service is not going to be as good as what we could have provided within the Council. So it's not as good service as it should be.

Others like the Business Manager, Environmental Services, wanted their secondees back as they felt they had lost the expertise from their department:

> I think we need to decide, particularly as I'm losing the business expertise within the Contact Centre. We need to form a view about what sort of calls the Contact Centre should be able to take. Is there a need for back-office? And indeed, when I found out that the secondees were going I said to Corporate Relations, 'If they're going, can I have them back please and we'll use them as a back-office here and we'll leave the Independent Company staff to handle the simple, quick-win enquiries and we'll have these people back'.

Staff stability was clearly an issue in the UKCC CRM initiative. As reported to us, several X CRM stakeholders left without seeing the project through to its completion. This was the case at all levels of the hierarchy, at senior level, middle management and floor level. Staff instability at the higher level of hierarchy also had a negative impact on user commitment (see below).

User Commitment

User commitment continued to decrease at the UKCC as the stakeholder base became narrower due to staff retention issues. We will now discuss this at different levels of hierarchy within the UKCC.

Initially the UKCC CRM initiative had senior management sponsorship in the form of the chief executive, who saw a CRM system in action on his trip to Brisbane:

> The Deputy Leader saw this as a good opportunity to kill two birds with one stone. One, this would eliminate the call answering

> issues that the city was having. The second, that implementation of a CRM system will be in line with the government directive. (CRM Programme Manager)

Both the Former Head of IT and Strategic Director of Resources of senior management bought the idea initially. However, as they started to work on the implementation plan, their differing opinions became more explicit and their psychological contracts became more individual than mutual. The Former Head of IT was perceived to be IT-led, whereas the Strategic Director of Resources wanted to focus on resolving the issue of public calls not getting through to the UKCC. They may have started with a mutual understanding on the surface (Anderson & Schalk, 1998) yet as they interacted more closely and creative abrasion took place, the implicit part of their psychological contract became more explicit, and, following (Makin *et al.*, 1996), more obviously misaligned. Where the psychological contract was previously implicit, this had resulted in a lack of clarity for both parties on the level of their disagreement (Makin *et al.*, 1996).

Creative abrasion can positively influence performance (Leonard-Barton, 1995). In this case, however, it created a divide which not only slowed down the progress of the CRM project development, but also resulted in the Former Head of IT's resignation, and subsequent suspension of the original X development in favour of the revised "Contact Centre X" solution with its call answering focus. The arrival of the new Business Manager reinforced the direction of the project towards a call answering focus and away from the integrated approach focus. The CRM Programme Manager did not share that view either and left the project. This narrowed down the stakeholder base further. Others were hoping to keep the customer contact centre internal:

> We'd been working on the assumption, all the way through, that the call centre would be set up, but it would probably be internally run and managed. And it was a bit of a shock to some people on the group that hang on, because I think some people had sort of seen roles for themselves within the subsequent development of the organization—and, 'I'm going to run this,' and, 'I'm going to be doing that,'—as we were sort of bought into it. And that was suddenly taken away, and it was going to be a managed service. So I think at that point a lot of people probably lost a little bit of interest. (Business Manager, Environmental services)

User commitment was also affected by the original CRM X decision having a narrow participant base. This narrow base has not expanded over the years and continues to cause frustration and dissatisfaction among the stakeholders of the system. Lack of stakeholder involvement has resulted in lack of commitment:

> Key players (I mean those that were actually involved in running the Contact Centres departmentally) should have been involved in the decision making process. (Business Manager, Environmental Services)

The Business Manager, Environmental Services further expressed his frustration:

> The Programme Manager . . . should have been involved and perhaps co-ordinated it whether or not we agreed with the decision to outsource the Division and you had a contract that was given to the Independent Company. That I would certainly never to have agreed to, I don't think Neighbourhood Advice would either, simply because it totally—the quality side of it—it just went on the number of calls handled and there are so many get-out clauses for the Independent Company. We were excluded from the process and as a result of that we lost the knowledge.

According to the Business Manager, Environmental Services, who was not involved in the decision making process:

> The quality, aspects have been ignored.

He further stated that his expectations of the CRM initiative were very low:

> It's because they weren't very high in the first place.

Quality had been an issue for Council Tax as well:

> My general feeling has been one of frustration and I'm sure that's shared by other management here. We've been conscious of more complaints coming through because obviously it has a knock-on effect. While people aren't getting through on the phone then it has an impact on our face-to-face enquiry service, so we had problems up there, we get more letters sent through. So rather than easing the burden, it's felt at times like they're contributing to the problem because there's not enough people answering the phones, people aren't getting a good service when they ring through. So hopefully that's behind us but that's my experience so far. (Council Tax Officer)

The above statements show lack of trust and shared understanding. This had a negative impact on user commitment at all levels. At senior management level, lack of commitment was evident in people not seeing the project through to its completion. At middle management level, managers were not happy due to lack of their involvement during pre- and post-implementation phases.

The secondees leaving the Independent Company managed Contact Centre were happy to leave due to their lack of commitment to CRM X. Their contract agreement did not allow them to be upgraded to a team leader position:

> I'm in a land where, when it suits certain people then we can be recognised, when it doesn't suit certain people we cannot be recognized... A lot of the secondees feel, here on site, that they're not wanted from both sides basically—so you have that disadvantaged group of people who, a year ago, outwardly were the people who were keeping the centre running technically and expert wise. (Secondee)

Secondees, however, were paid more than their non-secondee colleagues. This caused a lot of dissatisfaction among secondees and non-secondees, for example:

> The level of pay that I was on, to the level of pay that they were on, affected my colleagues because they felt they were sitting next to someone who was on £16,500 and they were on £11,000 but doing the same job as them. We assured them that because we are on more money than them it doesn't matter, we will still try to give them the knowledge that we had. As it grew to the end of the year, they became more knowledgeable—that the staff were getting really angry—that it was now 'us' and 'them'—we were divided—there came a division between us. One - it was about the money, two- it was about the knowledge that we had, and three—it was really listening to what we were saying about how we were treated—what we were doing, the flexi-time that we had, how we worked, having to structure was working through us, and we were being treated differently to the Independent Company staff, because we had been told that we could still have our flexi-time but the Independent Company staff couldn't have it. (Secondee)

At the Independent Company, management also expressed their opinion:

> I think there was a morale issue for a time. I wouldn't say that was the main common denominator, but there was certainly a morale issue which affected people's views on the contracts and on the company, and for a while we did lose some personnel because of that.

The above created a divide between secondees and non-secondees and their interaction lacked creative abrasion and a mutual perspective (Anderson & Schalk, 1998; Boland & Tenkasi, 1996; Makin *et al.*, 1996; Rousseau, 1995; Shore & Barksdale, 1998; Thibaut & Kelley, 1959). This resulted in a lack of shared mental space between the two groups (Newell *et al.*, 2002). The relationship deteriorated between the two groups due to the lack of reciprocity (Krogh, *et al.*, 2000). The conflict grew as both groups started to find out more about each other (Lawrence & Lorsch, 1967), for example the issue of sick leave:

> So there was a difference because we were still under the umbrella of the UKCC, so as a staff we still had to be treated as the UKCC staff which then affected the Independent Company staff. For example, sick on duty, there was a big issue about that. If you're sick on duty ('you' referring to a non-secondee) you've got to phone in by 10.30 am—well if you were sick on duty you had to do half of your shift. And there was an uproar about that. But then we (referring to secondees) had to go back to the UKCC. Because it doesn't happen under the UKCC staff, and not because we're seconded makes any difference, so again we were treated differently to the Independent Company staff. And that's where the conflict between myself and colleagues, well all of us I should say, grew. And it's worse now because they're saying now they can't wait to see the back of us. (Secondee)

Our secondee respondent further suggested that seven secondees left within one month after starting at the Independent Company. These were replaced with the Independent Company staff. Other secondees were not happy:

> We're very upset about it because we do want to be here in the first place, so we've been asked now to just carry on doing the job. (Secondee)

Secondees' expertise whenever exploited by the Independent Company did not get rewarded extrinsically. Secondees felt that their fundamental loyalty lay with the UKCC and wanted to move back to their previous jobs. The Independent Company did not feel responsible for their job situation as their (secondee's) employment contract was managed by the UKCC itself. This caused a lot of dissatisfaction among secondees and gave rise to an "employee under-obligation" type of psychological contract between secondees and the Independent Company management. Our respondent expressed her frustration further:

> I'm totally stressed, absolutely stressed. I enjoy my work so much. I enjoy what I do. I enjoy the environment that I work in, which is

> the building. I do not enjoy being treated like a child and going ten steps backwards. You treat your things to make things work—as I've always said the nail is not broken, if it's not broken why mend it—and they keep on mending things here that don't need mending. If they left the whole system as it was things would have worked better, but they keep on implementing new ideas—then we come back to the old ideas, it's just called a different name, and that stresses me out. I want to, I told them, I'm quite happy to be the trainer. I'm quite happy to train my colleagues, but they tell me they can't pay me. So I have to wait for the UKCC to find me a job.

The secondee psychological contracts, resulting from such mistrust, were of "employee under-obligation" type and lacked a mutual perspective with the Independent Company (Boland & Tenkasi, 1996; Shore & Barksdale, 1998). This is also evident through the comments made below regarding the re-employment of secondees who had no real job satisfaction at the Independent Company Contact Centre:

> Very recently an arrangement has been whereby they (secondees) can come back into the UKCC, and I think they have grabbed that with both hands and have been very keen to get back into the Authority, so I think that tells its own story. (Council Tax Manager)

Various changes at the senior management level influenced subsequent developments. According to the CRM Programme Manager, the Deputy Leader only remained in the picture for a while, and the Chief Executive Officer left prematurely. This again points towards a lack of stakeholder commitment at senior management level.

User commitment was also affected by the technical issues arising as a result of a lack of system integration between back-office and other e-business applications. This gave rise to data migration issues and duplication. End-users were using different systems. They used CRM X to answer and log a call and then logged in to a different system to follow through the customer's query. According to an end-user:

> CRM X duplicates more than complicates and in duplicating it complicates because you have to verify your customer, customer details when it comes to Benefits and Revenues anyway, but with CRM X you have to take all the details again, add them in first. So you get a repetitive state of taking the customer's details and sometimes that can cause delay which was already in a red zone to an elevated red zone. From the feedback I've had from CA's it duplicates.

A Corporate Customer Relations manager confirmed the duplication issues:

> An example being—customer phones in . . . we put their name and address details into X to check who they are . . . we go into MBAS to check their claim out . . . we've got to put their name and address in again, because there's no interaction.

One end-user further stated that the system was slow and had a lot of technical problems:

> I think it's slow. I think it has too many technical problems. It will produce a technical issue a day. It will produce an error message or it basically will error. It will break down here at least once or twice a day, because it's telephony linked as well . . . plus it has the CRM X aspect . . . plus it has the web link . . . plus it has the middle ware . . . plus it needs to talk to our back-office system. There are too many things going on with that and I think the other support functions that are coming in, all those other providers of information, i.e. the back-office system, the UKCC web site, the telephone, things along those lines, I don't think they're all being managed effectively. On a technical basis that would result in it having technical problems daily. I just feel that there's too many systems not actually talking to each other correctly.

The above analysis shows how user commitment suffered at all three levels, namely senior management, middle management and floor level. Relationships were not reciprocal and evidently lacked a mutual perspective (Boland & Tenkasi, 1996; Krogh *et al.*, 2000). This resulted in psychological contracts with mutually low-obligations between the groups (Shore & Barksdale, 1998). The system itself acted as an inhibitor due to its technical incapability and a lack of thorough integration with the back-office, resulting in lack of commitment and stress.

User Training Issues in the "Process" of Our Framework (Figure 5.4)

Under this section we will discuss the training issues that rose at the Independent Company managed Contact Centre. We will discuss this under the light of comments by different stakeholders regarding training quality.

The training provided by the Independent Company to the contact centre agents was more in the form of descriptive knowledge, which included what the system could do and how the written scripts could be used to answer the incoming calls (Herschbach, 1995;

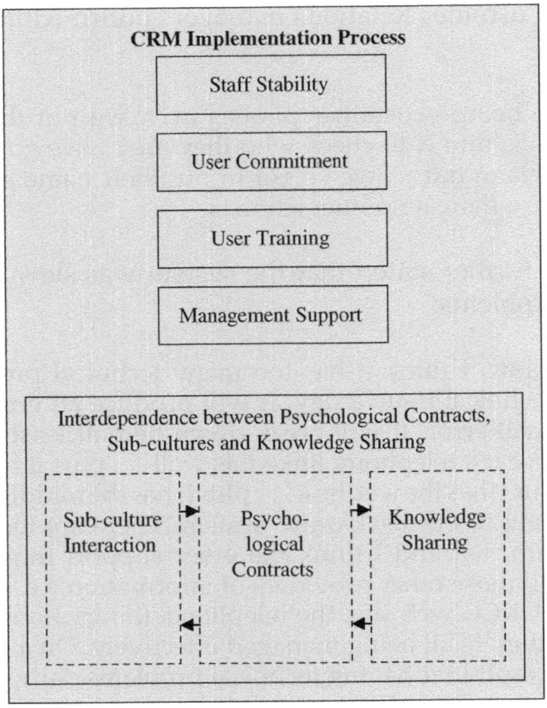

Figure 5.4 CRM Process including salient elements derived from the literature review

Nonaka and Takeuchi, 1995; Vincenti, 1993). However, there were some qualitative issues regarding the training:

> I felt it was inadequate. I felt it was poorly managed. I didn't feel that the trainers were aware of how to utilise the system any better than the people they were training. (Contact Centre Duty Manager)
>
> They hadn't for instance, (they didn't deliver) very high quality training materials to go with the training so the staff were, having been trained, walking away and not having anything they could refer to. (CRM Project Manager)
>
> I think we neglected . . . we could have spent more time on helping the Independent Company employees understand how the Council works. (Business Manager)

Training provided by the Independent Company did not impress the UKCC staff and management. However, in our analysis this was because the Independent Company did not have enough knowledge about the UKCC departmental cultures. Their interactions with the UKCC were not on a prolonged basis and did not allow creative abrasion to take place (Leonard-Barton, 1995; Newell *et al.*, 2002).

Following Boland and Tenkasi (1996), this resulted in a training not based on "mutual perspective taking". On our analysis, there was an agreement at senior management level that saw a mutual psychological contract in place. However, this agreement was not shared by the people on the floor. According to Leonard-Barton and Kraus (1985) it is important to plan for the sharing of knowledge from the old operations, in which people knew the materials and the product very well, to the new processes. They further argue that the developers of the new process often know their tools well, but rarely do they understand the materials and processes to which their software is applied or the people on the floor who have been working with both for years. In the UKCC situation secondees from the back-offices were put in the Contact Centre environment, but their knowledge was not exploited fully to complement and enhance the quality of the end-user training.

In our analysis, the UKCC senior management when signing the contract with The Independent Company had an illusion of consensus that failed to expose the innermost feelings of individuals involved (Gee, 1992). Hence it resulted in inadequate training material and lack of communication between the parties. The UKCC staff were more fully trained and experienced with considerable codified knowledge regarding the UKCC and its cultures. More than half of the Contact Centre staff were existing council staff (secondees) whose training needs were, in many cases, different from those of newcomers (non-secondees).

The window of opportunity for adoption continues to close (Orlikowski & Tyre, 1994)

As the users of the system became more familiar with the systems and its strengths and weaknesses, the work-arounds, the shortcuts and the "tricks of the trade" started to surface (Orlikowski & Hofman, 1997; Orlikowski & Iacono, 2001; Vincenti, 1984). According to one non-secondee end-user (in Contact Centre), initially the call centre agents tried to use the CRM system as much as they could. But as time passed they started to realize that answering the calls was taking too long. So they started to make notes while answering the calls, using the system as little as possible.

Interviews with the agents showed that they learned to take notes manually while on a call and then after the call put the logs on the system. This was the case especially with agents from the revenue and benefits section. A brief interview with the recruitment section in early 2004 showed that they used X CRM for salutation purposes only. They then had to log into the back-office system separately.

This was the case with both benefits and revenues departments. This showed that, as system adaptation time passed, people were finding new ways of working with the CRM system. One way was using it as little as possible. The system was getting adapted by the users rather than users adopting the system, as indeed Orlikowski and Tyre (1994) found in their study.

The Business Manager, Environmental Services reported that one benefit with the externally managed Contact Centre was, within the contract, clear quantifiable performance indicators that say, "Yes, X number of calls have got to be answered to hit a certain percentage call rate". However, there were other issues:

> What it hasn't addressed is the qualitative aspects. Whilst people now get through—and that was an initial huge win for the City because there was a lot of bad publicity around the fact that people couldn't get through to us and to other departments. . . . We'd got a big success with people now being able to get through, but I don't think—and I wasn't involved with the letting of the contract for the external service provider—I don't think there was much put in the contract around the qualitative issues, as I am now finding as a business user. (Business Manager, Environmental Services)

The Contact Centre managed by the Independent Company went live in March 2003. It was divided into three sections. Section one had advisors handling calls regarding environmental services and neighbourhood advice. Section two dealt with benefits and revenue. Section three (gone live early 2004) dealt with recruitment services. Advisors in all the sections used the new CRM system to read scripts, in order to use correctly the salutations.

According to the UKCC IT programmer, in handling the calls related to the environmental services the CRM system used a middleware to interact with the back-office system. The matters, regarding which the call centre agents were able to provide help to the callers, were information requests and specific issues such as programming the disposal of bulky waste items or missed bin collections. However, not all the call centre agents had access to the full version of the back-office system. Only the UKCC secondees were given full access (Business Manager, Environmental Services Department). Thus non-secondees with a customer query passed on the information manually to the secondees in order to achieve a resolution.

Secondees from the UKCC were trained separately from non-secondees in the new CRM system. A collective training of call centre staff could have provided an opportunity for the staff to interact with each other on an informal basis. Such interactions on an informal level might have helped to start the process of "mutual perspective taking" (Boland &Tenkasi, 1996) and a shared ownership, leading to "mutual high-obligations" psychological contracts thus facilitating knowledge sharing including the sharing of short cuts and "tricks of the trade" (Shore & Barksdale, 1998).

According to a duty manager, secondees carried with them the UKCC culture, whereas the non-secondees hired by the Independent Company to handle the incoming calls did not. Secondees were more aware of the process loop in handling incoming calls because of their UKCC background. This knowledge possessed by the secondees was not exploited fully. The training was short, only three to four weeks according to end users, and was different for secondees and non-secondees (Wathne *et al.*, 1996). "T-shaped skills" and "knowing of what others know" could not be fully developed due to the shortage of time and lack of prolonged cross-cultural interaction between secondees and non-secondees (Bakhtin, 1981; Iansiti, 1993; Krauss & Fussell, 1991; Lawrence & Lorsch, 1967). According to end users, there was very little interaction between the three sections present at the Contact Centre. The chances of creative abrasion taking place were limited. The common coffee or lunch room was mainly used by the recruitment services thus the limited interaction that took place was in more formal types of setting. Lack of informal settings worked as an inhibitor to the sharing of "tricks of the trade" at the Contact Centre. This, combined with lack of "mutual high-obligations" psychological contracts due to the departmental subculture (Shore & Barksdale, 1998), a lack of thorough system integration and vertical knowledge silos, undoubtedly inhibited the sharing of various forms of knowledge across the departments and between the front-office and back-office (Ross, 2003).

The eventual aim into late 2004 was that CRM X would be a fully integrated solution and then the UKCC would start to reap the benefits. By late 2003 training had improved. Some feedback from the staff has been picked up by the trainers and resulted in some improvements in training the new comers, as recommended for example by Vincenti (1993). However, as reported to us in late 2004, most of the Contact Centre advisors still did not see the CRM X as a facilitating tool in their work. They perceived it more as a burden. The CRM system was deemed slow and broke down at least once or twice a day. Contact Centre advisors also perceived that there were too many screens to juggle with and too many systems which fail to communicate with each other. Contact Centre staff also showed their concerns regarding the management of different systems in use:

> I think in England they use too many Chiefs and not enough Indians. (Secondee)

By late 2004 secondees were leaving the Independent Company managed Contact Centre and were applying for jobs within the UKCC. They did not feel committed to the CRM Project; their expertise was exploited in a limited way:

> We had a couple of their secondees here to iron out any wrinkles that the Independent Company trainers couldn't do because they, obviously, weren't familiar with the system, so we had about eight people, I think it was. Some of them are now going back into the main UKCC work field, but they were with us at that time and still with us up until today. (End-user)

Moreover, whenever their expertise was exploited by the Independent Company managed staff, it did not result in an extrinsic reward. As one of our respondent put it:

> I've been doing the supervisory role, as they call it a Technical Specialist. I've been a Technical Specialist for over one and a half years, so I've been looking after my colleagues as well as new staff. I have taken an escalated course, which is not part of my job as a CSA (Customer Service Advisor.) I have trained all new staff that have come in, along with my colleagues and I have set-up forum meetings—I am a forum representative as well as, so I do feel that we have been exploited because we haven't been paid for what we've been doing.

Non-secondees at the Contact Centre were not happy about the above situation where they had to do the same amount of work as their secondee colleagues and yet were paid at a much lower rate. This caused friction:

> They were obviously getting more money, but then again their knowledge base is greater than ours and their experience is greater than ours. We've just been introduced to this, whereas that's something that they've been implementing and doing for a number of years, so therefore I personally think that the difference in wages reflects that. What a lot of the Independent Company staff were hoping for as the years have gone by—especially by the 18 month mark—they were hoping that our wages would be more on a par with the UKCC staff, but that wasn't to be. And again that's started a lot more friction in that the Independent Company had to roll out different ways of promoting us as well as giving us more money for the skills that we had since obtained. But I don't think that the Independent Company will ever be able to match what the UKCC are doing in like for like positions. I don't think that they will because, I think, that the UKCC are more generous in that way.

There were other reasons why non-secondees felt they did not have as much access to the back-office systems as their secondee colleagues. Secondees—due to their loyal mutual obligation contracts with their back-offices—could log on the back-office systems using their user name pass word. However, non-secondees were deprived of this full access to the back-office. This made them dependent on their secondee colleagues. As a result, there was freer sharing of knowledge between the secondees and the back-office. Scholars (Gregory, 1983; Pettigrew, 1979, Riley, 1983; Schein, 1985; Strauss, 1978), further suggest that people tend to share assumptions, knowledge, and expectations with others with whom they have close working relationships. In the above case the "tricks of the trade" and short cuts did get shared to some extent due to secondees and non-secondees working in the same room.

The secondees' situation at the Independent Company managed Contact Centre put pressure on the non-secondees. They worried about the knowledge which they never got the opportunity to acquire and were aware that it would leave with their secondee colleagues quitting the Contact Centre. A lot of non-codified/tacit knowledge stored in the minds of secondees has already gone with them. One of the few secondees left behind at the Contact Centre as per end of year 2004 reported:

> The knowledge went with the majority of my colleagues. The service level, the calls coming in, the queuing system has gone tremendously out the door because the staff here—we haven't got the quality of staff to take the calls. So the majority of time we were training and getting them up to the level that they will need to be to take calls on a faster level. The quality is non-existent, so there's a lot of errors being made. There's people who will start today and leave tomorrow, so then there's no commitment to the job, where [whereas] the people that had left or were here for two, three, four, five, probably six years—so those that had more knowledge than myself, at that point, had left, so left [thus leaving] people, who had just started, to look after people who were coming in, the Independent Company staff. So my concept of it was that it was disorganised and it was all about quantity not quality. We had more complaints, irate callers.

As the secondees left the non-secondees realized the value of having them (secondees) around:

> The relationship in the beginning—it was very 'them and us'. Then when we realized their value as time has gone on, we're now . . . you see they were only here for . . . I didn't realize that they were here for an allotted time. They were seconded here just for an allotted time, which is now running out, and now they're realising that they've got

> to go back into the main UKCC stream of things. I personally am getting the feeling that a lot of the Independent Company, especially the older ones, who know the value of their [secondees] knowledge, that's going to be taken... so we're getting a little bit worried as to how we're going to cope, free on our own, because we have relied on them for a lot of background knowledge, a lot of in-depth knowledge that they've got, and how Environmental works. (non-secondee)

There were clear indications by November 2004 that the Independent Company management were trying to exploit the non-codified, tacit knowledge possessed by secondees at the Contact Centre. However, this left as the secondees continued to stream out. This created a knowledge vacuum at the Contact Centre. The people who replaced secondees in particular lacked the non-codified knowledge regarding the UKCC back-offices. There was no opportunity for "tricks of the trade" to get shared from secondees to non-secondees.

Management Support

Here we analyze the management support provided for CRM X at three levels of hierarchy, senior management, middle management, and floor.

Management support at the senior level

The Former Head of IT did not get enough support from his superiors to implement his system integration perspective. The Deputy Leader supported the Strategic Director's idea of getting the calls answered. However, the Deputy Leader did have a good working relationship with Former Head of IT:

> It got very political... The Former Head of IT had a good working relationship with the Deputy Leader—so did the Strategic Director of Resources, but obviously that was an issue as well. But the Former Head of IT left... because he felt that he was being stopped from doing what he needed to do to sort out IT by the Strategic Director of Resources. He didn't have the backing, the financial backing. He felt constrained and he just didn't feel that he could do the job that he was supposed to be doing. (Corporate Programme Manager)

Support at senior management level was more towards a call answering focus type solution. This was due to the fact that the public was not getting through and politicians wanted this issue to be resolved as quickly as possible. This, however, resulted in lack of business-IT alignment (Willcocks & Margetts, 1994). The knowledge shared at the senior management level regarding their innermost feelings created a negative type of abrasion between the senior management and caused division based on different approaches and differential interests. The stakeholders with a system integration approach were classified as "IT people" by the group that supported the Strategic Director of Resources. The group supporting the Strategic Director of Resources claimed to have the business perspective on the whole CRM situation.

According to Orlikowski and Gash (1991, 1994), to interact with technology, people have to make sense of it; and in this sense-making process, they develop particular assumptions, expectations, and knowledge of the technology, which then serve to shape subsequent actions toward it. While these interpretations become taken-for-granted and are rarely brought to the surface and reflected on, they nevertheless remain significant in influencing how actors in organizations think about and act toward technology. At the UKCC the Strategic Director of Resources's supporters had a mutual, shared understanding. This was also the case with the Former Head of IT supporters. They also had a shared understanding about an integrated solution, in which systems needed to talk to each other, in order to provide a "one-stop-service". The two groups, however, did not have a common frame. The innermost feelings, when revealed, created a divide instead of a shared understanding (Leonard-Barton, 1995).

Furthermore, Walsham (1993) confirms that contextual conditions of history and different stakeholder perspectives create the conditions for conflict at the level of "Process" in Pettigrew's (1985) five-fold framework. This was the case with the above two groups. Management support given to the middle management by senior management was coloured by their respective frames. Most of the key supporters of system integration strategy left the project. A "mutual perspective" (Boland & Tenkasi, 1996) was never achieved and thus knowledge, in particular tacit knowledge, did not surface or get shared in discussions. The above two groups lacked trust and loyalty (Janssens *et al.*, 2003). Thus the pattern of management proved to be more divisive and destructive than creative and unifying.

Support at middle management level

As discussed above, there was lack of trust and commitment between the CRM Programme Manager and Business Manager and the CRM Programme Manager left the project. According to Janssens *et al.* (2003), when investigating the employer obligation of long-term involvement and the employee obligations of personal investment, flexibility and loyalty are related to high affective commitment. Moreover, according to the CRM Project Manager, his expertise in the call centre environment was not exploited. The IT implementation team, formed with a limited involvement at departmental level, did not, however, continue as an on-going implementation team after the launch of the Contact Centre:

> They went for an implementation team, and instead of keeping that as an on-going implementation team, that team then had to be the team that were servicing it and supporting it. You should always have a situation where your support team is separate from the implementation team so you can keep the momentum and impetus going. What happened was, the implementation team ended up being the support team. And they're still having to give support, and they're being pulled from pillar to post from that point of view. So there hasn't been sufficient (I don't think) resources addressed and committed to it as an overall project to ensure the continued roll-out. (CRM Programme Manager)

The above also shows lack of continuity in the implementation scheme. The continuity was affected by the lack of commitment resulting in stakeholder resignations. The team now led by the Business Manager handed over the management responsibility to the Independent Company (outsourced agency) to manage the Contact Centre. Moreover, there were doubts expressed from our respondents from the UKCC regarding how the Contact Centre was being managed:

> What I'm saying is, given the fact that it's outsourced at the moment, we should be working more with the Independent Company to develop improvements to what they are doing. I don't think there's sufficient performance monitoring or management of the Independent Company. But again people that wrote the performance standards were new to the game—they weren't aware of what we call 'tricks of the trade'. To be quite blunt with you, there's lies, and then lies and statistics. (CRM Programme Manager)

Others had higher expectations not being met:

> I think we expected big things because, from a Public Sector perspective you expect a Private Sector company to come in, bring in it's expertise, make the sort of improvement that you can't make in Local Government because of the constraints with funding and I'd say it's been a sense of frustration. (Council Tax Manager)

A lack of trust was expressed by our research site respondents about the capability of the Independent Company managed Contact Centre. Walsham (1993) confirms that contextual conditions of history and different stakeholder perspectives create the conditions for conflict at the level of process. This conflict can be sensed in the above reports made by our respondents from the UKCC.

The above conflicting situation between the Independent Company and the council back-offices resulted in a withholding and denying of access to technology knowledge by the back-offices (Vincenti, 1993). The knowledge, in particularly non codified or tacit knowledge mostly remained buried in the back-offices and the owners of such knowledge were not ready to let it go. This is evident in the case where only secondees had been provided full access to the back-office systems and their colleagues non-secondees were not. This was due to the lack of trust and commitment expressed by our respondents in the back-offices at the UKCC. The psychological contracts resulting from such a lack of trust were of employee "under-obligation" type and lack a mutual perspective, which yield the poorest results (Shore & Barksdale, 1998).

Management support at end-user level

End-users (non-secondees) were not trained on the back-office systems. They had a limited access to the UKCC back-office systems:

> That's right, which we don't know; they didn't train us on back-office system at all. Only a certain... I think now a few individuals are going to be trained up to the standard of UKCC employee's, in that they can re-open jobs and stuff like that. (non-secondee)

This again confirms a lack of trust shown by the back-office in not allowing the non-secondees full access to the back-office systems. One non-secondee respondent added:

> I would like that. I would like to be able to re-open and close jobs ourselves. Yes, that would be a boom if we could access back-office system. Also the way in which it brings up the information on my own personal PC—I'd like it to be a lot faster. I can't think of anything else apart from accessing back-office system—that's the key, that's what made the UKCC staff so invaluable to us.

Secondees and non-secondees were also operating under different employment contracts yet managed by the same management, namely the Independent Company (in this research the real names have been removed for confidentiality reasons), at the Contact Centre. Moreover, secondees were earning much more than their non-secondee colleagues, yet doing the same job as them. According to several reports made by our non-secondee respondents, the friction caused by having different employment contracts has made non-secondees feel that they have an inferior employment contract compared with their colleagues who earn more due to their contract with the UKCC, know more due to their previous UKCC experience, have more access due to their loyalty to their back-offices and yet have the same work responsibilities as their non-secondee colleagues:

> The Independent Company probably wouldn't say this to you, but probably it would be easier to manage from their point of view if everybody was on the same terms and conditions. As a Manager myself, I'm sure that it creates issues if you've got people sat next to each other who are on totally different conditions of service. (Council Tax Manager)

The Independent Company management did try to even up the balance between secondees and non-secondees by taking away privileges like flexi-leave:

> The main perception behind all of it, I'd say, is with anyone in the Public Sector they would like to be managed by their own, by the Public Sector. Obviously there is a clash of two separate sectors. And obviously, you can quite easily see that here, the Independent Company could have quite easily, I suppose, adapted their policies slightly to suit the needs of the client, or to suit the needs of the UKCC. But, if you look at it, some of the issues like flexi-leave—which is something that the Independent Company don't do, whereas the UKCC do have—it's only on this site where the secondees where not given any flexi-leave. Whereas if you were working within the council you'd have flexi-leave, so they were taking things away from them. (Non-secondee Team Manager)

The taking away of privileges such as flexi-leave did not go down well with the secondees and their psychological contracts with the Independent Company management were weakened and became more of an "employee under-obligation" type (Shore & Barksdale, 1998). This was a significant reason why secondees did not want to stay at the Independent Company Contact Centre. There were other issues why secondees thought about leaving:

> The whole management process . . . because it's very hard to manage two sets of people . . . because you've got the UKCC policies and processes and then you've got the Independent Company policies and processes. So you've got two people side-by-side but yet they're on two different contracts, being managed on two different processes. One may be able to go off sick today, who might be on a UKCC

> process, which might not be as harsh as his colleague sitting next to him who is on the Independent Company contract, who might go off sick, who would then go through the benchmarks of that policy a lot more faster.

A non-secondee Team Manager further argued that there was a clash of contracts and policies throughout:

> An Independent Company's policies are different from a city Councli's. So realistically what they could have done on this side is, if they were looking at, like . . . an amalgamated contract is having one policy, whichever it was to be, but having it signed off from both parties. So it's having, like, a mutual agreement which really is probably what failed the whole UKCC process. There was no bridge in the middle; there was a big gap, so you were either a UKCC or you were the Independent Company staff. But what they should have really done here is have that bridge there—and had one contract, whether it was the UKCC policy or the Independent Company policy, and everyone's going by the same rules and guidelines. But when you're looking at managing two sets of different people, on different rules and different guidelines, obviously that has an impact on the floor.

This non-secondee Team Manager further reported sub-cultural gaps between secondees and non-secondees:

> It does cause friction between the secondee and a non-secondee because, obviously, that's again . . . that's splitting them up and again it's a contract like this . . . where you've got an outsourcing organization you need to have all of that inter-linked, you have to have one operation, or the one system, and you want to try and keep everything as single as possible, not having separate rules and regulations for one individual, something separate for somebody else, you need to have them all bridged off and all inter-linked.

But not only was there a clash of two contracts, but also a clash of two different cultures, namely public sector and private sector:

> Again I think any kind of issues where you've got a clash of two contracts, or you've got the simpler clashes of Public Sector and the Private Sector. (Non-secondee Team Manager)

However, the UKCC had a perception of the Independent Company being more knowledgeable than really was the case. They did not see the culture gap as being a big issue before signing the contract with them. The Independent Company's perspective is discussed by Non-secondee Team Manager. According to him the intention of the Independent Company was to bridge the cultural gap between secondees and non-secondees:

> We've always wanted to have access to the systems and train all of our staff to give them all that knowledge that our secondees are going to have. We've always known that secondees will always move on within the Council because opportunities within the Council are a lot more greater, and again the benefits within the Council, or any Public Services, are always going to be higher than the Private Sector. So we've always known that the secondees, at some stage, would, one-by-one, leave the contract anyway, because they were unhappy on-site. Taking that into account it's been . . . if you want to look at it from the UKCC side of it, we've had a lot of barriers put in place where we were unable to bridge those gaps.

These cultural gaps were due to a lack of creative abrasion and a mutual perspective which had its roots at senior management level (Boland & Tenkasi, 1996; Leonard-Barton, 1995). The conflict and lack of mutual perspective between the Former Head of IT and Strategic Director of Resources trickled down also to back-office (departmental) level. The stakeholders at the back-offices were not content with merely getting calls answered. They also wanted quality to be delivered to the public. The back-offices seemed to be more in line with Former Head of IT's system integration perspective.

According to Nonaka (1994) knowledge intensive firms, competitive advantage and product success are a result of collaborative, ongoing learning. Success depends not only on how effectively the diverse individuals are able to organize and develop their unique knowledge competencies but also how they can integrate and utilize their distinctive knowledge both effectively and synergistically (Nonaka, 1994). The synergy can be obtained if the aids/barriers to the knowledge sharing across the sub-cultures are understood. This synergy of integrating back-office/departmental knowledge with the front-office using X CRM was not achieved at the Independent Company managed Contact Centre. This was due to the fact that aids and barriers were not fully understood by the stakeholders involved. Non-secondee Team Manager concludes:

> Myself, I just wish that the Independent Company probably could have amalgamated this, like a core contract, where the UKCC employees were happy and the Independent Company employees as well.

The contract was not amalgamated and by the end of 2004 most of the secondees had already left the Independent Company managed Contact Centre.

End-users at the Independent Company managed Contact Centre also expressed their frustration

Respondents claim that they were not well informed, involved and equipped for new ideas and changes made at the Contact Centre, for example:

> No I'm not. I think we should be more informed. I think it should be as you . . . as when a new theory or the new things that they're bringing on . . . they should, I suppose, not just . . . they should roll it out to us over a longer period and not expect . . . and give people a chance to take on the idea. I think they give you something . . . they come up with a new idea and they expect us to take it on straight away, and not enough training is given, or not enough time to get to understand and digest it and know what it really means, is given to us. We hear these new things 'pathways'. We don't know what they mean, they're just names now and we don't know what they actually . . . what is the theory behind it. So I think they should be more in-depth. (A non-secondee)

Lack of end-user involvement resulted in lack of trust among the end-users towards CRM X and The Independent Company management (Janssens *et al.*, 2003). Moreover, management pressure on end-users, employing power based relationships resulted in "employee under-obligation" types of psychological contracts between the end-users and the Independent Company management. The X system was nominally in charge at the Independent Company managed Contact Centre; end-users were obliged to use the system to help the customers. When asked about who was in control a non-secondee end-user stated:

> The system is because everyone wants to get their bonuses and things so we have to do it.

There were other issues with the system that put extra pressure on the end-users:

> Well sometimes my system runs really slow and I've got someone on-line waiting whilst I'm saying, 'Well I'm watching this little blue line go across the page, so just bear with me'. I know that it's just the backing system or whatever they say 'that's booting'. So it just runs really slow, so that's an inhibitor in that it prevents me from dealing with that caller effectively, well quickly, and getting them off the line which is what they want. (Non-secondee)

This non secondee respondent further argued that there were more people at the Independent Company Contact Centre but less quality.

Management support was better in the back-office. She claimed that the services provided by her at the back-office had more quality:

> Yes it was, much better by management because they had more time to look after the staff, to see what the staff was doing, this is a more vast scale than when we had before. Although we had less people we had better quality people, which gave a better quality service.

Staff retention continues to be an issue at all levels including the Independent Company managed Contact Centre. There was a continuous change of management at the Independent Company, which further added to the pressures on the end-users at the Contact Centre, for example:

> We have new management now, which is the third one since I've been here, and it proves there's something wrong at the top—to have three different managers to run this ship and they keep on sacking this captain. Who's the next one? Do we believe? We've heard it all before. Are we going to believe this one? That is the question! Back to the question that you asked me . . . do I think it's going to be . . . it has to get worse before it gets better. (Secondee)

Our respondent suggested that secondees would have stayed had they been given higher status than their non-secondee colleagues:

> How the people work—the management team—how they deal with crisis, how they promote people off the floor, how they deal with staff pay. That's the biggest issue really, staff pay. They need to try and hold down the staff so they don't get such a high turnover of people leaving, so they've come a long way. They need more experience. They needed to have kept a lot of the experienced people from the UKCC in like a role, a higher role that what they're doing now, because then the knowledge would have stayed here, but they have still got Head Office to fall back on.

According to our secondee respondent, the Independent Company management has limited interaction with the end-users:

> The managers need to come from behind their computers and they need to do a lot more floor walking. They need to talk to the staff more. They need to keep their promises. They need to do their one-to-one which they promised. Don't start something that you're not going to finish!

Our respondent also claimed that management did not tend to keep their promises:

> An example, we are supposed to have one-to-one's each month, we're supposed to have coaching side-by-side each week, we're supposed to, what we call 'qualitest' on each staff, each month, and if you go out there and ask, ask three people, 'When was the last time you had a call quality??', they will say, (it's certain teams—I'm not speaking about every team) 'Six months ago' . . . 'two months ago' . . . or 'The other day". They need to keep their promise because that's what the Independent Company always said that they would do—so they have us in these meetings and meetings and meetings, all about a meeting about a meeting, and nothing is being done. Every time they say this is going to happen it doesn't happen. They've brought in trouble-shooters to sort out what is the problem here. Why is it not working—why is it working at other complexes and it's not working at this complex? These trouble-shooters were supposed to do A, B and C—we're still waiting to see A, B and C.

The trouble-shooters were told they should start with the management, according to our respondent:

> Well they came in to see where the problem lies, they had us in a group and they asked us questions about where we thought the problem was. We said, 'Well don't start with us, start with the management, because it starts from management and filters down into your staff. So if you haven't got someone steering the car then the car will go all over the place, so therefore you start with the steering and then work on the wheels, and then the engine, and the seats and the seat-belts.' So therefore they promised this is what's going to happen as from now. As far as this is concerned nothing has happened because on top of that a few more other staff have left. The environment that you work in has improved. It looks better out there, but they've had a 2 % rise, full-stop.

Interaction through the meetings with the management was not able to solve the issues:

> It's fine to have that meeting, but if we've come to a meeting to resolve a problem and we leave that meeting with the ideal—how we are going to resolve that problem—and we put a target on it, which it's supposed to have, we're coming back a month later to resolve the same problem. Then nobody took heed it what was said in the first meeting—because when you left that meeting that problem should have been solved. And now we're back in a second meeting, about the first meeting, that should have been resolved within that month . . . so there's something wrong, that is what I'm saying. (Secondee)

The above are examples of disappointments expressed by end-users regarding the Independent Company management. Our respondents were clearly dissatisfied with their job situation at the Independent Company managed Contact Centre. They lacked management support and felt excluded from decision making processes. The examples highlight lack of loyalty towards the Independent Company management. An "employee under-obligation" type of psychological contract resulted, as neither secondees nor non-secondees felt adequately rewarded either intrinsically or extrinsically (Janssens *et al.*, 2003; Shore & Barksdale, 1998). The Independent Company management, on the other hand, had staff retention issues and had their third manager in place in less than three years. However, they started to use the secondees in training non-secondees more effectively—but they were running short of secondees who continued to move back to the UKCC.

Krogh *et al.* (2000) describe how effective knowledge creation depends on the physical, virtual and emotional context of an organization. They discuss the importance of the notion of reciprocity of relationships. When a relationship is felt to be reciprocal then a trust develops which can work to overcome power-based relationships. Between the Independent Company management and secondees there was a lack of reciprocity of relationship. Secondees felt their potential was being exploited without any reward from the management. This resulted in lack of trust and loyalty between secondees

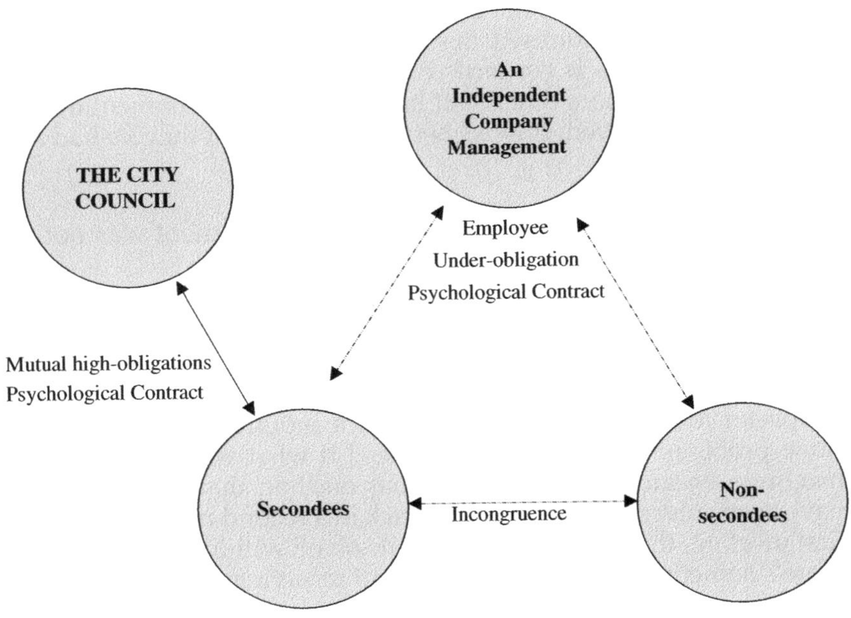

Figure 5.5 *The dilemma at the Independent Company Contact Centre involving secondees, non-secondees and the Independent Company management*

and the Independent Company management. Secondees also felt exploited by their non-secondee colleagues who were interested in the non-codified knowledge their secondee colleagues possessed.

There was also friction between secondees and non-secondees. Secondees were governed under a better employment contract. There was a lack of trust and lack of reciprocity between the secondees, non-secondees and the Independent Company management. Lack of loyal and "mutual high-obligations" types of psychological contracts restricted the non-codified or tacit knowledge sharing between secondees and non-secondees. The sharing of "tricks of the trade" even though encouraged by the Independent Company management, did not take place due to lack of reciprocity between secondees and non-secondees (Krogh *et al.*, 2000). Secondees also had a strong bond with the UKCC back-office and an underlying loyalty to the UKCC based on perceived benefits. We summarize this dilemma at the Independent Company Contact Centre graphically with the help of the diagram below.

The dilemma at the Independent Company Contact Centre involving secondees, non-secondees and the Independent Company management

Secondees

- Secondees showed lack of trust and loyalty towards the Independent Company management. They felt they were not well informed about updates and were excluded from the decision making process.
- Secondees also felt that their knowledge was exploited without any extrinsic reward.
- They claimed that although the Contact Centre had more people than the back-office, nevertheless the quality of service was comparatively low.
- Secondees claimed that management support was better in the back-office at the UKCC. They showed a lack of trust in the Independent Company management.
- Secondees were moving back to the UKCC and taking with them the non-codified knowledge/'tricks of the trade'.

The Independent Company management

- The Independent Company management tried to bridge the gap between secondees and their non-secondee colleagues by taking away the formers' privileges such as flexi-leave.
- Management also made efforts to exploit the "tricks of the trade" possessed by secondees by using them as trainers. However this

happened belatedly as the secondees were starting to leave the Independent Company.

- Moreover there was no extrinsic reward in terms of bonus or anything like that attached to the training provided by secondees.

Non-secondees

- Non-secondees felt inferior to their colleagues secondees who had full access to their back-office systems.
- They felt they lacked management support and that management interaction with them was limited.
- They also expressed their concerns on training and claimed they were not well informed.
- They felt stressed by the fact that they had to answer the calls as quickly as possible. However they felt that this reduced the quality of service delivery to the customers.
- They claimed that secondees would have stayed if they were offered a better position and status.
- Non-secondees would like to have had full access to the back-office systems and also acquired the knowledge possessed by the secondees.

Interdependence Between Psychological Contracts, Sub-cultures and Knowledge Sharing

In this section we discuss the interdependence between subculture interactions, knowledge sharing and psychological contracts at the UKCC (Figure 5.6). A special focus is given to the sharing of non-codified knowledge. Below we discuss the sub-cultures at different

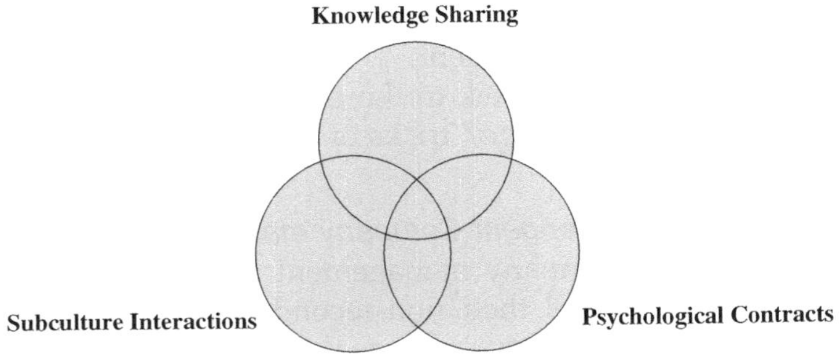

Figure 5.6 Interdependence between Subculture Interaction, Psychological Contracts and Knowledge Sharing

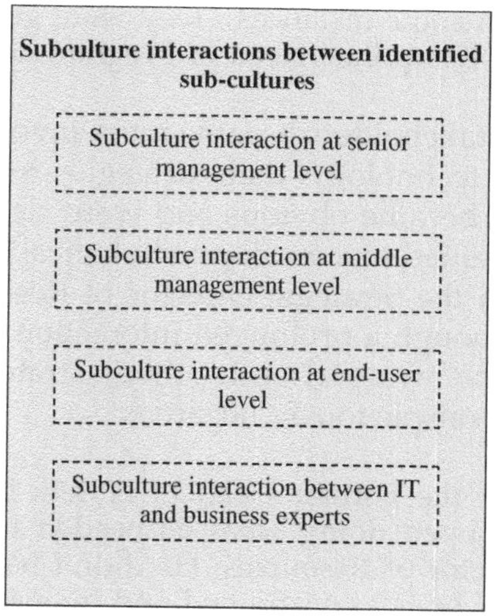

Figure 5.7 *Subculture interactions at various levels of hierarchy*

levels (Figure 5.7) and how they impinged on one another affecting the whole process of CRM X development.

Subculture interaction at senior management level

There were two groups at the senior level. One supporting the Former Head of IT's integration strategy and the other supporting Strategic Director of Resources's call answering focus strategy. The initial interaction between Strategic Director of Resources and Former Head of IT was not overtly problematic:

> The Deputy Leader was a politician who was very switched on into modern techniques. It was Andy that wanted me to do it, and he got me and the Strategic Director together and said, 'go and do it.' (Former Head of IT)

Initially the Former Head of IT was the driving force and the project was more IT led according to Corporate Head of Programme Management. To begin with, the Strategic Director did not object to a system integration strategy. However, problems started when creative abrasion (in this case destructive) began to take place and the innermost feelings of the stakeholders were revealed. This was also a time when individual frames and perceptions regarding the technology surfaced (Davidson, 2002; Orlikowski & Gash, 1994):

> There was a lot of friction between Former Head of IT and Strategic Director of Resources, to such a degree that, there was no

> communication in some instances—they were getting towards open hostility at times. (Corporate Head of Programme Management)

As the two senior stakeholders became more involved in discussions regarding the new technology, their strategies regarding the implementation of CRM became obvious and were clearly different from each other. This resulted in a weak psychological contract, lacking in mutuality, between the Strategic Director of Resources and Former Head of IT. Even though a prolonged interaction took place and the two subjects became aware of each other's strategies, the "creative abrasion" became conspicuously negative:

> My view of why the Former Head of IT left: because he felt that he was being stopped doing what he needed to do to sort out IT by Strategic Director of Resources. He didn't have the backing, the financial backing, he felt constrained and he just didn't feel that he could do the job that he was supposed to be doing. (Corporate Head of Programme Management)

The Former Head of IT, as a result, resigned to escape the prolonged interactions based upon negative abrasion between him and Strategic Director of Resources. There was some exchange of information between the Strategic Director of Resources and Former Head of IT. However, the weak psychological contracts between the two lead them to shut themselves off from each other, not listening to each other actively. Both promoted their individual agendas (frames) and gathered followers to support these.

Subculture interaction at middle management level

The UKCC's strategy to promote IT autonomy resulted in several software solutions, and systems were bought by each department to facilitate its departmental tasks. However, this was done without any consideration of overall system integration. The stakeholders of the systems within each department had acquired codified and non-codified knowledge over several years. This knowledge however remained in departmental silos. According to the CRM Programme Manager, the UKCC had departmental vertical silos. The Corporate IT Services interacted with departments sporadically without any in-depth prolonged interaction which could facilitate creative abrasion between the Corporate Services and departments. CRM X was supposed to facilitate integration. Limited departmental involvement could not achieve cultural integration, which in turn could have assisted in establishing mutual perspective and shared understanding. This lack of departmental involvement continued, resulting in "employee under-obligation" types of psychological contracts between Corporate Services and the various departments. Knowledge sharing among the stakeholders of CRM X was poor, for example:

> We suspect they (Corporate Services) don't want us to know, they don't want us to have access to it (CRM X). Maybe we'll find out something we're not supposed to know—I don't know. (Head of Community Initiatives, Neighbourhood Office)

As a result the departments are continuing to use their departmental autonomy to promote independent systems (such as NOSS+) to cater for their needs:

> I'd reached the point where I actually thought... if we could work towards either... we need to have consistent CRM... we may not [need] to roll out the Local Neighbourhood Office System, if we'd got something else that would do the job... alternatively then we would want to do that. It just seems to be now they (UKCC Corporate Services) want to develop an integrated system with someone else, and in the meantime I've got responsibility for Neighbourhood Offices and therefore we will push for an upgraded solution. (Head of Community Initiatives)

The Head of Community Initiatives further reported that the knowledge created in the departmental silos was not exploited and integrated in CRM X. This was also due to a limited degree of interaction between various departments involved in the CRM initiative. According to several respondents, the information regarding call handling sent to them by the Independent Company managed Contact Centre lacked qualitative information:

> We just get a little bit disappointed when we're supposed to be in partnership with people and we don't get the impression they have been as open as they could have been in terms of letting you know that the service is suffering. (Council Tax Manager)

The Business Manager, Environmental Services added:

> We undertake certain systematic sampling of data that is input in relation to business issues, e.g. a missed collection that is reported: we need basic information like location, what's been missed. And we sample, a rolling programme, 1 % of all the jobs that have been input through X through to the back-office system, and there are inaccuracies or errors in over 20 % of the jobs that are input. Similarly I hear, a lot of this is anecdotal, a fair number of complaints from elected members [of the UKCC], members of the public who come to Council

> Tax complaining about the way they were dealt with and what has been said to them via the Contact Centre. So quantity, quantitatively we've got it right, but the quality aspect is not all working.

There was a lack of trust between the departments and Corporate Services. The stakeholders of CRM X were also not happy with the Independent Company managed services at the Contact Centre. They would like to have seen more quality in the service delivery at the Contact Centre. Moreover, they would also have liked detailed qualitative information sent to them by the Independent Company Contact Centre management. This, they claimed, would have helped them to achieve a better quality control over services.

Due to departmental silos, knowledge sharing between the departments was minimal horizontally. Also, due to a limited interaction between the senior management (Corporate Services) and departments, a mutual perspective and shared understanding of CRM X was missing. There was also a lack of trust between the departments and the Independent Company management:

> The Managers at the Independent Company I don't know—as I say I'm on my third lot now—so you meet with them and you get the same stories about capacity planning and all the buzz words, whereas I'd just rather them get in there and try and turn the service round. But I don't know, I haven't got the answers for you, how they're going to do that. (Council Tax Manager)

This in turn gave rise to suspicions and lack of trust, as was reported to us by our respondents, resulting in psychological contracts that were not mutual and were of "employee under-obligation" type (Janssens *et al.*, 2003; Rousseau, 1995; Shore & Barksdale, 1998). The lack of prolonged interaction was not the only reason for the above. All the departments we spoke to, believed in a more integrated approach to building and running a CRM system. However, this could not be achieved without integrating the sub-cultures at middle management and senior levels. The departments felt they were not a part of the CRM initiative of their free will but were under obligation to participate in it (Shore & Barksdale, 1998). They felt that their opinions were not taken on board. Knowledge, in particularly tacit knowledge, resided in departmental (horizontal) and vertical (management hierarchical) silos.

Subculture interaction at the floor level (end-user sub-cultures)

As previously discussed in this chapter, there was friction between secondees and non-secondees caused by several factors. Secondees were paid more than their non-secondee colleagues and yet allocated the same roles. The secondment agreement was terminated according to Business Manager, Environmental Services (Environmental Services):

> The secondment has ended, as a result of, or at the request of, I think, the secondees themselves who had a conflict of interest between what they perceived as their loyalty to the Council and the business and the Independent Company, who perhaps had a different attitude and different managerial styles used in the private sector to that that they've been used to at the UKCC.

Secondee loyalty lay firsthand with the UKCC and their back-offices. They were obliged to interact and share knowledge (explicit) with their colleagues. Latterly the Independent Company management started to make effective use of their tacit/non-codified knowledge whilst using them as trainers for the newcomers. However, by this time secondees had already made their minds up about going back to the UKCC. Moreover, secondees perceived it as exploitation of their expertise without any financial reward:

> I've been doing the supervisory role, as they call it a Technical Specialist. I've been a Technical Specialist for over one and a half years, so I've been looking after my colleagues as well as new staff. I have taken an escalated course, which is not part of my job as a CSA. I have trained all new staff that have come in, along with my colleagues, and I have set-up forum meetings. I am a forum representative as well as, so I do feel that we have been exploited because we haven't been paid for what we've been doing. (Secondee)

Secondees delivered a high quality service using their informal connections and their invisible colleges within the UKCC (Krogh *et al.*, 2000; Kunda, 1991; Van Maanen, 1986). However, they were under pressure to be quick in delivering that service due to the Independent Company management's call statistics monitoring. Secondees perceived the Independent Company management relationships with them as more of a power based type. This resulted in an "employee under-obligation" type of psychological contract between secondees and the Independent Company management (Shore & Barksdale, 1998). The outcome was obvious; secondees started to leave the Independent Company and took with them the "tricks of the trade" and their non-codified knowledge regarding the systems and the UKCC culture. This reduced the quality of service delivery at the Independent Company managed Contact Centre:

> The knowledge went with the majority of my colleagues. The service level, the calls coming in, the queuing system has gone tremendously

> out the door because the staff here . . . we haven't got the quality of staff to take the calls, so the majority of time we were training and getting them up to the level that they will need to be to take calls on a faster level. The quality is non-existent, so there are a lot of errors being made . . . So my concept of it was that it was disorganised and it was all about quantity not quality. (End-user)

Management at the Independent Company tried to exploit the non-codified knowledge possessed by secondees. Secondees, on the other hand, did not have a mutual type of psychological contract with the management. They perceived the relationship between them and the management as a more power based type. According to secondees their skills were exploited without an extrinsic reward in the shape of a bonus. As a result they became more convinced of the desirability of moving back to the UKCC. Moreover, they also felt their relationship with the Independent Company management lacked reciprocity (Krogh *et al.*, 2000).

There was some knowledge sharing between the management and the customer service advisors at the Contact Centre. However it was mainly of a descriptive and prescriptive nature. Descriptive knowledge is in close proximity to explicit knowledge since it describes things as they are; it can be in the form of rules, abstract concepts and general principles, and it often has a consistent and generalisable structure (Herschbach, 1995; Nonaka and Takeuchi, 1995; Vincenti, 1993). Such knowledge had been shared during the training of customer service advisors at the Independent Company managed Contact Centre. Furthermore, prescriptive knowledge is based on efforts to achieve greater effectiveness, such as improved operations (Vincenti, 1993). This type of knowledge had been in the form of transcripts updated by the Corporate Services. Up to the end of 2004, tacit knowledge had continuously moved back to the UKCC as secondees made their way back to the UKCC.

Subculture interaction between IT and business experts

There was initially an illusion of consensus between the groups led by the Former Head of IT and the Strategic Director of Resources. Our respondents seem to agree on the fact that CRM X was initially an IT led project. It subsequently changed its direction and, according to the CRM Project Manager and Business Manager, became more business led. It is worth noting that "business led" at the UKCC meant simply having a call answering focus—not anything else. The interaction between the two groups was intense at senior management level. However, it produced a mainly negative type of abrasion. A "shared context for knowing" could not be reached between the Former Head of IT and Strategic Director. They had decided to not to share their frames with each other (Orlikowski & Gash, 1994). Furthermore, they were not going to move from their positions towards developing so called "T-shaped skills" (Iansiti, 1993). Consequently they developed a "mutual low-obligation" type of psychological contract, which indeed weakened as time passed. Former Head of IT finally resigned and left the UKCC. With him went knowledge, in particularly tacit knowledge relating to a system integration approach.

At a lower level of hierarchy the same scenario was repeated when friction arose between the Business Manager and CRM Programme Manager. The two interacted on a regular basis in steering group meetings, revealing their innermost feelings and their divergent approaches regarding CRM X. The CRM Programme manager supported the integrative approach, whilst the Business Manager wanted to promote the Strategic Director's "call answering focus" strategy. This resulted in a weak psychological contract between the two, lacking in mutuality (Rousseau, 1995). The CRM Programme Manager also left the project and took with him knowledge, particularly tacit knowledge regarding a system integration approach.

By the end of 2004 the UKCC still had limited IT expertise as most of the IT expertise was outsourced, that is with the supplier. El Sawy (1985) argues that if IT specialists are members of a corporation or are directly related to it, they are part of an organizational culture and none of them should be excluded from an analysis of organizational behaviour in the face of IT. The IT knowledge possessed by individuals at the UKCC had not been fully understood by the decision makers at senior management level. Interaction between the two sub-cultures, that is, the IT and business cultures had been limited. Furthermore the interaction had not been able to achieve a shared understanding between the groups. This resulted in weak psychological contracts lacking a mutual perspective and "shared context for knowing" (Boland & Tenkasi 1996; Rousseau, 1995; Newell *et al.*, 2002). As a result, knowledge sharing, particularly non-codified knowledge regarding system integration have not been shared and exploited fully by the UKCC.

Summary highlighting subculture interactions, knowledge sharing and psychological contracts

From the beginning of their CRM initiative the UKCC had differing frames and "sense making" of technology (Davidson, 2002; Orlikowski & Gash, 1994). Subculture interaction at different levels of hierarchies was limited. Even when prolonged interaction took place it resulted in negative abrasion. Weak psychological contracts lacking mutual perspectives and "shared context for knowing" at different levels of hierarchies emerged. This inhibited the sharing of knowledge across the sub-cultures. There was, nevertheless, some knowledge sharing in relation to descriptive and prescriptive knowledge at end-user level (Vincenti, 1993).

Non-codified tacit knowledge had not been mobile and remained in subculture silos (Bartlett & Ghoshal, 1998). The efforts made by the management at the Contact Centre to exploit the tacit knowledge possessed by the secondees and convert it into to a codified form did not pay off. Secondees were making their way back to the UKCC and did not feel a strong mutual obligation to share their personal knowledge and "tricks of the trade". Stakeholders at senior and middle management level also withheld their non-codified knowledge regarding an integrative approach. Negative abrasion resulted in "mutual low-obligation" types of psychological contracts (Shore & Barksdale, 1998). Consequently managerial stakeholders started to leave the project and took their non-codified knowledge and "tricks of the trade" with them.

Throughout the development of the CRM "Process" subculture interaction had been present, and to some extent even in a prolonged form. However, this did not result in a non-codified type of knowledge sharing. Rather, non-codified knowledge sharing was dependent on the types of psychological contracts resulting from subculture interactions.

Stakeholders left the project instead of being loyal to it. Tacit knowledge moved with the stakeholders. In the case of the Former Head of IT it (tacit/non-codified knowledge) went to the CRM vendor where he got a new job and was able to use his previous knowledge regarding an integrative approach as a CRM Consultant. In the case of the CRM Programme Manager, it (tacit knowledge) went back to his call centre where he continued to develop an integrative strategy. As for secondees, they took their invisible colleges (their strong networks) and "tricks of the trade" back to the UKCC. Their psychological contracts with the back-offices proved to be strong and of a "mutual-obligation" type. Back-office management were very happy to receive the returning secondees. The fact that secondees had thinned out and the lack of prolonged interaction between the back-office management and the Independent Company management had resulted in a "mutual under-obligation" type of psychological contract between them, which Shore and Barksdale (1998) claim is expected to attain the poorest results. Back-offices were in a process of planning alternate systems to patch up the loopholes in the service delivery at the Contact Centre. According to Head of Community Initiatives from neighbourhood advice:

> Earlier in the year (2004) we did some mystery customer's testing of the service. Well it was before I came back, somebody who actually now works for me as part of the Neighbourhood Offices support. And to a large degree that's borne out what I've just said. The service that's now being given is not the best of the service, which ideally we would want.

According to the Corporate Head of Programme Management, the Independent Company management did not take many steps to monitor the quality of its service. The service provided by the Contact Centre was of a more generalized nature, lacking the capacity to offer detailed responses to clients. It needed to be more differentiated according to the needs at the back-offices. A Senior Accounting Assistant from the Council Tax claimed that calls at the call centre were being abandoned prematurely:

> I can see the call abandoned—I can see that happening anyway. Yes I can see calls abandoned because they're not being answered quickly enough, and then, obviously, the calls answered are getting quicker because there's not as many calls coming through, do you see what I mean.

These examples show the background to a weak, "employee under-obligation" type of psychological contract between back-offices and the Independent Company management. Management at the back-offices according to the Business Manager, Environmental Services, would rather have their own systems and call centres with a virtual integration link between the departments. They also preferred to have an IVR (Interactive Voice Response) rather than ACD (Automated Call Distribution). When the ACD distributed an incoming complex type of call to the next available customer service advisor, and if that advisor was a newly appointed non-secondee with a limited knowledge of back-office culture and procedures, then the quality started to suffer as a result. This was the reason why back-offices preferred to see a differentiated and sophisticated service being provided at the Contact Centre.

However, as their comments were not taken on board, the back-offices' psychological contracts with both the Independent Company and Corporate Resources Management became weaker and of an "employee under-obligation" type. As a result they continued to pursue a non-integrative approach in developing new processes to improve their services. This acted as a barrier to the fulfilment of the UKCC's aim to establish a "one-stop-service" for their customers and meeting the latest government directives regarding e-government. Knowledge sharing, particularly non-codified knowledge sharing, became minimal between the groups. For an overview of our analysis see Figure 5.8.

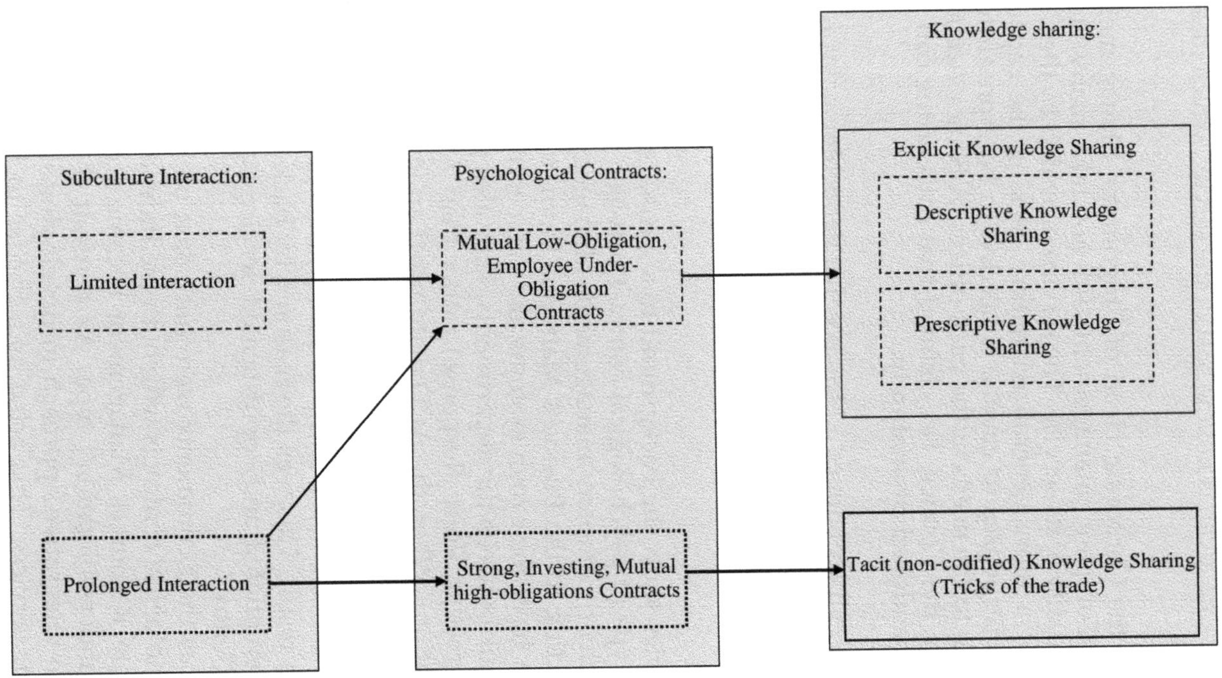

Figure 5.8 *Interdependence between subculture interactions, psychological contracts and knowledge sharing, showing Psychological Contracts playing a key role in sharing of "tricks of the trade"*

SUMMARY ANALYSIS—A UKCC CRM X IMPLEMENTATION

Summary

This research set out to investigate the CRM implementation at a UKCC (name of the council has been kept anonymous). The research focused on the implementation of CRM X at a UKCC. Case research methods were applied as the CRM application was still in a formative stage, and the experiences of subjects and their perceptions thus becomes vital (Benbasat *et al.*, 1987). In particular we wished to investigate the relatively neglected issues relating to knowledge management and sharing, and psychological contracts. Case research through interviewing and participant observation seemed particularly appropriate.

The research was structured firstly to describe the key events and subsequently to discuss the "how" and "why" questions relating to those events in terms of an exploratory analysis. We have included some preliminary analysis already in structuring the case history. Theories and learning from the relevant literatures were applied to enhance the understanding of the CRM system and its implementation at the UKCC.

In the final analysis section an improvised framework resulting from a refined literature review was adopted to structure, analyse and explain events and evidence longitudinally (Pettigrew, 1985; Willcocks and Margetts, 1994). The salient features that emerged from the literature review were used as a lens to focus on knowledge sharing issues linked with psychological contracts for final data analysis (Davidson, 2002; Orlikowski & Gash, 1991, 1994; Pettigrew, 1985; Willcocks & Margetts, 1994). The improvised framework adapted from Pettigrew's model (1985, 1991) contributed to developing a deeper insight into the contemporary situation and to understanding the phenomena at the research site.

As per November 2004, the UKCC CRM X implementation was at the adaptation and acceptance stage during which they were trying to develop systems to promote integration, and streamline the processes as much as possible. The impact of knowledge creation, retention and exploitation on the ongoing process of implementation has become highly important to the organization.

How knowledge, in particular tacit knowledge, is shared and exploited has been addressed in this chapter. The chapter has aided the discussion of the "tricks of the trade"—the short cuts and work-arounds that are born in the minds of the end-users of the system, their hands-on skills, including best practices and special know-how (Orlikowski & Iacono, 2001; Polanyi, 1973; Vincenti, 1984). The discussion has concluded that in order to understand the above, one needs to understand the micro-elements (psychological contracts in our project) in the process of mutual perspective formation (Boland & Tenkasi, 1996) which facilitate tacit knowledge sharing. Scholars argue that tacit knowledge sharing is dependent on prolonged interactions resulting in a creative abrasion type of environment where innermost feelings are revealed (Leonard-Barton, 1995). However, this research has highlighted the fact that a prolonged interaction does not necessarily result in a creative abrasion which was clearly the case at the UKCC senior management level. In this case a prolonged interaction resulted in progressively destructive abrasion leading to a weak "mutual low-obligation" type of psychological contract. This scenario was repeated at every level in the hierarchy.

In the UKCC case some knowledge was shared, but it was largely of descriptive and prescriptive nature. This research suggests in particular that tacit/non-codified knowledge sharing is largely dependant on a strong, investing and "mutual high-obligations" type of psychological contract.

Throughout this research the micro-elements (the psychological contracts in this research) leading to "mutual perspective taking" were investigated and critically analyzed. This enhanced our understanding of how the "tricks of the trade", the shortcuts, and work-arounds surface, and how they are shared across the sub-cultures, individuals and groups. We drew attention to the impact of psychological contracts on non-codified knowledge sharing, recognizing the inhibiting effects of "mutual low-obligation" and "employee under-obligation" types of psychological contracts resulting in knowledge hoarding and the formation of knowledge silos, both horizontally and vertically.

Emerging Issues

In many ways the case history demonstrates not only the importance of previously neglected areas of knowledge sharing and psychological factors in systems implementation, but in particular how lack of knowledge sharing, failure of non-codified/tacit knowledge sharing, and unconnected psychological contracts can inhibit systems implementation. Applying a longitudinal research approach also reveals the origins of these sub-optimal outcomes—at least sub-optimal from systems promoter, external customer and governmental stakeholder perspectives. Referring to Figure 5.9, the origins can be traced from the historical decision to give departments autonomy over IT decisions and purchasing. This resulted in the functional hierarchical structure of the organization developing both vertical and horizontal stratification in knowledge possession and psychological loyalties (invisible colleges) at every level. Outsourcing brought into play further differential knowledge bases and psychological contracts without sufficiently addressing the need to dissolve the resulting barriers to knowledge sharing, learning and mutual perspective-taking.

These fissures in organization led to the development of subcultures, each embodying differing perceptions, interests, loyalties and objectives. In such circumstances politics breed, and become particularly visible in times of technological change (Pettigrew, 1985; Willcocks *et al.*, 2003), and, as the case shows, during the development and implementation of a key system such as CRM. At the same time external contextual pressures forced organizational stakeholders into action, with one group clustered around the Strategic Director and Business Manager with what we have called a "call-answering" focus, winning over against the integration approach favoured by the Head of IT, and for the support of which the vendor had been originally selected.

In terms of the internal context, we identified many examples of knowledge hoarding in vertical silos and of "mutual low-obligation" types of psychological contracts resulting in subsequent non-cooperative, and less informed patterns of behaviour relative to systems implementation. All this made the process of systems implementation much more difficult than it could have been had the issues of knowledge sharing and enhancement, and shared psychological contracts been addressed through, for example, training and education, team-building, better communication and changed ways of working.

The process of change revealed real knowledge and psychological contractual issues. The project team at the UKCC went through its ups and downs. The CRM programme manager resigned soon after the new business manager's arrival. More people left, including the chief executive and the head of IT services as a result of a power struggle and conflicts (Jehn, 1995). Frequent changes of personnel may not have allowed the group to attain cohesiveness thus contributing to a less productive output (Kirkman & Shapiro, 1997). The Council re-aligned their strategy and moved back from a complete integration approach to having a call answering system with limited integration. These events can be related to knowledge and psychological contractual issues.

Knowledge silos found at the UKCC were at different hierarchical levels. At senior management level the sub-cultural gap between the Strategic Director of Resources's team and Former Head of IT's created a divide. The divide continued with CRM Programme Manager being replaced with a new business manager. Due to a lack of "mutual perspective taking" and "shared understanding" the psychological contracts were more imposed and "mutual low-obligation" rather than "mutual high-obligations" in type (Shore & Barksdale, 1998). This inhibited the process of developing positive creative abrasion, thus resulting in knowledge hoarding in the silos.

This research suggests that psychological contracts play an important role in knowledge sharing. It also suggests that imposed psychological contracts (employee under-obligation) tend to promote power based relationships (Shore & Barksdale, 1998). Explicit elements of psychological contracts between senior management and end-users include a sense of obligation to work, and job security. Importantly, implicit elements of psychological contracts remain hidden (Makin *et al.*, 1996) producing illusions of consensus, which influence and inhibit adoption and acceptance of the CRM system.

Outcomes

In this particular systems implementation it is interesting to look at what happened where the "Process" issues as listed in Figure 5.9 were not addressed. Knowledge sharing and development were delayed because of low staff retention, imposed, weak, "mutual low-obligation" and "employee under-obligation" types of psychological contracts, low user involvement in the process of change, lack of external user involvement, declining senior management commitment and limited user training. As Willcocks *et al.* (2003) and Walton (1989) have shown, these insufficiencies had knock-on effects in terms of the final outcomes.

The UKCC lost control of the end to end process. Two sets of management were involved (Corporate Services and the Independent Company management) in many transactions, leading to confusion over responsibility and service level achievement. The provision of another layer (the Independent Company) between the Council authority and the public may also have led to a perception of reduced accountability.

The system went live a year after the contract was signed with the vendor. A CRM vendor (manufacturer of CRM X) also brought in a third part middleware vendor to help with the integration of the back-office systems. Subsequently UKCC outsourced their call centre management to the Independent Company. The consequences of outsourcing included stakeholders resigning from the project and secondee/non-secondee relationship issues.

The outcomes from the case are summarized in Figure 5.9. Management support at senior management level was provided for the project. The support thinned out as secondees at the UKCC started to leave. In addition the training seems to have been rushed at the Contact Centre. This was done without taking into account the UKCC culture and its expectations. The initial motive behind bringing in the CRM system at the UKCC was to get the calls answered.

Subsequent user commitment was effected by a lack of involvement in the decision making process in buying the system initially. Decisions to buy the systems were taken at a senior management level. End-user involvement in the implementation process came at a later stage. No external user involvement was taken into consideration. User commitment was linked predominantly with imposed, "employee under-obligation" types of psychological contracts and power based relationships (Rousseau, 1995). At the UKCC users subsequently found work-arounds in the form of manual methods to answer a call rather than using the CRM X system. However, they ended up using the system in order to meet the job requirement. Users were not able to see the shared benefits fully and hence the psychological contracts were not of "mutual high-obligations" type (Shore & Barksdale, 1998).

User commitment has potential links with job security (Davenport *et al.*, 1998). "Mutual perspective taking" had not fully happened due to the secondee/non-secondee relationship situation at the UKCC (Boland & Tenkasi, 1996). Furthermore, the content of an apparently mutual perspective may not have been allowed to surface or be challenged thus avoiding any interpretations which could shake up the illusion of consensus between stakeholders of the system (Fahey and Prusak, 1998). As the project progressed and the innermost feelings were exposed, people started to leave the project. The achievement of a new definition of the situation in which all participants could share had yet (as of December 2004) to take place in its full capacity at the UKCC (Habermas, 1979).

Partly as a consequence of these factors, staff turnover at the floor level was very high. This did not allow staff interactions to come to a state of "mutual perspective taking" where shared learning leading to "mutual high-obligation" types of psychological contracts could take place (Boland & Tenkasi, 1996). At the Independent Company managed Contact Centre, the staff, in particular non-secondees, did not interact on prolonged basis with the back-offices (departments). The secondees felt excluded at the Contact Centre. Furthermore, their (secondee's) contract with the UKCC did not allow them to be upgraded to a higher position. Non-secondees, on the other hand, could get promoted. Relationships at the contact centre between the

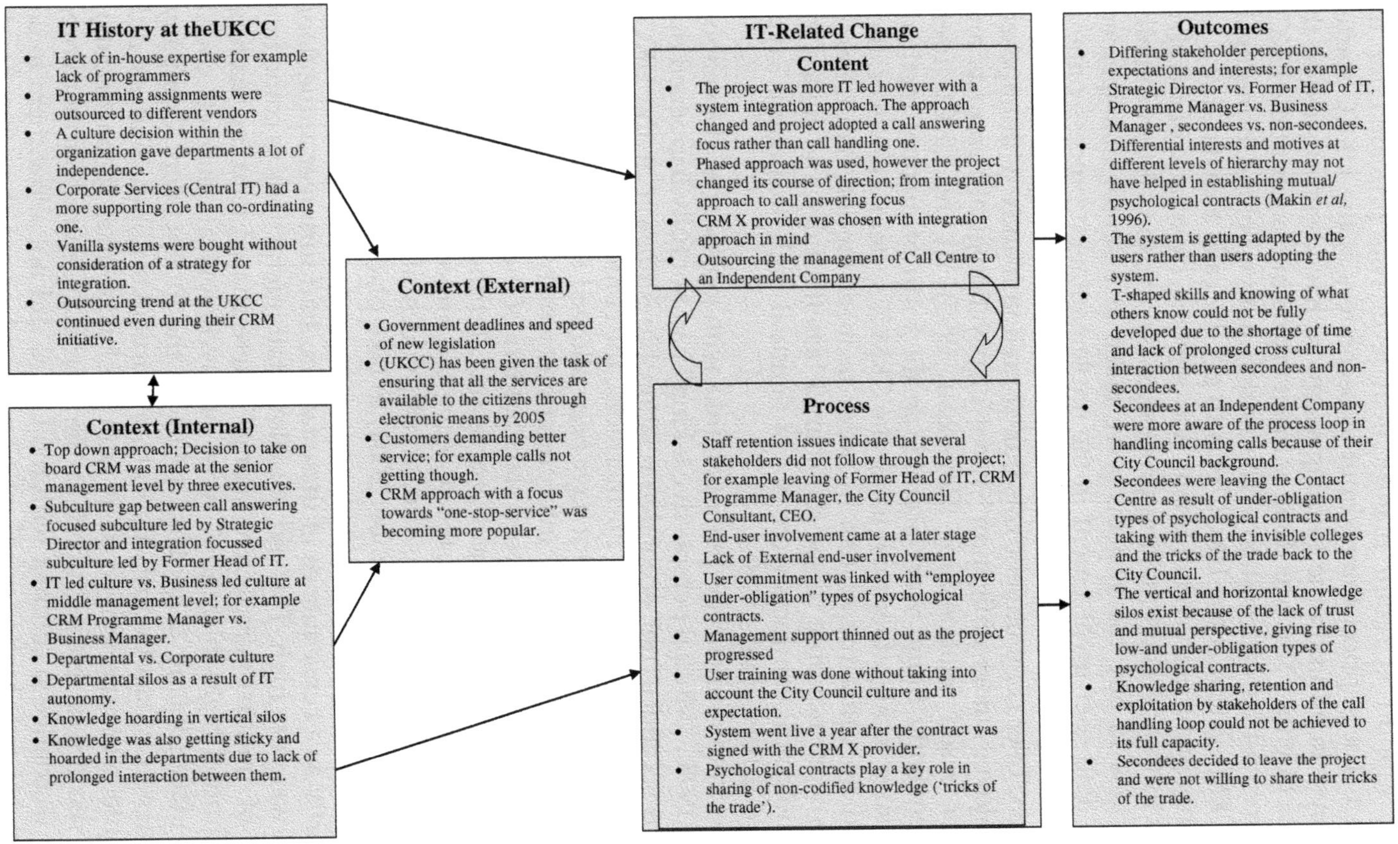

Figure 5.9 *Summary of the Analysis Using Pettigrew (1985, 1990) and Willcocks and Margetts (1994)*

secondees and the outsourced management were more power-based in style. This resulted in a scenario where the UKCC secondees with a lot of experience and the UKCC cultural knowledge felt inferior to their non-seconded colleagues. The high turnover of staff at senior level at the UKCC did not help the project to get stabilised or the new staff to settle. The resulting psychological contracts were more of an imposed than a "mutual high-obligations" type (Shore & Barksdale, 1998). The "creative abrasion" that could have facilitated the development of "mutual high-obligations" types of psychological contracts to help in sharing of "tricks of the trade", did not take place. Stakeholders at different levels of hierarchy interacted with each other from within their silos and the sharing of non-codified knowledge has tended to remain limited to the silos.

The micro mechanisms, (in this research the psychological contracts, underlying the development of "mutual perspective", "shared mental space", "T-shaped skills" and "knowing of what others know") upon investigation have been shown to play a key role in sharing of "tricks of the trade" and work-arounds across the sub-cultures of a post CRM implementation environment.

Wherever the psychological contracts were weak, as a result of lack of sharing of individual frames, and sense making of technology, knowledge sharing (particularly the tacit knowledge sharing) suffered greatly (Davidson, 2002; Orlikowski & Gash, 1994). People chose to leave the project. Moreover, secondees had full access to the back-office systems due to their trustful and loyal relationships (invisible colleges) with the back-office management. Secondees were also able to take advantage of their UKCC cultural knowledge and invisible colleges in order to deliver a high quality service to the customers. "Tricks of the trade" were shared through invisible colleges as a result of reciprocating "mutual-employee obligation" types of psychological contracts between the secondees and the back- offices. Secondees were given full access to the back-office systems due to their strong investing psychological contracts with the back-office management (Janssens *et al.*, 2003).

By the end of 2004, CRM project was at adaptation and acceptance stage where the UKCC were trying to develop the system further, promoting integration, and streamlining the processes as much as possible. The impact of knowledge creation, retention and exploitation on the ongoing process of implementation had become of high importance to the organizational promoters of CRM, as was the building of improved psychological contracts based on of the system. However, this had proven to be very difficult as the errors made by the optimal utilization management initially resulted in "employee under-obligation" types of psychological contracts. As a result staff retention, particularly knowledgeable staff retention (secondees), became an issue. According to the CRM Project Manager, CRM X project was "a ship no one wants to stay on". The quality of service delivery had suffered as a result of secondees moving back to the UKCC. Management had become aware of the need of system integration over time and was slowly moving towards it. However, their understanding regarding the relationship between system integration and cultural integration remained limited. The UKCC CRM project was still more focussed on call answering rather than call handling.

CONCLUSION

The research here has sought to extend the analysis of IT implementation to CRM systems, and to include in that analysis, knowledge issues—including tacit knowledge sharing, knowledge silos, psychological contracts. A longitudinal approach has elicited how contextual, cultural, political and structural factors have influenced propensity to share knowledge and pursue common cause in the CRM implementation and use at the UKCC, and the factors that could alleviate knowledge bottlenecks and facilitate more optimal utilization of the system. Our research has confirmed what our initial reading of the literature led us to believe—that knowledge issues, and what constructs them, are not just implicit in all systems implementations, but can be key reasons why a system optimises or fails in the light of its different stakeholders' interests. Our investigation of subculture interaction has shown that a prolonged interaction in some cases can result in a negative type of abrasion resulting in "mutual low-obligation" types of psychological contracts. This in turn acts as an inhibitor in the sharing of particularly the non-codified knowledge. The research concludes that micro elements such as psychological contracts play a key role in the sharing of tacit/non-codified knowledge.

6 CRM Implementation Case: An International Enterprise (IE)

INTRODUCTION

This chapter presents a chronological description for 1999–2004 with a thematic account of an International Enterprise's initiative to deploy a CRM Solution to promote system integration. It uses the analytical framework presented in Chapter 4, and in the first part discusses the history, context and content of the project. It then, in the second part, uses the "Process" part of the framework to carry out a within-case analysis of the implementation and post-implementation environment at the IE. The chapter also provides an end summary. The framework adapted from Pettigrew's (1985, 1990) six categories model is shown in Figure 6.1 and continues to contribute to the development of a deeper insight into the contemporary situation and understanding the phenomena at our research sites. In our pilot (see Chapter 4) throughout 2001–2004 we also observed sub-cultures prevalent at three levels: Senior Management level, Middle Management/Pre-Deployment Team (PDT) level and within the PDTs at end-user level. These sub-cultures are shown in Figure 6.1, and are discussed in detail at a later part of the chapter in the second part "Process"—part of the analytic framework.

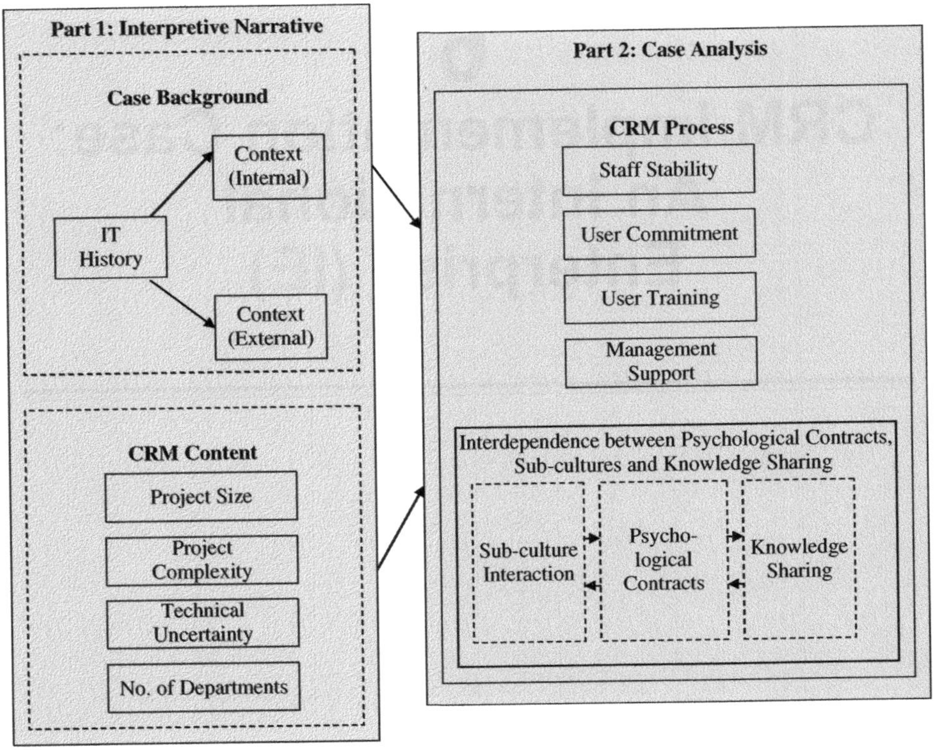

Figure 6.1 Framework for the final data collection and analyses

IE CASE PART 1—HISTORY CONTEXT AND CONTENT OF CRM

Case Background

This IE makes a broad range of computers, including PCs, notebooks, mainframes and network servers. It also develops software and peripherals. According to the reports stated in the company archives, during the 1980s and early 1990s, IE was thrown into turmoil by back-to-back revolutions. The PC revolution placed computers directly in the hands of millions of people. And then, the client/server revolution sought to link all of those PCs (the "clients") with larger computers that laboured in the background (the "servers" that served data and applications to client machines).

Both revolutions transformed the way customers viewed, used and bought technology. And both fundamentally rocked the IE. Businesses' purchasing decisions were put in the hands of individuals and departments and not the places where IE had long-standing customer relationships. Piece-part technologies took precedence over integrated solutions. The focus was on the desktop and personal productivity, not on business applications across the enterprise and system integration. By 1993, the company's annual net losses reached a record US$8 billion. Cost management and streamlining became a chief concern. It was then that IE considered splitting its divisions into separate independent businesses. However, this was done without giving any consideration to overall system integration in mind.

According to a Call Centre Manager at IE.COM, IE splits into three "geographies" namely: EMEA, Asia Pacific and the Americas. Furthermore, each "geography" is subdivided into regions. Our research focuses mainly on the North region. The North Region entails UK, Ireland, Netherlands and South Africa.

IE appointed their new CEO on April 1, 1993. He had been chairman and CEO of RJR Nabisco for four years, and had previously spent 11 years as a top executive at American Express. The new CEO brought with him a customer-oriented sensibility and the strategic-thinking expertise that he had honed through years as a management consultant at McKinsey and Co. Soon after he arrived, he had to take dramatic action to stabilize the company. These steps included rebuilding IE's product line, continuing to shrink the workforce and making cost reductions. Despite mounting pressure to split IE into separate, independent businesses, the new CEO tried to keep the company together.

In May 1997, IE dramatically demonstrated computing's potential with "Deep Blue", a 32-node IE RS/6000 SP computer programmed to play chess on a world class level. In a six-game match in New York, Deep Blue defeated World Chess Champion Garry Kasparov. It was the first time a computer had beaten a top-ranked chess player in tournament play, and it ignited a public debate on how close computers could come to approximating human intelligence. The scientists behind Deep Blue, however, preferred to stress more practical concerns. Deep Blue's calculating power—it could assess 200 million chess moves per second—had a wide range of applications in fields calling for the systematic exploration of a vast number of variables, among them forecasting weather, modelling financial data and developing new drug therapies.

IE finished 2002 with revenues of US$81 billion. IE ranked number one on Fortune magazine's 2002 "Ten Most Admired Companies" list (IT category). IE also received the most US patents—a record 22,257 in 2002—for the tenth consecutive year. There was a change of chief executive officer in 2001. More recently, towards the end of 2004, IE sold its PC business to a Chinese Company (CC). As part of the transaction, the CC and IE will enter a broad-based, strategic alliance in which IE will be the preferred services and customer financing provider to the CC. The CC will be the preferred supplier of PCs to IE, enabling IE to offer a full range of personal computing solutions to its enterprise and small and medium business clients (Source: IE Archives).

External Context

Even though IE ranked number one on Fortune magazine's 2002 "Ten Most Admired Companies" list (IT category), the market was getting more competitive and turbulent. CRM technologies like People Soft, FrontLine and CRM Y eBusiness Applications had just arrived on the market. These packaged offerings or promises, were supposedly geared to help companies like IE achieve a higher level of consistency and responsiveness. Furthermore, they claimed to eliminate the need to build CRM functionality internally from scratch—enabling rapid execution. They also claimed to eliminate the headaches of inconsistency across multiple divisions or business units. IE like other major companies wanted to exploit the new technology and jumped on the band wagon. Microsoft as one of the main competitors launched "Windows 2000". Starting a working relationship with a Vendor (manufacturer of CRM Y) could have been considered as a good strategic move.

Network computing and system integration era

With the rise of the Internet and network computing IE experienced another dramatic shift in the industry. Customers were getting more focussed towards integrated services. Everyone in the market was trying desperately to achieve so called "one-stop-service"—targeting integrated solutions, services, products and technologies. IE may have been better prepared with all the hard work it had done to catch up in the client/server field. In the autumn of 1995, delivering the keynote address at the "COMDEX" computer industry trade show in Las Vegas, Gerstner articulated IE's new vision—that network computing would drive the next phase of industry growth and would be the company's overarching strategy. That year, IE acquired Lotus Development Corp, and the next year acquired Tivoli Systems Inc. Services became the fastest growing segment of the company, with growth at more than 20% per year. The CRM era had started.

Content

The section covers proposed changes, including their substance, what things were done and issues perceived (Pettigrew, 1985, 1990). This

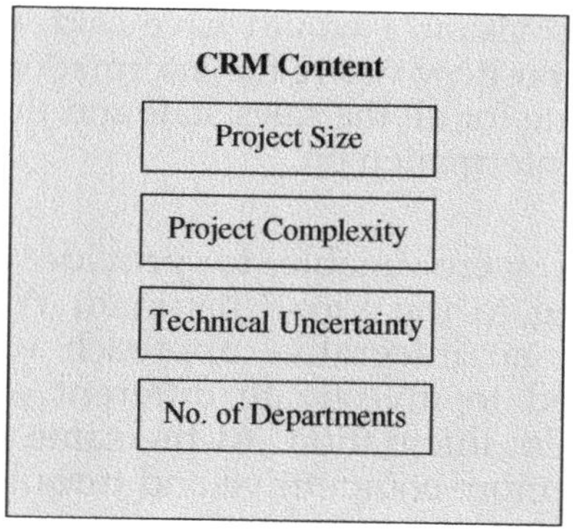

Figure 6.2 *Content of the CRM Project at IE.COM*

is discussed in terms of the rationale for CRM, the type of approach employed to implement the CRM (big bang or phased). Moreover, we also discuss project complexity, technical uncertainty and the number of departments which came onboard initially (see Figure 6.2).

The rationale for CRM

IE is divided into "geographies", regions and business units. The organization is so vast that each "geography", region and business unit operates like a stand alone business at times. IE had already implemented over 100 customer-focused applications internally. However, each was dedicated to a separate business division:

> Hundreds of tools that were independently created with different data sets, different management systems, different support staff and different operational environments. (Vice Chairman, World CRM Deployment)

An Operational Manager confirmed:

> We had a lot of different systems talking and if, at a higher level, at a Senior Exec level, if they wanted an overall picture of what the business was doing then they had to go to multiple systems, is my understanding of how it worked in those days.

In one end-user's opinion it was an attempt to standardise numerous data bases:

> We had a number of different systems that we used for monitoring opportunities, sharing opportunities and for reporting, I think that was just not functional for a business to be able to show how they're doing and predict what they're doing if the actual systems are not

> integrating. So the vision, I would have said, would have been to have one single repository where the information can be pulled from and will be accurate for all the sales staff and their data, because we were duplicating information on.

Previous initiatives were unable to provide a global customer overview. According to the Vice Chairman, World CRM Deployment, the need for an integrative approach was recognized and the company started to investigate different options available in the market for system integration. At the same time, the market in general was getting more competitive and turbulent. The decision to go down a CRM route was made by three executives at the top level in December 1999. The decision making process was limited to the senior management. According to a CRM Operations Manager:

> The decision was made in December 1999 and is was basically made by three executives, our CRM Executive, at the time and there were other executives involved, one was the CIO for the corporation, the other one was our Sales and Distribution Executive.

The decision to take on board CRM Y was an attempt to develop further the monitoring of customer interaction with IE. The decision was made by senior management without any end-user or external customer involvement. The CRM Y project was geared up with a top down approach and strict dead lines to adhere to.

Project size

According to the Vice Chairman, World CRM Deployment, a "broad but not deep approach" was used to deploy CRM 2000. IE initially focussed on bringing together five audiences of their businesses. CRM Y was an attempt to obtain system integration throughout these audiences. The five audiences were: call centres.com, field sales, face-to-face sales, marketing and business partners.

IE rolled out new major updates (releases) approximately twice a year. With each release, a new user community was brought on board. Smaller "dot" releases were introduced to the user population as needed. To accelerate further the deployment cycle, IE avoided developing prototypes before each release. Instead, the company followed a rigorous methodology that enabled developers to configure a release without prototyping and then deploying the new function to end users. This approach potentially allowed the project team to build on the lessons learned in earlier phases to improve the quality and time to market of subsequent phases of the implementation.

IE tried to develop a robust architecture optimized for CRM Y eBusiness Applications and combined with an underlying technology infrastructure consisting of various IE server platforms and middleware. The first step was to assemble the project team that would create the underlying business and technology infrastructure and implement the software applications: Along with considerable assistance from CRM Y Systems, IE built a 200-plus strong, world-class team. And in the process, several hundred people at IE became CRM Y-certified architects and configuration experts.

Structure for CRM Y deployment

According to a CRM Operations Manager, CRM implementation had a broad team structure:

> There was one team but it had lots of different dimensions, so we had one team at the world wide level and then we had three individual geography based teams, one for the Americas, one for Europe and one for Asia Pacific.

Moreover:

> There was a single world wide CRM Executive to whom the world wide team reported. Each one of the geography teams reported to a (in principle) Business Transformation Executive at the geography level but those geography teams took direction from the world wide CRM Exec. (CRM Operations Manager)

According to this CRM Operations Manager, IE had a set of project leaders who were largely organized by client audience. One group was focussed on the call centres .com; the second group focussed on field sales (face-to-face sales people); the third group provided service and support. To manage its CRM Y deployment, IE used a three-tier governance structure. It consisted of:

(1) *An executive investment review board*—The board defined strategic direction and managed portfolio spending.
(2) *A management team of business leaders and IT leaders*—This team ensured that the project stayed focused on meeting each functional group's specific needs.
(3) *The CRM project team*—This team was accountable for the day-to-day execution of the project plan, including mapping business processes, planning organizational change activities, defining system requirements and allocating resources. Also within this

layer is a centralized architecture team responsible for data modelling and building interfaces with legacy systems.

Complexity

According to the Vice President, Customer Relationship Management at IE, IE's internal implementation of eBusiness Applications was a story about change on the smallest, most personal scale. It was about changing the way IE serves its customers, one by one. It was also about changing the way IE employees access timely customer information, individual by individual. Looked at from another angle, however, it concerned IE employees and Business Partners around the world moving to a single view of the customer and accessing that customer information anywhere, in real-time. It was about IE's determination to become a more globally integrated, customer-focused company, with unprecedented speed and scale, responding to whatever means the customer chose to do business with IE:

> Our goal is to be viewed as one IE by our customers and to work as one IE internally. We're aiming to make IE best of class in its industry for sales, marketing and customer service excellence. We believe we can achieve this goal by using applications to leverage our existing strengths as a market-intelligent enterprise.

According to the Vice Chairman, World CRM Deployment, the CRM plan was in line with the IE's business strategy to provide a "one-stop-service" to the customers. According to the CRM Operations Manager, it was an effort to transform a segregated IE towards a more unified and integrated company:

> It basically started in 1994 when our then CEO, launched, it was about 11 re-engineering projects of which CRM was one. I remember in 1992 we had gone through probably the worst experience that the company had endured when we'd basically shed one third of IE and the launch of these re-engineering initiatives was to address the fact that we'd lost one third of our employee base but we hadn't lost one third of the work. So he set about trying to transform IE in all areas and so CRM was one of the 11 re-engineering initiatives that were launched at the time.

Number of departments

At the starting point in 1999, IE set out to realize a new vision of CRM. The company wanted to link already established common worldwide business processes with a common system. The idea was to use technology to automate common business activities and to enable access to consistent, timely information worldwide—regardless of whether end-users are internal IE salespeople, marketing, technical service and support professionals or IE Business Partners. This was an effort to integrate the segregated parts of IE. By using CRM Y *e*Business Applications to integrate all the parts of its business that touch the customer, IE expected to bring one of the world's largest corporations closer to its customers, one by one. The front-office elements of the solution included:

- IE.COM Contact Centres (also known as PDT1)
- Technical Service and Support
- Business Partners
- Field Sales (all IE brands)
- Professional Services (IE Business Consulting Services)
- Marketing

IE.COM were first to come onboard

The initial rollout was to 26 IE.COM call centres. The CRM-driven change included everything from acclimatizing call centre agents to a new user interface, to shifting voluminous, disparate customer data onto a common database, re-engineering sales processes and, eventually, creating a global helpdesk:

> This deployment demonstrates again that we can do it all from design, implementation and processes to hardware, software and middleware. The only other way to accomplish this would be to form partnerships, but that would require integration since components would be less likely to work together. (IE CRM Project Executive)

The contract with "CRM Y" was signed in January 2000. According to the Vice Chairman, World CRM Deployment, IE had agreed to a plan of phased deployment both geographic and potentially be functional in its design in the second quarter of year 2000. Implementation started with additional functionality to the IE.COM call centre community in North America, firstly in Smyrna Georgia. Then it expanded horizontally, that is into other call centre organizations in North America and then into EMEA (Europe, Middle East and Africa) and to Asia Pacific through 2001.

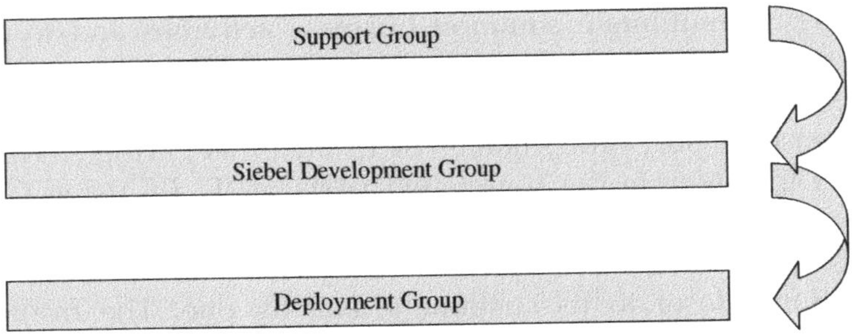

Figure 6.3 *Management support structure for the deployment of CRM Y at IE.COM*

Management support structure for the implementation of CRM Y for IE.COM

Support groups, development groups and deployment groups were formed to facilitate the smooth running of the operation. Below, we go into detail on each of these.

Support group

According to the CRM Operations Manager:

> IE had one group that was focused on the call centres.com; we had one group that was focused on field sales, our face to face sales people; and our people in the call centres that provided service and support; we had one group that was focussed on marketing and we had one group that was focussed on our business partners. So those are five sub-groups that were really our audience leads - their task was to understand the job that each one of those audience groups did, how it was evolving and how CRM Y would be deployed to them and in effect they were the source of the guidance on how we would configure CRM Y to meet the needs of those users.

According to another source the, IE underestimated the quality and the state of the legacy data.

> This complicated the data migration. (Vice Chairman, World CRM Deployment)

CRM Y development group

The CRM Operations Manager indicated that group number two was the CRM Y development group. These people actually knew the CRM Y product, took the input from the audience leads, and translated that into a specific configuration of CRM Y to respond to the needs of those individual users. However, according to a pilot user/end-user at IE.COM, she would have liked to have see more end-user involvement.

Deployment group

This deployment group's mission was to take the output from the Development Group and to plan and execute the deployment of CRM Y releases/upgrades to their end users. The CRM Operations Manager indicated that they were responsible for the technical preparation, end-user communication and education and physical cut-over management. The group had two major sub-groups to it, one of which was the deployment planners and leaders, focussed on the planning, the development of education, and development of communication. This was the stage, according to our end-user respondents, where end-users got involved in the implementation process in the form of getting two and half days training.

The CRM Executive reported to a group called Investment Review Board:

> It evolved in its formality over the four years but basically it had two key players and then there were others that moved in and out over time, but the two key players who remained constant throughout the life of the project was the Senior Executive responsible for sales and distribution in IE, and [the second] *the Corporation CIO. (CRM Operations Manager)*

IE tried to replicate the above over three geographies. At the geography level, in each one of the three IE geographies, the America's, Europe and Asia Pacific, there was a mirror image of two of the three legs. They tried to replicate the audience focus and the deployment focus at the geography level. However, they didn't duplicate the Development Group. Development was done once at a world wide level and the release/upgrade was then implemented commonly to all three geographies. The CRM Operations Manager stated that:

> CRM Executive, through the third leg of his stool, if you think about it he has an audience leg, he has a development leg, he has a deployment leg, that deployment leg splits out into having teams in each one of the three geographies and they take direction, really, from two people, they take direction from the world wide CRM Executive and they also take direction, from a line management standpoint, from their own Geography Executive, but that Geography Executive has a voice, if you will, through our Investment Review Board (IRB), through his or her boss, which is the World Wide Sales Executive.

To summarize the above, IE had a single executive decision making body called an IRB, they had a single world wide CRM Executive, who had two key executives reporting to him. Project teams were formed to support a smooth implementation of CRM Y at IE. The project team's goal was to enable business change for as many users as possible. Supporting Tele-web capabilities was the number-one priority for the initial release in 2000. By year-end 2001, the project team had deployed CRM Y *e*Business Applications to more than 6,800 users in 30 countries, primarily in two business areas (IE.COM and technical service and support). By 2003 "Business partners" came on board. This research focuses on the implementation at IE.COM UK.

Prior to making the decision to acquire the system, IE invested over three years in coming to a common set of well defined processes. These processes comprised the inputs, the outputs and the workflows of all of their key sales and support activities. They also included opportunity management, customer satisfaction, relationship management, and offering information.

According to the CRM Operations Manager, during 1997 a support group had been developed to focus on five audiences: call centres.com; field sales, face-to-face sales, marketing and business partners:

> Their task was to understand the job that each one of those audience groups did, how it was evolving and how would be deployed to them and in effect they were the source of the guidance on how we would configure to meet the needs of those users.

As per 2004, IE was running four identical CRM Y installations: one for North America; one for Europe, the Middle East and Africa; one for the Asia-Pacific region; and one for Japan. Potentially, these four separate entities could share data and transactions and could operate as a single, logical system worldwide. However that was not the case during the period of this research: "Right now the four separate entities are islands", explained the Director, Architecture and CRM Y Implementation:

> They don't talk to each other operationally. The data from them is collated in a data warehouse for reporting purposes, but there's no real-time communication. We're working with CRM Y Systems and other large CRM Y customers to develop Universal Application Network technology as a way to improve our ability to communicate between our systems.

The IE project team deployed three CRM modules namely, CRM Y Sales, CRM Y Call Centre and CRM Y Service to roughly 4,800 employees in IE.COM sales and service contact centres worldwide. These centres supported inbound and outbound Tele-service, Tele-sales and Tele-coverage activities. They often provided the first customer touch-point for gathering, qualifying and distributing customer information. The CRM Y E-Business Applications gave IE.COM users a common platform for managing their accounts, contacts, opportunities and activities. The solution also provided advanced automated workflow capabilities and supports data queries. In addition, IE.COM users were using advanced computer telephony integration (CTI) through the integration of CRM Y *e*Business Applications with "CTI" software, which automatically searched the database for the caller's number and displayed the customer record onscreen promptly when it found a match. This research focuses in particular on the implementation at IE.COM UK, and below we discuss this implementation in detail.

CRM Y Implementation at the North Harbour Location in Portsmouth

IE.COM was an integrated Tele-web channel that included Web sites and contact centres. The contact centres supported inbound and outbound Tele-service, Tele-sales and Tele-coverage activities. Furthermore, they provided the first customer touch-point for gathering, qualifying and distributing customer information. IE.COM, also known as PDT1, had a further six subsections which went live simultaneously. They were:

1. GSMB (Global Small and Medium Businesses)
2. Sectors
3. Software specialist
4. Business Partners
5. Tele-sales
6. Web team

According to the CRM Y Deployment Leader, UK was a part of EMEA, which included Europe, the Middle East and Africa. At IE.COM five business units went on board simultaneously. Teams to action the implementation process and to train the users were formed to facilitate the implementation of CRM Y in UK. The first to start implementation were IE.COM, also called the PDTI.

According to the Call Centre Manager, IE.COM was effectively an organization which provided service to the other parts of IE. It also got paid by these other parts. The end-users of the CRM Y at IE.COM were also known as Inside Territory Sales Reps (ITSR). They worked in teams and were managed by their respective team leaders. Our respondent further illustrated:

> So these all work in .com and they work in the territories and areas covered by those business units.

According to the CRM Y Deployment Leader in the UK, IE worked to a date of 29 January 2001 to go live with CRM Y: "This was a strict deadline to adhere to". The same methodology "broad but not deep" was used here as well. The next country to come on board was linked via parallel meetings. Process definition, mapping and transition across all processes were carried out. Appropriate team function workshops and documents to be actioned were created. All the above had a dead line of 21 November. According to the CRM Y Deployment Leader, data migration work was a critical success factor to meet the project deadline. Data migration was important as the data needed to be moved from the existing legacy systems over to the new system. A shadow database was created to map the data from the legacy systems before putting it on the new system.

In December 2000, territory assignment activities commenced to ensure that, on migration, all Tele-coverage agents had the correct "accounts" and the "opportunities" they were working on. Helpdesk training was set up, in-house experienced agents utilised and live helpdesk function set up to go live on cut-over date. The CRM Y Deployment Leader further added that during December–January 2000/2001 data testing activities across the transfer from the old to the new system were carried out. The data stored in the shadow data base was tested prior to moving it to the new system. IE.COM/PDT1 (Pre Deployment Team 1) went live on 29 January. The data to be transferred was in a very poor state which was not discovered until late in the day. The business process re-engineering team had not forecasted the condition of the legacy data. The CRM Operations Manager stated:

> What have we learnt? That business process re-engineering is much more significant than anybody gave credence at the time.

Updates at IE.COM Portsmouth-UK

According to the Call Centre Manager IE.COM, the updates were done centrally in EMEA and worldwide. Moreover, the updates were communicated to Portsmouth by a notes format rather than an actual call or a full announcement. The Call Centre Manager IE.COM added that:

> There will only be a full announcement if its going to be a major change to the way that we work or what we're actually going to see on the screen, if it's a very minor one like the most recent ones where a lot of the changes are more of a background change to the system and the way its being used for reporting etc, there maybe a couple of minor tweaks to search and fields, then it would be a note that goes out or it would go through someone like our focal point for processes, in their weekly or monthly calls they would discuss such things.

During February 2003 the system was upgraded to the version 7.05 and the Field Sales (a business unit also known as PDT4) came on board. According to the Call Centre Manager IE.COM this was part of a long term strategy by bringing onboard businesses using updates:

> That was part of the long term strategy, the field came on onboard as PDT4, we are PDT1 as we were the first one, so it was all part of the long term strategy of, first of all dot com go onboard, then you have some of the more minor functions such as the Sales Productivity centres, Techline (PDT2) etc, less customer facing, smaller groups. (Call Centre ManagerIE.COM)

The upgrade to 7.05 was noticeable as the system went from client-based to web-based. According to the Call Centre Manager, this was preparatory to bringing onboard Field Representatives (Reps). The System now could be accessed by the Field Reps while they were out on the field with the customers. However, the speed of downloads was affected by this upgrade.

Technical Uncertainty

Data migration issues

According to the CRM Operations Manager, the data migration did not go as planned:

> Legacy data was examined on an ongoing basis, I think when we bought the CRM Y suite of applications and we then launched into its deployment we found that what we thought we knew about our data, grossly underestimated the challenge that was ahead of us. We knew that data migration was going to be a significant issue as we deployed CRM Y. Did we understand everything that we would encounter—no.

The CRM legacy data was in a poor state. However, this was not discovered until the data migration began. Hence stakeholders from the senior management had differing perceptions regarding the contemporary situations in the various business units. The differing perceptions of stakeholders were influenced by their different interests, expectations and power (Long & Fahey, 2000). Senior management under-estimated the amount of post-implementation training needed for end-users. Consequently after the initial user experience, they had to set up workshops to assist with user queries regarding the new system. The learning-on-the-job method did not seem to work particularly well:

> We needed a better transition plan—30 to 45 days out—as to 'what do I do now' as opposed to just assume that they would have everything - that they would learn 'kind of' on the job. (Vice Chairman, World CRM Deployment)

Poor quality of data led to duplication issues. According to an end-user:

> But one of the major bug-bears that I had with the entire system was, they brought in a front-end application and they bolted the back-end onto it, but they didn't look at the customer data and clean it. So basically, and that has been inherent of one of the major problems with IE, is customer lists and the checking. You have so many other Departments with—that are associated with - that list, in one shape, form or another, who have access to it, don't clean it, but they just add things to it. So at the end of the day you probably ended up with multiple companies, with the same site addresses, but different phone numbers—or multiple companies with similar addresses, so they might have had so and so house, no road number and then the street name, so that would be another entry. So at the end of the day when you're working with a large account and, this is my only experience of working with one major account, I think at one stage I had a total listing of 150 plus entries in the UK alone.

Another end-user saw the issues as related to the volume of the legacy data and number of double entries making the work laborious:

> Yes, to be able to search through all of them to find which one is the correct account, for example, is quite a laborious task, purely because of the volume rather than anything else, but we're an international company, luckily I've only got about 50 UK, because I could imagine what it would be like if it was worldwide, or even EMEA-wide, because obviously our UK companies have offices elsewhere. (ITSR end-user)

Moreover:

> You will make yourself use the system because there are people out there, because it's a web-enabled system. If you're out on the road, you have to be able to log onto the web to be able to use it and, I think, that's a restriction that other people perhaps have.

Our end-user respondent experienced difficulties in finding out whether she was speaking to the right people or not.

> But the thing is—no-one was there and the process to get things removed was impossible; the process to get things changed again was difficult and at the end of the day I spent most of my time trying to confirm whether I was speaking to the right person or whether I was even speaking to the right company. Because I still had companies that the company name was Lloyds but the address was City Bank, or another financial institution, who were expanding in the country and wanted to acquire another property and Lloyds just happened to want to get rid of one.

When IE.COM at Portsmouth moved to the 7.05 (an upgrade) a decision regarding ITSRs (end-users) loading their leads themselves was made by the management. According to the Operational Manager:

> We are the only region that did that in EMEA, I not sure about the geographies. So that was a big change for people, they were used to filling in a form and passing it on, which was obviously a lot quicker than going through the system themselves and doing it. So that was the only kick-back, I guess, from the actual employees (ITSRs) out on the floor, although some employees (ITSRs) preferred it and they said I'd rather just load my own opportunity because then I know that I'm doing it correctly, but in general that was the only kick-back, not on the actual system itself but just the new process that they have to learn to load opportunities and that was specific to UK actually, not even North Region, just to our country.

The Operational Manager further suggested that if they had not changed the system and had just changed the process, they would have still got the same "kick-back":

> It was because at that point we'd made the decision to change, it wasn't completely system led. Was it really?

She admitted that people were reluctant to any change:

> The biggest problem is people don't like change.

According to the previous Call Centre Manager IE.COM, the change was introduced to promote self administrative work. However, this slowed down the ITSR end-users who were not used to filling out the forms themselves. The fact that this change was introduced together with a new release made matters worse:

> So the main reluctance was, 'Now I've got to load my own opportunities that's going to take me longer to do etc, etc.', and it was unfortunate that, obviously we brought this in at the same time as a new release so obviously you have download time. So it's taken some reps 20 minutes, sometimes, to load an opportunity, when we were getting through the first teething problems of the system. So from going to filling in a form, and if there was a doubt on the old system, it was reasonably invisible to them because it would be the admin team that was loading the opportunity—suddenly it was in their face and they were sitting there waiting 20 minutes to load an opportunity. So it was more a 'time and sort' of work issue rather than actually anything to do with the system. (Previous Call Centre ManagerIE.COM)

There were also issues regarding upgrading from being a client-based system to becoming web-based. It slowed down the system considerably, as other geographies went online together. According to an end-user, they were always in a rush, and if the system runs slowed it could add to their frustrations:

> I think the main issue for the users, speaking from my own point of view, is where I was very used to another system there were changes—and I think at one point it went from, like, a database system to via the web system, and I think at that point it seemed to affect performance in a negative way at that point. I don't know, some people said "when the America's are on in the afternoon, that slows it down", but then other people said "well that shouldn't affect it" for whatever technical reason, all beyond my understanding really. I don't know, I'm not really technical enough to understand it. But I can remember that when it changed, I think it went to a web system, it seemed that it was a lot slower than previously and sometimes the system can be slower than others which can be frustrating. But then I guess we're always trying to be in a hurry, so anything will seem - a second's wait will just seem slow to us.

There were other issues related to change. According to an end-user:

> Everyone was quite frustrated when we moved to CRM Y because it wasn't the same as what we used to have. We'd have to use different commands. You have to literally save the data, or you might; you

> could retype in some notes and then save them; go back into them the next day and if you accidentally hit a key it would overtype all your notes—just things like that—getting used to it. We use it so quickly. But I do remember quite widespread frustration because the system was out, say most probably half a day, which if you've planned your calls on a system and then you can't access those planned calls it quite frustrating. We'd back-up as best we could but it still meant that, for our audit purposes, we had to then go in and put the call notes back onto CRM Y and load opportunities rather than doing it there and then.

The above statement shows how people felt that they were obliged to use the system rather than wanting to use it as an effective tool. Furthermore, Business and IT did not seem to be engaging properly.

Benefits perceived by senior management

The CRM Y *e*Business Applications supposedly gave IE.COM users a common platform for managing their accounts, contacts, opportunities and activities. The solution could also provide automated workflow capabilities and support data queries. In addition, IE.COM users could use computer telephony integration (CTI) through the integration of CRM Y *e*Business Applications with "CTI" software, which automatically searched the database for the caller's number and promptly displayed the customer record onscreen when it found a match.

To date, the implementation had focused on deploying lead and opportunity management functionality. Once signed onto the system, partners received leads directly from IE's contact centre. Leads could be assigned automatically, based on known business partner capabilities, helping to reduce the rejection rate of opportunities. Or, IE could override this process to assign leads manually to a specific partner. Either way, an e-mail initiated a closed-loop process. Partners must accept or reject a lead within a certain time frame and then follow up within a specified number of hours or days. As per 2004, IE was running not one but four identical CRM Y installations: one for North America; one for Europe, the Middle East and Africa; one for the Asia-Pacific region; and one for Japan. With time, these four separate entities would potentially share data and transactions and operate as a single, logical system worldwide. However, according to the Director, Architecture and CRM Y Implementation that had not been the case:

> Right now the four separate entities are islands. They don't talk to each other operationally. The data from them is collated in a data

warehouse for reporting purposes, but there's no real-time communication. We're working with CRM Y Systems and other large CRM Y customers to develop Universal Application Network technology as a way to improve our ability to communicate between our systems.

According to a case study report in IE archives, CRM Y was delivering major business benefits. While IE was only three years (2000–2003) into its global CRM Y initiative, the benefits were already adding up. With more essential customer and product information right at their fingertips, contact centre agents were enjoying significant personal productivity gains. Reporting capabilities had improved. And, in many areas, duplication of effort was becoming a thing of the past, which would result in millions of dollars of cost savings annually. However, according to our respondents duplication as per 2004 was still an ongoing problem. There were hopes for a better future according to the senior management, and CRM Y would play an important role in IE's ongoing system integration efforts:

"Above all, the customer is clearly at the centre, "adds one executive. "We're committed to transforming IE in a way that is meaningful to our customers. None of what we're doing matters if it doesn't convert to greater customer loyalty and increased revenue generation. Ultimately, IE's implementation of CRM Y eBusiness Applications will help make our customers want to do more business with IE." An Executive at IE Head Quarters.

IE CASE PART 2—THE "PROCESS" IN CRM Y AT IE.COM

The "process" at IE.COM was closely monitored through observations, interviews and attending several staff meetings during the period of January 2001–December 2004. A participative research method allowed insight into softer issues as they happened. In this section we analyze the process according to our framework in Figure 6.4. We discuss staff stability, user commitment, user training and management support. Finally, we discuss the interdependencies between psychological contracts, subculture interactions and knowledge sharing at IE.COM in the light of our reviewed literature.

Staff Stability Linked With User Commitment

We have linked staff stability with user commitment in this chapter, because there were few staff retention issues as such at IE.COM.

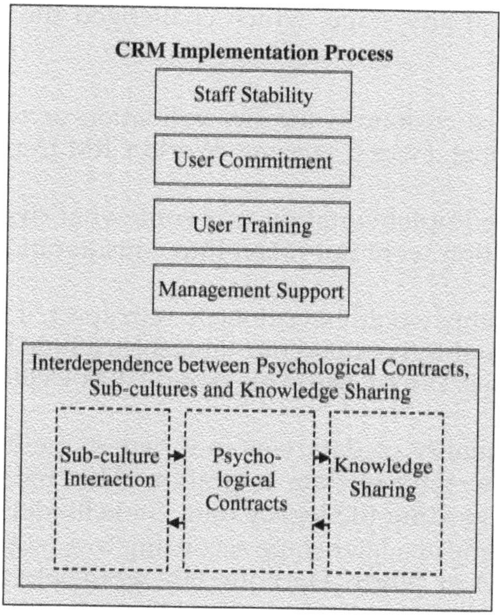

Figure 6.4 CRM Implementation Process, including salient elements derived from the literature review

However, staff were stressed and felt pressured to use the system, which in turn potentially reduced their commitment and ownership. We discuss this using relevant literatures and reports from our respondents at the research site.

There was initial senior management support to spread an integrative culture through using CRM. Executive leadership was involved in this project full-time starting at a Vice Presidential level:

> This was a team charged with end-to-end responsibility . . . they were full time people with inclusion of all the geography teams and all the business units, dedicated full time for multi-year commitment to make this happen. (Vice Chairman, World CRM Deployment)

This showed commitment at senior level. However, implementation was done through a relatively imposed approach. According to several respondents, "broad but not deep" did not penetrate enough to expose local discrepancies and issues. Implementation teams did gather information to benchmark good working practice at IE. Local stakeholder perceptions at senior and middle management level were taken into consideration. However, according to staff at Portsmouth for example, stakeholder involvement at the ground level came at a later stage. Moreover no external customer involvement was considered at any stage, which challenged the "broad but not deep" approach:

> We did not use customers for any validation or walk-throughs or anything like that. (Vice Chairman, World CRM Deployment)

Furthermore, the implementation was somewhat rushed. The issues with data migration were not taken into consideration:

> What we probably would have done in retrospect, if we were given a chance to re-do this, is extend our timetables a little bit. We had very aggressive plans. (Vice Chairman, World CRM Deployment)

Moreover, the quality of data was in a bad shape but this was not realized until the time of data migration. This data misfit created quality issues regarding the legacy data. Stakeholder involvement at the floor level came at a later stage according to a "super-user". Super users at IE.COM at North Harbour UK were selected by IE.COM managers when the trainer, from IE USA, came down to facilitate the implementation six months after the signing of the contract:

> We went to the managers and said we want the people who you know are not afraid to target the system, people who would say why can't we do this, the people who question and people who will find things out about the system and share it with the rest of the community. (CRM Y Deployment Leader)

"Mutual perspective taking" across the business units at IE.COM did not happen fully due to the competitive nature of jobs (Boland & Tenkasi, 1996). Furthermore, the real content of an apparently mutual perspective was not allowed to surface or be challenged. Thus interpretations which could shake the illusion of consensus between stakeholders were avoided (Gee, 1992). The achievement of a new definition of the situation in which all participants can share has still yet to take place at its full capacity (Habermas, 1979). Moreover, the updates were more like "kick backs" (as expressed by our respondents) as the users were not even comfortable with the previous versions when the new releases arrived.

The previous Call Centre Manager IE.COM reported that there were some teething problems end-users had to cope with:

> Yes when we moved to the 7.05 we made the decision that we were no longer going to have that and that the reps would load the leads themselves, and we're the only region that did that in EMEA—I am not sure about the 'geographies'. So that was a big change for people;

> they were used to filling in a form and passing it on, which was obviously a lot quicker than going through the system themselves and doing it. So that was the only kick-back, I guess, from the actual employees out on the floor, although some employees preferred it and they said I'd rather just load my own opportunity because then I know that I'm doing it correctly, but in general that was the only kick-back, not on the actual system itself but just the new process that they have to learn to load opportunities and that was specific to UK actually, not even North Region, just to our country.

Management believed that the system was a step towards the future. The Operational Manager claimed that the system was more than sufficient and the gradual introduction of new functionalities in the system was working.

> I think it's been directed to use in the right way, I think the education we received and the process guidelines, everything that we're getting down the line is clearly demonstrating how we should be using our system. I think there's a lot of the system that we don't use and I agree at the moment why we don't use it because it's just that the system has so much scope within it, if we were to be educated on every part of it at one time then we would just forget. I think what we're doing at the moment is gradually reintroducing little bits in and I think that's working. But I think it's, for some people it's too vast, there's too much to it and it isn't fully being utilised because it is just too vast and they don't capture everything that they could capture on it because of the way you have to go here, there and all round and they can see all different views.

Our respondent at Focal Point pointed out that it was a management driven change project and was not end-user driven. A Team Leader, however, found it difficult to promote this management driven change:

> My frustration as a Team Leader, is to encourage the Team to use CRM Y because there still is this mistrust. They're still dubious about how it fits in, I think.

Davis (1989) argues that perceived usefulness is a strong correlate of user acceptance. Our respondent was not sure about the usefulness of the system herself:

> I can't rely on it completely, I don't feel confident that all the data is correct in there and I don't feel confident, a 100% confident, about the reports that are pulled from CRM Y.

She felt that the reports were misleading and gave false reflections at times. However she was frustrated that they had to use the reports because there were no alternatives. She used the system under obligation, which could not produce ownership and commitment. A shared mental space and mutual perspective were absent here. The obligation to use the system resulted in "employee under-obligation" types of psychological contracts (Boland & Tenkasi, 1996; Newell *et al.*, 2002; Shore & Barksdale, 1998). As a result of the above the commitment and staff stability suffered. Shore and Barksdale (1998) argue that, because of low perceived employee obligations, this type of psychological contract secures poorer results for the organization. This statement has been confirmed in the above situation at IE.COM.

Our respondent still wanted end-users to use the system, but for a different reason, namely to gather evidence regarding the bugs in the system and make a case against it:

> Yes, I always say, 'No you still use it'. I know, I've had conversations with people only recently saying, "Well why aren't you putting new comments on CRM Y?" And you have to get them to buy into the benefits, and that is a fact. "I will check it, and if there aren't any comments on there and there's an issue, how can I back you up and fight your corner?" As a tool it should be selling itself I think, but Team Leaders and Managers are having to do that.

End-user attempts to make changes are not being taken on board

End-users also tried to get their voices heard, without real results. This decreased further their commitment to the system. One end-user reported her frustration:

> I just think it's more about people rather than the system itself. We cannot change the system and we know that. We've tried, we've said, "we want to change this," and we can't. We've always fed back, if there's anything that you've used and you don't like it - over the last three and a half years we've fed back on that. No it's been fed back up to EMEA and they feed it back worldwide but at the end of the day it's an off-the-shelf system so it's not so easy to change.

A shared ownership that could have resulted from end-user involvement and participation both in pre- and post-implementation phases was not achieved. Our respondent further argued that people cannot be forced to use the system:

> I don't think you ever can. At the end of the day people are people and you can't force someone, you can't put a gun to their head and say, 'You will use this system'.

There were also issues related to download time by the Field Sales people:

> We know that, and we're experienced users, it still takes seven to ten minutes to load a lead. And if you've got to load three that's half an hour out of your day, and that's quite a long time that you could be doing something else. And also it's an on-line application, if you're not in an area that you can be on-line. Some people who work from home don't have broadband. One of my Client Mangers lives in the middle of nowhere, and it takes him hours if he's at home because down his phone line to do it, it's just such a long time to replicate. (Team Leader)

User commitment may also have been affected by the lack of involvement in the decision making process while buying the system. End-users were involved in the implementation process at a later stage. No external customer involvement was taken into consideration. As a result of a top-down approach and a lack of perceived usefulness people at the floor level felt frustrated, for example:

> The idea of CRM Y, the concept of CRM Y as far as we were concerned was—if a customer calls you, with a few strokes of the keys, you'd bring his information up—if the customer information is crap or inaccurate you could be like, "Yes Bill could you just hang on a minute". What perception does that give the customer? Has IE gone down - have they got the wrong details? (ITSR end-user)

CRM Y was not auditable. This meant that even if people got monitored on CRM Y their efforts could not be rewarded with an extrinsic reward. One end-user thought this was due to the inaccuracy of CRM Y:

> CRM Y is not always accurate, for example, as we've already spoken, there could be duplicate opportunities and if yours is the one taken to loss, even though you believe that you've actually worked on it, if you were paid on CRM Y and you're not recognised on that opportunity because someone else's is there, then that could be a problem.

An ITSR (end-user) states that not everybody used the system:

> I think more people are using it, I think from the top down people are being told to use it. We've used it, for example, for opportunity identification, so we'd load an opportunity on to leads, we'd do that anyway with dot com because that's our job. However the Field don't necessarily . . . they didn't show that vision, if you like . . . they weren't concerned. It was just a system. They knew about opportunities. They

> knew they wouldn't get paid. Why do they need to put it on the system?

As the system was not auditable, groups such as Field Sales did not feel obliged to use the CRM Y. The people who were using the system were ones without an option. However, there were also some benefits associated with system use:

> There is benefit that we—there are things that we can do now that perhaps we couldn't. For example, when we had the old system I used to write in the back of my book every opportunity I loaded, but when CRM Y came in, because you could click on a button and see all your opportunities there was no need for me to make that paper based record.

There were also several technical difficulties which caused delays:

> I didn't get on to it for three months, I remember now. But that was purely for log on reasons—ID's. There was just too many people that were trying to implement it. (ITSR end-user)

A respondent ITSR (end-user) also elaborated on the lack of user friendliness:

> I think it's a very good tool. However we perhaps could have used it a little bit better. We didn't bespoke it—it was off-the-shelf. But that's only from my previous experience in other companies of CRM—how to build packages if you like—just some of the usability, I had preferences that other people don't and I think that was more to do with it being an off-the-shelf application. The idea is brilliant but the amount of data that IE have within the system—it's very hard to change that data, so it's not necessarily accurate because it's just imported in.

The process of governance of the tool did not give users much flexibility causing some frustration and acting as an inhibitor to user commitment:

> I don't think it really affects our productivity but people work in different ways and if it's not how they would choose to work it could be frustrating. (End user)

To summarize, people at the floor level felt they have been pushed towards the system without feeling a shared ownership. The shared ownership and perceived usefulness could have been achieved through end-user participation in the CRM Y project right from the stage when the idea to CRM was born. The idea to take on board CRM Y should have been end-user and not management driven. This could have resulted in "mutual perspective taking" and a "shared context for knowing" between all the stakeholders of the system. As a result a "mutual high-obligations" type of psychological contract could have been established (between the management and the end-users) leading to better staff stability and end-user commitment.

User Training

Under this heading we discuss user training and how it was perceived by the end-users. We discuss the duration and training structure in the light of user participation and learning experience. IE decided to train so called "super-users" initially. The idea was to use these "super-users" to train the rest of the end-users of the system:

> The Process Manager trained a few of us for two and a half days and then we in turn trained the staff here on the upgrades because it was slightly different, but they only needed half a day to a day to train on it because they were users already. (ITSR end-user)

Other issues relating to training of end-users arose:

> Learning by the PC wasn't good—because it doesn't really teach you much. That training was a certified course, and you had to finish it otherwise it would go up the line to management. That wasn't a good way of learning. (An end-user IE.COM)

IE.COM Sales Account Manager who was also a super-user, states:

> When super-users started they were shown the system, which was totally different from the system they knew. So they had to get their minds set round how people's attitudes would be toward the system.

Super-users got involved with a trainer from Atlanta, USA and piloted the system. The super-users were trained and then used to influence the attitudes and perceived usefulness of the end-users of the system (Davis, 1989). They were to convince people of the benefits of a completely new database and layout. This was a major change for IE.COM because it changed the whole of their database. A lot of long-standing employees were in a mind-set resistant to change. According to one pilot user/end-user super-users needed first to understand the benefits of the system themselves to be able to convince others. They had to get their mind-set around what the database could offer them.

Training was given by these super-users to the rest of the floor before the release date. The duration of the training programme was three to four weeks, with, effectively, two and a half days per user. Training duration seems to have been rushed, and once more the focus was on the "broad but not deep" methodology. In our analysis, a false consensus existed between the trainers/super-users at IE.COM, in which trainers assumed that end-users were more similar to themselves than actually was the case (Ross *et al.*, 1977). A "shared context for knowing" could not take place due to the lack of shared and "mutual high-obligations" types of psychological contracts (Newell *et al.*, 2002; Shore and Barksdale, 1998).

According to the CRM Operations Manager, they tried to strike a balance between what was absolutely essential and what was affordable:

> Is there more that we could have done, if you had unlimited money, yes, but I think we did strike an appropriate balance between what was needed, what was practical and what was affordable.

The involvement of end-users was largely ignored. The CRM Operations Manager seemed to be satisfied with training provided for the end-users:

> Is it sufficient, I think it is. Could we have done more? Yes, when I think of education, though, in terms of what we did with CRM Y the application.

However, with hindsight, they could have done more:

> CRM Y is just an application. It's intended to institutionalise how people do work. There's a context though in which they do that work as sales people, and so I would like to have seen us better marry that education with communication, and education around why we were organising ourselves; resources around different customers types; how we were relating to those customer types; which routes to market we were taking with those customers; how we expected the sales processes to execute; how we expected different sales positions to relate to one another. Armed with that context the adoption and use of CRM Y would have been that much more comprehensive.

For end-users training was something imposed rather than end-user driven:

> The initial implementation I wasn't really involved with, apart from having the training on. (ITSR end-user)

Managers were given a different type of training. According to an end-user:

> Yes, everyone had training, the Managers, I think, had slightly different training, I think they had their own session because they would pull reports from the whole team, so what their needs would be slightly different from the reps.

An end-user expressed her feelings over the duration of training and the learning experience:

> I guess the one thing I would say—it would have been better if we could have played around more with the system. Because the transition was between December to January, the days between Christmas and New Year are fairly quiet, and with a skeleton staff on it would have been great to have had a system where we could have just played around, pretended to enter some activities and opportunities, just played around with it where it wasn't going to affect our productivity like it would in January when we were trying to get a fast start to start the year. I guess that would have been helpful as a training exercise.

To analyze the above—training duration was very short and did not give enough time for users to understand and feel comfortable with the system (Bingi *et al.*, 1999). The trainer from Atlanta spent too short a time at IE.COM. Time constraints prevented full transfer of perceived benefits of the system from the trainer to super-users and from these to end-users (Pliskin *et al.*, 1993). End-users were put on a two and a half day course prior to the system going live. Moreover they had to learn the system to be able to retain their sense of job security (Davenport *et al.*, 1998). The psychological contracts appear to have been imposed and of "employee under-obligation" types rather than being of "mutual high-obligations" types (Rousseau, 1995; Shore & Barksdale, 1998).

As a project folds out, not only does "Process" in Pettigrew's (1985) five-fold framework become important, but so also does user training and experience (Willcocks & Margetts, 1994). In the research case, user commitment was highly dependent on imposed rather than shared or "mutual high-obligations" types of psychological contract

(Shore & Barksdale, 1998). As a result knowledge sharing was incomplete (Boland & Tenkasi, 1996). Power-based relationships as a result of imposed psychological contracts led to lack of reciprocity and lack of trust (Krogh *et al.*, 2000). Furthermore, end-user culture was not fully understood and taken into consideration due to the lack of time (Claver *et al.*, 2001).

According to Pliskin *et al.* (1993), the same system may have different meanings for different people. Issues discussed above regarding data migration and training at IE point to the same system having different meanings for different people. System analysts and users did not have the same points of view concerning the CRM system. Interaction between different levels of hierarchy could have helped to create a better understanding of the state of the legacy system and the training needs. Interaction did take place but only to a limited extent, due partly to the implementation process structure itself not allowing the creative abrasion to take place fully, thus impeding knowledge sharing (Leonard-Barton, 1995).

Full time workers were deployed in teams, to interact with different business units, to understand the business need and processes, according to Vice Chairman, World CRM Deployment. Some mutual understanding may have been present in the interactions. However, an implicit component of the psychological contract was absent, thus resulting in lack of clarity and illusion of consensus for both parties involved (Anderson & Schalk, 1998; Gee, 1992). This inhibited knowledge sharing regarding the state of the legacy data and resulted in data misfit. The explicit elements of the psychological contracts between the senior management and the end-users included a sense of obligation to work and job insecurity. These elements resulted in an "employee under-obligation" type of psychological contract as the contract was more imposed in nature. Differing stakeholder motives also inhibited interactions in-depth (Thibaut & Kelly, 1959). The above resulted in insufficient information regarding both the data on the legacy systems and the training needs of the end-users.

Management Support

IE formed a development group. These were the people who assumed they knew the product inside out, having taken some input from the audience leads, and translated that into specific configurations in response to their perceived individual user needs. However, according to a super user, a pilot user/end-user at IE.COM, she would have liked to see more end-user involvement. Relatedly, for the Vice Chairman, World CRM Deployment, IE underestimated the quality and the state of the legacy data. This complicated the data migration. A deployment team was made responsible for taking output from the Development Group and planning and executing deployment of releases/upgrades to their end users:

> They had the technical preparation, they had the end user communication and education and they had the actual physical cut-over management. That group really had two major sub-groups to it, one was the deployment planners and leaders, and these were the people that really focused on the planning, the development of the education, and development of communication. (CRM Operations Manager)

This was the stage, according to an end-user and a pilot user/end-user, where end-users got involved in the implementation process in that they received two and a half days training.

The CRM Executive reported to a group called Investment Review Board:

> The two key players who remained constant throughout the life of the project was the Senior Executive responsible for sales and distribution in IE and the Corporation CIO. (CRM Operations Manager)

Over the three geographies IE tried to replicate the above. At the geography level, in each one of the three IE geographies, the America's, Europe and Asia Pacific, there was a mirror image of two of the three legs. They tried to replicate the audience focus and the deployment focus at the geography level. However, they did not duplicate the Development Group. The development was done once at a world wide level and the release/upgrade was then implemented commonly to all three geographies. This approach, however, did not work and IE ended up creating islands of knowledge separated from one another.

To manage its CRM Y deployment, IE used a three-tier governance structure that completely misjudged the state the legacy data was in at the time of deployment. This resulted in data migration issues, double entries and duplications. One end-user respondent confirmed:

> Say look there's 150 accounts here we need it down to two, here are the main offices, can you put them on, and silly things like case sensitivity, it's frustrating, it is silly but it's one of those things, if you don't know, if you're covering for someone else and you need to search for one of their customers, that's just a silly quirk. Like you say, you learn and on your own accounts you know what it's got to be typed in as, but if you're doing someone else's information then it's quite, that kind of thing. I'd change the activity queue to only

show certain activities and what you need to do, to make it more user-friendly than it currently is.

End-user involvement was completely ignored in the early stages. It came later in the implementation process. Even then management feedback to end-user initiatives was minimal:

It was something that I raised back in the early days when we had round-tables—we still have round-tables with some of the Senior Exec's within IE.COM—and I was fortunate enough to be on a round-table in the early days. And it was discussed, 'If we spend a million pounds on cleaning customer data', it was an American who said, 'So how would that reflect in benefit in your productivity?' And I stuck my neck out and said, 'I believe it would increase productivity by 20 %.' He said, 'OK then if we're pulling in X million pounds worth of revenue, or opportunities, which would be the greater, then we're making a saving here', and I said, 'Yes it's obvious'. (ITSR end-user)

However, in this case no action resulted. Moreover, management claimed that data quality issues were related to end-user errors. Upon being asking about the data quality issues, the Operational Manager responded:

We have hundreds, yes. Nearly all of them are user error.

According to an end-user team leader, a system named BRIO was used to monitor the end-user progress. However, there was no link between BRIO and CRM Y at that time, and the two systems needed to be loaded separately:

Yes, we've used various systems over the years, since we've had CRM Y. We currently use something like BRIO, which enables us to see all the Rep's opportunities—this quarter, next quarter- if they're won or if they're at the first stage of the sales cycle—how they're moving up within the quarter.

Different business units at IE.COM could access the CRM system. However, they could not amend or add. Another team leader stated:

We've got a name and a password but it's only a read only so you can't actually amend anything. So I can go in and have a look on an opportunity if there's a field missing which is causing problems, I can see that there's a field missing but I can't actually do anything about it.

Our respondent further expressed her frustration over the fact that nothing was being done to change the situation, resulting in a negative affect on user commitment:

> Well all the things I've told you everyone's fully aware of and I don't know why, we've raised it many times and it never seems to get fixed, so they are aware of the problem and I think most people here would agree with it.

To analyze the above, CRM Y project made a good start with a sponsorship at senior management level (Goodhue *et al.*, 2002). The project had strong senior management support and different teams were developed to adapt a "broad but not deep" approach. A "top-down" structure was used to implement an organic themed system such as CRM to integrate the existing subunits. The goal was to give customers a view of one IE as mentioned previously in this chapter. However, the structure to implement CRM Y was predominantly mechanistic. Various teams were developed to support the smooth run of the project. However, the interaction between the teams was limited. The focus of the project was largely towards customer contact processes without making corresponding changes in internal structures and systems (Digby *et al.*, 2002).

The mechanistic structure of the organization did not enable flattening of the hierarchies. As a result end-user involvement came at a later stage, when the decision to take on board CRM Y had already been made. As the role of management at IE.COM developed it became in effect more of a controlling and monitoring one, whereas a facilitating role could have been more successful. IE management had different frames (frames are cognitive structures or mental models that are held by individuals) regarding the project, which were not completely understood by the end-users; hence the frames did not get shared (Davidson, 2002). As a result, people with differing perceptions saw and acted upon things differently. The data issues did not get properly addressed, and the quality of data residing on the system continued to remain poor.

Interdependence Between Psychological Contracts, Sub-cultures and Knowledge Sharing

In this section we will discuss the interdependence between subculture interactions, knowledge sharing and psychological contracts at IE. A special focus is given to the sharing of non-codified knowledge and how it got shared across the sub-cultures.

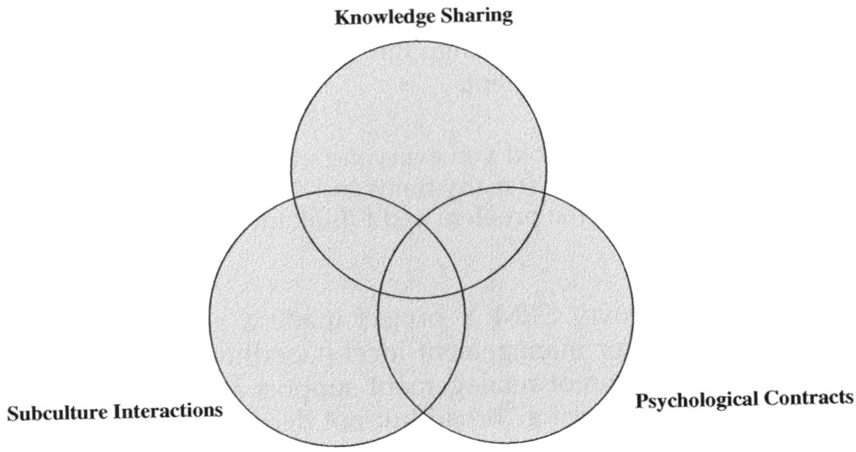

Figure 6.5 *Interdependence between Psychological Contracts, Sub-cultures and Knowledge Sharing*

Subculture interaction and psychological contracts

The subculture interaction at the senior management level remained limited to some interactions between the middle and senior management. There was very limited interaction between the senior management and the end-users of the system. Decisions were made at the senior level without any representation from end-users of the system.

Subculture interaction was also limited between the middle management and end-users. The interaction was more formalized within a mechanistic framework. Krogh *et al.* (2000) argue that an organization must actively pursue the work context as a learning organization where the individuals of that organization are attuned to learning new things. A learning organization environment was absent at IE.COM. Learning implies encountering and assimilating new facts. The end-users were not prepared to encounter CRM Y, and were getting stressed over the fact that data was in a poor state. Double entries to the systems were making matters worse. These double entries continued to occur at the end-user level as a result of inadequate subculture interaction. A Team Leader for the Internal Software Sales Rep Team in IE.COM commented:

> I don't think there's a trust in CRM Y. People use CRM Y in different ways. There's the standard approach that everybody is asked to use it. So for opportunity loading, for example, there is a set way we need to load it so that the data flows between CRM Y and ERW, which is the management matrix that we use, that's standard. In terms of searching for accounts and contacts, people use it for that because

that's logging activities; activity queues, some people use it, some people don't. We do encourage people to use it from a DQ (Data Quality) point of view, then if you're checking your activity queues and you're using that in that way, then it will help you; but a lot of people still use their calendars or their diaries just because they find that CRM Y can be a bit daunting and complex. They don't trust it still, they find it a slow tool and they don't trust it.

According to our respondent, the data quality was not up to the mark. She further argued that there was not much of a problem with the system itself:

I don't think it's distrusting the tool, I think the tool is good, I think the problem is that the data that's on the tool is not up-to-date and I don't think that's a CRM Y problem necessarily, I think that's an IE problem. But then therefore the perception is that it's CRM Y.

But also IE was using CRM Y as a forecasting tool:

The other thing is that IE are using CRM Y as a forecasting tool, they're not using it as a CRM tool. It's not a customer relationship management because you can phone a customer and not be aware that somebody the day before in another part of IE has called them. So the customer gets upset, they say "Don't you use CRM?', and then we're talking to them and IE are saying, "Have you thought about your customer relationship management?" But we're not actually doing it ourselves effectively.

Thus CRM Y was being used to log new opportunities and the data then flowed to the management matrix and other forecasting and monitoring systems such as SCOTT (SCOTT was the software which IE.COM management used to check the opportunities logged on CRM Y.). This shows again how the role of managing in a mechanistically structured organization led more towards control and monitoring of the end-users hooked to the systems with their head sets. However, the end-users were also IE.COM's internal customers. Their job satisfaction and how they related to the management was of vital importance. The management perceived CRM Y to be a tool that facilitated their interactions with the customers, and yet end-users saw it as a "forecasting tool" (Long & Fahey, 2000). Moreover, the bad data on the system caused frustration resulting in poor customer service:

It's not up-to-date, it's not updated. The process within IE to change the data on CRM Y is very long-winded, so people just don't have time to do it. So you've got to move on to the next call, you've got to close. Rightly or wrongly, it's not right, but people just leave it

> and that person's no longer there—so I'll put an activity in. I call this contact. He's no longer there! But they don't then do the stuff behind that to send off to the team that will update the record - so the data is not being updated as it should be. Contacts, you can phone in to customers and they haven't been there for two years. There's contacts that are missing on CRM Y CRM—IE know but they're not adding them on, so it's just not slick. (Team Leader)

Not everyone at IE.COM had access to the entire system. End-users individually log opportunities onto the system and were thereby creating frequent duplications that remain undetected:

> Not everyone has access, most of the field resource. I know that the Software Group have come onboard last years. I don't know about Sectors. And the Brands now have access, but I know that the most of IE doesn't—so you've got that problem. Plus, of course, you've got the limited access on an opportunity; you can't go into an opportunity unless you're one of the sales teams, so that doesn't help. Duplication, all the time, all the time, it's very, very difficult. (Team Leader)

Duplication continues

An ITSR (end-user) described the duplication at IE.COM as follows:

> The functionality, for example, within. I have got ten accounts—however on CRM Y . . . four of those ten accounts—they have 283 entries. And as a new person to choose, which account do you choose? You've got to know which ones are offers. There are duplicate entries, there are duplicate contacts, there are duplicates there that you can't just get rid of or sub-section it.

There was also rivalry between the business units at IE.COM:

> Well it's mainly between SMB and Large Enterprise—there's a rivalry between the two, and then within. I don't' know about SMB because I'm not exposed to that, but certainly within Large Enterprises there is also a bit of rivalry between the different units, Business Units. (ITSR end-user)

The sub-sections did not communicate well. This was partly due to the competitive nature of their jobs. As a result end-users within and across subsections failed to share information regarding opportunities. Knowledge sharing—implicit and explicit, codified and non-codified—suffered. Lack of interaction between the business units due to competition and confidentiality also resulted in double entries:

> Say for instance when we're logging our opportunity to someone within IE, a Business Partner would not be able to see that opportunity because then, obviously, they could compete. So that's one reason I guess, but I've never seen the Business Partner system—but they can also input opportunities, as we can. So it sometimes can get to the point where the Business Partner enters an opportunity and so do we—and there's duplication on that. So I guess just managing the data and keeping it correct and not duplicating it is quite difficult now there are a lot of people on the system. (End-user)

An Operational Manager confirmed this:

> So potentially you could be ringing the customer, inviting them to an event or asking them if they've seen the latest offerings, and they might already be aware of it and say, 'Well I spoke to someone yesterday about it', or, 'I've bought that'.

According to the CRM Operations Manager, not everyone used the system. Information regarding "tricks of the trade" remained buried inside the departmental/business unit silos. A Process Manager explained that there was no system available which could facilitate interaction between the PDTS and business units within dot com around CRM. However, she claimed that interaction did take place at her level (subject matter expert, trainer level).

The Operational Manager claimed that the double entries were captured by the reports that management pulled out while doing a compliance test. However as per 2004 no reports were pulled out directly from CRM Y. The Operational Manager claimed that the CRM Y analytics would develop further towards the end of 2004 and make it easier. However CRM Y analytics seemed to have its limitations:

> The only downside of that is it's not historical. I need to be able to pull a report that says to me, 'OK this time last week how much was loaded,' because if I pull it with the CRM Y analytics project that's coming, I can only see what's been loaded today. I don't want to know that. If I'm looking to see who's created the most opportunities I need to look at it maybe from last week, the week before, not just this week. So I need the whole picture and historical data.

An end-user continued to express her frustration over double entries:

> As sales people it's always, "Well you haven't done this on a lead." I think there are quite a lot of [duplications]. For instance—we log opportunities and we have to fill in what seems like the same information more than once.

She argued that duplication of entries was also closely related to duplication of effort and the time spent to submit the information. User commitment was negatively affected by the stress caused by duplication and double entries. Management, however, considered double entries as errors made by the end-users. The psychological contracts between the IE.COM management and the end-users appeared to be of "employee under-obligation" types. End-users saw the system as a hurdle slowing down the process of customer service, thereby decreasing its quality. Management, on the other hand, perceived CRM Y as a tool that facilitated interaction between the end-users and external customers.

The duplication of efforts at IE.COM continued:

> If you raise an opportunity, someone has called and raised an opportunity . . . Business Partners, they won't be able to see that opportunity.

According to the this end-user, if "Business Partners" then called the same customer, they would end up asking the same sort of questions again—thus not only duplicating the effort, but also potentially causing customer dissatisfaction.

According to Call Centre Manager IE.COM, information sharing across the sub-units was entirely dependent on access and control. This in turn prevented not only the sharing of experience and uncodified know-how, but also sharing of descriptive and prescriptive types of knowledge. According to Pliskin *et al.* (1993), the same system may have different meanings for different people. Issues discussed above regarding data migration and training at IE point to the same system having different meanings for different people. System analysts and users did not have the same points of view concerning the CRM system. Prolonged interaction between different levels of hierarchy could have helped to create a better understanding of the state of the legacy system and the training needs. Interaction did take place but only to a limited extent, due partly to the implementation process structure itself not allowing the creative abrasion to take place fully, thus impeding knowledge sharing (Leonard-Barton, 1995).

Davidson (2002) argues how frames and shifts in frame salience influence sense-making during requirement determination. This study helps to understand how interpretive power is exercised in an IS project. Moving on from frames to shared frames, Orlikowski and

Gash (1994) show shared frames as closely related to the concept of sub-cultures. Individuals—drawing on their shared frames—engage in symbolic action and thereby construct a social reality that reflects their common assumptions, beliefs and understandings and that includes particular rules, rituals and customary practice. According to Geertz (1973) and Van Maanen and Barley (1985), sub-cultures rely heavily on cognitive elements such as common frames of reference. A sharing of frames did not take pace across the hierarchies at IE. This was more evident at the lower level of hierarchies at IE.COM.—particularly as to how managers and end-users had differing perceptions regarding the usefulness of the system and data issues.

According to the Vice Chairman, World CRM Deployment, full time workers were deployed in teams, to interact with different business units, to understand the business need and processes. Some mutual understanding may have been present in the interactions. However, an implicit component of the psychological contract was absent, thus resulting in lack of clarity and illusion of consensus for both parties involved (Anderson & Schalk, 1998; Gee, 1992). This inhibited knowledge sharing and resulted in data misfit. According to Lawrence and Lorsch (1967) the particularities of the environment, task and technologies faced by an organization's sub-cultures are associated with differences in cognitive and emotional orientations among individuals in these sub-cultures. There was a lack of the sharing of cognitive and emotional orientations regarding data issues at IE.COM which widened the sub-cultural divide between the management and end-users. This resulted in "employee under-obligation" types of psychological contracts between the end-users of the system and the management.

The explicit elements of the psychological contracts between the senior management and the end-users included a sense of obligation to work and job security. However, this resulted also in an "employee under-obligation" type of psychological contract as the contract was more often of an imposed nature. Differing stakeholder motives also inhibited interactions in-depth (Thibaut & Kelly, 1959). These factors resulted in insufficient information with regard to both the data on the legacy systems and the training needs of the end-users. There may also have been a false impression regarding the state of data due to the lack of in-depth interaction between the partners. Different theories of meaning on the subject of data quality were not exposed. People from different backgrounds subject to normal discourse could have agreed unproblematically at the level of words while truly but erroneously believing that they were indicating the same referent domain of meaning, thus giving rise to an illusion of consensus regarding the state of legacy data (Gee, 1992).

Moreover, according to the Operational Manager, whenever an upgrade arrived, people in different PDTs got separate training. She also admitted that there was not much interaction between the PDTs themselves. However, there was some interaction between the trainer, CRM Process Manager at dot com, and another business unit, namely Field Sales:

> The Process Manager actually worked with the PDT4 to say, 'Here's what we did, here's our experiences'. She sat in on a lot of the clinics and workshops to help and work with the other people. So there was a bit of cross working there, but it was more just a general sort of agreement between myself and the person running that rather than structured. (Call Centre Manager IE.COM).

Evidently the higher one went in the hierarchy, the freer the interaction between individuals and across departments:

> I think the interaction wouldn't be at our level. If there were interaction with say different sponsors, different areas, and the area in which Alex Parsons (one of the executives) works for instance, the interaction would be at a higher level. It wouldn't be at our level, if you see what I'm saying. (Operational Manager)

Some interaction with mutual perspectives did take place at the senior management level. However, the environment at that level of hierarchy was less threatening and people had more mutual understanding and shared benefits resulting in "mutual high-obligations" types of psychological contract. The lack of interaction between PDTs could also be due to reasons other than competition. The Call Centre Manager IE.COM argued that the physical distance between the PDTs (business units) played an important role. He claimed that Marketing had been able to pick up some "tricks of the trade" from IE.COM from being physically nearer to them than other PDTs. The sub-cultures interacting face to face could have helped to generate a conflict of ideas. According to Leonard-Barton (1995) this creative abrasion can positively influence performance. However, interaction between the sub-cultures must happen over a prolonged period (Newell *et al.*, 2002). Thus creative abrasion across the PDTs had not taken place.

There was some interaction between some business units within IE.COM:

> For example they would find an opportunity and they might pass it to the software business person, so the person here will be on that opportunity as will the software business person, they will both be on that opportunity as identifier and owner of the opportunity. So

> the software business person will then be engaged with the customer, speaking to them on a regular basis to deal with that opportunity and then they will talk, interact, to say how this opportunity is progressing. (Call Centre Manager IE.COM)

This interaction took place because of the shared interest where a win-win (shared benefits) situation was an ultimate outcome. Both individuals sharing information in the above case received an extrinsic reward in form of a bonus. The interaction resulted in a "mutual high-obligations" type of psychological contract and generated a "shared context for knowing" and ownership (Newell *et al.*, 2002). The Call Centre Manager IE.COM further reported that the ITSRs and Software Specialists made joint calls, shared information and helped each other in obtaining a success outcome of their shared effort. This was not always the case:

> IE is a very big company and it has lots of points of contact into a customer and all those points of contact into the customer aren't always aware of all the other points of contacts. So you've got a marketing person, they might not be aware that there's an ITSR who's aligned to the account, a client manager and that there's two or three brand sales specialists who are currently working with that customer. So they can go and speak to that customer and not be aware of all this.

In any communication, the "knowing of what others know" is necessary for co-ordinated action to take place (Bakhtin, 1981; Krauss & Fussell, 1991; Mead, 1934). The presence of a mechanistic competitive culture at IE.COM resulted in the lack of joint efforts and shared ownership, which in turn resulted in duplications at IE.

The interdependencies between subculture interactions, psychological contracts and knowledge sharing continued

End-user involvement did not come until later, and even then the development of CRM Y was not end-user driven. One respondent expressed his frustration:

> We're the users, for god's sake someone up there speak to us! We have to use the tool on a day-to-day basis. We can tell you our likes, our dislikes. Let's have these round tables—let's take it to the top and explain the difficulties that we're having, not only with the application which were little things, but also those things that support it on the back-end, mainly the customer database.

Knowledge sharing increased to some extent. Previously there was some interaction between IE.COM and Field Sales. The old systems

(Marketing and Sales Management and Opportunity Management System) did not talk to each other. The Call Centre Manager IE.COM, claimed that the new system increased efficiency:

> The biggest sole major increase in efficiency and change was when the field sales reps came onboard to CRM. Up until then we had been using two separate sales management systems, so whereas before when we were on CRM they were on something called OM-Notes (Opportunity Management—Notes) and prior to that when we were on Emerson they were on something called OM System. The two systems didn't talk to each other, so it meant that every region, every country, had to have.

However it did not help if Field Sales did not use it:

> Field don't even put in notes whether they've seen a customer or not. And likewise Dublin, Dublin might put three words in there, 'Spoke to the customer.' OK, about what? Is the customer going to take it further? I've sent you an opportunity—at least give me a bit of information, how you got on with the customer. It is appalling! (ITSR end-user)

ITSR (end-user) confirmed the above with an illustration:

> The Field Sales, effectively, so when they came on board they'd never really used it. And that's another problem. There's not a problem at all with the system. However people don't use it in the way it's meant to be used, and therefore the information's not there. The tools are only as good as the people who use them. It's a great repository for information and because we use it so often we put in any contacts, any calls we have, data from what the calls were all about. However external field brands don't do that. They put the opportunity on but nothing else—it's great but it's also, it could be better. But that's not about the system—that's about people using it.

There was some interaction between GSMBs and Software Specialists because of the shared benefits. However, there was even less interaction between GSMBs and Sectors:

> To a certain extent although there's really no business need, no benefit for them to really interact in that level. Obviously with all systems—same office, so people know each other and they might talk about various different products that they've been selling in to a customer, and how well it's worked etc, etc... sharing best practice to that extent, but not sharing the information on the actual system itself. (Call Centre Manager)

This respondent suggested that overall knowledge sharing through what he called "best practices" and "tricks of the trade" at IE.COM was minimal:

> I'd say there's very little sharing of best practices in that way, to be honest with you because I'm not an out and out user of the system. There might well be that going on because it happens within the sub-cultures and between friends and informally and I might well not be aware of it, but it might well be happening in the management team.

To a certain extent the problem could be the rigidity of the system's access:

> Because you had to be named on an opportunity to see it sometimes, and now because everyone's on the system, you might have someone from marketing might load an opportunity but not put you on it. So therefore there will be an opportunity on the system but you wouldn't actually be able to see it and so that is an inhibitor to some extent.

The mechanistic culture and rigidity of the system did not allow non-codified knowledge to get passed around frequently. The interactions were generally in a structured and rigid environment. Such interactions even on a prolonged basis failed to overcome the power-based relationship barrier. Underlying psychological contracts tended to be of an imposed and "employee under-obligation" type restricting the revealing of innermost feelings:

> Now the other side of it is the way that the CRM system is set up—is—there are a lot of processes surrounding that control—how issues and so therefore the actual ability to have, sort of, best practices, short-cuts where you're doing things is limited very much because it is controlled so intensely. I'm sure there are probably, some people bound, they'll always find some short-cuts or some way of doing something, but I think it is limited quite a lot. (Call Centre Manager IE.COM).

There were control and monitoring mechanisms which, combined with a competitive business unit culture, allowed very limited creative abrasion to take place (Leonard-Barton, 1995). A lack of creative abrasion and prolonged interactions between the business units at IE.COM resulted in a knowledge silo environment (Iansiti, 1993; Newell *et al.*, 2002). Knowledge in these silos does become sticky (Bartlett & Ghoshal, 1998). According to Nonaka (1994) knowledge intensive firms, competitive advantage and product success are a result of collaborative, ongoing learning. Success depends not only on how effectively diverse individuals are able to organize and develop their unique knowledge competencies, but also how they can integrate and utilize their distinctive knowledge both effectively and synergistically (Nonaka, 1994). However, people holding information regarding any experiential know-how in the business units at IE.COM would not share them freely. In a competitive environment such as above, non-codified knowledge hoarding may give the individuals a sense of job security and power (Davenport *et al.*, 1998; Salancik & Pfeffer, 1978). However, there was some informal sharing of knowledge:

> Do we share best practices, these short-cuts etc, etc,—is there a team room, an intranet site or something, so people can find out that if you do X, Y, Z? (then you get through this a lot quicker). There isn't like that, so any passing of that knowledge would be done in the smoking room, or having a coffee or within your team—things like that—and it will be very rarely passed across formally to any other part of IE.COM, or outside to another PDT. So it will all be very informal - you know, my friend told me X, Y, Z—that sort of thing. (Call Centre Manager IE.COM)

Interaction and knowledge sharing was more along the vertical than the horizontal axis. There was a limited interaction across PDTs and within IE.COM (PDT1). Our respondent Call Centre Manager IE.COM further explained:

> But because you have different ways of working, I mean people in IE.COM have one culture and PDT 5, for example, or marketing, have their own culture—when you merge these cultures there is going to be a clash, a cultural clash. Now are there any plans or are you working towards, are all these PDT's having the same idea like yourself when you talk to them? Do they think in terms, we going to merge together in the future, why don't we get to know each other more and have more co-operation?

In summary, there was a need for more active collaboration between the business units to enhance their performance and efforts towards developing a better customer service.

System integration did not help subculture integration

IE.COM was finding it hard to share best practices and experiential know-how due to the competitive nature by which people are primarily watching over their own opportunities. At IE.COM the segregated, rigid structure resisted the CRM ideology of subculture integration and its aim to facilitate knowledge sharing with shared understandings and psychological contracts of a mutual type:

> But it's again that we're coming back to this idea of CRM, the structure of CRM itself is integrated. Let's gather the knowledge. Whereas IE still has this hierarchy that it has to follow, so it kind of contradicts this. Its in conflict with the CRM culture and as the CRM culture develops its going to take along time before the hierarchy start to flatten, and there will be more and more information spread out and be more balance of information sharing both horizontally and vertically. (Call Centre Manager IE.COM)

An ITSR (end-user) added that non codified knowledge only got transferred occasionally through informal conversations:

> Only if it comes up in conversation, but there's not a lot of work-arounds really to do because the system is quite rigid, you can't change what the system is, as it is off-the-shelf.

Our respondent had concerns regarding the company's image:

> Yes, but the thing is, is from how the system should be set up—the stroke of a few keys—it's there. My system, a stroke of a few extra keys, there's that 20 second delay—because you have to go into one screen, come out of that screen, into another screen. So we try to portray that IE is the cutting edge—they've come up with e-business, they've come up with on-demand and all this, and here we are running with a . . . it is a . . . don't get me wrong, it is an excellent application. There are a couple of little things that I don't like about it, but if the back-end is right, the front-end is brilliant, because it does what it's supposed to do.

Our respondent expressed his frustration over the quality of back-end data:

> If you have wrong information in the back-end, you are sitting in the front-end interacting with the customer, you're bringing up the wrong sort of information to give to the customer. Yes, because you might take a call from a customer you don't deal with, because for some reason he's got a direct line that he's dialling to the person that he normally speak to—they might be on the phone, so it jumps to you, then you're in the wilderness, particularly with . . . Now if it was straight forward . . . 'Can I check the spelling of your surname? Christian name?' . . . Press the button, whoosh, he comes up. He's got one template, that's it . . . He's on the system ten times under different names!

The IE CRM initiative expected the company to become more organic, more adaptable and a learning organization. However, lack of prolonged subculture interactions, "shared context for knowing" and "mutual high-obligations" psychological contracts across the business units in a mechanistic culture inhibited developing this type of environment. Krogh *et al.* (2000) describe how effective knowledge creation depends on the physical, virtual and emotional context of an organization. They discuss the importance of the notion of reciprocity of relationships. When a relationship is felt to be reciprocal then a trust develops which can work to overcome power-based relationships. It can be that the inability of an individual to deal with a new situation, new event, new context such as CRM Y or new information, is an obstacle to knowledge creation. IE needed to pursue actively the work context as a learning organization where the individuals in different PDTs were attuned to learning new things. Learning implies encountering and assimilating new facts. Differing cultures within an organization also affect the efficient sharing of knowledge. These cultures can arise from different educational backgrounds, differential interests, expectations and power (Long & Fahey, 2000). Differing opinions and cultural diversity in fact presented an excellent opportunity for creative abrasion at IE.

Psychological contracts and knowledge sharing

We learned from the previous analyses that there was some "mutual perspective taking" that took place at the senior management level. As the people at that level of hierarchy shared their cognitive frames regarding the particularities of CRM Y, their shared benefits and mutual understanding led to "mutual high-obligations" types of psychological contracts. Furthermore, this was also repeated at the end-user level. The interaction between GSMBs and Software Specialists had also shared interests and mutual benefit, bringing the two groups close in their working relationship. This also gave rise to "mutual high-obligations" types of psychological contracts. Based on mutual and not imposed psychological contracts they were then willing to share their innermost feelings and secrets with each other in order to achieve a successful outcome. The "mutual high-obligations" type of psychological contract based on shared benefits helped to facilitate the sharing of "tricks of the trade". On the contrary the interactions between the management and end-users prior to CRM Y deployment, even though on a prolonged basis, were not able to expose the data misfit issues. In these power based formal interactions, innermost feelings were not revealed and psychological contracts were predominantly imposed and "employee under-obligation" type.

Some prescriptive knowledge was shared over the web through the CRM Website and online team-rooms (Iansiti, 1993). People from IE could log in and access information available on CRM Y. They could also ask questions and get answers from the web administrator. According to the Operational Manager, there was nothing available at a local level to facilitate knowledge sharing across the PDTs and business units within them. Moreover, not everyone at IE.COM had access to the online team-rooms. Strong hierarchical enterprises prevent smooth cross-functional communication and consequently inhibit cross-functional cooperation or knowledge sharing (Nonaka, 1994). The rigid organizational structure did not allow a free sharing of knowledge at IE.COM.

The Operational Manager illustrated further with regard to access to team-rooms:

> No, not unless we give them access. But we have team-rooms and work-rooms. Work-rooms are . . . only a certain amount of people can go in and put information in them, and for everyone else it's just as a repository to read information. Then you have team-rooms and team-room pluses, dependent on the access people are given—depends on whether they get 'read only', 'author' or 'edit', and they can put comments in and that kind of thing.

The research on social information processing (Salancik & Pfeffer, 1978), power (Pettigrew, 1973; Pfeffer, 1980), process management (Burns & Stalker, 1961; Daft & Lengel, 1986; Lawrence & Lorsch, 1967), and organizational cultures (Gregory, 1983; Pettigrew, 1979; Riley, 1983; Schein, 1985; Strauss, 1978) further suggests that people tend to share assumptions, knowledge, and expectations with others with whom they have close working relationships. Some tacit/non-codified knowledge did get shared in the teams and with people who are physically close by at IE.COM:

> I suppose I'd say that, for instance, if I'm looking for a customer and I type in, for instance, British Homestores and BHS and I just can't find them on CRM Y, I might look up on a different system, like my spreadsheet, and say, 'Well they must be on CRM Y. I've got five customer numbers for them, so I'll search by customer number.' Now that sort of information, I guess, that I would share with my immediate team—but there'd be many other users across the other side of the floor and other countries that I wouldn't share it with. But I'd say anything that is a short-cut we would share amongst our immediate team, but someone diagonally across the other side of the room is not going to get that knowledge. (An end-user)

As the distance between the individuals and business units increased, the opportunities for prolonged interactions decreased. In relation to CRM Y there was no simple round table which could facilitate interaction and discussions on CRM Y and allow end-users to share codified (descriptive and prescriptive knowledge) and non-codified/tacit ("tricks of the trade") types of knowledge. This table could have acted as a neutral platform where people would feel less threatened and could share various forms of knowledge about CRM Y in order to maximize their performance.

Some descriptive and prescriptive knowledge got shared only through vertical silos because of the vertical reporting structure at IE. Any non-codified knowledge could get reported to the Process Manager and the CRM Focal Point Co-ordinator and the latter, in turn, could pass them on to the next level of hierarchy. This resulted in some knowledge residing in the vertical silos without travelling along the horizontal axis. However, there was knowledge sharing through informal channels that travelled in all directions. We discuss this under the next heading.

Sharing of knowledge through invisible colleges based on "mutual high-obligations" psychological contracts

Learning and experiential knowledge did get shared, but through informal contacts within and outside the sub-cultures. One end-user used the expression "scratch my back and I'll scratch yours" to illustrate the presence of invisible colleges at IE.COM. This also illustrates how reciprocal relationships with "mutual high-obligations" types of psychological contracts could act as vehicles to the sharing of "tricks of the trade":

> I've gone through the back door and I've got to use my own personal network of people . . . and when I've not been happy with something, or the record is totally incorrect, I've done the same thing. I've said, 'Give us a ring I need your assistance here.' We've gone through three or four changes or consolidations—he's done it at his end because he's in a position to do it—I haven't had to get any authorisation. (An ITSR end-user)
>
> I mean it's humans we're dealing with, not machines. (Team Leader)

People used their informal networks and gave favours to each other. Some issues did get resolved through these informal networks, or what we might call "invisible colleges":

> We do actually have to be a bit creative because otherwise we wouldn't actually, in the sales environment, get anything done at all, and that's something that everybody does. We don't break business, we don't trade audit, we work on our own and it is much more of an informal process. For example there's two teams within Software,

> there's another team leader, and we work together, for example on data quality perspectives. (A Team Leader)

Knowledge sharing through invisible colleges could also result in knowledge hoarding silos because people were not aware of each other due to lack of interaction and explicitness of contacts:

> The gurus will always pass ['tricks of the trade'] to the gurus. (CRM Y Deployment Leader)

Such "invisible colleges" gave rise to a new subculture—a "guru culture"—which may be even more isolated than other sub-cultures and can act as a clique, hoarding the "tricks of the trade". Individuals within these cliques have a strong "mutual high-obligations" type of psychological contract, but may not want to share their knowledge more widely in formal settings, thus weakening the organizational architecture. Hence knowledge in this case became sticky and a symbol of power (Davenport *et al.*, 1998; Salancik & Pfeffer, 1978; Sutton, 1999).

Knowledge sharing through moaning

According to Kunda, (1991) an informal setting may facilitate the sharing of non-codified knowledge. One respondent verified this:

> We do talk about it, it's inevitable. IE's fully like that—a lot of my friends, because I'm not from this area, and all my friends outside work are IEer's. You do slip into the business conversation and we also talk about CRM. And yes, I suppose people might come up and say, 'I've had a nightmare day today.' You say, 'Well why's that?', or' 'Bloody Steve!', or something like that. But, yes, you do—you don't avoid it. We try not to, but we do. (Team Leader)

Not everyone liked to talk about work on informal occasions though:

> It's not really something I try and talk about really, if I can help it. It's not a debate we have, like some work, it's something we use—and we get on with it. You can tend to find within the environment that you sit in that you can hear someone say, 'What are we doing with this? It's not working.' And you'll find other people will say, 'I know what to do with that,' or 'That's not working for me either.'—because we work very closely in our environment. (ITSR end-user)

The above shows that informal settings as argued by Kunda (1991) did not always facilitate the sharing of the "tricks of the trade". Especially, if a work environment is stressful, individuals may see informal interactions as a step back from the stressful environment. However, others in our case saw it as a place to complain and through this "moaning" some knowledge got shared.

Summary

The interaction at the senior management level was based on shared benefits and a mutual understanding, giving rise to "mutual high-obligations" types of psychological contracts. The decision to take on board CRM Y was made by three senior executives. The decision then trickled down to the middle management levels that were given the implementation task. There was no end-user involvement in the decision making process. Furthermore, no external user involvement was considered.

Subculture interaction was also limited between the middle management and end-users. The interaction was more formalized within a mechanistic framework. A "mutual high-obligations" contract learning organization environment was absent. Double entries occurred on an ongoing basis at the end-user level as a result of lack of subculture interaction. End-users did not trust the system. Their low trust led to not everyone using the system. Mistrust in CRM Y was mainly due to the data issues, in particular the double entries slowing down their service to customers, thus impeding their performance. Furthermore, the end-users saw CRM Y as a forecasting tool for the management whereas management perceived CRM Y as facilitating end-users' interactions with the customers. Differing perceptions showed that a mutual perspective and "shared context for knowing" between the management and the end-users were not prevalent.

The fact that not everyone used the system with its mechanistic rigid organizational structure, led to considerable non-codified knowledge remaining buried inside the departmental/business unit silos. There was no system which could facilitate interaction between the PDTS and business units within IE.COM in relation to CRM. In this context the sub-sections had no neutral platform/round table where prolonged interaction leading to creative abrasion could take place. Moreover, the competitive nature of their jobs did not allow such interaction. As a result, end-users within and across subsections had few information sharing opportunities. The psychological contracts between the subunits were more of "mutual low-obligation" type. Consequently knowledge sharing suffered—implicit and explicit, codified and non-codified.

Due to a strong vertical reporting structure, resulting in power based relationships at IE.COM, knowledge hoarding occurred in vertical silos.

The lack of interaction between the business units at IE.COM Portsmouth, due to competition and confidentiality, also resulted in double entries. Some of the double entries were captured by the reports that management pulled out while compliance testing. However as per 2004 no reports had been pulled out directly from CRM Y. There were plans to develop further CRM Y analytics. Duplication of entries was also related to duplication of effort and the time spent in gathering the information. User commitment was affected negatively by the stress caused by duplication and double entries. Management, however, considered double entries as errors made by the end-users. Not surprisingly, the psychological contracts between the IE.COM management and the end-users were of an "employee under-obligation" type.

IE.COM was finding it hard to share "best practices" and "tricks of the trade" due to the competitive atmosphere in which people were watching over their own "opportunities". The segregated rigid structure resisted a CRM ideology of subculture integration. IE.COM management admitted the need for active collaboration between the business units in order to enhance their performance and improve customer service.

There was some knowledge sharing through informal channels that travelled in many directions, through which "tricks of the trade" got shared across the sub-cultures and hierarchies. People used these informal networks and also exchanged favours. A "Guru Culture" was born as a result and became a knowledge silo in itself. Knowledge became sticky and resided within the élite "clique" type guru culture. It was shared between the "gurus" due to their "mutual high-obligations" contracts. Apart from guru to guru sharing there were also informal occasions and gatherings where some know-how and non-codified knowledge got shared. However, other people tried to avoid talking about work in these social gatherings in order to escape from their work related stress.

We have investigated the interdependencies between subculture interactions, psychological contracts and knowledge sharing. Our investigation of the contemporary situation at IE.COM revealed that prolonged interactions with mutual perspectives and shared benefits are associated with "mutual high-obligations" types of psychological contracts, which in turn facilitate the sharing of non-codified/tacit knowledge in the form of "tricks of the trade". In our case, imposed or "employee low-obligation" types of psychological contracts were

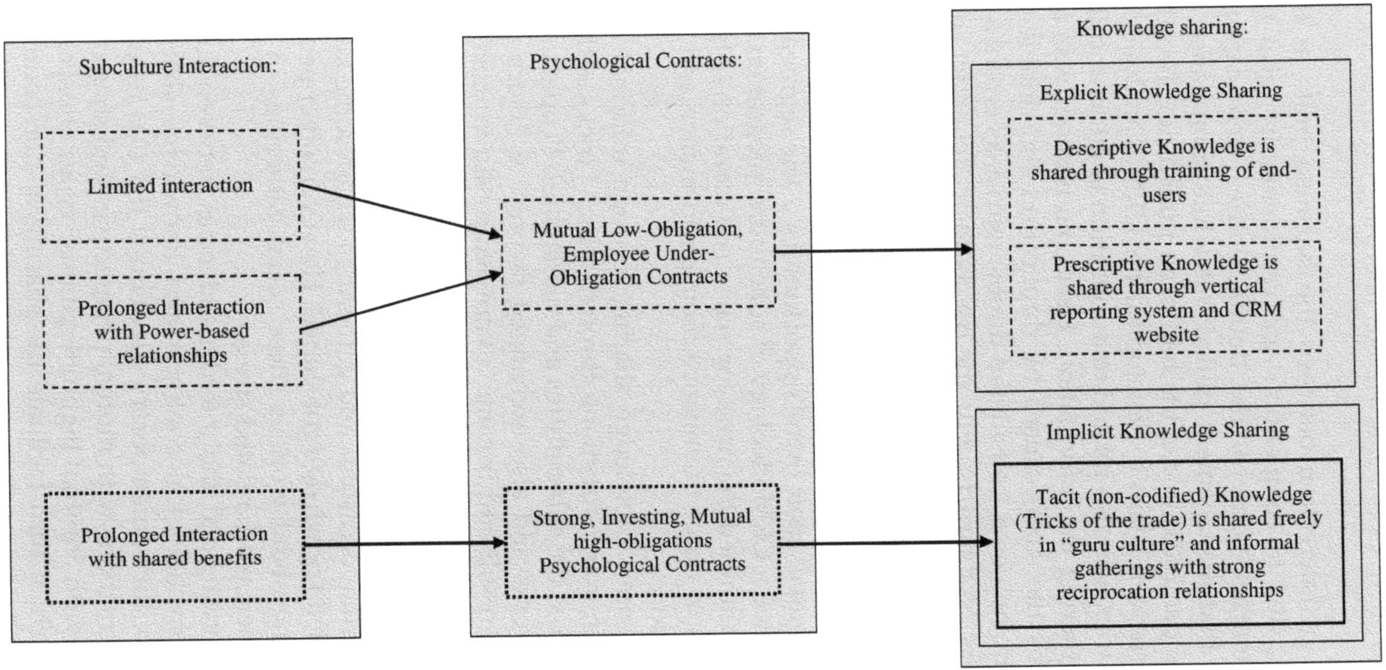

***Figure* 6.6** *Interdependencies between subculture interactions, psychological contracts and knowledge sharing*

linked with sporadic sub-culture interactions and lack of a shared mental space. For an overview of our analysis see Figure 6.6.

SUMMARY ANALYSIS

This chapter has focused on the implementation of CRM Y at IE.COM Portsmouth. It has taken a close interest in the post implementation environment at IE.COM Portsmouth in order to investigate further the adaptation and acceptance of the system by its users from a knowledge sharing perspective. It builds on the pilot chapter which was focused primarily on the implementation process of CRM Y at IE.COM.

The decision to take CRM Y on board was made at the senior management level and the system was implemented using a top-down approach without any consideration being given to end-user or external customer involvement in the "decision making" process. Support groups, development groups and deployment groups were formed to facilitate the smooth run of the operation. However, they were not able to expose the data misfit issues at IE.COM Portsmouth. All the six subsections at IE.COM went live simultaneously. According to the end-users it was an attempt to standardize numerous data bases in order, better to monitor and control their interactions with the customers. Management, however, hoped that the system would facilitate the end-user's interactions with customers and thereby enhance their performance and the quality of customer service. However, due to several data misfit issues, which were ignored during the implementation, the use of the system has become a stress factor. CRM legacy data was in a poor state. However, this was not discovered until the data migration began.

End-users were stressed and feel pressured to use the system, reducing their commitment and ownership. Not everyone used the system and duplication and double entries happened frequently. Due to the vast mechanistic organizational structure, end-user issues took a long time to receive any feedback. This led to people finding work-arounds in the form of social networks, to cope with issues arising from their use of the system—invisible colleges in the form of an élite "guru culture" emerged. These gurus, however, withheld their knowledge of "tricks of the trade" to ensure job security and power.

End-user involvement at the floor level came at a later stage. Super-users at IE.COM at North Harbour UK were selected by IE.COM managers when a manager from IE USA came down to facilitate the implementation, six months after the signing of the contract: A shared context for knowing and "mutual perspective taking" did not happen fully due to the competitive nature of jobs at IE.COM (Boland & Tenkasi, 1996; Newell *et al.*, 2002). Furthermore, the real content of an apparently mutual perspective was not allowed to surface or be challenged. Thus interpretations which could shake the illusion of consensus regarding data issues between stakeholders were avoided (Gee, 1992).

The achievement of a new definition of the situation in which all participants could share had yet to take place to its full capacity (Habermas, 1979). Moreover, the updates were more like "kick backs" (as expressed by our respondents) as the users were not even comfortable with the previous versions when the new releases arrived. As a result the psychological contracts between the management and end-user were of an "employee low-obligation" type. The low-obligation contract resulted in end-users finding and sharing work-arounds which in turn gave birth to a "guru culture". Knowledge sharing, in particular the sharing of "tricks of the trade", was minimal between management and end-users. Also, there was minimal sharing of "tricks of the trade" between the business units.

This chapter suggests that psychological contracts play an important role in knowledge sharing, particularly the sharing of non-codified or tacit knowledge in the form of "tricks of the trade". It also suggests that imposed psychological contracts ("employee under-obligation") tend to promote power based relationships (Shore & Barksdale, 1998) but may result in sharing of some descriptive and prescriptive knowledge. However, an "employee under-obligation" type of psychological contract does not facilitate the sharing of inner-most feelings and "tricks of the trade". Explicit elements of psychological contracts between senior management and end-users included a sense of obligation to work, and job security issues. Importantly, implicit elements of psychological contracts remained hidden (Makin *et al.*, 1996) producing illusions of consensus, which influenced and inhibited the adaptation and acceptance of CRM Y. As a result data issues became a major stress factor for the end-users at IE.COM.

Upon investigating micro mechanisms (in our example, the psychological contracts) underlying the development of "mutual perspective", "shared mental space", "T-shaped skills" and "knowing of what others know", we found that these psychological contracts inhibit or facilitate the sharing of non-codified knowledge across sub-cultures. Furthermore, psychological contracts, subculture interactions and knowledge sharing have strong interdependencies. Our case shows that where the psychological contracts were weak, the interactions and knowledge sharing were both limited, particularly the non-codified/tacit knowledge sharing. For an overview see Figure 6.7.

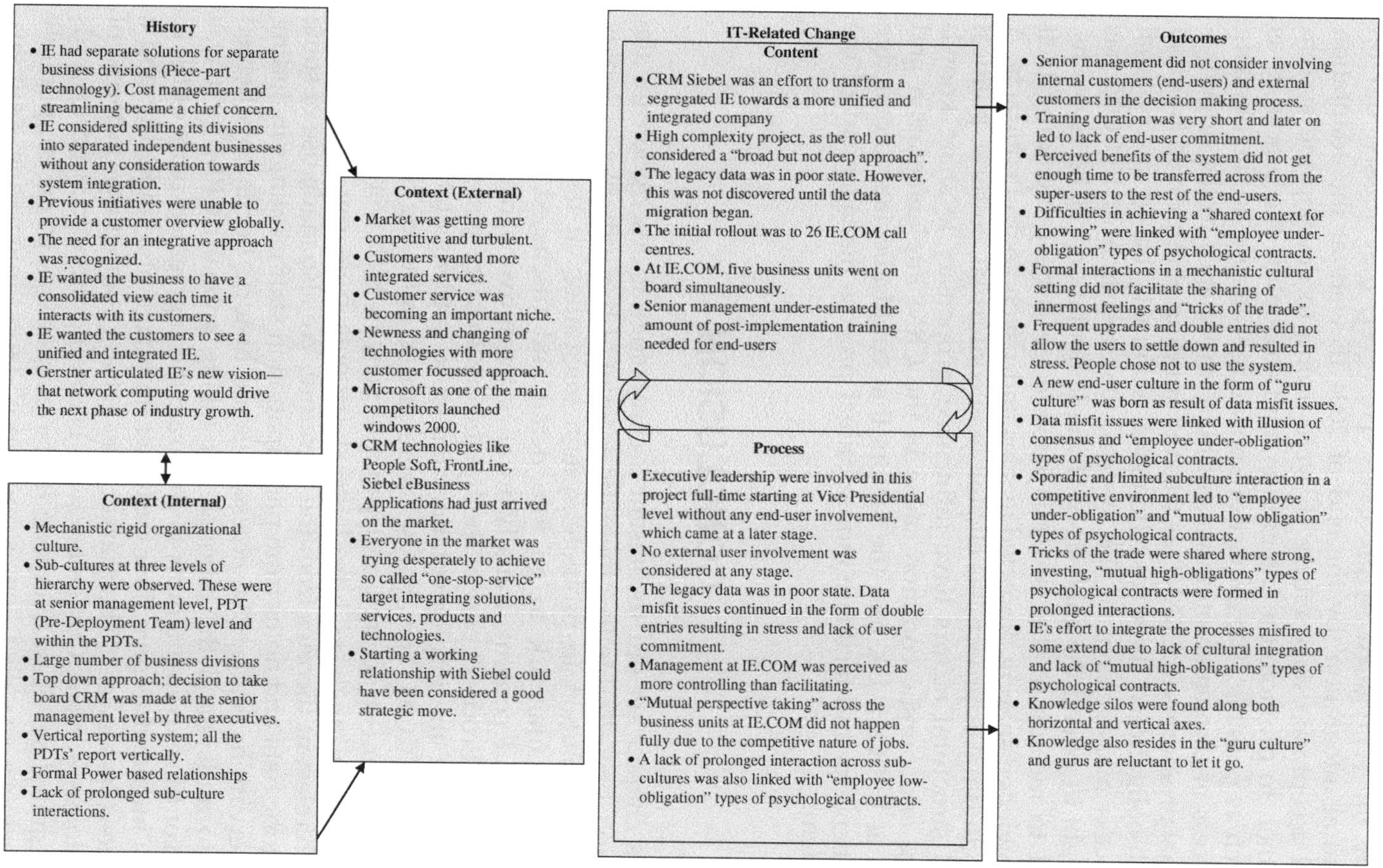

Figure 6.7 *A summary of analysis using Pettigrew (1985, 1990)*

According to our respondents at IE, CRM Y was an effort to integrate the segregated IE processes. However, they missed out on cultural integration. By the end of 2004 IE were at the adaptation and acceptance stage where IE were trying to develop the system further, to promote the integration, and streamline the processes as much as possible. The impact of knowledge sharing on the ongoing process of implementation was of high importance to the organizational promoters of CRM Y, as was the building of improved "mutual high-obligations" type psychological contracts based on optimal process management of the system. Our research at IE.COM has sought to extend the analysis of IT implementation to CRM systems, and to include in that analysis knowledge issues—including tacit knowledge sharing, knowledge silos and psychological contracts. A longitudinal approach has elicited how contextual, cultural, political and structural factors have influenced propensity to share knowledge and pursue common cause in the CRM implementation and use at IE.COM, UK and the factors that could alleviate knowledge bottlenecks and facilitate more optimal process management of the system.

CONCLUSION

This chapter set out to present a chronological description for the period 1999–2004 with a thematic account of IE's initiative to deploy a CRM Solution to promote system integration. It used a refined analytic framework to go into detail and discussed the history, context and content, initially in an interpretive narrative. It then used the "Process" part of the framework to carry out a within-case analysis of the implementation and post implementation environment at IE.COM. The analyses were carried out using data from the final 16 semi-structured in-depth interviews which were also taped. The critical analyses linked the statements from our respondents with relevant theories from the literature. We also made use of some historic data and notes from participation in staff meetings including observations made. The access to some historic documents helped us to understand the rationale for taking onboard CRM Y. It was one of the eleven attempts to integrate the segregated parts of IE. IE also intended to give their customer an image of a unified IE and a "one-stop-service". The market was getting competitive in terms of customer service. Customers were becoming more focused towards integrated services. Everyone in the market was trying desperately to achieve so called "one-stop-service" target integrating solutions, services, products and technologies. IE wanted network computing to drive the next phase of industry growth and this also became the company's overarching strategy. The IE CRM era had started, but, as we have seen, implementing effective CRM was proving to be a not inconsiderable challenge. In particular, our research has concluded that knowledge sharing issues, and what gives rise to them, are highly significant factors underlying the optimization or failure of a system in the light of its different stakeholder's interests.

In the next chapter we present a cross-case analysis comparing the "process" element from both cases. The deviating patterns and similarities in the adaptation of CRM systems are investigated and compared in order to gain further insight into the linkages between knowledge sharing, subculture interaction and psychological contracts in a CRM environment.

7 Cross-Case and Cross-Sector Analysis: What Can We Learn?

INTRODUCTION

Here we analyze the research findings from both cases in the light of the reviewed literature. The framework previously used in the "within-case" analyses is used to discuss deviating patterns and similarities across both research sites, in order to gain further insight into the linkages between knowledge sharing, subculture interaction and psychological contracts in a CRM environment. The analysis is carried out as depicted in Figures 7.1 and 7.2, using our derived framework, together with one from Willcocks and Harrow (1992) for cross-sector comparison. Initially we discuss and compare the "Process" in the first part of the analysis. In the second we analyze similar and deviating patterns, discuss our findings and relate them to distinctive contexts from Willcocks and Harrow's framework. The section concludes with a summary of the analytical findings.

PART 1: PROCESS COMPARISON

Under this section we discuss the "Process" from our framework as shown in Figure 7.1. We critically analyze and compare staff stability, user commitment, user training and management support. Additionally, we compare and analyze the interdependencies between subculture interactions, psychological contracts and knowledge sharing at both sites. We conclude the section with a summary.

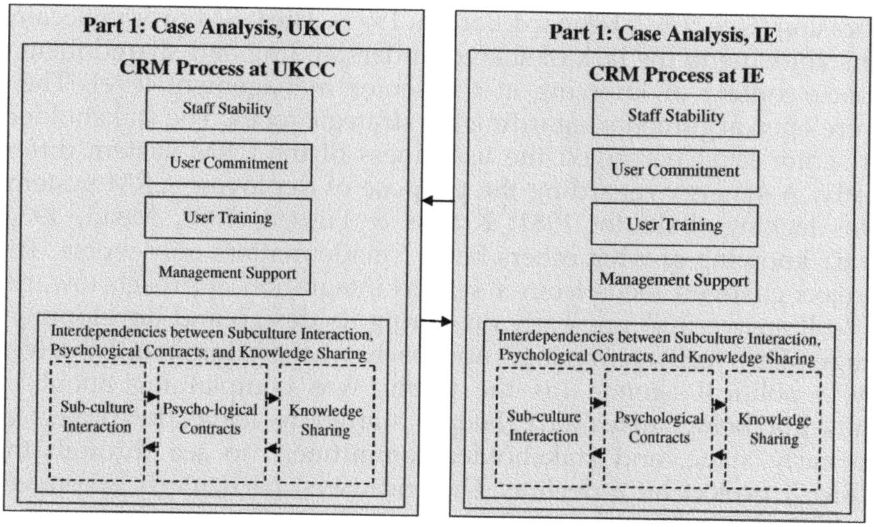

Figure 7.1 *Framework: Comparing "Process" at both research sites*

Part 2: Public/Private Sector Comparison using Willcocks and Harrow (1992)

- Differential customer base; as both the organisations have a differing clientele
- Differing goals; social goals vs. profit goals
- Complex and debated performance indicators vs. mainly quantitative financial measures
- More ill defined policy directives; complexity of policy implementation vs. relatively less ambiguous policy
- Relative openness of government and decision making; stress on representatives vs. relative secrecy; stress on business confidentiality
- Wide stakeholder base vs. primary focus on shareholders
- Extensive accountability vs. restricted accountability
- Primary resource base from public taxes vs. primary resource base from operational returns and borrowing
- Multiple values and goals; service, public interest, equity, professionalism, consumer participation,
- Complex trade-offs vs. relatively restricted
- Statutory and parliamentary regulation; codes of conduct vs. board of directors; company planning frameworks
- Needs of national economic management vs. market place signals, e.g. business lending rate

Figure 7.2 *Framework for assessing distinctive sectoral influences*

Staff Stability and User Commitment at UKCC and IE.COM

Staff stability suffered heavily at UKCC and the CRM project became "a ship no one wanted to stay on". The project ran into difficulties at an early stage after an illusion of consensus was shaken by discussions in the steering group meetings, resulting in a negative abrasion (Gee, 1992; Leonard-Barton, 1995). The CRM project became unstable due to the lack of shared understanding and shared mental space/context of knowing at the senior management level. There were open arguments regarding the strategic focus. The stakeholders at senior level perceived the usefulness of the CRM system differently. A synergy regarding the purpose of deploying CRM systems was lacking (Bakhtin, 1981; Krauss & Fussell, 1991; Mead, 1934) and "knowing of what others know" made matters only worse. The project changed focus from a system integration approach towards a "call answering" one early on during its design and development stage. The "call answering" approach was predominantly driven by a political agenda (as the public was complaining about its calls not being answered). People started to leave the project at an early stage, and stakeholder commitment to see through the CRM X project hit a decline. The end-users, particularly secondees leaving the Independent Company managed Contact Centre, were happy to leave the place due to their lack of commitment to CRM X. Their contract agreement did not allow them to be upgraded to a team leader position. Moreover, they had much stronger "mutual high-obligations" types of psychological contracts with their own back-offices and decided to move back (Shore & Barksdale, 1998).

In comparison, at IE, there was initial senior management support to spreading an integrative culture through using a CRM system. Executive leadership was involved on a full-time basis starting at Vice Presidential level. However, senior management did not understand the technical and cultural complexity of the project at an early stage. This resulted in data misfit issues. Moreover, senior management perceived the system as facilitating customer service and presenting a unified IE to its customers. The end-users saw it as a forecasting tool for the management. There was also an illusion of consensus regarding the state and quality of legacy data (Gee, 1992, Ross *et al.*, 1977). This illusion continued, and, as a result, data misfit issues affected the user commitment negatively at IE.COM. The end-users, moreover, perceived the system as being too rigid and slowing down the speed of their service to the customers instead of speeding it up. The updates to the CRM system were perceived as "kick backs". Even at a later stage end-user involvement was limited, which caused a lot of frustration and stress. The mechanistic and rigid organizational architecture did not make things easier either. Thus at both sites a learning organizational type of environment with reciprocity of relationships was missing (Krogh *et al.*, 2000).

Both CEOs left before the completion of deployment of the CRM systems at our research sites. The decision to deploy CRM was made at the top end at both sites. At UKCC the CEO saw a CRM system in Brisbane, and after his return wanted to introduce one for UKCC. At IE it was its CEO's eleventh integration initiative to integrate the segregated business units of IE. CRM projects at both sites were implemented using a top down approach without any end-user involvement in the decision making processes. No external user involvement was considered. As a result end-users did not feel any ownership of the project and felt stressed. At UKCC they eventually started to leave the Independent Company managed contact centre, whereas at IE.COM this gave rise to the birth of a "guru culture". The end-users at both sites felt under compulsion to use the system and many chose not to do so. As a result their commitment to the system suffered. The end-user psychological contracts at both sites were of "employee under-obligation" in type. User commitment was also affected by the technical issues arising at both sites. At UKCC it was the lack of system integration with the back-office and at IE.COM the double entries which respectively slowed down the end users in serving their customers effectively.

There was some prolonged interaction at the senior and middle management level at both sites. However, the psychological contracts were different. At UKCC stakeholders at senior management level lacked unanimity regarding the perceived purpose of the CRM project. Their differing perspectives resulted in negative abrasion and lack of "mutual perspective taking" (Boland & Tenkasi, 1996). Their psychological contracts as an outcome of the above were predominantly of "mutual low-obligation" type (Shore & Barksdale, 1998). At IE, on the other hand, there was shared and mutual understanding regarding the purpose of CRM Y at senior management level. This resulted in "mutual high-obligations" types of psychological contracts (Shore & Barksdale, 1998). Furthermore, the interaction took place in a non threatening environment enabling stakeholders to agree, resulting in shared mental space/"shared context for knowing" and shared benefits.

To summarize the above, staff stability was poorer at UKCC compared with that of IE at the senior management level. However, both sites lost their CEO before the completion of the project. End-user involvement was missing and external user involvement was not considered.

End-users at UKCC decided to leave, and go back to their back-office positions, in order to get away from the Independent Company managed Contact Centre. At IE.COM end-users found their own work-arounds through social networks using their invisible colleges, giving rise to a "guru culture" (Orlikowski & Iacono, 2001; Orlikowski & Tyre, 1994). User commitment at both sites was low, even lower at UKCC as the secondees did not even want to stay in the CRM project. The end-users at both sites established "employee under-obligation" types of psychological contracts with the management as they felt compelled to use the system. They also perceived the system to be more controlling than facilitating in nature. A learning organizational type of environment with reciprocity of relationships was missing at both sites.

User Training

The user training given at UKCC was by an outsourced organization, namely an Independent Company, which also managed the Contact Centre for UKCC. Training provided by Independent Company did not impress the UKCC secondees and management. Independent Company did not have enough knowledge about UKCC and its subcultures. Independent Company interactions with UKCC were not on a prolonged basis and did not allow creative abrasion to take place (Leonard-Barton, 1995; Newell *et al.*, 2002). Following Boland and Tenkasi (1996), this resulted in a training which was not based on "mutual perspective taking".

At UKCC there was an agreement at senior management level between UKCC and Independent Company that established a mutual psychological contract (Shore & Barksdale, 1998). This agreement was not shared by secondees. Secondees brought with them an immense wealth of experience regarding the UKCC culture in a non-codified form which was not exploited to its maximum capacity (Leonard-Barton & Kraus, 1985). Moreover where secondee expertise was exploited, it was done without providing any extrinsic reward, which resulted in "employee low-obligation" types of psychological contracts between the Independent Company management and UKCC secondees (Shore & Barksdale, 1998). There was also a "we and them" culture between secondees and non-secondees. Secondees as per end of 2004 were leaving the Independent Company managed contact centre and going back to UKCC where they felt at home. Their loyalties continued to lie at UKCC (Janssens *et al.*, 2003).

Training at UKCC was only three to four weeks long and was different for secondees as compared with non-secondees. At IE.COM it was even shorter. Super-users were first trained for two and a half days on the system and then used as trainers to train the rest of the end-users. The super-users were used to influence the attitudes and perceived usefulness of the end-users of the system (Davis, 1989). Their brief was to convince people of the benefits of a completely new database and layout, a task they found difficult. This was partly due to the fact that they had yet to get their own minds set around what the new system could offer them. Trainers of the super-users were convinced that this was the right thing to do and apparently had an illusion of consensus with the super-users without understanding the whole picture. They did not see the mistrust in the system perceived by the super-users was going to be passed on to the other users. The so called "T-shaped skills" and "shared context for knowing" were limited (Iansiti, 1993; Newell *et al.*, 2002). As a result many users—particularly from the Sales Section—did not use the system.

Management at UKCC admitted to the inadequacy of the training more openly. The CRM X training was provided by an outsourced company lacking in UKCC cultural knowledge. Departmental managers including the CRM project manager expressed their dissatisfaction over the quality of training. At IE comments regarding the short duration of training were made. However, IE.COM still perceived that, given the short amount of time, they did well. End-users including super-users at IE.COM openly expressed their feelings over the short duration and inadequacy of the CRM Y training (Pliskin *et al.*, 1993).

Unlike UKCC, IE.COM took steps to involve the end-users in the user training process. A longer training duration could have helped the super-users to master the system and get their mind set around it. This in turn could have helped them to communicate the benefits of CRM Y more effectively to the rest of the end-users. UKCC tried to exploit the non-codified knowledge possessed by the secondees when they realized that secondees did not want to stay at the contact centre anymore. A timely use of secondees' expertise in the training process could have helped in the sharing of experientially-based non-codified knowledge—in the form of "tricks of the trade", work-arounds and shortcuts—between secondees and non-secondees. Secondee involvement at an early stage could have resulted in enhanced user ownership and autonomy.

End-users at both our research sites were using the system under compulsion, and were not convinced regarding its benefits. At both sites the end-users would have liked to have had a longer training duration. Our findings suggest that end-users interacting with CRM systems under compulsion and time constraints chose not to use the systems. Moreover, power based relationships only resulted in illusions of consensus at both sites; people did not reveal their innermost feelings and agreed only at the level of words (Gee, 1992; Leonard-Barton, 1995). The resulting psychological contracts were "employee under-obligation" in type (Anderson & Schalk, 1998; Makin *et al.*, 1996; Rousseau, 1995; Shore & Barksdale, 1998; Thibaut & Kelley, 1959).

In summarizing the above, we find that training duration at both sites was short. It was much shorter at IE.COM. At IE.COM however, end-users were involved in the training process compared with UKCC, where secondee involvement in the training process was minimal. The training did not impress the management at UKCC and they criticized it very openly. While IE management admitted the limitations of the training yet they perceived it to be sufficient. End-users at both sites criticized the inadequacy of the training quite openly. Furthermore, the end-users felt compelled to use the system. There was also an illusion of consensus between the super-users and their trainers regarding the usefulness and duration of the training. A prolonged training programme with effective involvement of end-users could have helped better to communicate the CRM Y benefits to the end-users at IE.COM. At UKCC, Independent Company management could have been able to capture and exploit secondees' non-codified knowledge by involving them in the training process at an early stage.

Management Support

Mintzberg (1987) and Orlikowski and Hofman (1997) suggest that people talk about strategies in one way, that is as a plan with fixed steps to achieve a known goal, while implementing them, if at all, in another, more ad hoc way, to accommodate unforeseen circumstances. At UKCC, strong support was given to those who supported the "call answering" focus strategy. This was due to the fact that the public was not getting through and politicians wanted this issue to be resolved as quickly as possible. Senior management including the Former Head of IT and the Strategic Director of Resources agreed to take on board CRM X at the level of words. Their innermost feelings when revealed showed differing mind sets and frames resulting in negative abrasion (Orlikowski & Gash, 1994). People were reluctant to share their frames and did not change their perceptions regarding CRM X strategy. The project changed its focus from a system integration approach towards a "call answering" one. Business and IT were not aligned (Willcocks & Margetts, 1994).

Davidson (2002) argues that frames and shifts in frame salience (frames are cognitive structures or mental models that are held by individuals) influence sense-making during requirement determination. This study helps to provide an understanding of how interpretive power is exercised in an IS project. Moving on from frames to shared frames, Orlikowski and Gash (1994) show shared frames as closely related to the concept of sub-cultures. Individuals—drawing on their shared frames—engage in symbolic action and thereby construct a social reality that reflects their common assumptions, beliefs and understandings and that includes particular rules, rituals and customary practice. According to Geertz (1973) and Van Maanen and Barley (1985), sub-cultures rely heavily on cognitive elements such as common frames of reference. The Strategic Director of Resources's supporters at UKCC shared their frames and had a mutual, shared understanding. This was also the case with the Former Head of IT's supporters. They also shared their frames and had a shared understanding regarding an integrated solution, in which systems need to talk to each other, in order to provide a "one-stop-service". The two groups however, did not have a common shared frame (Davidson, 2002). The innermost feelings, when revealed instead of creating a shared understanding resulted in a divide between the partners (Leonard-Barton, 1995).

Bloomfield and Vurdubaki (1994) highlight the problematic nature of the boundary between the "technical" and the "social" and its consequences in respect of understanding the relationship between technological and organizational change. The power shown by the technical experts needs to be balanced by bringing in the social part of the organization. The knowledge shared at the senior management level regarding their innermost feelings created a negative type of abrasion between members of senior management and caused division based on different approaches and differential interests. The stakeholders with a system integration approach were classified as "IT people" by the group that supported the Strategic Director of Resources. The group supporting the Strategic Director of Resources claimed to have the business perspective on the whole CRM situation. The above shows that differing perceptions not only created a divide but also had a negative affect on the implementation process of CRM X at UKCC.

The survey done by Price Waterhouse (1991, 1992) states that 47% of the IT directors in UK saw that their main problem is the culture gap existing between IT and business professionals. Furthermore, 56% of IT directors believed that the culture gap was losing or seriously delaying IT opportunities for their companies to gain competitive advantage. Several authors have discussed the culture gap between systems analysts and computer specialists charged with information systems (IS) implementation and business users (Fincham, 1994; Grindley, 1992; Hinton, 1994; Kumar & Bjorn-Andersen, 1990). In an overview of the literature Willcocks *et al.* (2003) corroborate the persistence of these types of culture gaps into the new century. At UKCC the two differing perceptions created a sub-cultural divide which continued to affect the implementation of CRM project negatively at departmental and end-user level. At the departmental level managers perceived their senior management support in the project as poor. Poor management support was also perceived by secondees at the Independent Company managed Contact Centre. Management there was not able to establish a "mutual high-obligations" type of psychological contract between them and the secondees and thus were not able to exploit the non-codified knowledge in the form of "tricks of the trade" possessed by the secondees (Shore & Barksdale, 1998). As a result of "employee low-obligation" type of psychological contract between secondees and Independent Company management, the secondees decided to move back to their old back-office jobs at UKCC. Differing employment conditions for the end-users resulted in issues like "we and them" culture between secondees and non-secondees, creating yet another divide at end-user level. Secondees continued to maintain their "mutual high-obligations" types of psychological contracts with their back-offices and expressed happiness over their moving back to UKCC back-offices.

According to Orlikowski and Gash (1994), to interact with technology, people have to make sense of it; and in this sense-making process, they develop particular assumptions, expectations and knowledge of the technology, which then serve to shape subsequent actions toward it. While these interpretations become taken-for-granted and are rarely brought to the surface and reflected on, they nevertheless remain significant in influencing how actors in organizations think about and act toward technology. At IE senior management support was predominantly unified. This led to the creation of deployment teams, working on a full-time basis to assure the success of the CRM project. However, the Development team misinterpreted data misfit issues and perceived the data to be in a better state than was really the case. This in turn led to data migration issues. Furthermore, data misfit issues continued to cause trouble for the end-users in the form of double entries, duplications and duplication of effort. End-users openly expressed their distress over a lack of support regarding data misfit issues.

The rigid mechanistic organizational structure at IE did not allow any "creative abrasion" to take place during the pre-deployment phase. The prolonged interactions between the Development Team and the end-user were predominantly based on power based work relations and did not facilitate the development of "T-shaped skills" (Iansiti, 1993). This resulted in people agreeing on the surface avoiding conflicts. The innermost feelings regarding the quality of legacy data did not get revealed. The resulting psychological contracts were of "employee under-obligation" in type and did not facilitate the development of a mutual perspective (Boland & Tenkasi, 1996; Shore & Barksdale, 1998).

In a somewhat mechanistic IE culture, feedback from the management regarding end-user complaints was minimal. According to reports to us, the management at IE.COM were perceived as more controlling and monitoring than facilitating and enabling. Response time to end-user complaints was long and slow. Management perceived the CRM tool as facilitating end-users in their interactions with the customers. End-users on the other hand perceived it as a forecasting tool which was also used to control and monitor each move they made. The resulting psychological contracts were of "employee under-obligation" in type highlighting a lack of mutual perspective (Shore & Barksdale, 1998). The end-users expressed their distress over a lack of management support regarding issues such as double entries, duplications and duplication of effort. They ended up finding their own work-arounds and making an effective use of their invisible colleges, resulting in an élite "guru" culture.

In both UKCC and IE end-users used the system under compulsion and avoided using it in several instances when it suited them. At UKCC there were instances when end-users made hand notes while serving a customer and later on entered the data on to the system to fulfil a need regulated by the system. At IE.COM Sales Section decided not use the system at all making matters worse for the rest of the business units. At both sites the end-user psychological contracts with the management were "employee under-obligation" in type not allowing the establishing of a mutual perspective and "shared context for knowing" (Boland & Tenkasi, 1996; Newell *et al.*, 2002).

In summarizing the above, we conclude that management support at both sites was in general insufficient in several respects. IE senior management were more unified in their approach towards the deployment of CRM Y than were UKCC, where strong differing opinions and perceptions caused a sub-cultural divide which trickled down to middle management and finally to the end-user level causing severe staff retention issues. At IE.COM the role of management became more controlling and monitoring than facilitating. The mechanistic organizational architecture made matters worse for the end-users. Feedback to end-user complaints had a long response time which resulted in end-users finding work-arounds using their invisible colleges. End-user psychological contracts with the IE.COM management were of "employee under-obligation" in type and failed to create a "mutual perspective" and a "shared mental space".

Secondees at UKCC decided to move back to their back-offices having retained a good relationship with their previous management there. Independent Company management were not able to establish a "mutual high-obligations" type of psychological contract with the secondees and did not exploit the non-codified knowledge possessed by the secondees regarding UKCC back-offices. We conclude from our research findings that power based relationships and poor management support led to "employee under-obligation" types of psychological contracts. We also found that end-users at IE.COM stayed in the project discovering their own work-arounds through using their invisible colleges effectively. At UKCC the secondees chose to leave and move back to their old jobs in the back-office.

Subculture Interactions, Psychological Contracts, and Knowledge Sharing

Prolonged subculture interactions at senior management level were limited at both sites. At UKCC interactions at senior management level resulted in negative abrasion furthering the subculture gap between the social and so called IT domains. The resulting psychological contracts were "mutual low-obligation" in type. The sub-cultural gap continued to haunt the project life cycle even during the post implementation stage. At IE interactions at senior management level were predominantly formal and there was a shared understanding regarding the implementation of CRM Y. Their psychological contracts were largely "mutual high-obligations" in type.

The "mutual low-obligation" types of psychological contracts at UKCC's senior management level did not allow a sharing of frames and thus people remained stuck in their own understandings and perceptions of the strategic implementation of CRM X system. Stakeholders at senior management level did not reach a stage of

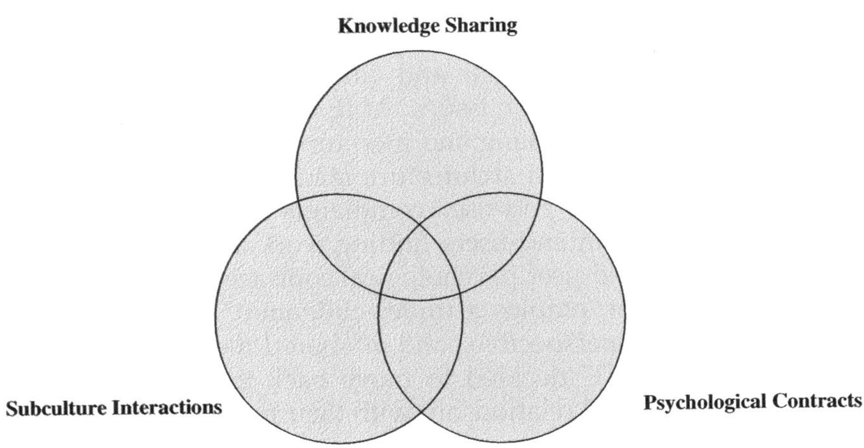

Figure 7.3 *Interdependencies between psychological contracts, subculture interactions and knowledge sharing*

"shared mental space" and "knowing of what others know". Their prolonged interactions only resulted in negative and destructive abrasion. The stakeholders at senior level were not able to resolve their differences and establish a shared understanding.

The above indicates that very little sharing of individual understandings took place. Success, it has been suggested, depends not only on how effectively diverse individuals are able to organize and develop their unique knowledge competencies, but also how they can integrate and utilise their distinctive knowledge both effectively and synergistically (Nonaka, 1994). This synergy can be obtained if barriers to knowledge sharing across key sub-cultures are understood. In our case at UKCC, the senior management did not reach a shared understanding and therefore a synergy which could have facilitated an open sharing of knowledge was not achieved. According to Boland and Tenkasi (1996), it requires a process of mutual "perspective taking" where distinctive individual knowledge is exchanged, evaluated and integrated with that of others in the organization. The presence of "mutual low-obligation" types of psychological contracts did not allow the development of a mutual perspective.

At IE, on the other hand, there was some shared understanding regarding the deployment of CRM Y and resulting psychological contracts were of "mutual high-obligations" type at the senior level. They had formulated clear guidelines towards training and piloting. The system was first tested and deployed in Smyrna Georgia. Senior management hoped that lessons learned from their initial deployment would make the deployment at IE UK easier. However, that was not the case. The project suffered drawbacks in the areas of data migration and training issues covered elsewhere in this chapter.

Attitudes of conflict avoidance and some conservative habits may have also prevented the sharing of knowledge regarding the state of legacy data. Scholars argue that if most leading members of an organization are not comfortable with change and not willing to take risks, different views and perspectives could remain hidden, and therefore knowledge not culturally legitimated may be suppressed (Fahey & Prusak, 1998). This happened during the implementation process of CRM Y and inhibited the development of individual opinions or ideas. Fahey and Prusak (1998) refer to the failure to establish, challenge and align a shared context for the members of an organization as "one of the eleven deadliest sins of Knowledge Management". This shared context requires engagement in open, honest, supportive, and critical dialogue to develop different and new views. A process that permits the surfacing and examining of interpretations can allow the shaking of the background of consensus and open the possibility of mutual interpretation. This can enable the achievement of a new definition of the situation in which all participants can share (Habermas, 1979). An informal setting—according to Van Maanen (1986)—can help in voicing the differences and facing the conflicts in a constructive manner. Communication between the Development Team and end-users lacked a creative abrasion type of environment, through which innermost feelings and truth about the quality of the legacy data could have been revealed. The teams also had a limited interaction between themselves. These limited interactions combined with a limited end-user involvement resulted in a false perception regarding the state and quality of legacy data.

The CRM Y deployment had a formal, rigid and mechanistic structure. Strong hierarchical enterprises prevent smooth cross-functional communication and consequently inhibit cross-functional cooperation or knowledge sharing. Breaking down hierarchies can enable knowledge sharing (Nonaka, 1994). Organizations such as IE, that maintain hierarchical levels and silos will not encourage it. Knowledge in such organizations frequently becomes "sticky"—that is residing in one area or silo and not easily moved to the other parts of the organization (Bartlett & Ghoshal, 1998). Knowledge regarding the state and quality of data remained buried in the minds of end-users and raised its evil head in the shape of double entries and duplications. The end-users may not have been honest in their opinions regarding the quality of the legacy data while interacting with people from the Development Team (Wathne *et al.*, 1996).

The competitive nature of the jobs at IE.COM did not facilitate an open interaction type of environment. A round table where informal discussions, creative abrasions and exchange of ideas could take place was missing. Furthermore, as discussed earlier in this chapter, the controlling and monitoring role of management only led to the establishment of "employee under-obligation" types of psychological contracts. Fear as an emotion is closely linked with the kind of psychological contract that exists between the two sub-cultures. Rousseau (1995) asserts that mutuality is key for a psychological contract to provide acceptable outcomes—she argues that it is only when both parties have something to gain that they will work to ensure a successful result. However at least part of such a psychological contract will be implicit (Makin *et al.*, 1996), resulting in a lack of clarity for both parties (Anderson & Schalk, 1998). Although each party has a clear and conscious view about the key elements of the exchange they expect (such as reward for achieving goals or the sense of obligation to work late to meet a deadline), other elements will be subconscious and therefore much harder to define (Makin *et al.*, 1996). In our case at IE.COM end-users felt under pressure to use the system to maintain their job security (Davenport *et al.*, 1998). However, Sales Section acted boldly to resist the pressure and decided not to use the system.

There were occasions when people from different business units worked together on the basis of shared benefits. These types of interactions facilitated a free sharing of "tricks of the trade" resulting in "mutual high-obligations" types of psychological contracts. The end results were in the form of saved effort and good team work. A joint effort eliminated the duplication of effort in the above case. There were also other cases where less codified knowledge was shared freely. This happened through invisible colleges resulting in a "guru culture" where information was shared as a favour towards each other.

Knowledge—particularly tacit knowledge in the form of "tricks of the trade" "work-rounds"—remained buried in the vertical and business-unit silos because of the mechanistic organizational architecture at IE.COM. Interactions in general were more formalized within a mechanistic framework. Krogh *et al.* (2000) argue that an organization must actively pursue the work context as a "learning organization" where the individuals of that organization are attuned to learning new things. A "learning organization" environment in IE's mechanistic organizational culture could not be achieved at IE.COM. Learning implies encountering and assimilating new facts. The end-users were not prepared to encounter CRM Y, and were stressed over the fact that data was in a poor state. As a result of inadequate subculture interactions at the end-user level double entries to the systems continued to occur making matters worse.

People who are able to control relevant resources, and thereby increase others' dependence on them, are more able to achieve the outcomes they desire (Salancik & Pfeffer, 1978). This happened in the "guru culture". Gurus or experts of the field shared knowledge through invisible colleges creating a yet another knowledge silo and a digital divide.

At UKCC managers in departmental silos withheld their non-codified knowledge through not allowing full access to the back-office system as a result of their mistrust in CRM X. Their mistrust was also related to lack of involvement in the implementation and decision making processes. As per 2004 they were very sceptical of the system and were constantly looking for better alternatives than CRM X. Departmental management, particularly Environmental Services and Council Tax, were pleased to have their secondees return to back-offices. According to our respondents from Neighbourhood Services, Council Tax and Environmental Services, the information regarding call handling sent to them by Independent

Company managed Contact Centre lacked quality. As a result of this the departmental managers had established an "employee under-obligation" type of psychological contract with the Independent Company management. This was also evident through their sympathetic comments towards the secondees in their return to the back-offices.

The research on social information processing (Salancik & Pfeffer, 1978), power (Pettigrew, 1973; Pfeffer, 1980), specialisation (Burns & Stalker, 1961; Daft & Lengel, 1986; Lawrence & Lorsch, 1967), and organizational cultures (Gregory, 1983; Pettigrew, 1979, Riley, 1983; Schein, 1985; Strauss, 1978) further suggests that people tend to share assumptions, knowledge, and expectations with others with whom they have close working relationships. Similarly, social interaction and negotiation over time create opportunities for the development and exchange of similar points of view (Brown & Diguid, 1998; Gray *et al.*, 1985; Isabella, 1990). There was some sharing of uncodified knowledge and ways of doing things between secondees and non-secondees where they sat next to or close to each other. This confirms what our literature led us to believe. Moreover, non-secondees felt slightly inferior to their colleagues because of their lower pay scale and lack of back-office knowledge. Management at Independent Company did not anticipate this and were unable to facilitate the establishment of "mutual high-obligations" types of psychological contracts between secondees and non-secondees. This resulted in an "us and them" culture as reported by our respondents. The "us and them culture" caused a divide and inhibited knowledge sharing in general.

In summarizing the above, we conclude that psychological contracts play an important role in the sharing of less codified knowledge relating to work practices. Interactions even though prolonged may end up in negative abrasion or an illusion of consensus at the surface of words. In the case of UKCC prolonged interactions created a divide and a destructive type of abrasion at the senior management level. In the case of IE.COM people withheld their innermost feelings to avoid conflict in maintaining their job security. Knowledge, as know-how, "tricks of the trade", and learning-from-doing was shared through invisible colleges and other informal settings. However, this informal sharing also gave rise to a "guru" subculture. In that type of élite culture information was shared in the form of favours towards each other. IE.COM did not exploit the "guru culture" effectively.

We also conclude that prolonged interactions with shared benefits led to "mutual high-obligations" types of psychological contracts facilitating a free sharing of "tricks of the trade". Further the lack of an effective end-user involvement led to "employee under-obligation" types of psychological contracts and lack of ownership. This in turn led to staff retention issues at UKCC and lack of trust and commitment to the CRM project at IE.COM. Our analysis has led us to believe that prolonged interaction combined with "mutual high-obligations" types of psychological contracts based on shared benefits can facilitate a free sharing of less codifiable but relevant forms of knowledge. Furthermore, sharing under these circumstances is not bound to a certain group of people but can take a new shape as it did in the case of IE.COM. There it took the shape of a "guru culture" where gurus shared information with other gurus from other hierarchies and business units.

PART 2: PUBLIC AND PRIVATE SECTOR COMPARISONS

In this section we compare and contrast the findings from our research sites. We show that although there may be several differences, this research has also identified a number of similarities across the two contrasting sectors. We base our analysis around the sectoral distinguishing features detailed in Figure 7.2.

Differential Customer Base

In this section we discuss the impact of different clienteles on the performance of CRM from a knowledge sharing perspective. We critically analyze the differential customer base at both sites in light of the literature.

At UKCC the customers were a general public not happy at the way UKCC was handling their calls. The urgency to have something done regarding people's inability to get through to the council was predominantly a political agenda. This changed the project focus from a system integration approach towards a short term solution. Mintzberg (1987), and Orlikowski and Hofman (1997), suggest that people talk about strategies in one way, namely as a plan with fixed steps to achieve a known goal, while implementing them in another more ad hoc way, to accommodate unforeseen circumstances. In our case at UKCC strategy did change, but not to accommodate unforeseen circumstances. It changed to accommodate a short term solution of getting the phones answered promptly. The "call answering" focus was not strategically thought through and had implications on the successful closing of delivery loops by the call centre agents. Management at the back-offices was satisfied with the quality of the service provided by the call centre. There was also a stress factor relating to the need to answer calls as quickly as possible at the Independent Company managed call centre. The problem arose when end-users, particularly the non-secondees, had to answer phone calls from the public in the shortest time possible without having enough knowledge regarding the back-office culture. Secondees, who possessed the non-codified knowledge regarding the UKCC back-offices, decided to move back to their old jobs because of the "employee under-obligation" type of psychological contract between them and the Independent Company management (Shore & Barksdale, 1998). According to reports from the departmental management, non-secondees, when not able to answer a query, redirected the public to the back-offices, thus taking away the main purpose of having CRM X system in the first place. Independent Company did not have an in-depth knowledge of the back-offices and the UKCC culture, which made matters worse. Independent Company as an outsource services company lacked "T-shaped skills" which could have helped them to understand the needs of secondees better. It would also have helped them to exploit the non-codified knowledge possessed by secondees in the shape of "tricks of the trade" (Iansiti, 1993; Orlikowski & Tyre, 1994; Vincenti, 1984).

Pliskin *et al.* (1993) point out that the same information system may have a different meaning for different people, such as system analysts and users who may not have the same points of view concerning the system. At IE.COM, management hoped the system would facilitate the end-users in their interactions with the external customers. End-users (as internal customers), however, perceived CRM Y as a controlling and monitoring device. This, together with the double entries, created technology bottlenecks and slowed down the customer service instead of speeding it up. CRM Y evolved over time as the users found new ways and work-arounds in working with the system (Orlikowski & Iacono, 2001, Orlikowski & Tyre; 1994). End-users at IE.COM discovered their short cuts and work-arounds using invisible colleges in getting their jobs done. At UKCC end-users did the same. Instead of using the CRM X system they answered the phone calls making notes and taking help from secondees wherever and whenever it was possible. A sharing of "tricks of the trade" happened but only to some extent. The sharing of "tricks of the trade" was free in the invisible colleges at IE.COM and was related to "mutual high-obligations" types of psychological contracts (Shore & Barksdale, 1998; Van Maanen, 1986).

In both cases the end-users felt an obligation to use the system but chose not to use it whenever possible. Furthermore, in both cases the external customer involvement was largely ignored. Business Process Re-engineering work done by the development team at IE had limited participation, acceptance and ownership, at the grass roots level. At UKCC and IE.COM, IT capabilities did not support business processes, and business processes were not in harmony with the capabilities IT could provide. Moreover, limited end-user involvement had a negative impact on user commitment.

We discovered that end-users at both sites worked under similar stressful conditions to answer customer queries. Moreover, the system, instead of creating a "one-stop-service", actually inhibited the service it was designed to provide. Knowledge hoarding occurred at both sites (Bartlett & Ghoshal, 1998). At UKCC, secondees withheld their share of non-codified knowledge and took it back with them to the UKCC back-offices. At IE.COM it remained buried in the business unit silos due to the competitive nature of their work. The "guru culture" added to yet another knowledge silo where knowledge got shared only between the gurus. The differing clienteles may have had differing implications for the management at both sites. However, in the case of both cohorts of end-users using the CRM system for customer interactions, it created a stressful environment. Statistics recorded in order to monitor end-user's call time acted as a stress factor. As a result the service quality suffered at both sites. Errors such as duplications and double entries due to a lack of cross-cultural interaction did not speed up nor facilitate a successful customer service. At both sites, the lack of sharing of "tricks of the trade" was also related to job security and power (Davenport *et al.*, 1998; Pfeffer & Sutton, 1999). People, who are able to control relevant resources, and thereby increase others' dependence on them, are able to achieve the outcomes they desire (Salancik & Pfeffer, 1978). Secondees and gurus held desirable non-codified/tacit knowledge. In the case of secondees it enabled them to move back to UKCC and in the case of IE.COM, gurus found a way out of the double entries and duplications without having to use a time consuming vertical reporting structure.

We conclude that although the customer bases in the two cases were different, the issues faced by the end-users were remarkably similar in nature. At both sites the end-users perceived that the system complicated and slowed down their progress in securing an efficient customer service. Furthermore, end-users at both sites felt under compulsion to use the system but decided not to use it when the opportunity arose. No external customer involvement was considered by the senior management at either site. We also found that tacit/non-codified knowledge hoarding issues were related to job security and power. At UKCC, secondees used this power as insurance to move back to their old jobs, whereas at IE it resulted in a "guru culture" giving rise to a clique type power structure where gurus only shared their "tricks of the trade" with gurus.

Differing Goals: Social Goals vs. Profit Goals

Despite the two organizations having different overriding goals in terms of social versus profit goals, this seemed to account for very little at the level of organizational functioning to implement CRM. According to our findings both cases had a history of "part technology" strategy. IT systems were bought and implemented without any consideration to overall system integration. IE wanted to integrate the segregated business across all their geographies. UKCC's CRM initiative was triggered by a political agenda with a "call answering" focus; however, "vanilla" applications seemed to be popular in UKCC as well because they required less in-house expertise, a general trend also found at IE (Parr & Shanks, 2000; Willcocks & Sykes, 2000).

Claver *et al.* (2001) also underline the cultural consistency which the implementation of an IS requires. They conclude by claiming that IT systems are implemented following technical analysis and considerations, with little if any regard for business needs. However, if the corporate culture of a company is dominated by the business experts with limited knowledge of IT the reverse can happen. In the case of UKCC business experts implemented a new system without understanding the implications of the implementation process. Our research findings indicate that whilst calls at UKCC were getting through the quality of service was suffering. While CRM X met the "call answering" focus objective to some extent it also raised further issues. These issues included the poor quality of information provided by call centre agents (non-secondees) at the Independent Company managed Contact Centre. The four stages of knowledge generation outlined by Nonaka and Takeuchi (1995) did not have enough time to take place. The leaving of secondees not only created a non-codified knowledge vacuum but also had a negative affect on the service quality at the Contact Centre.

The Former Head of IT's system integration approach—which was favoured at the departmental level as well—may have been an appropriate implementation strategy after all. El Sawy (1985) argues that if IT specialists are members of a corporation or are directly related to it, they are part of an organizational culture and none of them should be excluded from an analysis of organizational behaviour in the face of IT. Senior management at UKCC changed its course and ignored the implications of a "call answering" approach to knowledge sharing at departmental level. The CRM Project suffered from a lack of in-house IT expertise support as people such as the Former Head of IT and the CRM Programme Manager resigned from their posts. Their expertise was not taken on board and their integrative approach was completely ignored.

"Public getting through" at UKCC also increased demands on the resources available at the back-offices (departments). According to our findings the CRM project created extra workload for the departments. The fact that people could call in and get through also meant that UKCC had to provide back-office services to the public. These back-office services had not been pushed to their limits when the public was not able to get through to UKCC previously. Our research indicates that although UKCC may have met their goal concerning getting the phones answered by their CRM initiative, yet they have exposed their limitations at departmental level. The CRM project pushed departmental resources to their limits, which also acted as an inhibitor to management commitment at the departmental level. Furthermore, a continual limited involvement in the development of CRM X made departments fall back to their old thinking of "part technology" strategy. The movement of secondees back to UKCC left the "call answering" goal vulnerable to even more quality issues.

According to Herschbach (1995), tacit/non-codified knowledge is embedded in technological activity to a greater extent than is normally recognized. In addition, tacit/non-codified knowledge has not disappeared with the use of more sophisticated ways of manufacturing based on the application of science and descriptive knowledge: "On the contrary, new forms of know-how have appeared and all these non-codified techniques play an important role both in industrial production and in technical and technological innovation" (Perrin, 1990). Polanyi (1966) has demonstrated that all human action involves some form of tacit/non-codified knowledge (Nonaka and Takeuchi, 1995). In our case at UKCC the non-codified knowledge in the form of "tricks of the trade" returned, buried in the minds of secondees, to the back-offices. Non-secondees with their limited understanding of UKCC culture, back-office non-codified knowledge and lacking any support from departmental level at UKCC, were not able to secure an efficient customer service at the Independent Company managed Contact Centre.

IE wanted customers to get a unified view of the organization. The management also wanted CRM Y to facilitate end-user interactions in order to provide an efficient service to customers. Our findings indicate that discrepancies during the BPR prior to CRM Y deployment had negative consequences in form of data misfit issues. Davis (1989) argues that perceived usefulness is a strong correlate of user acceptance. User acceptance at IE.COM was limited. Our research findings reveal that double entries and duplications caused stress and slowed down the end-users' ability to serve their customers efficiently.

Innovation diffusion theory recognizes that while the technical attributes of innovation per se may not be significant, perceptions of technology do matter, and are important factors influencing technology adoption. Pre-existing structures and cultures (internal context) shape differing stakeholder perceptions regarding new systems and their implementation and performance ("Process" and "Outcome", Pettigrew, 1997). Our analyses confirm that many end-users were not against the system per se. It was their perceptions as to its usefulness and its objective, which caused the difficulties. CRM Y was interpreted as a controlling and monitoring device by the end-users.

Scholars analyze information systems and organizational culture as two closely related issues in any firm. Organizations with a mechanistic culture tend to standardize the system implementation compared to organizations with an organic culture, where the implementation process for an IT system is more culture led (Burns & Stalker, 1961). The mechanistic organizational architecture at IE.COM acted as an inhibitor to the knowledge sharing processes. Knowledge, particularly the tacit/non-codified knowledge, became sticky and resided in vertical and horizontal silos. According to our findings lack of cross-cultural communication across business units at IE.COM did not facilitate a "unified IE" view.

In conclusion, both sites missed their targets to some extent. UKCC secured the "call answering" target and helped the public to get through. However, this exposed discrepancies at the departmental level pushing their resources to their limits which resulted in a decline in commitment towards CRM X. At IE.COM a segregated and mechanistic organizational architecture continued to haunt the CRM project resulting in knowledge silos along the vertical and horizontal axis. A "unified view" was hard to achieve as the end-users struggled with data misfit issues and duplications.

Complex and Debated Performance Indicators vs. Mainly Quantitative Financial Measures

In this section we discuss various performance indicators at UKCC and compare them with those at IE.COM. We discuss how CRM system performance has been measured at both sites linking it with relevant theories from our reviewed literature.

At both sites there were very few qualitative performance measures in place. At UKCC call rate was monitored using the "Call Stats" (statistics), whereas at IE.COM in addition to call monitoring, a different system (a forecasting system named SCOTT) was also used to control and monitor the use of CRM Y. End users at both sites felt that they were being monitored and controlled. "Mutual high-obligations" types of psychological contracts were missing as a result of a controlling and monitoring culture (Shore & Barksdale, 1998). This affected their user commitment negatively. Our findings indicate that people tied up with their headsets to their work places felt under pressure and were complaining about the stressful environment.

The CRM project at UKCC, according to our research findings, was all about quantity. The "call answering" focus strategy ignored the qualitative issues related to knowledge sharing between the front and back-offices. Creating a call centre to get the calls answered had qualitative consequences. These were not taken into consideration and inhibited successful implementation and post implementation processes. Moreover, the departmental managers were not happy with the quantitative measures. They wanted qualitative performance indicators and were not provided with such from the Independent Company management. This resulted in dissatisfaction on the managers' part. They actively started to look for parallel alternatives to CRM X.

At IE.COM CRM Y was not auditable. This was due to the fact that the system was still in its teething stages and was not perceived as reliable according to our reports. As the system was not auditable, there were groups such as Field Sales which did not feel obliged to use CRM Y. The people who were using the system were the ones without an option. Furthermore, the reports taken from the systems lacked qualitative information for the management at IE.COM. IE.COM had hopes for improvement regarding the system analytics as per 2004.

Our findings show that the methods used to measure the performance of CRM systems at both sides were predominantly quantitative. Qualitative measures to assess the knowledge created and shared were not in place. According to Nonaka (1994), strong hierarchical enterprises prevent smooth cross-functional communication and consequently inhibit cross-functional cooperation or knowledge sharing. Breaking down hierarchies can enable knowledge sharing. Organizations that maintain hierarchical levels and silos will not encourage it. Knowledge in such organizations frequently becomes "sticky" that is, residing in one area or silo and not easily moved to the other parts of the organization (Bartlett & Ghoshal, 1998). Perrin (1990) argues that the non-codified techniques play an important role in industrial production and in technical and technological innovation. There were no knowledge management systems in place at either site that could capture, retain and exploit knowledge, particularly less codified knowledge in the form of "tricks of the trade". Boland and Tenkasi (1996) argue that, in order to develop new products, the separate domains must interact and learn from each other in ways that will yield new insights into a problem, and new ideas for the successful production of improved products. At our research sites, there were no CRM team rooms or round tables where current CRM issues could be discussed and dealt with. Knowledge continued to reside in departmental and hierarchical sub-cultural silos. Scholars like Mumford *et al.* (1978) vote for user participation. However, in our cases, user participation was very limited and in some cases completely ignored. According to our findings, end-user involvement in the decision making process was completely ignored at both sites and otherwise when participation occurred, it was on management's terms and conditions and highly regulated. Our respondents at both sites openly admitted a lack of intrinsic satisfaction in relation to the CRM project.

In summary, both sites used predominantly quantitative measures to control and monitor the system usage. The quantitative measures did not include any financially related audits at IE.COM. At UKCC the quantitative measures led to a dissatisfied departmental management. The managers at the departments started to look for alternative systems. End-users at both sites felt controlled and monitored by the management. This had a negative affect on their commitment and resulted in "employee low-obligation" types of psychological contracts. Knowledge became sticky and remained in departmental and hierarchical sub-cultural silos. No knowledge management systems were in place at either of the sites. A round table or a neutral platform for discussing and resolving CRM issues was missing at both sites.

More Ill-defined Policy Directives; Complexity of Policy Implementation vs. Relatively Less Ambiguous Policy

At UKCC, around 1994, the senior management made a decision to move from a centralized IT structure to increased autonomy over buying in and outsourcing IT services by departments. As a result, the role of central IT became that of a support function. According to Willcocks and Margetts (1994), the newness and attractiveness (convenience/pricing) of technology led many public sector organizations to expose themselves to consultancy and supplier markets.

Various applications developed without consideration of a strategy for integration. IT solutions were bought in by different departments with little regard for cross departmental integration resulting in technology bottlenecks (Holland & Ben, 1999). Knowledge silos resulted from an ill-defined "part technology" policy through which Central IT ended up facilitating the development of departmental knowledge bottlenecks. According to our research findings the pattern of outsourcing the programming to a Third Party and the buying of hundreds of solutions continued for many years.

In 2000 came the UK government directive dictating a new policy, according to which UKCC were given the task of ensuring that all its services were available to citizens through electronic means by 2005. This government directive was intended to modernize the way public sector delivers policies, programmes and services to its customers/citizens. The above illustrates the government deadlines and speed of new legislation that Willcocks and Margetts (1994) talk about as pressure factors exposing organizations to consultant and supplier markets.

The purpose of IEG (Interactive Electronic Government) was to build local government services around customer/citizens' needs rather than the organizational structures of service providers, giving its customers a "one-stop-service". All levels of government were being encouraged to make full use of the potential for electronic service delivery to improve the responsiveness and quality of services.

The CRM Project at UKCC was an effort by the senior management to implement the IEG government policies. According to the new directive the role of central IT was to facilitate integration in order to achieve the objective of "one-stop-service". However, implementation of such an objective needed a high level of in-house IT expertise. According to our findings UKCC had very limited in-house IT expertise. Outsourcing was yet again a popular option available to the senior management. However, the CRM initiative missed the "one-stop-service" objective as they moved away from their initial integrative approach towards a "call answering" strategy. At the political leadership and senior management level the CRM initiative had succeeded in increasing public access to UKCC. Nevertheless, at departmental level it did not remove the knowledge bottlenecks and ended up re-enforcing the departmental silo mentality (Holland & Ben, 1999).

IE was similar to UKCC in their "part technology" strategy. Different business units at IE.COM operated as separate businesses without any consideration of system integration. CEO wanted to integrate the islands of businesses within IE. CRM Y was supposed to unify IE and facilitate customer interactions with IE. However, their CRM initiative could not facilitate a sub-cultural integration. According to our findings knowledge bottlenecks created by a segregated mechanistic organizational architecture continued to develop even during the post-implementation stage at IE.COM. Louis (1985) argues that the sub-cultures are the set of understandings or meanings shared by a group of people. The meanings are largely tacit among members, are clearly relevant to a particular group, and are distinctive to the group. Mechanistic hierarchical sub-cultural silos at IE.COM developed further, giving birth to a "guru" type subculture. The anticipated unifying of IE did not occur as CRM Y could not facilitate cross-cultural communication in a competitive and rigid environment (Boland & Tenkasi, 1996).

CRM Y was implemented mechanistically, without any deep understanding of sub-cultural and knowledge management issues. This resulted in data misfit issues which had an adverse affect on data integration. Double entries and duplications ended up creating more "prescriptive knowledge" silos. The data misfit issues combined with the strict and rigid work environment resulted in "employee low-obligation" types of psychological contracts (Shore & Barksdale, 1998). End-users perceived CRM Y as a forecasting tool used to monitor and control their actions and IE again fell short of achieving its unifying objective.

In conclusion, both sites suffered from "part technology" syndrome. Both considered CRM to be a means of integrating the separated departmental and business unit silos. At UKCC, the CRM project changed its direction and become focussed on short term results re-enforcing the departmental bottlenecks and failing to integrate the sub-cultural silos. At IE, it could not integrate and unify distinctively mechanistically isolated business unit structures. In both cases there was a lack of cross-cultural communication based on "mutual high-obligations" types of psychological contracts. As a result, knowledge sharing was very limited. We conclude that both sites faced severe difficulties in the implementation of their policies. At UKCC the role of Central IT changed from a "part technology" support function with the aim of facilitating system integration. However, this role did not get a chance to develop fully as the project changed its direction and became focussed on short term results. The inherent ambiguity of the above situation had an adverse effect on the departments. At IE the policies also led to ambiguity in that CRM was supposed to unify and facilitate, and yet the end-users perceived it to be predominantly a controlling and monitoring device.

Relative Openness of Government and Decision Making; Stress on Representatives vs. Relative Secrecy; Stress on Business Confidentiality

At UKCC and IE the decisions were made by the senior management without involving any internal or external end-users of CRM systems. Both sites had a narrow stakeholder base initially. More departments and business units were added on with time, and usage of the CRM system was given a high priority at both sites. However, at the Independent Company managed Contact Centre end-users whenever possible, made manual notes in helping the customers. They then later on logged their calls onto the system thus fulfilling a system need. At IE.COM even though the system was highly regulated, nevertheless end-users declined to use it whenever possible.

At IE.COM the competitive nature of the business resulted in duplication of efforts and double entries. However, when occasionally the possibility of working across the sub-cultural boundaries manifested itself, the resulting cross-cultural team work ended up saving effort and increasing efficiency. The rigidity of IE's mechanistic organizational culture did not allow many prolonged interactions across the business units (Burns & Stalker, 1961). This gave rise to information and knowledge bottlenecks. Non-codified Knowledge sharing when possible occurred within the business unit silos without being shared across the business units. The resulting psychological contracts established in such a competitive work environment were of "mutual low-obligation" type, where both partners were not willing to share any non-codified knowledge. This impeded the development of an environment enabling "mutual perspective" and "shared context for knowing" (Boland & Tenkasi, 1996; Newell *et al.*, 2002; Shore & Barksdale, 1998).

At UKCC the governance of the project was very much dominated by the "call answering" focus and did not allow an integrative approach. This divide, resulted in reinforcement of departmental silos (Bartlett & Ghoshal, 1998). The departments ended up planning their own independent alternatives, in parallel to the CRM project. The closed nature of the project governance persists, with its continuing narrow stakeholder base. Closed governance similarly presented itself at IE.COM, the lack of end-user involvement resulting in weak psychological contracts between the end-users and the management (Janssens *et al.*, 2003). Consequently issues regarding the poor quality of the legacy data were not exposed until a later stage of the implementation process.

Meyer and Rowan (1977) argue that sub-cultures at the periphery of an organization may not share information fully with sub-cultures at its technical core. A small team from UKCC's technical core (Central IT) worked with the Independent Company management without any involvement from the departments. This alienated the stakeholders, particularly secondees and departmental management, inhibiting the development of "mutual high-obligations" types of psychological contracts. This consequently had an adverse effect on tacit knowledge sharing, inhibiting the sharing of "tricks of the trade" (Orlikowski & Tyre, 1994; Shore & Barksdale, 1998; Vincenti, 1984). The above highlights the significance of micro-elements in the closed governance at UKCC.

According to Janssens *et al.* (2003), when investigating the employer obligation of long-term involvement and the employee obligations of personal investment, it was found that flexibility and loyalty are related to high affective (sic) commitment. Affective commitment was mainly found in clusters of strong, investing and loyal psychological contracts. Secondees at UKCC withheld their non-codified knowledge regarding the UKCC culture resulting in a knowledge vacuum after their departure from Independent Company managed Contact Centre—an outcome of closed governance.

In summary, both CRM projects had relatively closed governance throughout the project life cycle. At neither site was end-user involvement considered in the decision making process. At IE.COM the competitive nature of the work led to "mutual low-obligation" types of psychological contracts between the business units. At UKCC the alienation, of secondees and departmental management in the project governance resulted in reinforcement of a knowledge silo type of culture. Moreover at UKCC closed governance produced weak and non-reciprocal types of psychological contracts (Janssens *et al.*, 2003). Knowledge sharing particularly the sharing of non-codified/tacit knowledge was limited at both sites.

Wide Stakeholder Base vs. Primary Focus on Shareholders

Under this section we discuss and compare the type of stakeholder base CRM Projects had at our research sites. We analyze the impact it had on subculture interaction, psychological contracts and the sharing of non-codified/tacit knowledge.

IE claimed to have a "broad but not deep" approach towards the implementation process of CRM Y. However, the end-user involvement at our research site, namely the IE.COM, was very limited. Decisions were made at the top level and the system was deployed with a top down approach. The implementation process was steered from the top and had a rather rigid and mechanistic structure. Interestingly we found that UKCC used a similar top down approach for the implementation of their CRM X. Here also departmental and end-user involvement was limited. Sponsorship of CRM according to Goodhue *et al.* (2002) is initiated by senior management. Project sponsorship was initially strong at both sites; however, it died out as both CEOs left their respective projects before completion, narrowing further the stakeholder base.

According to our findings, both sites used a top down mechanistic approach towards implementation without understanding thoroughly the pre-existing environment. At IE.COM this resulted in data misfit issues, and lack of trust in the system. At UKCC the results were similar as secondees and departmental managers showed very little trust in the system. In both cases it led to interactions displaying weak, imposed and "employee low-obligation" types of psychological contracts (Anderson & Schalk, 1998; Janssens *et al.*, 2003; Makin *et al.*, 1996; Rousseau, 1995; Shore & Barksdale, 1998; Thibaut & Kelley, 1959). Consequently knowledge sharing in all forms suffered. Less-codified knowledge did get shared in closed groups or subcultures where, however, it remained trapped, reinforcing the silos.

According to Nonaka (1994) knowledge intensive firms, competitive advantage and product success are a result of collaborative, on-going learning. Success depends not only on how effectively diverse individuals are able to organise and develop their unique knowledge competencies, but also on how they can integrate and utilize their distinctive knowledge both effectively and synergistically. Such synergy could have been achieved if the aids/barriers to knowledge sharing—in particular non-codified knowledge sharing—across the sub-cultures were understood. According to Boland and Tenkasi (1996) this synergy requires a process of "mutual perspective taking" where distinctive individual knowledge is exchanged, evaluated and integrated with that of others in the organization. In essence, developing a comprehensive knowledge base amongst a community of highly differentiated yet reciprocally dependent individual specialists requires an ongoing process of "mutual perspective taking" where individual knowledge and theories of meaning are surfaced, reflected on, exchanged, evaluated and integrated with others in the organization. Much of social behaviour is predicated on assumptions an actor makes about the knowledge, beliefs and motives of others. This is the beginning of the process of "mutual perspective taking", and is fundamental to communication. Pervasive weak psychological contracts in our cases did not allow creative abrasion to take place where innermost feelings could be revealed and a mutual perspective could have been reached. On the contrary, lack of trust in a mechanistically driven project structure resulted in non-reciprocal relationships and knowledge bottlenecks.

In conclusion, sponsorship at senior level lacked some continuity as both CEOs left their projects prematurely. Weak and low-obligation types of psychological contracts between the stakeholders failed to develop reciprocal relationships. A mutual perspective and shared understanding regarding the usefulness of CRM system was missing at both sites. Knowledge sharing, particularly the non-codified/tacit knowledge in the form of "tricks of the trade", did not get shared across the sub-cultural boundaries. Both projects had a narrow stakeholder base and the system deployment was carried out without a thorough understanding of the pre-existing environment.

Extensive Accountability vs. Restricted Accountability

Senior management accountability at UKCC was to the elected politicians and eventually the public. They, however, did not take a long term strategic route and chose a short term solution to the "call answering" problem. The project was implemented without any deep understanding of the back-office integration issues. Also UKCC were not aware that by having calls answered they would expose their resource limitations in the back-offices. This overstretched the limited resources in the back-offices, which in turn did not please the managers who had to cope with an increase in demand without an increase in their resources. Hence the management at the departmental level were not satisfied with the CRM X solution.

Departmental autonomy at UKCC had been promoted prior to the CRM initiative, Central IT at that time having a supporting role. This changed with the CRM X. Departments were now expected to align themselves with a corporate system. Thus the CRM project increased departmental accountability and expected departments to adjust themselves to the needs of the project. They responded by finding their own work-arounds and exploring the idea of having a separate solution. Increased accountability negatively affected departmental interactions with the Central IT. The fact that departmental involvement was limited in the decision making process regarding the CRM project made matters worse. Departments felt alienated and pressurized to use a system which they did not have a strong faith in and consequently chose to withhold their non-codified knowledge.

IE senior management wanted to integrate the segregated parts of IE and present a unified view of IE to their customers. Senior management was responding to the current market needs to improve their service by providing a "one-stop-service" to their customers and thus improve their ROI and consequently please the shareholders.

Segregated parts of IE acted as separate businesses without any prolonged interactions across the business units. Middle management at IE.COM found themselves in an odd position. They were supposed to promote integration methodology in a mechanistic organizational structure (Burns & Stalker, 1961). Their perception regarding the system as a facilitating tool was not taken on board by the end-users.

Accountability at the end-user level was limited. End-users at both sites chose not to use the system whenever opportunity presented. However, at both sites end-users felt obliged to use the system—not because of its usefulness, but because of the top down regulations. Our findings show that the system caused some stress and slowed down end-user interactions with customers. This resulted in end-users withholding their non-codified knowledge and sharing it only among people with whom they had reached "mutual high-obligations" psychological contracts (Shore & Barksdale, 1998).

In summary, both sites had limited accountability because of the "part technology" strategy which allowed and promoted IS autonomy without any consideration of system integration. Recall Ciborra's blunt statement: "CRM seems to have no built in mechanisms by which it acquires its own momentum and the diffusion becomes a self-feeding process" (Ciborra, 2000). CRM initiatives, according to our findings, were intended to improve integration. However, with a top down approach the implementations only resulted in alienation and sub-cultural silos at both sites.

Primary Resource Base from Public Taxes vs. Primary Resource Base from Operational Returns and Borrowing

In this section we discuss the impact of resources on the departments and business units as a result of both CRM initiatives. At UKCC CRM X was supposed to facilitate a "one-stop-service" by getting the public through and effectively helping them with their queries. However, it ended by slowing down the service due to the lack of a thorough back-office system integration, and understanding of UKCC cultural knowledge. Moreover, it exposed the limitations in back-office resources, as when the free furniture removing service, which was accessible via the Independent Company managed front-office, resulted in strains being put on hard pressed personnel at the back-office. Those managing the resources in the back-office were not pleased, as joining the CRM X project had increased the demand without taking into consideration its impact on back-office resources. Consequently Central IT as at 2004 was desperately trying to improve integration whilst back-offices were investigating alternative options in parallel to CRM X in order to meet their customers' demands.

At IE.COM CRM Y was not auditable. Team leaders of various end-users were not sure about the usefulness of the system themselves. Managers who took out the reports claimed that it only gave them a snapshot and not a comprehensive report over a period. They were hoping for the analytics to improve. The double entries were an ongoing problem. This combined with a rigid hierarchical organizational structure, where interactions across the business units were minimal, also caused a duplication of efforts and some waste of resources (Nonaka, 1994).

The full time working teams that were supposed to see through a smooth implementation were unable to discover the poor state of legacy data prior to the implementation. This data misfit issue had a negative affect on the CRM project. A closer interaction involving the end-users at an early stage could have enabled an effective use of the available resources. It would have also helped in creating a shared understanding based on "mutual high-obligations" types of psychological contracts (Shore & Barksdale, 1998). This in turn could have facilitated end-user ownership.

In both cases, we conclude, the CRM systems were implemented without a thorough understanding of their impact on the available resources. An in-depth business analysis could have saved time and effort. In the case of UKCC the resources from public taxes came under pressure as demands in terms of personnel in the back-offices increased. At IE.COM data misfit issues made things worse resulting in double entries and duplication of efforts. The resources were thus stretched at both our research sites as a result of a poor implementation planning.

Multiple Values and Goals; Service, Public Interest, Equity, Professionalism, Consumer Participation, Complex Trade-Offs vs. Relatively Restricted

Under this heading we discuss the values and goals at UKCC comparing them with those at IE.COM. We critically analyze the multiple goals at UKCC in terms of how the CRM project has taken into consideration the public interests and consumer participation in order to achieve their "one-stop-service" target in a professional manner. We then compare this with IE.COM, analyzing any deviating factors.

At UKCC the public was interested in getting access to UKCC. CRM X was an initiative that was supposed to provide increased public access and ultimately achieve the government directive of a "one-stop-service". There was some trade-off in terms of the increased access to UKCC by the public who now needed to dial just one number in accessing UKCC. The public was getting through to UKCC via the Independent Company managed Contact Centre; however, the quality of service suffered due to a lack of system and cultural integration. Professionalism was missing, as the CRM project was rolled out without any comprehensive analysis of the existing environment. As at 2004 UKCC Central IT were working to achieve improved system integration. Back-office managers—as a result of weak and "employee low-obligation" types of psychological contracts—were not happy with the system and felt excluded from the CRM X development process (Anderson & Schalk, 1998; Janssens *et al.*, 2003; Makin *et al.*, 1996; Rousseau, 1995; Thibaut & Kelley, 1959). They were actively looking for a better system that would meet their departmental needs more specifically. Consumer (in this case the public) involvement in the CRM project was minimal. Davis (1989) argues that perceived usefulness is a strong correlate of user acceptance. Dissatisfied end-users (secondees) were moving back to their back-offices as per 2004.

Secondee contract terms with UKCC put them on a higher scale compared with their non-secondee colleagues. The fact that they were given the same working status as their non-secondee colleagues under Independent Company management caused friction in form of "us and them" culture. The outsourcing of the Call Centre management to Independent Company lacked professionalism in terms of understanding the consequences of having secondees and non-secondees under different employment contracts. The outsourcing contract seemed to have been rushed through without any creative abrasion which could have resulted in the achieving of so called "T-shaped skills" and a "knowing of what others know" type of environment. Davidson (2002) argues how frames (frames are cognitive structures or mental models that are held by individuals) and shifts in frame salience influence sense-making during requirement determination. In the above case sharing of frames between UKCC central IT and Independent Company did not take place fully.

At IE.COM, the ultimate goal of unifying IE was not fully achieved. Customer service suffered as the end-users struggled with the new system and the poor quality of transferred legacy data on it. The competitive nature of their work and a lack of prolonged interactions across the business units could not present a unified IE to their customers. Professionalism in terms of a lack of a thorough investigation of the existing environment prior to CRM Y deployment was missing. Moreover, the project was launched to promote integration in unifying the segregated parts of IE. A rigid mechanistic organizational structure did not allow free sharing of knowledge (particularly the non-codified/tacit knowledge in the forms of "tricks of the trade") across the business units and different levels of hierarchies (Orlikowski & Iacono, 2001; Polanyi, 1973; Vincenti, 1984). End-user involvement was limited and consumer (customer) involvement was not considered.

In summary, UKCC had been successful to some extent in providing telephonic access to the public. However, they had not achieved their ultimate target of "one-stop-service". At IE.COM a unified service could not be achieved due to the competitive nature of the work. Moreover their service suffered from poor data quality and the duplication of efforts. At both sites there was some lack of professionalism as neither investigated the existing environment fully prior to the implementation. At both, non-codified knowledge sharing was limited. Both sites had dissatisfied end-users as per 2004. Furthermore, a lack of external customer involvement hindered the establishment of a broad stakeholder bases at both sites.

Statutory and Parliamentary Regulation; Codes of Conduct vs. Board of Directors; Company Planning Frame Works

Under this heading we discuss the impact of statutory regulations on the CRM project at UKCC and compare that with the regulatory framework at IE.COM in the implementation of their CRM initiative. According to the Office of the Deputy Prime Minister (2002), UKCC was given the task of ensuring that all its services were available to the citizens through electronic means by 2005. The fact that the public was complaining and wanted a "one-stop-service" from UKCC put pressure on UKCC senior management to prioritize and take the quickest route. Hence the "call answering" focus strategy was prioritized over the "system integration" one. This illustrates how government deadlines and speed of new legislation, which Willcocks and Margetts (1994) talk about as pressure factors, push organizations towards consultant and supplier markets.

The code of conduct was very much dictated by the "call answering" focus strategy, which caused divisions, not only at senior management level, but also at middle management and grass root levels. The perceptional divide where partners were not willing to share their "frames" prevented the integration of departmental knowledge silos and hindered the development of a "shared context for knowing" (Davidson, 2002; Newell *et al.*, 2002; Orlikowski & Gash, 1994).

At IE a mechanistic organizational structure could not facilitate the unifying of IE through their CRM Y initiative. At our research site IE.COM people had very strict deadlines, and training seemed to be rushed through to get the system running. The vertical reporting structure could not facilitate a free sharing of non-codified/tacit knowledge in the form of "tricks of the trade" across the sub-cultures at IE.COM. Knowledge, particularly the tacit/non-codified knowledge remained buried in different business-unit silos (Bartlett & Ghoshal, 1998). New sub-cultures (guru culture) took shape and furthered the knowledge silo mentality.

In both cases, whether the directives were from the government or from the Board of Directors, they ended up delivering a solution without carrying out preliminary comprehensive business and cultural investigations. The implementation seemed to have been rushed through without covering such issues such as back-office data integration at UKCC and data misfit issues at IE.COM. Moreover, as a result of a top down implementation approach both organizations suffered in terms of stakeholder commitments at middle management and end-user levels. Lack of commitment was also found at the senior management level at UKCC. This was due to differing perceptions and competing interests (Long & Fahey, 2000).

Needs of National Economic Management vs. Market Place Signals

In this section we discuss how the CRM project implementations at our research sites were affected by the needs of economic management and market place signals. The purpose of IEG (Interactive Electronic Government) was to build local government services around the needs of customer/citizens rather than the organizational structures of service providers, giving its customers a "one-stop-service". UKCC were encouraged to make full use of the potential for electronic service delivery to improve the responsiveness and quality of their services. This was intended to result in different departments of UKCC working together seamlessly to deliver services more effectively and efficiently. The idea of "one-stop-service" was also, supposedly, going to save time and resources to have information integrated and available when required. At UKCC the CRM X project was heavily reliant on limited time and financial resources. The Strategic Director of Resources, with her financial background, steered the project towards a cheap and effective solution to satisfy public complaints. However, a mutual perspective and shared understanding where the sharing of frames could have taken place to establish a "mutual high-obligations" psychological contract between the Strategic Director of Resources and Former Head of IT did not take place (Bartlet and Goshal, 1998). Thus CRM X was deployed without a thorough understanding of system integration and its effects on the implementation process.

Within IE, the part technology strategy was proving to be expensive and systems were bought and implemented without any consideration for overall system integration. CRM Y was supposed to integrate the segregated parts of IE. At our research site, IE.COM, the project had a tight budget and strict deadlines to adhere to. The data quality issues, such as duplication and double entry, were perceived to be user errors by the management. According to our reports there were limited funds available as per 2005 to ensure data quality at IE.COM. CRM Y was supposed to save time and increase efficiency in facilitating a quick customer service by its end-users. According to our findings the project was still going through its teething stage and had still to win end-users" trust. However this was also the case at UKCC, confirming Willcocks (1991).

In conclusion, both projects were launched without covering the major issues of data migration and information integration thoroughly. There were no extra financial resources available at either site and projects were not able to secure a large stakeholder base. The departments at UKCC and business units at IE.COM were hesitant in volunteering their resources to obtain an overall system integration due to the lack of "mutual high-obligations" types of psychological contracts. Very little "float" was given in both projects due to time constraints.

SUMMARY ANALYSIS

The CRM Implementation Process: Comparisons

We summarize the first part presenting the summary of our analyses regarding staff stability, user commitment, user training, and management support, interdependencies between subculture interactions, psychological contracts and knowledge sharing.

We found that staff stability at the senior management level at UKCC was poorer compared with IE. However, both sites lost their CEO before the completion of the project. End-user involvement was missing and external user involvement was not considered. A "learning organization" type of environment with reciprocity of relationships was missing at both sites.

User training duration at both sites was short. It was much shorter at IE.COM. However, at IE.COM, end-users were involved (as super-users) in the training process compared with UKCC, where secondee involvement in the training process was minimal. The training did not impress the management at UKCC and its inadequacy was openly criticized. While IE management admitted the limitations of the training yet they perceived it to be sufficient. Management support at both sites in general was limited. IE senior management were more unified in their approach towards the deployment of CRM Y than UKCC, where strong differing opinions and perceptions caused a sub-cultural divide which trickled down to middle management and finally to end-user level causing severe staff retention issues.

We found that power based relationships and poor management support led to "employee under-obligation" types of psychological contracts. We also found that end-users at IE.COM stayed in the project discovering their own work-arounds through using their invisible colleges effectively. At UKCC the secondees chose to leave and move back to their old jobs in the back-office. We conclude that psychological contracts play an important role in the sharing of non-codified/tacit knowledge. Interactions even though prolonged may end up in negative abrasion or an illusion of consensus at the surface of words. Our analysis has led us to believe that prolonged interaction combined with "mutual high-obligations" types of psychological contracts based on shared benefits can facilitate a free sharing of non-codified know-how. Furthermore, sharing under these circumstances is not bound to a certain group of people but can take a new shape as it did in the case of IE.COM. There it took the shape of a "guru culture" where gurus shared information with other gurus from other hierarchies and business units. For an overview of our findings see Figure 7.4.

Public Versus Private Sector Implementation: Comparisons

We used Willcocks and Harrow's (1992) framework to present the similarities and dissimilarities in our analytical findings from both research sites from a knowledge management perspective. We conclude that although the customer base in the two cases was different, the issues faced by the end-users were remarkably similar in nature. At both sites the end-users perceived the system to complicate and slow down their progress in securing an efficient customer service. Furthermore, end-users at both sites felt under compulsion to use the system but decided not to use it when the opportunity arose. No external customer involvement was considered by the senior management at either site. We also found that tacit/non-codified

Staff Stability, User commitment, User training and Management support

- Staff stability at the senior management level at UKCC was poorer compared to IE. Both sites lost their CEO before the completion of the project.
- End-user involvement was limited and external user involvement was not considered.
- End-users at UKCC decided to leave and returned to their back-office positions in order to get away from the Vertex managed contact centre. At IE.COM end-users found their own work-arounds through social networks using their invisible colleges, giving rise to a "guru culture" (Orlikowski & Iacono, 2001, Orlikowski & Tyre, 1994).
- User commitment at both sites was low, even lower at UKCC as the secondees did not even want to stay in the CRM project.
- User training duration at both sites was short. It was much shorter at IE.COM.
- End-users at both sites criticised the inadequacy of the training quite openly. Furthermore, the end-users felt compelled to use the system.
- Management support at both sites was poor in general. IE senior management were more unified in their approach towards the implementation of their CRM project than UKCC, where strong differing opinions and perceptions caused a sub-cultural divide which trickled down on to middle management and finally to end-user level causing severe staff retention issues.
- End-user psychological contracts with management at both sites were of "employee under-obligation" type and failed to create a mutual perspective and a shared mental space.

Interdependencies between Subculture Interactions, Psychological Contracts, and Knowledge Sharing

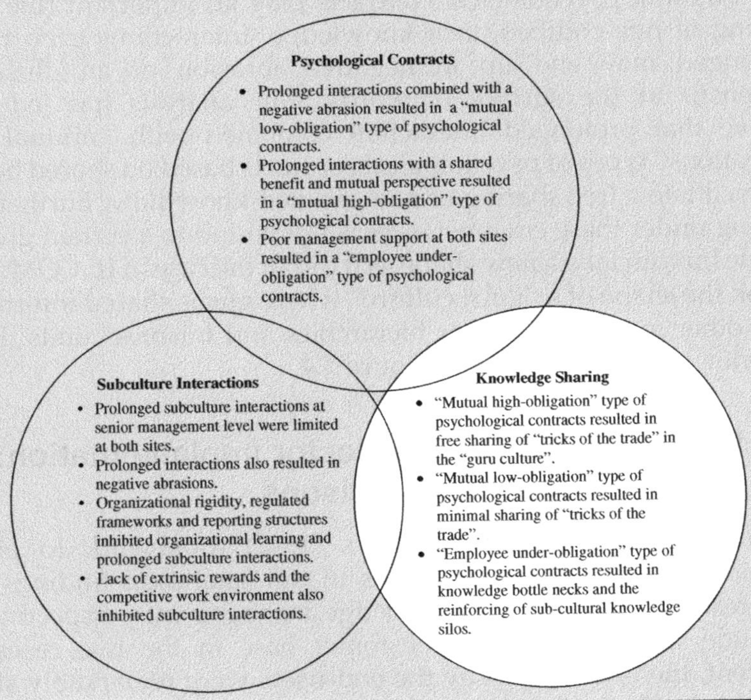

Figure 7.4 *Summary of the first part: Process analysis UKCC and IE.COM*

knowledge hoarding issues were related to job security and power. At UKCC secondees used this power as an insurance to enable them to move back to their old jobs, whereas at IE it resulted in a "guru culture" giving rise to a clique type power structure where gurus only shared their "tricks of the trade" with other gurus.

As at end of 2004, both sites were still in the process of securing their goal of providing an effective and faster service using a CRM system. UKCC secured the "call answering" target, helping the public to make speedy contact with the Council. However, this exposed discrepancies at the departmental level and pushed resources to their limits, resulting in a decline in commitment towards the CRM X project. At IE.COM a segregated and mechanistic organizational architecture continued to haunt the CRM project resulting in knowledge silos along vertical and horizontal axes. A "unified view" was hard to achieve as the end-users struggled with data misfit issues and duplications slowing down their progress.

We found that both sites used predominantly quantitative measures to control and monitor system usage. The quantitative measures did not include any financially related audits at IE.COM. At UKCC the quantitative measures led to a dissatisfied departmental management. Knowledge became sticky and remained in the departmental and hierarchical sub-cultural silos. No knowledge management systems were in place at either site. A round table or a neutral platform for discussing and resolving CRM issues was absent at both sites.

We conclude that both sites faced severe difficulties in the implementation of their policies. At UKCC the role of Central IT changed from a support function to a facilitator of system integration. However, this role did not get a chance to develop fully as the project changed its direction and became more focused on short term results. The ambiguity of this dilemma had an adverse affect on the departments. At IE the policies were ambiguous in the sense that CRM was supposed to unify and facilitate, and yet the end-users perceived it to be predominantly a controlling and monitoring device.

According to our analysis both CRM projects had relatively closed governance throughout the project life cycle. No end-user involvement was considered in the decision making process at either site. The competitive nature of the work at IE.COM led to "mutual low-obligation" types of psychological contracts between the business units. At UKCC the alienation of secondees and departmental management in the project governance resulted in reinforcement of a knowledge silo type of culture. At UKCC closed governance produced weak and disloyal types of psychological contracts (Janssens *et al.*, 2003). We found that both projects had a strong senior management support initially. However, it lacked continuity as both CEOs left the project before its completion. Weak and "employee under-obligation" types of psychological contracts between the stakeholders failed to produce reciprocal relationships.

Both projects had a narrow stakeholder base and the system deployment was carried out without a thorough understanding of the existing environment.

Limited accountability used to be a feature common to both sites because of the "part technology" strategy which allowed and promoted IS autonomy without any consideration of system integration. CRM initiatives according to our findings were designed to improve integration and accountability; however, implementations, with a top down approach only resulted in alienation and sub-cultural silos at both sites. Fulltime working teams employed to see through a smooth implementation were unable to discover the poor state of legacy data prior to the implementation at IE.COM. This data misfit issue had a negative affect on the CRM project. In both cases we conclude that the CRM systems were implemented without a thorough understanding of its impact on the available resources.

We found that UKCC has been successful to some extent in providing telephonic access to the public. However, it has not secured a "one-stop-service". At IE.COM a unified service was not possible due to the competitive environment. In both cases CRM solution was delivered without preliminary comprehensive business and cultural investigations. Implementations seem to have been rushed through without uncovering potential issues such as back-office data integration at UKCC and data misfit issues at IE.COM. Moreover, as a result of a top down implementation approach both organizations suffered in terms of stakeholder commitments at middle management and end-user level. Lack of commitment was also found at the senior management level at UKCC.

In conclusion both projects were launched without thoroughly covering the issues such as data migration and information integration. There were no extra financial resources available at either site and projects were not able to obtain a broad stakeholder base. The departments at UKCC and business units at IE.COM were hesitant in volunteering their resources to obtain an overall system integration due to their lack of reciprocal and "mutual high-obligations" types of psychological contracts. For a further summary see Figure 7.5.

CONCLUSION

This chapter set out to compare, discuss and analyze the research findings from both cases in the light of the reviewed literature. The framework previously used in "within-case" analyses was used to discuss deviating patterns and similarities from both research sites.

Contextual analysis at UKCC and IE.COM using Willcocks and Harrow (1992)

- Although the customer base in our two cases was different yet the issues faced by the end users were remarkably similar in nature. At both sites the end users perceived the system to complicate and slow down their progress in securing an efficient customer service.
- Both sites are working towards their goal to provide an effective and faster service using a CRM system. However, both sites have knowledge bottleneck issues and have not been able to deal with them successfully.
- We found that both sites used predominantly quantitative measures to control and monitor system usage. No knowledge management systems were in place at either site. A round table or a neutral platform for discussing and resolving CRM issues was absent at both sites.
- Our findings indicate that both sites suffered from part technology syndrome although CRM was deployed with the intention of integrating the separated departmental and business unit silos. In both cases at lack of cross-cultural communication based on "mutual high-obligations" types of psychological contracts was absent. As a result knowledge sharing, particularly the sharing of "tricks of the trade", was limited.
- We found that both CRM project had relatively closed governance through out the project life cycle. No end-user involvement was considered in the decision making process at either site.
- We found that both projects had strong senior management support initially. Sponsorship at the senior level lacked continuity as both CEOs left the project without seeing it through to completion. A mutual perspective and shared understanding regarding the usefulness of CRM system was absent at both sites.
- Both sites had limited accountability because of the "part technology" strategies which allowed and promoted IS autonomy without any consideration of system integration. CRM initiatives according to our findings were designed to improve integration; however implementation with a top down approach only resulted in alienation and sub-culture silos at both sites.
- In both cases we conclude that the CRM systems were implemented without a thorough understanding of their impact on the available resources. Resources were thus overstretched as a result of a poor implementation planning.
- There was some lack of professionalism at both sites in that they did not investigate the existing environment fully prior to implementation. Both sites had dissatisfied end-users as per 2004. Furthermore, lack of external customer involvement did not help in establishing a broad stakeholder base.
- In both cases whether the directives were from the government or from the Board of Directors, they ended up delivering a solution without preliminary comprehensive business and cultural investigation.
- Furthermore, both projects were launched without investigating key issues such as data migration, information and cultural integration adequately. There were no extra financial resources available at either site. Very little "float" was given in both projects due to time constraints.

Figure 7.5 *Summary of the second part: Contextual analysis of UKCC and IE.COM using Willcocks and Harrow (1992)*

The deviating patterns of the adaptation phase of CRM implementation and their similarities were investigated, and compared to gain further insight into the linkages between sub-culture interactions, knowledge sharing, psychological contracts and the existing theories regarding IT implementation in a CRM environment. The analysis was carried out using our refined frame work together with Willcocks and Harrow's (1992) framework detailing distinguishing features of public and private sector organizations. An interesting finding has been that the distinctive contexts of the two cases have had less effect than the distinctive nature of CRM Systems and the implementation processes adopted. The study shows that irrespective of sectoral backgrounds the two organizations failed to address fully a range of common issues related to human behaviour, psychology, organizational characteristics, sub-cultural interactions and knowledge sharing. In our judgement these factors have greater explanatory power for the results achieved than the distinctive contexts in which the two organizations operated.

In the next chapter we discuss the main findings relating to the micro elements, namely psychological contracts and their impact on the success of the implementation of CRM systems from a knowledge management perspective. We summarize the theoretical, methodological and managerial contributions of our work. Finally, we summarize the limitations, possibilities and scope for future research, building on the foundations established by this study.

8
Conclusion: CRM Developments

INTRODUCTION

This chapter points to the contributions of this study and possible future directions for CRM research and practice. Within the large context of implementation studies described in Chapter 2 we focused on the implementation of new technology in the form of Customer Relationship Management (CRM) systems, from a knowledge perspective in contemporary (1999–2004) situations within a UK City Council and IE.COM. A specific focus was given to areas neglected in previous CRM studies: sub-culture interactions, psychological contracts, how tacit knowledge—including in the form of what Orlikowski, Vincenti and others have called "tricks of the trade" "work arounds", "short-cuts", "special know-how"—surfaced and were shared, and with what effects on implementation. The research, using two case studies, investigated how CRM system stakeholders and the system itself evolved through encountering barriers, sharing knowledge, finding new uses and inventing work-arounds. A rich picture emerged of sub-cultural silos of knowledge linked with psychological contracts and power-based relationships influencing and inhibiting adoption and acceptance of the CRM system.

In this final chapter we discuss the main findings relating to these micro elements, by summarizing the theoretical, methodological and practice-based contributions. We also summarize the limitations and the possibilities and scope for future research, building on the foundations established by this study.

RESEARCH CONTRIBUTIONS AND IMPLICATIONS

This research attempts to provide a contribution towards understanding the implementation of Customer Relationship Management (CRM) systems from a knowledge management perspective. Our study of previously neglected areas (psychological contracts, subculture interactions and less codified knowledge sharing) and their interdependencies presents an enhanced understanding regarding the implementation of a new technology. A rich picture, consisting of sub-cultural silos of knowledge linked with psychological contracts and power-based relationships influencing and inhibiting adoption and acceptance of the CRM system, seeks to make a fresh contribution to this area of research. The three main contributions—theoretical, methodological and practice-based—are discussed below.

Theoretical Contributions

This research—by integrating existing IS implementation literature with sub-cultures, less codified knowledge sharing and psychological contracts in the implementation of a new technology—provides a novel lens through which to demonstrate the importance of the micro elements in implementation. Many even quite recent implementation studies, such as Ross (2003) provide only another phased approach at a macro level. Our study has attempted to investigate the process of implementation at a micro level and has demonstrated the importance of underlying psychological contracts in sub-cultural interactions from a knowledge sharing perspective. We chose to investigate the above mentioned micro elements in a CRM system implementation environment, where it emerged that knowledge sharing forms a vital element to effective system integration.

Furthermore, we investigated Roger's (1995) "complexity" concept from an implementation perspective that is the degree to which a CRM (Customer Relationship Management) implementation is perceived as difficult to understand. Different sub-cultures may not be able to communicate with each other if the implementation is not communicated and understood. Examining this communication from a knowledge perspective has helped us to assess the knowledge sharing barriers that inhibit the sharing of knowledge across sub-cultures and thus delay a successful implementation of a technical innovation.

In the implementation studies so far, the importance of knowledge sharing and shared psychological contracts is implicit, but rarely fully explicitly stated or researched. Davidson (2002) argues how frames (frames are cognitive structures or mental models that are held by individuals) and shifts in frame salience influence sense-making during requirement determination. Our study has helped with the understanding of how interpretive power is exercised in an IS project. Moving on from frames to shared frames, Orlikowski and Gash (1994) show shared frames as closely related to the concept of sub-cultures. Individuals, drawing on their shared frames, engage in symbolic action and thereby construct a social reality that reflects their common assumptions, beliefs and understandings and that includes particular rules, rituals and customary practice. According to Geertz (1973) and Van Maanen and Barley (1985), sub-cultures rely heavily on cognitive elements such as common frames of reference. The perception of different stakeholders regarding the success of the implementation process of the CRM system is an important factor, and proves the usefulness of this research.

While the literature on organizational culture is large, that referring explicitly to IT and CRM implementation is surprisingly small. The management literature is replete with various subsequent attempts made to improve communication and participation between the sub-cultures in order to enable a successful implementation of an IT system (Wright-Cummings, 1997). However, these efforts have rarely investigated the factors enabling and inhibiting communication across sub-cultures from a knowledge sharing perspective.

Our study has investigated the implementation process of CRM with a special focus on the "transformation" part. Chapter 2 provided an overview of extant knowledge on how implementation could be accomplished effectively. Our more micro study used existing theories of IT implementation, and probed the adaptation and acceptance of the CRM systems by its stakeholders. That is, how the stakeholders of the system and the system itself were evolving through finding new uses, workarounds, upgrades, patches, cookies, viruses and failures in the so called societal and organizational transformation process. The study has investigated how the "tricks of the trade" and know-how born in the minds and bodies of the stakeholders of a system are shared across the sub-cultural boundaries and the impact of such sharing on the successful implementation of a new technology. The present research thus contributes to the field of cultural studies by analysing in-depth sub-cultural interactions at a micro level and its resulting distinctive perspective on the implementation process that might result.

Previous IS studies do talk about the importance of a "mutual perspective", "T-shaped skills", "knowing of what others know", "shared context for knowing", "prolonged interactions" and

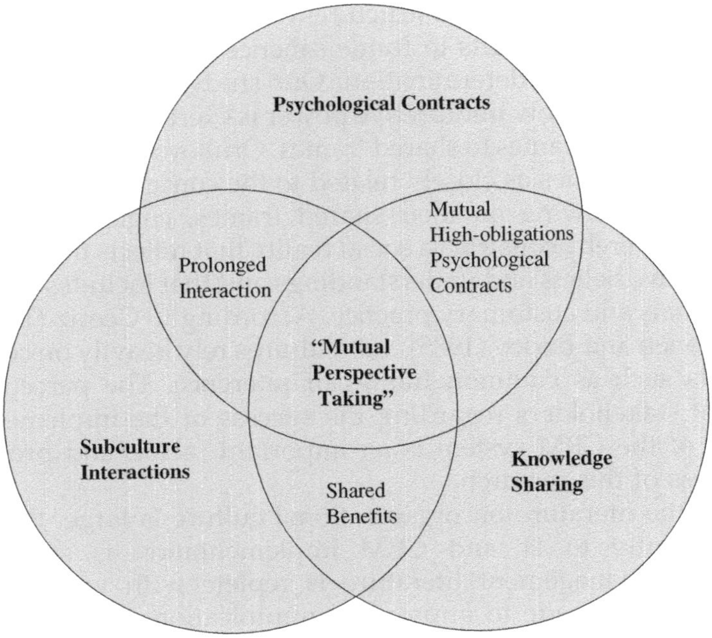

Figure 8.1 *Close relations between Psychological Contracts, Subculture Interactions and Knowledge Sharing*

"creative abrasion" in the sharing of less codified knowledge. However, they do not fully address the micro processes that lead to the above. This study fills the knowledge gap by investigating psychological contracts and uses them as a lens to probe into and obtain an improved understanding surrounding the process of a "mutual perspective taking". We expanded the investigation of probing further the process of a "mutual perspective taking" by taking into consideration the interdependencies between sub-cultural interactions, less codified knowledge sharing and psychological contracts.

By integrating findings from scholars like Shore and Barksdale (1998) and Janssens *et al.* (2003) we have thus enhanced our understanding concerning the significance of micro elements (in our case psychological contracts)—those elements that lead to a "mutual perspective taking" in facilitating a free sharing of "tricks of the trade" "work arounds", "short-cuts" and "special know-how" across sub-cultures in the implementation of a new technology. We found that prolonged interactions can also result in negative abrasion and result in "mutual low-obligation" types of psychological contracts thereby inhibiting the sharing of less codified knowledge across the sub-cultural boundaries. Figure 8.1 provides an overview of the research and one part of its conceptual contribution.

The present study leads us to believe that prolonged interaction combined with "mutual high-obligations" types of psychological contracts based on shared benefits can facilitate a free sharing of personal, tacit knowledge. Furthermore, sharing under these circumstances is not bound to a certain group of people but can take a new shape as it did in the case of IE.COM. There it took the shape of a "guru culture" where gurus shared information with other gurus from other hierarchies and business units. We also found that power based relationships led to "employee under-obligation" types of psychological contracts which consequently reinforced the knowledge silos.

Finally, we used our integrated lens based on our multidisciplinary approach to probe the implementation of a CRM system. CRM in the form of a new technology is emerging as a key element in system integration. It has attracted a lot of attention but also a high failure rate. CRM systems also remain relatively understudied academically. Linkages between knowledge sharing, sub-culture interactions and psychological contracts also remain understudied in the implementation of a CRM, or indeed any other, system. Our study fills the above gap by using our integrative probing approach in investigating the knowledge sharing mechanisms involved in the implementation process. A CRM environment suited the investigation of knowledge sharing issues. Thus our study provides a novel theoretical contribution by using a multidisciplinary approach and enhances understanding of the underlying factors—also known as micro elements in this research—in the process of knowledge sharing across sub-cultural boundaries.

This study focused on the process of "adaptation and acceptance" of the system, covering both the internal and external customers as part of the stakeholder analysis. The research in particular, studied the knowledge sharing loop between the front and back-office of the CRM project in order to identify and investigate the knowledge silos. Sponsorship of CRM, according to Goodhue *et al.* (2002), is initiated by senior management. This research investigated the involvement of senior management and the grassroots/end-users (internal customers) including the external customer and its impact on the "adaptation and acceptance" of the CRM implementation. Our findings show that the window of opportunity to adopt the system closes fairly quickly if the project fails to establish "mutual high-obligations" types of psychological contracts between the stakeholders. Not only did the stakeholders withhold their "tricks of the trade" "work arounds", "short-cuts" and "special know-how" but it also resulted in a narrowing of the stakeholder base as the stakeholder commitment to the project decreased reinforcing the departmental/business-unit knowledge silos. This study also found that sub-cultural silos act as an inhibitor to overall system integration and that subculture integration is an important element in achieving a so called "one-stop-service". We also found that the success of prolonged interactions in achieving a free sharing of less codified knowledge is strongly related to underlying psychological contracts.

Methodological Contributions

This study was conducted using an in-depth longitudinal approach, effectively an adapted-for-use, extended version of Pettigrew (1990, 1997). This research has been of a processual type investigating the CRM implementation phenomenon using two case studies. The five guiding assumptions for processual research proposed by Pettigrew (1985, 1990 and 1997) provided an appropriate framework for gathering data using altogether fifty semi structured in-depth interviews. The implementation process was studied and critically analyzed over a period of three years both along the vertical (hierarchical) and horizontal (cross-organizational) axes. It helped us to investigate sub-cultural interactions at different levels of hierarchies. We critically analyzed the development of psychological contractual issues responsible for the sharing of "tricks of the trade". The process of implementation of a CRM system was also studied analysing the historical context and linking it with the present contemporary situations at our research sites. We found the processual approach suited this research well as it helped in understanding the knowledge sharing issues in a holistic dimension. The longitudinal approach also helped in gaining insight into the micro mechanisms of subculture interactions at different levels of hierarchies at both research sites. This approach enabled us to maintain a continuous close contact with the data and the subjects thus enriching our findings.

We piloted our data collection at both research sites using general types of research questions arising from our initial literature review using a data triangulation, combining retrospective and real time analysis. Data was then analysed using Pettigrew's six fold framework to enhance our preliminary understanding of the phenomenon at both research sites. We chose the manual colour coding of data in order to maintain our closeness to the collected data. By coding the data manually we were able to identify and better present the emerging issues under relevant themes in our analytical framework. The pilot study helped in refining our reviewed literature, research questions and our analytical framework, in better preparing us for the final data collection and its analysis. This research, unlike many others, shows the development of our research process by showing its stages of probing the surface of CRM implementation phenomenon at different intervals. The probing of our sites at different intervals over a period of two years helped us to present a holistic view of knowledge issues and their interdependencies with sub-cultural interactions and psychological contracts. This research was able to follow the stakeholders and how their perceptions regarding the system changed over time, thus confirming the closure of the window of opportunity as described by Orlikowski and Tyre (1994) in our reviewed literature.

Different industrial sectors were chosen (private and public sector). Using a theoretical justification provided by Pettigrew (1989) polar types to exploit planned opportunism was followed. This approach produced an excellent opportunity for comparison and contrast. In order to increase the ecological validity of the findings two different organizations were chosen—one public and one private sector. The deviating patterns and similarities of the phenomenon were investigated and critically analyzed using Willcocks and Harrow (1992).

An interesting finding has been that the distinctive contexts of the two cases have had less effect than the distinctive nature of CRM Systems and the implementation processes adopted. The study shows that irrespective of sectoral backgrounds the two organizations failed to address adequately a range of common issues related to human behaviour, psychology, organizational characteristics, sub-cultural interactions and knowledge sharing. According to our research findings these factors have greater explanatory power for the results achieved than the distinctive contexts in which the two organizations operated.

This research has applied a multi-disciplinary approach in order to produce a rich picture revealing knowledge issues in the implementation process of a CRM system. The whole research process has worked to get a closer and better understanding of the micro elements that lead to a "mutual perspective" and "shared context for knowing". We have been able to probe deeper using the longitudinal approach over a long period in order to understand the strengths and weaknesses of CRM projects at both research sites. The holistic and processual approach has attempted to produce an enhanced understanding of the phenomenon and has secured a deeper insight into issues leading to technology and knowledge bottlenecks at a micro level in the implementation of a CRM system.

In summary, the study process has confirmed the strength of processual, longitudinal, historically and contextually sensitive, qualitative case research. In Information Systems studies the dominant preference for more quantitative styles that tend, in their less flattering manifestations, to be ahistorical, acontextual, aprocessual, and that lead to what C. Wright Mills (2000) has called an Abstracted Empiricism—can be usefully contrasted against what can be found out through the methods adopted in the present study.

Practice-based Contributions

We have studied organizational practices in the light of existing academic theories. We see this research as making a useful contribution at the level of practice. This research has several implications. We discuss each one of them in detail.

Broad/narrow stakeholder base

This study has attempted to investigate the implementation process of a CRM system with a special focus on the "transformation" component. By using existing theories of IT implementation it attempted to investigate the "adaptation and acceptance" of the system by its stakeholders. That is, how the stakeholders of the system and the system itself are evolving through finding new uses, work-arounds, upgrades, patches, cookies, viruses, and failures in a "so called" societal and organizational transformation process (Orlikowski & Iacono, 2001).

The decision makers need to have an understanding of the inhibitors to the implementation process of an IT system and of how to work their way around those inhibitors. They need to interact as flexibly as possible both formally and informally so as to understand the perception of other stakeholders regarding a new system. It is not the formal meetings that necessarily give valuable information regarding the perceptions of the users of the system, but rather the informal conversations that can remove misunderstandings and give an insight into any perceived implications and difficulties other stakeholders may be experiencing. To unleash the power of tacit knowledge in an organization the sharing of such tacit knowledge must be managed differently from explicit knowledge. Many of the traditional methods of knowledge diffusion like manuals and lectures are unsuitable for tacit knowledge sharing. Different methods like apprenticeship, direct interaction, networking and action learning which include face-to-face social interaction and practical experiences are more suitable for supporting diffusion of tacit knowledge. Decision makers can facilitate focus groups, steering groups and interest groups to enable regular meetings to improve face to face interaction between the stakeholders of the system. The interactions between the decision makers, internal as well as external users of the system and experts of the system such as CRM are vital for the system development. This study also signified the need for educating stakeholders in understanding how they can play a part time marketers' role thus facilitating the process of implementation.

Both internal and external customers were kept in focus in this study. Most post-mortems of CRM failures trace the problems back to the alignment of incentives and metrics, and the absence of a customer-facing organization. Another pitfall has been to concentrate on the customer contact processes without making corresponding changes in internal structures and systems (see for example, Digby *et al.*, 2002). This study focussed on the process of "adaptation and acceptance" of the system, covering both the internal and external customers as part of the stakeholder analysis. The research, in particular, studied the knowledge sharing loop between the front and back-office to identify and investigate the knowledge silos. Sponsorship of CRM, according to Goodhue *et al.* (2002), is invariably initiated by senior management. The study investigated the involvement of senior management and grassroots, including the external customers, and the impact of their respective involvement on the "adaptation and acceptance" of the CRM implementation.

Previous studies on CRM have emphasized the importance of having a broad stakeholder base. However, they have not been able to discuss the details regarding micro mechanisms enabling/inhibiting the establishment of a broad stakeholder base. Previous studies point out the importance of a project champion playing a key role in the successful implementation of a CRM implementation. Our research points out how the discontinuation or leaving of such a project champion can have adverse affects on the success of the project. Our study also points out that, psychological contracts play an important role in stakeholder commitment to the CRM project. We found that "employee under-obligation" contracts not only inhibit the free sharing of less codified knowledge but also weaken stakeholder commitment. We saw how stakeholders at different hierarchical levels of UKCC left the project as a result of their weak and "employee under-obligation" types of psychological contracts with the management; also at IE.COM how weak psychological contracts again led to users finding their own work-arounds and establishing new subcultures.

This study highlights and confirms previous IS studies in emphasizing internal and external customer involvement. In our study a broad stakeholder base was not achieved as the stakeholders at the lower levels of hierarchies lacked a sense of ownership of the system and the entire "change" project. End users and lower management felt alienated as a result of a predominantly top down approach. This research suggests the use of both "push" and "pull" methods in order to establish a broad stakeholder base and promote ownership at all levels. This study further suggests that the success of a CRM System implementation depends on all users sincerely believing in the system and its benefits. Users involvement in the decision making process is thus highly recommended. We found that the system remained highly dependent on the input of data by its users. The fact that end-users are ultimately the process owners cannot be denied, and must be addressed rather than neglected, as at both our research sites.

We also found at both sites that lack of clarity of objectives and differing stakeholder perceptions at different levels of hierarchies gave an illusion of consensus. This research suggests that realistic goals should be set and objectives discussed in a creative abrasion type of environment in order to establish clarity towards the company objectives. Factors such as the degree of technical proficiency of employees, effectiveness of current systems and processes, and management commitment will impact both the timeline to, and the degree of, success. The objectives and underlying benefits of deploying a CRM system need to be understood by all the stakeholders prior to an implementation.

System integration

Most sources, certainly managerial sources, agree that system integration is desirable. However system integration can also have downsides. The challenge is to understand and manage the negative aspects of integration to minimize the adverse effects. Doing this requires an awareness of the potential problems. This study points out that system integration is a great deal more than an integration of hardware. EAI (Enterprise Application Integration) is not limited only to hardware. Our study promotes integration where it is in response to a business need strongly favoured by the existing organizational sub-cultures (see also Chapter 3). Our research suggests that without a sub-cultural integration based on "mutual high-obligations" types of psychological contracts the implementation of a CRM system has less chance of success. We also conclude, from our findings, that prolonged sub-cultural interactions based on shared and mutual benefits and strong mutual psychological contracts result in a free sharing of less codified knowledge. The promotion of such a free sharing is highly important to cultural integration to accomplish system integration.

Further, we suggest that management needs to facilitate the above sub-cultural integration by providing formal and informal neutral meeting places. These neutral meeting places can be in the form of CRM sponsored clubs, discussion groups, round tables or formally organized weekly/monthly CRM discussion days. The above neutral places can act as non-threatening platforms to discuss CRM issues. Managers should act as facilitators to grasp the knowledge created through the above neutral meeting places and then exploit it, effectively reinforcing the cultural and system integration. Our study shows how a lack of sub-cultural integration resulted in knowledge silos and digital divides. To overcome such technology and knowledge bottlenecks, a sub-cultural integration based on shared benefits needs to be promoted and rewarded.

A competitive environment where business units withhold information and less-codified knowledge inhibits sub-cultural integration. A learning organizational type of environment needs to be promoted where team efforts are rewarded, both extrinsically and intrinsically. Working in teams across the sub-cultural boundaries can overcome the technology and knowledge bottlenecks. In the same way, and by the same methods by which individuals find their work-arounds, the teams will be able to find their own work-arounds to overcome the technology bottlenecks, by using their invisible colleges to support a successful resolution of any business issues. As a result the creation of a business intelligence type of environment, where individuals will be willing to share their "tricks of the trade" based on shared benefits and rewards can be made possible.

Psychological contracts

Our study probed the implementation process of a CRM system using the lens of psychological contracts and their interdependencies with sub-cultural interactions and knowledge sharing. We found that psychological contracts play an important role in the sharing of less codified knowledge. We also found that prolonged sub-cultural interactions when combined with a "mutual low-obligation" type of psychological contract can also result in negative abrasion. This negative abrasion impedes a free sharing of less codified knowledge.

According to our findings prolonged interactions where individuals do not feel threatened by each other and have shared benefits, result in "mutual high-obligations" types of psychological contracts. These types of contracts facilitate a free sharing of knowledge across the cultural boundaries, assisting in cross-cultural communication. As the current literature says little about the role of psychological contracts in a CRM environment, our study will be useful to CRM Project Managers in understanding the micro elements important in the sharing of less codified knowledge and information across business unit boundaries. This will help in reinforcing an holistic EAI strategy.

The findings of our study which investigated various scenarios and how they result in different types of psychological contracts will also be useful to senior management in enabling them to understand the implications of psychological contracts thus equipping them to better understand issues related to data migration, staff retention and end-user commitment.

Finally, our study investigated the relationship (R) part of CRM. It points out the importance of paying attention to the needs of the stakeholders including internal and external customers. Managers ought to facilitate the reciprocity of relationships across the business unit boundaries and facilitate relationship building not only with the external customer but also within the organization, not forgetting the internal customers who are also the end-users of the system. An ultimate goal is to build strong enough bonds with internal and external customers so that all share common values and purposes, and want to work together in achieving such goals. This will lead to the development of a "mutual high-obligations" type of psychological contract which is an integral component of mutual commitment enabling people to work together so that everyone benefits.

Once trust between the managers and the end-users is established, it can lay the groundwork for a "mutual high-obligations" type of psychological contract. Such a contract will be based on mutual understanding/benefit and reciprocal trust and commitment. The end-users will thus be able to see the managers as enablers and not as controllers of their work. The more this happens, the deeper the psychological contract will become. The violation of such a contract as shown by our findings results in mistrust and non-reciprocal relationships leading to work-arounds and short cuts discovered to fulfil the needs of the system and in order to carry out the jobs. Managers need to align their mission, vision, values and purpose with a service orientation. They need to grasp and understand the end-users' perceptions, by looking at things from their perspective, rather than only from their own perspective.

Motivation and commitment as important components of a strong psychological contract are, according to our findings, related to the provision of both intrinsic and extrinsic rewards. We saw how end-users at IE.COM worked together on their own initiatives across the business units when they had shared benefits related to their teamwork. Not only did it produce commitment but also intrinsic rewards in the form of job satisfaction sharing freely their "tricks of the trade" with each other.

CRM Managers need to enable a close relation between the psychological contracts, subculture interaction and knowledge sharing. In order to promote the above three elements, a facilitative style would be more preferable to a monitoring one.

Facilitating interactions across the business units both formally and informally with shared benefits attached can produce "mutual high-obligations" types of psychological contracts and consequently a non-threatening environment. This non-threatening environment can act as an arena for a free sharing of less codified knowledge in the form of "tricks of the trade" work arounds, short cuts and favours, all working towards the goal of a successful resolution of an issue. The ensuing results when rewarded extrinsically by the management will continue to preserve and promote a learning organization type of environment where people feel free to admit to making mistakes and are encouraged to learn from them. This will contribute to a sense of intrinsic reward. The above cross cultural relationships with strong underlying psychological contracts will act as a catalyst promoting the overall success of system integration within an organization.

LIMITATIONS AND REFLECTIONS

Under this section we identify the limitations of this research and discuss them as opportunities for future research. Even though we covered both public and private sectors in order to provide a set of similarities and dissimilarities related to IT implementation, the limitation of its confinement to only two case studies, and to two sectors in developed economies cannot be denied. We also focussed more closely on the implementation process rather than the CRM technology itself. Future studies could focus more on the CRM technologies and probe further into issues relating to its architectural design and whole project life cycle.

The overall research challenge in our comparative longitudinal study was to examine the linkages between content, contexts and process over time in order to obtain the rich picture of the knowledge sharing phenomenon. This study sought to capture the reality of non-codified knowledge sharing, in the introduction of a new technology, in flight. We amalgamated our theoretical framework with Pettigrew (1985) in revealing the process ingredients of tacit knowledge sharing across the identified key sub-cultures. This can be seen as a weakness. However, in doing so we were able to link the process with internal and external contexts and elucidate the history behind sub-cultural knowledge silos. We were able to disentangle the origins of these silos and identify patterns/continuities.

The study used a qualitative approach due to the nature of the research subject and questions. The questions using "how" and "why" could not be answered satisfactorily using quantitative techniques. The data gathered through the qualitative approach using semi-structured in-depth interviews contained qualitative information and the analysis of such information is a complex issue. However, the results obtained relate to real life situations and as such are a valuable source of information. The processual or longitudinal approach used by us had to cope with personal bias and "subjectivity" versus "objectivity". We had to struggle through to maintain the data as bias free as possible. This study could have expanded the data collection triangulation by doing additional surveys using quantitative methods. As it was, a vast amount of data was collected, there were time limitations, and it was unclear what further major insight quantitative surveys, for example, could have given us, given our research focus.

The literature using a multidisciplinary approach was chosen under five themes; IT implementation, culture, knowledge management, psychological contracts and CRM. The knowledge management covered mainly the tacit knowledge barriers. It did not go into detail to discuss the explicit part of the knowledge sharing. The use of a multidisciplinary approach did enable the investigation of micro elements such as psychological contracts although this made the literature vast. Other themes discussing the fusion regarding technical innovation could have been included. We could also have expanded the CRM part and discussed it in a greater detail. However this would have made the literature review even lengthier. The initial literature review resulted in broader types of questions which needed to be refined. This was achieved by conducting a pilot/initial case study. This helped us to refine not only the research questions but also helped in testing the appropriateness of our chosen methods.

The semi structured in-depth interviews undertaken took much longer than anticipated due to the absence of key stake holders during the summer breaks. The qualitative data collected needed a thorough analysis which was time consuming and put pressure on time management. Interview dates had to be changed several times to suit the availability of the subjects. However a good relationship and professional attitude was maintained throughout the interactions, before during and after interviews. Manual colour coding, though cumbersome, was preferred to a computerized method, because this sharpened the awareness of the researcher to the interrelated issues involved.

Despite the above mentioned limitations, our research was able to gather rich data, and using our lens of psychological contracts penetrated major underlying factors influencing knowledge sharing across the identified key sub-cultures at our research sites. Our study has also helped us to realize the importance of conducting research in such a way that the real issues faced by practitioners out in the field are addressed, and linked with the existing academic theories from several disciplines through a rigorous analysis thus producing a rich picture of the phenomena.

The longitudinal research form adopted to conduct this study helped us to gather the perceptions of the stakeholders of the system over a period of three years. We found that perceptions regarding the CRM project changed over time as stakeholders interacted on a prolonged basis with one another. We were thus able to identify the factors that promoted or impeded the establishment of "mutual high-obligations" types of psychological contracts in these interactions and their impact on the success of the CRM projects at UKCC and IE.COM. The research findings highlighted the importance of psychological contracts in understanding the factors leading to technology and knowledge bottlenecks.

CONCLUSION

There was a time when IT was looked at as a gadget and nothing much else. If during the 1990s we learned more about the importance of organizational, managerial and political factors and their relationships to IT implementations, nevertheless the dot.com boom re-installed in the general pysche an irrational faith in information and communication technology as a silver bullet. This gave rise to the dot.com bubble. When the bubble burst, one would like to think that an era seeing IT as an essential part of business systems arrived, giving rise to business process re-engineering and desirable enterprise applications, managed in to promote system integration. The present study suggests that, even as IT-based systems enter into the core of organizational functioning, still stakeholders neglect to take into account a range of factors other than the technical. It is important therefore to continue to carry out studies like the present one that manifestly demonstrate the complex issues inherent in the implementation of modern systems.

Looking specifically at CRM and its role in organizational attempts at system integration, this is a much talked about, yet relatively under researched area. We are heading towards an era where the fabric of CRM needs further clarification. Dispute over cultural boundaries was highlighted and discussed in this research using the lens of psychological contracts, showing continuing cultural gaps between technical and other cultures in systems implementation. It is becoming crucial to look again at the "techno-culture" itself in greater depth, that is what one might call the "culture behind the clicks". This research did not explore the technological fabric of CRM in any depth. This fabric does in fact deserves to be explored further, as Orlikowski and Iacono (2001) have suggested. It would be interesting to highlight the technological issues faced at a micro level in the CRM project. This will be a way to work against the fear of IT and enhance our understanding regarding technological issues from a technical perspective that is from the viewpoints of members of the techno-culture. We also propose further research using a multidisciplinary approach in testing the psychological contracts and its interdependencies with sub-cultural interactions and knowledge sharing from an international perspective. This research was limited to the UK only. It would be useful to compare the interdependencies between psychological contracts, subculture interactions and knowledge sharing across the high context and low context culture nations. A comparison with what have been referred to as relatively high context culture nations like Japan and China will enhance our understanding concerning enablers and inhibitors to the sharing of tacit knowledge in the implementation of CRM systems.

A final word on studying knowledge. It would be foolish, with a subject like knowledge, to end on a high note of somehow having solved the problem. We have attempted to catch the reality of knowledge sharing issues in flight and yet are very aware of the fact that we have managed to capture only so much of what after all is a socially constructed reality. Our findings were based on observations, historical data gathering and semi-structured in-depth interviews. We visited our research sites frequently. However, we were not able to live the experiences of the stakeholders fully. Our interactions and data gathering had their limitations and are by no means perfect. It was difficult to get hold of subjects at both sites and even though a good working relationship was maintained at all times, there were issues such as time constraints that could not be ignored. It may well be that, in practice, we have only communicated half-knowledge. As Mary Coleridge once said, half-knowledge is very communicable, not so knowledge.

There are also issues regarding incommensurability of knowledge. The distinction between tacit/non-codified knowledge and explicit/codified knowledge is not clear but problematic. According to scholars such as Polanyi it is impossible to separate tacit/non-codified knowledge from explicit knowledge. Polanyi (1966) has pointed out that, "These two are not as sharply divided as we might think. While tacit/non-codified knowledge can be possessed by itself, explicit/codified knowledge must rely on being understood and applied in a tacit/non-codified manner. Hence all knowledge is either tacit/non-codified or rooted in tacit/non-codified knowledge." Also, the attempts to separate these two dimensions of knowledge may only produce perceptive information regarding a very specific situation. One could also ask whether it is beneficial at all to promote the integration of knowledge across the sub-cultural boundaries. The adoption of common practices and artefacts may enable knowledge integration in the near term but may fail to address significant underlying differences. It can be useful to understand these underlying differences in promoting what Thompson and Walsham (2004) call "knowing", and yet, from another perspective again, an attempt to integrate or share tacit knowledge may reduce the compatibility and overall performance of individuals within an organization.

Going further down the political route detailed in Chapter 2, we saw in the case studies how divergent interests supported or inhibited the creation, sharing, and use of different types of knowledge. This leads to the proposition that knowledge is not just a power resource, but that power itself can create forms of knowledge, in terms of classifying, allowing, forbidding and legitimating what is called knowledge. One can see elements of this in our two rich case studies, in terms of how players at different levels allowed certain knowledges to be public and accepted, others to be excluded or hidden, while we also uncovered orphan knowledge, that is, knowledge that existed and was potentially helpful to the implementation but was detached from any power structure or mode of legitimation. Clearly there is no end in sight to the riches in store for pursuing further the subjects we have chosen to concentrate on. But books, said Albert Camus, are never completed, only abandoned.

Appendices

Appendix A: Interview guidelines for the Pilot/Initial Analysis

Appendix B: Interview Guidelines for Final Data Collection

Appendix C: A Note on Processual Analysis

Appendix A: Interview guidelines for the Pilot/Initial Analysis

PERSONAL BACKGROUND

1. What is your position?
2. How long have you worked in that position?
3. How long have you worked with CRM System?

IMPLEMENTATION

4. In what way were you involved in the implementation process of CRM System?
5. Describe the process of implementation from your perspective: how you were involved, dates, what happened, main issues why they occurred?
6. What were the strengths and weaknesses of the implementation of CRM System?
7. Have external end-users of the system been involved in the implementation process? Please elaborate how.
8. How would you implement it differently, if you were given free hands?

KNOWLEDGE MANAGEMENT

9. Is there any explicit knowledge management process operating?
10. Does it cover how knowledge is created, shared, retained and exploited?

11. On what basis would you share knowledge and with who?
12. What sort of knowledge you would expect and what is not you getting?

KNOWLEDGE SHARING

13. Have you learned any tricks of the trades; any workarounds during the implementation of the system?
14. Do you share the tricks of the trades with other stakeholders of the system?
15. Please describe the way in which you interact with other stakeholders of the system?
16. Do you socialize with other stakeholders of the system outside the working hours?
17. Is the knowledge captured on the operational side shared with the analytic/back-office side? Please elaborate how?

KNOWLEDGE RETENTION

18. Are their any experts of the system and how is their expertise being take advantage of?
19. Has the system changed over time?
20. Has the knowledge created through the interactions been captured to facilitate the changes in the system?
21. Is the system evolving according to the needs of your job?
22. Are the changes in the system acting as an enabler or as an inhibitor?

EVALUATION

23. Which of the following statements describes the effectiveness of the system?

    1. CRM system is an effective tool for the management to get an overview of customer care.
    2. It has helped me with improving the speed of the work, accuracy, integration of customer information and customer intimacy.

3. It has improved the speed and accuracy considerably and has helped to integrate customer information.
4. CRM System has promoted customer centric connectivity, consistency and responsiveness.
5. CRM System has helped to provide a personalized and consistent customer care
6. CRM System has helped to create a 360-degree view of the customer.
7. If none of the above applies, please elaborate.

24. In what way have you been benefited by your involvement with the system?
25. Could you please describe a working loop for example right from the stage a customer contacts UKCC/IE to the stage when a service has been delivered?
26. What, in your opinion are the inhibitors (sub-optimizing factors) of the CRM System?
27. Who is in control, people or the system? (Technical determinism)
28. Does the system meet the requirements of the job?
29. In what way do you think has the system enhanced/facilitated the quality of work?
30. Is the system meeting your expectations? Please elaborate.

Appendix B: Interview Guidelines for Final Data Collection

PERSONAL BACKGROUND

1. What is your position?
2. How long have you worked in that position?
3. How long have you worked with the CRM system?

IT HISTORY AND EXTERNAL CONTEXT

4. How much of the IT has been in sourced and how much has been outsourced and why?
5. What are the past successes and failures? Please elaborate
6. What environmental pressures were/are there and how are they effecting the IS strategy?
7. Has the technology matured?
8. How has the CRM market changed over time?
9. Is there anything distinctive and more difficult about CRM implementation?

INTERNAL CONTEXT

10. Has the in-house expertise increased over the past year?
11. What sort of reward systems are at place?
12. Has the interaction between the sub-cultures increased over time and why?
13. What methods are at put to practice to facilitate prolonged interactions between the sub-cultures?

CONTENT ISSUES

14. **Nature of Technology**—refers to people's images of the technology and their understanding of its capabilities and functionality.
15. **(ii) Technology Strategy**—refers to people's views of why their organization acquired and implemented the technology. It includes their understanding of the motivation or vision behind the adoption decision and its likely value to the organization.
16. **(iii) Technology in Use**—refers to people's understanding of how the technology has been used on a day-to-day basis and the likely or actual conditions and consequences associated with such use.
17. Size, complexity, definitional uncertainty of system, technical uncertainty, no. of departments / units affected—effect on knowledge issues below.

PROCESS OF CHANGE

18. How is the change being managed in the post CRM implementation environment? For example, user involvement, project management, evaluation, application of learning, knowledge creation/retention, training, staff stability, levels of different stakeholder commitment.

KNOWLEDGE MANAGEMENT

19. Is there any explicit knowledge management process operating?
20. Does it cover how knowledge is created, shared, retained and exploited?
21. On what basis would you share knowledge and with who?
22. What sort of knowledge you would expect and what is not you getting?

KNOWLEDGE SHARING

23. Have you learned any tricks of the trades; any workarounds during the implementation of the system?
24. Do you share the tricks of the trades with other stakeholders of the system?

25. Please describe the way in which you interact with other stakeholders of the system?
26. Do you socialize with other stakeholders of the system outside the working hours?
27. Is the knowledge captured on the operational side shared with the analytic/back-office side? Please elaborate how?

KNOWLEDGE RETENTION

28. Are their any experts of the system and how is their expertise being take advantage of?
29. Has the system changed over time?
30. Has the knowledge created through the interactions been captured to facilitate the changes in the system?
31. Is the system evolving according to the needs of your job?
32. Are the changes in the system acting as an enabler or as an inhibitor?

EVALUATION

33. Which of the following statements describes the effectiveness of the system?

    1. CRM system is an effective tool for the management to get an overview of customer care
    2. It has helped me with improving the speed of the work, accuracy, integration of customer information and customer intimacy.
    3. It has improved the speed and accuracy considerably and has helped to integrate customer information.
    4. CRM system has promoted customer centric connectivity, consistency and responsiveness.
    5. CRM system has helped to provide a personalised and consistent customer care
    6. CRM system has helped to create a 360-degree view of the customer.
    7. If none of the above applies, please elaborate

34. In what way have you been benefited by your involvement with the system?

35. Could you please describe a working loop for example right from the stage a customer contacts the front-office to the stage when a service has been delivered.
36. What, in your opinion are the inhibitors (sub-optimizing factors) of the CRM system?
37. Who is in control, people or the system? (Technical determinism)
38. Does the system meet the requirements of the job?
39. In what way do you think has the system enhanced/facilitated the quality of work?
40. Is the system meeting your expectations? Please elaborate.

Appendix C: A Note on Processual Analysis

This research used a longitudinal comparative case study approach to collect and critically analyze empirical data. The nature of this research was essentially of a processual type. The five guiding assumptions for processual research proposed by Pettigrew (1990, 1997) provide an appropriate justification of our approach. They are:

- embeddedness; studying processes across a number of levels;
- temporal interconnectedness; studying processes in past, present and future;
- a role in explanation for context and action;
- a search for holistic rather than linear explanations;
- a need to link process analysis to the location and explanation of outcomes.

We discuss these in detail below.

EMBEDDEDNESS

According to Pettigrew (1997) social processes are deeply embedded in the contexts that produce and are produced by them. Part of the interactive field is the analysis of how outer and inner contexts surrounding the firm shape this process. Outer contexts include the economic, social, political, competitive and sectoral environments in which the firms are located. In our cases the environment may have been the same and yet how people from public and private sector made sense of it varied.

Inner context refers to the inner mosaic of the firm; the structural, cultural and political environments which in consort with the outer context shape features of the process. Processes according to Pettigrew (1997) are embedded in contexts and can only be studied as such. We have attempted to study the micro elements of a CRM system implementation in this research from a knowledge perspective. In order to understand the micro elements such as psychological contracts, it was vital to take into account the inner and outer contexts of the organizations studied. The above principle is also favoured by Walsham (1995) and Klein and Myers (1999). Furthermore, we investigated and took into account the differing perceptions at different levels of hierarchies at both research sites.

TEMPORAL INTERCONNECTEDNESS

We provide briefly an organizational history and IS strategy background of the research settings so that the intended audience can see the emergence of the knowledge sharing phenomenon. Pettigrew (1997) argues that understanding the sequence and flow of events over time is a crucial requirement for the process scholar. Our pilot/initial analysis was instrumental in studying longitudinally the micro mechanisms of knowledge sharing processes in CRM implementations at our research sites.

Our research attempts to show how antecedent conditions at our research sites have shaped the present and are influencing the emerging future. Beneath the surface events and chronology we have searched for the recurrent patterns, structures and underlying logics in the processes of CRM implementations. According to Pettigrew (1997) there is no assumption of predetermined time tables, of ordered and inevitable sequences or stages. As we saw in our research process, the trajectories of CRM implementation strategy process were probabilistic and uncertain because of changing context and human action. This coincides with Loasby (1976) who so eloquently put it: "If choice is real, the future cannot be certain; if the future is certain, there can be no choice."

A ROLE IN EXPLANATION FOR CONTEXT AND ACTION

According to Pettigrew (1997), context is not just a stimulus environment but a nested arrangement of structures and processes where the subjective interpretations of actors perceiving, learning and remembering help shape the process. The above reinforces the suitability of Pettigrew's processual approach in our research. Our processual approach has been instrumental in highlighting how differing perceptions of CRM system stakeholders shaped the process of implementation at our research sites.

This research attempts to reinforce what Pettigrew (1997) stated so elegantly—that organizational processes are both constrained by features such as tradition and technological commitments and also shape contexts, by for example preserving or (as in one of our cases) altering technological strategies.

A SEARCH FOR HOLISTIC RATHER THAN LINEAR EXPLANATIONS

Links between multiple levels of contexts can only be established by exposing actions and recurrent patterns in the investigation over a long period of time. Time is captured in our study of the CRM implementations through a combination of retrospective and real-time analysis of the contemporary situations. As stated by Pettigrew (1997), our processual comparative case study approach has a natural advantage over other comparative methods as it has provided the opportunity to explore holistic explanation through within-case and cross-case analysis. We were able to use the processual approach in examining real time issues linking them with intersecting conditions of context and theories from our multidisciplinary literature (Ragin, 1987). We have attempted to enhance the understanding towards micro-mechanisms in the implementation of a CRM system by linking the context (both internal and external) with the process.

A NEED TO LINK PROCESS ANALYSIS TO THE LOCATION AND EXPLANATION OF OUTCOMES

Finally we have attempted to link the process with outcomes in our study. As Pettigrew (1997) states, building an outcome into process research design has a number of advantages. The outcome both simplified and complicated our study by providing a focal point, an anchor for the whole investigation. Furthermore, we were able to compare the "how" and "why" variations across cases. We have achieved this by comparing the results in a cross-case analysis to highlight the similarities and differences from a knowledge perspective. We have attempted to show how policy outcomes are shaped by the process and context and their impacts on the knowledge sharing mechanisms in our study of CRM implementation. We concur with Pettigrew (1997) and attempt to confirm that processual research is capable of generating reliable knowledge not only of processes and outcomes but also of why and how outcomes are differentially shaped by processes.

We have been able to implement the deduction and induction cycle as stated by Pettigrew (1997) in our research. The cycle consists of the core questions of study leading to related themes and questions. Preliminary data collection then takes place resulting in early pattern recognition and early writing (our pilot chapter) disconfirmation and verification (testing of our methodology and refining the reviewed literature). This leads to elaborated themes and questions (our initial analysis in Chapter 4) resulting in further data collection (Chapters 5 and 6), further pattern recognition and comparative analysis (Chapter 7) ending in a more refined study vocabulary (Chapter 7), and scope for further research (Chapter 8).

CHOICE OF SECTOR AND SITES

Data was collected from the previously mentioned two organizations using a data triangulation (data collection from multiple sources) and combining retrospective and real time analysis. Different industrial sectors were chosen (private and public sector). Using a theoretical justification employed by Pettigrew (1989), choosing of polar types to exploit planned opportunism was used and this approach produced an excellent opportunity for comparison and contrast. In order to increase the ecological validity of the findings two different, polarized organizations were chosen—one public and one private sector. The deviating patterns of the phenomenon under investigation between UKCC and IE.COM were as follows:

- Differential customer base; as both the organizations have a differing clientele.
- Differing goals; social goals vs. profit goals.
- Complex and debated performance indicators vs. mainly quantitative financial measures.
- More ill defined policy directives; complexity of policy implementation vs. relatively less ambiguous policy.
- Relative openness of government and decision making; stress on representatives vs. relative secrecy; stress on business confidentiality.
- Wide stakeholder base vs. primary focus on shareholders.
- Extensive accountability vs. restricted accountability.

- Primary resource base from public taxes vs. primary resource base from operational returns and borrowing.
- Multiple values and goals; service, public interest, equity, professionalism, consumer participation, complex trade-offs vs. relatively restricted.
- Statutory and parliamentary regulation; codes of conduct vs. board of directors; company planning frame works.
- Needs of national economic management vs. market place signals, e.g. business lending rate.

Source: Willcocks and Harrow (1992)

There were also similarities. These will minimize extraneous variations and help to clarify the findings in a specific environment (Eisenhardt, 1989; Willcocks & Harrow, 1992).

- Both are UK based.
- Both are using a "Vanilla" (off the shelf) type package.
- Both have used the CRM system for about more than a year.
- Both the organizations come under B2C category.
- Both are also large organizations with a large customer base.

The sites IE.COM and UKCC were chosen as both the sites are using CRM systems to improve interactions with their customers. At the start of this research, both the sites had used the systems for more than a year. The deviating pattern of the adaptation pace of CRM implementation at both sites were investigated and compared to gain further insight and linkages between the existing theories regarding IT implementation in a CRM environment at a micro level.

References

Ackoff, R.L. (1989) From data to wisdom. *Journal of Applies Systems Analysis* **16**, 3–9.

Agar, M. (1994) *Culture Shock: Understanding the Language of Conversation.* Morrow, New York.

Alvesson, M. (2002) *Understanding Organisational Culture.* Sage Publications Ltd, London.

Anderson, N. and René S. (1998) The psychological contract in retrospect and prospect, *Journal of Organizational Behaviour*, **19**(Special Issue), 637–647.

Argyris, C. and Schön, D. (1996) *Organizational learning II: Theory, Method and Practice.* Addison Wesley, Reading, Mass.

Avison, D.E. and Myers, M.D. (1995) Information systems and anthropology: An anthropological perspective on IT and organizational culture. *Information Technology & People*, **8**(3), 43–56.

Avgerou, C. (2000) IT and organisational change: An institutional perspective. *Information Technology and People*, **13**(4), 234–262. London School of Economics, London, UK.

Bakhtin, M.M. (1981) Discourse in the novel. In *The Dialogic Imagination.* Holquis, M. (Ed.). University of Texas Press, Austin, TX.

Bartlett, C.A. and Ghoshal, S. (1998) *Beyond Strategic Planning to Organisation Learning: Lifeblood of the Individualized Corporation, Strategy and Leadership.* Harper Business, UK & Maxima, Paris.

Bell, J. (1992) *Doing Your Research Project.* Milton Keynes: Open University Press.

Benbasat, I., Goldstein, D.K. and Mead, M. (1987). The case research strategy in studies of information systems. *MIS Quarterly*, **11**(3), 369–386.

Bennett, R. and Gabriel, H. (1999) Organizational factors and knowledge management within large marketing departments: An empirical study. *Journal of Knowledge Management*, **3**(3), 212–25.

Bingi, P., Sharma, M., and Godla, J. (1999) Critical issues affecting an ERP implementation. *Information System Management*, **16**(3), 7–14.

Bloomfield B.P. and Vurdubaki T. (1994) Negotiating the boundary between the technical and the social in the development of IT systems. *Information Technology and People*, **7**(1), 9–24.

Boland, R. and Tenkasi, R. (1996) Exploring knowledge diversity in knowledge intensive firms: A new role for information systems. *Journal of Organizational Change Management; Bradford;* **9**(1), 79–91. MCB University Press.

Boland, R., Tenkasi, R.V. and Te'eni, D. (1994) Designing information technology to support distributed cognition. *Organization Science*, **5**(3), 456–475.

Bose, R. (2002) *Customer Relationship Management: Key Components for IT Success*, Industrial Management, **102**(1/2), 89–98.

Bostrom, R.P. and Heinen, J.S. (1997) 'MIS problems and failures: A socio technical perspective PART 1: The causes', *MIS Quarterly*, **1**(3), 17–32.

Brown, J.S. and Diguid, P. (1998) Organizing Knowledge. *California Management Review*, **40**(3), 90–111.

Burns, T. and Stalker, G. (1961) *The Management of Innovation*, Tavistock, London.

Bygstad, B. (2003) The implementation puzzle of CRM systems in knowledge based organizations. *Information Resources Management Journal*, **16**(4), 1–33.

Carr, N.G. (2003) *IT Doesn't Matter*, Harvard Business Review, May 2003. Available at www.hbr.com, also check his website http://www.nicholasgcarr.com where you will find some other responses to his ideas.

Chalmeta, R. (2006) Methodology for customer relationship management. *Journal of Systems and Software*, **79**(7), 1015–1024.

Checkland, P.B. (1981) *Systems Thinking, Systems Practice*. John Wiley & Sons, Ltd, Chichester.

Choi, C. and Lee, S. (1997) A knowledge-based view of co-operative interorganizational relationships. In *Co-operative Strategies: European Perspectives*. Beamish, P. and Killing, J. (Eds). The New Lexington Press, San Francisco.

Choo, C.W. (1998) *The Knowing Organization: How Organizations Use Information to Construct Meaning, Create Knowledge, and Make Decisions*. Oxford University Press, New York.

Christensen, C. and Overdorf, M. (2000) Meeting the challenge of disruptive change. *Harvard Business Review*, March–April, 75–83.

Churchman, C.W. (1982) *Thought and wisdom*. Intersystems C.A.

Chung, R., Marchand, R. and Kettinger, W. (2004) Citigroup's CEEMEA Sales and Trading Unit. IMD paper 3-1306, June, IMD, Lausanne.

Ciborra, C. (2000) *From Control to Drift*. Oxford University Press, Oxford.

Ciborra, C.U. and Failla, A. (2000) Infrastructure as a process: The case of CRM in IBM, in ciborra, C.U. and associates. *From Control To Drift—The Dynamics of Corporate Information Infrastructures*, Oxford University Press, Oxford.

Ciborra, C., Hanseth, O. and Associates (2000). *From Control To Drift*. Oxford University Press, Oxford.

Clark P., Bennett, D., Burcher, P. Newell, S. Swan, J. and Sharifi, S. (1992) The decision-episode framework and computer aided production management (CAPM). *International studies of Management and Organisation*, **22**(4), 69–80.

Claver, E., Llopis, J., Gonzlez, M.R and Gasc, J.L. (2001) The performance of information systems through organization culture. *Information Technology and People*, **14**(3), 247–260.

Cooper, R. and Zmud, R. (1990) Information technology implementation research: A technological diffusion approach. *Management Science*, **36**(2), 123–39.

Daft, R. and Lengel, R.H. (1986) Organizational information requirements, media richness and structural design. *Management Science*, **32**(5), 554–571.

Darke, P., Shanks, G. and Broadbent, M. (1998) Successfully completing case study research: Combining rigour, relevance and pragmatism. *Information Systems Journal*, **8**(4), 273–289.

Davenport, T.H. (1993) Process innovation: Reengineering work through information. *Journal of e-Government*, Harvard Business School Press, Boston, MA.

Davenport, T.H., DeLong, D.W. and Beers, M.C. (1998) Successful knowledge management projects. *Sloan Management Review*, **39**(4), 43–57.

Davidson, E. (2002) Technology frames and framing: A socio-cognitive investigation of requirements determination. *MIS Quarterly*, **26**(4), 329–358.

Davis, F.D. (1989) Perceived usefulness, perceived case of use, and user acceptance of information technology. *MIS Quarterly*, **13**(3), 319–339.

Davis, G.B. and Olson, M.H. (1985) *Management Information Systems: Conceptual Foundations. Structures and Development*, (2nd edn), McGraw-Hill, New York.

Denzin, N.K and Lincoln, Y.S. (2000) *Handbook of Qualitative research* (2nd edn) Sage, London.

Digby, D.K., Reichheld, F.K., and Paul Scheffer (2002) Avoid the four pitfalls of CRM. *Harvard Business Review* (February), 101–109.

Drucker, P.F. (1999) *Leadership Challenges for the 21st Century*. Butterworth Heinemann, Oxford.

Dutton, J.M. and Thomas, A. (1984) Treating progress functions as a managerial opportunity. *American Management Review*, **9**(2), 235–247.

Dutton, J.M. and Thomas, A. (1985) Relating technology change and learning by doing. In *Research on technological innovation, Management and Policy*. Richard S. Rosenbloom (Ed.). **2**, 187–224.

Eisenhardt, K.M. (1989) Building theories from case study research. *Academy of Management Review*, **14**(4), 532–550.

El Sawy, O.A. (1985) Implementation by cultural infusion: An approach for managing the introduction of information technologies, *MIS Quarterly*, **9**(2), 131–40.

Fahey, L. and Prusak, L. (1998) The eleven deadliest sins of knowledge management, *California Management Review*, **40**(3), 265–276.

Fincham, R. (1994) Computing occupations: Organisational power, work transitions and collective mobility. *New Technology, Work & Employment*, **9**(1), 43–53.

Gee, J.P. (1992) *The Social Mind*, Bergin and Garvey, New York.

Geertz, C. (1973) *The Interpretation of Cultures: Selected essays*. Basic Books, New York.

Geib, M., Kolbe, L. and Brenner, W. (2005) Customer relationship management in business networks: Lessons from the financial services industry in Germany and Switzerland. *MISQ Executive*, **4**(1), 247–258.

GMAC 2002 (2002) http://searchcrm.techtarget.com/qna/0,289202, sid11_gci811687,00.html.

Goldenberg, B.J. (2002) *CRM Automation*. Prentice Hall, NJ.

Goodhue, L., Wixom, H. and Watson, J. (2002) Business benefits through CRM, *MIS Quarterly Executive*, **1**(2), 79–96.

Gray, B., Bougon, M. and Donnellon, A. (1985) Organizations as constructions and destructions of meaning. *J. Manage*, **11**(1), 83–95.

Gregory, Kathleen, L. (1983) Native-view paradigms: Multiple cultures and culture conflicts in organizations. *Administrative Science Quarterly*, **28**(3), 359–376.

Grindley, K. (1992) The culture gap. In *Information Technology Review*. Grindley, K. (Ed.). Price Waterhouse.

Grönroos, C. (1994) Quo vadis, marketing?—toward a relationship marketing paradigm. *Journal of Marketing Management*, **10**(6), 347–360.

Gummesson, E. (2002b) Relationship marketing in the new economy. *Journal of Relationship Marketing*, **1**(1), 37–57.

Habermas, J. (1979) *Communication and the Evolution of Society*, Beacon Press, Boston, MA.

Hakansson, H. and Snehota, I. (1995) *Developing Relationships in Business Networks*. Routledge, London.

Herschbach, D.R. (1995) Technology as knowledge: Implications for instruction. *Journal of Technology Education*, **7**(1), 31–42.

Hewson Group (2002) *CRM in the Public Sector*, Hewson Group Publication, www.hewson.co.uk.

Hinton, C.M. (1994) *Technology Assimilation: Understanding the User—IT Professional Relationship*. Ph.D., Innovation and Technology Assessment Unit, Cranfield University, Cranfield.

Holland, C. and Ben, L. (1999) A Critical success factors model for ERP implementation. *IEEE Software*, **16**(3), 30–35.

Hyde, Kenneth F. (2000) Recognising deductive processes in qualitative research. *Qualitative Market Research: An International Journal*, **3**(2), 82–89.

Iansiti, M. (1993) Real-world R and D: Jumping the product generation gap. *Harvard Business Review*, **71**(3), 138–47.

Isabella, L.A. (1990) Evolving interpretations as a change unfolds: How managers construe key organizational events. *AccLd. Manage J*, **33**(1), 7–41.

Janssens, M., Sels, L. and Van den Brande, I. (2003) Multiple types of psychological contracts: A six-cluster solution. *Human Relations*, **56**(11), 1349–1379.

Jehn, K. (1995) A multimethod examination of the benefits and detriments of intragroup conflict. *Administrative Science Quarterly*, **40**, 256–82.

Kay, J. (1993) *Foundations of Corporate Success: How Business Strategies Add Value*. Oxford University Press, Oxford, 416.

Keen P. (1981) Information systems and organizational change. *Communications of the ACM*, **24**(1).

Kilmann, R. (1989) *Managing Beyond the Quick Fix*. Jossey Bass, San Francisco.

King, N. (1994) The *Qualitative Research Interview*. In *Qualitative methods in organisational research*. Cassell, C. and Symon, G. (Eds). Sage, London.

Kirkman, B.L. and Shapiro, D.L. (1997) The impact of cultural values on employee resistance to teams: Towards a model of globalized self-managed work teams effectiveness. *Journal of International Business Studies*, **22**(3), 730–757.

Klein, H.K. and Myers, M.D. (1999) A set of principles for conducting and evaluating interpretive field studies in information systems. *MIS Quarterly*, **23**(1), 67–93.

Kolb, D. and Frohman, A. (1970) An organizational development approach to consulting. *Sloan Management Review*, Autumn, 25–33.

Krauss, R.M. and Fussell, S.R. (1991) Perspective-taking in communication representation of others' knowledge in reference. *Social Cognition*, **9**(1), 2–24.

Krogh, G.V., Ichijo, K. and Nonaka, I. (2000) *Enabling knowledge creation: How to unlock the mystery of tacit knowledge and release the power of innovation*. Oxford University Press, Oxford.

Kumar, K. and Bjorn-Andersen, N. (1990) A cross-cultural comparison of IS designer values. *Communications of the ACM*, **33**(5), 528–538.

Kunda, G. (1991) Ritual and management of corporate culture: A critical perspective. In *Cultures in Organisations: Three Perspectives* M. Joaanne (Ed.), Oxford University Press, Oxford.

Kwon, T. and Zmud, R. (1987) Unifying the fragmented models of information systems implementation, In *Critical Issues in Information Systems Research*. Boland, J. and Hirschheim, R. (Eds). John Wiley& Sons, Ltd, Chichester.

Lam, W. (2005) Investigating success factors in enterprise application integration: A case-driven analysis. *European Journal of Information Systems*, **14**(2), 175–187.

Lawrence, P.R. and Lorsch, J.W. (1967) *Organisation and Environment*, Harvard Graduate School of Business Administration.

Leonard-Barton, D. and Kraus, W.A. (1985) Implementing new technology. *Harvard Business Review*, **63**(Nov–Dec), 102–110.

Leonard-Barton, D. (1985) Experts as negative opinion leaders in the diffusion of a technological innovation. *Journal of Consumer Research*, **1**(3), 914–926.

Leonard-Barton, D.A. (1988) Implementation as mutual adaptation of technology and Organisation. *Research Policy*, **17**(5), 251–267.

Leonard-Barton, D. (1995) *Well-springs of Knowledge: Building and Sustaining the Sources of Innovation.* Boston, Mass.: Harvard Business School Press.

Lewin K. discussed in Schein E. (1980) Organizational Psychology, Prentice Hall, New York.

Loasby, B.J. (1976) *Choice, Complexity and Ignorance: An enquiry into Economic, Theory and Practice of Decision Making.* Cambridge University Press, Cambridge.

Long, D.W.D. and Fahey, L. (2000) Diagnosing cultural barriers to knowledge management. *The Academy of Management Executive; Ada*, **14**(4), 113–127.

Louis, M.R. (1985) An investigator's guide to workplace culture. In *Organizational culture.* Frost, P., Moore, L.F., Louis, M.R., Lundberg, C.C. and Martin, J. (Eds). Sage, Beverly Hills, CA, 73–93.

Maanen, J., Van, S.R. and Barley (1985) *Cultural Organization, Fragments of a Theory.* In *Organizational Culture.* Frost, P.J. *et al.* (Eds). Newbury Park, California. Sage, 31–53.

Makin, P.J. Cooper, C.L. and Cox, C.J. (1996) *Organizations and the Psychological Contract.* British Psychological Society, Leicester.

Mangham, I. (1979) *The Politics of Organizational Change.* Greenwood, London.

Marchand, D., and Meadows, R. (2006) Customer relationship management: challenging the myth. *IMD Perspectives for Managers*, **131**, 1–4.

Markus, M.L. (2004) Technochange management: Using IT to drive organizational change, *Journal of Information Technology*, **19**, 4–20.

Markus, M.L. and Robey, D. (1988) Information technology and organisational change. Casual structure in theory and research. *Management science*, **34**(5), 583–598.

Mead, G.H. (1934) *Mind, Self and Society*, University of Chicago Press, Chicago, IL.

Meyer, J. and Rowan, B. (1977) Institutionalized organizations. Formal structure as myth and ceremony. *American Journal of Sociology*, **83** (September), 340–363.

Meyer, M. and Kolbe, L. M. (2005) Integration of customer relationship management: status quo and implications for research and practice. *Journal of Strategic Marketing*, **13**(3), 175–198.

Mintzberg, H. (1987) Crafting strategy. *Harvard Business Review*, **65**(4), 66–75.

Mumford, E. Land, F. and Hawgood, J. (1978) A participative approach to the design of computer systems. *Impact of Science on Society*, **28**(3), 253–256.

Myers, M. (1997) Qualitative research in information systems'. *MIS Quarterly*, **21**(2), 241–242.

Myers, M.D. (1995) Dialectical hermeneutics: A theoretical framework for the implementation of information systems, *Information Systems Journal*, **5**(1), 51–70.

Myers, M.D. (2003) *Qualitative Research in Information Systems* [Online]. Available: http://www.auckland.ac.nz/msis/isworld/ [2003, June 16].

Nelson, K.M. and Cooprider, J.G. (1996) The contribution of shared knowledge to IS group performance. *MIS Quarterly*, **20**(4), 409–432.

Newell, S., Robertson, M., Scarbrough, H. and Swan, J. (2002) *Managing Knowledge Work.* Palgrave, Houndsmills, Basingstoke, Hampshire.

Nonaka, I. (1994) A dynamic theory of organisational knowledge creation, *Organisational Science*, **5**(1), 14–37.

Nonaka, I., Takeuchi, H. and Umemoto, K. (1996) A theory of organizational knowledge creation. *International Journal of Technology Management, Special Issue on Unlearning and Learning for Technological Innovation*, **11**(7/8), 833–845.

Nonaka, I. and Kono, N. (1998) The concept of "ba": Building a foundation for knowledge creation. *California Management Review*, **40**(3), 40–54.

Nonaka, I. and Takeuchi, H. (1995) *The Knowledge-creating Company: How Japanese Companies Create the Dynamics of Innovation*. Oxford University Press, New York, NY.

Office of the Deputy Prime Minister (2000) *"e-Government Delivering Local Government Online"*, http://www.local-regions.odpm.gov.uk/egov/delivery/index.htm.

Office of the Deputy Prime Minister (2002) *Implementing Electronic Government: Draft Guidance*, http://www.odpm.gov.uk/stellent/groups/odpm_localgov/documents/source/odpm_locgov_source_605194.doc.

Orlikowski, W.J. (1993) CASE Tools as organizational change: Investigating incremental and radical changes in systems development. *MIS Quarterly*, **17**(3), 309–340.

Orlikowski, W.J. and Gash, I.C. (1991) Changing frames: Understanding technological change in organizations. Working Paper 3368, *Massachusetts Institute of Technology*, Cambridge, Mass.

Orlikowski, W. and Gash, D. (1994) Technology frames: Making sense of information technology in organizations, *ACM Transactions on Information Systems*, **12**(2), 174–207.

Orlikowski, W.J. and Hofman, J.D. (1997) An improvisational approach to change management. *Sloan Management Review*, **38**(2), 11–21.

Orlikowski, W.J. and Iacono, C.S. (2001) Desperately seeking the "IT" in IT research—A call to theorising the IT artifact. *Information System Research*, **12**(2), 121–134.

Orlikowski, W.J. and Tyre, M.J. (1994) Windows of opportunity: Temporal patterns of technological adaptation in organizations, *Organization Science*, **5**(1), 98–118.

Parr A. and Shanks G. (2000) A model of ERP project implementation. *Journal on Information Technology*, **15**(4), 289–303.

Parvatiyar, A. and Sheth, J.N. (2001) Conceptual framework of customer relationship management. In *Customer Relationship Management—Emerging Concepts, Tools and Applications*. Parvatiyar, A., Sheth, J. N., Shainesh, G. (Eds). Tata/McGraw-Hill, New Delhi, 3–25.

Payne, A. & Frow, P. (2005) A strategic framework for customer relationship management. *Journal of Marketing*, **69**(4), 167–176.

Peppers, D. and Rogers, M. (1993) *The One to One Future*. Piatkus, London.

Perrin, J. (1990) The inseparability of technology and work organizations. *History and Technology*, **7**(1), 1–13.

Piercy N.F. (2001) *Market-led Strategic Change: Transforming the Process of Going to Market*. Butterworth-Heinemann, Oxford.

Pettigrew, A. (1985) *The Awakening Giant: Continuity and change in ICI*. Blackwell, Oxford.

Pettigrew, A.M. (1973) *The Politics of Organisational Decision Making*. Tavistock, London.

Pettigrew, A.M. (1979) On studying organisational culture. *Administrative Science Quarterly*, **24**(4), 570–581.

Pettigrew, A.M. (1989) *Issues of Time and Site Selection in Longitudinal Research on Change,* Harvard Business School Research Colloquium: The Information Systems Research Challenge: Qualitative Research Methods, (1), 13–19.

Pettigrew, A.M. (1990) Longitudinal field research on change: theory and practice. *Organisation Science,* **1**(3), 267–292.

Pettigrew, A.M. (1997) *What is a processual analysis? Scandinavian Journal of Management,* **13**(4), 337–348.

Pfeffer, J. (1980) *Power in Organizations.* Pitman, Boston, Mass.

Pfeffer, J. and Sutton, R.I. (1999) *The Knowing-Doing Gap; How Smart Companies Turn Knowledge into Action.* Harvard Business School Press, Boston, MA.

Pliskin, N., Romm, T., Lee, A.S. and Weber, Y. (1993) Presumed versus actual organizational culture: managerial implications for implementation of information systems. *The Computer Journal,* **36**(2), 143–52.

Polanyi, M. (1958) *Personal Knowledge Towards a Post-critical Philosophy,* Routledge and Kegan Paul Ltd, London.

Polanyi, M (1966) *The Tacit Dimension.* Routledge & Kegan Paul, London.

Polanyi, M. (1967) *Knowing and Being.* University of Chicago Press, Chicago.

Polanyi, M. (1973). *Personal Knowledge.* Routledge & Kegan Paul, London.

Quinn, J.B., Anderson, P. and Finkelstein, S. (1996) Managing professional intellect: making the most of the best. *Harvard Business Review,* **74**(2), 71–80.

Ragin, C.C. (1987) *The Comparative Method.* University of California Press, Berkeley, CA.

Reinartz, W., Krafft, M. and Hoyer, W.D. (2004) The customer relationship management process: Its measurement and impact on performance. *Journal of Marketing Research,* **41**(3), 293–305.

Rigby, D.K., Reichheld, F. and Schefter, P. (2002) Avoid the four perils of CRM. *Harvard Business Review,* February, 101–109.

Rigby, D.K. and Ledingham, D. (2004) CRM done right. *Harvard Business Review,* **82**(11), 118–129.

Riley, P. (1983) A structurationist account of political culture. *Administrative Science Quarterly,* **28**(3) 414–437.

Rogers, E.M. (1995) *Diffusion of innovations* (4th edn). The Free Press, New York.

Ross, L. Greene, D. and House, P. (1977) The false consensus phenomenon: An attributional bias in self-perception and social perception processes. *Journal of Experimental Social Psychology,* **13**(3), 279–301.

Ross, J.W. (2003) Creating a strategic IT architecture competency: Learning in stages. MIT Sloan Working Paper No. 4314–03; Center for Information Systems Research Working Paper No. 335.

Rousseau, D.M. (1995) *Psychological Contracts in Organizations,* Sage Publications, London.

Salancik, G.R. and Pfeffer, J. (1978) A social information processing approach to job attitudes and task design. *Administrative Science Quarterly,* **23**(2), 224–253.

Scarbrough, H. and Corbett, J.M. (1992) *Technology and organization power, meaning and design.* Routledge, New York.

Schein, E.H. (1985) *Organizational culture and leadership.* (1st edn). Jossey-Bass Publishers, San Francisco.

Schwartz, M., Schliebs, O. and Wyssusek, B. (2002) *Focusing the Customer: A Critical Approach towards Design and Use of Data Warehousing in Corporate CRM.* DMDW Workshop at CAISE, Toronto.

Shanks, G., Seddon, P. and Willcocks, L. (2003) ERP-The quiet revolution? In *Second-Wave Enterprise Resource Planning Systems*. Shanks, G., Seddon, P. and Willcocks, L. (Eds). Cambridge University Press, New York, 1–19.

Shore, L.M. and Barksdale, K. (1998) Examining the degree of balance and level of obligation in the employment relationship: A social exchange approach. *Journal of Organizational Behaviour*, **19**, 731–744.

Sprint (2002) http://www.sas.com/news/success/sprint.html.

Stanmark, D. (2001) Leveraging tacit organizational knowledge. *Journal of Management Information Systems*, **17**(3), 9–24.

Stefanou, C.J. and Sarmaniotis, C. (2003) CRM and customer-centric knowledge management: An empirical research. *Business Process Management Journal*, **9**(5), 617–623.

Strauss, A. (1978) *Negotiations: Varieties, Contexts, Processes, and Social Order*. Jossey-Bass Publishers, London.

Tafti, M.H.A. (2002) *Analysis of Factors Affecting Implementation of Customer Relationship Management Systems*. IRMA, Idea Group Publishing, Seattleh.

TDWI Industry Study (2000) *Harnessing Customer Information for Strategic Advantage: Technical Challenges and Business Solutions*. The Data Warehousing Institute.

Thibaut, J.W. and Kelley, H.H. (1959) *The Social Psychology of Groups*. John Wiley & Sons, Inc, New York.

Thompson, Mark P.A. and Walsham, G. (2004) Placing Knowledge Management in Context. *Journal of Management Studies*, **41**(5), 725–747.

Tornatzky, L. and Klein, K. (1982) *Innovation Characteristics and innovation adoption implementation: A Meta-Analysis of Findings*. IEEE Transactions on Engineering Management, February, 28–45.

Trice, H.M. and Morand, D. (1991) *Cultural Diversity: Sub-cultures and Countercultures in Work Organizations*. G. Miller (Eds). *Studies in Organizational Sociology: Essays in Honour of Charles K. Warriner*. Jai Press Ltd, Greenwich, Connecticutt, 69–106.

Van Maanen, J. (1986) Power in the bottle: Drinking patterns and social relations in a British police agency. In *Executive Power*. Sirvasta, S. (Ed.). Jossey-Bass, San Francisco, 204–239.

Van Maanen, J. and Barley, S. (1985) Organizational culture: Fragments of a theory. In *Organizational Culture*. Frost, P., Moore, L., Louis, M.R., Lundberg, C. and Martin, J. (Eds). Beverley Hills, CA: Sage Publications, 31–53.

Vargo S.L. and Lusch R.R. (2004) Evolving to a new dominant logic for marketing. *Journal of Marketing*, **68**(1), 1–17.

Vincenti, W.G. (1984) Technological knowledge without science: The innovation of flush riveting in American airplanes, ca. 1930–ca. 1950. *Technology and Culture*, **25**(3), 540–576.

Vincenti, W.G. (1993) *What Engineers Know and How They Know It. Analytical Studies from Aeronautical History*. The John Hopkins University Press, Baltimore and London.

Walsham, G. (1993) *Interpreting Information Systems in Organizations*. John Wiley & Sons, Ltd, Chichester.

Walsham, G. (1995) Interpretive case studies in IS research: Nature and method. *European Journal of Information System*, **4**(1), 74–81.

Walsham, G. and Waema, T. (1994) Information systems strategy and implementation: A case study of a building society. *ACM Transactions on Information Systems*, **12**(2), 150–173.

Walton, R. (1989) *Up and Running*. Harvard Business Press, Boston.

Waterhouse, P. (1991, 1992) The culture gap, *Information Technology Review*, London, 16–19.

Wathne, K., Roos, J. and Von Krogh, G. (1996). Towards a theory of knowledge sharing in a cooperative context. In *Managing Knowledge: Perspectives on Cooperation and Competition*. Von Krogh, G. and Roos, J. (Eds). Sage, London, 55–81.

Watson, R., Piccoli, G., Brohman, K. and Parasuram, A. (2005) Customer managed interactions: A new paradigm for firm-customer relationships. *MIS Quarterly Executive*, **4**(2), 319–335.

Willcocks, L. (1991) Information systems and human resources in the 1990s—integration through culture, *Paper at the Fifth Annual British Academy of Management Conference, Bath University*, 22–24 September.

Willcocks, L. and Graeser, V. (2001) *Delivering IT and E-Business Value*. Butterworth Heinemann, London.

Willcocks L. and Harrow J. (1992) *Rediscovering public services management*. McGraw-Hill Book Company, London.

Willcocks, L. and Margetts, H. (1994) Risk assessment and information systems. *European Journal of Information Systems*, **4**(1), 1–12.

Willcocks, L. and Mason, D. (1987) *Computerising Work: People, Systems Design and Workplace Relations*. Alfred Waller Limited, Henley-on-Thames.

Willcocks, L. and Plant, R. (2001) Pathways to E-business leadership: Getting to bricks and clicks. *Sloan Management Review*, Spring, 84–93.

Willcocks, L. and Sauer, C. (2001) (Eds.) *Moving to E-Business*. Random House, London.

Willcocks, L. and Sykes, R. (2000) The role of IT function. *Communications of the ACM*, **41**(4), 32–38.

Willcocks, L., Petherbridge, P. and Olson, N. (2003) *Making IT Count: Strategy, Delivery, Infrastructure*. Butterworth, Oxford.

Yin R.K. (1994) *Case Study Research: Design and Methods*. Thousand Oaks, CA: Sage Publications.

Yu, L. (2001) Successful customer-relationship management. *MIT Sloan Management Review*, **42**(4), 18–19.

Index

Printed and bound by CPI Group (UK) Ltd, Croydon, CR0 4YY
16/09/2026
14963379-0004

Praise for *Medicine for All People*

"In *Medicine for All People*, Dr. Geeta Maker-Clark carries forward the essential work of redefining health care for our times. Through her vast clinical experience, beautifully shared with clarity, compassion, and scientific grounding, she invites us to see medicine not as a narrow set of interventions, but as a living system rooted in nourishment, ancestral connection, and care. A must-read."

—**Dr. Andrew Weil**, #1 *New York Times*–bestselling author; founder, Andrew Weil Center for Integrative Medicine at the University of Arizona

"With courage and conscience, Dr. Geeta Maker-Clark takes us on a healing odyssey—from a tribal village in India to the medical tents of Standing Rock to her patient table in Chicago—to learn the keys to wellness and collective liberation. Grounded in Indigenous knowledge and scientific rigor, she reimagines medicine to include our relationship to food, earth, and community. The result: a manifesto for healing the wounds of separation that keep us sick—and a blueprint for returning to our bodies, our ancestral wisdom, and each other. I will forevermore see medicine as an act of revolutionary love."

—**Valarie Kaur**, bestselling author of *See No Stranger* and *Sage Warrior*

"*Medicine for All People* is a remarkable and timely work. Geeta Maker-Clark beautifully bridges individual and collective health, understanding that they are deeply interconnected—much like a mycelial web. Her call to action, which began in her living room through the Mycelium Collective, is a living example of this principle in action. Dr. Maker-Clark reminds us that mycelium is not just a metaphor, but a foundational system of life—supporting the exchange of nutrients and information across ecosystems. In the same way, she invites us to recognize our shared responsibility for one another's well-being. The health of each person is inseparable from the health of the whole. This book is a meaningful contribution to our evolving understanding of holistic living, blending science and ancient wisdom with clarity and purpose. I highly recommend it."

—**Paul Stamets**, author; inventor; earthling

"In *Medicine for All People*, we are reminded that public education has the potential of reaching all children globally. If we teach human values at the lunch table, we can address climate change, community, and the livelihood of regenerative farmers."

—**Alice Waters**, founder, The Edible Schoolyard Project and Chez Panisse restaurant in Berkeley, California

"*Medicine for All People* is a powerful reminder that our minds, souls, and bodies are all one, and that to be healthy, we need to pay attention to all the elements that make us human. How much healthier we all can be if we heed this book's prescriptions!"

—**Sandro Galea,** MD, DrPH, author of *Well* and *Within Reason*; Margaret C. Ryan dean of the School of Public Health, Washington University in St. Louis

"What if medicine isn't something you take—but something you live? In *Medicine for All People*, Dr. Maker-Clark, a leading voice in integrative medicine, weaves science and ancestral wisdom into a deeply human vision of healing, revealing how food, nature, movement, and community can guide us back to vitality, wholeness, and a more intimate relationship with our health. I highly recommend this book."

—**Tieraona Low Dog,** MD, founding director, Integrative & Functional Medicine Fellowship, UC Irvine Susan Samueli Integrative Health Institute

"*Medicine for All People* is a love letter to every one of us. It cuts through the negativity and doom of our times to remind us that ancestral wisdom is not only relevant to modern life but deeply needed and fiercely powerful. In a time of confusion and difficulty, Dr. Maker-Clark offers us a path forward, grounded in thousands of years of knowledge and infused with the spirit of seva. This book is a gift."

—**Simran Jeet Singh**, bestselling author of *The Light We Give*

"Reading this book is medicine in and of itself. Rooted in Dr. Maker-Clark's belief that true healing begins with justice, *Medicine for All People* is as captivating in its powerful stories as it is instructive in its meaningful practices for strengthening our well-being. The author embodies ancient practices, making her stories relevant, personal, and inspiring. Her vulnerability invites us to find our own sacred place in community. So much more than a simple list of remedies, this richly woven offering reminds us that healing is integral to cultural and community life. A treasure for every home and medical practice."

—**Kat Maier**, author of *Energetic Herbalism*

"Against an orthodoxy that permits only white-coated strangers and insurers to administer your health, Geeta Maker-Clark offers a beautiful counterproposal. *Medicine for All People* moves between the clinic and the kitchen, the garden and the protest, to recover a truth of which capitalism has robbed us: that our bodies are not puzzles to be solved but relationships to be tended. This is a book of rigorous science and radical memory, written in the conviction that the most powerful medicines were never for sale—because they were ours in common all along."

—**Raj Patel**, author of *Stuffed and Starved*

"*Medicine for All People* is not a trendy protocol but a disruptive manifesto and a cultural homecoming written by a visionary physician of rare brilliance and deep empathy. It invites us to see the body as a living archive and our kinship with plants, movement, and community as the fuel for true wellness, the kind that brings joy and vibrancy. In a world that too often medicalizes our existence, this book is a breathtaking reclamation of what it means to be truly well. Geeta has drawn the definitive map for our journey to collective liberation."

—**Erika Allen**, CEO, Urban Growers Collective, Green Era Campus

"What is medicine? You may think it's what's behind that mirror in your bathroom, but in her evocative book, Dr. Geeta Maker-Clark shares a new way of thinking about medicine as the natural healing properties of the world around us—from the food we eat to the communities we connect with to how we move our bodies when no one is watching, and more. Maker-Clark provides a new framework for thinking about medicine, knitting together a systems view that doesn't falsely put the burden of self-help on our shoulders, showing us the powerful ways we can reclaim our own health *and* demand the changes needed so that all people have access to the multifaceted medicines our bodies and minds deserve."

—**Anna Lappé**, author of *Diet for a Hot Planet*;
executive director, Global Alliance for the Future of Food

"This is a truly solid and sensible holistic approach to health and longevity. Through personal experience and stories, Dr. Maker-Clark has laid down a solid path of social justice in health care. Here is well-seasoned advice from a medical doctor that promotes time in nature, social connection, love, diet, and herbs. Dr. Maker-Clark is teaching us how to truly be in partnership with nature. This is revolutionary work."

—**Dr. Rosita Arvigo**, founder, The Abdominal Therapy Collective;
author and international speaker

"As a community physician, Dr. Maker-Clark returns us to the path of humanity's healing through timeless ancestral medicines, including food. *Medicine for All People* skillfully redirects us from a culture of stress and sickness toward a society rooted in belonging and equity. This beautiful work of healing arrives perfectly on time for a world that is transitioning into awareness and wholeness."

—**Maya Tiwari**, spiritual teacher; Ayurvedic healer;
author of *The Path of Practice*

"Drawing on a unique mixture of ancient wisdom, modern science, lived experience, and her medical practice, Geeta Maker-Clark makes a compelling case that our orientation must change if we are to sustain the planet in all its biodiversity and realize global social, spiritual, and physical human healing. Rather than offer a single or dogmatic prescription for how we turn to an inclusive, collective, ecological, and equitable orientation as our starting point, she draws on different cultural traditions to suggest a 'medicine pouch' that we can fill with a variety of remedies and carry with us. A masterful integration of philosophical and evidence-based practical advice—including healthy recipes—Maker-Clark's critique helps us fill up our pouch, rather than leaving us holding the bag. Truly a book for all people."

—**Dr. Arline T. Geronimus**, author of *Weathering*

"Never underestimate the healing power of food, plants, dance, song, friendship, play, and purpose. In *Medicine for All People*, Dr. Geeta Maker-Clark brings this message boldly and beautifully to life—revealing that healing originates in the kitchen, the garden, and the embrace of community, and that too many people have been excluded from what makes us well. With personal stories, clinical expertise, a vast heart, and deep ancestral and cultural wisdom, she reclaims this truth with a joy that is itself an act of justice."

—**Victoria Maizes**, MD, author of *Heal Faster*; founding executive director, Andrew Weil Center for Integrative Medicine

"Reading *Medicine for All People* by Dr. Geeta Maker-Clark is like getting a house call from the local village physician who arrives with a treasure trove in her medical kit, carrying the wisdom of the ages."

—**Katrina Blair**, author of *The Wild Wisdom of Weeds*

"I love all the interesting things that Dr. Maker-Clark puts in her medicine bag. I plan to recommend such a pouch to all my students, colleagues, and patients."

—**Daphne Miller**, MD, clinical professor, UC San Francisco; author of *Farmacology* and *The Jungle Effect*

MEDICINE FOR ALL PEOPLE

MEDICINE FOR ALL PEOPLE

SCIENCE *and* ANCIENT WISDOM *for* REVOLUTIONARY HEALING

GEETA MAKER-CLARK, MD

Illustrations by Nicole DeBarber

Chelsea Green Publishing
White River Junction, Vermont
London, UK

First published in 2026 by Chelsea Green Publishing | PO Box 4529 | White River Junction, VT 05001 | West Wing, Somerset House, Strand | London, WC2R 1LA, UK | www.chelseagreen.com
A Division of Rizzoli International Publications, Inc. | 49 West 27th Street | New York, NY 10001 | www.rizzoliusa.com

Publisher: Charles Miers
Deputy Publisher: Matthew Derr
Project Manager: Natalie Wallace
Developmental Editor: Anna Bliss
Copy Editor: Ashley Davila
Proofreader: Nancy A. Crompton
Indexer: Shana Milkie
Designer: Abrah Griggs

ISBN 978-1-64502-337-1 (paperback) | ISBN 978-1-64502-338-8 (ebook) |
ISBN 978-1-64502-339-5 (audiobook)
Library of Congress Control Number: 2026018944 (print)

Our Commitment to Green Publishing
Chelsea Green sees publishing as a tool for cultural change and ecological stewardship. We strive to align our book manufacturing practices with our editorial mission and to reduce the impact of our business enterprise in the environment. We print our books using vegetable-based inks whenever possible. This book may cost slightly more because it was printed on paper that contains recycled fiber, and we hope you'll agree that it's worth it. *Medicine for All People* was printed on paper supplied by Marquis that is made of recycled materials and other controlled sources.

Authorized EU representative for product safety and compliance
Mondadori Libri S.p.A. | www.mondadori.it
via Gian Battista Vico 42 | Milan, Italy 20123

Printed in Canada.
10 9 8 7 6 5 4 3 2 1 26 27 28 29 30

FSC www.fsc.org MIX Paper | Supporting responsible forestry FSC® C103567

For Todd—who tends to our roots with love and care,
creating the steady ground from which I can be brave

For Sahaara, Sachin, and Devika—who are rising from
that steady ground into their own light and courage

CONTENTS

For if medicine is really to accomplish its great task,
it must intervene in political and social life. It must point
out the hindrances that impede the normal social functioning
of vital processes, and effect their removal.

*Rudolf Virchow, "Report on the Typhus Epidemic
in Upper Silesia" (1848)*

Most of us lead far more meaningful lives than we know.
Often finding meaning is not about doing things differently;
it is about seeing familiar things in new ways.

Rachel Naomi Remen, MD, My Grandfather's Blessings

PROLOGUE

The Call to Remember

Summer of 1992, Rajasthan, India. I was sitting under a dark sky awash with stars, beside a flickering fire. There were many of us encircled here, in a rural village in this desert state gathered around to listen to a woman only known as Ma. The scent of cumin and coriander seeds wafted up from iron plates laid on the fire, and the crackle of burning wood was the only sound between breaths. I was happy to be included, as Ma's wisdom was known far and wide and sought out by villagers and city people as well. People came from many miles away, seeking remedies, advice, and empathy from Ma, and just to be near her kind and spiritually elevated presence. During the day, word spread that she would be speaking in the evening, and by nightfall, people gathered, eager to hear whatever she chose to offer. Her stories were often filled with deep, sacred knowledge, and were also quite entertaining.

This particular night, she was speaking about herbs, and why seeds like fenugreek and cumin were so important for good health. Then, seemingly out of nowhere, her gaze turned directly to me. I think she knew I was an American college student, but she had never spoken to me during the many times I had attended her circles. "*Beti* (daughter), what heals the body?" she asked me in Hindi, looking straight into my eyes. I was so nervous that my mind went blank. Quickly I said what I imagined she would like to hear: "Herbal tonics and seeds and foods?" It was quiet. She didn't say anything, and I shifted my eyes from her deep gaze. She sang a few lines of a song as she swept the roasted seeds off the plate and into her hand and then looked back at me. "What do you want to do, *beti*?" "I want to be a doctor . . . to help people be healthier," I answered, the words trailing off as soon as they left my mouth. Was that really what she meant with that question? I was only nineteen—how much could I truly know about what I wanted to do?

Ma then said, waving up at the millions of stars above us, "Don't spend your time looking for answers. Our people have always sought orientation.

Look for that." Again, she looked deep into my eyes. "Your work here is not to fix what is broken, but to nourish what is forgotten."

And there it was, just like that: my work was laid out for me. It resonated so deeply that I had chills. I said it again to myself. I wrote it down later that night in my journal. And over the whole of my medical career, I have read it, and reread it, and said it out loud.

Nourish what is forgotten.

In my years as a physician, I have come to see how true this is: You cannot "fix" people, especially with narrow tools that ignore the complexity of their lives. Health is not created in the exam room—it begins in homes, neighborhoods, and workplaces. It takes root in childhoods, in food systems, in housing and labor policies, in whether schools are well funded and families feel safe. Real health depends on whether people are seen, heard, nourished, and protected. As I moved onward from Rajasthan, and into the deep groove of medical training, again and again, I returned to the same questions: What is medicine? What do we call medicine now, and what did our ancestors understand it to be? What does it mean, not just to prescribe or to intervene, but to truly *practice* medicine?

It is a truly beautiful word, born of Latin roots: *medicina*, the healing art, a remedy, an act of restoration. Too often, what we call medicine today is only reaction: chasing symptoms in individual bodies while ignoring the deeper forces that shape entire communities. And as long as we keep practicing this way, we will keep creating the very same results.

My work in the culinary medicine and food justice movements has shown me that the global food system is deeply tied to why chronic disease overwhelms US health care. Both operate on business models that create inequity, excluding those who cannot afford premium food, health care, or insurance. An estimated 112 million (44 percent) American adults are struggling to pay for health care, and more than double that number (93 percent) feel that what they do pay is not worth the cost, adding further worry and dysfunction to this system of sick care.[1] Meanwhile, rising food prices strain household budgets, leaving many families unable to afford nutritious meals.[2] These are the realities that my patients face—and that have long been concerns of mine, coming from my own roots in a rich food and health tradition.

I am a first-generation Indian American woman. My parents were both born and raised in India, and that shaped everything about how I came to understand the need for more inclusive healing in our medical system.

While I knew I had the privilege of holding two cultures, on most days I felt like I was on the outside of both. Navigating my dual identity as a Hindu Indian teenage girl in a wealthy, white suburb where I was clearly not welcomed was a full-time emotional job. My father, a surgeon who had trained in India and would continue his training in Chicago, arrived with my mother, with only eight dollars, the maximum allowed for many immigrants of his generation.

In the 1960s, the United States was experiencing a physician shortage and actively recruiting the brightest medical graduates from India. Thousands left their small towns for the first time to come here, stepping into an entirely foreign world. My father worked for every dollar he earned, eventually moving us to a suburb with one of the best school systems he could find. When I was eleven, we left a working-class immigrant neighborhood where neighbors understood each other's struggles and moved to a tree-lined suburb on Chicago's North Shore. The lakefront was beautiful, the houses grand, the schools well-funded—but the message to us was clear: we did not belong. My mother was excluded from neighborhood women's gatherings. I was one of the few students not invited to the school dances. My name was mocked, mispronounced, and twisted into cruel jokes. Our house was egged. Day after day, I felt the sharp edges of not fitting in, physically, culturally, or emotionally.

And yet, inside our home, I was held by something deeper. Indian homes smell of food—onions frying, cumin and coriander blooming in hot oil, turmeric staining the air gold. Our walls held the scent of meals that carried centuries of memory. The soundscape of my childhood was mustard seeds crackling in the pan, vegetables chopped rhythmically, pressure-cooker whistles. This atmosphere mortified me when friends came over, and it also grounded me in who I was. Food was my first medicine. When I was sick, the first response from my mother was not a pill but home food: khichdi to soothe an upset stomach, turmeric milk for colds, spices chosen not just for taste but for their healing properties. Ayurveda, the ancient wisdom and medical science behind Indian cuisine, teaches that food is medicine and that balance is the foundation of health. Rooted in the rhythms of nature, it recognizes that each ingredient carries its own energy, season, and purpose. Through the careful blending of herbs, spices, and foods suited to one's constitution, Ayurveda nourishes not only the body but also the mind and spirit. While Ayurveda is very sophisticated, the food itself is simple.

When I began medical school, this truth—that food is one of the most powerful medicines—felt invisible. I was chosen to be part of a small, specialized, and experimental curriculum at Rush Medical College in Chicago, one of the oldest and most respected medical schools in the United States. I loved medical school, and I excelled in it. I became president of the honor society, and was exalted as a student who could thrive in competitive fields like neurosurgery and surgical oncology. It was exhilarating, being on a bullet train moving toward my goals. I memorized metabolic and disease pathways, yet not a single lecture was devoted to nutrition, to food, to the very source of the nutrients in those pathways. The absence was staggering. I felt the tension between what I was learning and what I knew to be true.

Few of my mentors understood or celebrated my decision to go into family medicine, a medical field full of brilliant, empathetic, kind people who are undervalued and overworked in the health care system. It was seen as a less glamorous field, a step down from the glory of specialization. Family medicine was the first true field of medicine, born from the idea that healing begins with knowing the whole person and their families. Before specialization, all physicians practiced this form of medicine—caring for patients across ages, illnesses, and generations, "from cradle to grave." It called to me. Family medicine offered the chance to care holistically for people and their entire families, to understand the ecosystem of a patient's life, to practice medicine as listening, witnessing, and walking alongside. Here, I found a space for wholeness rather than fragmentation, for community rather than hierarchy. Later, fellowships in both Maternal Child Health and Integrative Medicine deepened my commitment to community health, women's health, nutritional science, herbal medicine, and mind-body healing.

Since then, my path has been to weave the wisdom I grew up with—the smells of our kitchen, the resilience of my immigrant family, the lessons of exclusion and belonging—into a vision of medicine that is not just about bodies, but about people, communities, land, and culture. I have worked to create healing paths that honor authenticity, that connect food to the land, the body to the spirit, the individual to the community. The conditions that keep us from thriving—racism, poverty, disconnection, inequity—are not natural laws. They are barrier walls built by human hands, and they can be changed. I believe we can rise to a paradigm of abundance and connection, of joy and aliveness. We can change the paradigm of what we believe medicine to be and restore it to what it truly is—a healing force.

The way forward begins not in products or quick fixes, but in reclaiming the simple medicines that have always been with us: nourishment, story, belonging, and love.

A Return to Ancestry and Agriculture

The Partition of 1947 displaced my family from their ancestral farmlands in Punjab and Sindh. After two centuries of colonization, Britain exited an India it had divided, exploited, and left to recover from the wreckage of colonial rule. India, specifically the state of Punjab, was split into two, and my grandparents became refugees in their own country. With their young children, they fled by train, bus, and boat from Karachi to Delhi and Jaipur, leaving behind the fertile lands where their forebears had planted and harvested in rhythm with the seasons. My maternal grandfather sold incense to feed his family; my paternal grandfather worked for an airline. They rebuilt lives in India's cities, far from the soil that had once sustained them. In Punjab, my father's homeland, "the land of five rivers," and in Sindh, my mother's homeland, where the Indus Valley meets the mountains, their kin had known the earth by touch and by scent, planting and harvesting, drumming and dancing in rhythm with the soil.

By the time I was born, those ancestral lands were a story more than a reality. My parents had moved from urban India to suburban America. Our ties to the earth had been severed even from the family that stayed; no one knew anything of farming or rural life anymore. I visited India often as a child, but always to see relatives in the bustle of Mumbai or New Delhi, and they had little sense of the mud huts, the weary hands, or the thin, soil-dusted children bent to labor in fields. I deeply longed to know myself and my origins, and to better understand where I belonged. I was very sure it wasn't Glencoe, Illinois.

Visiting India as a young adult without my parents was a chance for me to understand my country of origin—outside of the fast urban life of my cousins and the worldview of my middle-class family. In college, I joined the School for International Training in Rajasthan. The program focused on learning across cultures and communities, and it offered me my first chance to see India beyond my relatives' urban worlds. We traveled to rural villages where activists were restoring forests, fighting erosion, and testing biodiesel, which opened my eyes to the vastness of my homeland. For my final project, instead of arts or history, I chose something more ancient: the fundamentals of human survival. I wanted to learn Indigenous ways of living and how farming traditions were passed down, hoping this would guide me in becoming a better physician. A local environmental activist we had worked with, Dr. Raj Bhanti, agreed to help me. She was scholarly, fierce, and grounded, with a voice both scratchy and commanding, her simple cotton salwar kameez worlds away from the fashionable women of Mumbai. I asked her if I could spend my independent study in Undari, a village she often visited, home to around seventy Adivasi Indigenous tribal families. The villagers lived with deforested hillsides, depleted soil, and long commutes into the city for labor. Raj welcomed my request and introduced me the very next morning.

At first, the villagers greeted me with laughter and bewilderment—an American girl who looked Indian asking to join their daily lives. An odd request, but they allowed it, unsure what exactly they were agreeing to. For four weeks I rose at dawn, took the bus into the valley, and went from hut to hut working with the women. My Hindi was clumsy, but some words landed in the local dialect.

Life in Undari was grueling. The men left before sunrise for roadwork or stone-splitting in the cities while the women hauled clay pots of water for miles, cooked over coal, cut grass for the animals, and tended crops in the searing heat. They wore thin cotton saris, heads draped in bright scarves, silver nose rings and necklaces glinting. Dark-skinned and sun-drenched, they bore themselves with amazing strength, their bangles clinking as they worked. Day after day, I appeared, and after the initial giggles, stares, and sideways looks, they let me work.

I learned to cut grass with a machete, sometimes with a baby strapped to my back, swept mud floors with grass brooms, shooed feral pigs from doorways, and carried water jugs alongside younger girls who laughed with me about my Hindi. We rested under trees in the heat of midday, and went back to work together, without ever consulting a watch. Nights in the village were thick with smoke, as rotis and vegetables were cooked over open coal stoves inside mud huts, walls blackened by years of meal making. Women across India die young from pulmonary disease caused by these daily inhalations of carcinogens.[3] I slept curled in a corner with the family, my backpack for a pillow, pigs occasionally nosing me awake in the dark.

There was also the discomfort of my own role. I could not forget that I was a visitor, moving through their days for a few short weeks, while their lives demanded endless repetition of these life tasks. I asked myself constantly: What was I giving back? What was I taking? Was I there to learn, or to perform some version of rural life for myself? The complexity of community work—the danger of extraction—was becoming clear to me even then, and those questions have followed me into my life as an activist and doctor.

I don't in any way mean to romanticize my experience in Undari. It is trite and easy to spend a few days or months walking in the shoes of another and find it beautiful and fabled. Here, survival was precarious, bodies thin, and illness ever-present. Every task was backbreaking, each day focused only on survival and getting all the daily tasks done by nightfall. Life expectancy was low, and both acute and chronic illness were common. One terrible afternoon, I was called for help and witnessed the death of an infant from a simple skin infection—a condition antibiotics could have easily cured, but, in the village, was fatal. The ordinariness of this loss was devastating. It reminded me that only two generations earlier, this had been my family's life in Punjab and Sindh, where death was always close, survival never guaranteed.

While living with the Adivasi community, I felt the deep connection to land and the interdependence with animals. I watched the balance unfold each day: the animals' need to graze matched against the careful measure of grass the women cut, leaving enough for the future. I began to move with the rhythm of time itself—the rising and setting of the sun and moon, the cycles of harvest, the shifting heat of day, the gift of monsoon rains. This was a culture of kinship, a living biological ecosystem. As a young woman, I was learning ways of life far removed from my own, and in my heart I recognized that while the Adivasi in Undari endured hardship, their lives were centered on what mattered most: clean water, food, shelter, community care, the sharing of resources and stories, rest, and alignment with the rhythms of light and season. To live here was to live within our ecosystem, not apart from it, and I felt myself deeply woven into that experience. On many levels, this return to ancestral ways, to the elemental needs of life, was a kind of healing, a mending of the trauma of separation from the place I was really from. At nineteen, it changed the path of my future.

Emerging research in fields such as epigenetics, neuroplasticity, social epidemiology, and psychoneuroimmunology affirms what many ancestral traditions have long known: that the body is not separate from its environment, and that healing is deeply relational. The nervous system responds to safety, story, song, and silence. The gut responds to justice, and twists and hurts when stressed. The spirit responds to belonging and cries from loneliness. Stress is often a source of disease not easily measured by tests, and many physicians end up feeling demoralized by a system that treats chronic disease primarily with pharmaceuticals. This model drives doctors away from whole-person care toward more "sustainable" specialty jobs, leaving prevention and true healing behind.

A 2023 American Medical Association survey found that more than one-third of physicians were considering leaving or reducing hours, including many in early or mid-career.[4] The highest intent to leave was among physicians working in internal medicine, family medicine, OB/GYN, hospital medicine, emergency medicine, and pediatrics—the very doctors every family depends on. This isn't just about physician burnout—it's about the unraveling of the relationship between healer and community. Where medicine goes from here depends on whether we can reclaim care as something human, relational, and whole.

Chasing the Wellness Dream

Physicians see the harm in a system that commodifies chronic disease while ignoring the roots of unwellness. But too often, the wellness industry's response is a quick-fix add-on—green juice, detox cleanses, boutique fitness—that shifts responsibility entirely onto individuals. Lifestyle changes like eating well, exercising, and sleeping are important, but the wellness industry has turned them into products to be bought, not practices to be lived. The result is a seductive but misguided promise: that health can be purchased. Meanwhile, companies profit, knowing that people are quite desperate to feel better. The wellness industry thrives on our desperation and is now a $6.3 trillion market, with an annual growth of 5 to 10 percent. Most of this spending is on products, apps, foods, and apparel that insurance does not cover.[5] While these tools can support change, they cannot resolve the deeper causes of illness—structural racism, economic inequity, lack of shelter, and poor access to healthy food. For those already excluded from mainstream health care, the costly alternatives of the wellness market only deepen the divide.

Over the years, I bought into it, too—pricey powders in my smoothies, yoga classes where my mother's language was mispronounced, teas that promised unmatched energy and glow. Some were helpful, yet none of them could outsmart my exhaustion. Beneath all my purchased wellness practices, I carried the same anxieties, the same unhealed wounds, the same disconnection. It took years of close listening—to my patients, the land,

and my own spirit—to learn that the real medicines can't be purchased. They grow from nourishment, connection, and the hard work of tending to what really matters.

Back in college, when I thought of the life I was returning to after Undari, I felt a metaphysical dread, and I could not connect the here to there. But now I see that it was in Undari that I learned for the first time that humans had lost connection to the natural world, and that what we need to heal may not be inside of a building or a textbook. I learned through my own connection with my ancestral roots and culture that getting back to these basics of survival can indeed help us heal. Since then, I have been on a journey of remembering and visioning us back to ourselves and to the roots of healing.

In the following chapters, I share a wealth of statistics, academic research, scientific data, and explorations of complex social justice ideas. I invite you to think and reflect and join me on this journey of discovery, where integrating science with ancient wisdom reveals why so many ancestral healing practices work. But above all, I want to share the stories of people who have let me help them, and bring you into these intimate places where awe, courage, pain, and hope all live. The rawness of these patients' stories has stirred me, and I hope their stories will also move you. We are meant to tell them, to listen, and to recognize ourselves in their patterns—and to witness how they repeat, unravel, and transform us again and again. May this work serve as both a compass and a companion on your journey toward healing that is both personal and planetary.

INTRODUCTION

The Medicine Pouch

Most of the people who come through my office door have a big story to tell, and it is my job to listen. The stories have revealed a pattern of language over time:

"You are my last hope."

"I have been everywhere, and no one knows what is wrong with me."

"No one can figure out why I feel so much worse than I did ten years ago."

"I don't even recognize myself anymore."

The details of each patient's experience are devastatingly different, but the bedrock of despair is the same. Many are from historically disenfranchised, marginalized, and immigrant communities, though patients who are resourced, advantaged, and from the dominant culture also feel terrible and abandoned. Most feel that they have lost their connection to their own health and healing, having lost touch with their ancestral practices through the ravages of immigration and assimilation. They all hold a space with me that contains faith, but it is a space pregnant with anguish, fear, and longing for someone to hear them, feel with them, and diagnose them—all at once. In their eyes, I recognize the gaze of a warrior and self-advocate looking for something they cannot name but know that they need. They still have some hope.

They have waited months for this appointment, after having seen many other doctors for whom they also had to wait. I have these few moments to sit with them, to listen to the story of who they are now, to understand what is happening so that we can start a partnership and find a way forward. It is a very precious time for me to have my hands in the soil of this new relationship and to plant some seeds, and it goes by quickly.

Laura's Story

Laura, a thirty-eight-year-old first-generation Mexican American nurse who worked full-time in a mental health facility, is one of thousands of patients I have been fortunate to meet and care for. She came to her appointment with her husband, still dressed in her scrubs, with impeccable makeup and her hair pulled back in a tight ponytail. A mother of four young children, including her nine-month-old baby who she was still nursing, she told me that she was exhausted and had a "constant feeling of anxiety" centered in her chest.

Laura was homeschooling her three older kids in a local group, initially during the pandemic. They lived in a community with few Hispanic families, and each of her kids had encountered racism from teachers, which went unchecked even after she complained. Laura, like all of us, wanted her kids to have a great education without being bullied, or discriminated against, or othered. Her husband was supportive of her decision but did not share the homeschooling responsibilities and worked full-time as well at a car dealership. Laura had some support from her parents, who lived nearby, but she continued to work full-time shifts. Adding to her heavy workload, she had recently been diagnosed with postpartum depression and started on an antidepressant, which helped a bit with her mood, but didn't relieve the fatigue and anxiety.

Laura's circumstances were enough to explain the exhaustion and the low energy. When I asked what the anxiety felt like to her, she explained it as "a feeling of dread." Something was not right with her life, but she couldn't pinpoint it. Her parents believed that her life had wavered off course on many levels and thought she needed warmer foods, more meat in her diet, and should be spending more time at home and less at work. They did not believe that she needed to be making more money or homeschooling her kids when she worked nights.

In the Mexico of their younger years, a new mother would stay home for forty days after giving birth, for what is known as *la cuarentena*, to bond with her baby and heal her body with medicinal herbs and foods. I was very familiar with this ritual as we have the same postpartum recovery in India, forty days during which a mother and baby stay together in the home for care and rest. Laura took as much time off as she could after each baby but did not get the full forty days of rest before she had to go back to work and manage her household and her kids' schooling. She was back working in the hospital in three weeks.

"Can you imagine staying in your home for forty days without working or doing anything?" she said. I reminded her that mothers are doing a lot during that time: nursing the baby at all hours, changing diapers, feeding themselves, taking care of their bleeding and body's recovery, showering, resting when they can. Laura looked at me with deep fatigue in her eyes. "Yeah, I don't know much about rest."

Laura's story echoed that of so many immigrants. She shouldered the unseen weight of countering a racist gaze that cast Mexican people as not enough, pushing herself to work longer and harder than her coworkers to prove she belonged. Having grown up with parents who both worked full-time in factories, sharing a small home with her five siblings, Laura was constantly aware of how different her family was from the others in her neighborhood. She had been working in overdrive mode since she was in high school—going to school, caring for her younger sisters, and working two jobs. By the time she was twenty, she was overweight, had prediabetes, and was perpetually stressed. Despite her polished appearance, Laura was weathered.

In her book, *Weathering: The Extraordinary Stress of Ordinary Life in an Unjust Society*, Dr. Arline T. Geronimus argues that health and aging have more to do with how society treats us than how well we take care of ourselves. She describes "weathering" as the health deterioration that comes from cumulative exposure to social, economic, and political adversity. Decades of research substantiates the devastating effects of perpetually living in survival mode, reflecting what we see in our clinics and hospitals. People of color are substantially more affected by weathering. Black mothers die at a rate nearly three times higher than that of white mothers and only about half of Black sixteen-year-olds in high-poverty urban areas and half of white sixteen-year-olds in Appalachia who live to age fifty, will still be able-bodied. Middle-aged Mexican immigrants like Laura are more likely to suffer stress-related chronic diseases if they've lived in the United States for more than a decade than if they've lived here for less time, even as their incomes increase. This evidence-based definition of weathering clearly aligned with Laura's story, and with so many of the stories of my patients. It also explained her symptoms of profound exhaustion, anxiety, and general poor health. Her spirit was so tired. No one person could do everything she was doing or fight everything she was fighting and maintain a baseline of health.

I ordered basic labs to check her iron levels, her vitamin B12, her hemoglobin, and her thyroid function, but I intuitively knew that she really needed soul restoration and rest. The ancient wisdom of most cultures calls for forty days of bonding and adjustment to the radical new stage of life that comes with childbirth. Yet American work culture has translated this ritual period to one or two doctor visits after discharge from the hospital and one six-week postpartum visit, after which many women go fully back to their entrenched lives. While the Family Medical Leave Act allows up to twelve weeks of leave with job protection, this is unpaid and few can afford it. The United States remains the only high-income country without paid maternity leave.[1]

In Ayurveda, the ancient science and philosophy of living that originates from Vedic thought in India, the expression "forty days for forty years" means that what the new mother does in the first forty days postpartum will affect her health for the next forty years. The recovery period after pregnancy and birth is vital to her ability to go forward in her new role; her body needs to heal from the physical traumas of pregnancy and delivery, while she bonds with her baby and adjusts to life in an inseparable dyad. Modern pressures, financial and social, deny mothers the space for true recuperation. Instead, they recast the early return to work as a badge of honor, proof of devotion to career and a strong, loyal work ethic.

Like Laura's parents, I believed that she was suffering from fatigue and anxiety because her restoration was incomplete. Her body, mind, and spirit never had a chance to fully adjust to mothering, and could not keep up with so many other heavy responsibilities. Laura agreed to a plan for the next forty days. She would eat warm foods—soups, cooked vegetables, oatmeal and other cooked grains, and herbal teas. In Mexico, new mothers are offered *caldo de pollo*, a chicken soup, after birth, as well as chia seeds soaked and then added to a glass of water with fruit for hydration. Laura's mother and aunty would be particularly happy to engage in these traditions with the many recipes that they had offered unsuccessfully to Laura when she had her first babies. She would take a break from homeschooling on her days off and pass the role onto another parent in the homeschooling group.

Laura's husband agreed that she was carrying a daunting load, and now that he understood its effect on her health, he suggested that when she got home from work, she should immediately go upstairs and lie down for some quiet decompression time before engaging with the family. He offered to feed their daughter with her pumped milk while Laura rested, or to be with their other children if she wanted to quietly nurse. While Laura could not stop working or even take a break from her job, simply talking about the increased rest and warming homemade ancestral food felt nourishing to her and visibly changed her posture.

After we laid out this restorative plan, Laura started to cry, and deep sobs released from her chest and heart, as she held her head in her hands and leaned forward, back rounded. Her husband placed his hand on her back, and I came closer and lightly held her hand. "You are doing the best you can," I said. "I know you will feel better again. Your body knows exactly what to do."

Six weeks later, I saw Laura again. Her face looked more open and relaxed, and her eyes seemed clearer. She smiled and said that her mother and aunt had made enough *caldo de pollo* to feed her for months. She felt stronger and less exhausted. The feeling of impending doom also had lessened considerably with the support from her family and homeschooling community. She wasn't carrying as much psycho-spiritual responsibility on her back and *felt* the support in her body. Laura had begun a ritual that Irish poet David Whyte invokes: the "daily acts of undoing over doing that can become an integral and emboldening part of our practice and our daily lives."[2]

She was most enthusiastic about eating the food made by her family. Food is the earliest and most intelligent of medicines, particularly when prepared in ancestral ways. Traditional Mexican food often combines iron-rich foods like chicken with a Vitamin C–rich lemony broth that improves the absorption of the iron. Laura's labs had indicated that her iron stores were low, so now she was eating more iron-rich foods and taking an herbal iron supplement. Her appreciation of her mother's offerings had also improved their relationship, in loving ways. She was also drinking a daily evening tea of lavender, tulsi, lemon balm, and chamomile—all herbs that slow down the heart, decrease blood pressure, and support the parasympathetic nervous system to bring the body back to a state of rest, calm, and connection. Laura also used the breathwork practices that we reviewed to support the vagus nerve—the pilot of the parasympathetic nervous system.

Pranayama is the ancient yogic practice of breath regulation, and it is considered one of the most powerful tools for healing, clarity, and connection in the Indian tradition of yoga. The word *pranayama* comes from Sanskrit: *prana* means life force or breath, and *ayama* means to expand or direct. Pranayama, then, is the conscious expansion of life energy through breath. Even one minute of slow inhalation and extended exhalation can activate the body's relaxation response.

Breathwork reaches into the autonomic nervous system (ANS), housed in the brainstem and connected to the body through the vagus nerve. This ancient

BREATHWORK PRACTICES

Box Breathing (4-4-4-4 Breath)

This technique is simple and excellent for calming the mind and body, especially during moments of stress or anxiety, and it's easy to remember!

Instructions

1. Sit in a comfortable position with your back straight.
2. Inhale deeply through your nose for 4 seconds.
3. Hold your breath for 4 seconds.
4. Exhale slowly through your mouth for 4 seconds.
5. Hold your breath again for 4 seconds.
6. Repeat this cycle for 5 to 10 minutes, or until you feel calm.

Benefits

- Reduces stress and anxiety
- Promotes mental clarity
- Helps regulate the nervous system

Alternate Nostril Breathing (*Nadi Shodhana*)

This ancient yogic technique balances the left and right sides of the brain, helping to clear the mind and bring a sense of calm. This was taught to me in India as a teenager and I still use it often to focus before work.

Instructions

1. Sit comfortably with a straight spine and relax your shoulders.
2. Close your right nostril with your right thumb and inhale deeply through your left nostril.
3. Close your left nostril with your ring finger and release your right nostril, exhaling through the right side.
4. Inhale through your right nostril, close it, and release your left nostril to exhale through the left.
5. Continue alternating for 5 to 10 minutes.

Benefits

- Balances energy in the body
- Improves focus and concentration
- Promotes relaxation and emotional stability

4-7-8 Breathing (Relaxing Breath)

This technique helps reduce stress and promotes relaxation, especially before bedtime. Dr. Andrew Weil taught this to us during the Integrative Medicine Fellowship at the University of Arizona.

Instructions

1. Sit or lie down comfortably.
2. Inhale quietly through your nose for a count of 4.
3. Hold your breath for a count of 7.
4. Exhale completely through your mouth, making a whooshing sound, for a count of 8.
5. Repeat this cycle 4 to 8 times.

Benefits

- Promotes relaxation and sleep
- Calms the nervous system
- Can lower blood pressure

system governs survival functions like heartbeat, digestion, breath, and pupil dilation—processes that react instantly to stress or safety, often before we are aware. The ANS has two branches: the sympathetic system, which mobilizes us for fight, flight, or freeze, and the parasympathetic system, which restores calm and healing. Because the ANS is rooted in the body's oldest wiring, its healing requires practices that speak its own primal language. Breathwork, chanting, humming, safe touch, movement, warmth, and eye contact all stimulate parasympathetic tone, signaling safety and allowing the body to repair and restore. This is not just psychological; it is a biological remembering. So when we care for the autonomic nervous system, we are not simply managing stress. We are tending to one of the oldest forms of wisdom in the body: the part of us that knows how to survive, and also how to soften and heal.

Laura had so little of this traditional, primal nourishment in the last decades that she was hungry to learn more. With optimism, trust, and love, we embraced, and scheduled a follow-up in two months. We were on the path together, and she was feeling better, slowly but steadily. And from this place, she could continue the work she wanted and needed to do for herself and her family. Her ancestral medicine pouch was starting to fill.

Transforming Our Vision of Health and Healing

Of course, every woman deserves a *cuarentena* and much more, and for this to happen, entire systems and societies need to be transformed. We need a radical reimagining and remembrance of times in our human culture when the deep support that Laura and so many others need was the operative currency. The intuitive healing modalities that have worked for people for thousands of years have been reduced and eroded, and replaced with the capitalist, colonized corporate food, health, and education systems. This contributes not only to environmental destruction, but also to the overall disease burden that lands people in the doctor's office, where we provide "sick care."

After decades of holding space for patients within the sterile confines of biomedicine, I long for a shift toward life-centered ways of being—like the webs, ecologies, and root structures of nature. I envision hospitals, schools, and companies that emphasize relationships, healing, and belonging over rigid roles and fragmented systems, and I have seen them. After completing medical school, a family medicine residency, and two fellowships, I traveled around the world as a community builder, physician, educator, speaker, and activist for social justice in Indigenous, marginalized, and disinvested cultures and communities. Over the past twenty-five years, I've worked with and learned from esteemed physicians, midwives, migrant farm workers, Indigenous elders and healers, public health scientists, citizen activists, griots and master dancers, herbalists, artists, psychologists, health coaches, yoga gurus, bench scientists, community chefs, and thousands of patients all over the city of Chicago and the world.

Most of my expertise has come directly from what these experiences taught me, and from the wisdom of so many teachers, some of whom I am honored to say are also now my patients. In my work and in this book, I draw deeply from the collective wisdom of this incredibly diverse, smart, and dedicated community of experts. True expertise is not just technical ability; it is the doorway into a space of trust, where healing plans are shaped together. I honor the many teachers who have guided me throughout my career. But most of all, I honor the profound wisdom that has come from apprenticing myself to my patients, one by one, and to the living earth itself. That journey of learning is still unfolding.

Preparing Your Medicine Pouch

Through these experiences, I have found that there are many paths to real, profound healing that are freely available to us all. In many of the cultures I have worked with, there is a beautiful way to hold these medicinal paths: the medicine pouch. It has been used for centuries across many Indigenous traditions as a sacred, personal container of healing, protection, and spiritual connection. Medicine pouches can hold herbs, stones, or natural elements believed to protect the wearer physically and spiritually. A sprig of sage or sweetgrass, tobacco, medicinal leaves, small prayer scrolls, sacred powders, feathers, a lock of hair, a small bone, a bead, a symbol of a clan or nation might all be carefully placed inside. I also view medicine pouches as a way to hold a bundle of practices, stories, and objects that sustain a person or community.

This book dives into the healing medicines that are carried in the pouches of every community and culture I've worked with—and includes the scientific research that backs up why they work. These practices and medicines embody people's essential loving, joyful nature and resonant ancestral wisdom, no matter the traditions. They are the biological and sociological underpinnings that secure us to ourselves, to each other, and to the earth. Like other species, such as starlings, mushrooms, butterflies, and bees, humans are healthiest when using the power of the community and the natural world around us to thrive. When we gather in community and care for one another, we share what we have, protect what we love, and create safety together. In that circle of belonging, the body softens, the nervous system exhales. We move from the edge of survival—fight, flight, or freeze—into the quiet work of rest, digestion, and repair.

To be healthy in an unjust world, we need to feel a sense of belonging, have guides and helpers, and trust our communities to be protective. Social activist Grace Lee Boggs, author of *The Next American Revolution: Sustainable Activism for the Twenty-First Century*, writes: "The only way to survive is by taking care of each other." No one heals or prospers in isolation; wellness and wealth alike are woven from the care and labor of many. Modern culture may glorify individualism, but in truth we depend on one another to get through each day. It's time for healers to speak the truth to those in power, to partner with the community, advocate for healing on a personal, societal, and planetary level, and to offer our wisdom and knowledge to support the co-creation of a deeper vision of health and well-being. We can adopt a daily practice of reconnecting ourselves to the sacred circle of life, and carry that healing energy to our families, workplaces, and communities.

Before you step further into these pages, I invite you to imagine carrying a small pouch, like those our ancestors might have tied to their belts, tucked close to their hearts, or worn around their necks. A medicine pouch is more than a container; it is a place of reverence, a vessel for what sustains and protects us. As you read this book, think of each teaching, each practice, each story as something you can place gently into your own medicine pouch. Some medicines will feel familiar, like favorite foods prepared by loving hands or the comfort of community. Others may surprise you—practices you had not thought of as medicine at all, like play, plants, or dance. Each one is offered for you to hold, examine, and decide whether it belongs in your pouch.

A medicine pouch is deeply personal. No two are alike, because no two lives are alike. You may choose to carry only a few medicines that resonate most with you. You may add to it as you continue your journey, or even remove what no longer serves. What matters is not how much you carry, but that what you carry feels true, life-giving, and grounding for the road ahead. In preparing your medicine pouch, you are not just gathering tools—you are making space for remembering. You are honoring the medicines your ancestors carried, the ones that have been passed down through bloodlines, cultures, and communities, as well as those newly rediscovered or reimagined in your own life. You are reclaiming the right to be whole, to be connected, to live with joy, balance, and reverence.

About This Book

This book is a call to expand our definition of healing. It is not a wellness protocol with a trendy name, or a detoxification strategy, a biohacking manual, or a set of quick fixes. So, if you are here for those things, I am afraid that you will have to look elsewhere.

It is a call to see the body not just as a site of diagnosis, but as a living archive of experience—cultural, emotional, political, and ecological. To imagine food, plant relationships, nature kinship, dancing, and community gatherings as medicines that connect us to our past and our future and fuel our resistance against a painful world. *Medicine for All People* is a refusal to accept that wellness should be a luxury. It is a practice of remembering: that healing is relational, that health is political, and that the wisdom we need is already among us, in our ancestors, in our kitchens, in our movements, and in the land we live upon. This book offers stories, frameworks, and practices, each a kind of medicine—rooted in science, shaped by culture, and guided by a belief that every person is worthy of care and can access deep healing.

We will awaken to what we already know from our ancestors about healing and health, whether through lived experience or in our cellular memory. *Medicine for All People* is a manifesto that reminds you who you are and how you are meant to live. In this manner, it is disruptive. It will gently ask you to look at your life with kind and honest eyes and expand your current idea of what it means to be healthy. It will remind you that you deserve to learn and know how your ancestors healed themselves and each other, and that many traditions have been marginalized or excluded from dominant narratives. These are time-tested best practices that tie us to our humanity and the natural world that we live within.

To be healthy is not a privilege. It is a birthright. And yet, every day, in America and around the world, countless lives are shortened, not solely by disease, but by the cumulative health impacts of social inequities and systemic racism. This was not directly taught in the didactics of medical school, where we learned about the prevention of diseases only as primary and secondary. True medicine is much more than avoiding the onset of disease by reducing exposure to risk factors or detecting diseases in their earliest stages, when intervention can halt or slow progression and improve outcomes.

While still a student, I attended a talk at an American Public Health Association conference, where I learned about primordial prevention. Primordial prevention protects health by shaping the social, environmental, and cultural foundations of life so that risk factors *never take root.* This is structural protection against disease, protecting people before biological risk factors even arise, by creating the conditions for health to flourish and uplift. This kind of medicine is not limited to hospitals or clinics—it lives in kitchens, gardens, forests, rituals, community centers, community fridges, and on dance floors. This is where the real medicine lives. Primordial prevention is in fact *ancestral* protection, and is what this book is all about.

So *Medicine for All People* begins with a simple but radical premise: True healing cannot exist without justice. Real health is not something to be found only in pills or procedures, but in relationships, in traditional knowledge, in nourishment, rest, movement, connection to the land and to each other.

My career thus far has been a transformative journey of doing and undoing, learning and unlearning, and has left me at various times raw, vulnerable, depleted, and exhausted. In the biomedical model of medicine in which I was trained, disease is viewed primarily as a biological process, resulting from physical, biochemical, or physiological abnormalities in the body. Pathogens, genetic defects, chemical imbalances, and structural damage are the key causes. Generally speaking, this model assumes a separation between body and mind, and deems mental and emotional states as secondary to physical illness. The primary goal is to identify the disease through diagnosis and eliminate or manage it, or try to cure it. It is an extraordinary model that works for many conditions and has saved countless people from chronic illness and death.

However, I found that the patient's subjective experience of pain and suffering, and their search for understanding and meaning, took a back seat to the search for biological markers in the blood and external tests. The whole person—their life and their story and their complex quilt of social context—got lost in the biomedical shuffle. And yet, it was those aspects of human life that had inspired me to become a doctor in the first place. What has always called to me is the work of understanding people's hearts and digging down to the roots of their dis-ease, so we can walk together toward healing. I don't know the right path for everyone—but I believe nature does, and that life itself offers powerful medicines. Some are ones I've long practiced and carry with some skill. This book doesn't cover them all; there are so many more—sound, music, water, touch, breath, to name just a few—that are also part of this wide cosmology of healing.

I have seen firsthand that when we widen our understanding of what medicine is—and whom it belongs to—we begin to uncover powerful, often overlooked tools that restore both individual and collective well-being. And we begin to ask new questions:

What does it mean to be well in a world that is unwell?

What would it look like to design systems that center dignity, culture, and care?

The medicines I share here are not offered as a sunny escape from the harms created by the cruelty of our social structures. I believe deeply in resisting and dismantling the hierarchies that uphold extreme wealth, patriarchy, ableism, and cisgender and heterosexual norms as the status quo. This is the work I continue to do in both my professional and personal practices. I do not believe that dancing or feeling gratitude can resolve the injury and harm inflicted by lifelong poverty, unsafe housing, or contaminated water. What I do believe is that these embodied practices are powerful—not as substitutes for justice or as accommodations to an unjust world, but to sustain the stamina, clarity, and grounding required to keep working toward what we are called to do. They are a form of primordial prevention. These medicines cannot cure structural violence, but they can nurture resilience, kindle joy, and stand as acts of resistance. They help us survive, and even bloom, while we fight for a world in which all people can truly thrive.

This book is not another "call to action." We are already pressed on all sides to strive, to improve, to become more than what we are, until even our own longing for wholeness feels unsustainable. What follows is not another demand but an offering. As you move through these pages, imagine your medicine pouch filling slowly with gentle practices—ancestral wisdom carried forward, waiting to be remembered, not mastered. My hope is that you will gather and carry forward a bundle uniquely your own, to support and sustain your life's journey.

Revolutionary healing of our society is possible. It is time to create a movement in health and medicine that speaks for an ecology of healing—one that takes root in both health care and communities, and champions medicines that are regenerative, restorative, and life-giving. We can choose to seek out, create, and practice the medicines that work for ourselves, our families, and our communities. Healthy ecosystems are resilient, adapt to change, and recover from disturbances. Just as healthy soil thrives with diversity, balance, and resilience, likewise, human well-being must be intentionally cultivated to nourish mind, body, and spirit in right relationship with the world that holds us.

It *is* possible. You carry resilience within you, woven by your ancestors, who prepared you for change simply by bringing you to this moment.

You are ready.

Come, let us remember together.

—GEETA MAKER-CLARK

Evanston, Illinois, unceded land of the
Potawatomi, Ojibwe, and Ottawa

REMEMBRANCE ONE

Medicines of the Earth

Nature, Food, Plants

MEDICINE ONE

Nature

The Original Teacher and the Ground of Belonging

You only have to listen to nature in order to experience the harmonies and rhythms of the universe.
Maya Tiwari, Ayurvedic teacher and healer

The Earth is what we all have in common.
Wendell Berry

Summer of 1999, West Side of Chicago. I lay belly-down on sun-warmed earth, my cheek pressed into dirt and grass and my breath syncing with the rhythm of wind through the maple trees. I closed my eyes and almost fell asleep in the calm of the moment, feeling so immediately unburdened. My toes felt awakened by the soft grass and I spread my arms wide to feel it under my arms. The light cotton of my blue scrubs was thin enough that I could feel the warm soil through them and I could hear my heartbeat against the earth . . . as if I were melting into it. I felt almost euphoric with calm.

Soon, I heard someone running and screaming. "Dr. Maker, Dr. Maker, are you okay??" A fellow resident leaned over and put her hands around my arm to flip me. I suppose seeing a doctor face down, white coat splayed, on the tiny lawn outside the back of the hospital seemed pretty alarming. I lifted my head up and smiled. "Yeah, yeah, I'm good, don't worry," I said, and laid my head back down. She must have thought I was hungover or drugged, but I was relieved that she left me there.

I wasn't seeking healing in that patch of grass; I just needed out. That day, something shifted in me. Years of the fluorescent lights of the hospital, the rattling pings of my pager, and the giant whiteboard of lists of patients on clinical rounds had numbed something inside me. The night before, I had attended a laboring woman caught in the grip of cocaine addiction and unbearable pain. Her body flailed against mine, and her sudden kick to my stomach left me doubled over, stunned, before I gathered myself and stayed with her through the long hours until her baby was born. The baby needed emergency care after delivery, as did the mother. By morning, I was emptied out, with lingering abdominal pain, drifting through the day like a ghost in my own skin.

But outside, barefoot and prostrated to the bit of park behind the hospital, I felt the rhythm of life again, and I felt it quickly. It was like a sudden electrical awakening that mirrored the jolt I had delivered to a patient's heart days earlier, when I pressed paddles to their chest during the scary choreography of a code blue. The earth didn't offer sympathy or words; it simply held me and let me be. In that stillness, I remembered I belonged, not just to a role or a hospital, but to the living world that first taught me joy. Pressing my face into the soil, something shifted. It wasn't dramatic, just a quiet remembering of being a child lying in the grass, sun-warmed and unburdened. My body knew I had been held like this before—long before the charting, the overnight shifts, and the endless stream of patients whose pain I carried more deeply than my own. The earth offered presence, and that, in my world built on productivity and proof and constant doing, felt radical. Time slowed to a halt, and I felt expansive, happy, and restful. Ever so quickly, I was back home in the arms of the earth.

That's where we will begin, not with data points or research (though we'll get there), but with a remembrance of a more ancient form of knowing. One that lives in our skin, in our senses, in the ways our ancestors walked and touched the land. The living world is not a pretty backdrop to our healing; it is a participant, a relation, a part of our very cells. This is the medicine we cannot live without. It is not outside of us—*it is us*.

The Earth is always ready, always waiting. Even a short time beneath the open sky can awaken something ancient in us. The wind gently loosens the knots in our minds. The sun presses warmth into our skin like a perfectly weighted blanket. Cool, autumn air stirs us up more surely than a cup of coffee. Our feet remember the ground, barefoot and unhurried, like we were meant to. Nature really asks nothing of us. Even the ordinary sounds of children playing outside—their laughter, their shouts rising and falling—feel like a quiet invitation to return to the moment we are in. So, can we get outside for a few hours a week? Before we collapse on the ground in exhaustion at work? Can we? Yes. But do we? That is another question entirely. What are our obstacles to doing this? Some barriers are practical: schedules too full, pressing commitments, lack of safe, green space nearby. Others are invisible but just as real: our own habits, our own forgetting, the threat of real harm, the illusion that there is not enough time.

Most of us consider nature as an escape rather than a home, a place we visit instead of a place we belong. We spend so much less time outside than we ever did in the history of human life that even our art and our literature is reflecting the deficiency. The disappearance of nature words such as *river*, *moss*, and *blossom* from books has been noted in a study by Miles Richardson, a British professor of nature connectedness at the University of Derby. He identified the disappearance of natural words from books between 1800 and 2020, which peaked at a 60.6 percent decline in 1990. The modeling predicts an ongoing "extinction of experience" with children losing an awareness of nature and parents no longer passing on an "orientation" toward the natural world. More significant than the disappearance of words is that this mirrors people's connection to nature, which has also declined by more than 60 percent since 1800.[1] This movement toward an indoors-centered life is a bad move for our health. It's unnatural for us to be separated from nature. Our bodies, minds, and cultures evolved in direct interaction with natural environments, and our biology still reflects that origin. The human brain evolved within nature; it has been shaped by our deep sensitivity and instinctive connection to it. In other words, our entire conscious universe is based on the ecology of the natural world.

The act of opening the door, of choosing to step outside, of remembering our place in nature among other living beings, takes some effort. But in an unjust world, the greatest obstacle is perhaps the simplest: access.

Green Space as Healing Space

We don't need studies to tell us that having access to green neighborhoods with trees and parks feels and looks good. However, studies do show that exposure to green spaces is associated with wide-ranging health benefits, including decreases in diastolic blood pressure, salivary cortisol, heart rate, and even the incidence of diabetes.[2] Higher levels of neighborhood green space are associated with significantly reduced symptoms of depression, anxiety, and stress, lower levels of income-related health inequality, and better self-reported physical health.[3] Residents in low-income urban areas often face barriers to accessing these benefits due to a lack of nearby parks and green spaces.

Trust for Public Land (TPL) is a national nonprofit organization that works to create parks and protect land for people, with a mission rooted in equity, health, climate resilience, and community connection. TPL focuses on ensuring everyone—especially in historically under-resourced areas—lives within a ten-minute walk of a quality park. They design parks with community input to reflect the needs, culture, and aspirations of local residents. According to an analysis by TPL, at the height of the pandemic, more than 1.1 million New Yorkers lacked access to a park within a ten-minute walk of where they lived. And in poor neighborhoods, the average park size is less than half of those in wealthy neighborhoods. For families living in disinvested neighborhoods where there is higher crime, fewer kids are outside playing. When parents perceive their neighborhoods as unsafe, they are less likely to allow their children to play outside, leading to reduced physical activity among preschool-aged children. This reduction in outdoor play can have long-term health implications, including increased risks of obesity and related health issues. It is a cycle of diminishing returns that I see every day, as my patients contend with what should be the simple question of when to get outside.

My patient Imani is twenty-five, a single woman who works as a line cook at a Mexican restaurant. She is also a recent immigrant from Ghana. She came to me for help with her feelings of loneliness and sadness, as well as for relief from muscle pain from standing long hours at work. Since moving to Chicago and settling in Rogers Park, Imani found herself getting very little physical activity. On the Cape Coast of Ghana, where she had lived most of her life, the ocean had shaped her days—walking the shoreline, moving in and out of the water, and spending little time indoors. Her life in Rogers Park was a striking contrast. It is one of Chicago's most diverse neighborhoods, known for its immigrant history and the more than eighty languages spoken within its borders. The neighborhood stretches along Lake Michigan, holds Loyola University, and is alive with culture, old brick apartment buildings, murals splashed under the El tracks, and grocery stores from every corner of the world. It is one of my favorite places in the city for all these reasons, but for Imani, it meant a very different rhythm: more time inside, less natural movement, and a strained relationship with her environment than the one she had always known. We've talked about this during her visits, how the combination of living mostly indoors and her justified fear of venturing out has taken a toll on her health.

In Ghana, Imani's life was the opposite. "All of our social life happened outside," she told me. "In the street, on the beach, at the park." Now, from her street, reaching the lake meant taking a path where she didn't feel safe walking alone as a woman, and that fear kept her from the places she longed to be. In many American cities, crime is a significant danger, particularly for women alone, and the weight of this is more than physical; it presses on the soul, shaping choices, freedoms, and health in ways most women understand all too well. We carry an ancestral longing to walk without hesitation under open sky, to feel the ground steady beneath our feet. But alongside that longing lives a constant shadow—a sense of unsafety that lingers with every step, a fear carried in the body, passed quietly through generations in stories, warnings, and habits: keys between fingers, glances over the shoulder, listening for footsteps too close. Walking alone is a birthright, a simple communion with the world, but for so many women it feels too risky. Our most radical act, then, is to walk anyway. Not recklessly or without caution, but with intention, presence, and quiet defiance against the idea that the world was not meant for us to move through freely.

The simple act of stepping outside, something many wellness prescriptions take for granted, is tangled up in a complex web of systemic neglect: underfunded schools, lack of green space, hyper-digitalized time, overpolicing, gun violence, broken sidewalks, and generations of disinvestment. We often talk about health as an individual matter, but health is deeply environmental. When people fear harassment, violence, or neglect just by stepping outside, we cannot ask them to "just go for a walk" without addressing the deeper harm. Together, Imani and I searched for a safe and feasible way for her to get outside. We talked about how there is something sacred in reclaiming a path where the fear quiets and the soul expands. She said she didn't want to pretend the threats weren't real, but sometimes she felt her ancestors' strength in her veins, giving her courage. I suggested she try her nearby park in the mornings or early afternoons, when it's brighter, busier with families, and safer with a friend or group. We also talked about spending time outside at trusted places like the library, community center, her church, or even the neighborhood school—spots that often have gardens or courtyards that are easy to enjoy. Luckily, even though she was new to the city, she had already made a few friends.

Imani did join a neighborhood walking group that heads to the forest preserves on weekends, which made her feel safer and more connected. To reach the lake, she bought a used bike, which helped her feel quicker, more secure, and able to arrive at the water's edge with more ease. Lake Michigan, she told me, reminds her of the ocean in Ghana and brings her so much joy. I hope that with these changes she may be more likely to step into nature without hesitation, knowing she belongs to the open, breathing world.

In our cities, we have built a world around nature in a way that makes some neighborhoods calm and pleasurable to be in, and others more dangerous and ominous to navigate. Community-led safety models like Bogotá, Colombia's *Ciclovía* have created increased trust in public space. Each Sunday, over seventy miles of streets are closed to cars, allowing two million people to walk, bike, dance, and play freely across the city. This long-standing tradition has inspired other cities worldwide and proves that policy can create culture. In Chicago's North Lawndale neighborhood, Equiticity organizes joy-based community rides and walks that double as civic engagement and healing communion. They center transportation justice as racial justice, and shift who gets to be seen as a planner, a healer, or a public space user. When safety is reimagined by communities themselves, walking becomes not just about movement, it becomes a form of belonging, dignity, and freedom. We can reconfigure our ways to reconnect with what has been twisted and sometimes broken. To ensure that engagement with the natural environment is safe and restorative, we must reimagine neighborhoods as true homes—places where children can play, elders can walk without fear, and joy can return to public spaces.

Engagement with the natural world has historically been regarded, across diverse cultural traditions, as a foundation for spiritual vitality and human flourishing. In Indigenous North American worldviews, the land is not separate from the self—mountains, rivers, and trees are seen as relatives and teachers, offering and speaking to us with guidance, healing, and balance. In Hinduism, nature is revered as divine, with rivers like the Ganges, referred to as Ganga Ma—the mother goddess—considered so sacred that to bathe in her waters is to be cleansed of all impurities and to bring wishes to manifestation. And trees like the banyan, *Ficus benghalensis*, with its vast aerial roots that grow into thick, columnar trunks, symbolize wisdom and safe, blessed shelter. Its canopy is a space for worship, storytelling, and meditation.

Traditional Chinese philosophies like Taoism view humans as part of the natural flow of the universe (the Tao), emphasizing harmony with nature as a path to well-being. Taoism teaches that well-being comes from living in balance with the Tao, or the natural flow of the universe, and

Taoist practices like qigong and tai chi are designed to align the body's energy with the rhythms of nature—slow, flowing movements that mirror the cycles of water or wind. This harmony with nature is seen not just as exercise, but as medicine for both body and spirit.

In the Celtic traditions of pre-Christian Europe, groves, springs, and animals were believed to carry spiritual significance and healing powers. Sacred groves of oak, ash, and yew were not only gathering places for ritual but were also seen as portals to the divine, spaces where the human and spirit worlds touched. Springs and wells, believed to be sources of healing and prophecy, were often dedicated to goddesses and later became sites of Christian pilgrimage.

And in Andean cosmology, Pachamama—Mother Earth—is honored through rituals that express reciprocity, gratitude, and protection of the land. Offerings known as *despachos* are made with flowers, coca leaves, grains, sweets, and other sacred items, arranged in intricate patterns and burned or buried as a way of feeding and thanking the earth. For the Quechua and Aymara peoples, Pachamama is not symbolic but a living presence—one who sustains life and who must be cared for as kin. These practices embody a worldview where well-being is inseparable from harmony with the land, waters, mountains, and sky. Across these and many other traditions, the natural world is an active, living force—one that sustains, transforms, and connects us to our health.

Urban Nature

At 111th Street and South Shore, you are still hugging Lake Michigan, headed south toward the bend leading into Indiana, but deep in South Chicago. The land along the lake has the vestiges of the industries that once occupied the area—electrical towers, an overgrown railroad with rusted tracks, vacant warehouses, discarded machinery parts. Next to a small park filled with wildflowers, and across from a row of worn 1940s brick apartments, lies a large stretch of open land enclosed by a chain-link fence. Step inside the fence and the land opens into rows of abundant greens, herbs, heritage vegetables, and even an orchard of fruit trees. A geodesic dome greenhouse brims with trays of seedlings, hardening in preparation for the weather outside. Nearby, a cobalt-blue shipping container has been transformed into an office, while a city bus covered in colorful murals announces Fresh Moves—a mobile market that brings produce to dozens of neighborhoods across Chicago's South and West Sides. Goats graze on grass and vegetable scraps, while young apprentice farmers pull weeds, water beds, and transplant herbs. Under a gazebo, a few community elders sit together, enjoying the space and each other's company.

Urban Growers Collective runs this fourteen-acre farm, offering herbalism and grower apprenticeships and job training to create economic opportunities for youth and beginner BIPOC farmers in Chicago. The farm also distributes community-supported agriculture food boxes that serve hundreds of local families, a beautiful model that is increasingly found in many urban communities across the country. My dear friend Erika Allen is the CEO, master innovator, and thought leader behind this organization. She has won nearly every major award in food and social justice, from the James Beard Leadership Award to the Chicago Prize, a multimillion-dollar investment in her work. During the lush summer growing season, talking with her is a reverential experience as we walk through the rows of sacred tobacco, hibiscus, and tulsi, an herb that's sacred to many cultures, including my own.

Something wildly important is happening here, and it goes beyond the obvious fact that this woman and her team are growing healthy, nutrient-dense, fresh food for our city. The farm flourishes here in a once abandoned lot. The soil is alive and healthy from years of careful tending, boosted by compost made in an anaerobic digester that turns food waste into rich "black gold." The youth program trains BIPOC youth to become land stewards, herbal apprentices, farmers, and community leaders, repairing and reimagining a deeply fraught relationship with growing food that stems from the terrible legacy of American slavery. These young people are learning to grow food, communicate with each other on the team's daily tasks, feed the goats, make compost, set up irrigation systems, and decide what to harvest and what to leave. They've got mud all over their shoes, clothes, and hands. Honestly, it feels like a holy thing to see, in a time when most kids are indoors with their hands clutching devices.

Like many urban farms, there is life in this oasis, apparent in the smell of the soil and the terroir. The plants move with the wind in a dance that feels celestial and more beautiful than anything happening inside a building anywhere. There is a feeling of peace and release, and my breath fills deeply here with the synchrony of the plants breathing. It is a relationship, developed immediately, by just inhabiting and beholding the simple beauty of growing things. There is also a connective frequency that is notably different. What is that feeling of aliveness that comes from fresh air? Where does it come from? What creates the petrichor, the smell of the wet earth? It feels like a wash of new, wild energy, like a first breath, something nourishing and deep. It is a whisper to our senses that we are meant to spend *some* of our time in shelter … and most of it outside. Beyond the feeling, there is a primal molecular technology behind the magic.

Forest as Pharmacy

Shinto, the traditional spiritual practice of Japan, also sees nature as sacred, and many Shinto shrines are located in dense forests, where visitors are encouraged to walk mindfully and absorb the healing energy of the land. The practice of forest bathing is based on this deep cultural reverence for trees and the belief that spending time in forests cleanses the spirit and rejuvenates the body. Forests, mountains, and rivers are believed to be inhabited by *kami* (divine spirits) and were noted by the Japanese as vital—so much so that, in Japan, the practice of forest bathing is a deep-seated and codified part of the culture.

In 1982, long before the term "climate anxiety" entered our vocabulary or "burnout" was a clinical diagnosis, Japan's Ministry of Agriculture, Forestry, and Fisheries introduced a practice called Shinrin-yoku, translated as "forest bathing."[4] It was not a passing wellness trend; it was in fact a national health policy. The goal was to encourage people to spend more time in forests to counteract the increasing stress, anxiety, and urbanization that came with modern Japanese life and the rapid industrialization of the 1980s. Japan's government recognized the therapeutic potential of forest and garden walks and sought to integrate this practice into preventive health care. The premise was simple: Spend time walking slowly, quietly, and mindfully in the forest. The point was not to exercise, or to conquer a trail, but to bathe the senses in the atmosphere of the trees. The Japanese government went beyond encouraging forest time as a lifestyle tip. It designated over sixty certified "Forest Therapy" bases across the country—places where physicians, public health workers, and foresters collaborate to support physical and mental well-being through structured time in nature.[5] Today, doctors in Japan prescribe forest bathing as a therapeutic intervention for stress, high blood pressure, depression, and immune dysfunction.[6] It is a publicly supported form of preventative medicine, and the science supports it.

Ancestral knowledge always precedes laboratory science, but we have the biochemical science to back this practice up too. When you walk into a forest, you may notice the air smells different—earthy, crisp, a little spicy, almost citrusy in some places. That scent is not just pleasant, it's medicine. You are breathing in phytoncides, the aromatic oils released by trees and plants, particularly in evergreen forests. These volatile organic compounds (VOCs) are part of the forest's immune system—used to protect trees from insects, fungi, and harmful bacteria—while also playing a role in plant communication. You might know that some VOCs are harmful toxins, released from paint, perfumes, and cleaning products. Phytoncides, however, have a powerful effect on our cells, enhancing our mood, strengthening the immune system, and lowering blood-sugar levels. The strong and pungent smells of the forest are in part alpha-pinene, beta-pinene, limonene, and camphene—the phytoncides that we inhale. When humans intake phytoncides, whether inhaled through the nose or absorbed through the skin, the compounds enter our bloodstream and begin to gently modulate our own immune and stress responses.

The mechanism appears to be both direct and indirect. The VOCs interact with receptors in our respiratory system and olfactory pathways, which in turn influence autonomic nervous system activity, helping shift the body out of "fight-or-flight" sympathetic dominance into "rest-and-digest" parasympathetic tone. Simultaneously, these compounds seem to enhance immune surveillance, reducing systemic inflammation and improving resilience to infections. Dr. Qing Li, an immunologist at Nippon Medical School and one of the world's leading researchers on Shinrin-yoku, has spent decades measuring what happens to the human body when it reconnects with the forest. His findings are stunning: Cortisol levels drop, along with heart rate and blood pressure, after just two hours in a forest environment. Natural killer (NK) cell activity, a vital part of the immune response, increases for up to a week after a forest bathing experience. Participants also report improved mood, reduced anxiety, and greater clarity of thought. This research was transformed into policy; a short, leisurely visit to a forest became a Japanese government initiative, and is now a widely adopted holistic lifestyle-based approach to health.

Forest therapy programs, nature retreats, and even corporate wellness initiatives integrate Shinrin-yoku to promote mental, emotional, and physical well-being, and have spread to many other countries. Japan's initiative is an incredible example of how public health policy can significantly and meaningfully impact the health of a population. The forest bathing policy is not just a public health success; it is a reminder that medicine can be quiet and does not always require a pill or a screen or a protocol. Sometimes, the prescription is simply this: Go outside, and let the forest remind you of who you are.

Other Japanese researchers discovered that phytoncides not only boost the activity of natural killer cells, which play a key role in fighting infections and cancer, but also increase the levels of important immune proteins inside NK cells, helping them attack unhealthy cells more efficiently. When NK cells were weakened by exposure to a toxic pesticide, phytoncides helped *partially restore their strength and function*. This suggests that spending time in nature and breathing in the forest air can support immune health, especially in environments where toxins may weaken the body's defenses. This study showed a rise in the number and activity of natural killer cells among people who spent three days and two nights in a forest, compared to people who took an urban trip. This remarkable benefit lasted for more than a month after the trip concluded. Such a wonderful immersion is not always feasible, but other exposure-response research from the UK suggests that people who reported spending 120 minutes or more in nature a week had consistently higher levels of both health and well-being than those who reported no exposure.

So just a couple of hours a week outdoors in nature helps, and it doesn't have to be all at once or in large doses. Shinrin-yoku is a modern embodiment of an ancient knowing: that we are not separate from the forest. Our nervous systems recognize the language of leaves rustling and the scent of tree perfume. Our breath slows in rhythm with the trees. When we immerse ourselves in wild, living spaces, we remember something cellular, ancestral, and sacred, and our bodies align biologically.

Unlike the sterile air of climate-controlled rooms, forest air is chemically alive, carrying messages, immunity, and intelligence. You may not realize it, but your nervous system is recalibrating, your immune cells are awakening, and your stress hormones are literally dissolving into the forest's exhale. Dr. Yoshifumi Miyazaki of Chiba University, whose book *Shinrin Yoku: The Japanese Art of Forest Bathing* brought the practice to global attention, reminds us of the heart of the practice:

> Pay attention to any areas of stiffness or pain in the body and consciously relax them. Become aware of your present mental and emotional states. . . . Pay attention to the experience of walking and keep your awareness engaged in this experience. Be aware of the beginning, the middle, and the end of your stepping. Walk as silently as possible.[7]

Most of us spend our lives in manmade boxes, breathing recycled and canned air. Too much gray, black, and white—and not enough immersion in greens and blues. In fact, both the Environmental Protection Agency and the World Health Organization found that Americans and Europeans spend about 90 percent of their time indoors, where the concentration of some air pollutants can be two to five times higher than outdoors.[8] City gardens, forests, and urban farms all release phytoncides and generate cleaner air. Phytoncides are more than just chemical defenses; they are the spiritual breath of the earth, embodying the consciousness of the natural world, and offer balance, renewal, and connection. In many ancient traditions, the fresh air of forests, gardens, and green spaces are considered the primal energy. In Ayurveda, the air we breathe carries life force, *prana*, and the phytoncides of plants can be understood as a concentrated form of prana, imbuing us with their protective energy.

While forests have a particularly high concentration of phytoncides due to the density of trees—and it is particularly easy to forest bathe in Japan since forests occupy 67 percent of the land—even small gardens, herb patches, wild meadows, and urban farms like Erika's, contribute to the air's biochemical richness. Here, the energy immediately changes my mood. Spending time in any biodiverse natural space—not just deep forests—can provide exposure to these beneficial compounds, these out-breaths of the earth, supporting both physical and spiritual well-being. When you are outside in green, open spaces, the air breathes you back; it fills your lungs and your blood and your life force with an untamed energy that reminds our animal bodies that we need to roam. It heals.

Take the break, open the window, step outside. The most beautiful, complex, and sophisticated medicines await in the outdoors, where our bodies were made to thrive.

Spanda

One of the greatest challenges I have faced practicing medicine in the United States is the constant push and pull between what I know might truly help a patient, and what is considered "real medicine" within the health care system. So often, if no prescription is written, if no test is ordered, it can feel—to the patient, and to the institution—as though the doctor has not done their job. But some of the most powerful forms of healing don't come in a bottle or through a lab test, and while I am very comfortable and respectful of the many pills and tests that I utilize in my practice, I think that we have the definition of what makes a real medicine all wrong. Only after many years of practicing medicine am I comfortable guiding others toward a truth I had to uncover step by step: The medicine of nature opens us to the rhythm of life itself.

There is a rhythm to everything that lives. Our breath is moving in and out, the seasons turn and merge, the waves rise and fall, we wake up and go to sleep, seeds grow into plants that flower and then seed again. The primordial pulse of life is a thread that ties us to our source energy and to all of the ancestors who felt it too. *Spanda*, a concept from yogic and tantric philosophy, speaks to this primordial pulse, the subtle vibration that underlies all of existence. It is not just movement, but the divine trembling of consciousness itself, the sacred dance between stillness and action, emptiness and fullness, potential and creation. As was explained to me in the beautiful dance work "Spanda" by famed bharatanatyam classical dancer Mallika Sarabhai, in the vast silence of the universe, spanda is the whisper before sound. It is the ripple before the wave, that stirring in the soul before an idea takes form. It is the felt sense that life is not static but alive, pulsing with creative energy, guiding us toward expansion, expression, and deepening awareness. This subtle, dynamic vibration of consciousness, the primal throb that initiates all movement, perception, and creation, is movement between absolute stillness and dynamic energy. The eye of the storm, or the impulse that gives rise to a thought. That this concept exists, and has a word to describe it, is one of the miracles of human consciousness!

The ancients believed that when we immerse ourselves in nature, we step into the purest expression of spanda—the sacred, living pulse of the world. The rustling of leaves, the flow of water, the rise and fall of the wind, the sway of the wildflowers—all of these reflect the dynamic stillness of spanda. Nature is never truly still, nor is it truly chaotic; it moves in waves, cycles, and patterns, much like the subtle inner vibration that spanda describes. This subtle inner vibration exists within each of us as well. The constant hustle and push toward productivity has made us masters of efficiency, excellent consumers and workers, adept at keeping pace with a different rhythm that was never meant to sustain us. The modern world hums with urgency from emails, deadlines, notifications, schedules packed so tightly that even rest becomes another task to complete. It is a rhythm designed for machines, not humans.

In this rhythm, it's hard to feel the spanda, or even distantly sense it. In my practice, I talk about the rhythm of life with every patient. Often we start with the rhythm of sleep, mostly so that I can ensure that it is actually happening. Most people don't sleep enough, and they suffer for it. Sleep is one of the most significant parts of the rhythm of life, and without enough of it, we actually die earlier. I deep-dive with patients into the prelude before sleep, the obstacles to a restful sleep, and how many hours they are getting. So many of my patients with chronic fatigue, requesting a workup for an autoimmune or post-viral disease are, in fact, simply not sleeping enough or well enough. Prescribing sleep, and good sleep hygiene, is one of the foundational pillars of integrative medicine practice. Even when sleep patterns are not ideal, prioritizing periods of rest and restoration during the day is vital.

Unlike the steady pulse of nature—the slow unfurling of a flower bloom, the rhythmic pull of the lunar tides—our artificial pace leaves little room for deep breaths, space for pause, or permission for stillness. My soul sister, Hemalayaa Behl, and I lead a beautiful women's health retreat every year in Costa Rica, on the land where she lives, and one of the built-ins in the schedule is the "sacred pause." This time is not intended as just a break; it is an intentional pause from the busy mind, and a chance to ground into your present needs—closing your eyes if they are strained, eating and drinking, taking deep, slow breaths and practicing breathwork, stretching, splashing water on your face, or stepping outside. The sacred pause is about remembering that we don't have to fill every gap with noise or activity. It's a chance to slow down and notice the moment.

What if we let go? What if we softened? What if we stepped out of the noise and attuned ourselves to a different rhythm—the one that has always been present beneath the rush? The spanda. This is where nature can be our teacher. The forest doesn't rush to grow faster and the river doesn't force itself to flow. They follow the rhythm that is true to them, steady, unhurried, purposeful but without force. In complete attunement with spanda. We can mimic this sweet flow by deconditioning and decolonizing ourselves from the pressured pace of production, understanding and relearning that we all belong outdoors. Even the term itself, as practical and easy to understand as it is—*out of doors*—is one that does not exist in Indigenous wisdom. Indigenous languages have no direct translation for wilderness, but rather view our relationship with the wild world as that of kin. Indigenous cultures all over the planet see and acknowledge that land, water, trees are relatives, part of our human family. Kincentric Ecology, as defined by Ráramuri scholar and anthropologist Dr. Enrique Salmón, posits that humans are not separate from nature, but rather are part of a larger system where everything is related, including plants, animals, and natural forces like fire and water.[9] In *Braiding Sweetgrass*, Potawatomi scholar and botanist Robin Wall Kimmerer also emphasizes that the more-than-human world is not made up of "things" but of beings, kin with whom we are in reciprocal relationship.[10] In this cosmology, where we are kin and where spanda is expressed in the pulse of the wild world, we can remove the guilt and separation that we feel when we take time for a "break" to "go outside."

Indigenous teachings emphasize that daily time on the land nourishes the spirit. The land holds memory and medicine. Walking it, touching it, and listening to it allows people to stay rooted in ancestral relationships and to receive the wisdom of place. To walk with intention, to observe the changing sky, to feel the pulse of the earth beneath one's feet: these are ways of staying attuned to the cycles of life, and to the balance that sustains health. Many Indigenous traditions hold that daily engagement with the natural world is necessary not only for physical health but for emotional, mental, and spiritual wellness. To breathe the air of the morning, to greet the sun, to touch soil or pick up stones, to move under the trees or stars—these acts restore harmony within the self and with the greater web of life. I think that much of the anxiety that we feel to keep up with the unnatural pace of human busyness is actually our heart speeding about in scattered directions, looking for that spanda, that source.

We can move into sacred pause, feel the sacred pulse, and be our wild selves. At our essence, we are truly wild, by which I mean we are shaped by webs of life. Not the opposite of civilized, but the opposite of domesticated. Like many animals, humans have been domesticated, and that has suppressed our most primal and basic needs to be outside, in favor of other activities.

Are You "Outdoorsy"?

One of my favorite comedians, Jim Gaffigan, jokes often about his distaste for the outdoors. "I am what you call 'indoorsy.' I am surprised we can even get people to camp. 'Wanna burn a couple of vacation days sleeping on the ground outside?' Uh, *no*."

Many people feel that they are not "outdoorsy types" because of mistaken beliefs about what it means to be outdoorsy. If you walk into an "outdoor" retailer, you mostly find things like waterproof backpacks, specialized hiking pants, kayaks, tents, and lanterns. I love browsing and imagining the trips I'd have to plan just to justify buying some of it! Certainly, I do own some gear that has made my life more comfortable in all kinds of challenging weather. But I do think that this popular and particular retail lens is narrowing, and can make us feel that spending time outdoors needs to be a grand adventure to somewhere distant and magical with vast forests, towering mountains, or untouched landscapes, which require specific equipment. Adventures are great—don't get me wrong. But for most of us, who do not have the time, resources, ability, or access to this kind of immersion, we can focus on nearby nature. Experiences like walking around the neighborhood, getting on the swings at the playground, or having a family picnic at the park, forest preserve, or beach are meaningful ways of connecting with nature that can bring great mental and physical benefits. Adventures do not need to be far-flung.

When more than 20 percent of Americans and one in six Europeans are contending with a mental health disorder,[11] the importance of getting out into green space cannot be underestimated. The barriers are different for different people. But no matter what our neighborhood or income level, we can all relate to the barrier of time poverty, and the real loss of choice over how we spend our time. With jobs, kids' needs, school, grocery shopping, cooking, family priorities, it can feel impossible to fit outdoor time into the day. A simple idea that can help is to do any activities outside that you can, such as reading, doing homework, or having a snack or meal. Step out on the porch, in the backyard, or go to a nearby park. When my kids were younger, we would on occasion walk our full dinner plates to the benches at the park across the street—just to be in community and get some fresh air. The sounds of happy kids on the playground and the sight of dogs and babies and elders together all made for a great reset, and sometimes it changed the energy of our family entirely. It wasn't a mountain hike, but it was an immersion in open air that proved transformative. Fresh air can do that. Fresh air, however, is not guaranteed, even when outdoors.

For people living near highways or high-traffic corridors, daily outdoor time is a topic I approach with great care, cultural humility, and environmental awareness. Air pollution from vehicle traffic puts fine particulate matter (PM2.5), nitrogen dioxide (NO_2), and ultrafine particles into the air and is highest near highways. The air quality is also exacerbated by larger and more frequent wildfires in the age of climate change. These things can lead to significant health risks like asthma exacerbation, cardiovascular strain, neurocognitive impacts, and oxidative stress. Several of my young asthmatic patients cannot safely go outside of their homes without worsening symptoms. It is heartbreaking and a failure of our society on many levels that a situation exists where fresh air is not medicinal but rather can threaten our health because of our own human actions. Everyone deserves access to nature and fresh air, and time outdoors remains important for mental, emotional, and spiritual health, especially in disinvested neighborhoods where stress levels are high and green space is limited. How might someone safely get fresh air and outdoor time in this context? How to take in this medicine?

First, we need to acknowledge the grave injustice that people in parts of the world and this country do not have a safe space to breathe. In the 1930s, the US government, through the Home Owners' Loan Corporation (HOLC), created maps of American cities to guide mortgage lending. Neighborhoods were color-coded based on perceived "risk" for investment. Areas with high proportions of Black, immigrant, or low-income residents were marked in red and considered "hazardous," and thus denied loans. This practice didn't just block homeownership; it segregated cities and concentrated disinvestment in communities of color. Because redlined neighborhoods were denied financial investment, they were often located in less desirable parts of cities, like near factories, railroads, or, later, highways; and when the interstate system expanded in the mid-twentieth century, planners bulldozed through Black and immigrant communities at disproportionate rates. These highways cut neighborhoods apart and exposed residents to massive levels of car-related air pollution.

New polluting industries, freeways, and transportation hubs have historically been placed in low-income and BIPOC neighborhoods, where political resistance was weaker and land was cheaper. These communities became sacrifice zones for regional transportation and economic "development" and were exposed to air pollution, noise, and toxic stressors for generations.[12] On top of this, affordable housing shortages force many families to live in high-pollution areas, often next to freeways or major traffic corridors, while wealthier, whiter communities successfully resist freeway expansion near their homes, further entrenching unequal exposure to pollutants.

Redlining laid the groundwork for environmental racism, defined as the ongoing unequal distribution of pollution and environmental harms across racial and low-income lines, beyond mere economic variables.[13] Agrochemicals, introduced after slavery as so-called labor-saving tools, cannot be regarded as value-free technologies intended only to enhance productivity. Their use created sacrifice zones, most often in communities of color, exposed to pesticide drift, chemical manufacturing, and toxic waste. The same pattern of exploitation persists today, as AI datacenters are strategically sited in vulnerable neighborhoods, often without consent or adequate protections. Market-driven gentrification sometimes "beautifies" these corridors without reducing pollution or displacement risk, continuing the cycle.

Globally, the dependence on cars, particularly in urban and suburban regions, has locked communities into patterns of high fuel use and high emissions, and environmental impact statements often fail to address cumulative exposures and historic injustice. Air pollution mitigation is still treated as an afterthought, not as an essential matter of health equity and public health. The Children's Respiratory and Environmental Workgroup (CREW) consortium, established through funding from the NIH's Environment and Child Health Outcomes (ECHO) program, conducted research that focused on 202 cities around the United States, and looked at year-2010 levels of the two regulated air pollutants I mentioned—nitrogen dioxide (NO_2) and fine particulate matter (PM2.5).[14] The authors found that areas that were redlined in the 1930s consistently had higher levels of pollution today than areas that received favorable treatment. Strikingly, air pollution disparities associated with historical redlining status in these cities were even larger than disparities associated with race and ethnicity.

They also found that children who were raised in redlined neighborhoods are still paying a price in the form of higher risk of developing asthma. I have noted this for years in my practice. Asthma is the most common form of chronic childhood illness, affecting more than 4.6 million children in the United States. It is one of the most common reasons for children being hospitalized, resulting in 150 child deaths each year. Asthma is terrifying to live with, when wheezing can quickly progress to air hunger, and the albuterol and steroid inhalers that help relieve symptoms are expensive for families, and need steady refills.

My eleven-year-old patient Anna suffered from asthma and allergies, greatly worsened by her home's proximity to three major highways on Chicago's West Side. She walked to school with her brother. I discussed several options with her parents. Air pollution levels fluctuate during the day, so I advised them to avoid outside time during peak traffic hours (rush hour mornings and evenings) when pollutant concentrations are highest, and if unavoidable to wear masks. Midday or late morning, after traffic patterns settle, often has cleaner air, though this depends on local conditions.

There are real-time air quality apps such as *AirNow* and *PurpleAir* that empower patients to track and choose lower-exposure times. I encouraged them to seek outside streets, pocket parks, courtyards, schoolyards, or church grounds that are set back from major roads and to look for nearby urban tree canopies and shrubs that can act as partial barriers, as walking routes near more vegetation have measurable air quality benefits. Anna and her mother were interested in the idea of a window garden on the opposite side of the home from the highway, which could offer safer semi-outdoor spaces in their home. Even indoor nature exposure, through plants, natural light, nature videos, and audio of natural soundscapes can confer some mental health benefits when outdoor access is limited. A HEPA air purifier in Anna's bedroom and closed windows on high air pollution days helped.

Ultimately, no amount of individual adaptation replaces the need for policy change. My goal is empowerment for patients and systemic advocacy for communities—not individual blame for the great injustices they suffer. Green buffers; urban reforestation; highway traffic caps; air filtration subsidies for affected communities; and equitable investment in accessible, safe parks in environmental justice zones are all necessary for a just society. Prescribing nature without acknowledging structural air pollution is an incomplete practice, and it is vital to name these injustices out loud.

On a systems level, there are ways we can align our schools and workplaces and communities to make it easier to be outside. Some companies have instituted "green hour policies" and encourage walking meetings and outdoor coworking spaces to integrate nature into work life. Doctors in the United States, Canada, and the United Kingdom are starting to prescribe time in nature as a medical intervention to address stress, anxiety, and chronic illness. Programs like Park Rx America and Canada's PaRx initiative connect patients with nearby outdoor spaces for healing. There are over eighty local Park Rx programs in the United States, with new initiatives continuously emerging. Park prescriptions are a way to explicitly acknowledge that nature is medicine, that true health care sees that we deeply need nature to survive.

Dr. David Victorson is a psychologist, professor of medical social sciences, and director of the Flourishing in Society and Health Research Lab in the Feinberg School of Medicine at Northwestern University. He is also principal cofounder and director of a nonprofit for young adults and caregivers affected by cancer called True North Treks, an organization whose mission is to support young adults and caregivers affected by the "Big C" of cancer to find direction through "the Big C" of connection—connection to nature after the incredibly unnatural experience of cancer at this age; connection to peers who have walked a similar path and get it; and connection to oneself through the compass of mindful awareness practices. Dr. Victorson has led dozens of treks with young cancer survivors who often describe them as life-changing. I asked him what his research reveals about the need for humans to be outside.

> Being in nature isn't just nice—it's necessary and fundamental to who we are. Of our three hundred thousand years of existence as modern Homo Sapiens, we've spent roughly 97 percent of that time living directly in nature. . . . Our nervous systems and brains evolved over hundreds of thousands of years to sync our regulatory bodily processes and systems, which is how we respond to or recover from stress, with open, non-threatening, viewable landscapes and horizons that signal safety and survival. This is one of the reasons why we feel good when we're looking out over an open body of water. This is what the co-regulated biological dependency of nature looks like.[15]

For Dr. Victorson, we are not only living in an environment, we *are* the environment: interconnected ecosystems embedded within larger ecosystems.

Aligning with Cycles of the Day and Season

Shaped by centuries of observation, philosophy, and healing practice, Ayurvedic medicine is both a medical system and a way of living in harmony with nature. So immense is this cosmology that one could spend a lifetime exploring it and still only touch the surface of its sophistication and science. While I have studied under Ayurvedic scholars both here and in India, I will forever be an infant student of a tradition this intricate and wise. Ayurvedic health pedagogy is based on the five elements of ether, fire, air, water, and earth combining as three primary energies, or life forces, called *doshas*. All of us have a combination of these doshas, and by knowing and understanding them, we are given a map of self-care that can guide us to our best health.

Like every tradition rooted in ancient wisdom, in Ayurveda, we see humans as part of Prakriti (nature), not separate from it. Spending time outdoors is considered essential for balance for all doshas, as exposure to the sun, fresh air, and natural elements nourishes both body and mind. Prakriti Sthana is the alignment of oneself with nature's cycles through daily and seasonal rhythms. This includes waking with the sun, eating seasonal foods, being attuned to natural seasonal changes, and respecting that the body has different needs at different times of year. Just as animals hibernate in the winter, we, too, need to slow down, get more sleep, and attune to the lessened light and earlier bedtimes.

Here in the Midwest, when it is dark by 4 p.m. in the middle of winter, I often feel ready to go to bed by 7 p.m., though my schedule does not usually allow for it. This feeling is largely because our circadian rhythms, controlled by the tiny pineal gland in the brain, keep us aligned to Earth cycles, whether our daily routines do or not! The pineal gland is linked in yogic and Ayurvedic tradition to the Ajna Chakra (third eye center), governing not just circadian rhythm, but also intuition and higher consciousness, which are supported by rest, dreams, and sleep. Enter the main character of the circadian rhythm: melatonin.

Melatonin is an incredibly sophisticated and beautiful molecule that exemplifies just how tied to nature we are. It is the master regulator of our sleep-wake cycle, acting as an internal clock that aligns our bodies with the rhythms of light and darkness. This hormone signals when it's time to sleep and when to wake, helping to orchestrate the body's natural twenty-four-hour cycle that governs sleep and metabolism. It supports immune function and cellular protection, as it is an antioxidant that scavenges damaged cells. Melatonin also supports gut function, digestion, and menstrual cycles, among numerous other important roles.[16] I think it is one of the most overlooked and most important hormones in the body, reduced to the supplement aisle of the drugstore where it is underregulated, undervalued, and overdosed. Like a queen who deserves a robe of silk but has been relegated to a wear a grape-flavored gummy jacket. I make it a point to teach my patients about how melatonin works to keep us attuned to nature, if we let it do its work. It is a true guardian of health.

Dr. Satchidananda Panda at the Salk Institute is one of the world's leading researchers of circadian rhythm, and much of what we know today about blue light, melatonin, and daily rhythms builds on his discoveries. Here's a short academic lesson from his research on this one incredible part of your machinery: Melatonin is predominantly controlled by exposure to light and dark. When light, especially blue wavelengths (460–480 nm) from sunlight or artificial screens, is detected by specialized cells called intrinsically photosensitive retinal ganglion cells (ipRGCs) in the retina, melanopsin, a light-sensitive protein, then sends a signal to the optic nerve. This signal goes to the suprachiasmatic nucleus (SCN), the master clock located in the hypothalamus in the center of the brain. In response to the intensity and brightness of the light, the SCN activates neural pathways that suppress melatonin production. So the brighter and bluer the light, the less melatonin is being produced.[17] With melatonin levels suppressed, wake-promoting neurotransmitters like cortisol, serotonin, norepinephrine, and dopamine remain active, keeping the brain in an alert state. Body temperature rises, metabolism remains active, and cognitive function stays sharp, far from a state of sleep.

When darkness sets in, assuming that you are witnessing the light change with your eyes (not in a windowless room, or on a screen), the SCN stops sending inhibitory signals, allowing the pineal gland to resume melatonin production. Melatonin levels rise, signaling the body to lower core temperature, slow metabolism, and prepare for sleep. Drowsiness sets in, and brain activity shifts toward sleep-promoting pathways. This entire light-melatonin network ensures that our biological clock stays synchronized with the natural day-night cycle, helping regulate energy levels, immune function, and overall health. Thus, staying in synchrony with the cycles of light and dark not only improves sleep but also leads to better mental health, better-functioning mitochondria, healthier cellular functioning, and longevity.

At this moment in modern living, the consequences of ignoring the cycles of light and dark are steep—and reaching emergency levels. Our rhythms are often so altered from the light-dark flip-flop of screen time that we are perpetually fatigued and sleep-deprived, as melatonin levels aren't given the chance to rise. Chronic sleep deprivation increases mortality risk anywhere from 14 to 34 percent.[18]

It certainly wasn't always so. In the olden days, when the sun set, we lit candles and started fires, gathered round and told stories, or knit or wrote letters while the light lasted. Firelight, which emits primarily red-orange wavelengths, has minimal impact on melatonin, so it still settled us down for bed. When electricity entered human life in the 1800s, a certain ease came with it. No more candles. Bulb lights could be switched on as the daylight waned and could stay on as long as one could afford to keep it on. Of course, before electricity, work schedules were governed by daylight, and most labor ended at sunset, with minimal nighttime activity. There was no widespread concept of night shifts, only occasional work by firelight or gas lamps in some industries.

But by the early twentieth century, electricity allowed businesses to run twenty-four seven, and shift work became common in industries like manufacturing, mining, transportation, and health care. And the rise of electric streetlights made night commuting possible, reinforcing the feasibility of night shifts. Having done many years of these myself delivering babies, and being married to an ER physician who works nights, I can say with confidence that routinely working through the night with the intensity of daytime energy is incredibly destabilizing to one's health. This is an important and well-studied area in medicine. Large cohort studies like the Nurses' Health Study II and the Japan Collaborative Cohort show significantly higher all-cause mortality in long-term rotating shift workers.[19] In fact, the World Health Organization classified night-shift work as a probable carcinogen (Group 2A) in 2007 due to circadian disruption and melatonin suppression.[20]

Then the widespread adoption of television in the 1950s to 1990s kept people awake longer. Though TVs did not emit significant blue light, television culture did push bedtime later. If you didn't stay up for the ten o'clock news, how would you know anything about what was going on in the world? I still remember how amped up my parents would be after watching all the bad news at ten. How were we all supposed to go to bed peacefully after that? So, while electricity has allowed incredible advancements, electric lighting was the beginning of our disconnection from natural light-dark cycles. In truth, we are addicted to artificial light; it is part of the blueprint of modern and colonized societies, and it extends the day unnaturally.

And now? We have blown our electricity use out of the water! Screentime: In the 1990s and 2000s, the rise of computers, email, and internet usage meant that people began staring at bright screens for extended periods, often at night. The early screens emitted significant blue light, but awareness of circadian disruption and its significance was low at the time. Then in 2007, the launch of the iPhone and the rise of LED screens led to constant exposure to artificial blue light, particularly before bed. Unlike TVs or computers, smartphones and tablets are held close to the face, intensifying their effect on melatonin suppression. Social media, streaming services, and twenty-four seven connectivity have made nighttime screen use habitual and completely normalized. Evening time use of blue-blocker glasses, dimmer apps, and night modes are helpful, but they do not reduce screen time engagement—and much of what we read and watch is activating, stimulating, and straight-up distressing.

As little as thirty minutes of tablet or smartphone use before bed has been shown to significantly suppress melatonin onset and delay sleep. Two hours of screen exposure, especially from tablets and phones held close to the face, can suppress melatonin by 20 to 22 percent and delay our circadian rhythm by about 1.5 to 2 hours.[21] Night after night, this can significantly alter our circadian rhythm, which affects the functioning of all of our systems, leading to a profound impact on our health. Dr. Panda's work suggests that we dim lights two to three hours before bed, and reduce overhead and bright LED lighting, using lamps, candles, or warm-hued bulbs. If you must look at a screen, use blue-light filters or glasses. We can and should pay closer attention to the brilliance of melatonin, by remembering that we are animals of the natural world. My guess is that our pets are likely sleeping much better than we are.

Dusking

Our relationship with sunlight is far more intimate than we realize. When light enters our eyes, it allows us to literally see the world around us and also triggers powerful biological processes. Specialized photoreceptors in the retina send signals through the optic nerve, not just to the visual cortex, but also to regions of the brain that regulate hormones and mood. Morning sunlight in particular stimulates the release of serotonin, which stabilizes mood, supports our focus, and helps us feel calm and present. It's wildly important to step outside in the morning and let natural daylight reach your eyes—without sunglasses—while avoiding staring directly at the sun. Then we can return our attention to the light at the end of the day as well.

Melatonin is one of the millions of primal molecules that remind us that we are tied to Earth cycles, no matter what we choose to do with our time. When we are chronically out of sync, our bodies let us know. One of my remedies is to prescribe dusking. I like to think of dusk not just as a time of day, but as an activity. Dusk is the slow exhale of the day, a liminal space between light and dark, doing and being. To walk or sit in the natural world at dusk is to re-enter and remember ancient rhythms. The practice of dusking entails mindful observation of the transition from day to night, serving as a respite from hyper-production. It is an exercise in mindfulness, offering a break from consumption and encouraging contemplation. Just as our ancestors once did, under fading sunlight and firelight, we can decide that it is time to change the rhythm of the day.

Science affirms what Indigenous and ancestral traditions have long known: Dusk is a biologically sacred time. As the light begins to dim, our physiology begins to shift. Melatonin secretion begins in response to decreasing blue light. The sympathetic nervous system winds down, and parasympathetic activity increases. Cortisol naturally drops, reducing alertness and anxiety while signaling the body to prepare for rest. Just twenty to thirty minutes of exposure to sunset tones can shift our entire hormonal and neurological state toward calm, balance, and restoration.

Dusking can help us reconnect with nature, appreciate the subtleties of twilight, and understand the cyclical processes of our existence. I think it may hold something uniquely grounding, a return to our biological truth. In one study, participants who spent evenings outdoors reported lower anxiety, greater sleep satisfaction, and a stronger sense of spiritual connection to the land.[22] Psychologically, dusk invites integration, a chance to metabolize the day, and move from the now into the next. As the shadows lengthen, we soften, insights might stir, and the nervous system settles. For some of you, dusk might be a portal to safety and somatic peace, particularly when accompanied by birdsong, breeze, or familiar smells of soil and air.

Simply go outside at dusk and witness the change of light. Walk the dog, walk yourself, get out of your office and away from your computer and desk and take in the grandeur of the evening sky. The purplish pinks and light and bright blues, the light greys and whites. Notice the birds making their way across the sky toward warmer, safer resting places. Dusking is more than a biological shift; it is an intentional return to presence. It is the moment where the day eases into quietude, where the body is allowed to exhale fully, where the world surrenders to stillness. To dusk is to honor the wisdom of darkness, to trust that not all hours must be filled with light, and to remember that the body thrives when we allow it to follow the rhythm of the Earth. If nothing else, notice the dusk from your window, and take the time to truly sink into the waning light—with your breath, your eyes, and your mindful noticing. Even if you have to keep working, dusk can still program the brain and body to ready you for sleep several hours later. Gradually dim the lights and slow activities in the evening when you are able.

We can restore this lost rhythm! Consider it an act of resistance: a refusal to believe that every moment must serve a purpose, a rejection of rigid, binary thinking, a pushback against the relentless pursuit of growth and improvement that defines so much of modern life.

Earthing

Of course, we are creatures of the sun! Our bodies and rhythms are bound to its warmth, its rise and fall. For me, being barefoot feels like one of the great glories of summer. To feel the grass, sand, soil, beneath our feet is to feel connected, and can feel like freedom. It also can just make you feel more alive! The Earth is not passive ground beneath our feet; it is humming with energy, pulsing with electromagnetic force and a spiritual vitality. Across cultures and traditions, the Earth is considered a source of healing, grounding, and renewal, and to walk in harmony with it is to tap into an ancient, unseen current that nourishes both body and soul. The electromagnetic field (EMF) of the planet was long felt, worshipped, and celebrated before modern science defined it. But now EMFs have been well studied in biofield medicine and geoscience, and the research shows that you don't have to travel to specific coveted places to benefit from them.

I learned about the practice of earthing through my own health challenges. For years, often during the seasonal change in Chicago, I would struggle with headaches that did not subside with any of the usual treatments. The headaches weren't tied to typical triggers like sleep, menstrual cycles, stress, or diet, and I tracked them for years. They weren't debilitating but drained my energy, and remedies—whether medications or herbs—barely helped. Strikingly, the headaches vanished in summer and on trips to warm places, suggesting stress or barometric pressure as factors. The headaches especially dogged me in the fall-to-winter transition, even on sunny days.

Many of my patients also report relief in warm climates, which has always intrigued me. While the "vacation effect" is frequently invoked to account for the health gains of time away, I did not find it sufficient to explain what I was noticing. At one point, after explaining that walking barefoot had helped his own musculoskeletal pain, a patient of mine gave me a book called *Earthing* by Clinton Ober, Martin Zucker, and cardiologist Dr. Stephen Sinatra, and I went ahead and read it. (I have stacks of articles and books my patients give me to read, and I try to read them all, though it's slow going.) It was fascinating to learn the Earth gives off electrons, natural currents of energy that are all around us, everywhere. When we touch the ground or step into rivers, lakes, or oceans, those electrons move into us, where our own bodies absorb and respond to them. Ober and his coauthors write, "Grounding or earthing the body is having direct contact with the natural electric charge of the earth. . . . Your planet is a six sextillion (that's six followed by twenty-one zeroes) metric ton battery that is continually being replenished by solar radiation, lightning, and heat from its deep-down molten core."

The humming of the energetic surface of the Earth can be felt in the body, because the human body is electrically active. Looking further into the research, one finds the Earth has a slightly negative electrical charge, creating an electromagnetic field. Electron transfer occurs when a person comes into direct skin contact with the Earth and electrons from the field are transferred into the body, which help to neutralize positive ions, restoring our bioelectrical balance. To my great surprise and delight, electrons also act as antioxidants that neutralize reactive molecules, reducing inflammation and protecting cells from damage. Research suggests that this may improve blood flow by reducing the body's natural electrical resistance and improve sleep quality by reducing static electricity in the body.[23]

So what does direct skin contact mean? Being barefoot on the earth. That was something I could do, and love to do, and do whenever it is not too cold. Being barefoot has always been one of my favorite things. Even as a kid, I never wanted to wear shoes and fought tooth and nail when forced to smoosh my feet into what felt like little jail cells. When I started to make a point of being barefoot even in my yard for a few minutes, and then for longer times as it got warmer, my headaches improved. Sometimes they improved rather quickly after standing on the earth. Of course, when the ground is cold, my earthing is quite brief. And now it made sense that the headaches went away on a vacation—as we usually travel to places where it is warm enough to swim in open water, hike barefoot along rivers, dirt paths, or sand, or have our feet in the soft grass. I was completely floored by how well earthing worked for me, and also by the irony of having to relearn from a book that it feels wonderful to be barefoot outdoors! We know these things already. We know deep in our cells that to be outside, and to be in relationship with the ground and the earth, feels right and good. We simply need to remember.

Since our bodies are bioelectrical systems, and direct connection with the Earth allows us to absorb its natural electromagnetic charge, earthing can help to balance our overactive nervous systems and reduce pain. I am particularly interested in the reduction in inflammation that results from this electrical conduction through our bodies, since all chronic disease stems from inflammation. In modern life, we have become disconnected from the Earth's natural electrical field due to rubber-soled shoes, concrete, and constant exposure to artificial electromagnetic frequencies from wi-fi, screens, and devices. So, this has become a vital part of my nature prescription for patients: Get outside, in direct contact with the Earth.

While many of the studies backing this practice are small, not always double-blind, and often rely on self-reported outcomes, the reported physiological effects are compelling and, in my worldview, deserve discussion. The evidence-based practical guides I recommend aim for thirty to sixty minutes of barefoot or grounded contact per day, when possible. Try to do this on natural ground, or in water, if available to you. Submersion in water or being wet gives better surface connectivity to the Earth's EMF. Stick with it regularly, for weeks to months, to allow the cumulative effects to manifest, which could be better sleep, less inflammation, and less stress.[24] (Patients ask me about grounding devices and indoor grounding systems like grounding mats, sheets, and patches, and while I think they can mimic some effects of outdoor grounding, there isn't a lot of research.)

If you can't ground with your feet, get your hands in the soil! Gardening is also a beautiful and joyful way to earth. Digging in the soil with your bare hands provides tactile connection with microbes and minerals in the earth, while also allowing your body to absorb the Earth's electrons. Where green space is limited, even small-scale gardening—on balconies, community plots, or windowsills—can be healing. So many of us are trafficking in systems that are shaped by disconnection, struggle, and chronic stress, so earthing is truly an act of radical reclamation.

Especially for my patients who have been shaped by the injustices of poverty, touching the earth can be a return to something that cannot be taken away. Poverty doesn't just deprive people of material resources—it often severs access to rest, joy, nourishment, and green space. It floods the body with stress hormones, erodes dignity, and isolates people from beauty and stillness. Lying on the earth, walking barefoot on grass, and sitting against a tree are not luxuries. They are ancestral practices, encoded in our biology, that regulate the nervous system, reduce inflammation, and restore a sense of place. For those facing housing instability, job precarity, or generational trauma, earthing is a way to return to a sense of belonging that capitalism cannot sell and colonialism cannot fully erase. It is a medicine for everyone.

Water's Healing Ions

What is it about the sound of the waves gently tumbling over the shoreline, or the way mist rises like breath from the earth at the edge of a waterfall, or even how a neighborhood fountain splashes water onto pavement that brings a sense of joy? Why did our ancestors pray to, make offerings of, and drink from holy waters as representations of God? I think it might have to do with one of the marvels of human physiology, that our bodies mirror the planet itself; just as Earth is two-thirds ocean, we, too, are two-thirds water. Nearly every cell in our body is filled with fluid; about two-thirds of that water lives inside our cells, keeping us alive at the most basic level, while the rest flows around them as blood, lymph, and plasma. Water carries oxygen, nutrients, and waste; cushions our joints; regulates our temperature; and even helps generate the electrical signals that allow our hearts to beat and our brains to think, and for our bodies to experience earthing. We are not separate from water—we are living, breathing expressions of it. We feel it resonate within us as we witness it. If there were space enough in this book, I would give water its own chapter as a medicine for all people, because being around water is chemically nourishing on a cellular level.

Flowing water releases negative ions: tiny, charged particles that move unseen but are felt deeply, shifting mood and physiology. Where water rushes, collides, and breaks into spray, negative ions abound. So that crash of waves against a shoreline, the steady current of a mountain stream, the soft spray that lingers in the air—all of these environments create a field of energy that contrasts sharply with the stale, positive-ion-heavy air of traffic, screens, and fluorescent rooms. Studies link this natural abundance of negative ions to lower stress, improved alertness, and lifted moods, affirming what our ancestors already knew: that water in motion is more than beauty; it is a real balm.

Negative air ions may influence serotonin levels in the brain, which plays a major role in regulating mood, sleep, and stress response.[25] They can also improve blood oxygenation and circulation; better oxygen delivery to the brain supports alertness, focus, and cognitive function, which indirectly improves mood and reduces fatigue.[26] In cities and crowded spaces, these currents of water are harder to come by, but not impossible. A walk along a lakefront, time spent by a fountain, and even the steam of a shower can offer small doses of this elemental energy.

For me, a walk to the lakefront is a daily necessity, even when it is mostly frozen over and the waves are slow with plates of ice. I also rely heavily on showers for water medicine. I often "prescribe" showers to patients as a quick way to shift mood, not only because flowing water releases negative ions, but because the warmth, rhythm, and enclosed environment activate the parasympathetic nervous system, calming stress and resetting the body. A shower is also a sound bath, the percussion of water on tile soothes the mind as much as it cleanses the body. Across cultures, people have long recognized this: the Japanese *onsen*, Roman bathhouses, Indigenous sweat lodges, and Ayurvedic rituals of oil and water all honor bathing as medicine. Within that cocoon of steam and rhythm, a simple daily act becomes sanctuary, a ritual of renewal that washes away heaviness and makes space for lightness again. We need water to survive, we feel better near water, and we are water.

Brazil Backwaters

Working in multiple countries, climates, and conditions made clear to me that health is not a one-size-fits-all model—it is shaped by place, tradition, access, and systemic inequities. Practicing medicine and studying in St. Lucia, Brazil, Cuba, India, Venezuela, Senegal, Italy, inner-city Chicago, and with migrant farm workers in Southern California exposed me to a spectrum of health care facilities, from high-tech hospitals to mobile health trucks, to community-led, traditional healing centers.

When I tell Brazilians where I worked, they're usually stunned. I have yet to meet anyone who's been there. My last Uber driver from São Paulo laughed, "Piauí? What were you doing *there*?" Piauí, in northeastern Brazil, is a state of river plains and rising *chapadas* (large plateaus), hot lowlands, and dry highlands. It's rural, agricultural, and among the country's least developed regions—where health care is scarce and distances vast. During my family medicine training, I spent six weeks in Piauí with a health assistance NGO, treating patients in its most remote corners. This was global health in the pre-internet era—no itinerary, few details, just a start date, an end date, and the promise that someone would meet me at the airport. Back then, global health ran almost entirely on trust.

After four flights and over twenty-four hours of travel, I landed in Teresina and was greeted by my translator—Haroldo, a six-foot-four man with blond hair, a booming laugh, and a presence that filled the room—and our driver, Santi. We squeezed into a tiny two-door car beside my oversized suitcase of medications and drove five hours north to Barras, a small town in the Parnaíba Delta where I'd begin my medical service. I was only a few years into residency, preparing to assist a visiting surgical team from Seattle. But when I arrived, I learned the team wouldn't be coming for several weeks. Until then, it would be just me—evaluating patients and deciding who needed surgery once the team finally arrived. "We'll set up a table and chair in the village clinic," Haroldo said. "You can start tomorrow."

My bag never arrived, so Haroldo's girlfriend kindly lent me her clothes. The next morning, I showed up in a micro-miniskirt, stilettos, and a clingy tank top—sweating in 102-degree heat, my hair tripled in size from humidity. Following Haroldo through the narrow streets, I felt absurdly un-doctorlike. Thankfully, no one seemed to notice or care. Then I saw the line. It stretched down the block and around the corner. "Wow," I said, "this clinic must be busy! How many doctors work here?" Haroldo burst out laughing. "No one works here! They're all waiting for *you*! The American doctor! I told them on the radio you were coming. Every day this week."

Over five weeks in six remote villages, I examined nearly a thousand patients on my own. Most days, I didn't know exactly where I was—just that I'd set up a desk wherever the team dropped me and begin seeing the long lines of people who gathered for care. I was the only doctor for many miles, and soon my makeshift clinic ran efficiently. I even trained our driver, Santi, to take vital signs and track patients. As we traveled between villages, the scenery unfolded—vast tropical savannas at the edge of the Amazon, both dry and lush, their beauty grounding yet surreal. On the sun-scorched plains of Piauí, where heat shimmered and dust hung in the air, I saw waves of respiratory illness: asthma, allergies, bronchitis, thyroid goiters, skin diseases, and tumors later confirmed malignant in the United States. Why was this land making people so sick? After several weeks, I found that the answer lay along the roads—miles of deforestation where green gave way to barren, chalky soil that lifted into the air like talcum powder.

When the Seattle team finally arrived, I felt proud to have identified enough patients for more than fifty surgeries. During our long drives, I often saw Indigenous women farming, harvesting, and carrying water. Weeks passed before I realized none of them ever came to my clinic. On my day off, I asked to visit their villages, and Haroldo finally took me to one. Haroldo, a lifelong Brazilian, had never set foot on these remote farms. He humored my requests for quiet mornings to meditate and for meatless meals, shaking his head and laughing. "You are a very wild person," he'd say. "Different from other doctors." I never asked what he meant, but I sensed he'd never considered that the stories of the rural poor were part of their health. Together, we sat with a few of the women farmers, talking about the illnesses I'd been seeing—the wheezing, the coughs—and what they believed caused them.

These women helped me see what I'd sensed but hadn't fully understood. The expansion of export agriculture had brought land-grabbing, deforestation, and even violence to their homeland. The health problems, they explained, stemmed from the loss of trees and native plants. "Trees are our mothers," one woman said. "They clean the air, bring rain, and give us shelter. We do what we can to protect them—planting cover crops, shading the soil, and keeping our plant medicines alive." They showed us bottles of tinctures made from *jatobá* and *copaíba*, beautiful Amazonian trees, for respiratory ailments, and pastes crafted from barks and roots. At dusk, we followed them barefoot across the land, gathering herbs once used by their ancestors for fevers and infections. The air was thick with smoke—a reminder of trees lost to logging and fire. Still, they taught the young to honor sacred forests, care for the soil, and catch rain when it falls.

In this overlooked corner of Brazil, the land once offered abundant medicine, and its destruction has left deep human suffering in its wake. These women, like Indigenous land stewards all over the planet, know that survival here is not just resistance but an act of devotion, a promise to the land that, despite everything, it will still be cared for, and still be honored. In that short chapter of my life in Brazil, the connection between land rights and sovereignty, nature and humans, health and disease forever informed my perspective as a physician. We are not living in a vacuum. We are a part of the ecosystem, and the downstream consequences of our environmental destruction are often immediate—and always show up in the body.

In an unjust world, it becomes all the more urgent to draw strength from our ancestral wisdom. If paradise is paved to put up a parking lot, we can crack the concrete with our ancestral roots, let the wild things push through, and remember that the land still holds its memory beneath the asphalt. We can gather the seeds of what was stolen and replant them, both in the earth and in ourselves. We can carry forward the knowledge that was slated to be erased. We can walk the land that tells our stories, swim in the waters that hold our healing, witness the sun rising and setting and synchronize to that untouched rhythm, align with spanda, get outside of our boxes, and refuse to let industrialization sever our relationship with the sacred. Because no matter how much is taken, the land and water remember, and so do we.

Medicines to Carry

Tap into spanda often. The ever-present rhythm of life can be tapped into anytime. Time outside nourishes the spirit. The sacred pause can be an intentional practice integrated into your daily routine.

Take moments out of your day to notice the natural world around you. Start small and get hyper-local. For example, observe what is going on in a patch of grass right outside your door. Crouch down and get close to really notice the dew on the grass, the insects and their activity, the fallen leaves and their colors, the snow's contrast. Spend time observing birds, insects, or other wildlife in your area. Set up bird feeders and bird baths; it's mutual aid!

Walk near trees. Bathe in their phytoncides, which improve your immune system's balance. Choose walks that are meaningful to you. Remember, you *are* an outdoor person! You are biologically built in ways that respond to nature.

Practice dusking. Return home to your animal body. Pause from doing; become available to dusk and let the twilight colors bathe your senses.

Enjoy your meals outdoors whenever possible. A simple lunch in a park, or on a bench outside your workplace, can help you feel more connected to nature.

Practice earthing. Walk barefoot on natural surfaces (grass, dirt, sand, rock, shoreline, shallows) twenty to thirty minutes a day, if and whenever possible.

Lie on the ground. Take some deep breaths and feel the earth supporting the full length of your body. Stay for as long as you can! Or take your yoga or meditation practice outside.

Garden with bare hands. Receive Earth's electromagnetic charge through the soil by tending to the earth, a community garden, or your own patch.

Get close to moving bodies of water, or take a shower. Bathe in negative ions to elevate your mood, reduce fatigue, and increase oxygenation to your brain. A relaxing and immediate medicine!

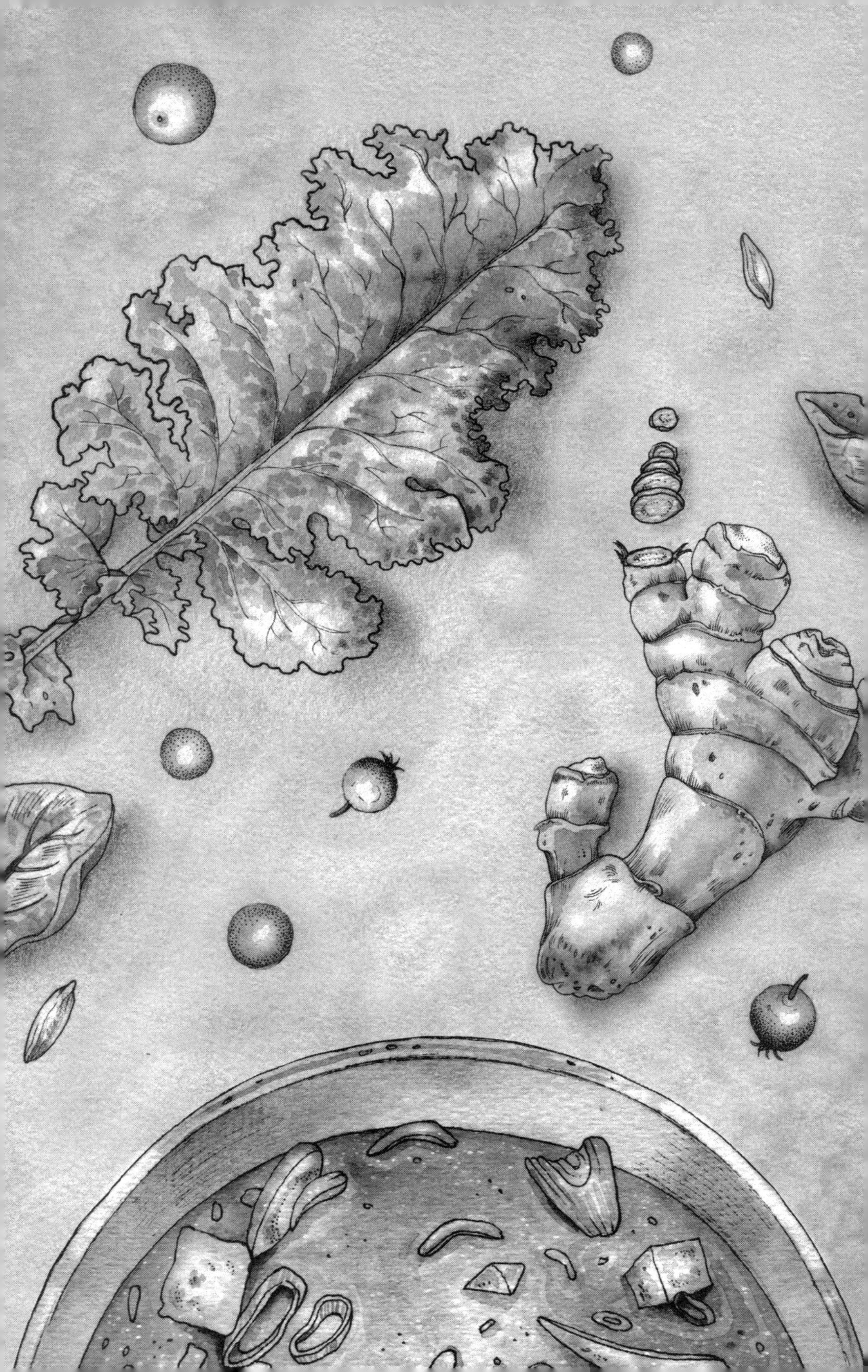

MEDICINE TWO

Food

Nourishment as Memory, Power, and Ceremony

Nature provides us with the medicine we need in the form of traditional foods. It's our responsibility to honor this gift.

Indigenous Wisdom

Food is not just fuel. Food is about family, food is about community, food is about identity. And we nourish all those things when we eat well.

Michael Pollan

Raised in the traditions of Punjabi Indian food culture, I always understood food to be a medicine, a framework that has shaped my entire worldview. Being a first-generation Indian American came with its challenges, but I was always keenly aware of the uncommon privilege of belonging to two rich cultural traditions. The smells and the tastes of food at home always provided me with a strong connection to my family, my heritage, and to the medicine of our Ayurvedic cuisine.

Cooking Indian food at home is an art—a labor of love that demands time, patience, and instinct. Ask any Indian person born or raised outside India if they cook as well as their mother or grandmother, and few will claim they do. Our recipes live in memory and muscle, not on paper. I watched my mother cook, never the same way twice, never by a book. Each dish carried a nuance and essence—impossible for me to recreate. The layering of spices and the play of salt, butter, and heat were a reflection of her mood, our family, our story. Each household, each hand does it differently—and that's the beauty of it.

My mother's food was always a kind of cure. If your stomach ached, she would prepare *kitchari*, a simple alchemy of rice, moong beans, cumin, and onions. Soft on the body, rich in fiber, protein, and minerals, it soothed and strengthened, the perfect medicine disguised as a meal. Headaches? Depending on the location and nature of the pain, cumin, coriander, and fennel tea, or a cucumber salad, could help. Cold coming on? Chopped up turmeric root, honey, and garlic in a generous and overflowing spoonful. Beyond the cultural significance and the health benefits, which I was not aware of as a child, the food itself was delicious and really satisfying. And the remedies worked, too! Even as I ventured into the diverse culinary landscape of the United States, Indian home food remained a source of comfort and nostalgia, a medicine for my body and my heart.

But taking Indian food to school was impossible—too fragrant, too much attention for a brown girl who just wanted to blend in among classmates eating baloney sandwiches and drinking from their cold milk cartons. There was no escaping the pull and draw of American life for me, the culture of eating on the go, eating out, and eating whenever there was time. Soon enough, the medicinal food of my childhood was a memory.

In college and medical school, eating—once one of my life's great joys—became just a means to survive. I received no formal nutrition education, not even an hour on how food supports health. Though I knew the basics, I often skipped breakfast or grabbed a cellophane-wrapped muffin between lectures, then ate the same limp cafeteria sandwich each day, the only vegetarian option. Evenings were spent studying, barely pausing to eat whatever a friend brought back from a nearby restaurant or the hospital's night café.

Inevitably, my perfectionism and poor health habits would betray me. My weight dropped, my menstrual cycles stopped, I developed anemia, and I was perpetually exhausted. I exercised intensely but never recovered, becoming riddled with severe neck spasms that eventually led to steroid injections into my cervical spine. I was clearly far from well.

It took years—through several more injections, pain medications, failed fertility treatments, a miscarriage, and physical therapy—to rebuild my relationship with food, and to understand that food had to be the beginning of my health journey and not the end. Only when I was happily pregnant during my grueling OB fellowship, delivering several babies every third night, did healing truly begin. My daughter's small kicks inside me urged me to eat, to rest, to care for both of us. Food was no longer an afterthought—it became the foundation of my family's health. Nothing if not a good student and patient, I began a reclamation of my health and my relationship with food.

My Return to Food as Medicine

The path back to my family's food roots and wisdom was eased considerably when we moved to the city of Ventura, on California's coast, months after our daughter was born, for our first jobs as attending physicians at the county medical center. I felt reconnected to something I hadn't known I was missing, maybe to the cellular memory of my ancestors. To a joy that felt deeper than the present but that flowed in my blood. It was there that I began to garden, and grow food, and cook, and to remember that I am a daughter of land stewards, farmers, and food makers. My body responded well to this new place, and being surrounded by fields of fresh produce and regular farmers' markets meant I ate more fresh, colorful food. The processed hospital food I was so accustomed to was replaced by dark green leafy chard and spinach, bright red peppers, yellow tomatoes, and avocados fresh off my neighbor's trees.

The more time I spent outside near the ocean, the more my nervous system calmed from decades of hustle, and the more I began to feel and look like a healthy person. My menstrual cycles regulated for the first time, my anemia resolved from my improved diet, my weight was healthy for me, and my sleep was more restful, even with a young baby. How could you hold fresh, colorful vegetables from a farmers' market, or pick your own lemons, and not feel yourself fall a little in love with the earth? I sure did. The farmers' market became my temple of worship, and I went several times a week. I cried there sometimes, so overcome by the beauty of all the bounty, grown from this abundant land. I fell deeply in love with the earth and my place in it. It was the remembrance of things past. A remembrance that food is medicine.

In Sickness and in Health

I tell every patient that food is the medicine we take daily, from our first breath onward. It is among the strongest medicines—or poisons—depending on what we choose. For many, this is a wake-up call: Our very cells are built from the nutrient density of what we eat, and little can be made without those raw materials. Each meal is an act of self-love and repair, a chance to build vitality from within. Yet most people don't think of food this way; they focus on flavor and texture, not its impact on body, mind, and emotions. Patients rarely expect to discuss food with their physician, but I invite them to see it as a profoundly powerful medicine. Even that shift in perspective—asking ourselves, *Will this meal uplift my health? How will I feel afterward?*—can change what we choose to eat.

My patient Sabrina has been successful in overcoming the pain and disability that come from fibromyalgia, a poorly understood condition I see very often. This difficult disease typically affects women more than men, and is characterized by widespread musculoskeletal pain, fatigue, and heightened sensitivity to pain. It is challenging to treat and can be terrible to live with, as there is no single remedy or medication that works well. Additionally, fibromyalgia has a wide range of complex symptoms, many of which overlap with other conditions like chronic fatigue syndrome and irritable bowel syndrome, so it is often misdiagnosed. Sabrina visited me after seeing many doctors, and she was on several medications, still not feeling well or even consistently better. We dove into her lifestyle quickly, where I knew we could do the most beneficial work.

Sabrina's diet was guided by cravings, not by how food made her feel—yet much of it worsened her pain, fatigue, and heaviness. For her, the flavors of Puerto Rico were unmatched, though the dishes she loved most were often fried, meat-rich, and heavy with starch. Together, we tracked her meals and symptoms with a food journal, building awareness over several months. Through this mindfulness, she learned to notice what foods eased her pain and how to honor her body's hunger and fullness cues, eating only when hungry and stopping when satisfied. I offered the Ayurvedic wisdom on quantity: to eat until satisfied, not heavy, and to keep balance in the stomach—one-third food, one-third liquid, and one-third left open for digestion. Paying attention to how different foods made her feel, both physically and emotionally, allowed her to make connections that she hadn't made before. She told me, "I love my *pan sobao*! But I noticed it triggered pain flares. So I slowed down, tuned in to how I'd feel later, and chose something else. I stopped buying so much of it, and even found a great substitute at the bakery."

Over several months of this practice of mindfulness, Sabrina was able to avoid foods that worsened her physical symptoms and intentionally choose ones that didn't. She felt better and unintentionally lost weight, which motivated her to stay on this path. "You changed the way I thought about food," she said, "and after my mind changed, I didn't go back." This was one of those aha moments that patients have, where a perceptual shift translates to action. Recognizing the profound effect food has on the body gives us real agency over both illness and health. At the beginning of my integrative medicine career, I shared this idea with one patient at a time. Later, as interest grew, I shared it with larger groups of people at all types of professional conferences, libraries, community centers, festivals, and schools, then at corporate think tanks, national and international medical conferences, news media, podcasts, on NPR, and through teaching in medical schools. It seems to be universally interesting, since we all eat food.

Most people have grown up eating for pleasure or survival, not for well-being. Again and again, I have seen how powerful the "food is medicine" message can be. Almost everyone can understand it instantly, even children and teenagers. Beyond nourishment, food is information, fueling our cellular engines with what they need to detoxify, energize, and rebuild the body day after day. When we treat food as medicine, it can transform everything. It's a catalyst for change.

Why Are We Wondering What to Eat?

With so much media interest in diets, and so much information available to people, much of it conflicting, it is no wonder that people are thoroughly confused by the topic of food. It makes sense to ask your doctor what you should eat, but many doctors don't have enough nutrition education or time to answer the question deeply. Meanwhile, everyone else—from Instagram influencers, actors, and podcasters with no medical background, to athletes and yoga teachers, to your neighbor—has an idea about what you should eat, and suddenly you are back to relying on your own common sense, or what is left of it after all these people have told you something different. People are waiting for someone to tell them what to eat, and most of the time, I've found, it's not someone who should be.

I have scoured research and walked through kitchens and markets across cultures and continents, searching for the roots of our relationship with food, and how it has come to this—that people wait months for an appointment to ask me the simplest of questions: "What should I eat?" "What can I eat to be healthy?" "How much?" "When and how often?" "Keto, paleo, low-carb, high-protein, or intermittent fasting?" I, too, need to verify and interpret the information that magazines and social media are broadcasting on any given day about gluten, dairy, sugar, eggs, greens, protein, or nightshade vegetables. Widespread confusion is the best way for the food industry and various purveyors of the latest ultra-processed foods to gain business.

When all ancient cultures relied on food and herbs as their first medicines, how have we arrived at a time when most doctors are trained to know far more about pharmaceuticals than about nutrition?

Losing Our Way: A Brief History

Back in the seventeenth and eighteenth centuries, advancements in chemistry, biology, and physiology led to significant breakthroughs in understanding the human body and disease. Germ theory, developed by Louis Pasteur and Robert Koch in the nineteenth century, revolutionized medicine by identifying microorganisms as the cause of many diseases. This led to the search for drugs to combat specific pathogens, such as antibiotics, rather than relying on the age-old preventive and holistic medicines like food and diet.

The discovery of penicillin by Alexander Fleming in 1928 and its widespread use in the 1940s marked a turning point in medicine. Penicillin was the first antibiotic that could cure previously fatal bacterial infections, leading to an explosion in drug discovery and pharmaceutical research. This antibiotic revolution fueled the belief that specific drugs could cure or control diseases more effectively than traditional approaches, including dietary interventions. The success of antibiotics was real: mortality and morbidity rates from infectious disease went down, and life spans went up, which encouraged a focus on developing new pharmaceuticals for a wide range of conditions. Unlike food and herbs, which can vary in strength and effect based on growing conditions, how they are prepared, and individual metabolism, drugs could be created with consistent doses and effects. This appealed to both doctors and patients, as it made treatment more predictable and measurable. Drugs provided quick results, while dietary changes and herbal medicines often took longer to show their benefits. Pharmaceuticals were seen as a faster, better, and more efficient option for managing acute and chronic conditions, not just infectious disease.

Also during the twentieth century, the focus of agriculture shifted from small-scale, diverse farming to industrialized monocultures. Crops such as corn, wheat, and soy became the backbone of the food system, and processed foods made from these subsidized crops became cheaper and more accessible than fresh, whole foods. The rise of processed foods—high in sugar, refined grains, and unhealthy fats—contributed to the increase in chronic diseases like diabetes, obesity, and heart disease. As food quality diminished, pharmaceuticals became the go-to solution for treating diet-related illnesses. You might see where this is going.

As people's diets shifted toward processed foods, the role of food in preventing and treating disease diminished in mainstream culture. Medicine and food became separated entities, with pharmaceuticals taking the lead in managing health. The pharmaceutical industry became a major economic force during the twentieth century. Pharma companies were able to patent drugs, giving them exclusive rights to sell their products and generate large profits. Food and herbs, being natural products, cannot be patented, which made them less financially lucrative for large corporations, and this economic reality drove research, investment, and development toward drugs, and away from food and botanicals. As a result, food-based treatments and preventive medicine were deprioritized in favor of pharmaceutical research, which was more profitable for both pharmaceutical companies and health care providers.

The rise of pharmaceuticals also shaped medical education. Pharmaceutical companies began funding medical research and educational programs, creating a strong bias toward pharmacological treatments. Nutrition and diet-related education received little attention in medical schools, with students, like me, receiving minimal training in using food as a tool for prevention and treatment. Instead, I was trained to diagnose diseases and prescribe medications, reinforcing the idea that pharmaceuticals were the primary solution to health problems. The culture of convenience has grown in lockstep—people want quick fixes for health problems, and pharmaceuticals seem to provide that. Dietary changes, on the other hand, require more effort, planning, and time. They require a depth of awareness and commitment that a culture obsessed with speed and efficiency tends to erode. Food choices are also deeply influenced by marketing, food-industry lobbying, and social norms that promote processed and ultra-processed foods as normal and desirable.

When people are constantly exposed to conflicting messages—"Eat this, not that!" "No, really, you can eat this again!" "I know we said you could eat that, but not anymore!"—and add to that fad diets and miracle supplements, it becomes even harder to know whom to trust. At the same time, doctors often feel ill-equipped to guide patients on how to use food as medicine, lack the time to dive into it, and are not supported by a working system that allows us to easily prescribe food, which many of us would like to be able to do. Instead of empowering people with the knowledge and skills to nourish themselves, the health care system keeps us dependent on prescriptions and quick fixes. This widespread confusion leaves patients and physicians alike struggling to navigate a food landscape that is more profit-driven than health-driven. Unfortunately, the food, pharma, and health industry are all basically run the same way.

Big Pharma and Big Food

At the height of the COVID pandemic, twelve thousand Americans were dying every day from the virus and its consequences.[1] What was most appalling and less known was that Americans have been dying from mostly preventable diseases at this same daily rate for the past twenty years. This is squarely because, compared to other wealthy nations, the United States has inferior health care despite the best access to the latest medical treatments.[2] We spend 17 percent of our GDP on health care annually, when most other wealthy countries spend closer to 10 percent.[3] While there is no single culprit on whom to place the blame, the most powerful driver of the imbalance of health care outcomes and costs is Big Pharma's influence on our health care. As Dr. John Abramson writes in his book *Sickening: How Big Pharma Broke American Health Care*:

> The reason the pharmaceutical industry has been able to achieve this tail-wags-dog position is that over the past forty years, public funding for clinical research and federal support of university-based medical research has declined, allowing drug companies to fill in the gap. This has led to increased commercial influence over much of the information that doctors rely on to determine optimal treatment for their patients.[4]

Our most trusted resources for scientific evidence have become increasingly dependent on drug-company funding, because the peer reviewers and journal editors do not have access to the real data from the drug trials, only unverified data summaries that are prepared by the drug companies. I have many smart colleagues who work in this industry, and while I don't believe that Big Pharma is out to harm people, its primary job is to maximize profit. And that is the problem. Food is not researched at nearly the same volume or with the same rigor as a treatment or cure for chronic disease. Since, as I mentioned before, pharmaceuticals are patentable, and food—especially whole, natural, traditional foods—can't be owned in the same way, there is little financial incentive for large-scale clinical trials that cost tens of millions of dollars. A kale leaf can't be patented. Neither can turmeric, ginger, or collard greens. Food is complex and context-dependent. It's hard to isolate and study one food in a vacuum because diet involves cultural habits, microbiome responses, preparation methods, and synergy between nutrients. This makes it harder to design "clean," randomized trials that fit the gold standard of pharmaceutical testing.

Academic institutions and medical journals are largely shaped by a biomedical model. Funding agencies, such as the National Institutes of Health, devote far more resources to drug development than to nutrition, and so clinical nutrition often takes a back seat in medical training. The pharmaceutical industry has powerful lobbying arms and well-funded pipelines to support clinical trials and influence public policy. The industrial food system, meanwhile, often funds research that supports ultra-processed foods, rather than whole-food, traditional, or plant-based interventions. And food is not just biochemical; it's social, ancestral, ecological, and political. Researching it requires cross-disciplinary approaches that are harder to fund and coordinate within the narrow silos of modern science. Physicians work in an evidence-based paradigm that requires us to follow a standard of care that is largely determined by those important clinical trials. I am not arguing against an evidence-based paradigm or standard of care, but there needs to be room at the head of the table to include treatment that causes the least harm, the deepest benefits, and is time tested: food.

The tide is turning. Movements in culinary medicine, food justice, Indigenous foodways, and planetary health are reclaiming food as a critical subject of study, not just as "nutrition," but as medicine, memory, and resistance. More researchers, practitioners, and communities are conducting research that honors the complexity of food and the people it feeds. There is a growing and popular public movement to revitalize the food-as-medicine mindset and practice, as people recognize the limitations of pharmaceutical interventions in addressing long-term health and wellness. Medical education is increasingly including nutrition. I have been speaking, teaching, and talking to anyone who will listen about this for a long time, so I am deeply excited to see the movement so vibrant and robust.

I invite you to join in. Cook something from the earth where you live. Ask who grew it. Share a meal that carries meaning. The food-as-medicine movement isn't happening somewhere else—it's happening right here, in the small, daily acts of care that feed you and your family and your community. Make a meal from a few simple, local ingredients, and remember where you come from.

Culinary Medicine

There is, in fact, robust, large-scale research demonstrating the profound impact of diet on health. A 2018 study published in the *Journal of the American Medical Association* found that a poor diet—defined as high in calories but deficient in essential nutrients—was the leading risk factor for premature death in the United States, surpassing tobacco use, high blood pressure, and obesity.[5] This evidence makes clear that prevention cannot wait until adulthood; it must begin early—through the nourishment of children and young people, and through medical education that treats food as foundational to health.

In several of the South Side Chicago neighborhoods surrounding the University of Chicago where I teach, the average life expectancy is as low as sixty years, compared to more than ninety years in affluent areas a few miles away—a nearly thirty-year gap, one of the widest in the nation. Many South Side neighborhoods are also considered food apartheid zones, with limited access to fresh produce and healthy food outlets. (I prefer the term "food apartheid" to "food desert." Unlike "food desert," which suggests a natural condition, "food apartheid," coined by farmer-activist Karen Washington, points to intentional policies, disinvestment, and structural racism that create these inequities.) Here, residents are more likely to rely on corner stores and fast food, contributing to higher rates of diet-related illness.

In 2015, my colleague and friend Dr. Sonia Oyola and I set out to bring meaningful nutrition education to the University of Chicago's Pritzker School of Medicine. Together, we piloted a program in culinary medicine—a field that weaves nutrition science with the art of cooking, helping people use food as medicine for chronic disease prevention, healing, and joy. The idea took root years earlier, when my friend Dr. John La Puma, who first defined the field, gave me his *ChefMD's Big Book of Culinary Medicine*. His work inspired us to move beyond lectures and PowerPoints toward something more experiential: teaching nutritional medicine by cooking food in a kitchen and then eating together. We began with grant support from the Women's Board of the University of Chicago, partnering with chef-teachers to create hands-on sessions where medical students learned clinical nutrition, meal prep, cost balancing, and patient counseling while chopping, sautéing, and tasting together. The students set down their heavy backpacks, tied on aprons, and entered a classroom filled with warmth, laughter, and the beautiful scent of garlic warming in olive oil.

What started as a lofty vision and after-school experiment has become a cornerstone of our curriculum, and a dynamic, communal space for hands-on learning. A decade later, culinary medicine has become more than a course; it is a living laboratory in a teaching kitchen, cooking with a trained chef, and learning the science of functional nutrition directly from integrative medicine physicians. Every graduating Pritzker School of Medicine student learns not only where nutrients come from, but how food shapes health—through the sensory experience of cooking alongside other medical students. Hundreds of graduates have carried their culinary medicine training with them to nearly every specialty. What began as a bold experiment has become a transformative movement that helps new doctors to understand that food is medicine.

Our culinary medicine classes are mostly plant-based. We make dishes like sweet potato and black bean tacos, quinoa and veggie bowls, chickpea and garden veggie salad, and spiced lentils and rice. These are affordable, quick, and simple dishes that reflect many traditions and can be easily prepared with ingredients most grocery stores carry. Our classes focus on balancing the three macronutrients—protein, fat, and carbohydrates—rather than eliminating one of them or vastly exaggerating the importance of one over the other. Each meal averages around two dollars per serving, making it accessible and realistic for the communities we serve.

For example, in our Heart Health class, we begin with what every medical student needs to know: Heart disease is fueled by high blood pressure, high cholesterol, smoking, diabetes, obesity, and inactivity. Food is both a risk and a remedy. We reach for omega-3–rich foods, low-salt meals, fiber that strengthens the gut and lowers cholesterol, and antioxidant-rich vegetables that help the body heal—the foundational elements that can shift the course of heart health.

Our quinoa salad with vegetables and lemon tahini dressing (see recipe below) is an example of how to combine whole grains, colorful vegetables, and heart-healthy fats into a balanced meal that supports cardiovascular health, reduces inflammation, and provides a variety of nutrients. Quinoa is a complete protein and high-fiber whole grain that is affordable and relatively easy to find. It is also easy to customize to many cultures, and can be swapped for other nutrient-dense grains. The dressing has olive oil and tahini (a sesame seed paste favored in Middle Eastern dishes), both sources of heart-healthy monounsaturated fats and anti-inflammatory compounds, which are covered in class. This balanced, flavorful dressing is delicious without excessive sodium or sugar.

QUINOA SALAD WITH GRILLED VEGETABLES AND LEMON-TAHINI DRESSING (Middle Eastern-Inspired)

Serves 4 to 6

For the Salad

1 cup quinoa, rinsed
2 cups water
2 zucchini, sliced lengthwise
2 bell peppers (any color), cut into strips
1 red onion, thickly sliced
1 eggplant, sliced
3 tablespoons olive oil (for grilling vegetables)
Salt and pepper to taste
Fresh parsley and mint (chopped)

For the Lemon-Tahini Dressing

¼ cup tahini
2 tablespoons lemon juice
1 clove garlic, minced
2 tablespoons olive oil
1 teaspoon honey (optional)
Salt and pepper to taste
1 tablespoon water to thin the dressing

Optional Add-Ins

½ cup crumbled feta
¼ cup toasted sesame or sunflower seeds
½ cup chickpeas (for added protein)

Cook the Quinoa: In a medium pot, combine the quinoa and water. Bring to a boil, then lower heat, cover, and simmer for 15 minutes or until water is absorbed. Fluff with a fork and set aside.

Grill the Vegetables: Preheat a grill or grill pan at medium-high heat (375°F–400°F). Toss the zucchini, bell peppers, onion, and eggplant with olive oil, salt, pepper, and herbs. Grill for 5–7 minutes on each side, until tender and slightly charred. Remove from heat and chop into bite-sized pieces.

Prepare the Dressing: In a small bowl, whisk together the tahini, lemon juice, garlic, olive oil, honey, salt, and pepper. Add water to thin the dressing to desired consistency.

Assemble the Salad: In a large bowl, combine the quinoa, grilled vegetables, fresh herbs, and optional add-ins. Drizzle with the Lemon-Tahini Dressing and toss to coat evenly. Serve warm or chilled.

Vegetables of every kind are the foundation of the course. Simple cooking methods can enhance both their taste and their nutritional value. We teach the basics—how to hold a knife, how to chop an onion, how to heat olive oil, how to mix a quick lemon-garlic marinade—so students can bring these skills straight into their own kitchens. With high blood pressure as the greatest risk factor for heart disease, and heart disease the leading cause of death worldwide, we also point out that we all tend to rely too much on salt for flavor. Most heritage diets and traditional cultures lean on spices and herbs rather than salt. Our teaching kitchen is fragrant with thyme, oregano, basil, parsley, coriander, cumin, fennel, and za'atar—ancestral herbs that season food with both richness and history.

In the spirit of strengthening community food systems, and after successfully launching the culinary medicine program for medical students, I founded Food Is Power, a culinary medicine program for middle schoolers on Chicago's South Side. I was struck by how few medical students had ever studied food or cooking, a realization that deepened my conviction that this learning must begin much earlier, in childhood. Designed with an intentionally Afrocentric and decolonized lens, the yearlong curriculum blends food as medicine with food justice. Each class combines hands-on cooking, nutrition science, and food justice narratives using a syllabus that

I cowrote with Julia Hesse-Fong, a brilliant young food activist. When I first launched the class, I named it, "Food as Medicine." When I asked the kids what "medicine" made them think of, hands shot up. Their answers? Pills! Shots! Sick people! That night, I changed the name. For now, *medicine* is not a word that kids think of positively. "Food Is Power" better reflected what food truly is—powerful information for the body, shaped by the choices we make.

We transform school cafeterias into teaching kitchens, where each student dons an apron and handles a chef's knife (under close supervision), cooking, tasting, and learning where their food comes from. The recipes are simple, healthy, and adventurous, meant not just to nourish but to open conversations about culture and history. Kids learn the "why" behind what they eat—including how additives, marketing, and access influence their health and energy—and, in the process, they reclaim the power to choose for themselves.

For me, this is justice: giving children the tools to choose powerfully, even as we work to dismantle the systems that keep them unwell. Children are smart, and they deserve to understand the food system and how to make empowering choices within it. We teach them in the language of color, arranging our lessons by the rainbow. In our Orange lesson, we explore how color connects food, health, and culture. The recipes—sweet potato fries and mango salsa—are simple, bright, and nutrient-rich, showing how real food can replace fast food with flavor and power. Students learn that orange and yellow foods are full of vitamins A and C, antioxidants that protect cells, support immunity, and strengthen skin, bones, and eyes. Food, we remind them, is medicine made visible. We also talk about why Doritos taste so good—how the "bliss point" of sugar, salt, and fat is engineered to keep us hooked. Once kids realize this is by design, they can reframe the narrative around "irresistible" junk food and start reclaiming their power of choice.

This is where social change begins. Not with judgment and shame, but with the knowledge that food is power, and that knowledge itself is power. And in our classrooms, change is joyful—we cook, we taste, we talk freely, and in that safe space, kids not only learn from us, but we learn from them as well.

Decades of systemic racism and structural inequities have created conditions that lead to early inflammation, which leads to chronic disease. Our program is a humble attempt to help our local communities prevent early inflammation. Starting kids early in their food education is one of the missions of many incredible US organizations such as Pilot Light,

Cooking Matters, Wellness in the Schools, Growing Home, The Edible Schoolyard Project, Common Threads, FoodCorps, the National Farm to School Network, and the WIC program (Supplemental Nutrition Program for Women, Infants, and Children), as well as international efforts such as Slow Food International and the Global Alliance for the Future of Food. Supporting organizations like these are great ways to contribute to the movement.

What Should I Eat, Doc?

As lifestyle-related diseases are more prevalent, the importance of whole foods and lifestyle and nutrition interventions are now, finally, in the limelight. It has been a long time coming for those of us who have been working on this revolution for many years. After twenty-five years of clinical practice and review of the complex data as it comes in, I can truly say that knowing what to eat can be relatively simple.

Here is what the research shows. There's a clear consensus: Healthy diets tend to be plant-forward and low in ultra-processed foods.[6] Diets that are rich in fruits, vegetables, whole grains, and lean proteins, with limited intake of processed foods, red meat, and added sugars, are optimal for health. There have been numerous studies on the Mediterranean diet, DASH Diet (Dietary Approaches to Stop Hypertension), Blue Zones (regions in the world where people have a significantly higher-than-average life expectancy and a higher proportion of centenarians),[7] and whole-foods, plant-based diets—and they all show that a diet that is plant-forward and nutrient-dense can prevent and even reverse chronic diseases and improve overall health.[8] If this is all you learn here, it is enough to build a diet from!

Fresh and Colorful Produce

Decades of research also back up the foodways of many traditional plant-forward diets around the world. I encourage every patient I meet to build color and variety into their daily intake of fruits and vegetables, as this is where most of the minerals, vitamins, phytochemicals, and antioxidants are found, all of which repair and build our cells. Each color represents a different chemical compound that can scavenge old, damaged, or sick cells from the body. They are natural housekeepers! Specific types and colors of fruits and vegetables—such as leafy greens, berries, and cruciferous vegetables—are associated with distinct and meaningful reductions in cardiovascular disease and cancer risk, supported by robust epidemiological and clinical evidence.[9]

The recommendation of at least five servings of colorful vegetables and fruits (three vegetables and two fruits) a day works for almost everyone. However, patients with digestive problems might be better served with warmed and cooked vegetables over raw, cold ones. Most of us do better with vegetables that are broken down a bit by heat, whether by steaming, grilling, or sautéing. Since people generally do not eat enough fresh produce, it's a good idea to shop on the periphery of the grocery store, where the fresh food is, and spend less time and money in the aisles, where the processed food is. Precut and prepped produce is a great investment and time saver, if you can spend a bit more. If your cart doesn't have lots of natural colors in it when you are checking out, go back to the produce area and get the colors and veggies that call to you! This guidance can provide the base layer of your diet.

Carbs

No matter what anyone tells you, there is no formula as to how much of each of the three macronutrients—carbohydrates, proteins, and fats—is right for you. Macronutrient ratios should be tailored based on individual goals, health conditions, and lifestyle. However, I do recommend balancing macronutrient distribution, not just focusing on getting mostly one at the expense of the other two. The quality of carbohydrates (whole vs. refined), fats (unsaturated vs. saturated), and proteins (plant-based or lean vs. red or processed meats) is more important than specific macronutrient quantities. Focus on slowly digested carbs like whole grains, vegetables, and legumes—all excellent sources of fuel for your brain and body, easily utilized, which can be prepared in a variety of ways that suit your cultural and personal preference.

You want minimally processed, nutrient-dense carbs that provide a steady release of energy without causing significant blood sugar spikes. What are those? Whole grains such as quinoa, brown rice, oats, barley, bulgur, farro, whole wheat. Whole grains contain all parts of the grain kernel, including the bran, germ, and endosperm. This means they're packed with fiber, B vitamins, antioxidants, and trace minerals like iron and magnesium and can regulate blood sugar levels, improve digestion, and promote heart health. If you are gluten-free, some whole-grain choices that are safe are: quinoa, all varieties of rice (including white, brown, wild, and black), buckwheat (despite its name, it's gluten-free), amaranth, millet, teff, sorghum, and corn. Legumes such as lentils, chickpeas, black beans, kidney beans, and peas are high in complex carbohydrates, protein, and fiber—triple greatness. They are also rich in essential nutrients like folate, iron, and potassium. These foods alone make up so many of the most delicious, simple dishes around the world.

It's best to choose seasonal vegetables and fruits. In the fall and winter, I recommend beautiful and colorful starchy vegetables such as sweet potatoes, squash, carrots, beets, and parsnips. They are full of fiber, vitamins, and minerals like potassium and vitamin A. Unlike refined carbs, they offer a slow, steady release of glucose into the bloodstream, and provide a grounding energy as we head into the quieter, darker months. Nonstarchy vegetables like leafy greens (spinach, chard, arugula, lettuce, kale), broccoli, cauliflower, bell peppers, and zucchini are great for high nutrient density and are packed with fiber, vitamins, minerals, and phytonutrients. They have minimal impact on blood sugar levels and are anti-inflammatory.

The carbs to minimize are white bread, pastries, all-purpose flour-based pancake and waffle mixes, sugary cereals, plain bagels, white rice, white-flour pasta, and other processed foods that have been stripped of their fiber and nutrients. Leaning heavily on these items as breakfast foods will weaken your energy and concentration for the day. The quick spike of blood sugar is followed by an equally rapid decline of blood sugar and insulin levels, which leads to fatigue, irritability, decreased concentration, and hunger. Sodas, energy drinks, and other beverages high in added sugars contribute to rapid blood sugar spikes and dips and are linked to obesity and diabetes. Fresh-pressed juice can also spike the blood sugar, though there are countless more nutrients in a juice than a soda. Refreshing, healthy options can be water (plain or with lemon or fruit slices), flavored water, sparkling water, kombucha, kefir, herbal teas, green or black tea, coffee in moderation, and diluted fresh juices.

Proteins

After the age of thirty, we lose muscle at a rate of 5 to 10 percent per year, so it's vital to build muscle with strength training and plenty of protein. If you eat meat, opt for lean animal proteins like wild-caught fish, pasture-raised organic chicken, and other lean meats. If you are vegetarian or wanting to incorporate more plant-based proteins into your diet, tofu, beans, legumes, nuts, and seeds are great choices. Certain foods, such as quinoa, eggs, fish, and soy, provide all nine essential amino acids needed for muscle growth, tissue repair, and overall health. I also recommend organic tofu and tempeh, which are made from soybeans. Tempeh is also rich in probiotics due to its fermentation process. Edamame are young soybeans packed with protein, fiber, and healthy fats, and can be bought frozen and organic for a low price. Almonds, walnuts, chia seeds, flaxseeds, pumpkin seeds, and hemp seeds are powerhouses of protein and some also contain omega-3 anti-inflammatory fats. I love seeds, for their nutritional power and their profound spiritual significance across many cultures and spiritual traditions. They symbolize potential, growth, regeneration, the cycles of life, and provide the source energy of all our food.

There is a tremendous surge toward increasing protein consumption in the popular culture right now. Protein is a dietary buzzword, and every day in my clinic, I have patients asking me about how to get more protein in their diets. Products marketed as "high-protein" have significantly increased, and in the United States, the percentage of people seeking to consume more protein rose from 59 percent in 2022 to 71 percent in 2024.[10] Platforms like TikTok and influencer culture are fueling a craze for high-protein diets that are detached from personalized nutritional needs. The current protein boom is fueled more by market trends and media narratives than by new nutritional necessity. When you look at the full scope of human history with respect to protein consumption, along with the latest data, here is what I believe to be the bottom line: For the majority of healthy adults, current evidence suggests a daily protein requirement of roughly 0.8 grams per kilogram of body weight. For a healthy adult weighing 70 kg (about 155 lbs), that would be 56 grams of protein per day, which could look like two eggs, one cup of Greek yogurt, three ounces of grilled chicken breast, half a cup of cooked quinoa, half a cup of lentils, and 1 cup of sautéed vegetables.

Higher intake becomes relevant for older adults (over 60–65 years), when age-related muscle breakdown begins to blunt muscle protein synthesis. One to 1.6 grams per kilogram of body weight per day can maximally stimulate muscle protein synthesis and promote greater muscle strength and function.[11] Higher protein intake is also relevant for athletes; people intentionally working to maintain, lose, or regain weight; those recovering from illness; and pregnant or lactating women. These are all estimates and may be different depending on your medical conditions.

What About Meat?

We may have eaten plenty of meat as early humans, but it wasn't processed, and it bore little resemblance to the meat available today. While animals raised for meat consumption can also be a part of a healthful diet, reports from the UN's Food and Agriculture Organization (FAO) indicate that industrial livestock operations account for much of global meat production, especially in industrialized nations.[12] Industrial farming practices often involve intensive confinement and poor living conditions for animals. Globally, the majority of antibiotics are used in animal agriculture, followed by human health care. This high use of antibiotics contributes to the development of antibiotic-resistant bacteria, posing a significant public health risk.

Several years ago, when I successfully pushed for more plant-based food options in our hospital cafeteria, the infectious disease department singularly backed my recommendations, as factory-farmed meat can lead to antibiotic resistance in humans. So, industrially produced meat comes with a big dose of antibiotics, as well as saturated fat, estrogen, and cortisol. As a teenager, I visited several factory farms, and witnessing the terrible conditions made such a profound impression on me that I never went back to eating meat.

Meat consumption remains a controversial topic in nutrition. Studies have consistently shown that high consumption of red and processed meats is associated with an increased risk of coronary heart disease, stroke, heart failure, type 2 diabetes, and colorectal cancer, which is another reason why I point people to diversify their diets and eat more plant-based foods.[13] Eggs, fish, and dairy are also well-loved sources of animal protein, with organic options as a healthier choice. Sustainable, humane, and responsible animal care leads to better animal sources of food for humans, too.

If you choose to eat meat, make sure that it is organic, which means that animals are not receiving antibiotics or hormones, their health and natural behaviors are prioritized, and they are fed 100 percent organic feed and forage. In the United States, the USDA Certified Organic label encompasses these practices, but many local farms that cannot invest in the certification also meet these criteria. Talk to your farmers at your farmers' market to be sure! Good quality animal protein can absolutely be a part of a healthful diet. But, if you can't afford organic or local sustainable options, I would prefer that you avoid meat altogether, as industrially produced meat is truly dangerous. What is good for our individual health is good for community health, and ultimately should be aligned with planetary health. When it comes to environmental impacts, industrial animal agriculture is a mega business that consumes far more than it produces. Our current food system is responsible for around 30 percent of global greenhouse gas emissions, and industrial animal agriculture is responsible for 57 percent of those emissions.[14] Producing animal-based meat, dairy, and eggs consumes one third of the world's freshwater stores and occupies a majority of the world's land resources.[15] Despite taking up nearly 80 percent of agricultural land, industrial animal agriculture produces less than 20 percent of the world's supply of calories.[16] Animal agriculture leaves an enormous footprint. And from a nutrition perspective, 83 percent of the world's calories and 63 percent of its protein actually come directly from plant-based foods.[17]

Fats

Fats have been demonized for so long that many people avoid all foods with fat. The truth is that obesity rates went up during the low-fat craze of the nineties because people were not satiated by synthetically created low-fat foods, and ate more carbs to feel full. We need healthy fats. Polyunsaturated fats, like omega-3s and omega-6s, and monounsaturated fats are associated with lower risk of total and cause-specific mortality, including cardiovascular disease and cancer.[18] We tend to eat more omega-6s than we need, so I focus more on omega-3s for patients.

Prioritize omega-3 fats that are found in avocados; walnuts; chia, flax, and hemp seeds; purslane; fatty fish; and olive oil. These omega-3 fatty acids are the building blocks of hormones and neurotransmitters and cell production. Unlike most saturated fats and trans fats that are found in processed foods and meats, omega-3 fatty acids decrease inflammation on a cellular level. Omega-3 fats can also be found in enriched eggs (the chickens are fed flaxseed) or wild-caught fatty fish.

Unlike their farm-raised counterparts, wild-caught fish are caught in oceans, rivers, and lakes using nets, poles, and other methods. Because they are not confined to small spaces or fed a diet of manufactured foods, wild-caught fish are often healthier than farm-raised fish. They also have a more natural diet of plankton, algae, and other aquatic plants and are typically higher in nutrients than farmed fish, and tend to have a lower mercury content, as they are not exposed to the same pollution levels as some farmed fish. Wild-caught fish also can have a lower environmental impact, and their populations are not as at risk of being depleted by overfishing. Salmon, herring, sardines, mackerel, and cod all have high levels of omega-3 fatty acids.

Please, at all costs, avoid trans fat. When I teach middle schoolers in my Food Is Power class, I call this a "red light" food. A hard stop. Trans fat is a disaster for human health, as it's synthetically created to keep food shelf-stable, but you are not a shelf! These hydrogenated oils have an extra hydrogen bond that keeps the oils solid at room temperature, and they are very pro-inflammatory. Look on the labels of crackers, cookies, chips, cereals—if you see hydrogenated oils there, do yourself a favor and put it back on the shelf. One of my mentors in nutritional science, Dr. Walter Willet, professor of Epidemiology and Nutrition at the Harvard School of Public Health, said many years ago that hydrogenated fats were the worst thing to ever happen to our food supply. Those are strong words coming from a nutrition legend. We should listen!

Fiber as a Nutrient

People are woefully undernourished in fiber, which is a bigger problem for our health than we think. I grew up with folks eating a bran muffin or Grape Nuts cereal and thinking they were done for the day for fiber needs. Our bodies don't digest fiber, but the trillions of bacteria that populate our gut microbiome do. Fiber feeds these beneficial bacteria, which produce short-chain fatty acids. Short-chain fatty acids fuel the cells of the gut, reduce inflammation, strengthen the intestinal barrier, and help regulate metabolism and the gut-brain axis. A healthy gut microbiome also lowers inflammation, regulates blood sugar, and helps keep cholesterol levels balanced and digestion effective. The recommended daily fiber intake is around 25 to 38 grams, but the average person gets only around 15 grams per day. Historically, it was much higher. Our hunter-gatherer ancestors had a fiber intake more like 75 to 100 grams per day, from wild plants, tubers, seeds, and fruits. With the industrialization of food and creation of agriculture, traditional agrarian diets moved down to around 40 to 60 grams daily. Now we are just hoping people will eat a couple of veggies and fruits a day.

Here's what happened: Preindustrial diets, even in Europe and Asia, were naturally high in fiber, rooted in grains like millet, barley, brown rice, rye, and oats, along with legumes and seasonal produce. The Industrial Revolution introduced new milling technologies such as steel roller mills in the 1800s, which stripped bran and germ from wheat to produce refined white flour. White bread became fashionable and much desired, but fiber content plummeted. Colonized countries shifted from diverse, fiber-rich subsistence crops like millet, legumes, and tubers to export cash crops like sugar, cotton, tobacco, tea, and coffee. This reduced local access to traditional high-fiber foods.

People often think that India, for example, is a country where rice is the most popular grain, but actually India's millet-rich diet was replaced by refined rice and wheat during British rule. The twentieth century saw the explosion of processed, packaged, shelf-stable foods. Refining grains and sugars extended shelf life but removed fiber, so we saw more items like white flour, white rice, fruit juices without pulp, canned foods, and sweetened cereals on the shelves. Of course, marketing has always been about creating desire in the customer, and by the mid-1900s, processed foods were marketed as modern and superior to "old-fashioned" whole foods, so breakfast cereals, white bread, and instant foods became staples. Fiber was viewed as unimportant "roughage" rather than essential nutrition.

In medical education too, we focused on protein, fat, and calories as markers of nutrition, not fiber. The dramatic drop in fiber intake contributes to the modern epidemics of constipation, obesity, diabetes, cardiovascular disease, and colon cancer. When researchers observed that rural African diets, which are very high in fiber, were protective against colon cancer, heart disease, and diabetes—all diseases much more common in high-income countries—fiber started to come back to view.

Fiber comes in two forms: soluble and insoluble. Soluble fiber are foods that feel a little sticky or gel-like when cooked or chewed, such as oats, beans, lentils, apples, and flaxseeds. They slow the digestive process and help keep blood sugar steady. This is why eating whole foods—fruits and vegetables with their skin intact, or the stems and leaves of greens like spinach, kale, and lettuce—keeps blood sugar balanced in a way that juicing those same foods does not.

Insoluble fiber, on the other hand, adds bulk to the stool and helps food move efficiently through the digestive tract, supporting regularity and overall gut health. Together, the two types of fiber keep digestion balanced and resilient. One way that a teacher taught this to me years ago was through the kitchen sponge analogy. The kitchen sponge has a green scratch pad on one side and a yellow sponge on the other; the scratch pad is the insoluble fiber, scrubbing and cleaning your digestive system. The yellow sponge is the soluble fiber, absorbing and mopping things up. For people with constipation, adequate hydration and increased fiber often makes a significant difference.

In Ayurveda, a healthy gut is the cornerstone of good health, and fiber-filled cooked vegetables are a cornerstone of the diet. Since our gut bacteria play an incredibly powerful role in our gut health—strengthening the gut-based immune system, producing mucus to shield the gut lining, and maintaining balance within digestion—we need to feed them plant fiber, at every meal, every day. The trillions of bacteria that live in our intestines cannot thrive without it, and the vitality of this microbiome is deeply tied to our overall health and longevity. By choosing a whole-food, plant-forward diet, fiber becomes abundant without effort.

To embrace food as medicine is also to honor the earth it comes from. Plant-based diets can reflect the wisdom of regenerative agriculture, a system of farming that restores soil health, biodiversity, and ecosystems by working with natural processes, using practices like cover cropping, crop rotation, reduced tillage, and managed grazing to rebuild soil, capture carbon, and strengthen the resilience of the soil. These are hardly new ideas, though some of the concepts and terminology are new and trending among non-Indigenous people. Indigenous communities have always known that land, water, plants, animals, and people are inseparable, and that tending soil fertility and diversity is essential for the health of all beings.

Dr. Lydia Jennings, a Pueblo soil scientist, argues that restoring this foundation is critical for ecological and human survival, and entirely within reach through regenerative, holistic practices. The nutrient-dense foods I recommend—fruits, vegetables, legumes, nuts, and seeds—benefit directly from the improved soil health promoted by regenerative agriculture. The better the soil—the more alive and abundant with microbes, humus, and minerals—the higher the nutrient density of the food. Our human health and our earth's health are deeply connected through the precious soil under our feet, from which all our food and nourishment comes.

All of the above recommendations are evidence-based and time-tested; they reduce risk of chronic disease, cancer, can improve digestive health, increase longevity, and enhance planetary health by preserving biodiversity and ecosystems. To me, they are the foundation for a personalized, culturally respectful, and delicious path for healthy living, with strong and ancient medicines. True wisdom is making choices that sustain your own life and leave a legacy worthy of future generations.

Decolonizing Nutrition and Honoring Foodways

In Ayurveda, and many other ancient traditions, like Chinese medicine and Indigenous herbalism, there is no one way to eat. Your best diet is determined by your constitution, your natural energy patterns, and the principles that govern the physical and mental processes in the human body. This perspective allows for more individualized care and guidance around diet and lifestyle, which I incorporate into patient care.

While my work is deeply rooted in teaching people that food is a medicine, therapeutic for illness, as well as protective and preventative, I bridge ancestral wisdom with modern understanding. Patients, parents, and even teenagers frequently ask me about "superfoods." Which are the best? Blueberries, açaí, hemp, maca, mushrooms? The fascination says much about our culture of convenience and celebrity trends. For years, I've given the same answer: "Focus on a plant-based diet rich in nutrient-dense fruits and vegetables." I stand firmly by this advice. Yet true health is not about the perfect eating plan, or about glorifying one cuisine or the latest exotic ingredient; it is something larger and deeper.

In my own professional nutrition education, the Mediterranean diet has been hailed as the epitome of optimal eating. The Mediterranean diet is the most studied and, in many ways, the most prescribed dietary pattern in the world. Born from the traditional foodways of countries bordering the Mediterranean Sea—rich in vegetables, fruits, legumes, whole grains, olive oil, nuts, fish, and modest amounts of dairy and wine—it has been the subject of thousands of clinical trials, observational studies, and meta-analyses. Over the past four decades, it has been linked to reduced risks of cardiovascular disease, diabetes, cancer, depression, and even improved cognitive health. Because of this robust evidence base, physicians, nutritionists, and public health organizations frequently recommend it as the "gold standard" of healthy eating.

The PREDIMED trial in Spain, one of the largest randomized controlled nutrition studies ever conducted, showed dramatic reductions in cardiovascular events among people following a Mediterranean dietary pattern supplemented with olive oil or nuts.[19] Those results and several others like the Lyon Diet Heart Study, the NIH-AARP Diet and Health Study, and EPIC Study have positioned the Mediterranean diet at the center of dietary guidelines across Europe and the United States—by demonstrating a statistically significant lowering of all-cause and cardiovascular mortality, reduced incidences of certain cancers (colorectal, breast), and a lower risk of type 2 diabetes.[20] It deserves accolades as a very healthful and delicious model on which to base a great diet.

However, as a trusted member of my patients' health care team, recommending a European diet as the healthiest and most superior choice to non-Europeans also perpetuates harmful colonial practices. Promoting one specific dietary pattern as the ultimate solution does not serve individual patients or honor traditional foodways. While the Mediterranean diet remains a powerful model, especially for chronic disease prevention, it must be understood as one of many nourishing traditions, rather than the sole best dietary prescription for human health. Sacred traditions are erased when people are separated from their cultural heritage and nourishment, and taught to eat "better" foods that they are not connected to. Food sovereignty, defined as the right of people, communities, and countries to define their own food systems, emphasizes local control over how food is produced, distributed, and consumed, centering cultural, ecological, and community needs rather than corporate or market-driven demands.

Camille Dungy, author of *Soil: The Story of a Black Mother's Garden*, writes about her choice to grow food as she pleases in her essay "From Dirt":

> On the property of Thomas Jefferson's retreat home, Poplar Forest, archeologists have discovered caches of food that give insight into the diet of the enslaved men and women who lived on that property. . . . Archeologists have found the remains of wheat, oats, rye, sumac, blackberry, purslane, pigweed, poppies, and more. . . . But Jefferson made sure his son-in-law "put an end to the cultivation of tobacco" by the people he called property, who were growing it in their gardens. "There is no other way of drawing a line between what is theirs and mine," Jefferson admitted in a letter, than to forbid these men and women from growing for personal use the same crops they cultivated in his fields.
>
> Don't think I don't have histories like this in mind when I insist on growing what I please in the soil that surrounds me. There is power to be generated from cultivating whatever might sustain me, in whatever way I wish.[21]

For Dungy, food is a form of power—having the freedom to grow what she wants, how she wants, for her family. It's a freedom that her ancestors, like so many people oppressed by slavery and colonization, were stripped of. Unfortunately, the medical profession often unintentionally contributes to this process, as well.

Our medical training is designed to keep us focused on identifying physical and laboratory indicators for diagnosis and treatment, which is vital training that teaches us to be great detectives and diagnosticians, and to keep searching for answers. Yet the holistic nature of our humanness—including the deeply rooted traditions that shape our foodways and our communication styles, and which provide insight into the sources of pain and ailments—is not always considered. This is partly why health care professionals create dietary plans that fail to integrate with individuals' unique food heritages and cultural practices.

During the era of European colonial expansion and cultural destruction, settlers brought their own food traditions, crops, and livestock to new territories of unfamiliar foods, cooking techniques, and agricultural practices, while outlawing and decimating food traditions that had existed for thousands of years. The introduction of crops like wheat, rice, potatoes, coffee, and various fruits, as well as the raising of cattle, pigs, and chickens, significantly altered local diets and agricultural landscapes. This systematic disruption of Indigenous food systems overran and often destroyed the local cuisines and ecosystems as well as ancestral ways of growing, tending to the land, and communal eating.

This forceful imposition of dietary practices had a profound impact on human societies as well as on the ecosystems and biodiversity of these regions. The very seeds, crops, and livestock became unwitting participants in these harmful practices, in contrast with many Indigenous traditions that value kinship with the beings we share space with. For instance, the Indigenous values of the Lepcha people of India emphasized reciprocity and solidarity with the natural world, evident in their sharing and exchanging of seeds and the planting of new saplings after tree felling. A few years ago, I visited natural foods expert Tom Newmark at his farm, Finca Luna Nueva, in Costa Rica. He shared that the plants and trees that they were growing on the land were being "liberated" from their histories as being an essential part of the trade that led to colonization of so many countries, trafficking of enslaved people, and human suffering. He felt that the plants, not just humans, deserved a different story, too.

To truly honor the healing power of food as a medicine, we must acknowledge the historical injustices perpetrated by colonial forces that disrupted ancestral food systems and imposed foreign dietary practices. We must recognize the interdependence of cultural heritage, traditions, and well-being. By fostering an understanding of diverse foodways and integrating them into our approach to nutrition, we can forge a path that celebrates the wisdom of ancestral connections and nourishes both body and soul. Remember, you can eat in a way that honors your cultural food traditions. By following plant-based diet recommendations and adapting them to your family's cuisine, you can eat healthfully and in a way that fits your style.

The food and nutrition nonprofit organization Oldways has been a great staple resource for my patients, providing food pyramids for Asian, African, Mediterranean, Latin American, and vegan diets that are easily understood, and available on their website at oldwayspt.org.[22] (For more on Oldways, see Appendix B.) As stated on their website, they believe that "traditional diets also differ from the Western style of eating in that they emphasize the cultural aspects of eating, such as cooking meals at home, and enjoying food in the company of friends and family. Rather than succumbing to mindless eating, microwave meal plans, or munching in front of the television, embracing the community aspect of traditional diets can help cultivate wider support for a healthy, happy life."

Many nonprofits create tools to support health care providers who are offering excellent patient care. We need all the help we can get in the time we have! This kind of work helps people make informed choices about real, whole foods across culinary traditions.

Food Justice and Primordial Prevention

Social determinants of health are the nonmedical factors—such as income, education, employment, housing, and food access—that shape health outcomes. When these conditions are insecure, people are far more vulnerable to sickness. Improving social determinants is critical to preventing disease and supporting community health. Among all the medicines I write about in this book, food is the one we rely on to live, and the one that touches every layer of our health. And when it comes to the importance of food as a medicine, we move into primordial prevention. As I've mentioned before, primordial prevention looks to the source, addressing the conditions that create risk factors. When it comes to food, it pushes us to examine how our systems—food supply, economic policies and subsidies, city design, school curricula—could be reshaped so that healthy choices are built into daily life, while harmful ones fade from reach. At its heart, primordial prevention is about changing the upstream currents of health so that whole generations grow up with fewer risks before they even appear. It represents the most holistic and justice-oriented form of prevention, aligning with current efforts in public health to integrate equity, environmental sustainability, and systems-level change.

Most conversations about food as medicine focus on the primary prevention of using diet to reduce risk of diabetes, hypertension, obesity; or on the secondary prevention of treating disease through medical nutrition therapy, food prescriptions, or medically tailored meals. But primordial prevention asks that deeper question: What would it take for entire populations to grow up in conditions where the risks of diet-related disease barely exist in the first place?

This is possible in a multitude of ways. Instead of leaving families to struggle against fast-food saturation, sugary-beverage marketing, and ultra-processed-food dominance, primordial prevention calls for reshaping the food environment itself, zoning policies that support local grocers and urban farms, restrictions on predatory junk-food advertising to children, and subsidies for fresh produce over industrial meat and refined grains.

The question I keep hearing from colleagues and patients is: If organic and regenerative food costs more, how will families with limited means ever access it? It's the right question to ask. My fellow advocates for food security are absolutely right to demand affordability. And farmers are right to insist that their labor and care for the land, especially as they convert to regenerative agricultural practices, not be devalued. Food distributors are right to say that food won't sell if no one can buy it. And everyday people, already carrying the weight of inflation and thinned paychecks, are right to feel exhausted by the impossible math. But this is not a debate between types of agriculture or the fault of farmers, or the fault of consumers. This is the problem of a broken food system, one that requires us to rethink how value, labor, and access are structured from the ground up.

Addressing poverty and inequitable access to health care is central to improving health for all people. In the United States, this could mean expanding SNAP, the Supplemental Nutrition Assistance Program that provides forty-two million low-income individuals and families with monthly funds to buy groceries, into farmers' markets, strengthening school food programs to include fresh and culturally relevant meals, and challenging agricultural subsidies that prop up corn syrup and industrial animal feed, which come up in the Farm Bill every five years. At this time, the United States subsidizes the wrong "foods"—the top five being corn, soy, cotton, wheat, and forage. Corn was the most-subsidized crop in 2024; corn farms received $3.2 billion, or 30.5 percent of all federal farm subsidies.[23] Corn makes up 95 percent of all US-produced feed grains.[24] Most Americans don't realize crop corn is not used not as a source of whole food but rather for livestock feed, ethanol production, and food products like sweeteners, corn oil, beverages, starch, and alcohol.

We must restore food sovereignty by supporting seed-keeping, land access, and intergenerational transmission of food knowledge in Indigenous and diasporic communities. This allows people to grow up nourished by culturally appropriate diets that strengthen both body and spirit, rather than eroded by imposed systems of cheap, unhealthy calories. Primordial prevention in food justice isn't only about giving people healthier meals; it's about reshaping the soil of society so that future generations never inherit the risks we carry today. This is possible. For example, in the 1970s, Finland had the highest cardiovascular disease rates in the world. Much of this was linked to very high salt intake through bread, cheese, and processed meats. The Finnish government strategy included a national campaign called the North Karelia Project, which didn't just tell people to "eat less salt." Instead, they worked with food manufacturers to reduce salt in products, required front-of-package salt labeling, launched public media campaigns, and partnered with schools and communities to further the education and the message. Over twenty years, Finland's average salt intake dropped by one-third, and cardiovascular deaths fell by more than 80 percent in some regions.[25] This is an elegant and revolutionary example of primordial prevention, which reshaped the food environment so that everyone benefited, not just those with resources to seek healthier diets.

My dear friend Chef Michel Nischan is a food justice warrior and a primordial prevention warrior. He is a four-time James Beard Foundation Award winner, the cofounder and chairman of Wholesome Wave, and the cofounder of the James Beard Foundation Chefs Boot Camp for Policy and Change. Nonprofits like Wholesome Wave pioneered the Produce Prescription Program, where doctors prescribe fruits and vegetables that patients can purchase with vouchers at grocery stores and farmers' markets.[26] A produce prescription is a medical treatment or preventative service for eligible patients due to diet-related health risks or conditions, food insecurity, or other documented challenges in access to nutritious foods, and are referred by a health care provider or health insurance plan. These prescriptions are fulfilled through food retail and enable patients to access healthy produce with no added fats, sugars, or salt, at low or no cost to the patient. When appropriately dosed, they are designed to improve health care outcomes, optimize medical spending, and increase patient engagement and satisfaction. This tackles the root cause of poor diets, which are economic and access barriers, before disease progression requires more intensive medical interventions. Early studies show increased produce consumption, improved hemoglobin A1C (a marker of blood sugar control) in diabetic patients, and reduced household food insecurity.[27] These programs work, and we can expand them nationwide with federal funding.

My frontline colleagues agree that solutions are not only reachable but right in front of us: Shift subsidies and food program dollars toward local, regenerative growers. Grow produce prescription programs and value-based care so that health care systems cover food as medicine. Instead of paying trillions of dollars to try to fix health problems, spend less money to actually feed people fresh, nutrient-dense food. Anchor markets by having big buyers like schools, hospitals, and institutions buy nutrient-dense food grown in good soil, knowing the savings will show up in fewer ER visits and hospitalizations for chronic disease. Build sliding-scale and blended pricing models so costs are shared fairly and access is widened. This is the framework we need for a food system where nutrient-dense, healing food is the accessible, affordable option for all. A better food system means your insurance costs go down, your community becomes safer, your tax burden shrinks, and your children grow up in a healthier society. Everyone wins.

Mindful Eating

Finally, while I am a proponent of the healthiest possible food choices—whole food over processed food, locally grown over imported, plant-based over animal-based, organic and regenerative over conventional—I am the greatest proponent of all for eating without your phone, peacefully and mindfully, either by yourself or with others whose company you enjoy. Your enjoyment at the table can be more important than what you are eating. There is something so rich and restorative about eating for pleasure.

Mindful eating is the act of eating while being in a state of nonjudgmental awareness, shifting our attention to the food and the mind-body connection. No matter how busy we are, we can prioritize daily meals as a reverent time to receive medicine, no matter what we are eating. We have the power to honor and enjoy our food, whether we can set aside ten minutes or a full hour. Mindful eating is a daily slow-motion act of care.

When we are distracted while eating, we tend to make poor food choices and overeat. Researchers consistently show that using a phone or any screen while eating distracts people from their food, leading them to eat more than they realize. One study published in 2012 found that distracted eaters consumed up to 25 percent more calories at a meal and were more likely to snack later. Eating while distracted shifts attention away from the sensory experience of food (taste, smell, texture) and seems to blunt the brain's ability to process satiety signals. Eating in the car, at our desks while working, or while scrolling are all ways to undermine our enjoyment of our food.

Family dinners in our house are not a farm-to-table Instagram post, but they are very much a reflection of my family and our time together. My family can be loud, as we all have things to share and tend to interrupt each other, and some of us eat quickly while others eat so slowly that they never finish at all. When my parents join us, they tend to obsess over how much everyone is eating and are always offering more once the plate clears, so we have to contend with listening to our own appetites while honoring the primal Indian way of being overfed. It is a bit wild, but it is how we commune and bow to our tradition of honoring each other for a little while every day. Someone always says a blessing before we eat, to thank the chef, the farmer, the land, or the cooks at the takeout restaurant. To me, it is all part of what makes sharing food a spiritual moment for savoring the daily nourishment of body and mind, after a full day.

Medicines to Carry

To reconnect and begin a more loving relationship with food, consider what is possible in your life, budget, and time. There are many ways to bring honor and true nourishment back to eating. Here are some ways to start:

Stock up on whole, inexpensive foods. Introduce staple foods such as beans, lentils, brown rice, oats, sweet potatoes, and frozen vegetables, which are cost-effective and packed with nutrients. These foods provide a strong foundation for affordable, balanced meals.

Emphasize beans and lentils. These are inexpensive, versatile sources of protein, fiber, and vitamins. Dishes like lentil stews, bean soups, or bean salads are delicious and easy to make. Almost all cultures and cuisines feature these foods, and you can explore how your family heritage included them.

Consider frozen and canned options. Frozen vegetables and fruits are often cheaper than fresh, and they are still nutrient-dense. Canned beans, tomatoes, and fish (like sardines or salmon) can also be healthy, affordable options, especially when well rinsed to reduce sodium and gas-producing carbohydrates.

Emphasize plant-based foods. Eat plant-based foods such as vegetables, fruits, whole grains, legumes, nuts, and seeds. Plant-based diets

NOURISH WITH EASE

Oven-roasted veggies only requires chopping your favorite vegetables, drizzling them with olive oil, and seasoning with salt, pepper, and herbs. Roast at 400°F for 20 to 30 minutes, and you've got a healthy side or base for a meal!

Smoothies are also simple to make: Blend fruit (bananas and berries work well) with a leafy green (like spinach), a spoonful of nut butter, and water or organic nondairy milk for a nourishing breakfast or snack.

Overnight chia pudding requires no appliances: Just combine chia seeds with your choice of milk and a dash of vanilla, and let it sit in the fridge overnight. In the morning, let it come to room temperature and add fresh or dried fruit, nuts, granola, or a drizzle of maple syrup for a ready-to-eat healthy breakfast.

generally have a lower environmental footprint, are more affordable, and more nutrient-dense compared to diets high in animal products.

Gradually reduce processed foods. You don't have to give up everything at once. Start by swapping one processed snack a day with something that keeps you full longer. Pick options that require little or no prep, like a handful of nuts (almonds, walnuts, cashews, or pistachios), which offer healthy fats, protein, and fiber. If you need something more substantial, hard-boiled eggs travel well and can be seasoned with a little salt, pepper, or paprika. If you eat dairy, plain Greek yogurt with a drizzle of honey or maple syrup gives you protein and a bit of sweetness without the crash. Even small changes—one snack at a time—can make a big difference over time.

Cook more at home. Preparing your own meals gives you control over ingredients, portion sizes, and cooking methods. It also deepens your connection to the food you eat. Start with simple recipes and build confidence in the kitchen, even if that just means making one easy dish on repeat until it feels natural.

Learn where your food comes from. Take a moment to notice where your food was grown and how it was made. Reading labels or looking up the country of origin can help you feel more connected to the roots and routes of what nourishes you.

Celebrate mealtime. Create a ritual of enjoying food. Set a nice table, play great music, use the good plates! Beauty slows us down. A friend of mine uses an exquisite embroidered placemat she bought on a trip to Michigan whenever she eats alone—it carries good memories. Make eating a joyful experience, whether you're alone or with loved ones. I love to light a candle at dinner, to bring an element of ceremony. In the summer, fresh flowers from our garden are always on the table, too. What a privilege to eat!

Eat seasonal and local. Incorporating seasonal, local foods connects you to the rhythms of nature and provides fresher, more nutrient-dense meals. Farmers' markets are great places to commune with food and farmers, and they often accept SNAP and WIC (a federal assistance program that provides healthy food and other supports to low-income pregnant women, new mothers, and children under five who are at nutritional risk). I treat our farmers' market like our temple—as a weekly place of worship to the earth!

Practice mindful eating. Savor and appreciate your food, and grow awareness of how your food choices impact your health, the environment, and other beings. Try not to eat in your car, while walking, or scrolling. Reserve a few minutes of time for yourself to eat with intention.

Buy into community supported agriculture (CSA). Consider signing up for a CSA program, where you get a weekly box of seasonal produce straight from a local farm. It's a great way to support small farmers and eat fresh, nutrient-rich food. Many farms even offer donation-based shares—just ask.

Support food justice initiatives. Advocate for policies and initiatives that promote food justice, including access to healthy and affordable food for all communities, regardless of income or location. Learn about the Farm Bill and advocate for subsidy shifts to your elected officials.

MEDICINE THREE

Plants

The Healing Intelligence of the Living Earth

The plants have enough spirit to transform our limited vision.
Rosemary Gladstar, master herbalist, founder, California School of Herbal Studies

Where do I get my breath? From the trees, the plants,
the green leaves, they are the condition of my life, they are me.
That lake is me, I get my water from there. There is no separation
from the soil, the seed, and the sun transformed into food,
and the plant . . . and the body. The body is consciousness.
Vandana Shiva, scholar, environmental activist

Some years back, my fascination with the question of how the foods we eat today differ from those of our prehistoric ancestors took me to the Dolomites Mountains in Northern Italy, to the South Tyrol Museum of Archaeology, a remarkable place. The Dolomite region is a stunningly beautiful area, with shockingly bright-green meadows of wildflowers and rolling hills with paths to walk and bike through. Many years before I ever set foot in Italy, I had torn a picture from a magazine—jagged, gray peaks thrusting skyward from fields of luminous green—and pinned it to my vision board. For a decade that image hung above my desk, a window into a dream I hadn't yet lived. When I finally hiked in the Dolomites years later, at one point, I looked up to the peaks and froze. The edge line of the mountains matched the picture exactly. My dream had crossed over into the real. Vision boards really work: they are a way of calling in your future. It's not magic; it's alignment!

I insisted on stopping at this museum that I'd first read about in a *National Geographic* article back in the nineties, when those glossy pages were my passport to the wider world. (I still have that bright-yellow-bordered issue, along with dozens I can't bring myself to recycle.) After navigating Bolzano's one-way streets and cryptic parking signs, we found it—a former 1912 bank with a grand stone façade in the city's historic center. Spotting the long winding line, I assumed it was for the nearby gelato shop. But the crowd snaked around the block for the museum itself. Apparently, everyone was there for the same reason I was: to meet the legendary ice man, Ötzi.

High in the Alps in 1991, two hikers stumbled upon what they thought was a fallen climber. It was soon revealed to be Ötzi, a Copper Age man emerging from melting ice—his body preserved for over five thousand years. Believing him to be a modern victim, rescuers chipped him from the glacier, unknowingly damaging priceless artifacts: a copper axe, leather and hide, bits of string and hay, a long wooden bow. Ötzi's body, perfectly desiccated by centuries of ice, offered scientists an unprecedented window into prehistory. Through CT scans and genetic analysis, they've pieced together his life—his last meal, his diet the week before, the blow to his head that killed him, and the many ailments he endured: heart disease, arthritis, rotted teeth, Lyme disease, intestinal parasites, and ulcers. What fascinated me most, though, was not the science of his death but the beauty of the way he survived—with his small satchel of plant medicines, carried across the mountains as tools for healing.

Among his belongings were herbs, mushrooms, and plants that scientists believe his people used for healing. I was most moved by Ötzi's preserved medicine kit—a calfskin pouch once tied to his waist, filled with tools and small treasures. Inside were a scraper, bone awl, flint flake—and two pieces of birch polypore, a mushroom with antibiotic, anti-inflammatory, and antiparasitic properties. Analysis revealed traces of it in his digestive tract, proof he had been using it as medicine. He also carried horse hoof fungus, a tinder for catching sparks, and bog moss, likely used as a natural antiseptic. Dried sloeberries—tiny blue fruits from the blackthorn tree—were found as well, rich in vitamin C and now known for easing inflammation and healing wounds. The interior of one of the small, cylindric bark vessels that he had on the belt was blackened and contained freshly picked Norway maple leaves and charcoal fragments. Researchers believe Ötzi kept charcoal embers wrapped in leaves inside a birch-bark container, enabling him to carry fire for hours and rekindle it in moments. This pouch tells the story of a man who traveled through the mountains carrying medicine, warmth, and wisdom—our earliest known medicine man.

His clothing, meticulously sewn from leather, hide, and braided grass, revealed both artistry and function. Each piece was joined with sinew, fibers, and strips of tree bark, with no woven fabric in sight. His knee-length coat, crafted from alternating bands of goat and sheep hide, was stitched with sinew and worn fur-side out. On his feet were lace-up leather boots built for alpine resilience—functional, yes, but strikingly stylish. Honestly, I'm surprised no one has revived this Neolithic sustainable chic.

In many ways, Ötzi's beautifully made and preserved medicine pouch, along with the functional and decorative pockets in his hand-hewn clothing, inspired me to write this book. For as long as we've existed, humans have needed plants, not only for nutrition and survival, but for their medicinal and spiritual gifts. Five thousand years ago, they were the only medicines we could rely on, and our early human ancestors clearly held a sophisticated knowledge of which plants could heal. I found myself wondering, *Who taught Ötzi about birch fungus? His mother? His companion? Or his own experiments, testing plant after plant until he discovered its power?* We will never know. But in that little museum, where Ötzi was preserved for modern humans to gaze at with awe (and fright, as he's quite unrecognizable), I was struck again by how much our Neolithic ancestors understood about medicine, and how fundamentally we still depend on plants for our health and survival. They witnessed and understood the power of the medicine all around them, the medicine for all people, and cherished it as the most prized of all relations. They kept plant medicines with them at all times, a reminder that the land grows what we need, always near and abundantly helpful. Ötzi's medicine pouch was life-giving and likely saved him many times.

Plants, the Real Big Pharma

Midwestern winters arrive as a cascade of white-gray skies, interrupted now and then by a sudden burst of blue joy. There is also the long brown season, when snow turns dirty and slushy, and the landscape feels tired and mucky. Still, beauty lingers in the stubborn greenery that pushes through, on those days of fleeting warmth and sunlight. It has taken me a lifetime to train my gaze toward that quiet beauty, and to soften my inner voice that told me my brown, melanated, Indian body belonged only in tropical climates, not in this cold Midwestern landscape.

When we moved back to Chicago after many years in southern California, a pragmatic friend gave me all sorts of advice to help me ease back into that first winter. My body had forgotten about down coats, wool socks, and shivering, and I was often lamenting the cold with her, and questioning the decision we made to move back. Among the many bits of wisdom she tossed my way as we stood on the playground waiting for dismissal, one line stayed with me. "Pretend you're a frontierswoman," she urged. "Wake each morning ready for a day outdoors on the land, and know you were built for this." With that, she whisked away in her thick wool coat and tasseled green hat, corralling her three children into the car.

For me, those words became a turning point. I've always seen myself as fierce, always trying to grow fiercer, and so I rose to the challenge. I began to dress not for the weather I longed for, but for the one I had. And I spent more time outside as a result, noticing what was actually happening underfoot in the winter. There is a whole world of beauty, and memory, underfoot.

Here in the Midwest, one of my dearest plant companions is the snowdrop, *Galanthus nivalis*, a delicate, wild spirit that braves the cold. They are among the first spring blooms that decorate our forest floors, meadows, lawns, and gardens with a carpet of white, precious flowers that look like tiny bells. Sometimes we even see them poking through in January, but more often in March, where they are a sure sign that spring is coming soon. Whenever I see them, I always crouch down and give them a moment of thanks and love for reminding me of what is coming and what is coming to an end. In the ancient language of flower meanings, they were thought to symbolize consolation and new beginnings, both of which feel accurate. Snowdrops also contain a substance called galantamine, which can treat the symptoms of dementia. Dementia is a progressive, fatal neurological disorder characterized by degeneration of the cerebral cortex and loss of nerves under the influence of a key neuromodulator involved in memory and learning pathways called acetylcholine, in the anterior part of the brain.

Alzheimer's disease is the most common form of dementia, a disorder characterized by memory loss, impaired reasoning and judgment, language and communication difficulties, changes in mood and behavior, and eventual loss of independence in daily activities. Alzheimer's disease accounts for 60 to 80 percent of all dementia cases, and its symptoms are linked to disruptions in brain cell communication, metabolism, and repair, particularly in areas involved in memory and cognition such as the hippocampus and cerebral cortex. In 2021, approximately fifty-seven million people worldwide were living with dementia, with over 60 percent of them residing in low- and middle-income countries. This disease affects not only individuals but also entire families, altering the emotional landscape of homes, relationships, and futures. It is devastating, it breaks my heart to witness, and I do my best to treat it, as there currently is no cure. Watching a loved one disappear slowly, memory by memory, while their body remains, is a kind of grief that has no name and no clear ending.

Any medicine that can improve these catastrophic symptoms is a blessing. Enter the snowdrop. The snowdrop's chemically active compound galantamine blocks an enzyme called acetylcholinesterase. By inhibiting this enzyme, galantamine increases acetylcholine levels in the brain, which can help improve cognitive function. Uniquely, galantamine also modulates nicotinic receptors in the brain—receptors that respond to acetylcholine and are central to neural signaling. By enhancing their response, galantamine improves communication between neurons and offers neuroprotective effects.[1] Under the brand name Razadyne, it remains one of the only drugs used for the symptomatic treatment of Alzheimer's disease. While it cannot reverse the illness, it can help sustain cognitive function and quality of life, especially when combined with supportive care, nutrition, and meaningful engagement. For those affected, it is a pivotal medicine. How extraordinary, then, that this compound comes from the humble snowdrop, *Galanthus nivalis*, the first flower to pierce through frozen ground, long held as a poetic symbol of hope, that winter will end and spring will return.

Galantamine is also found in the bulbs of daffodils and other members of the *Amaryllidaceae* family. Daffodils are another beloved flag of joy in the late winter, so sturdy and papery in appearance, and so very stolid in their posture, despite the winds. In 2022, a farmer in Wales found that daffodils grown under stress in heavy-wind conditions produced more galantamine, which could help increase production of more transformative treatments. For this plant, the more stress, the stronger the medicine. To think of these flowers as "medicines of memory" feels deeply fitting: small, delicate blooms that carry the power to preserve the fading light of recollection. These flowers are a memory keeper, a quiet guardian reminding us that what seems lost can sometimes still be held, at least a little longer. In the sweet white blossoms lie both resilience and remembrance, a light for those needing a reminder that spring is coming, and for those who need hope that even in the coldest winters of the mind and spirit, renewal is possible.

Most modern pharmaceutical drugs exist on the foundational backbone of plants. Aspirin comes from the bark of the willow tree. The chemotherapy drugs used for leukemia, lymphoma, and breast cancer originated in plants: vincristine from the Madagascar periwinkle plant and taxol from the bark of the Pacific yew tree. The antimalarial drugs, chloroquine and hydroxychloroquine, come from the bark of the cinchona tree. Whenever colleagues or patients balk at the suggestion that they take herbal medicine, I remind them that most of the time they already are taking some form of plant medicine, and that all medicines were originally derived from food and plants. I think the spiritual and intellectual disconnection from the plant roots of pharmaceuticals is a fundamental reason why we are more likely to take a Tylenol for a tension headache than apply peppermint oil to our temples, even though the oil can have better results.

Modern medicine often presents pills and prescriptions as if they were conjured from thin air in a lab, divorced from the living plants that first inspired them. This severing of lineage distances us not only from the earth, but also from the embodied wisdom of generations who knew how to work with plants as allies. When we no longer recognize the mint leaf as kin to the menthol in our cough drops, or the willow bark as the ancestor of aspirin, we lose both reverence and agency. The pharmacy of plants becomes invisible, and we are trained to trust only what comes in a bottle. Reconnecting with these plant origins is not about rejecting pharmaceuticals, it is about remembering that medicine was, and still is, rooted in the earth. To see plants as teachers and healers restores a sense of relationship, gratitude, and choice, allowing us to blend ancestral knowledge with modern science for fuller healing. I regard plants as true partners in care, trusting my training to guide me in knowing when a pharmaceutical is essential and when the gentler strength of plants can carry the work.

Ancestral Plant Allies

Plants and herbs offer a powerful way for me to connect a person's health with the traditions and culture that shape them. When Dionna, a first-generation, fifty-three-year-old Jamaican woman, came to see me, she was generally healthy, but she was experiencing physical and emotional difficulties that she attributed to menopause—hot flashes, irritability, and fatigue. She didn't want to take pharmaceuticals or hormones, as she had tried hormone replacement therapy (HRT) and it had not suited her well. So she sought out my help to see if an integrative medicine approach might be a better fit for her values and symptoms. I do prescribe HRT for women who see me with similar symptom constellations, and know it to be a very effective and important plan of care for many, but it is not the right, or desired, choice for all peri- and post-menopausal women.

After talking with her and better understanding her cosmology (values and beliefs) and culture, as well as her health goals to help mitigate the various symptoms that were causing her some distress, I prescribed maca, black cohosh, and lemon balm, as well as red clover from her African heritage. These medicines can be helpful for the symptoms she had. I made sure they were not contraindicated or interactive with the medications that she was taking for her psoriatic arthritis, and then we began them one at a time, some in the form of supplements and others as teas and tinctures. She responded well to the botanical medicines and noticed improvement in the following four to six weeks. Dionna felt that she was regaining the power she had given away to the medical establishment when she was taking medicines that she did not want to take but were the only ones offered to her.

Honoring her heritage also supported her reconciliation with her changing body, and restored her faith in the wisdom of this transition as a time for moving into her wise mind, a time of rebirth and renewal, to reflect, rest, and reconnect with her deeper purpose and spirituality. Her culture values the elder women, as sages and kinkeepers, and she felt that by accepting the transition with confidence as she had seen her grandmother do, she was following her proud lineage. I suggested she ask some of the respected elder women in her family about their beliefs about this time of life, and what remedies they recommend. We also talked about getting to know plants better and bringing them into her life as friends and allies for her health. This resonated with Dionna, as her grandmother had kept many personal favorite plants.

We discussed the practice of noticing and observing plants in her neighborhood parks and gardens, and she dived into this on her daily walks. Dionna was deeply drawn to the bushes of catmint that abounded in the parks near her home; she smelled them, tasted the leaves, and brought branches home. Her research revealed that the nepetalactone content in catmint is a balm for the stressed and sleep-deprived, offering a mild sedative effect, and in spiritual practices, catmint is used to soothe the soul. Her attraction to this plant ally very much reflected her needs at this time of her life. Through traditional plants and acknowledgment of her cultural beliefs around menopause, she could walk a path that was truly healing and authentic to what she wanted and needed. And while botanicals and herbs may not be the only treatments required for a person to achieve their health goals, they are allies that are too often forgotten and buried in our pasts.

Growing Native Plants

Our front yard is only eight by twelve feet, but it stands out on the block. Instead of grass, there's a raised bed catching the morning sun and a small stone labyrinth ringed with native plants. It's the wild child of the neighborhood—a little *Lord of the Rings*—and I love it for that. We rarely water it; the prairie plants are built for Midwest extremes, weaving into each other as they grow—coneflower, bluestem, rattlesnake master, black-eyed Susan, milkweed, yarrow, and columbine. Creeping thyme softens the labyrinth's edges, and new volunteers appear each summer. It took years for these plant relatives to root deeply, and for us to understand that bright annuals did nothing for the soil. The shift came as we watched others water their perfect grass lawns: lush but empty of life.

After living in Southern California, where lawns were discouraged and water was scarce, it felt gluttonous to squander this abundant, precious living resource in the Great Lakes region. Research from the Rodale Institute and local native plant groups taught us that lawns, often a single non-native grass, offer little habitat or food for pollinators, birds, or insects. Without biodiversity, there's no life buzzing, fluttering, or nesting. So we traded our lawn for something wilder—a living, breathing patch of native prairie. It's been imperfect. Some plants thrive, others vanish, sometimes eaten or overtaken. Yet, through seasons of trial, the prairie persists.

Now, I love that the path to our door hums with life—bees, butterflies, hummingbirds, robins, chipmunks, and more bunnies than a city yard should hold. In summer, standing there feels like stepping into a small island of joy, like I am a Disney princess with fluttering all around—a reminder that when we make space for life, life fills it.

Tending native plants teaches balance—not just taking, but giving back, rematriating seeds and species that belong to the land. It cultivates patience, humility, and gratitude. In caring for native plants, we engage in mutual medicine-making: healing the soil, and being healed. Though this is not the land of my ancestors, my family has lived here for over sixty years, and it is home. Without a living tie to our ancestral soil in India after Partition, replanting our yard with native species has become an act of decolonization and remembrance. Each rooted stem restores our relationship to the land; to the Potawatomi, Ojibwe, and Ottawa whose stewardship shaped it; and to our own lineage. Being among native plants reminds the body what belonging feels like—that it, too, is home.

Sacred Plants

There are so many stories to tell about our medicine plant allies, it is a quandary for me to consider which ones to include here, especially since there is a vast pantheon of research to support their use, and the energetics of each plant are so unique and different. Also, there are many wild medicinal plants that are now threatened from overharvesting by the herbal supplement industry, so I remain cognizant and careful about what I choose to use and from where. Like my mentor herbalists, I decided to become deeply familiar with a smaller apothecary and its range of power, rather than work with hundreds of different plants. In this more contained manner, I have been able to learn about the many attributes, qualities (hot, cold, damp, dry), and actions of specific plants that help us heal. Partnering with plants is part of every culture, from the Mapuche people in Chile, who revere medicinal plants as a gift from the Creator, to the Celts in Ireland and Scotland, where herbs such as mugwort, meadowsweet, and vervain were gathered in alignment with moon cycles and solstices. I've found that herbal healing is as much about our relationship with the plant spirit as it is about the biochemical action.

One of my favorite allies is a beautiful example of the rich heritage, traditions, and multifaceted healing powers of plants. Tulsi, *Ocimum tenuiflorum* or *Ocimum sanctum*, is the most beloved plant in my apothecary, and also the queen of my summer garden. (Tulsi is honored as a goddess-like plant in many traditions, so I use feminine pronouns to reflect that respect.) Tulsi's stems are tinged with a blush of purple, and her leaves are small, oval, and edged with the faintest serrations; when your fingers graze their surface, a tiny, sweet breath of clove and pepper is released. When the sun warms her, the air holds a sharp, sweet fragrance, and the delicate spires of tiny lavender or white blossoms rise above her leaves, drawing bees, butterflies, and hummingbirds to her. Tulsi has been cultivated in India for over three thousand years—for its sacred place in Hindu households and its healing role in Ayurveda. Revered as both a living medicine and a divine being, tulsi is planted at the heart of courtyards across India and worshipped daily as a guardian of the home. Every part of the plant—roots, stems, leaves, even soil—is considered blessed.

Tulsi embodies a feminine energy that sanctifies new beginnings and symbolizes union and devotion. In the ritual of Tulsi Vivaha, the symbolic wedding of tulsi and Vishnu, the monsoon ends and the wedding season begins. Each day, people light lamps, offer flowers, chant mantras, and wear tulsi seed malas for prayer, purification, and protection. I planted her at the center of our garden—a small act of devotion, a thread connecting me back to that sacred rhythm of care and reverence.

While there isn't a particular malady that calls tulsi to mind, she is a relative and a part of the cosmology of my family's spiritual life. Many other plants, such as neem (*Azadirachta indica*), sandalwood (*Santalum album*), brahmi (*Bacopa monnieri*), and amla (*Phyllanthus emblica*), are revered as medicines as well as deeply symbolic and spiritual. Of course, the ancients didn't idolize every plant; there is always an incredible phytochemical medicinal power in these chosen ones that was carefully listened to and used with caution and high regard for their power.

Tulsi has been rigorously studied and consistently found to offer a remarkable range of health benefits. I use it in my practice as an anti-inflammatory, an analgesic for pain, as an adjunct helper for blood glucose stability in diabetes, to aid with lipid balance, and as a support for individuals experiencing significant stress. Clinical trials reinforce these traditional uses. A systematic review of twenty-four studies highlighted tulsi's effectiveness against chronic, lifestyle-related conditions—such as diabetes, metabolic syndrome, and psychological stress—without serious adverse effects.[2] Additional studies show that tulsi can reduce inflammatory markers, which may mitigate neuroinflammation linked to depression, lower cortisol levels, and improve subjective stress and sleep quality.[3]

Tulsi is one of many herbs defined by herbal medicine as adaptogens, a class of plants and mushrooms that help our bodies manage stress and restore balance. Tulsi is considered a *sattvic* herb in Ayurveda, which promotes clarity of mind, calmness, and spiritual upliftment, as well as a *rasayana*, or rejuvenative, herb, so it is often taken as a tea or simply by chewing fresh leaves in the morning to promote mental balance for the day. If you can grow the plant in a pot for access to fresh leaves, that is a beautiful start to the day. Otherwise, drinking tulsi tea can also be a beneficial morning ritual. Since tulsi is believed to strengthen prana, reduce mental fog, and protect against the *tamasic* states of depression and lethargy, it can be a great ally in all seasons, as a tonic. We can also use tulsi as a remedy when we are overworked, have many ongoing stressful events, and need more tender care. Tulsi is the sister that tends to your heart, strengthens your mood, and never steals your clothes or makes fun of you!

Healing is not owned, patented, or locked behind a prescription pad. It is rooted, growing, and in the soil beneath our feet. With a bit of time and intention, you can reconnect with the plants and herbs in your own lineage, pay attention to what calls to you on your walks, or choose a plant from the apothecary at the end of this chapter—and begin a sweet, healing relationship. Before pharmacies, there were grandmothers with bundles of herbs, midwives with roots and teas, farmers with victory gardens and farms that fed not just the body, but our health. Plants remind us that medicine can be relational, not just transactional; that medicine is not only what comes through pharmacies, but also what sprouts from the land we live on. Plants offer soul-rooted, practical forms of medicine that are abundant and affordable. Embracing them is not only an act of healing but an act of decolonization, challenging the idea that knowledge of plant medicine should remain locked away in academic halls, rather than in the hands of the people who need it most.

I am reminded of Harriet Tubman, best known as a courageous conductor on the Underground Railroad. Fewer people know that she was also a skilled herbalist and healer, a woman deeply connected to the land and the medicine it offered.[4] She spent much of her life outdoors, first enslaved on Maryland plantations and later guiding hundreds to freedom through forests and swamps. Tubman learned to read the land not only for direction, but for survival. Along with an immense and steely courage, Tubman carried with her botanical knowledge passed down through African and Indigenous traditions.

According to Leah Penniman in her beautiful book *Farming While Black: Soul Fire Farm's Practical Guide to Liberation on the Land*, enslaved herbalists fought to keep their traditions at great costs; slave owners so feared being poisoned by the people they enslaved that herbal practices were banned altogether. Tubman used remedies passed down from her grandmother to treat fugitive slaves, keep babies quiet on the Underground Railroad, and heal soldiers in the Union during the Civil War. Herbalism wasn't separate from her activism but part of her resistance, a way to care for her people when no one else would, and to restore dignity through the act of tending, nourishing, and healing. She reportedly grew and gathered her own herbs, making teas, salves, and tinctures, all without formal medical training.[5] In a time when enslaved people were denied access to care, Tubman used the land itself as a source of empowerment and survival. Her knowledge kept people alive—physically, spiritually, and culturally.

Starting a relationship with plants does not require a full herb garden, clinical training, or an herbalism diploma; it simply requires curiosity, reverence, and the willingness to slow down and listen. As a physician with dual fellowships, several teaching certificates, and plenty of letters after my name, I was trained in a culture that prizes expertise and certification. I honor that training—it gave me the rigor and standards essential for excellent care. Expertise matters. Yet certifications alone cannot define knowledge of plants. When they do, we risk dismissing the wisdom held in lived experience, ancestral teaching, and community-rooted practice. True knowing comes from tending, enduring, and carrying wisdom through generations. In many traditions, the most trusted healers weren't certified by a board—they were recognized by their community, apprenticed by the land, and guided by lineage. They knew the medicines not through exams, but through reverence, use, and relationship.

Today, as influencers with weekend herbalism certificates advise millions on social media, it's vital we honor the quiet, trusted practitioners who've learned through time and care—just as our ancestors did, as far back as Ötzi. Your relationship with all the medicines in this book will grow as you live with and share them. And we develop a relationship with plants by being with and around them, tending to them, and listening to our spirit, to what we enjoy deeply. While social media may oversimplify these sacred medicines, waiting until you've "learned enough" before beginning serves no one. If you're inspired by a reel to plant an herbal garden, start now and learn by doing!

From the perspective of the ancients and the Indigenous, plants are not limited to curing disease. Many plants, like tulsi, are used to balance energies and emotions, cleanse and protect, communicate with the divine or spirit world, mark transitions and rites of passage, and align the body with the seasons, cosmos, and elements. Even plants that aren't ingested can be

PLANTS VS. HERBS

A plant is a category that includes all types of vegetation—trees, shrubs, grasses, flowers, vines, mosses, ferns, and more. It's a general term for any living organism that belongs to the kingdom Plantae. Herbs are specific types of plants—usually nonwoody, with soft stems that die down at the end of the growing season—used for their flavor, fragrance, or healing properties, and often associated with culinary or medicinal use. All herbs are plants, but not all plants are herbs. While not all plants or herbs are considered medicines, I think we just don't know enough about them to know that for sure.

burned, worn, planted, or prayed with. This holistic view of healing sees every plant as part of a living system of reciprocity. This frees us to start our relationship with plants in any place and in any way that aligns with our lifestyle. The important thing is that we start.

Find plants that you like, and start spending some time with them. You might find that you are drawn to exactly what you need. My patient Miriam, who suffers from significant seasonal allergies, told me that she had always been drawn to nettles since her childhood and planted some in her backyard garden years ago. The nettles grew with intensity all over her backyard, and she learned from an herbalist friend that they are wonderful for alleviating allergies. They are now an irreplaceable medicine for her. The nettle tea she makes for her allergies is one of her most effective remedies, and she feels that the nettle in her yard grows in proportion to how much she needs it. It's beautiful, and it's no longer surprising to me when I hear stories like this. Our connections to the living world are multiple and profound.

Your Apothecary

Creating a kitchen apothecary is one common and practical way to begin. I think it is easiest with herbs, fresh and dried. With most patients, I recommend they start with a simple tea ritual. Everyone can boil water, and it does not require much time.

Choose herbs that support your current needs, such as chamomile for calming and sleep induction; tulsi for resilience, stress management, and gentleness; peppermint for clarity; nettles for allergies and deep nourishment. You can learn more about which herbs to start with from your integrative medicine physician, your local herbalist, or your relatives, the older the better! I lean heavily on my expert mentors Dr. Tieraona Low Dog, Dr. Rosita Arvigo, Rosemary Gladstar, Dr. Vasant Lad, Karen Rose, and Dr. Lise Altshuler—all of whom have robust online presences and are great resources for botanical and Ayurvedic medicine baby steps. All of these healers have taught me that to know plants and plant medicine is not to have hundreds of plants in your apothecary, but rather just a few that you know really well. We can discern wisely and learn slowly as we familiarize ourselves with the plant and herb pharmacopeia.

Plants grow in cracks and corners. They break through concrete and persist in forgotten places, much like the communities that rely on them. They are resilient, generous, and adaptable—and in this, they model how healing can be shared. It is a practice, a remembering, and a relationship. In a world where health inequities are deeply systemic, the practice of turning to plants is a way of returning to what is communal, ancestral, and abundant. It doesn't mean every plant is safe or every illness can be cured by a leaf, but it does mean that knowledge, empowerment, and healing are not reserved for the few. To speak of plants as medicines accessible to all is to reclaim a birthright and remember that well-being is not a privilege. And the earth, in its quiet generosity, still offers it freely.

Let your process be slow. Boil the water, steep your herbs in a bag or a tea ball with intention, inhale the steam, sip with presence. This is medicine, after all, and it is gentle and sweet.

Medicines to Carry

Get curious about the plants in your immediate world. Notice the plants growing along the streets and sidewalks, in the parks and playgrounds, and near the buildings in which you work or routinely visit. Observe the number of leaves on each stem, the color of the stem and leaves, the difference between the upper and underside of the leaf, how the leaves affix to the stem, and if there are different neighboring plants. Approach the plants with a sense of curiosity and a willingness to learn. Set an intention to be present and attentive, or even dedicate specific times for observing plants, whether daily, weekly, or as often as you can. Spend a moment in the wonder and mystery of it.

Connect, identify, and grow. Allow yourself to be drawn to certain plants, preferably in their outdoor habitats. Look for any symbiotic relationships the plant may have with fungi, other plants, or animals. Gently smell the leaves, flowers, or fruits; scent can be a significant identifier and connects you more deeply to the plant. If you are curious about a plant, you can identify it with a *Peterson Field Guide* or plant ID app. Consider growing it from seed in a pot and tending to it regularly to deepen your relationship.

Communicate and deepen your connection. Get to know your chosen plant on a deeper level. Sit with it, introduce yourself, get to know it—even talk to it out loud if you like! Then do some research. Learn more about the plant's native habitats and characteristics and how it is used around the world. In these ways, and with guidance and time, you can learn how to use plants as allies in your health journey as your ancestors have.

Consider adding native plants to your garden. By bringing in plants that belong to the land you live on, you help restore ancestral healing to your soil and your home. Many beautiful insect visitors will come through and help ensure that you continue to have a healthy habitat for the future. If you are not indigenous to the place you live, your lineage began in another landscape. Planting native species can help you build a relationship with the land you're on now, offering a sense of belonging even far from your ancestral home. If you don't have lawn or garden space, natives can also be grown in pots on balconies, patios, and porches.

Create your own apothecary! If possible, plant herbs in clusters and let some of them flower to attract pollinators. Pairing herbs with native flowering plants provides nectar sources throughout the whole season. If you don't have outdoor garden space, feel free to do this in pots on a stoop, porch, balcony, community garden, or windowsill. Some of my patients cut up milk cartons as pots and start seeds in takeout containers. It all works.

SOME HERBS AND PLANTS TO CONSIDER FOR YOUR APOTHECARY

Tulsi (*Ocimum tenuiflorum*): Also known as holy basil, tulsi is revered in Ayurvedic medicine and Hindu spiritual traditions as a sacred plant with profound healing properties. Spiritually, tulsi is believed to purify the mind and spirit, support devotion, and invite clarity and protection. In India, many people keep a tulsi plant near the home altar or in the central planter of the courtyard, and offer her ablations daily to foster peace and spiritual grounding. Physically and biologically, tulsi acts as an adaptogen (helping the body manage stress) and has powerful anti-inflammatory, antimicrobial, and antioxidant properties. She supports respiratory health, blood sugar balance, and immune function, making it a revered tonic for both body and spirit. She is native to the Indian subcontinent and parts of Southeast Asia and has been introduced to tropical and subtropical regions around the world, where it can grow easily. However, tulsi is not generally classified as invasive in most areas, because she tends to require specific care or favorable climates to thrive and does not aggressively overtake native plant populations like true invasive species do. Tulsi can be grown from seed and kept in a pot that can be moved in and out with the seasons. Teas can be made from the sweet leaves and aromatic seeds.

Basil (*Ocimum basilicum*): Basil is rich in antioxidants and has properties with a range of anti-inflammatory effects. Basil contains eugenol, a compound that reduces production of proinflammatory prostaglandins. This, in turn, helps soothe the digestive tract and reduces symptoms of inflammation such as gastritis and irritable bowel syndrome (IBS). Add fresh basil leaves to salads, sandwiches, and wraps to incorporate its digestive benefits into your meals. Brew basil leaves in hot water to make a soothing tea that can help alleviate digestive issues like bloating and indigestion. Add fresh basil leaves to smoothies for a refreshing, digestion-friendly drink.

Rosemary (*Salvia rosmarinus*): Rosmarinic acid also has anti-inflammatory and antioxidant properties and protects neurons from oxidative damage, which is a key factor in neurodegenerative diseases. It also helps to increase levels of acetylcholine, a neurotransmitter important for memory and learning. You can bring rosemary into your routines in the form of the essential oil, which contains 1,8-cineole and is associated with improved cognitive performance and mood. Use rosemary-infused oils for scalp massages, or apply diluted rosemary essential oil to the temples, staying away from the eyes. Rosemary essential oil, or just a bundle of fresh rosemary from your garden in the shower, creates a decongesting steam bath when you have a cold. Add fresh or dried rosemary to your meals, such as roasted vegetables, lean and clean meats, soups, and bread. It grows slowly and stays where it's planted because it doesn't spread aggressively by seed or underground runners. It also does well in pots and will survive in colder temperatures.

Mint (*Mentha* spp.): Mint stimulates digestive enzymes, which facilitate better absorption of nutrients from food. The menthol in mint helps reduce spasms in the gastrointestinal tract. Drinking mint tea can help relieve digestive issues like bloating, gas, and indigestion. Peppermint in particular can help relieve indigestion by relaxing the muscles of the gastrointestinal tract, allowing gas to pass more easily and reducing bloating and discomfort. Peppermint oil capsules are commonly used to treat IBS and other digestive disorders. Always consult with your integrative health care professional before starting any new supplement like this, though the side effects (heartburn, nausea, stomach discomfort) are minimal here.

I use these capsules often in my practice. Aromatherapy with peppermint oil can be effective in reducing nausea and vomiting, especially in pregnant women and after surgery or during chemotherapy. Mint is considered invasive in home gardens and in certain wild habitats, so consider planting it in containers or raised beds with barriers, and regularly trim to prevent flowering and seeding. Consider choosing native wild mint (*M. canadensis*) or mountain mints (*Pycnanthemum* spp.), which support local pollinators, and which won't take over your whole garden or overwhelm other native plants. These native mints preserve the incredible aroma and culinary uses of mint, as they provide scents and flavor notes similar to peppermint and spearmint.

Cilantro (*Coriandrum sativum*): Known as a great detoxifier, cilantro is rich in vitamins A, K, and C and helps support digestion when used in Indian chutneys and garnishes, Mexican salsas, and Middle Eastern rice dishes. Cilantro has dodecenal, a compound with strong antimicrobial properties that can fight against harmful bacteria and fungi, and has also been shown to bind to heavy metals and facilitate their excretion from the body, a process known as chelation. This makes it a great topping that can add medicine to any meal. Cilantro tea can also be made by steeping fresh or dried leaves in hot water, which can help with digestion and detoxification. Cilantro is generally safe to grow without worrying about ecological damage, though in very mild climates it may naturalize in disturbed soils if allowed to reseed freely. Grow cilantro in a pot on your windowsill, or in your garden, where its umbel flowers will attract beneficial insects.

Coriander seeds (*Coriandrum sativum*): These are the seeds of the leafy plant cilantro! They contain bioactive compounds such as cineole and linoleic acid, which have anti-inflammatory effects and are very helpful for digestion and reducing gas and bloating. One of my favorite go-to prescriptions is jeera, dhaniya, and saunf water—also known by its English translation CCF tea—a simple Ayurvedic preparation that involves boiling equal parts of coriander, cumin, and fennel seeds and then straining it into a tea. This ancient preparation is excellent to sip all day or to have after meals to facilitate digestion, and so simple to make. This tonic is a foundational prescription for all patients I see. (For recipe, see page 215.)

Oregano (*Origanum vulgare*): Oregano contains carvacrol and thymol, compounds with strong antibacterial, antifungal, and antiviral activity. Oregano oil has demonstrated inhibitory effects on E. coli, Salmonella, and Candida in vitro, and the herb ranks high among antioxidants thanks to compounds like rosmarinic acid.[6] Antioxidants help neutralize free radicals and protect against cellular damage.

I rely heavily on oil of oregano as an antiviral medicine. It is in my recommended list of items that should go into every handbag. A few drops in water during cold and flu season and before every airplane trip truly helps prevent and curtail the length of colds. Even my college kids swear by it, though it's strong stuff and no one loves drinking it. Eating oregano is also a great idea, for the same reasons. In herbal medicine, the leaves can be plucked and used in oregano tea or steam inhalation to ease coughs and mild respiratory infections. It's native to Europe, the Mediterranean region, and parts of Central Asia, but it's generally noninvasive and an excellent pollinator plant, especially for bees and small butterflies.

REMEMBRANCE TWO
Medicines of Connection

Community, Seva, Trust

MEDICINE FOUR

Community

We Heal in Relationship, Not in Isolation

You cannot change any society unless you take responsibility for it, unless you see yourself as belonging to it and responsible for changing it.
Grace Lee Boggs

At the beginning of my medical career, my priority was to give the very best care to each person who sat across from me. Caring for whole families gave me glimpses into their interconnected lives, but I still focused on the physical struggles of each individual. Those struggles were often so immense that I rarely paused to consider the wider web of relationships and circumstances shaping their health. Even with a deep foundation of work in community service and commitment to whole-person health, I continued to frame health as an individual issue. I believed my task as a physician was to help each patient take personal responsibility and somehow rise above the inequities of the society around them.

As my work in community health and grassroots advocacy deepened, I came to recognize that the real work of health and healing is in fact never solitary, but rather always collective. Just as rivers converge and become something larger than themselves, our health is entwined with the health of our communities and the planet; each is sustained by the others. Serving as a doctor-activist at Standing Rock made this truth visible, embodied, and undeniable.

Standing Rock

In January 2016, Energy Transfer Partners, a Texas-based company, began digging the Dakota Access Pipeline—a 1,170-mile project to carry oil from North Dakota to Illinois. The pipeline's route cut through the sacred lands and rolling hills of the Standing Rock Sioux Nation in South Dakota. Called "the black snake" by Indigenous communities, it stretched from the shale oil fields of the Mandan, Hidatsa, and Arikara Nations, through South Dakota and Iowa, to an oil terminal near Patoka, Illinois, crossing beneath two major rivers along the way. The Standing Rock Sioux warned that any leak could poison their primary water source, Lake Oahe, and threaten the entire Missouri River system—lifeline to more than seventeen million people—across the Midwest. A single spill could contaminate not just local wells and aquifers, but the very waters sustaining communities, farms, and ecosystems downstream.

In early 2016, Indigenous activists on the Standing Rock Indian Reservation launched a peaceful protest against the multibillion-dollar Dakota Access Pipeline. By April, the protest had grown into full-time encampments on and off the reservation, with thousands joining from around the world. It was Indigenous youth who coined the hashtag #NoDAPL (No Dakota Access Pipeline) in solidarity with the first water protectors. The phrase spread rapidly across social media, illuminating the dangers pipelines pose to land and water and underscoring the enduring fight for Indigenous sovereignty.

The movement expanded into marches, divestment campaigns, bank shutdowns, and blockades. People from Hawaii, Sweden, Mongolia, Mexico, Polynesia, and dozens of other nations traveled to Standing Rock in solidarity. This movement stirred me deeply—it echoed the same struggles for land and water rights my Punjabi ancestors faced for centuries under British rule and beyond. Native peoples have long fought to keep their lands sacred and uncontaminated. Now, they face not only governments but also massive corporations driven by profit and deadlines, capable of bulldozing through resistance in minutes, literally and metaphorically. In the summer of 2016, I joined a circle of Indigenous healers, physicians, nurses, bodyworkers, and organizers, calling ourselves the Medic Healer Council—a collective providing medical care, healing, and people power for the thousands who had committed themselves to living on the land. We met a few times a week on a call to organize the effort.

LaDonna Brave Bull Allard ("Auntie LaDonna" as she was known by her community), respected citizen of the Standing Rock Sioux Tribe, shared her land as the heart of the movement. Thousands camped there, forming an intentional community. By fall, the Dakota winds turned bitter, and I grew concerned about infections spreading through the crowded camps, a pattern I had seen in India. At home, with three young children and a full clinic schedule, I felt torn. But after weeks of restless nights, I woke one morning with clarity: I needed to go. My son, Sachin, eleven at the time, had been listening to me speak about Standing Rock for months, and was also learning about the movement at school. When I asked if he wanted to come, he immediately said yes. There's something ancient between us, a quiet knowing. I knew I could keep him safe, and he would be both helper and companion. He began collecting coats at his school for the trip.

Through the Medic Healer Council, I connected with Linda Black Elk—respected ethnobotanist, Standing Rock–based food sovereignty activist, and coordinator of the Council—who shared exactly what was needed: snowshoes, blankets, tarps, rope, socks, and bags of healing herbs. Together, we all planned a clinic grounded in Indigenous healing, built not to replace Native medicine but to support it—to keep activists strong, honor traditional ways, and avoid the colonial patterns of saviorism that cause harm. I brought a few essential Western medicines, but our true work was guided by the wisdom of the Očhéthi Šakówiŋ healers and the spirit of service to the land and people we came to stand with.

On November 11, 2016, just days after Donald Trump's first election, Sachin and I left for North Dakota, knowing the new administration would soon greenlight every aspect of the pipeline. Our dear friend, poet and scholar Rachel Webster, joined us, continuing her work gathering oral histories from Pine Ridge and standing in solidarity during this crucial moment. I rarely traveled heavy, even on international relief trips, but this time I checked in four large suitcases of supplies. In Bismarck, we loaded a rental car and drove across rolling, brown hills, vast and seemingly infinite as they rose to meet the blue sky, where thin, white clouds stretched in delicate waves. These were Native lands—wild, beautiful, and fiercely defended and stewarded through generations of struggle. Remembering that history filled me with reverence and humility. And then it appeared, like a black snake, a raw tunnel tearing through the gentle hills, flanked by mounds of upturned earth. The pipeline.

I felt a choking rise in my throat, as if I might vomit. The gash of the pipeline reminded me of the first time I cared for a woman in the ER who had been shot, the unbelievable sight of her smooth skin surrounding the explosive damage of blood and tissue at the bullet entry, the irreparable harm that had been done to her soft body. The same violence now carved through the soft earth. I gasped, the air catching in my chest, and called to Sachin. "This is what a pipeline looks like before they bury it so you can't see it," I said.

For the next two hours, Rachel, Sachin, and I drove in silence beside the black snake, bracing ourselves for what lay ahead. No news story or hashtag could have prepared us for the devastation before us—the desecration of sacred land, the poisoning of waters that sustain life for thousands. As the drills and bulldozers tore into the hills, I felt, deep in my body, the weight of centuries of violence against Native lands and peoples—and a grief that reached beyond words for what we have done to the earth.

Collective Action

When we arrived at the hilltop over the Ballard land, we could see thousands of people working. Several tent clinics were spread across multiple encampments, with tents, teepees, and wigwams spread over many miles. We connected quickly with the Sacred Stone camp and the medic tent. It was one of the most organized movements I have ever engaged in. People were busy, building shelters and gathering wood, posting signs with the times and places of direct actions. In front of many tents were signs and banners that read "Mní Wičóni," a Lakota phrase meaning "Water is Life." In Lakota cosmology and the many Indigenous traditions represented at Standing Rock, water is a relative, not a resource. It carries spirit, memory, and healing. The community's energy was palpable, and we felt united by a common purpose: the greater good, the best possible outcome for the most people.

The pipeline was not only a blatant act of disrespect toward Indigenous nations, but also a direct threat to the life-sustaining water we all depend on. In that way, the camp's rhythm of purposeful, determined activity stood in sharp contrast to America's culture of hustle and grind, with its fixation on individual wealth and health. Not long after we arrived, a school bus pulled in carrying hundreds of winter coats and blankets collected from communities in Kansas, two large cases of honey donated by beekeepers offering their medicine to the cause, and fifteen more people ready to lend their bodies to the resistance. Though we were new, we were immediately woven into the fabric of this community. People kept arriving, by car, bus, RV, motorcycle, bringing all kinds of supplies, and a contagious spirit of purpose. The energy of collective care was invigorating, even as it was heartbreaking that this kind of solidarity was needed at all.

Before we made our way to the clinic, we spoke with many folks who had been at Standing Rock for weeks and months. They described intense confrontation on the front lines. Law enforcement deployed militarized tactics, armored vehicles, rubber bullets, sound cannons, tear gas, concussion grenades, and high-pressure water hoses even in freezing weather. Hundreds of water protectors were injured, and mass arrests were common. Standing Rock was a convergence point for movements against environmental racism, police brutality, and corporate exploitation. The elders we spoke to compared it to Selma and other watershed moments where marginalized communities demanded justice in the face of overwhelming state power. I worried that I should not have brought my son. But we were there, and we were there to work, so we made our way to the medic healer clinic.

The small clinic was crowded with people waiting to be seen. Two herbalists were busy brewing teas and preparing tinctures. We introduced ourselves and asked how we could help. "We need more water boiled," Lena said. So we filled several pots with bottled water and set them on the convection stove. I imagine Sachin expected that being a doctor there would be more eventful, but in those first few hours we boiled a lot of water for healing teas to ease coughs and congestion. Almost everyone was coughing, and because I was worried about the contagion in this small clinic, I asked them to wait outside and get their medicines one at a time.

The following day, Sachin and I set out from Sacred Stone camp, walking a few miles to Rosebud camp to deliver the medicine and supplies we had carried from our community in Chicago. The clinic there was created by Daphne Singingtree, a deeply respected Lakota healer from Oregon. On that frigid winter day, we sat with her inside a teepee she had raised after driving cross-country with her trailer packed full of clinic equipment and the basics she needed to live and work on the land. Despite the long journey and the limited space to bring her clinic to the prairies of North Dakota, she had elegantly covered the floor with handwoven rugs and placed several small, wooden bookcases stacked with glass jars of herbal medicines. The sweet smell of burning sage filled the space. A majestic woman with a knowing and grounded presence, Daphne is a deeply knowledgeable herbalist and friend of plant medicine. She immediately made us feel like we were protected and welcome as friends. From her perspective, this NoDAPL resistance movement was simply a longer moment of public visibility in her people's steadfast journey of resistance for the last several hundreds of years.

Daphne acknowledged her appreciation of the masses, and the vitality that community can bring to a movement. The world was finally listening, for the first time after many other pipelines had been laid down in native land, and after hundreds of years of battles against land grabs fought with no support. After helping her sort and organize the medicine we had brought, we stepped outside for fresh air as the sun began to set. About a hundred yards away, a group of teens gathered outside another teepee from which came the sound of drumming and men's voices singing and chanting. Sachin joined them to kick around a ball, and the teens kindly accepted him into their kick circle. Curious, I asked what was happening in the teepee. A teen explained the elders were helping a young man "falling into bad ways" by staying with him, checking in daily, even accompanying him so he wouldn't feel alone. My throat tightened, eyes filled with tears. In the Sioux community, there was always a circle, and no one was left alone.

Collective Care

We are meant to be in community, not only as a way of feeling secure, but as a means of survival. Our loneliness epidemic is largely a lack of community and connection. I could hear in the low, soulful singing and drumming that the young man was no longer alone on his path. This elder circle was saving—if not his spirit, possibly his life. That moment of communal grace has stayed with me as a reminder of the connection all people should know, a connection many once lived by, and one we must bring back into medicine, education, and the ways we shape our public spaces. It feels like our shared responsibility to remodel and relearn the ancient wisdom of caring for one another. Our culture's prized fable of individualism and making it on one's own is a lie, one that has fooled us into believing that we don't need each other to survive. We do.

Mainstream health and wellness culture often demands that individuals shoulder the responsibility for their own well-being, neglecting the generations of wisdom carried by cultures that are often marginalized. Individualism, a defining feature of American culture, applauds self-reliance over communal bonds, and this emphasis on personal achievement and independence often leads to social isolation and loneliness. Real strength in any community comes from collective care, especially for the youth, who require guidance, protection, and nurturing. And our youth are silently suffering.

Teens in the United States are increasingly lonely. Even before the pandemic, researchers consistently showed that loneliness in children and adolescents confers a risk for poorer well-being; it is longitudinally related with depression symptoms in young people. Considering that over 50 percent of mental health problems develop during childhood and adolescence, poorer well-being that results from loneliness may have long-term implications for health and wellness well into adulthood. It is not only preventive but also therapeutic to have people who "have your back" in these formative years, people who can gently hold a young person's spirit as they explore and migrate. The research verifies that supportive, healthy, and meaningful social relationships should be prioritized across societal sectors, which demands that we have policies that support our needs for better parks, schools, safe places to gather, and public transportation.

Dr. Vivek Murthy, the nineteenth and twenty-first US surgeon general, has become a leading voice linking loneliness to public health. In his book *Together* (2020), he reframed loneliness as a medical and societal crisis: "Loneliness is the feeling the world doesn't care about you. But connection is the cure, because human relationships are the foundation on which we build healthy, fulfilling lives."[1] As surgeon general, he observed that beneath chronic illness, addiction, and mental health crises lay a common thread: lack of connection. He declared loneliness an epidemic—its health risks akin to smoking fifteen cigarettes a day—fueling heart disease, dementia, anxiety, and depression. In 2023, he issued a Surgeon General's Advisory calling for a national framework to rebuild connection across workplaces, schools, infrastructure, and health care. Murthy's work frames love and belonging as medicine, urging us to treat loneliness with the urgency of infectious disease and reweave the relational fabric of our lives.

This power of connection was central to the historic Standing Rock civil rights action. The movement at Standing Rock, like all mass efforts, was not free from controversy. Critiques emerged: some felt the land was overwhelmed by the sheer number of people, while others argued that outside activists brought in political agendas that overshadowed the Standing Rock Sioux Tribe's original concerns. There were many injuries on the frontlines, some severe. And after the camp was forcibly dismantled, many supplies remained scattered on the land, leaving behind unintended waste. Ultimately, the Dakota Access Pipeline was laid down, and oil is currently running through it. But from my perspective, working as a physician there and standing on the front lines with hundreds of other water protectors when law enforcement faced off, I believe that the people who participated in this resistance supported the principles of Indigenous sovereignty, environmental protection, and the rights of the Standing Rock Sioux Tribe. The protests ultimately brought national and international attention to issues related to tribal sovereignty, environmental racism, and the role of fossil fuels in the United States, sparking a broader conversation on these topics. The community that grew there over several months was a powerful reflection of what is possible when people unite over collective beliefs.

This civil rights protest embodied the creation and spirit of community that is vital to invigorating our modern culture and protecting our shared human rights. In this communal living environment, people shared meals, lived in close quarters, and worked together to meet the daily needs of the massive camp, which strengthened bonds and fostered a deep sense of belonging among diverse people. The shared experiences of facing adversity and potential danger from law enforcement and private security also created a bond among us. It was a community forged by a shared belief, that water is life, and that the Standing Rock Sioux should have sovereignty over their land. But it was also a community that people created by choice, and came into with free will. Creating community is grounded in choice. We can choose our communities: chosen family that is just as vital and important as, and potentially even more binding than, biological family. Belonging isn't about external validation or fitting in, but about reclaiming the forgotten parts of ourselves and returning to who we truly are.

Communal Healing Rituals

Art, music, and creative expression were everywhere—beautifully handmade paintings, banners, flags, trailers, and makeshift dwellings. These forms of expression allowed people to connect on a cultural and emotional level, fostering a sense of community through shared artistic experiences. We also felt supported by spiritual and healing practices, which were an integral part of the protest. With private industry helicopters flying overhead most of the day and night, intentionally creating a constant loud buzz that was difficult to sleep through and designed to break us down, the rituals were very helpful. Fire ceremonies, prayer circles, and traditional rituals were conducted several times a day by elders of the Standing Rock nation. We circumambulated the large fire every morning with other activists, elders, and youth beating skin drums and singing in the ancestors, and we listened to the morning messages over the bullhorn. The rituals allowed people to connect and find solace in shared faith and spiritual learning that Indigenous citizens of the land so generously offered. The NoDAPL movement, like so many movements before it, was a historic moment when humans shone in our abilities to come together over shared values.

With Sachin as my assistant, and beside a cadre of young herbalists and wise tribal elders, I treated a lot of respiratory infections, lacerations, asthma exacerbations, skin infections, and injuries incurred from confrontation with the security personnel of Energy Transfer Partners. It was a drop in a river of care that emanated from many people and locations. I was deeply humbled as a mother and a physician to witness and participate in what I count as one of the most extraordinary movements and community creations of modern times. It solidified my understanding that community is a bedrock of health and well-being, an ancestral need, and a salve for loneliness, one of the most deadly diseases of modern times. I was convinced that this medicine needed to be in every human's medicine pouch, and that I needed to be the seed of community creation for my family. As the days passed, I was increasingly aware of my responsibility as a mother to keep my son safe, especially as we came closer to the front lines. I decided it was time to go home. It was a choice that came from privilege, and a choice that I made.

When Sachin graduated from high school many years later, and headed off to college and out of our home and neighborhood, I felt some fear about what would come next for a young brown man in our times, with the many pressures, dangers, and stresses that this generation faces, which feel different and more heightened than those of mine. A material graduation gift did not meet our desire to give him something he could truly lean on beside our family's moral support. Reflecting back on Sachin's and my time together at Standing Rock, my husband and I were moved to give him the lasting gift of a wisdom council of elders who could be there to support his mental health and decision making as he grew into adulthood. A chosen group of men in our community, mostly family friends whom we deeply trusted, agreed to meet with Sachin periodically, on Zoom or in person, to take him on a walk or for a meal, to just share their unique wisdom and special skills and to listen to his needs and his concerns. We printed out their names and messages for him and gave them to him with the hope that it would serve him in the way that the elder council circle supported the young man at Standing Rock.

The lessons from that time of humble service became a chapter of deep learning for me, a reminder of what matters most on the path of healing. True health requires resilient communities that can hold us as individuals, creating a network of support to lean on. The culture of urban and suburban America lacks such structures, unlike many other cultures, where they are woven into daily life. Community building is an essential part of supporting health and wellness. "Health care is not health itself," Dr. Sandro Galea writes in his book *Well*. "Health results from a constellation of forces, and we must have the freedom to do things we want, like be healthy, and also freedom from other things we don't like, such as being lonely." Collective care can and should be the focus of how we build our communities. Ideally, as a culture, we can create more community and wisdom councils for all of our youth, not just for our own children.

Community Care in the Wild

Examples of community care abound in the wild world around us. Mushrooms are often relied upon in integrative medicine for their adaptogenic properties (which help cells adapt to stress) and for immune support, while certain specific species have also been used historically in ceremonial psychedelic contexts associated with deep healing from trauma. Not a day goes by that someone does not ask me about whether they should be eating, supplementing with, or engaging with mushrooms. I have long been interested in the botanical complexity and intriguing science of the underground world of mushrooms, and I'm further fascinated by their use as a path of connection and healing from trauma. Mushrooms are incredibly sophisticated organisms that communicate a wide variety of information to each other through a mycelium network—signaling everything from the presence of a nearby predator, to their own nutritional needs, to weather changes—ensuring the survival of the entire interconnected system.

The work of my friend and mentor, citizen scientist and expert mycologist Paul Stamets, has greatly enhanced our knowledge of mushrooms and their complex life systems. Beneath the surface of the earth, mushrooms live through an intricate underground network. They exist as mycelium, a dense mat of threadlike hyphae that spreads through the soil like silken sensory webs. The mycelium seeks out food, breaks it down, and gathers nutrients and water, eventually producing the mushroom above ground that carries spores to future generations. Unlike the roots of a flower, mycelium can extend laterally for miles, interweaving and communicating across vast distances. Mycelium mats that span over thousands of acres have been noted in the Pacific Northwest. This hidden network functions as a community, exchanging resources, offering protection, and sustaining growth for the entire organism.

In his book *Mycelium Running*, Paul Stamets reveals that mushrooms communicate through chemical signals moving across underground webs so vast that beneath every step lie some three hundred miles of mycelium. He notes that they may even "speak" to one another, using as many as fifty words conveyed through electrical pulses.[2] So, if a mushroom is growing in an area that is water- or nutrient-depleted, for instance, the mycelium can communicate and redistribute resources to areas where they are most needed. These networks are called mycorrhizal networks, from the Greek words for fungi (*myco*) and root (*rhiza*). Through these networks, trees also exchange water and valuable nutrients with one another and have a symbiotic relationship with mushrooms, which keep some carbon and sugars for their own growth. Trees feed mycelial networks, acting as the protective mothers of the forest floor, the mushrooms being the only evidence of what lies beneath. What emerges from the studies is that trees can communicate with each other through these mycorrhizal networks and can send chemical signals that detect distress, deliver nutrient resources to trees in need, or even create chemicals that make the tree or the mushroom unappealing to a predator. This deep and constant communication is happening all around us, all the time, ensuring that no tree or mushroom is alone in its journey to survive and thrive on this planet.

Suzanne Simard, in her lovely book, *Finding the Mother Tree*, frames the mycorrhizal network as a kind of memory system, a living archive of shared information, holding knowledge of past stresses and guiding future forest resilience. Her work reminds us that forests behave more like communities than collections of individuals and that these networks actually mirror human social systems: with families, elders, and communities caring for one another. Her work challenges the old idea of forests as places of pure competition; I think it can also challenge our belief in self-reliance as an unquestioned virtue.

Mushrooms and mycelium model how human communities can uplift and support each other. There are so many other beautiful models in nature as well. Social insects like ants, bees, and termites exhibit complex social structures that enable them to divide labor, defend the colony, and share resources. These social connections enhance their chances of survival in various habitats. Migratory birds, too, often involve thousands of individuals traveling together, which provides protection from predators and enables them to find seasonal food sources. These beings are all around us and offer remembrances and reminders of how we might live again. Like the systems that sustain plants and animals, community and connection are vital medicines for us as humans. Even brief moments of connection—a day, an hour, a week—can be deeply protective. We, too, need our own mycorrhizal networks, unseen webs of support that carry nourishment and resources to us when we most need them, allowing us to rise above the soil line.

These networks must be cultivated at every level, from public policies and social systems to the intimate, local circles of care we create in our daily lives. Small, even micro-level change is effective. A study in the journal *Nature* argues that the turn toward community and social living was a key survival strategy for our primate ancestors. When they moved from foraging under the cover of night to carrying out their activities in daylight, they became more vulnerable to predators, and collective bonds became essential for protection.[3] The protective element of community has always been vital to our survival. In these times, when chronic disease and loneliness are some of the greatest threats to our longevity and vitality, social connections are a vital medicine. Being in community improves our ability to recover from stress, anxiety, and depression; eat healthier foods; be more physically active; lose weight; improve sleep and well-being; reduce the risk of violent and suicidal behaviors; and even prevent death from chronic diseases.[4] It is how we are meant to live.

It is increasingly clear that solutions to our health problems must encompass more than reforms to health care systems. Our health is a function of far more than medical care, and the data repeatedly reflects that our health behaviors and the social and physical environment in which we live and work has a stronger influence on well-being than clinical services alone. From the gatherings at Standing Rock to ancestral wisdom council circles, and even the ways plants and animals organize themselves, a pattern emerges. What sustains life is never a rigid, linear hierarchy, but a softer circle, braided together by care.

Many communities hold this wisdom within their cultural and spiritual traditions. In Okinawa, the practice of *moai* embodies it: a lifelong circle of friends who walk together through life, offering mutual support. Dan Buettner discusses this group in his research on Blue Zones. *Moai* (pronounced "mo-eye") is a Japanese term that means "a group for meeting for a common purpose." Originally, moais were formed as informal social support networks, often for financial help. Over time, they evolved into lifelong social groups that provide emotional, social, and even physical and financial support. Typically formed in childhood, moais consist of about five to ten people who commit to one another for life. Members meet regularly to catch up over shared meals, celebrate joys, and support one another in hardships. They often pool resources, help in times of illness, and provide a reliable safety net. Moais help protect against loneliness and social isolation, and the emotional support reduces stress and promotes mental health, both of which are crucial for longevity. A moai is not just a friend group, it's a lifelong commitment to showing up for each other in every season of life. By creating a culture of mutual accountability and belonging, moais encourage healthy behaviors like staying active, eating well, and engaging in community life. While formal moais are unique to Okinawa, the principle of building strong, dependable social circles can be applied anywhere.

In Kenya, too, the community spirit lives in the concept of *harambee*. Harambee, a Swahili word meaning "all pull together," is a powerful Kenyan tradition of collective action and community self-help. In practice, neighbors and community members come together to pool financial resources, labor, and support for shared goals, such as building schools, funding medical treatments, or helping a family in crisis. It embodies the spirit of unity and shared responsibility, reminding people that individual well-being is deeply tied to collective welfare. By fostering deep social bonds and a sense of belonging, harambee strengthens community resilience and empowers people to thrive together.

A Mycelium Collective of One's Own

The biological brilliance of mushrooms and their quiet genius, worthy of worship on its own, is only part of their gift. What moves me even more are the symbolic and spiritual truths in the way they live and connect. I truly long for all humans to feel that same web of belonging and support, and I have never quite understood why we would want to glorify a story of our singularity. I had a remarkable dream one night of a long table with abundant food and flowers and people, that extended infinitely. There were people I recognized in the dream, and many I didn't, and there were certain details, like a tree growing through the center of the table and a girl from my kindergarten class serving the drinks, that told me I was dreaming. Regardless, I loved the imaginary event even after I awoke, and I decided to make a version of it manifest.

In October of 2019, I gathered thirteen people at a long table in my living room for what became the first meeting of the Mycelium Collective. We were thirteen activists from across Chicago, spanning medicine and law, prison reform and urban farming, poetry and psychology, creative nonfiction writing, world music, yoga, visual art, leadership coaching, and ministry. Not everyone knew each other, and in fact I didn't even know some people that well, but I knew of their work. Some people I had long admired from a distance, and some were a few degrees of separation but known to me through friends. I invited them anyway, not knowing how the group would come together. Nearly everyone said yes. When we met that first time, I explained the vision: to be there for each other. That was it. This was to be a place of rest. A place to feel cared for, in ways that people who care for others by nature and profession don't always get to receive. No networking, no presentations, no need to impress or shine.

I chose mushrooms as our compass, these fierce and fantastical beings that speak in threads and webs, underground and above, teaching us the sacred art of connection. In the Mycelium Collective, we enjoy meals together, decompress, and share ideas. We just gather, and give each other safe space and time, one at a time, to share what is on our minds and in our hearts. We just listen and be, rather than do. No one needs to be anything more than present. At any given gathering, there are folks who don't want to talk much, and that is part of the rest that the collective nurtures. At its heart, the collective is about care, holding one another so we can return to the world and our work with courage and resilience. We reject the hustle culture, and restore some strength together.

Over time, our gatherings at the long table have woven us into something like a forest floor, linked by filaments of interconnection and profound soul-sharing. Out of these threads have grown deep, unexpected bonds among people who began as strangers. Like mushrooms that can detoxify poisons and transform toxins into nourishment, we, too, metabolize one another's struggles and grief, collectively holding them until they become something we can all carry. And from this shared ground, incredible and unpredictable growth has emerged: new books, great works of art, pieces of music, inspiring talks and sermons, and new friendships all have emerged from that long table. Nature's example offered us a beautiful solution to loneliness during the pandemic, one that has evolved into a lasting community of care.

At its heart, a community is a shared sense of belonging, a web of relationships, and a commitment to mutual support. It's the gathering place where diverse individuals unite under a common purpose. Communities can form around neighborhoods, cultural identities, shared experiences, or common goals. And while social injustice inflicts visible and invisible wounds on individuals and marginalized groups, I know that true healing can happen within the embrace of a caring community. If there is an antidote to loneliness, it is in the deep medicine of community. In these spaces, people find understanding, empathy, and the courage to confront their pain and trauma. Community is the heart of humanity. In fact, it is the heart of all living beings.

There is no separation between us and nature. We require the protection and care that the powerful medicine of community can provide. Whether we realize it or not, we are all bound together by a mycelium network. It is already there, ready to be activated.

Medicines to Carry

Start your own mycelium collective. This kind of simple gathering can allay loneliness and isolation as well as create a support network upon which you can lean emotionally and spiritually in times of need. Invite people you know along with those you'd like to know. You never know who will say yes.

Host gatherings at your place or at another comfortable location. All you need is three people. You can quietly read books together, talk about a TV show you all like, or have dinner regularly. Just be there for each other. It doesn't have to be fancy or cost anything, and you don't need an agenda. Your mycelium network can just be people you'd like to get to know better, like neighbors or work acquaintances.

Create a wisdom circle for your children. You may be surprised by how readily people, even those you don't know well, will show up to share their stories and guidance. Invite individuals whose qualities you admire: those with a strong work ethic, a generous heart, gentle speech, meaningful contributions to their communities, or authors whose words have moved you. The insights they offer can shape your child's life in quiet, enduring ways, enriching the circle of care and influence that already surrounds them. This is a gift that grows deeper over time.

Consider making a *moai* for yourself. Decide what you want the group to center on, whether friendship, health, activism, spiritual growth, parenting, or simply shared life support. A *moai* thrives on a clear shared purpose. Agree that this is a safe place to share challenges, grief, joys, and hopes without judgment. Shared rituals like weekly potlucks, morning coffee circles, or seasonal celebrations can anchor a community together over time. Even if attendance fluctuates, keeping a steady rhythm of connection through monthly meals, group text check-ins, or seasonal retreats allows the relationships to deepen over time.

Evolve as needed. Let your community shift with life's seasons. Mycelium's intelligence is implicitly trusting, generous, and adaptable. We can be like this.

MEDICINE FIVE

Seva (Service)

Healing through Purpose and Interdependence

Service is the rent we pay for being. It is the very purpose of life, and not something you do in your spare time.

Marian Wright Edelman

If you have come here to help me you are wasting your time, but if you have come because your liberation is bound up with mine, then let us work together.

Lilla Watson, Murri visual artist, activist, and academic

The clang of steel plates echoes loudly under the clamor of conversation and the warm thrum of barefoot footsteps on the marble floor of the gurdwara (Sikh temple). The air is rich with the scent of simmering lentils, onions, cumin, turmeric, and chapatis puffed golden on the hot, black iron plate of the *tavaa*. A grandmother ties on an apron and gets to work, sautéing spices in the cook line. Families sit on the floor of the giant hall with large stainless-steel plates, thin ribbons of people in parallel carpeted rows, while some of the elders slowly walk around the room greeting each other. A young boy, his head tightly wrapped in a saffron-colored cloth *pagri* (turban), carefully and quickly pours water down the line of shiny steel cups. Right after him, a woman with a giant ladle pours steaming dal onto the plates. Next comes another woman with a heaping ladle of rice, followed by another with potato and peas sabzi. Within minutes from the start of serving, plates are full to the edges. Every volunteer has also received this generous and loving food. No one here is paid to work, and no one is turned away from a meal. Here, in this sacred kitchen hall of the Sikh faith, everyone eats together—whether devout or uncertain, experienced or newcomer—all seated cross-legged on the same floor.

Langar is the Sikh practice of preparing and serving a free, nourishing meal from a community kitchen, rooted in the principles of equality, *seva*, and non-judgment. It was begun in the fifteenth century by Guru Nanak, the founder of Sikhism, who believed all people, regardless of caste, gender, religion, or wealth, should sit together as equals and share a meal. At every gurdwara around the world, a langar hall serves freshly cooked vegetarian meals, prepared and served by volunteers, free of cost. It is both literal and symbolic nourishment, breaking down social hierarchies, affirming dignity, and embodying the Sikh value of *sarbat da bhala* ("the well-being of all humanity").

In this beautiful tradition of langar, service to others reaches an astonishing scale; at the Golden Temple in Amritsar, Punjab volunteers prepare and serve fifty thousand to a hundred thousand meals every single day. There is of course the business of washing the thousands of dishes, and the chopping of thousands of pounds of tomatoes and potatoes, and everyone who comes to gurdwara is invited, but not required, to participate in this logistical feat. Even without a formal system of sign-ups, it all gets done, several times a day, every day of the year. To sit at langar is a holy thing. Everything one needs to live is here: loving care wrapped in warm food, shelter, conversation, laughter and the pulse of community. At langar, service is not an act of rescue, it is about sitting side by side and remembering that we belong to each other.

Reach Outward, Restore Within

Seva is a Sanskrit word that means more than just community service or to serve. Pronounced "say-vaa," it is the cornerstone of the Vedantic Hindu philosophy of yoga, and it means to serve without the existence of one's own identity; in other words, service rooted in humility and love. In yogic, Sikh, Hindu, and many South Asian spiritual traditions, seva is a sacred duty, a way of honoring the divine in others by caring for their needs, especially those who are vulnerable or overlooked. Seva can be expanded to include animals, plants, rivers and lakes, mountains, gravel streets and concrete sidewalks, the earth itself . . . to treat the entirety of our surroundings as a community of life that can benefit from our service. It's a recognition that we are interconnected, and our liberation is bound together.

Extending to Ayurveda, health is defined not just as the absence of disease, but as *svastha*, being rooted in the self, in harmony with the rhythms of nature, in balance with one's *prakriti* (constitution), and in right relationship with community and spirit. Seva is one of the ways we express that health outwardly, through actions aligned with compassion, humility, and connection. When we are in balance physically and spiritually, we naturally feel called to give, uplift, and support others. It's a form of nourishment, actually. Ayurveda teaches that true wellness includes how we show up in the world. Seva becomes a reflection of *sattva*—clarity, purity, and harmony in the mind. And it can be a path to health as well, not as an obligation, but as a flow of loving energy, even, or especially, when it feels we don't have much to offer.

In my clinical work, I've observed that too much self-focus can strip us of something essential: the human need to feel useful and connected. While caring for ourselves is necessary, when self-focus tips over into preoccupation with the self, it often isolates us from the web of mutual support we most need. People come to the clinic with pain (physical, emotional, generational), chronic illnesses with no clear cure, family tensions, ancestral trauma, and the relentless consequences of overwork. In such conditions, it is understandable to zero in on survival. Chronic pain in particular can wear away energy, interest, excitement, and hope over time. Many patients can't see past it, and their brains become overwhelmed by persistent pain signals that are nearly impossible to manage over time. And I've seen that the deeper we collapse into the individuality of our suffering, and the further we drift from the connections that offer relief, the heavier our suffering grows. When we lose our connection to a larger purpose, and from our incredible capacity to be of service, we slip from the fabric of community and with it, the beauty, warmth, and safety that belonging provides.

Our ancestors knew this. They wove tapestries not just with fibers on the loom, but through acts of care and mutual support, understanding that every thread is essential to the larger design. The warp gives the fabric its strength, while the weft weaves through to shape pattern and depth; each depends on the other to become whole. Their measure of success was not personal triumph but the flourishing of the community that shaped one's character. As colonization and industrialization emerged as defining forces of culture that benefited the few and not the many, the resulting capitalist framework that evolved encouraged self-interest and competition. These misaligned values teach that success is a personal achievement, not a shared sense of well-being, and that fulfillment is found in personal consumption, not collective connections. I don't think I am oversimplifying by stating that capitalism has led many to be alone in our misery, and miserable in our aloneness. One of the hallmarks of capitalist culture is the tendency to measure how well we treat others by what we stand to gain from them. This predatory mindset, quietly woven into the very fabric of socialization in a profit-obsessed society, trains us to approach human connection through the lens of transaction rather than care. The loving invitation is to rejoin the loom through seva, weaving ourselves back into the larger design, in an ever-available medicine of connection and creation.

The connection between service and human flourishing is undeniable, and truly heartening. A recent umbrella review of the impact of volunteering on social, mental, and physical well-being highlighted two standout benefits: lower mortality risk and better physical functioning. Yes, reduced mortality! There was also consistent evidence to support many other benefits, including psychological well-being, pride and empowerment, motivation, self-efficacy, life satisfaction, positive affect, reduced depression, purposefulness, improved self-reported health and physical activity, and improved social support, sense of connectedness, and community.[1] According to more recent epigenetic data, volunteering may even reduce age acceleration, an accessible and free longevity medicine.[2]

From our earliest beginnings, humans have been wired for service and care. Unlike many other species whose young fend for themselves right after birth, human infants arrive utterly dependent, unable to walk, feed, or protect themselves. Survival is only possible through the attentive care of others. This reliance doesn't end in infancy; it becomes the seed of reciprocity that continues throughout our lifespan. Parents nurture their children, teachers guide their students, neighbors look after one another, adult children tend to their aging parents. These daily acts of service are not just practical responses to need, they are the building blocks of trust, safety, and belonging.

Across history, it has been this same impulse, to extend care beyond the self, that has fueled transformative change. Movements for justice, equality, and liberation have always been carried forward by people who see service as the path forward. The Zapatista movement in the mid-nineties was rooted in the struggles of the Indigenous Maya peoples of Chiapas, Mexico, who demanded recognition of Indigenous sovereignty, land rights, cultural preservation, and self-determination. They emphasized *mandar obedeciendo* ("to lead by obeying"), a model of governance in which leaders are accountable to the community and which rejects traditional top-down political systems. They built community schools, clinics, and farms, all rooted in collective self-governance and mutual aid, not top-down aid.

The Black Panther Party's Free Breakfast Program was a revolutionary act of service by hundreds of community members, meeting basic needs for the community while resisting and refusing systemic neglect. It was one of the most influential community-based initiatives in United States history, and it reshaped the national conversation around hunger, education, and justice. Panthers and volunteers would rise before dawn, gather donated food, cook hot meals, and serve them in church basements, community centers, and neighborhood kitchens. Within a year, the program had expanded to more than thirty cities across the United States, serving tens of thousands of children every day.

The independence movement in India that set my parents and grandparents free from British colonial imperialism, led by Mahatma Gandhi, was grounded in *sarvodaya*—the uplift of all through small acts of service like spinning khadi (handwoven cloth), promoting village sanitation, and building schools—and in *satyagraha*, or "truth-force."

And during the height of the COVID-19 pandemic, my husband, Todd—an ER physician—and his colleagues worked shift after shift in hazmat suits, facing a constant stream of severely ill patients while risking their own lives and that of their families. It was the work of their profession, but also an act of service, showing up when other doctors became sick and staying hours after shift end when the patient load was far too great for a smaller core of physicians and nurses to manage alone. This same scenario unfolded in small and large ways in emergency rooms, intensive care units, operating rooms, and primary care clinics across the world, where the call to service outweighed the risk of that service. (Sadly, the World Health Organization estimated that between 80,000 and 180,000 health and care workers died from COVID-19 globally between January 2020 and May 2021, with a central estimate of about 115,500 deaths.[3])

Through service, we find the strength to question the status quo, dismantle systems of inequality, and build a more just and equitable world through care. And this instinct to serve, to support each other, is not only human.

Together, We Go Farther

Again and again, nature shows us models of resilience and cooperation. Biomimicry—the practice of designing human systems after nature's time-tested patterns—provides a way forward rooted in solutions that have already proven successful. The models of seva are all around us. As I write this during a spring dusk beside Lake Michigan, flocks of geese traverse the evening sky in a V formation. It is a beautifully ordinary experience, the honking of the geese as they soar above, heading swiftly to their sleeping spot. In the miraculous V that keeps every bird in the peripheral vision of the other, they make sure that no one leads for too long or gets left behind. Except for the leader, each bird rides the upwash generated by the wingtips of the one in front. This lift reduces air resistance, helping the birds conserve energy, and creates a swirling vortex of air behind each set of wings. By flying slightly above and behind the bird in front, geese ride the lift.

Like a peloton, geese draft in each other's wake, shifting positions whenever one grows weary. The lead goose meets the headwind first, so the flock takes turns at the front. When the leader's strength wanes, another steps ahead, and in this rhythm of shared effort, they travel safely to their destination. This collaborative effort helps the whole flock conserve energy over long migrations. Because of this formation, geese can fly up to 70 percent farther together than alone.[4] There is less burnout, more belonging, and deeper purpose. Geese don't fly in a V for a beautiful show; they do it because it works. Because together, they can move through storms, cross continents, and protect each other along the way. This is what mutual aid looks like. What a community looks like. What sacred seva looks like.

With my patients, especially those who are feeling disconnected and depressed, I often prescribe seva in their local community, and tailor it to what I know about them. Estrella was a fifteen-year-old girl in my practice. I have known her since she was four, and she's quiet by nature. Her social anxiety intensified as she moved into her preteen years. Entering the large public high school, she felt overwhelmed by crowded events and found it nearly impossible to join clubs or sports. Concerned by her daughter's isolation and emerging depression, her mother brought her in to explore what options beyond therapy might offer support. She had already seen a psychiatrist, was formally diagnosed with social anxiety and depression, and was started on medication. While these interventions helped, Estrella was still not engaged in any communities or friends' circles and spent most of her nonschool time in her room and at home.

I knew Estrella's heart belonged to her dog, and truly to all dogs. She and I often met in conversation on this topic, a shared affection that opened her up. I suggested that service might be a way to help her feel grounded again and more connected to those around her. Still, she shrank from the thought of joining the community service club at school. "How about volunteering at the animal shelter?" I suggested. "There are so many dogs there that need a lot of love from a person like you." She liked the idea of being around lots of dogs and we laughed about how much more fun lots of dogs might be than lots of humans. (It is a popular opinion!) Her mom helped her apply to the animal shelter volunteer group, and within weeks she was accepted into orientation.

At Estrella's follow-up, she excitedly told me about all the ways she was contributing to the shelter—by doing laundry, helping organize crates and blankets, cleaning spaces, and taking the dogs into the yard to play. At the shelter, Estrella met two other teens she connected with over a shared interest in anime. She laughed as she told me about a litter of three playful puppies, all adopted by one family, and how she was asked to take on extra shifts because of how well she supported the shelter's work. The impact of this seva was profound; it became a path of self-discovery for her, and a way to feel connected to something larger than herself . . . a higher, universal power beyond her individual mind and its struggles.

Seva, though selfless by definition, carries medicine for the one who serves. For Estrella, it was the path back to herself, a space where she felt genuinely needed, valued, and purposeful. What began as an act of service soon became her weekly ritual, and ultimately, her way out of despair and the endless tangle of her own thoughts. When I see her now for her yearly check-ins, I see a young person who provides so much for our community and is confident in who she is. She was recently admitted as an undergraduate to University of Illinois, a huge state school that she might never have applied to due to its size, but that she was thrilled to be accepted into as a major in veterinary sciences.

Estrella remains a quiet soul who deeply dislikes crowds and struggles with anxiety, for which she continues therapy. She still avoids large social settings, but rather than seeing this as a flaw, she has learned to accept it as part of who she is right now. What has shifted is that she now sees her gifts clearly and knows that her strengths are useful and valued by others. And she is out in the world, sharing those gifts, sharing her heart and her passion for animal health, excited for her future. For her, seva is a medicine that healed some emotional wounds, mended her sense of self, and led to personal transformation.

Seva allows us to gain a deeper understanding of the challenges and struggles faced by others. Increasing our well of empathy leads to greater compassion and improved communication with those who are different from us, and in that way seva can lead us to more harmonious relationships. In a time when extremes and polarities are more normalized than embodiment of nuance, seva can be the salve that leads to a higher consciousness of our oneness.

Mutual Aid as Seva

Service, offered freely and collectively, is one way we can begin to restore what has been lost and rebuild systems of care that sustain us all. Meanwhile, mutual aid has always been the backbone of human societies and its erosion under the capitalist model has fueled much of the suffering we see today. My stance on capitalism may differ from the mainstream, but I have personally witnessed how a culture that prioritizes individuals as consumers rather than members of a collective can profoundly erode human health. I agree with Nancy Fraser's view that unregulated capitalism is cannibalistic, "programmed to devour the social, political and natural bases of its own existence—and consequently of ours."[5] The medicine to cure at least some of this destruction comes from seva and collective care.

Mutual aid is defined as an organizational model where voluntary, collaborative exchanges of resources and services take place among community members to overcome social, economic, and political barriers to meeting common needs. In movement work we often say that it reflects "solidarity, not charity," human-to-human support and collective action. Examples of mutual aid are collecting and distributing food to people who are experiencing food insecurity, providing direct financial support to individuals or families in need, offering temporary or long-term housing solutions, providing access to health care services, including first aid, medication, and transportation to medical appointments, offering legal advice and assistance to people facing legal challenges, or responding to natural disasters and other emergencies by providing immediate support and long-term recovery assistance.

Unlike charity, mutual aid is horizontal, not hierarchical; no one is "the helper" and no one is "the helped." It's about building collective power and trust. This is not new, nor a trend. It is an ancestral tradition rooted in how our communities have always survived, healed, and thrived together. Long before governments or institutions offered care, people cared for one another through forms of seva like this—help freely given, without hierarchy or expectation of return. This model is as old as humanity, alive in nearly every culture, and foundational to homesteading communities around the world. We tend to glimpse it only in times of crisis as an emergency strategy, but it is the unseen mycelial web of our civilization. It is the ancient way we have always endured, always made it through together.

When my parents arrived in Chicago from India in the late 1960s, they were completely on their own—no family, no friends, no welcoming crowd at the airport. At the time, the United States faced a physician shortage and actively recruited top medical students from India to train here in residency programs. They were part of a broader wave of "recruited migration" of health care workers from India, the Philippines, and the Caribbean; industrial and service laborers from Mexico, Puerto Rico, Poland, and Greece; and technical professionals from Korea and Taiwan—all shaping Chicago's labor force and communities in that decade. Unbeknownst to them, the airport that day was probably filled with many others also arriving alone to a vast unknown.

My parents were fortunate compared to many immigrants, as my father arrived with a promised job that included housing. They found solace in the company of a few Indian couples in their building, also young doctors, who quickly became their chosen family. Together they created a small circle of belonging—speaking Hindi, sharing meals and spices, lending clothes to weather their first winters, learning how to balance assimilation with their memories of home. Yet outside those walls, they encountered the sharp edge of racism: rude remarks, mocking questions about their names and traditions, offensive questions like, "Are you a dot Indian or a feather Indian?" At times, they felt unmoored, especially my mother, who bore the brunt of isolation while my father disappeared into tough hundred-hour weeks at the hospital. After my mom and her friends had babies, they shared childcare, kids' clothing, cooperative cooking, prayer ceremonies, home supplies, and cassette tapes of Hindi film songs; and they often cried together, missing their parents and siblings who were not there for these big life milestones. Those friends are still their primary community and support structure sixty years later. These are sacred systems built on trust, traditions, and kinship that reach far beyond blood—and must if we are to endure. When systems failed or excluded them, my parents and other immigrants like them turned toward one another, not away.

Mutual aid often rises to the surface in times of crisis, such as the one happening now as I write. A new US administration has slashed food assistance and affordable housing programs, unraveling decades of progress meant to protect the most vulnerable. In response, we are once again called to show up for one another through seva—to prioritize collective care and to help meet each other's needs. Some of the most powerful expressions of mutual aid are small and informal: a meal train organized by email for a friend in treatment, a church drive distributing winter coats before the cold weather hits, a neighborhood garden whose overflow feeds more than one family. Mutual aid matters now more than ever, because the crises we are facing are constant, layered, and global. Wars and violent conflicts displace thousands of people, forcing families to flee with nothing but what they can carry. Climate disasters, wildfires, floods, droughts, and hurricanes are growing in frequency and intensity, threatening food systems, water access, and entire homelands. Economic instability widens the gap between the wealthy few and the struggling many, while many governments cut the very programs meant to provide relief.

In moments like these, mutual aid and seva are not luxuries or optional kindnesses; they are required for survival. Mutual aid is making sure neighbors have food in their fridge if they cannot get outside of the house. It is strangers pooling funds for refugees they will never meet, halfway around the world. It is grassroots aid groups getting medicine to communities abandoned by official channels. Solidarity networks remind us that the fabric of society does not unravel entirely when institutions fail, because people still have the will and capacity to care for one another. Most importantly, mutual aid builds resilience. Each act of shared care, local or global, creates the relationships we will need to face whatever is ahead. In times when world events feel distant and indifferent to human suffering, it is these networks of compassion that keep us tethered to hope, to justice, and to each other.

Organizations like Border Kindness in Tijuana, Chicago Mutual Aid Network, Bed-Stuy Strong in NYC, and Cooperation Jackson in Jackson, Mississippi, are built entirely on volunteer coordination and trust-based giving. Delivering medical care, groceries, prescriptions, and housing support to neighbors, especially the elderly, immunocompromised, and low-income residents, based on mutual respect and solidarity, not saviorism, is the modus operandi of this work. And during times of crisis like the COVID-19 pandemic, citizen- and community-led responses were vital to the early response and likely prevented thousands of deaths. The data now reflects that these responses were so widespread that, in the early stages of the pandemic, they constituted a crucial source of immediate support and awareness, evolving alongside what was offered by authorities and health care professionals around the world.[6]

Tens of thousands of food parcels and soap bars were mobilized by a multitude of grassroots groups in *favelas* across Brazil and other parts of Latin America. In Cape Town, South Africa, a coalition of activist networks offered instructions for safe food and water distribution to communities on the frontlines. Restaurant Workers' Community Foundation offered relief funds and mental health resources to food service workers laid off or exposed during lockdowns. EveryoneOn and Human-I-T worked to close the digital divide by providing low-income households with internet access and refurbished devices so students could continue remote learning.

I was fortunate to meet renowned chef and humanitarian José Andrés, founder of World Central Kitchen (WCK), when we both presented at SXSW in 2024, and his talk was gripping. In the wake of the 2010 Haiti earthquake, he created World Central Kitchen, redefining what it means to provide emergency relief through food. Guided by the philosophy that food is not only nourishment but also a tool for dignity and resilience, WCK brings chef-driven, locally sourced meals to communities in crisis. Unlike traditional food aid models reliant on pre-packaged goods, WCK partners with local restaurants, farmers, and chefs to activate food economies even amid devastation, whether after natural disasters, war, or pandemics. During the COVID-19 pandemic, WCK rapidly mobilized in cities across the United States and around the world to address widespread food insecurity and restaurant industry collapse. By paying struggling restaurants to cook for their own communities, WCK offered a dual model of relief and recovery, feeding millions while preserving jobs and supporting local food ecosystems. In 2020 alone, the organization served over forty million meals in more than four hundred cities, proving that seva can be swift, culturally relevant, and rooted in justice. WCK's work walks the talk that service is not charity, but in fact solidarity. As Chef Andrés says, "We show up. We cook. We feed people. It's that simple." By showing up with hot, thoughtfully prepared meals in times of crisis, WCK reminds us that care is a right, not a luxury, and that feeding one another is one of the oldest and most sacred forms of human service.

These people-driven movements filled a vital vacuum, when government authorities and larger national and international NGOs reacted more slowly, taking weeks or months to implement programs around the world. Many of the pandemic mutual aid works were women- and youth-led responses. Although seva cannot lift the full weight of need, and citizen-led responses surely need robust federal and international backing, seva is the medicine that heals and restores, and it is how humanity survived this terrible chapter of human history.

Mutual aid is ancestral care in motion. In ways big and small, we can carry forward the "we keep us safe" ethos from generation to generation. It is in the actions of recipe sharing, food sharing, community fridges where people take what they need and leave what they can, tool libraries where tools are borrowed and donated, healing circles where mindfulness practices, yoga, and massage can be shared. This is how we reclaim the world we want to live in, the one that belongs to us all.

Seva as Preventative Medicine

At Northwestern University in the 1990s, I ran the youth division of the Northwestern Volunteer Network. I sought out service opportunities to continue the work I had started in high school with Students Working Against Poverty, as a coach with Special Olympics and as a teaching assistant for students with intellectual disabilities. For me, volunteering felt like an integral part of my identity as a person interested in the well-being of others, and as a young person looking to find where I fit in the world. I knew I felt best when I was doing this work, could share my empathic ability to listen and care for people, and could get out of my own head. It offered me a much-needed respite—from the relentless grind of being a pre-med and English major, the pressure of social climbing, and the peculiar intensity of college life itself, where thousands of young people live side by side yet apart from the rhythms of ordinary family life in the surrounding city.

The Northwestern Volunteer Network organization was huge—with over five thousand students participating in weekly volunteer activities around Chicago, partnering with dozens of organizations. It was a testament to the hope, power, and immense quantity of labor that college students lend to their surrounding communities all over the world, and I was so proud to lead a division that had fifteen programs for Chicago youth. I went to at least a few sessions at each of them every year to supervise, and very regularly to one, the Misericordia teen program. Misericordia is an organization that offers a community of care that maximizes potential for people with mild to profound developmental disabilities, many of whom are also physically challenged. Misericordia also serves the families who want the best for them, yet cannot provide services at home, by providing a full-care living environment. The demands on the staff there are immense, as the residents need full support to bathe, use the toilet, eat, and do any kind of activity. Many of the teens at Misericordia used wheelchairs, and on Wednesday nights our NU group would join them for wheelchair basketball. We were all roughly the same age but living in very different circumstances. The games were fierce—the residents were incredibly skilled at maneuvering the court, while we were often huffing and puffing just to keep up, hoping to make a pass or sink a shot. Those nights became some of my most meaningful college experiences, taking me off campus and out of the library, playing ball with people who became my friends and family over the years. (To this day, I'm still not much of a basketball player, but I definitely remain a better wheelchair basketball player.)

On any given day in Chicago, thousands of college students were out in the community—tutoring middle schoolers, swaddling and rocking babies born with drug dependencies, mentoring high schoolers preparing for college, or assisting overburdened teachers in crowded classrooms. These kinds of volunteer activities are invaluable, and communities across the globe depend on them. Seva of this kind fills critical gaps in services, offers care and support to vulnerable populations, strengthens community organizations, and often provides much-needed relief to overworked staff. Volunteers provide essential services that otherwise might not be available, improving the quality of life for individuals and enhancing the overall well-being of the entire community.

Some of the most difficult problems that we face in communities can be greatly helped with seva. Crime reduction is a lightning-rod topic, sparking heated debates that often reveal deeper tensions around race, class, policing, and the meaning of safety in our communities. Community organizers and researchers have reported for decades that one of the most effective ways to prevent crime is to provide more resources and support to low-income communities. In a panel study of 264 US cities from 1990 to 2013, researchers found that for every ten additional community nonprofit organizations in a city with a hundred thousand residents, the murder rate fell by approximately 9 percent, the violent crime rate by about 6 percent, and the property crime rate by about 4 percent.[7] These organizations play a significant role in reducing crime rates not by changing justice system policy but by providing more support for individuals who lack economic resources and rely heavily on volunteer-dependent community services, like after-school programs, leadership development, and substance-abuse treatment.

As a restorative justice approach, community service has long been a source of healing. Instead of focusing solely on punishment, this approach aims to repair harm and rebuild relationships between those who caused harm and the communities or individuals affected. Through service-based projects, like cleaning public spaces or restoring damaged public property, it offers meaningful opportunities to make amends, restore trust, and foster healing for everyone involved. Community service can be an effective alternative to incarceration. By engaging individuals in meaningful community projects, it provides a chance for reflection, accountability, and hands-on contribution.

This practical involvement not only supports personal growth and positive life changes, but also can help lower the likelihood of reoffending. Restorative justice is the functional and integrative medicine of crime—looking at root causes and prescribing solutions to solve them. If the medicine for collective thriving lies in the policies we fight for and the leaders we elect, then seva is the deeper remedy—a root-cause solution that nourishes all.

Medicines to Carry

Let seva free you from the isolation of hyper-individualism. Seva can be the path that draws you back into something bigger, truer, and more communal than the self alone. In this space of care, you will discover a lightness that softens your heart and the edges of your spirit. Seva is our evolutionary inheritance.

Practice mutual aid in both big and small ways. Mutual aid is not a radical emergency plan; it's how humankind has always made it through tough times. When you commit to meeting the needs of a community, you are not practicing saviorism but strengthening mutually sustaining bonds. Think about the ways you would most like to contribute.

When you feel lonely or depleted, reach for seva. If you feel that your heart energy is depleted, volunteering or practicing even the smallest acts of community care is a medicine that will always help you and those around you. No act of seva is too small, and you will notice over time that the more you engage in seva, the more you'll notice your own energy, mood, and sense of well-being rising.

Show up for others using your voice, time, or skills. Opportunities for civic engagement—for building a more just and thriving community—abound. For example, you might help people register to vote, volunteer at the local library, participate as an election judge, join or start a community garden, or help at the local food pantry. Providing necessary help and connections in the mycelial networks of the community will fill your own heart and spirit.

Practice small acts of kindness. Even small, everyday gestures—carrying groceries, lending a hand with yard work, or checking on an older person—support others and nourish you too, without requiring a big time commitment. Even putting your grocery cart back in the rack in the parking lot helps to create a sense of responsibility and loving-kindness for people who work at the store and those who are parking there.

SEVA SELF-ASSESSMENT

Assess your emotional compass:

- What breaks my heart?
- What brings me joy to help with?
- What communities or causes do I feel called to stand with?

Assess your gifts and capacity:

- What skills or knowledge can I offer?
- How much time and energy do I have to give consistently?

Assess impact and need:

- Where will my efforts genuinely serve others, not just feel good?
- Which community-led efforts value collaboration, not saviorism?
- Which local organizations or initiatives embody trust, accountability, and love?

MEDICINE SIX

Trust

Reclaiming the Body's Wisdom and the Truth of Connection

Move at the speed of trust. Focus on the critical connections more than critical mass—build the resilience by building the relationships.
adrienne maree brown, Emergent Strategy

Many of the patients I see have already given up on the health care system. They've cycled through doctors, collected diagnoses that don't quite capture their experience, and endured treatments that only partially worked. When they turn to integrative medicine, it is usually with the hope that something beyond the conventional biomedical model might finally bring some relief. By then, trust in the medical system has eroded, worn away alongside their hope.

When Mateo Sanchez walked briskly into my office, he sighed loudly as I pulled out my wheelie stool and sat down.

"Hello, Mr. Sanchez. How might I help you today?"

"Well, I doubt you can. Dr. Singh sent me to see you since nothing has helped my back pain for the last ten years, and he gave up," he said.

I scanned his list of appointments over the last few years. There were close to ninety, including physical therapy and rehabilitation, neurosurgery, rheumatology, pain management, primary care, orthopedics, and many more.

"I am a professional patient—I go to doctors for a living," he continued. "And they give me pills to try that don't work, but I take them and then I get all the side effects. So, who are you and what do you have in store?"

The wall of distrust was already high between us, but I was going to have to scale it, and I had to start immediately. I knew I would not have many chances.

"Thank you for sharing that with me, Mr. Sanchez. I can tell you must be incredibly frustrated and frankly exhausted from all of these appointments," I said.

"Yes, I am . . . I really am," he answered. His shoulders slumped a bit. "It's a lot of pain I'm in," he said.

"Yes, I hear you. It looks like you have been working so hard to find a way to improve your pain. I am so sorry that it's been so hard."

He looked up at me, and I met his eyes.

"I hope we can find a way together that can help."

"Well, me, too. . . . Me, too."

And so it begins. Before any history is elicited, before any diagnosis made, I sit and listen. That moment of presence is the first medicine. Healing asks for slowness and for attention. I am planting a small seed of trust. And it takes care and patience and time to grow it from a seed to anything more. This script represents an amalgam of hundreds of conversations I've had with patients.

"I have nowhere else to turn. I've been to the rheumatologist, the neurologist, the gastroenterologist . . ."

"I've had every test—MRIs, CT scans, endless blood work, scopes. And still, no one can tell me what's wrong."

"I can't accept that there's no explanation for why I feel this way."

"I am half the person I was ten years ago."

In each case, I see a person who's fighting hopelessness and despair and is continuing to advocate for themselves. After months of waiting, they arrive for this appointment, and I have a window of time to sit with them, to listen closely, to understand and interpret their story, and to mine for clues that might reveal a diagnosis or a path forward. The space is one of trust-building, sacred and heavy with cautious optimism. They wonder if I can help when so many other brilliant physicians have not, and I wonder this, too. This is where our work together begins.

First, this is not my story. It's not about my credentials, talent, or skills, though I have them. It's about the work of holding space—of offering trust and presence so another person can activate their own deepest healing. That work takes time. It cannot be rushed, written onto a prescription pad, or reduced to a quick-fix pharmaceutical. And only rarely does a test or procedure provide the answer. When I am with a patient, I am working within a field of energy—trying to understand where someone has been, standing with them in their pain, listening, holding, and, dare I say, simply being a friend as a relationship takes shape. My recommendations may or may not be accepted, but if I can offer something that helps them feel even a little better, then together we have begun to create a path toward healing.

In truth, the real medicine in this space is trust, which is critical to health. Trust is fragile, for doctors and patients alike. I've written from the physician's seat, but I know that patients, too, carry frustration, skepticism, and fear into every visit. They deserve transparency, curiosity, and partnership, not hierarchy. I always advise to bring your full humanity to the room. Ask questions. Share your story. Let your doctor see *you*, not just your symptoms. Healing begins in that mutual recognition, where both doctor and patient reclaim agency in a system that often takes it from us. The trust and the connections we build with our physicians about our most vulnerable and pressing concerns can determine outcomes. Trust is the foundation of effective care and without it, no protocol works.

But how do you build trust with someone you have never met? How do you build trust in a health care system where trust has eroded on both sides? Historical harms like medical racism and colonialism have broken trust in systems, especially in marginalized communities, and this legacy extends far beyond the United States. In India, the forced sterilization campaigns of the 1970s left a deep scar on public trust in medicine and government health initiatives. Millions of men and women were coerced or deceived into sterilization procedures, often without adequate information or consent. The legacy of these programs persists today, fostering generational wariness toward public-health campaigns, family planning initiatives, and even vaccination drives, as people question whether such efforts truly serve their interests or mask coercive population control.

The Erosion of Trust

Across much of Africa, legacies of colonialism continue to shape public mistrust of health interventions.[1] Memories of unethical medical experimentation—such as syphilis and vaccine trials conducted without consent—as well as the extraction of natural resources for European markets while local populations were left in poverty, inform a skepticism toward contemporary global health initiatives. Many communities still question whether international programs prioritize local well-being or primarily serve foreign interests and pharmaceutical markets.

In Latin America, structural inequalities are reinforced by extractive industries such as mining, oil drilling, and industrial agribusiness. Communities displaced from ancestral lands often face toxic exposures from mercury, pesticides, and other pollutants that contaminate water supplies and contribute to rising rates of respiratory disease, cancer, and birth defects.[2] Despite these health burdens, displaced populations are frequently left with fragmented or absent medical infrastructure, revealing the imbalance between corporate profit and public-health protection.

And within the United States, entrenched inequities similarly manifest in access to care. Indigenous communities continue to face chronic underfunding of the Indian Health Service and geographical isolation from hospitals and specialty providers, resulting in disproportionately high rates of preventable disease. Migrant farmworkers, whose labor sustains the nation's food supply, often lack legal protections, health insurance, and safe working conditions, making it difficult to secure timely medical attention. Meanwhile, urban neighborhoods—particularly those populated by Black and Brown residents—have been disproportionately affected by hospital closures and the withdrawal of trauma centers, leaving residents without emergency care and perpetuating cycles of health disparity.[3]

These wounds make clear that rebuilding trust in medicine and public health is local and global work. But research has also shown that it is actually the interactions with staff and medical professionals that can erode trust the most. Patients report skipping or avoiding care because they did not like the way the health care provider or their staff treated them, and after an experience where they lost trust, four out of five participants say there was nothing the provider or health system could do to make them return.[4] Having a provider who has empathy, is culturally competent, and/or looks like them is a top priority, and many are willing to trade off access to convenient, in-person care for longer-distance travel or virtual visits to get to that provider.[5]

So how did we get here? From where I sit, I hear several repeating themes: medical gaslighting, dismissing of lived experience, emphasis on data over story, and speed over listening. One of my most beloved patients of many years, Mrs. Graham, is now in her mid-nineties. Whenever I start to type into her chart, she always says, "Yes, make sure you take good notes, honey. This is important stuff and I know lots of people want to read about it!" or "There she goes again, writing her little book about me and my troubles, for who, god knows!" Her sharp wit makes me laugh, but it also reminds me of the absurdity of the level of documentation I am required to do now. From her perspective, she has come to see me so I can listen and try to help her, not type.

When my patients share their frustrations with the health care system, I believe them completely. I've lived through many of the same challenges as a patient myself. I also know my colleagues in medicine deeply—the ones I've trained with, learned with, and learned from—and I carry great respect for their dedication and humanity. I believe in them, and I love this profession. The journey to becoming a doctor is grueling: twelve years of focused study in high school, college, and medical school, followed by three to ten years of residency and fellowship, then eighty-hour work weeks in one's twenties, and staggering six-figure debt. Most who commit to this path are motivated not by prestige or money, but by a sincere desire to be of service, both to humanity at large and to each person who comes under their care. Ask any doctor why they are in medicine and I promise you the story will go back to a passion for caring for others, a desire to improve their quality of life. Among all the people in this world, doctors are not the ones seeking to undercut others, complicate lives, or disrupt anyone's peace of mind.

But the intense pressures that we all face to provide great care, in a system that demands a level of productivity better suited for a meat-packing factory than a medical clinic, has changed the way that medicine is practiced. The push to see more patients, and the demands to do so in ways that are dictated by the clock rather than the needs of the individual, means that some of the art of medicine has been lost. With the loss of time comes the loss of listening. Doctors do not feel protected by the systems they work for, and health care systems negotiate reimbursement with insurance companies that often do not cover the costs of the delivered care.

In Australia, over a third of physicians surveyed in 2025 reported facing retaliation from hospital administrators when raising safety or workplace concerns, with only 25 percent feeling respected by management—highlighting a significant breach of trust in institutional support.[6] In the United States, a 2025 AMA poll revealed that 48 percent of American physicians continue to experience burnout, with systemic issues, such as low Medicare reimbursement rates and escalating administrative burdens, cited as primary contributors. This indicates a health care system perceived as unsupportive of provider well-being.[7] And for patients, this translates to a doctor who might be rushed, distracted, or exhausted.

Before a doctor can build trust or extend a healing hand, the sacred work of listening and caring is already halted at the door. Insurance companies, the faceless empires of profit, have become gatekeepers to care. The questions from them are not "What do you need to heal?" but "What can we afford to cover?" Bodies are reduced to charts, time to quotas, pain to percentage scales, and health and healing to an allowable cost. And this is how trust, the most vital medicine in health care delivery, is eroded. I have come to see that trust is actually the altar upon which all medicine is laid. You just cannot progress on the path to well-being without it. But when care is brokered by institutions designed not to heal, but to delay and deny, the altar cracks.

Insurance, Trust, and the Soul of Healing

A patient cannot truly surrender their story when they feel the clock ticking in the room. A health care professional cannot listen deeply when thoughtful diagnostics must be translated into the language of CPT codes, ICD-10s, pre-authorizations, and denials. And care cannot flow freely when fear of litigation or the constraints of reimbursement are woven into the relationship. Insurance imposes the question of what will be covered over what is possible. Healing is not a commodity—it is a birthright that can't be preapproved or denied by an algorithm! It lives in presence, in relationship, in trust. To reclaim these medicines for all people, I must name this wound, not just as policy failure, which it most certainly is, but also as a spiritual betrayal.

And then I, and we, must dream beyond it.

Trust is the certainty that we will be cared for. That when we are most vulnerable, grieving, bleeding, unraveling, we will not be left alone, denied, or dismissed. If you are told by your insurer that your pain is not covered, your healing is too expensive, and that you must prove you are suffering enough to deserve help, this erodes something deeper than policy. It erodes the belief that care is a right. And for healers, too, that kind of a system hurts. Most of us do enter the path of medicine with open hearts, only to be pushed into roles that might resemble technicians more than witnesses, data recorders more than listeners. We are asked to practice with one eye on the chart, one eye on the clock, while fearing that the system will penalize us for giving too much time or services.

Insurance, in this context, is not neutral. It is an instrument of disconnection that can turn every encounter into a transaction, every patient into a potential denial, every healer into a time-bound provider. At the end of 2024, the terrible murder of the CEO of a health insurance company long known to be a top denier of claims led to an outpouring of stories on social media from patients. The stories felt both familiar and shocking: surgeries canceled at the last minute; surgeons forced to justify procedures to nonphysician insurance reviewers; cancer medications costing thousands a month despite coverage; and stroke patients denied hospital admission because insurance agents claimed they could be treated as outpatients. According to a recent survey by KFF, a health policy watchdog organization, nearly one in five insured adults in the United States experienced claim denials during a twelve-month period.[8]

If we are to reclaim medicine for all people, we must name this problem plainly: The current system profits from distrust. It divides and delays and devalues human life. I have seen how, due to the surge of distrust over the last decades, patients are less likely to accept recommendations that doctors make. And when it comes to public-health measures—such as cancer screenings, certain vaccines, and test or medication suggestions—doubting the information often leads to poor health outcomes. Edelman, a global communications firm that partners with businesses and organizations, completed in-depth research in 2021 showing that trust enables acceptance of evolving science. As health experts update their recommendations based on developing information, those with higher trust in the health ecosystem are 21 percent more likely to willingly accept the new guidance (72 percent vs. 51 percent). Those with lower trust are more likely to doubt the experts.[9] And so, we must not only reform our system of clinical care, but reimagine it entirely. We must dream up care rooted in relationship, reciprocity, and reverence. In many ways our lives depend upon it.

On top of a widespread loss of trust in the health care system, we're now facing an overreliance on social media "experts," where anyone can position themselves as a health authority, peddling medications, ordering unnecessary blood tests they don't know how to interpret, and prescribing what people should smear on their skin or drink each morning. The rise of these wellness influencers has only complicated this landscape. Being a wellness influencer can mean cherry-picking a twenty-person study, declaring a miracle cure for fatigue or brain fog, dismissing doctors as gatekeepers of hidden truths, and then selling a product with zero accountability. By contrast, being a physician with training and experience means something very different: it means guiding the person in front of me with care, discernment, and responsibility, not playing the role of supplement cheerleader to millions.

Many of us do enjoy wonderful, trusting relationships with our patients despite this challenging climate. These relationships come from presence before protocol, collaboration in care plans, honoring the stories and the tests of time. My eighty-year-old father's patients still travel from states away to see him. Many no longer need surgery, but they trust him to provide excellent, loving care because of the lived truth of their past experiences with him. He is often running behind schedule, and every patient knows why: he gives each person the time they truly need, and they themselves have been on the receiving end of that attention. They don't mind waiting.

Now, in my own practice, I experience similar trust and joy, the kind that comes full circle within families. I see young adults, some of whom I delivered as babies, preparing to start families of their own or even heading to medical school. I still remember caring for their mothers during pregnancy, and now here they are, all grown up! These moments are the most extraordinary part of medicine. These patients are like family to me, and I am like family to them.

Cultivating Trust-Based Ecosystems

The births, deaths, weddings, and funerals that are part of the life of a family doctor are some of the most rewarding parts of this work. There is so much good, so much growing in the garden of trusting relationships. They are the foundation upon which we can build health ecosystems that trust people to know their bodies, and trust healers to honor their calling. We must create spaces where healing is not dictated by insurance formularies, but by what the person in front of us truly needs to be whole. And we must shape governments that truly support scientists and health care experts, allowing them to carry out the work they are trained and entrusted to do. Because medicine is more than a science—in its deepest sense, it is a promise of care.

Health care settings are not the only places where we can cultivate a garden of trusting relationships. Rebuilding this trust requires a deliberate shift from the transactional care of getting people in and out, to relational care that is deeply individualized and personal. The data shows that culturally concordant providers, empathetic communication, and consistent follow-through can restore some of the relational bonds that patients most value.[10] Practical approaches include using plain language instead of technical speak and "teach-back" methods to confirm understanding, creating avenues for patients to voice concerns when errors occur, and ensuring care teams reflect the cultural and linguistic diversity of the communities they serve. Trust, in this sense, is the medicine, the medium through which information is received, treatment is accepted, and healing becomes possible—for both individuals and the communities. As Brené Brown writes in her book *Dare to Lead*, "When you think about trust, remember that it's a slow, steady practice of showing up for people, not a grand gesture."[11]

Cuba's community health system offers a strikingly different but equally powerful example of how trust can be embedded into the very architecture of health care. My studies of public health in Cuba in medical school changed the way that I imagined health care delivery. Unlike systems that primarily respond to illness, Cuba's model is explicitly prevention-oriented, rooted in neighborhoods through the *consultorio* (a family doctor and nurse's office that also serves as their home). Each physician is assigned to a defined geographic area, usually covering 120 to 150 families, and is expected to know not only the medical histories of their patients but also their social conditions, daily struggles, and strengths.[12] This relational continuity fosters deep trust: The doctor is a neighbor, a consistent presence, living in the same community as those they serve. Trust here is not an abstract ideal but a practical tool of public health. Because patients trust their local physician, vaccination campaigns reach nearly universal uptake, chronic illnesses are identified early, and prevention strategies, such as promoting exercise or food security initiatives, are woven seamlessly into daily life. I watched elders gather each morning for stretching and light exercise classes led by a government worker. I saw neighbors bringing food to families who couldn't make it to the market. During crises, this trust becomes even more vital. For instance, when Cuba faced dengue outbreaks and later the COVID-19 pandemic, the close relationship between community physicians and families allowed for rapid mobilization, contact tracing, and community compliance with public health measures. For health care systems worldwide, Cuba's approach offers a spiritual lesson: Trust does not emerge from glossy patient experience campaigns or technology alone but from embedded relationships cultivated over years, grounded in community life. It suggests that scaling trust requires not only reforming policies but reimagining care delivery so that the doctor is not just a provider but a trusted ally, given the autonomy their expertise requires, walking alongside patients in the context of their lives.

Indigenous, African, Asian, and diasporic healing systems all rely on relational healing. In these systems, trust is community-based and often spiritual in nature. Trust is woven into relationships, cultivated over time through presence, reciprocity, and care. In many ancestral traditions, the healer was not a stranger in a long coat, but a known member of the village, the one who knew your mother's name, your birth story, your childhood illnesses and your grief. When you sought their care, you brought your whole self—not just your symptoms. And you were *seen* as a whole person, not just as symptoms.

To rebuild trust today, especially in a world where modern health care has grown distant, fast, and extractive, we must return to these older ways of being with one another. In the case of Mr. Sanchez, we eventually got to a place where our work together felt grounded in ancestral wisdom. After I met his daughter and son-in-law at a few visits and connected with them on shared goals, pivoted to a telehealth visit on a day he was unable to get to the office, and provided some promising ideas and integrative treatments that had no side effects, he started to trust me. And from there, we were able to forge a path that could, and did, relieve his pain.

Lessons from the Natural World

Trust is not only a human-to-human practice, but something deeply mirrored and taught by the natural world. In nature, trust is not a contract written in ink or words; it is a quiet agreement, renewed each day in the rhythms of light and soil, wind and seeds, predator and prey. It is a living force, seen in the deep interdependence that allows entire ecosystems to thrive.

Many species engage in symbiotic relationships, where two or more organisms depend on each other for survival. Seva and trust go together. Snorkeling is a rare gift, one I don't often experience, but once in a while on a family vacation I get to slip into the sea and float above a reef. It always feels like a privilege—to hover, weightless, between sky and ocean, invited into this secret world. Below me, corals bloom like an underwater garden, fish flash by in sudden bursts of color, and the muffled silence of the water holds me in a kind of reverent stillness. Each time I lift my head to look up, I'm reminded that this glimpse into another universe is a borrowed moment of wonder, of life revealing itself in abundance. In the ocean, I feel both respect and caution, and move with gentle reverence.

In the magical blue waters of Hanauma Bay State Park in Hawaii, I once witnessed something extraordinary: the ritual of a cleaner fish. These small, brilliantly colored wrasses or gobies make their living by removing dead skin and parasites from other fish. Their "clients," often enormous and potentially dangerous species like groupers, eels, and even sharks, approach the cleaning station and wait, mouths open, gills flared, bodies stilled. They trust this tiny creature, fragile enough to be swallowed in an instant, to do what it has always done: offer care. And the cleaner fish, in turn, trusts that the client will not devour it, that within this moment aggression will be set aside for a mutual exchange. What unfolds is one of nature's most intimate dances—the client surrendering its most vulnerable parts, the mouth, gills, and skin, to the careful touch of another. The cleaner moves with precision, fulfilling its role, and when the ritual is complete, the client drifts away. For that brief time, the reef is a sanctuary for them, built entirely on trust.

There is something profoundly touching about witnessing animals trust each other without the language we rely on, guided instead by what is encoded in their primal DNA. It might seem like I'm anthropomorphizing here, but take a moment to consider that that this level of trust is written into their very being. Among these animals, trust is not a prize to be earned but is in the water they swim in; it's the assumption from which their interaction begins. Imagine if we started from that same place, with trust as the baseline, instead of suspicion. The whole way we relate to each other could feel lighter, less about proving ourselves and more about simple connection.

My family and I are great supporters and believers in the National Park Service. I love spending time with my family on public lands and waters because they are a shared inheritance, wild places that belong to all of us. On another journey, the five of us traveled to the vast, untamed expanse of Denali National Park in Alaska, where wolves, intelligent and deeply social beings, move through the snowy wilderness as a single, breathing organism. We were fortunate to witness a pack crossing the tundra in a steady, purposeful jog, both beautiful and unnerving, like a gang you wouldn't want to encounter by chance. The Denali park ranger explained that within the pack, every wolf knows its place and purpose. During cooperative hunts, they operate with stunning coordination, strategizing silently, flanking prey, anticipating each other's moves with an intelligence that seems both ancient and intuitive.

This isn't just instinct; it is embodied trust, forged from the first moments of life. From birth, wolf pups are nourished by the presence of elders who teach them how to listen, how to wait, how to protect, and how to hunt. Trust is not cognitive for a cleaner fish or a wolf; it is built into their nervous systems, honed by ritual and necessity, reinforced through play, discipline, and an unspoken understanding that no individual survives alone. Wolves pass down wisdom through generations traveling together across vast terrain, each member playing a vital role. The strong protect the young, and the experienced lead. The tired are waited for. And all are held by invisible agreements that they will not be left behind and that survival depends on the pack.

In the world of wolves, trust is not earned through dominance but lived through cooperation. It is the quiet, steady heartbeat of the pack. There is no illusion of individualism or "lone wolf" in the wilderness. There is an embodied knowing that "my survival is tied to yours." This truth, so natural to the wolf, is one we as humans are being called to remember: Healing, protection, and collective thriving are only possible when we choose to trust each other again. No one can be truly healthy unless all of us are.

Restoring Trust, Together

It is a difficult task to restore trust, but it is possible. When my patients have lost trust in doctors, hospitals, and the health care system, I do take it personally. Meaning, I take responsibility for how I am going to show up to rebuild their trust, even if I wasn't the one who broke it in the first place. I listen and make sure I validate what they have experienced, and I squarely agree that the system is indeed broken in many ways. Then I promise to do what I can to be of service. That is a promise I can keep.

As David Brooks writes, "Falling trust in institutions is bad enough; it's when people lose faith in each other that societies really begin to fall apart."[13] We can do our part to hold up our ends of our commitments, especially when we work in institutions. Restoring trust in our institutions and in one another requires deliberate, sustained action rooted in transparency, accountability, and community participation. Trust cannot be mandated; it must be earned through visible commitments to justice and equity. Here in the United States, for instance, the renewed push for police reform following the murder of George Floyd illuminated both the urgency and complexity of rebuilding institutional trust.[14] Programs like the Community Violence Intervention Collaborative, which was supported by the Biden administration, attempt to bridge this divide by investing in local leaders and community-based public safety solutions rather than relying solely on law enforcement.

CAHOOTS (Crisis Assistance Helping Out On The Streets) in Eugene, Oregon, is a mobile crisis-intervention program that dispatches trained mental-health professionals instead of police officers to respond to nonviolent crises, such as mental-health emergencies, homelessness, or substance use. Operating for over thirty years, CAHOOTS has become a national model, demonstrating how redirecting certain calls away from police can reduce harm and build public trust.[15] And in 2013, the town of Camden, New Jersey, dissolved its city police department and replaced it with a county-run force. The restructuring emphasized community policing, foot patrols, and de-escalation training. Since the overhaul, the city has reported a decline in both violent crime and use-of-force complaints, and the new force has focused on building neighborhood relationships rather than maintaining aggressive enforcement.[16] Each of these local reforms addresses a different aspect of the systemic crisis in policing, whether it's reducing the scope of policing, increasing transparency, or redistributing safety work to better-suited and trained professionals. When paired with investments in community health, housing, and education, these reforms can begin to restore trust, particularly in communities long harmed by over-policing and under-protection.

In health care, the pandemic revealed deep fractures in public trust, especially among Black, Indigenous, and immigrant communities. Initiatives like the Black Doctors COVID-19 Consortium in Philadelphia directly addressed this by bringing vaccines to trusted spaces like churches and barbershops and centering culturally competent care. Similarly, the Community Health Worker model, widely used in Latinx and rural communities, has reemerged as a powerful tool to restore relational trust in public health through peer-based education and advocacy. Civic engagement efforts also offer models for institutional repair. Participatory budgeting, implemented in cities like New York and Chicago, gives residents direct control over public funds and decisions, fostering transparency and a renewed sense of agency.

In education, the movement for student-led curriculum reform, as seen in campaigns to include ethnic studies and climate justice in schools, reflects a growing demand for institutions to be more inclusive, honest, and responsive to the people they are built to serve. When we are betrayed by a person or institution, what becomes clear is that maintaining trust is an ongoing practice that requires vigilance, transparency, and accountability. Without consistent reinforcement, even the strongest reforms and promises can unravel. We are also witnessing in real time that governments interested in their own self-serving agendas can rapidly break down the trust that takes decades to build.

Rebuilding interpersonal trust, meanwhile, is being nurtured in spaces like the mutual aid networks I described. Community-building efforts build trust. Hyperlocal, volunteer-driven systems of care, from grocery deliveries to rent assistance, demonstrate that when institutions fail, communities can and do show up for each other. Those meal trains, GoFundMe donations, check-ins, and other acts of charity all build trust between people. Their continued presence challenges us to rethink what governance could look like if it were built on relationships rather than bureaucracy. Restoring trust is not a passive return to the status quo; it is a radical and necessary reimagining of how we live and lead together. It demands we honor lived experience, share power, and build systems that reflect the interconnectedness of our futures. With trust, democracy and health care becomes participatory on the most personal level. Without it, even the most well-designed policies will always fall short.

Medicines to Carry

Deepen the medicine of trust in your life through grounding rituals. You can slowly and steadily improve wounds or betrayals that have made it difficult to trust others (or even yourself) through practices that rebuild trust. Trust grows from repeated experiences of reliability, and rituals can calm the nervous system and create safe containers for connection. Share weekly meals with friends or family. Take regular walks with a loved one: side-by-side conversations are often easier and calmer than face to face. Begin group gatherings with a moment of breathing or gratitude. Rituals build predictability, and predictability builds trust.

Be honest with yourself about your feelings related to trust. Journaling, as well as working with a skilled therapist, can help you process emotions and ease the distrust that keeps you feeling isolated. While certain life experiences may have taught you to be cautious, try to give trust a chance to grow in new relationships and situations, as difficult as it is.

Build self-trust by following through on the promises you make to yourself. Begin with simple habits—like making your bed each morning, stepping outside for a few breaths of fresh air, journaling for five minutes, or turning off screens before bed—and then move toward larger health or fitness goals. When you miss a day, be gentle with yourself and recommit. With consistency, your confidence and self-trust will grow.

Surround yourself with trustworthy people. Choose to spend time with people who are reliable, supportive, and trustworthy. Nurture the relationships that are grounded in mutual respect, honesty, and care. If you don't yet have people like this in your life, start by seeking out spaces where healthy connection is more likely to grow: community groups, classes, volunteer settings, support circles, faith communities, or interest-based gatherings. Healthy relationships can be built over time, even if you're beginning alone.

Practice empathy. Try to understand others' perspectives and motivations. When you respond empathetically over time, you become emotionally predictable, which can then help reduce misunderstandings, soften your heart, and build trust with others. (My friend Debi sends blessings to those who cut her off in traffic, trusting that they are in a rush due to an emergency. That is serious loving-kindness, and it protects her from feeling rage!)

Be willing to forgive past mistakes and move forward. When you hold onto grudges, it becomes harder to build trust—and it can take a toll on your body. Stress from unresolved hurt can lead to inflammation, pain, and a sense of being emotionally stuck. Be open to forgiveness.

Grow trust in the work that you do and the organizations to which you belong. Communicate more openly with colleagues and collaborators. Hold regular communication circles where individuals can openly discuss concerns, challenges, and ideas for improvements in a structured and respectful environment. Practice forgiveness if mistakes are communicated.

Establish a ritual for apologizing and making amends. Make space in your life for apology and repair. Many traditions, such as the Jewish holiday of Yom Kippur, set aside time specifically for reflection and forgiveness. We can create our own moments to reflect, take responsibility, and mend the trust that may have been broken.

REMEMBRANCE THREE

Medicines of the Spirit

Dance, Gratitude, Play

MEDICINE SEVEN

Dance

Movement as Memory, Joy, and Resistance

In many shamanic societies, if you came to a medicine person complaining of being disheartened, dispirited, or depressed, they would ask one of four questions: "When did you stop dancing?" "When did you stop singing?" "When did you stop being enchanted by stories?" "When did you stop being comforted by the sweet territory of silence?"

Gabrielle Roth, American dancer and musician, founder of the 5Rhythms approach

If I can't dance, I don't want to be in your revolution.

Emma Goldman, Lithuanian-born anarchist, revolutionary, political activist, and writer

When I pull up to the fieldhouse for Ayodele rehearsal, I can feel the drums before I even open the door—the air itself vibrating, summoning me closer. The rhythm catches my pulse and quite literally drowns out the noise of the day and the long drive. I step out of the car, and no matter how tired I am, my body somehow remembers. On the dance floor we start slowly, then gather heat—arms carving through the air, feet striking the wood floor until joy starts to rise up and lead. That is the medicine of dance: the rhythm does the remembering.

Ayodele Drum and Dance is a rare company composed entirely of women, drummers and dancers both. In a tradition where men usually lead the rhythm, we drum our own stories, layering djembe and dundun into a living pulse that shakes the walls and mends the heart. Each rehearsal feels like ceremony—where movement is memory, and joy is resistance. I feel deep gratitude for being invited into circles where Black joy is celebrated, where the shared stories are rooted in different ancestries than mine yet woven from the same human experiences. It is a privilege and honor to be welcomed into this collective expression with my sisters. Most Tuesday evenings, after long clinic hours under fluorescent lights, my head pounding, the ritual is that I tell my husband I feel too tired to go, and he always reminds me, "You'll feel better once you're there." He's right. I sigh, change, and drive an hour through traffic to the other side of the city. Because dance is the medicine that lets me do everything else—it keeps me whole.

I didn't dance much as a child. My parents didn't see it as a sport, and they felt "American dance" was too suggestive. Still, I loved dancing alone in my room, moving to my boom box and dreaming of a stage I never stepped onto. In high school, surrounded by girls who had trained since childhood, I finally found my way in through a daily dance class that counted as a physical education credit. For the next two years, I trained every day for forty minutes with a professional dance teacher and a live drummer. It was incredible. I stopped worrying about how I looked and let myself move freely, and was encouraged by my dance teacher to continue. At Northwestern, I squeezed in a dance class here and there between my pre-med and English Literature studies. I joined an amateur dance group and performed a solo piece that I choreographed to a Joan Baez song. My future husband came to see the performance that night. I had dinner with him after, and we have been together ever since, which I think had to do with him seeing me at my most creative and vulnerable, and his ability to bake pretty extraordinary cookies.

After graduation, I longed to keep dancing, but my father, ever practical, urged me to stay on the path toward medical school and keep dancing as a hobby. My twenties were a long stretch of training—four years of medical school, three years of residency, another year of fellowship. The day it all ended, I delivered my first child at thirty. Two more babies followed soon after. By the time I got my head up over the waterline—aware again of my body, my mind, my spirit—I was forty. I hadn't danced since college, except at the occasional wedding or dimly lit party. For a while, I felt sorry for myself, convinced the best days of my life were behind me, that I was trapped by my own choices in a life that had no room left for my own deep desires.

Then one morning, for no grand reason I could name, I told myself that chapter was over. After tiring of the self-pity, I admitted that the reason I wasn't dancing rested entirely with me. That week, I dropped into a West African dance class with Baba Idy Ciss, a teacher I had loved in college. When I returned to my car afterward, I cried for twenty minutes. It felt like an unearthing of a part of myself I had buried beneath the responsibilities of adulting. Then, on my phone, I quickly signed up for a two-month weekly session before I could change my mind, not knowing how I would ever make it work with three young children and a very demanding work schedule. But with the help of my mom and my husband, for the next six years, I went to that dance class every week. It became my temple, my place of accountability to my own heart, and a disciplined practice of soul tending.

There, I danced through grief, worry, and the dizzying weight of motherhood, returning to my body as more than just a tool of service. I reconnected to this incredible vessel that had birthed three children, to the hands that had delivered countless babies, performed emergency surgeries, and offered a healing touch to many others. My body felt like mine again, if not for the first time. A few years later, I screwed up the courage to audition for the prominent African dance company Ayodele Drum and Dance in Chicago. I mostly went to prove to my kids that I also take 100 percent of the shots, as I was always telling them to do—as in, you miss 100 percent of the shots you don't take. When Ayo Alston and Imania Detry, the directors of Ayodele Drum and Dance, called me afterward to offer me a spot in the company, I was completely floored. Knowing the company was mostly young women in their twenties and thirties, and even some teenagers, I told them, "I think you should know that I am forty-eight years old." There was a pause on the other end of the line. I hung in the silence, quite sure my confession was the end of that dream. Then Ayo said, "Well, girl, there is no time to waste. Let's do this."

Dance is not an escape; it is a return to the intrinsic connection between body and spirit and spanda. It is a necessary excavation of the self from the layers of dirt, dust, and judgment that have collected on our souls. Dance connects us to our source energy, the primal, animating force from which all life flows. Source energy is not confined to one religion or name; some may call it God, Spirit, Great Mystery, Prana, Chi, Creator, or simply Love. But whatever the name, source energy is the unseen current that moves through all things—trees, oceans, ancestors, galaxies, the breath in your lungs. It is what was here before your wounds, our collective wounds, before fear, before forgetting. It is the place we return to when we are fully aligned, fully alive, fully home in ourselves. Our ancestors carried immense resilience because they drew on countless practices that connected them to source energy. Dance was one of these, a medicine so powerful that it was among the first to be stripped away by forces of control.

Dance as Resistance

In the colonized and oppressed communities most of us come from, dance is a form of resistance and storytelling, carrying the truths that were forbidden to be spoken out loud. Enslaved African people braided their histories and stories into rhythm and footwork, and like Indigenous people around the globe, they danced in secret to preserve their connection to spirit and land. Even in exile and terror, people danced to remember who they were.

Traditional dancing, shaking, and chanting—essential forms of prayer, grief, joy, and connection in many cultures—were punished and dissolved by colonizers, oppressors, and enslavers. In West Africa, drumming and communal dance were central to spiritual ceremony and resistance, and banned by enslavers in the Americas who feared its immense power to unify and mobilize.

In Indigenous North America, powwow ceremonies—including the intricate footwork of Hopi and Navajo hoop dancing and the Ojibwe jingle dress dance, among many other traditions—were violently outlawed, viewed by colonial authorities as mysterious and threatening expressions of resistance. In Haiti and throughout the Caribbean, Vodou rhythms and possession dances became targets of Christian colonizers, who condemned them as dangerous prayers to another god. People accused of practicing Vodou (later anglicized to "voodoo") faced brutal punishment, their spiritual traditions met with fear and violence.

Bharatanatyam, one of the oldest classical dance forms of India, was a sacred temple offering, an embodied prayer performed by devadasis, women who served as spiritual conduits between the human and divine. Through intricate mudras (gestures), footwork, and facial expression, bharatanatyam told stories of gods, love, cosmic cycles, and moral truths. But during British colonization, the dance was condemned as immoral, primitive, and un-Christian. The devadasi system was dismantled, temple dancing was outlawed, and an entire spiritual lineage was nearly erased under colonial notions of purity and control.

In a parallel history across the ocean, capoeira emerged in Brazil as a martial art disguised as dance, created by enslaved Africans as a form of resistance, defense, and cultural survival. Its flowing, rhythmic movements—executed to music and call-and-response—allowed practitioners to train for defense while under the gaze of oppressors. Fearing its power, Portuguese colonial authorities criminalized capoeira in the nineteenth century, forcing it underground for generations.

Tango, too, carries a similar history. When tango emerged in the late nineteenth century in Buenos Aires and Montevideo, it was born in the port districts, shaped by immigrants from Italy and Spain, formerly enslaved Afro-Argentinians, and working-class communities. Its music and dance reflected a fusion of African rhythms, European instruments, and criollo (local) traditions. Because tango came from marginalized neighborhoods, it carried the stigma of being "low-class," its sensuality and intimacy signaling that it was morally suspect. The Catholic Church denounced it, and it was banned from public dance halls and respectable salons.

In all of these cases, colonizers recognized what these art forms truly were: movements of freedom, repositories of ancestral wisdom, expressions of deep emotional freedom, and spiritual practices that could not be fully conquered by anyone. They also recognized what they feared: that movement is medicine, and that in the collective joyful movement of our bodies, people remember who they are and remember their power. Though outlawed, most of these dance forms survived through resilience, adaptation, and the fierce determination of many strong individuals and entire communities to remember. Your ancestors, all of them, had to fight, hide, and persist, to keep these dances alive. When I dance with Ayodele, and for the decades that I have taken my daughters to their bharatanatyam and hip-hop rehearsals, I am acutely aware that our dances are not just for show or performance, but are part of reclaimed ceremony, decolonial practice, and embodied resistance. We feel this in our blood, in our bodies, and in our ancestral memory. What we cherish so casually now was hard-won, gifts literally wrestled into being by the struggles and committed joy of our ancestors.

These hundreds of years of destructive imperial practices did have consequences, and they took their toll on the psyche of our communities. This is a root reason so many of us are no longer connected to dancing, and why many communities no longer gather to dance during many rites of passage, or seasonal change, or harvest celebrations. These remembrances are no longer part of the weavings of everyday human life for many people. Sometimes we cannot even hear the call to dance, let alone the call to move when we hear music. Yet as children, we danced spontaneously when we heard music. I loved watching my little ones jump with joy when they heard the songs that they loved, no matter where we were. Think of your favorite songs—the ones that lift your mood instantly. Your body can't help but want to move with them!

Sadly, too many of us consciously hold back the call to dance or overthink it. Deep down, we are still the children who were taught we weren't "good" dancers, that moving our hips was inappropriate or provocative, that boys shouldn't dance, or that dancing with passion isn't cool. These lessons separated us from our ancient birthright: to move our bodies expressively. Our brains are wired to move when we hear music. If you lower your defenses and listen to the music—not to the mind, but to the music—your body will naturally move. Let it. Music and dance are the medicine!

Entrainment

At the heart of dance lies a powerful and primal physiological phenomenon called entrainment: the ability of separate beings to synchronize their rhythms, movements, or biological functions simply by being in shared presence. In physics, entrainment occurs when pendulum clocks gradually synchronize their swings; in biology, it appears when clusters of fireflies flash in unison, or when women's menstrual cycles align through pheromonal signaling. Entrainment emerges most vividly through music and dance. Neuroscience has shown that when we dance together, especially to a strong beat, we don't just move *with* the music, we move *with each other*. Our breathing, heart rates, and brain waves actually begin to synchronize.[1]

Even before we have language, we have rhythm. (This remains true despite evidence to the contrary at office parties.) Neuroscientific data shows that synchronized movement increases feelings of trust, social bonding, and cooperation. Infants as young as five months old can bounce to a beat, suggesting that rhythm and synchronization are hardwired into the human nervous system.[2] This ability to move together in time is not just enjoyable, but evolutionarily vital. Synchronized movement builds social cohesion, enhances cooperation, and reduces perceived pain and isolation.[3] It's why people dance at weddings, at funerals, in protest marches and healing ceremonies. In entrainment, our bodies remember their place in the web of belonging, and that web is rhythmic, relational, and healing. Moving together is an evolutionary protection that creates safety and cohesion within communities. Entrainment in dance conducts a spiritual and emotional resonance, a felt knowing that we are not alone. When our bodies move in rhythm, our nervous systems remember what colonizers tried to make us forget: that we are connected, that joy is communal, and that healing happens in the shared pulse of movement.

In 2024, after teaching about the neuroscience of dance at several conferences, I had the opportunity to teach a workshop I called "DanceMedicine: A Doctor's Rx for Joy, Movement & Healing" at South by Southwest (SXSW). This creative mega event is held annually in Austin, Texas, and celebrates the convergence of technology, film, music, education, and culture. It's a place where someone building wearable health tech might sit next to a poet or a DJ, and where new ideas are born in the liminal space between disciplines. In the midst of all this creative energy, I was invited to bring something ancient, embodied, and deeply human: the medicine of movement. I was delighted to share my message with so many in this space of cross pollination and cultural convergence.

When I arrived, the room was set up like a lecture hall, rows of chairs lined up neatly, signaling that perhaps they expected a talk, a slide deck, maybe an audience-centered discussion. But dance doesn't live in the rows of academia; it lives in circles, in rhythm, in breath, in eye contact, and in sweat—so we shifted the space, moved the chairs aside, and made room for a different kind of doctor-led workshop. Participants came from diverse backgrounds, representing many ages, abilities, and cultures. Some people had not danced in many years. I began with a short presentation on the research and power of dance to prevent neurodegenerative disease (which I will explain later) and how trust, rhythm, and joy help rewire the brain. I spoke about how movement isn't just exercise, it's a return to connection, a tool for regulation, a form of resistance, a ritual of remembering.

Then, we turned on the music. I had readied myself for the possibility of needing to coach and encourage people to stand up and move, but it was not necessary. At all. Within the first twenty seconds, every single person, from age twenty to eighty, was on their feet. Some were hesitant at first, gently swaying, while others jumped right in. But very quickly, something shifted. Shoulders dropped. Smiles emerged. The energy softened and rose up at the same time. You could feel the room exhale, almost a sense of relief and ecstasy taking over. It was a palpable and rapid shift. Many people met eyes and danced with each other for seconds or minutes, mirroring each other's movements, and entraining their dance vocabulary without words or thoughts, only joy.

Dance is the kind of medicine that works really fast, because it speaks a language older than caution and fear. It bypasses the thinking mind and goes straight to the spirit. It taps into our primal urge to move, to connect, to release. In that workshop, in the middle of one of the world's most cutting-edge thought festivals, something deeply ancestral unfolded. A room full of strangers were moving in unison, laughing, letting go, completely uninhibited. I invited some vocalizations into the space, and soon whoops and hollers and trills filled the room. Dance, in that room, was not art or therapy, but communion, a radical act of trust and remembrance.

As our time together drew to a close, it felt like everyone was flying, in the middle of the day in a carpeted hotel conference room. After we regrouped in circle, I reminded everyone to remember what this moment felt like in their body, and how they could feel this anytime they chose, simply by dancing. When the doors opened, people were laughing and talking with one another and sharing phone numbers, and loads more people were standing outside the room wondering what they had missed, what magic had transpired in conference room three. The workshop made the Day One B reel, and when SXSW started up the next day, the video clip of our wild dance party was everywhere. The collective effervescence—the healing uplift from shared resonance and the release of endorphins, oxytocin, and dopamine that comes with it—restored belonging, connection, and emotional vitality on that wonderful day. It was one of the most special workshops that I have taught, and it spurred me to continue spreading this message of just how effective dance medicine can be, if we simply open ourselves up to it.

Dance as Neuroprotective Medicine

Neurodegenerative diseases like Parkinson's, Alzheimer's, and other forms of dementia are marked by the gradual breakdown of brain cells and communication pathways. Many of my patients express to me that their main concerns about aging are firstly about losing memory then next falling and getting injured or hospitalized, and losing quality time with loved ones. These are very real concerns. Dementia can affect younger people, but it is far more common in those over sixty-five, with incidences rising dramatically with age. Until a cure is found, prevention remains our best hope and is what I focus on with my patients.

In our integrative clinic, we consistently recommend regular sleep schedules, a predominantly plant-based, anti-inflammatory diet, ongoing intellectual engagement, and routine physical activity. While these measures are unquestionably preventive, current research has not demonstrated transformative or groundbreaking effects from any single intervention. Because there is no single cure for neurodegenerative disease, growing research highlights the power of movement-based interventions—especially dance—to slow cognitive decline, enhance memory, and promote neuroplasticity, the brain's natural capacity to adapt and rewire itself.

A landmark study out of Germany by Katrin Rehfeld and her team compared elderly adults who participated in regular dance classes versus those doing conventional fitness training. Only the dance group showed increased hippocampal volume—a brain region critical for memory and balance—and improved white matter integrity, which supports communication between brain regions. The author states, "Dance challenges both body and mind, especially through constantly changing movement patterns . . . this may explain its neuroprotective effects."[4] While all exercise and movement can have powerful health outcomes, and should be a daily part of one's routine, only dance has been shown to improve this area of the brain. A meta-analysis by Dr. Teixeira-Machado in Brazil reviewed multiple studies and found that dance enhances cognitive performance, particularly in working memory, spatial awareness, and executive function—skills critical for navigating daily life and decision-making.[5] Unlike repetitive exercise, dance demands mental agility, coordination, and learning new patterns, which keeps the brain active and adaptable. In other words, when we do the same activity over and over, it may strengthen the muscles, but it does not create neuroplasticity, the brain's incredible ability to adapt and reorganize itself throughout a person's life. I think it is one of the most remarkable and awe-inspiring aspects of our biology!

Your brain is not fixed. It's always learning, reshaping, and responding to experiences, movement, emotion, injury, and even intention. The brain continually creates new connections between neurons and strengthens or weakens existing pathways, depending on how often they're used. It can even reorganize itself after injury or trauma, as seen in stroke recovery. Old patterns fade when they go unused, while new ones grow stronger with practice and reinforcement. You might notice that when you practice something new like an instrument or meditation, new neural pathways are forming and strengthening, which might make the skills feel hard to learn initially. But you can indeed "teach an old dog new tricks" if you keep stimulating your brain. Likewise, if you stop doing something you once did for a long period of time, like speaking a foreign language or riding a bike, the related brain connections do weaken, but they can be reactivated. We have one of the most sophisticated, divinely designed machines on earth in our skulls, weighing only three pounds, controlling our every thought and move. You never have to stay stuck, because your brain is well designed to change. It's a real miracle.

For people with neurodegenerative disease like Parkinson's disease (PD), dance is another medicine to add to their support system. More than one million people in this country are living with Parkinson's disease, and, according to the Parkinson's Disease Foundation, each year another sixty thousand are diagnosed with it. PD belongs to a group of conditions called motor-system disorders, which develop when the dopamine-producing cells in the brain are lost. The chemical dopamine is an essential component of the brain's system for controlling movement and coordination. As Parkinson's disease progresses, an increasing number of these cells die off, drastically reducing the amount of dopamine available to the brain. The primary motor symptoms of PD include slowed movement, stiffness of the limbs and trunk, tremors, and impaired balance and coordination. It is these very symptoms that dance may help alleviate. And while there is a lot of research on dance and disease, much of it is observational and not in the form of randomized controlled trials, the holy grail of medical research. Still, there is a plethora of significant observational science in this field, and any risks associated with dancing are miniscule compared to the benefits.

The acclaimed dance company Hubbard Street Dance Chicago offers the oldest Parkinson's dance program in the Midwest. The Parkinson's Project uses contemporary dance techniques to slow the progress of the disease, while providing a community of support for students. Classes are free and open to all, on Zoom, every week, and recorded in case anyone is unable to attend the live class. Most, but not all, of the instruction is from a sitting position, allowing for bold, expressive movement that does not compromise balance, often an obstacle for many people with PD. According to one participant, "The exercises increase range of motion, get you using muscles and joints that PD stiffens and cripples with tremors, and reminds you that, in spite of PD, you are still a creative, expressive and physically capable person. You'll also interact and dance with other friendly and encouraging PD sufferers."[6] Dance provides an invaluable outlet for joyful expression that PD can take away as facial and muscular rigidity sets in. When so much of our emotional expression lives in our gestures and movement, conditions like Parkinson's and dementia can narrow the ways we communicate and shape how others see us. Dance becomes a salve for the spirit.

One of the studies I rely on most in my workshops on dance as medicine is more than twenty years old, from long before the other studies I mentioned earlier. Published in 2003 in the *New England Journal of Medicine* by researchers at the Albert Einstein College of Medicine, it showed that dance has a unique impact on brain health. The study examined how leisure activities affected dementia risk in older adults. Of eleven popular physical activities—ranging from cycling and swimming to golf and tennis—*only* dance was linked to a reduced risk of dementia! The researchers stressed that no other activity combines cognitive demand, neuroplastic transformation through movement, and rich social interaction quite like dance. This multidimensional stimulation makes it one of the most powerful known lifestyle factors for reducing dementia risk.[7] While all exercise offers some neuroprotective benefit, this finding about dance is remarkable. Decades later, I still believe it deserves to be headline news: Dance—which is free, enjoyable, accessible, and something you can do anywhere, anytime—has the power to help prevent a disease for which there is no cure? That is a medicine, indeed!

A Radical, Accessible Intervention

For communities facing barriers to clinical care or systemic neglect, dance offers a low-cost or no-cost, culturally adaptable, nonpharmacological health support. And when grounded in ancestral movement practices—such as Afro-Caribbean, Indigenous, South Asian, Latinx, and diasporic traditions—dance is more than a brain exercise; it is a radical medicine of identity and remembrance, a return to lineage and belonging. From powwows on Indigenous lands and in community centers, to queer dance parties, to somatic healing circles rooted in ancestral movement—we can reclaim our power to speak, to grieve, to praise, and to heal.

Dance is where we process trauma that words just cannot reach. It is where we rewire the nervous system, reawaken pleasure, and return to collective rhythm. In healing justice movements, dance serves as both release and repair—a way to come back into relationship with land, lineage, and each other. Dances like Afro-Brazilian samba, Punjabi bhangra, Greek sirtaki, Palestinian dabke, Irish barn dance, and street-dance cyphers reclaim space and rewrite narratives of survival, affirming that our ancestors are still here with us and that we still remember how to come together. Dance becomes a form of embodied sovereignty, an insistence that we are more than what was done to us. Joy and movement are not luxuries, but medicine. And in every twirl, spin, jump, sway, and strut, we are becoming whole and embodied.

Dancing with others is a joyful experience, and the best part is, you don't need a community already in place to join in and feel connected. Many neighborhoods and towns have YMCAs, community centers, or religious organizations that hold group dances or DJ'd parties that are open to all. If you do not have a particular dance tradition from your family culture, these are great opportunities to join in. They are often nonhierarchical, nonperformative, inclusive, and rooted in the belief that movement is medicine. They hold space for grief, joy, ancestral memory, and liberation—especially for those whose bodies have been marginalized or politicized. At a recent cypher following my daughter's dance competition, I was delighted to see a ten-year-old girl jump into the center circle, right after an adult who had just won the competition exited. She was jumping and shaking and flailing her limbs about, owning her moment. The crowd went wild. We all recognize freedom when we see it.

One of my favorite movie scenes is from the epic 1997 film *Titanic*. Jack (Leonardo DiCaprio) brings Rose (Kate Winslet), who comes from the elite upper class, down to the third-class quarters to experience a wild, joyous Irish dance party. The room bursts with immigrant travelers moving to a driving, live Celtic fiddle; beer sloshes, boots pound, and partners spin in ways that echo the barn and ceilidh traditions. The scene couldn't be more different than the rigid, formal ballroom above; this is dancing that's loud, alive, and defiantly communal—a working-class celebration of freedom. They're unquestionably having a better time than the rich folks on the higher floors. It's also a moment when Rose tastes real joy and autonomy, briefly breaking free from the constraints of her aristocratic life, and seems to understand what she has been missing. Think of the cinematic dance scenes in *Footloose*, *Pride and Prejudice*, *La La Land*, *Slumdog Millionaire*, *West Side Story*, or *Bridgerton*. Even in the high-society dance scenes, there are defining moments of mystery and longing. They're the inflection points, where freedom of the soul and spirit enters the plot and bends it in a new direction. All Bollywood films have many dance numbers in them—it is an integral part of Indian culture!

My patient Jon's favorite community dance is the square dance, though he came to it late. A religious culture that frowned on dancing kept him away for decades, until his sixties, when he finally stepped in and found the joy he never knew he'd missed. Square dancing evolved from European folk dances brought to the Americas by settlers, particularly the English quadrille, French cotillion, and Irish and Scottish reels. As these forms blended and borrowed African rhythms, a uniquely American tradition emerged. By the nineteenth century, square dances and contra dances were central features of rural life, particularly in Appalachia and the Midwest, often taking place in barns, hence the term barn dance. Barn dances were informal, intergenerational, and community-based affairs. These events were one of the few places where people of all ages and backgrounds could come together to celebrate, flirt, socialize, and build a sense of local identity. Music was typically live, played on fiddles, banjos, and guitars, with a "caller" guiding dancers through steps—especially helpful since most participants were not trained dancers.

Today, square dancing and contra dancing are still thriving in many communities in rural and small-town America as well as in cities, and they are much more inclusive than they were in previous chapters in history. They are sometimes included in physical education classes in the South, Midwest, and parts of the West; as well as in Canada, Europe, and Japan, where enthusiastic niche communities keep the tradition alive. LGBTQIA+ square dance clubs are the latest arrival on the scene. Queer-friendly clubs have brought new energy and inclusivity to the traditions of this dance form. Jon enjoys square dancing because it requires no memorized choreography—just listening to the caller, following along, and having fun with people of all ages.

My friend Radha Agrawal created Daybreaker, a morning dance movement that channels nightclub energy—at daybreak. It's all about dancing hard before work with great music and community, but without drugs or alcohol. Costumes and playful outfits add to the joy, and Radha fully embodies its spirit. Now held in cities worldwide, Daybreaker is pure celebration. If it comes near you, go dance your heart out.[8]

Dance as Art and Storytelling

Some of you, like my daughters and I, may be dancers who perform for audiences. There is certainly a different sensibility as a performer than when dancing for fun, exercise, and as a medicine. The energy is directed *outward*, and we shape our movement to be witnessed, received, and interpreted. The dance becomes a communication, a crafted message meant to tell a story, convey emotion, or showcase form and technique. When you are working as an artist, you are learning choreography that requires precision, synchrony, and an aesthetic that your company and choreographer are trying to convey through movement. It is hard work, and requires hours and hours of rehearsal.

When we arrive at performance venues, our assistant director, Imania Detry, has taught us to walk the stage to understand where we will be positioning ourselves physically and mentally, attuning to the space's energy and developing a relationship with the stage and the empty seats, well before people arrive. There are strict call times hours before the show, elaborate makeup and costumes, and the inevitable adaptations that need to be made last minute that can be very stressful. While performance is deeply sacred, powerful, and vulnerable, it also carries pressure, and invites a certain amount of self-awareness and control, even when emotion is raw. The beautiful balance of these forces is what we work so hard to achieve in rehearsal. Every performing dancer knows the phrases "dancing full out" and "this time, with feeling!" Or, as Ayo says, "You got the steps, now dance it!" This means to move with full energy and extension, no marking or half-steps, committing to the emotional tone and physical demands of the choreography, and taking up space with confidence and clarity, as if you are moving like you're on stage. It's a whole lot to manifest.

To witness an Alvin Ailey performance is to enter a soul temple—where movement speaks beyond words, carrying history, grief, joy, and truth. Since its founding in 1958, the Alvin Ailey American Dance Theater has embodied Black resilience, beauty, and cultural memory while speaking to the universal human soul. Ailey, born in Jim Crow Texas, transformed the rhythms of Black Southern life—gospel, blues, spirituals—into a living vessel of art. He believed Black bodies, so often marginalized, could be sacred instruments of truth on stage. "Dance is for everybody," he said, "born from the people and always to be returned to the people." His most iconic work, *Revelations*, created in 1960, is a cornerstone of modern dance and is the soul of the Ailey company. It is the company's signature work and a masterpiece of spiritual storytelling. Set to African American spirituals, gospel, and blues, it weaves a journey from grief and bondage to release and redemption. It is more than choreography; it is a ritual of spiritual survival, a sweeping journey through suffering, baptism, transcendence, and communal release, and it becomes a kind of collective remembering—of ancestors, of migration, of the sacred bond between dance and deliverance.

The company so reveres this piece and it is so beloved that it is the last piece performed for every single concert. I cannot contain my emotion after *Revelations*, even after the twenty times that I have felt and witnessed it. It is the power of dance as a medium of communication, change, and vivid storytelling that makes it an extraordinary art form. The movement, the music, the lighting, the vividly embodied stories, the dancers' incredible technique and athleticism are all heart-opening and sometimes heart-shatteringly beautiful, in ways that words cannot describe.

Now, dancing for fun—or as daily practice, release, or spiritual care—is a dance of freedom. It's a movement for joy, for release, for no reason at all. It doesn't need to be seen to be valid, and there is no one to impress or necessarily anything to communicate. There are no steps to remember or an artistic vision to uphold, or such a thing as being good or bad at it. This kind of dance emerges from intuition, not choreography, and allows the body to lead, and the mind to follow.

When I bring up the idea of dance as a medicine into the patient room, I make sure to be clear that free dance welcomes silliness, slowness, and sweat and is often healing, playful, emotional, and deeply *felt.* When you dance for yourself, it can be wild, quiet, primal, awkward, ecstatic, or tender. It may look like swaying in your kitchen, jumping around in your underwear and socks, or even crying while you move your hips in circles to release tension. This is a medicine dance, not for display, but for remembrance, joy, and release. There's no hierarchy between dance for performance or dance for oneself. Both are powerful. Both are joyful. Both can heal. Both invite you to express and feel. You can choose whether you want one or both forms of dance in your life.

When Hemalayaa and I teach movement practice together at our retreat in Costa Rica, we invite people to move their hips first. We store so much of our trauma, our ideas of what is provocative or suggestive, or not for us, in our bodies. The hips in particular are often so tight after decades of use only for walking and sitting and rarely opening up. They are a storage center for emotions, especially deep feelings like stress, fear, sadness, and even old memories. This is partly because physical tension builds up there. We tend to tighten our hips when we're stressed, anxious, or trying to protect ourselves and over time, these small, repeated contractions cause the muscles and fascia (the connective tissue) to hold tension. The hips also connect to the pelvis and lower body, which is tied to our sense of safety, grounding, sexuality, and creativity.

The sacral chakra, known as Svadhisthana in Sanskrit (which means "one's own dwelling place"), is the second chakra in the traditional chakra system of yogic energy.[9] It's thought of as the energy center of emotions, creativity, sensuality, and flow, and is located in the lower belly and pelvic area, just below the navel. It connects to the hips, reproductive organs, and lower back. This chakra is all about our ability to feel, express, and process emotions, and our drive to create—whether that's art, new ideas, or even new life. It is also where we connect to physical pleasure, intimacy, and joy in the body. When we move our hips in big circles, back and forth, and get energy flowing there, the movement actually increases our ability to adapt, change, and "go with the flow" rather than get stuck in our minds. So beginning with the hips offers a beautiful gateway into dancing with yourself—into feeling the pleasure of movement and music while opening into a deeper sense of joy and release. Experiencing that expansion so quickly is a profound and fantastic medicine.

Medicines to Carry

Begin with a space where your spirit can move freely. To begin a daily dance practice, you do not need mirrors or specific skills. You only need a space where you feel safe to unfold—without judgment, without performance. This practice is for *every* body, in *every* shape, in *every* season of life. You are invited just as you are. Have the audacity to just dance for no reason!

Choose music that stirs something in you. Songs that carry memory, make your heart swell, or that feel like home or like fun—whatever music you choose, let your body hear it, and let your spirit rise to meet it. If you are more comfortable when seated, dance seated. If you are still, begin from that stillness. Movement can bloom from the smallest place—a fingertip, an eyebrow, a breath.

Commit to the 5-Minute Dance Meditation Practice every day. I offer this practice to every person I care for. We can all spare just five minutes a day. Let it be sacred, let it be silly, let it be alive! You will feel the shift. The lifting of mood, the softening of the chest. Within one week, you will feel lighter and more free and more joyful.

5-MINUTE DANCE MEDITATION PRACTICE

1. **Begin grounding.**
   Take a few slow breaths.
   If standing, plant your feet hip-width apart.
   Feel the earth beneath you.
   Gently bounce your knees; let your arms shake loose.
   Soften your jaw, shoulders, and spine.
2. **Let rhythm move you.**
   Feel the pulse, music, or silence rising through your body.
   Let your hips circle and your spine sway gently.
   Expand or contract as you wish.
   Move honestly, wildly, tenderly.
3. **Make sound.**
   Sigh, hum, laugh, cry, howl.
   Sound is medicine, too. Let it move through you.
4. **Keep moving.**
   There's no choreography, no wrong way.
   Your dance is the language of your aliveness.
   When self-judgment appears, keep moving.
   Breathe. Let rhythm lead.
5. **Remember and return.**
   This practice is not about perfection—it's about presence.
   Close your eyes if you need to go deeper.
   Each movement is remembering, returning to your body.
6. **Dance with others.**
   When you can, dance in circles, in community.
   Belonging is its own kind of medicine.
7. **Close in stillness.**
   When you are ready, come to stillness.
   Place one hand on your heart, the other on your belly.
   Breathe. Feel your aliveness.
   Thank your body. Thank your breath.
   Thank the rhythm that found you again.
   Go back to the world—refreshed, restored, and free.

MEDICINE EIGHT

Gratitude

Daily Practices of Sacred Reciprocity

Stormy or sunny days, glorious or lonely nights,
I maintain an attitude of gratitude.
If I insist on being pessimistic, there is always tomorrow.
Today I am blessed.
Maya Angelou, Letter to My Daughter

Whenever I saw my patient Anita in the clinic, both of us would cry. Our relationship was the holy grail of family medicine: we had become family. In the fourteen years she was in my practice, there was very little that wasn't said. She came to me in her late twenties, with her new life partner Miguel and a new job in museum design, hoping to start a family. Anita felt as a Black woman that her concerns had been minimized in the past, so this time she insisted that her doctor be a woman of color, and I was fortunate that she found me.

For Black women, the overlapping forces of racism and sexism continue to shape life-and-death experiences in health care. These structural inequities—not individual behaviors—drive the alarming rates of maternal and infant mortality. Her lived experience deepened this generational vigilance and caution in the face of care.[1] Being a brown woman myself, I was particularly attuned to her concerns and felt honored to have the opportunity to provide her the excellent care she deserved. Initially, Anita shared that she needed spiritual support as she navigated the emotional challenges of infertility, and we discussed bringing loving-kindness meditation from Buddhist philosophy into her daily practices. This meditation, widely known as metta prayer, is first practiced toward oneself, reflecting the ancient understanding that we often have difficulty loving others without first loving ourselves. Here are the simple steps:

1. Sitting quietly, mentally repeat, slowly and steadily, the following phrases: *May I be happy. May I be well. May I be safe. May I be peaceful and at ease.*
2. After a period of directing loving-kindness toward yourself, bring to mind someone in your life who has deeply cared for you, or someone who has caused pain and challenge.
3. Then repeat phrases of loving-kindness toward them: *May you be happy. May you be well. May you be safe. May you be peaceful and at ease.*

This practice resonated deeply with Anita. She gained considerable ease from it and told me that she added this to her already strong gratitude practice from her family lineage, which had grounded her through difficult times. Her practice, which had been passed through generations of her family, honored her African ancestors and was expressed as: "I give thanks to my ancestors, those who walked before me and made a way. I thank the spirits who protect and guide me. May I honor your sacrifices through my actions and keep your light alive in my life." She wrote this in a card she gave me and I tacked it up in my office, where I look at it often. Together, we co-created plans of integrative approaches to healing and medical care that supported her spirit, mind, and body, and were hopeful that they would carry her through a desired conception, pregnancy, and birth.

Her long-held dream of a family became real when I delivered her daughter, Imani. I continued to care for them both, and supported Anita through the early struggles of breastfeeding. Months later, when she found a lump while nursing, we quickly pursued testing. The diagnosis of advanced metastatic breast cancer was crushing. Side by side, we faced the hard decisions for urgent surgery and treatment, in what became one of the most painful times for us both. I never tire of the miracle of a new life arriving, nor do I ever grow numb to the anguish of reading the report of an "advanced cancer." It shakes the ground beneath us, altering everything at once. Anita came to it with fierce resolve, committing to an aggressive treatment plan in hopes of more time with her daughter. Previously, Anita would not even take a Tylenol for a headache, but now she gratefully received chemo twice weekly for months, enrolled in a clinical trial, and had the most invasive and expansive surgeries that were offered—all for an opportunity for more time.

As Imani grew into a toddler and suffered severe food allergies, we created plans for both of them to eat nourishing food that was simple to prepare during Anita's treatments and surgeries. We worked together on a plan for colorful, fresh, and lightly cooked foods for the whole family, and botanicals like saffron and chamomile that would alleviate the depression that was disrupting Anita's sleep. She managed very well, for many years. Anita met her treatment with clean food, daily movement, acupuncture, therapy, dancing, and the love and visits of friends. To her own surprise, she said she had never felt better. For a time, the cancer receded, and Anita's light poured out of her, uncontainable. She went to all Imani's school performances and recitals, designed large museum events and created beautiful exhibits, and enjoyed her partner and her extended family.

Whenever I saw her, she would always update me on the family and say that she was so grateful for all the blessings in her life. She was also grateful that cancer had given her the vision to change some unexamined habits and to see that her life was so very precious and deserving of gratitude. Her struggles remained, too: anger at the cancer, grief over the life she had envisioned but could not have, the reality of a shorter horizon. The diagnosis reshaped her ties with her husband, friends, and family, sometimes in tender ways, sometimes in ways that hurt. All of it lived side by side.

Over the years, I became Miguel's doctor, too, and cared for Imani as she grew from toddler to preteen. Anita made sure that she was at every appointment for her family and would always express how grateful they were to have health insurance and a doctor who knew them all so well. When her cancer returned, we moved quickly to get her into care. Unfortunately the cancer moved quickly as well. Within months, I was coordinating her care for in-home hospice with comfort care. With music playing and her family close—Imani and Miguel beside her—we cried together, laughed about Imani's bold fashion choices, and remembered how, as a baby, her cries were so loud Anita feared something was wrong, and after my thorough examinations I diagnosed her as a loud little baby. Anita continued to focus primarily on her gratitude for this life, this family, the incredible things she had done in her forty-four years, including being the first person in her family to go to college, overcoming infertility and raising a wonderful girl, holding her dream job in a museum and starting her own design business, and having a connected and loving marriage.

After Anita passed away, I mourned for her, for her family, and was depressed and angry over my inability to do more for her, so early in the fullness of her life, when she was so happy to be alive. It felt completely unjust. I have lost many patients to cancer, and it remains one of the most heartbreaking parts of this work. In Anita's case, our journey together had felt like a lifetime. The loss of someone who shone so brightly with love was devastating. Yet even in her passing, the depth of her gratitude for the life she was able to live reshaped my understanding of gratitude as medicine.

What Is Gratitude?

Gratitude is difficult to define. It is more than being thankful for what you have. It's not just a polite etiquette or a fleeting emotion. To me, it is a way of seeing, a way of breathing, a way of walking through the world, in relationship with what is. Gratitude is a conscious choice to focus on appreciation. It's also potent ancestral medicine. Long before gratitude journals and neuroscience studies, our ancestors practiced gratitude as prayer, as protection, and as manifestation prophecy. They gave thanks not only for what was abundant, but also for what was scarce. They gave thanks to the rain and the drought, to the harvest and the loss, to the visible and the invisible. Gratitude was a rhythm, a way to stay aligned with the sacred. Across every faith, in every sacred text, under every sky where people have lifted their voices to the divine, gratitude is present. It is a core spiritual technology, a way to remember what is holy and much bigger than us, to anchor ourselves in humility, and to speak the language of reverence. It is a revolutionary medicine.

There are people who have worked to understand the potency of gratitude, and why it is so important to our health. Psychologist Robert Emmons, one of the leading scholars in the positive psychology movement and perhaps the world's leading scientific expert on gratitude, explains that gratitude has two key components.[2] The first is affirmation of goodness. Gratitude invites us to recognize that there is goodness in the world—gifts and blessings we have received. It doesn't mean denying the hardships, complaints, or struggles, or pretending life is perfect. But when we step back and see the whole picture, gratitude helps us notice that alongside the burdens, there is also beauty and abundance woven into our lives. The second component he points to is figuring out where that goodness comes from. We learn to recognize that much of the goodness in our lives comes from beyond ourselves. It's not simply the result of our own efforts or something we can claim with pride. True gratitude carries a humility, a deep awareness that others, and perhaps greater forces beyond us, have offered gifts, guidance, and support along the way. It is a quiet acknowledgment that we are held, helped, and blessed by a web of relationships far larger than our own making.

In a series of studies, Emmons and his colleagues helped people systematically cultivate gratitude, usually by keeping a "gratitude journal" in which they regularly record the things for which they're grateful.[3] This is one of the most simple and basic prescriptions that I have adopted from this body of research for my patients. The journal could be your phone's notes app, a special little journal, or just a plain notebook. (I am partial to getting a special journal just for this purpose.) Set aside a few quiet moments each day to reflect on ordinary events, personal strengths, or the people you cherish. By returning to gratitude again and again, even in small ways, you begin to weave gratitude into the fabric of your life—until the practice becomes a way of being. Emmons's research reminds us that it is helpful to remember the hard times that you have had as well. When you remember how difficult life used to be and how far you have come, you set up an explicit contrast in your mind, and this contrast is fertile ground for gratefulness.

While most research studies on gratitude have been conducted with mentally well-functioning people, there is growing research showing benefits for those seeking mental health assistance as well. Emmons studied college students seeking counseling for anxiety and depression and randomly assigned study participants into three groups. Although all three groups received counseling services, the first group was also instructed to write one letter of gratitude to another person each week for three weeks, the second group was asked to write their deepest thoughts and feelings about negative experiences, and the third group did not do any writing activity.

They found that compared with the participants who wrote about negative experiences or only received counseling, those who wrote gratitude letters to another person each week reported significantly better mental health four weeks and twelve weeks after their writing exercise ended. This suggests that gratitude writing can be beneficial for both emotionally healthy individuals and those who struggle with mental health concerns. In fact, practicing gratitude on top of receiving psychological counseling seems to carry greater benefits than counseling alone, even when that gratitude practice is brief. Other studies affirm that expressing gratitude in this way rewires the brain to think more positively, which helps to improve our mental health.[4]

These simple practices, echoing those of our ancestors, affirm that frequent offerings of gratitude are a powerful salve for the spirit.

Gratitude as Prayer, Across Cultures

In many Indigenous and ancestral traditions, gratitude is the foundation of all ceremonies. You do not ask for anything until you have given thanks for what you already have. You do not harvest food or water until you have offered your prayers of appreciation. Gratitude is what opens the doorway—it is the bridge between the human world and the more-than-human world. The Haudenosaunee people begin gatherings with the Thanksgiving Address, which offers thanks to the waters, the winds, the moon, the animals, and the ancestors. In this way, gratitude is not transactional but relational, affirming our belonging to the wider world. As Robin Wall Kimmerer writes in her beautiful book, *The Serviceberry*, "Gratitude and reciprocity are the currency of a gift economy, and they have the remarkable property of multiplying with every exchange, their energy concentrating as they pass from hand to hand, a truly renewable resource. Can we imagine a human economy with a currency which emulates the flow from Mother Earth? A currency of gifts?"[5]

In African diasporic, Andean, Christian, and South Asian spiritual lineages, gratitude is often embedded in movement, food offerings, song, and daily rituals. Pouring libations, lighting incense, singing the names of those who came before—these are all forms of embodied thanks. Gratitude is a remembrance that we are not the beginning of our story. We are the continuation of our ancestors who brought us here and we are a part of the living lineage that can give thanks to those forebears, and also do better by them. In Andean traditions, Pachamama (Mother Earth) is honored through offerings of coca leaves, cornmeal, and breath, to say thank you for what has already been given, not for transactional purposes but as a ceremony of relationship. Gratitude is also at the heart of Christian prayer. The Greek word for Eucharist, *eucharistia*, itself means thanksgiving in Greek. The central ritual of communion is one of giving thanks for nourishment, sacrifice, and divine presence. Many Psalms are songs of gratitude and testimonies of faithfulness.

My family's spiritual path is rooted in Hinduism, where rituals have remained consistent for generations. Gratitude is expressed through puja, the offering of prayers and gifts like flowers, food, incense, ghee, and water to deities, ancestors, and natural forces. Whether it's my simple morning puja of lighting incense and a flame, or our larger *havan* fire ceremonies marking seasonal shifts and special occasions, where *samagri*, a mix of herbs and plants, is offered to the fire, and water is placed on the body to honor its service—we are offering thanks. Into the flames, our family and friends place the *samagri*, whispering "Idam na mama"—"This is not mine"—a humbling reminder that nothing we hold is truly ours. These offerings are acts of reverence, a way of returning something to the universe, a gesture of recognition for all that has already been given. In the ancient Vedic traditions, the sacred *yajna* fire rituals extended gratitude to the elements themselves: Agni, the fire; Surya, the sun; Varuna, the waters; Vayu, the wind. Gratitude is also carried in the rhythm of mantras, repeated chants to the gods and goddesses, each recitation not just a call to the divine, but a quiet offering of thanks. Every repetition is an act of devotion, a way of weaving gratitude into the fabric of daily life.

Food is prepared with sacred intention and offered first to the deity, then received back as *prasad*, a sanctified gift. This act transforms eating into a reciprocal ceremony of gratitude, recognizing that nourishment is a divine blessing, not an entitlement. Before every meal, it is common to give thanks not only to the divine but also to the plants, animals, cooks, and unseen forces that brought the food to the plate. Another widely held custom is touching the feet of elders, teachers (gurus), and spiritual guides as a gesture of deep gratitude, thanks, and respect. Touching the feet is symbolic of humbling oneself and honoring the path that others have walked before you, as a way of saying *I bow to your wisdom.* While I grew up with this tradition, when I joined the African dance community, it was a lovely resonance to learn that we close our time together the same way, touching the ground in front of the drummers and teachers to give thanks and honor for their service.

In many Indigenous traditions, before a meal begins, a small portion of food is set aside on a separate plate, leaf, or small bowl as an offering to the ancestors. This food is not touched. It is placed on an altar, by a tree, in the fire, or on the earth. It is not wasted; it is returned. This practice is an act of ecological gratitude and communion that acknowledges that our nourishment is made possible by those who came before: those who sowed and foraged, cooked and sang, fought and survived.

And in Buddhism, gratitude is cultivated as a way to soften the ego and deepen compassion. The metta prayer that was so beloved to Anita centered the healing power of this compassionate lens in the face of challenge. When practiced with breathwork, it brought mindfulness to the precious, fleeting present moment.

Breath, Rhythm, and Repair

Over our years together, Ms. Linda has told me the stories of growing up shelling peas on her grandmother's porch in Alabama, barefoot in red clay soil, listening to the rhythm of cicadas and church hymns. Now, decades later, she sits in the clinic with high blood pressure, arthritis in her knees, and a worn-out spirit from caregiving for her grandchildren and grieving the recent loss of her sister. When I ask how she's doing, she shares that every morning, she gets out of bed, stands up, and thanks the universe out loud for "giving her another day." Her body carries stories of hardship, but also memories, resilience, and rituals, and she remains steadfast and committed to living her life fully. Despite her financial stressors, limited access to fresh foods, and ongoing health challenges, she has a deep practice of gratitude rooted in her Southern upbringing and spiritual life. Her appreciation for being alive always inspires me.

In a world addicted to chasing more and faster, gratitude slows us down. It shifts the focus from what is missing to what is already there. It interrupts the myth of isolation and returns us to what Zen Buddhist Master Thich Nhat Hanh called "interbeing," the idea that all things are interconnected and exist in a state of mutual dependence. Nothing exists in isolation. Gratitude does not erase pain but holds it with kindness. To practice gratitude today is also to push back against a culture that tells you that you are never enough, never safe, never full. It allows us to see the beauty, name the gifts, and honor the sources of nourishment in our lives, and it works so well because it allows us to celebrate the present and be an active participant in our own lives.

Research in newer fields such as cardiac coherence, psychoneuroimmunology, and neuroplasticity have shown that cultivating gratitude can significantly alter heart rhythms, breathing patterns, and autonomic nervous system balance. When we are in a state of gratitude, measurable positive physiological changes occur, particularly in the heart and nervous system. One of the most significant markers of health is heart rate variability (HRV), which refers to the variation in time intervals between consecutive heartbeats. Higher HRV is an indicator of greater adaptability and flexibility in the autonomic nervous system, reflecting a healthy balance between the sympathetic (fight-or-flight) and parasympathetic (rest-and-digest) branches. In a grateful state, the heart's rhythm shifts from erratic or disordered patterns to a more coherent, smooth, and sine wave-like pattern—a state sometimes called "cardiac coherence."[6] This ordered rhythm has real implications for health. High HRV is associated with improved emotional regulation, enabling individuals to better manage stress and recover more quickly from negative emotional states, and enhanced resilience, allowing the body and mind to adapt to challenges and maintain balance under pressure.[7]

Dr. Rollin McCraty at the HeartMath Institute has demonstrated that cardiac coherence, often stimulated by feelings of gratitude and appreciation, also leads to better cardiovascular health, including lower risk of hypertension, arrhythmias, and other heart-related conditions. Improved immune function is another amazing side effect, since coherent heart rhythms influence hormonal and immune system responses via the neurocardiac axis. Through this axis, the brain influences cardiac function, and signals from the heart also feed back to the brain, shaping stress responses, emotional states, and overall cardiovascular health. Gratitude literally brings the body into greater harmony with itself, creating internal conditions where healing and clarity are more likely to arise. A real medicine for the mind, body, and spirit.

Gratitude can become a full-body experience that changes us at a physiological level. On a cellular level, gratitude initiates profound shifts toward healing. Chronic stress, which keeps the body locked in a sympathetic fight-or-flight mode, suppresses immune function, promotes inflammation, and slows down tissue repair. This is one of the greatest pressure points toward chronic disease. In contrast, states of gratitude and appreciation reduce levels of cortisol (the body's primary stress hormone) and increase DHEA, a hormone associated with immunity, and longevity. Individuals who cultivate regular gratitude practices have lower markers of systemic inflammation (such as C-reactive protein) and higher levels of protective antibodies like IgA.[8] These biological responses are not trivial! My practice is filled with people with chronic inflammation, a state that underpins most diseases, including cardiovascular disease, diabetes, depression, cancer, and autoimmune disorders. A gratitude practice provides a profound positive cellular shift.

Gratitude serves as an internal signal of safety, telling the body that it can shift from survival mode into recovery and restoration. When we dwell in gratitude, even briefly, we create conditions where cellular repair, digestion, immune resilience, and mental clarity are enhanced. Emerging evidence also shows that gratitude is associated with cognitive resilience. The NEIGE Study in Japan found that higher levels of gratitude among older adults were positively correlated with cognitive functioning and linked to larger volumes in brain regions implicated in memory and emotion regulation.[9] These findings suggest that gratitude may serve as a protective factor in the aging brain, even if the precise mechanisms are still under investigation.

On top of this tremendous data, gratitude also impacts the vagal tone—an indicator of the health of the vagus nerve, which governs many automatic bodily functions including heart rate, digestion, and emotional regulation. Studies led by Dr. Stephen Porges on polyvagal theory suggest that gratitude, by activating the ventral vagal complex, helps create a sense of safety and social engagement.[10] In simple terms, gratitude tells the ancient animal parts of the brain: *You are safe now. You can rest. You can connect. There is no emergency here.* This transformation affects not only our inner chemistry but also the quality of our relationships, our ability to attune to others, and our openness to joy. Thus, gratitude is not merely a mental attitude; it is a physiological reorientation toward wholeness.

Gratitude reminds us that no matter what we may be experiencing, we are not lacking, not cut off. It draws our attention to what is already here: breath, sunlight, a glass of water, a bowl of food, a good memory, the simple miracle of another day alive. When we say thank you with our whole body, we call ourselves back from despair. When we come to understand gratitude this way—as a biological, emotional, and sacred phenomenon—we can approach it with greater reverence. Gratitude is no longer a duty to fulfill, but a medicine to receive. It becomes a river that runs through the body: stabilizing the heart, deepening the breath, strengthening the immune defenses, and expanding the capacity for connection. Each moment of gratitude we allow ourselves to truly feel is a moment of healing, pattern-shifting, and cellular renewal. Gratitude moves us from scarcity to sufficiency, from fear to belonging, from contraction to expansion—at every level of our being.

For Anita, who daily grieved the terrible situation of being a dying mother with a young child, who cried and screamed and confided in me her feelings of guilt and anger, there was so much tenderness and connection to be found in her gratitude. She remembered that even in grief something beautiful was still holding her here, to her life.

Gratitude as a Bridge, Not a Bypass

It's important to recognize that spiritual medicines like gratitude can sometimes be used to sidestep, rather than face, the harder and more painful work that real healing requires. It's when gratitude becomes a shield against feeling grief, anger, injustice, or sadness, rather than a bridge to deeper truth and wholeness, that it can be a bypass. This can sound like:

"I should just be grateful. I shouldn't feel upset."

"Other people have it worse, so my pain doesn't matter."

"If I focus only on the good, the hard things will disappear."

These statements are not gratitude; they are dismissals dressed up in language that can actually suppress the parts of us that are hurting. An expression of true gratitude allows you to hold both grief and gratitude, anger and awe. This matters.

In a culture where mottos such as "Live, Love, Laugh," "It's all good!" and "Don't Worry, Be Happy" (for those of us who are a little older) can sound hollow, we need to get real about what goodness truly means. Especially when many things are definitely not good. How do we stay in the medicine of gratitude while there is so much suffering and injustice all around us? What if it seems like there is nothing to be grateful for? When I say my gratefuls at night with my family, I often wonder what my sistren and brethren around the world who are rattling from the day's bombings, killings, floods, earthquakes, and fires are saying at that moment. Do I deserve to be grateful when they are suffering? Can I be grateful for anything during a genocide? Should I be even more grateful that today it's not me? And pay it forward? I don't know. Perhaps gratitude in these moments is less about comfort and more about responsibility, to let it move us toward compassion and action. A medicine to fortify and sustain us, even in our rage and sadness.

But if we use gratitude to cover up pain, trauma, or injustice, we cut ourselves off from true healing. We also risk upholding systems of harm by saying "everything happens for a reason" when some things absolutely should be grieved, resisted, or changed. Gratitude practiced without honesty can silence necessary mourning. It can delay necessary action. It can erase real suffering, both personal and collective.

Gratitude practiced with open eyes and an open heart becomes a powerful medicine. It helps us stay rooted in beauty without denying the brokenness of the world. It gives us strength to heal not by numbing, but by loving more fiercely and fully. And it can change us and our relationships.

Gratitude is not meant to be a bypass—it is a deep grounding, a re-rooting in what sustains, and a bridge to wholeness.

Hardship: A Light We Carry

It is easy to speak of gratitude when life is smooth, when there is abundance, good health, and peace in the home or community. But the real medicine of gratitude reveals itself when life breaks open, when we face grief, injustice, illness, betrayal, or the slow, painful grind of loss. Modern life carries deep wounds: the loneliness of disconnection, the violence of inequality, the harms of systems built to value profit over people. For most, gratitude can feel distant in times like these, almost like a betrayal. But true gratitude is not a way of denying pain or pretending everything is okay. It is about finding, even in the hardest places, something worth honoring, as our ancestors did. It's a way of holding pain and blessing in the same trembling soul and heart.

A few years ago, years into my career in family medicine, I found myself walking through a season of deep exhaustion and chronic pain—the kind that doesn't just live in the body, but in the spirit. I was pulled in every direction, caring for patients, raising my children, managing severe and chronic musculoskeletal pain that I hadn't had the time to look into, all while trying to hold up a community of fellow healers and seekers. My salary had been cut dramatically due to budget cuts in medical education, and I didn't feel that my work in food justice and community health was supported or even acknowledged by my institutions. I love being a physician and I love my patients and my work deeply, so while I was starting to lose enthusiasm, I did not want to walk away from any of it. I wondered where the good feelings had gone. Day after day, I showed up for others, but inside I was bone-tired, and a little bit lost.

One frigid January morning, I sat in my car before clinic and couldn't open the door. For the first time, I didn't want to go in. My chest was heavy, my breath shallow, as the quiet edge of despair settled in. Through the windshield, I saw a young mother crossing the lot, her baby wrapped tight against her chest. The baby's hand reached up and brushed her face. She looked down, their eyes met, and she laughed, the kind of laugh that rings like a bell in a still room. It was fleeting, but it cracked something open in me. I cried and laughed at once—not from relief, but from remembering that life was still shimmering, even in the ache. I literally said out loud, "Thank you." Thank you for this simple reminder of beauty, even now. There was still so much to love—this moment, this chance to witness tenderness. I got out of the car and went into my clinic. In the next few weeks, I went on a temporary medical leave, to avoid the kind of burnout that might require leaving medicine altogether.

When we live through profound loss—losing a loved one, a home, a partnership, a marriage, a dream, a part of ourselves—gratitude just does not come easily. It comes slowly, like green shoots pushing through scorched ground. It blooms like purple fireweed after a fire has burned the forest down to ashes. It is not loud or triumphant, but rather quiet, private, sacred, a little hand reaching for warmth in the dark. It reminds us that even in loss, we are still tethered to life, to each other, to something enduring. We are still being carried, even when we feel like we are falling.

In the face of injustice and systemic harm, gratitude can also feel really complicated. When the world is so often unfair and cruel, feeling grateful seems like accepting the unacceptable. But real gratitude does not ask us to condone oppression or pretend away suffering. It asks us to see clearly: to name what is broken, and also name what is still beautiful, still brave, still worth fighting for. Gratitude can be a daily revolutionary medicine when it fuels resilience, when it reminds us that joy, care, and solidarity are still possible even under a heavy sky. Giving thanks for a single meal, a kind neighbor, or a glimpse of the sunset is not naive, or toxic positivity; it is an act of fierce defiance against a culture that would rather keep us numb, bitter, or alone. That numbness, bitterness, and aloneness are the very places from which we can do regrettable things, and also get very sick.

There are times when surviving itself is an act of gratitude. When someone has lived through abuse, through trauma, through unbearable darkness, gratitude may come later, in whispers. It might sound like: *Thank you for my body, even the scars. Thank you for the strength it took to stay alive.* Gratitude after harm is not about excusing what was done; it's about reclaiming life, about honoring the flame within us that kept burning when the winds tried to put it out. It's about remembering that we are worthy of healing, of softness, of good things, even if the world has not always treated us that way. In his book *The Myth of Normal*, Dr. Gabor Maté writes that healing from trauma involves reconnecting with one's authentic self, and that gratitude can emerge despite the trauma, through the resilience and deeper awareness it brings. He emphasizes that gratitude in this context is not about being thankful for suffering itself, but about appreciating the growth, insight, and relationships that can arise in its aftermath. He writes, "Gratitude is not a response to getting what we want, but to recognizing what we have."[11]

So gratitude during hardship is not a platitude. It's actually a survival tool. It's a light in the fog. It doesn't erase hardship, but it prevents hardship from erasing joy. Gratitude can be found in the smallest acts: a breath you chose to keep taking, a meal shared between two tired souls, a song you sang yourself to sleep with. For me, gratitude for my work gave me the strength to leave it for a while to get stronger. For Anita, gratitude kept her heart open enough to stay present with her family and her life's great joys, even in her grief and discomfort. For Ms. Linda, it kept her eyes on the beauty of her life, not solely focused on the pain of it. Gratitude keeps us human, even when so much can harden us. This is the medicine that remembers, even here, even now, that life is offering itself to me and I can choose to see the light still flickering.

I share this blessing as it was given to me. In Arizona, my family and I spent time on Navajo Nation land, guided through Antelope Canyon by a Native steward, where water and wind have carved sandstone into breathtaking forms. Walking through the canyon felt like sliding into a sunset-colored seashell, the sunlight angling in from above in narrow, bright columns. I whispered to our guide that I felt like crying from the intensity of being so deep in the earth, like in a technicolor womb of spirit. She said to me, "This is the Beauty Way," and then she recited this prayer of the Diné/Navajo:

In beauty I walk
With beauty before me I walk
With beauty behind me I walk
With beauty above me I walk
With beauty around me I walk
It has become beauty again
It has become beauty again
It has become beauty again
It has become beauty again

Medicines to Carry

Invite gratitude into each day. You might write a few lines in a journal, speak your thanks aloud with family, or hold a quiet moment of appreciation before bed. At night, let your heart sweep back through the day and gather the moments, subtle or bright, that reminded you that life is still offering beauty.

Start small. Identifying three to five things you are grateful for. Big things, small things—whatever feels healing to you is worthy of your gratitude. A single moment of appreciation—your breath, a warm mug, a kind word—can soften stress and reorient the mind toward possibility.

Reach for gratitude during difficult moments. This free elixir is especially healing in moments when you feel overwhelmed by anxiety, anger, or depression. You don't have to feel grateful to begin; you just have to pause. The feeling grows from the practice. Consider what you still have, what is not lost or broken, and what goodness is yet to come and worth fighting for.

Teach children gratitude from a young age. This helps them grow up with awareness of their joys and privileges. Start small. Help them to notice the warmth of the sun, water flowing from the tap, a good meal, a friend's kindness. Teach them to express thanks whenever someone does something nice for them. Each day, ask them to name things they're glad for and encourage them to express their gratitude out loud. Over time, gratitude will become part of their worldview.

Find your own personal ways to record gratitude. There is no right or wrong way to do this. Write, speak, sing, create something beautiful. Allow your intuition and your heart to guide you. Relieve yourself of judgment and stress, as gratitude is a daily practice, not a personality trait. This is a living ritual that will evolve with you over time. This revolutionary medicine is for you.

MEDICINE NINE

Play

Liberation Through Joy, Creativity, and Wholeness

Children need the freedom and time to play.
Play is not a luxury. Play is a necessity.
Kay Redfield Jamison,
American clinical psychologist and author

The drive to play is as fundamental
as our drives for food and sleep.
Dr. Stuart Brown, child psychiatrist,
founder, National Institute for Play

In West Africa, the elder storytellers and musicians who hold the oral traditions and genealogies of the tribe have the esteemed position of the griot. Living repositories of history and culture, the griots of the villages tell their stories through music and with beautifully expressive instruments. They might begin with the steady rhythm of the kora, a twenty-one-stringed harp-lute, plucking out melodies that sound like rain meeting sun. Or the beat of a talking drum, whose tones mimic the human voice, rising and falling with emotion. Then the griot speaks, or sings, and their words are not just words—they are poetry, genealogy, praise, and politics all at once. They speak of kings and warriors, of migrations and family marriages, of heartbreak from deaths and diseases, and the resilience of the survivors.

While continuing my dance training in Senegal with my teacher, Baba Idy Ciss, I was honored to learn several origin stories of the dances I was learning from the griot of his village, all told to us in joyful song and ecstatic dance. Baba Conde was not just a historian or praise singer, he was an improviser, a humorist, a trickster, and a musical genius. There was teasing of the village elders mid-song, mimicking of the gait of a child learning to walk, and sly proverbs slipped into a love story. There were times when all the women would stand up and dance and laugh together, and others when the little ones would be cracking up laughing and falling over. Baba Conde's voice would rise in mock-seriousness one moment and drop into an inside joke the next. A griot can make the entire village laugh, then cry, then remember something they had forgotten they knew, all in a single sentence. He even brought some of us who were just visiting the village into his stories, and pulled us up into the dance circle to play along with the fun.

This was incredible entertainment, but not only that. It was embodied wisdom. These origin stories became stored in my body and mind. A griot's gestured and expressive sharing of myths and legends taps into living rivers of memory, music, and ancestry. In many West African traditions, including among the Mandé, Wolof, and Fulani, the griot understands that laughter, joy, and play are sacred forms of release. They are medicine for people who have endured, for a community that must keep its spirit alive through hardship. This kind of play was not childish. It was the heart of the community, a form of deep connection and release. Nothing in those moments of play felt serious, because the griot reminded us that life can be really silly and unserious, and that it is often better that way.

We can witness playful behavior across the animal kingdom. Social media is filled with reels of animals having all sorts of fun. Ravens sled on their backs down frozen roofs and, once they reach the bottom, go back to repeat the ride. Crocodiles give smaller friends piggyback rides. Baby elephants use riverside embankments as waterslides to splash into the currents. Above Lake Michigan, the seagulls sometimes drop shells while flying and then catch them again midair. Play is one of the ways that we human animals can connect with our younger selves and experience a sense of innocence and purity. So many of my patients don't get a chance to play and laugh and feel some freedom from their struggles. This can contribute to our sense of being automatons that eat, sleep, work, and worry on repeat. And for activists working toward justice and equity, it may feel like it is against the code of conduct to play and have fun amid so much strife.

I learned a lot about this balance from my father, who is now eighty. He has been a cancer surgeon for fifty-eight years, and having treated thousands of people with advanced cancers, he has seen more death and suffering than most people. He has worked continuously for over half a century without any significant breaks, and he has no plans to retire. His playful spirit always shines through in his interactions with patients and the world. Pop is always telling jokes and loves pranks and general mischief. While his jokes don't always land with a zinger, he thinks they are hilarious and laughs heartily at them, which usually makes everyone else laugh, too. I've seen his silliness make even the most hardened people smile. The jokes don't change the prognosis, but they do remind his patients that it is okay to take moments during their day to laugh and feel joy. When sounds of laughter emanate from his clinic and ripple out into the hallway, the energy of the healing environment lifts. He has patients who have seen him for decades, even if they are no longer sick and do not need surgery. They just like the way that he makes them feel . . . like they are alive. Like they can still find joy and lightness in their lives, even when there is no apparent reason to be feeling joyful and light.

What Defines Play?

It may seem paradoxical to try to define play, as there are so many ways to interpret the experience. And yet, play has been intensely researched and defined. The foremost researcher in this field is Dr. Stuart Brown, founder of the National Institute for Play. He has dedicated much of his career to the study of human play: what it is, how it affects our health, and the devastating consequences if it is suppressed. Dr. Brown has studied animal behavior and conducted more than six thousand "play histories" of humans from all walks of life—from serial murderers to Nobel Prize winners. He is of the conviction that we are "built to play and built by play." His groundbreaking book *Play: How it Shapes the Brain, Opens the Imagination, and Invigorates the Soul* defines play as a state of mind that one has when absorbed in an activity that provides enjoyment and a suspension of sense of time. An activity can be anything from painting a picture to building a cabinet to raking leaves to shooting hoops. The key is that there is enjoyment and flow and no pressure. I think of it as a state of being where the imagination leads, the stakes are low, and joy has room to grow. It's easy to forget about play, but we need to bring it back to the medicine pouch.

Child's Play, Food for the Spirit and Brain

If you are a parent or teacher, you know that play is basically the work of childhood. Kids wake up ready to play! Anything goes: singing, playing board games, creating art, kicking or throwing a ball, running back and forth, jumping over a stick, car games . . . Kids play so much, and desire to play so much, that they wear us out. The appetite for joy and entertainment, curiosity and delight seems insatiable. Why? This medicine is a biological, emotional, and spiritual necessity. Play is how children discover the world and learn to practice being in relationship. When kids chase each other through a park or build castles out of couch cushions, they are doing more than "having fun." They are learning resilience—falling, failing, and trying again in a space where the stakes are low but the lessons are long. They are practicing courage, inventing rules, breaking them, and learning how to find their way back to each other.

I always say that my first friend was a middle-aged man who loved sweaters and singing—Mr. Fred Rogers. *Mister Rogers' Neighborhood* originally aired from 1968 to 2001 on PBS, and it was a gentle revolution in media, a sanctuary for childhood, and a timeless example of how kindness, presence, and emotional intelligence can be radical. Fred Rogers was an ordained minister, musician, puppeteer, and fierce advocate for the emotional lives of children. He spoke directly to children in his show, and he certainly spoke directly to me. He was the one I would play beside in front of the TV at home, in the mid-to-late seventies and early eighties, and he was the one who taught me that I was unique, that my feelings were normal and manageable, and that he liked me just the way I was. Songs like "You Are Special" helped me create a sense of self-worth that I craved. Fred Rogers revealed just how deeply being present with children can shape lives, while embodying a gentle, powerful vision of positive masculinity.

To this day, I change out of my "outside clothes" into home clothes when I get back from work, because of him. One of the most enduring lessons he taught us is that play is a vital, rich, and necessary part of life. "Play is often talked about as if it were a relief from serious learning," Rogers said. "But for children, play is serious learning. Play is really the work of childhood."[1] Mr. Rogers believed that play was not just a pastime, but a biological, emotional, and cultural necessity for humans across the lifespan. A medicine for all people.

Our children were fortunate to have their earliest school experiences in a play-based preschool, Oak Grove School in Ojai, California. They spent hours in meadows of tall grass, exploring the hilly land and large, flat glacial rocks; climbing and swinging on the playset; enjoying simple snacks in the teahouse while singing songs together; playing with sweet, uncomplicated toys like push wagons and blocks; and shoveling in the sand. Their day was busy and tiring and filled with learning. The surrounding pomegranate and plum trees and the lovely tilt of the morning sun shining through the live oak trees lent a certain magical feeling to the preschool playground.

Our eldest child, Sahaara, was a quiet toddler, ever observant and very happy to be on the periphery rather than in the center of a group. She never went down the shiny metal slide, but she absolutely loved watching the other kids go down with abandon. She seemed as joyous as they were, standing at the top watching her friends slide down, or at the bottom laughing as they fell into the sand. We worried, as parents do, that she was not confident, that she was fearful of taking a small risk, and, worst of all, that she did not feel she deserved to have fun. The incredible school psychologist and teacher Carol Castanon reassured us, "What a gift that she can get so much enjoyment from being in community and from her place of safety! This is how she is learning!" As a new mother, I had to write this on a Post-it and keep it on the wall above my desk so that I could keep reminding myself of this perspective. And it did turn out to be true.

Sahaara was soaking it all in, through observation, through joy, through proximity to the experience of others. She was practicing relational play, the kind that doesn't need to be loud or center stage to be meaningful. She was watching how others moved, how they laughed, how they landed. She was gathering data, storing courage, building her own readiness from a place of deep attunement. And she was happy, radiantly so. In time, she did go down the slide. No fanfare, no prompting. Just a quiet morning, a moment of her own choosing. Her joy in that moment wasn't greater than before; it was simply different, and rooted in self-trust. And she has continued exactly like this through her childhood and adolescence—with no fanfare or prompting—right to this moment as she graduates from college. Her play personality taught me more about quiet joy and inner readiness than any book or lecture ever could.

Developmentally, play is how we grow. For children, play is the foundation of learning. Through make-believe, role-play, sports and physical games, they learn boundaries, language, problem-solving, and social skills. It is vital that children have safe spaces to play and opportunities to socialize with other children. Extensive research has demonstrated the critical importance of play for children's development across different areas, with some experts considering it to be as important as basic needs like sleep, water, and nutrition. Under the United Nations Convention on the

Rights of the Child, it has been codified that children have a right to play.[2] Considering the neurodevelopmental impact play has on children, the COVID-19 pandemic was a particularly devastating time for young ones, when play was predominantly limited to the home environment. Studies from several countries, including England, Korea, Mexico, Canada, and the United States, confirmed that children had much less play time during the pandemic, when outdoor activities were more restricted, and that older children had more screen-time play than outdoor play.[3]

As silly as it sounds, sometimes we really do need a reminder that play is fun. Daily life doesn't always leave much room for fun. I laughed one day at the grocery store when I saw a young woman wearing a hoodie that said it best: "It's not that serious."

Your Brain on Play

Play is hardwired into us. Our ancestors engaged in sport and physical play like wrestling, play-fighting, and other forms of physical contact, which also served as ways to connect through touch. Like all mammals, humans have an ancient biological drive to play that evolved over millions of years. Deep in the midbrain are specialized neural circuits designed just for this purpose, waiting to be lit up by something playful in our environment. The late neuroscientist Jaak Panksepp was a pioneer in the study of emotions—not just in humans, but across species. His groundbreaking work revealed that play is not a luxury or a learned behavior, but something deeply rooted in the brain's most ancient structures. He showed that play arises from the subcortical regions of the brain—the areas responsible for our most basic instincts—suggesting that the drive to play evolved very early in our history and is as fundamental as the need for food or sleep.[4]

In the 1990s, Panksepp helped establish the field of affective neuroscience, which explores how emotions are generated in the brain. His 1998 book *Affective Neuroscience* became a foundational text in the field, mapping out the primal emotional systems that underlie human experience. Over his career, he published more than three hundred scientific papers exploring how emotion, especially play, shapes learning, development, and social connection. In his 2013 TEDx talk, Panksepp explained that from birth, our brains carry seven primary emotional circuits: seeking, rage, fear, care, lust, love, panic, and play. These primal emotions are with us at birth, pre-wired in our midbrain, an ancient part of the human brain.[5] Known as the "rat tickler," Panksepp's most famous research focused on rats, where he observed that they not only played together, but even emitted high-pitched vocalizations—what he called "rat laughter"—during playful wrestling. He also showed that when deprived of play, animals experienced frustration and stress, much like they would when denied food or water.

Panksepp's investigations of the behavior of rats revealed that play impulses emerge primarily not from the neocortex, the latest addition to our thinking human brain, but from deep within the ancient brain stem. These primordial impulses to play thrived and deepened with social evolution. Panksepp discovered, for example, how rats that had been isolated for a time played with a special verve when rehoused with their rodent society. And what I found most fascinating and troubling was that rats deprived of nurture and playful experience in their infancy grew up as particularly unsuccessful adults who were unable to recognize threat from play-signaling and were awkward at or even incapable of mating. These emotional deficits would have threatened their survival and their ability to pass on their genes in the natural world. These findings challenged the long-held belief that play was trivial or optional. Panksepp argued that play is essential for healthy brain development and emotional regulation. His work suggested that it plays a key role in building social bonds and fostering cognitive growth, and may even help children with ADHD by promoting focus, flexibility, and emotional balance.

Ultimately, these scientific inquiries reveal that we are deeply wired to play, in our oldest cellular memory. And if we don't get enough of it, there can be consequences for our health and healing.

Play Deprivation

When the brain circuits are triggered by the sight of a ball, the wiggle of a puppy, or the spark of a fun companion, they send signals that pull us toward interaction. We feel a natural urge to reach out, to laugh, to move, to connect. We toss the ball, cuddle the puppy, or banter with a friend, not because we're told to, but because something in us knows *this is good*. Play is life-giving. When we don't get it, our brains and our lives seem to make up for the lack in unconscious, maladaptive ways.

The eminent play scholar Joe L. Frost, in his powerful book *A History of Childhood Play and Play Environments*, warns that the disappearance, suppression, or over-regulation of play in the late twentieth and early twenty-first centuries has created a crisis that threatens not just the well-being of individual children, but the very social fabric of future generations.[6] Frost meticulously traces how economic shifts, urban development, fear-based parenting, and academic pressures have squeezed unstructured, imaginative play to the margins. Children no longer have the time, space, or cultural permission to play freely or to wander and then get lost, to create, to make a joyful mess of their own learning.

But the consequences are not limited to children. When play disappears, emotional flexibility, social trust, and problem-solving shrink. Rates of anxiety, depression, and isolation increase, not only in young people, but in the adults they become. The "play deficit" shows up in rigidity, emotional numbness, poor impulse control, and a disconnection from community. In a particularly disturbing example, Dr. Stuart Brown echoed these findings when he traced the life of the University of Texas tower mass shooter, Charles Whitman, and discovered a childhood largely devoid of healthy, joyful play. Brown's subsequent research into incarcerated individuals involved in reckless or violent behavior revealed a common thread: a longstanding absence of play.[7] In contrast, people who had experienced rough-and-tumble, imaginative, and relational play often displayed greater emotional regulation, adaptability, and social connectedness. One can't help but question how much play some of today's world leaders ever knew as children, given the devastating consequences of power wielded by those who never learned emotional regulation.

Play deprivation is not just about a lack of recess or fewer toys; it is a deeper loss. It is the absence of self-guided wonder, of relationships built through laughter and risk-taking, of learning that comes through freedom instead of fear. It represents a wound to our collective nervous system, and if left unaddressed, it shapes entire generations to be more anxious, less collaborative, and less able to navigate uncertainty with grace. To heal this wound, we must re-sanctify play, not only for children, but for everyone. We must restore the spaces, time, and trust that allow curiosity, movement, and imagination to flourish. As we see from the research, play is not childish; it is primal, biologically coded, and developmentally irreplaceable. Reclaiming play is a necessary act of cultural repair.

Screen Time as Play?

For many people, but especially adults, screen time is the closest thing we get to play. Scrolling through funny dog memes and laughing, watching a favorite series, playing Candy Crush, or getting lost in online shopping rabbit holes can feel like moments of exhale, a reprieve from the grind of work, caregiving, or burnout. In a world that so often demands constant productivity, screen time can feel like a refuge, resting the body while keeping the mind engaged. It is a form of modern escapism that can be comforting, even joyful. Sometimes screen time carries the spirit of play: a game that delights, a viral video that sparks laughter, or a live-streamed dance party. I love learning dance sequences from my favorite dancers on Instagram, playing family Wordle with my kids who are in different states, and watching hilarious voice-over dog videos.

For adults who didn't grow up with permission to play freely, or who live with chronic stress or isolation, these moments can offer connection, imagination, and even healing. Experts note that social play through digital platforms—particularly among older adults and people with disabilities—can improve mood, foster connection, and reduce feelings of loneliness. Online games, group video calls, and interactive digital experiences create opportunities for laughter, collaboration, and shared achievements, even across long distances. For populations that may face mobility limitations or reduced access to in-person gatherings, digital play offers an accessible and often joyful form of engagement. Older adults who participate in online gaming communities often report greater psychological well-being and reduced feelings of social isolation.[8] Likewise, research with people living with disabilities shows that digital play environments can do more than lift mood—they foster agency and create a sense of belonging within a wider community.[9] In this way, technology, so often maligned for its isolating effects, can also serve as a bridge to belonging and fun.

Of course, screen time does not always equal play. What looks like joy can, at times, mask itself as numbing, endless scrolling, or distraction. True play is active, embodied, creative, and relational. It engages the imagination and regulates the nervous system. Prolonged screen use, especially passive scrolling, often has the opposite effect: draining attention, reducing movement, increasing fatigue, and lowering mood. It offers the illusion of rest, but not the repair that real play can provide. Observing others dancing, making music, or sharing laughter offers a glimpse of joy through the screen, but it will never match the full-bodied experience of moving, creating, and connecting yourself.

I'll always champion play in real life, but it's clear that TikTok has sparked a new wave of playfulness. Dance challenges, jokes, lip-syncs, voice-overs, and silly scenarios invite people to invest in joy. Some of my patients have even rediscovered the fun of moving their bodies through these social media trends. In countless ways, social media has brought play right into our hands. People get to move their bodies without pressure—just for fun, with laughter, and without worrying about being perfect. Personally, I love the fast art tutorials on upcycled fashion, clay miniatures, or thrift-store makeovers. It's everyday creativity—messy, fun, and available to anyone who wants to try. Think of BookTok, "cottagecore," PlantTok, or quirky humor groups, where people gather around their interests, sharing affection, irreverence, and playful rituals (like arguing about the best pasta shape or staging history skits with pets). They are like community centers for oddly specific hobbies. A joke or sound becomes a canvas for everyone to play on, remixed and reimagined into endless variations, like one big, global improv game.

TikTok works best when it feels like a digital playground, not a stage. When used intentionally, it can reawaken playfulness, break routine, and connect us to others through laughter, rhythm, and generally shared silliness. So the invitation here is not to demonize screen time, but to discern its function. Is it soothing? Creative? Shared? Or is it compulsive and disconnecting?

Excessive screen time is associated with poorer sleep quality, diminished face-to-face interaction, and increased symptoms of anxiety and depression in young people.[10] And excessive or unbalanced use of screen-based play may contribute to fatigue or displace opportunities for in-person interaction, highlighting the need for moderation and mindful engagement.[11] It's not too surprising that putting an electronic device a foot away from our faces that emits blue light twenty-four seven and contains all of the information of the universe could mess up our nervous systems. The more time we spend in a dissociated digital trance, the less time we spend moving our bodies, connecting with others, or doing activities that bring lasting nourishment.

Can we use technology with intention—to support joy, connection, or learning—while also making space for real-world play: dancing in the living room, biking with no destination, kicking around a ball, learning a new sport or playing an old beloved one, gardening, storytelling, painting, singing, or simply doing something spontaneous and silly? Play is a sacred right, not just for children. And the kind of play that brings us back to ourselves is the kind that invites us to be present, curious, and alive.

The Serious Work of Clowning

In Beirut, where echoes of conflict remain, Sabine Choucair whips around her curly black hair, wearing a sequined dress, red clown nose, and oversized tie, pretending to run from a monster. As Lebanon's pioneering humanitarian clown, she uses clowning and laughter to help communities grappling with adversity.

I met Sabine through her brother, Dr. Bechara Choucair, a dear colleague and former public health commissioner of Chicago. Sabine grew up during Lebanon's civil war and felt deeply angry and hopeless about the loss of her childhood. She found a safe and inspired career in theater and later was introduced to clowning in New York. She described the experience as "magical," a rare lightness and relief from life's heaviness that came, as she put it, "from people laughing at me and me being able to laugh at myself." Her work has since spanned continents. In India, she worked with survivors of gender-based violence, blending play, storytelling, and therapy to foster resilience. As Sabine melded her performances with empathy and trauma-informed therapy, she has crafted a unique approach to social activism.

In 2008, Choucair cofounded Clown Me In, a Beirut-based troupe dedicated to bringing joy to marginalized communities. Their performances aim to help audiences discover the healing power of laughter, and most importantly, to tackle their problems through clowning and play. Her storytelling approach is rooted in participation and often engages with urgent realities: violence, human rights, war, displacement, and the loss of safety. The performances are highly visual and physical, designed to transcend language and speak directly to the human experience. It gives people a chance to be out of survival mode, to feel joy and laugh, which she says "switches something in the mind, something clicks in the imagination that moves us out of deep despair. Even at funerals, people feel an urge to laugh, because it is a way of expressing and reminds us that even in dark times we are worthy of joy. We offer a small space of possibility, a place to reconnect and remake ourselves." She goes where she is needed.

In the wake of the 2020 Beirut port explosion, which left thousands dead and many more displaced, Sabine and her team of thirty took to the streets within days. Their red noses have appeared in refugee camps across Jordan, Iraq, and along the Balkan route to Sweden and Greece, sometimes performing in forests where families were hiding. After the earthquake in southern Turkey that claimed fifty thousand lives in just ninety seconds, her group arrived three weeks later, when survivors were still living in tents, to offer brief, vital moments of happiness.

Wearing her sequin dress and blowing a kazoo, fake teeth in, her players put a rope down in a circle and start playing music and dancing. The kids come first, running to the clearing and sitting at the circle, with the mothers following. The men arrive last, and by the end everyone is laughing, in on the game. She invites people into various scenes, often ending the performance with a wedding scene, where she pulls the grumpiest looking man in the crowd and pretends to marry him. This strategic move allows her to soften and lighten the most hardened people in the crowd, which lightens everyone.

One poignant moment in rural Lebanon involved a young girl, rendered mute by trauma, whose mother came to Sabine after the performance, telling her in tears that her daughter had not spoken in nine months and had gleefully recounted the whole performance to her father, laughing as she spoke—a testament to the transformative power of joy and play. Sabine says, "Play is based on failure, and getting up and trying again. Like in tag, you run and you catch someone, so they failed, right? And then they go to catch someone else! So many games are based on failure and then continuing. Clowning is based on this, too. It's very simple. When we are kids, we learn by failing, and fighting in clownish ways with each other. When we grow up, failure becomes a bad thing and we don't enjoy it anymore."

Transforming real-life trauma from war-torn communities into performance can be a powerful path to healing. In the places Sabine visits, death is a constant presence, a daily horrifying reality. She recounts a scene from a play where a clown dies, then slyly peeks at the audience with one eye open, signaling that he's not truly gone. Laughter ensues. Overhead, the hum of a drone begins to play, a noise all too familiar to refugees that so often comes before destruction. The audience instinctively looks up in fear. Then Sabine spots something in the air, studies it carefully, and claps it between her hands. A mosquito. She grins and brushes it away. The crowd erupts into laughter, relief, release. For once, it wasn't the terrible thing.

Sabine and her group work for ten to twenty days at a time, clowning up to six performances a day. Then in their week off, they try to restore and rest, integrate their experiences, and receive therapy for themselves to process the tragedies that they witness. Bringing play to people who need it so desperately is very serious work. Sabine is a facilitator of healing, a portal to the medicine that we all have available to us but rarely lean on for comfort. Her work gives permission to find joy even in the worst of human circumstances, and recognizes that fleeting moments of joy are required to survive them.

Play Personalities

Luis had been living with Parkinson's disease for almost five years by the time he came to see me. The tremors had set in, and the stiffness; his movements were slow and deliberate. His face carried the "mask" of the disease, a reduced expressiveness that often comes with muscle rigidity, making it hard to read his emotions. Yet the first thing I noticed was not his symptoms but the sparkle in his eyes, and the crazy baseball cap he had on, with a rubber duck glued proudly on top. When I asked about it, he lifted his hand with great care, pointed to the duck, and said with a slow smile, "This is my prescription."

Luis had worked as a children's hospital janitor for most of his life, and in those long fluorescent hallways he had learned the sacred art of play. Over his career, he saw so many kids with devastating diseases, bedbound and stuck watching TV instead of being outside and going to school, that he began to carry small toys and finger puppets with him to create micro moments of fun while he was mopping or sweeping. Luis was also a physical comedian; his shtick involved jumping up and down, pretending to slip and fall while he mopped and pulling scarves out of kids' ears. He was a beloved member of the hospital community, and a welcome face in the room. When the tremors came, and then the rigidity, he was unable to move nearly as fast as he had. He said he felt boxed in and like people were treating him as fragile, pitiful, or invisible. But Luis refused to disappear, and kept working, less as a janitor and more as a laughter worker. He created what he called his "joy toolkit," a small bag he carried everywhere with him, both at work and in the world. Inside was a tiny horn, a set of vampire teeth, stickers, a fake plastic nose, and a bubble wand. He made it his mission to get at least one person to laugh with him every day. "If I can't move like I used to," he told me, "I'll move people instead."

Dr. Stuart Brown stated that there are eight different types of play personalities—archetypes that describe the unique ways we each experience joy, curiosity, and self-expression. He says that the way people play is deeply individual. Recognizing your play personality is like finding the doorway back into joy that feels most natural to you. The eight types he mentions are: the joker, the kinesthete, the explorer, the competitor, the director, the collector, the artist/creator, and the storyteller. The Joker finds delight in silliness, humor, and laughter. They love making others laugh and being a little ridiculous—think class clowns, pranksters, or stand-up comedians at heart. The Kinesthete loves to move, dance, play sports, practice yoga, climb. For them, movement itself is a pleasure. The Explorer is drawn to new experiences, ideas, or sensations. This can be through travel, learning, or even exploring new feelings or relationships. The Competitor thrives in games and contests. They find joy in structure, strategy, and the thrill of friendly rivalry. The Director loves planning, organizing, leading—putting together events, productions, or group experiences where things come to life. The Collector finds joy in gathering objects or experiences: rocks, records, memories, recipes, or even rare facts. The Artist/Creator comes alive while making, crafting, painting, designing, building, baking, or inventing. The Storyteller expresses play through imagination and narrative, through writing, acting, or even conversation that brings stories to life.

Luis was definitely a joker. My family is made up of many different archetypes: My son and husband are competitors, and playing board games with them is a howling, wild blood sport! I cannot handle it, actually, and can get really overwhelmed, because I am more of an explorer and director. Planning an adventure and then going on it is my kind of fun. My daughters are collectors and artists who love to play music and craft, and find little treasures in vintage stores or on the beach. My father is definitely a storyteller, winding up tales that are infused with humor and the half-truths that all good stories are full of.

Sometimes we're a mix of types, but usually one or two shine through. Noticing what kind of play makes you forget time, or what you'd do even if no one else joined, is a great clue. Play is the kind of medicine that uplifts the soul, softens the heart, and keeps our nervous system flexible and regulated.

Medicines to Carry

Determine your type(s) of play personality. If you are not sure, ask yourself:

What did I love doing as a child when no one was watching?

When do I feel most alive, engaged, and free?

What absorbs me and makes me lose sense of time?

Which types of activities most energize me or make me laugh?

You can also ask family members or friends who know you well what type of play personality they think you are!

Once you know your play type, begin to make space for it again. If you're a Kinesthete, take short dance breaks or try a new sport. If you're a Joker, follow comedians, share memes, play with little kids who love silly jokes! If you're a Director, host themed potlucks or game nights. If you're a Storyteller, turn ordinary moments into mini-stories. Waiting in line? Invent backstories for the people around you. Walking your dog? Imagine the quest you're on together.

Play doesn't need to be loud or public—it just needs to be true to your spirit.

Revisit hobbies or activities you enjoyed as a child. Did you enjoy any creative activities like drawing, painting, or crafting? Did you dance or play sports? Perhaps you loved to build with Legos or play card games. (I love to play Go Fish even now with my young adult children.) These activities can help you relax and express yourself, relax without expectation of perfection or productivity. Recalling your favorite childhood activities, or the ones you wish you had been able to do, can lead you to activities that you'll enjoy now.

Go for a skip or bike ride—for fun, not fitness. If you have a bike, go for a ride to nowhere in particular, just to feel the breeze on your face. Go for a walk on a different path, looking for a new adventure, with a friend, a family member, or with your dog for companionship. Or skip instead of run—it will immediately make you smile! Move your body just for the fun of it.

Adopt a playful attitude toward everyday activities. Find joy in mundane tasks by adding playful twists, like dancing while cleaning or singing in the shower. Watch funny movies, read humorous books, or spend time with people who make you laugh. Avoid heavy, violent movies and people who are angry and are "energy vampires." You can make your life feel more light, fun, and playful by bringing those positive energies in and creating boundaries to limit exposure to negative influences.

Prioritize play in your life. There is much we cannot control, but in countless small ways we can bring a spirit of play into our lives, no matter how busy or burdened we are. Play isn't childish. It makes us healthier and more resilient to life's difficulties. It also reminds us who we are. Now, go make a little space for it!

EPILOGUE

The Medicines of Love and Justice

Justice is what love looks like in public.
Dr. Cornel West, American philosopher, activist, intellectual

When I moved with my family to Ventura, California, to work at the county hospital, I was thirty years old. My hope was to train the next generation of family doctors in one of the country's strongest family medicine residency programs, while also learning from the legendary attending physicians who had built its reputation. Each day I was struck by the beauty that surrounded me: the vast blue skies opening over the Pacific on one side, the mountains rising on the other, and all of it set in one of the most abundant agricultural valleys in the world.

With its mild temperatures and fertile soil, Ventura offered near-perfect growing conditions, and crops thrived in abundance. Yet within days I realized how little I understood about the complex system that brought food from the fields to the people it was meant to nourish. Before moving there, I had never seen a strawberry plant, or known that one head of broccoli grows alone on a stalk, or noticed that, mile after mile, fields of food lined Highway 1. Avocados, which I had only known sliced on plates, appeared to me like oversized green drops hanging from wide, draping trees. I hadn't grown up with a vegetable garden, and aside from a brief chapter in my twenties when I lived and worked on a cashew farm in India, I knew very little about how crops were cultivated, or sadly even what many fruits and vegetables looked like before they were harvested, processed, and packaged. Nor had I understood that much of this food was harvested by migrant workers from Mexico and Central America, people whose backbreaking labor sustains our food system, while wages, exploitation, and exclusion leave them with almost no ability to fight for the dignity and protections they deserve. In the fields, I never saw anyone besides migrant workers doing this work. Even with all my travels and international work, spending most of my life in cities had kept me from really seeing what it takes to grow food in America.

My office hours at the county clinic in Oxnard filled quickly. Because I am a brown-skinned woman, speak Spanish, and provide prenatal care, word spread fast, and before long my practice was composed almost entirely of women farm workers from Oaxaca, Mexico. It was, in many ways, a beautiful chapter in my career. My enduring passion for obstetrics was a defining factor in my choice to practice family medicine. I wanted not only to care for mothers and babies through pregnancy and birth, but also to remain part of their lives as the babies grew. I cherished caring for the young Mixteca women in my practice. Their quiet, proud culture required me to listen more closely and ask more carefully about pains or struggles they might be facing. Over time, many of the women opened up, and together we built trusting relationships.

To me, there is nothing more sacred than being invited into the space of pregnancy and birth, to witness and support the incredibly poignant and miraculous passage with care and gentleness. Drawing from both my surgical training and my background as a prenatal yoga instructor, I taught yoga, provided prenatal care, attended births, and, when needed, performed cesarean sections. I was finally practicing the comprehensive women's care that I had envisioned and trained for over so many years, and it nourished me to build such deep bonds with my patients. What I loved most was teaching residents to view hospital birth differently. I emphasized to every resident who worked with me that unlike other patients in the hospital, a pregnant woman is not sick, but usually a healthy individual undergoing a normal and natural process. Our job was to protect a safe birth experience, not control every aspect of it. This perspective proved more controversial than I anticipated, as some nurses frowned when I dimmed the lights, lowered the monitor alarms, or asked for everyone to lower their chatter to whispers. My labor rooms were quiet except for the sounds of women in labor, and I guarded that silence for my patients who would never demand it as wealthier, more resourced women might. The gratitude of my Mixteca patients was unmistakable, and in its presence I felt a deep, cellular sense of purpose and joy.

Within a year of practicing, I noticed a pattern: The babies of farmworkers I delivered often showed slower developmental milestones than others in my care. I would ask simple questions, such as, "Was the baby crawling, rolling, exploring at home?" Sometimes the answer was yes, but often there was only silence. I began to wonder if pesticide exposure, unsafe water, or environmental toxins like lead or mercury were playing a role. It seemed to me as though something critical was being missed, and that perhaps my patients knew more than they could share. So I started making house calls—a return to the old ways of family medicine—hoping to witness up close the homes and neighborhoods my farmworker patients went back to after long, exhausting days in the fields.

Today, house calls are nearly extinct, and with them we have lost the invaluable insight that comes from seeing patients in their own environments. What I witnessed during mine left me deeply shocked. Families were often confined to substandard, overcrowded housing, with three families sharing a small home and each paying disproportionately high rents for a single room. Even laundry rooms and garages were rented out as "living spaces," forcing entire families to sleep on the floor. These arrangements reflected systemic exploitation, where landlords profited while basic necessities—such as heating, cooling, and safe, dry floors for children to play and crawl—were absent. In many homes, mattresses covered the entire floor of a room, serving as sleeping space for one or more families. This meant that a mattress was the only safe surface for babies when they weren't being held. One family lived in an oil-stained cement garage, an environment wholly unsuitable for a crawling infant. Without safe, hard floor space, babies cannot build the muscle strength required to roll over, crawl, or eventually walk.

In just one day of house calls, the whole preceding year of my observations made terrible sense. What I saw felt like an emergency, and it changed me. Witnessing my patients in conditions so incompatible with health fundamentally altered how I practiced medicine from that point on. I realized none of the remarkable women I cared for would ever volunteer that six of them were sleeping in a laundry room hallway. Dignity is one of the few things you can hang on to when everything else has been taken away.

To care for a person in an unjust world is an inherently political act. As we have seen, health is shaped as much by nonmedical factors as by clinical care. These social determinants of health—the conditions in which people are born, grow, live, work, and age—include access to clean air and water, safe housing, fair wages, education, food sovereignty, health care, and freedom from violence. These are the real foundations of health. Yet they are not shared equally. They are shaped by policies and power, and those inequities decide who has the chance to thrive and who is left behind. When someone can't get their diabetes under control, it's often not about personal discipline but about whether they can afford insulin or oral medications. As we saw with eleven-year-old Anna, a child's asthma may have less to do with family history and more to do with mold in their apartment or air pollution in their neighborhood. And mothers like Laura—who was not only low on iron, but stretched thin by two jobs, with no paid leave or childcare—are deeply and gravely exhausted. These aren't unlucky circumstances; they're the predictable health consequences of systems built on neglect. We need compassion, and we need transformative change.

Justice is not an accessory; it is the foundation of care.

For the women I cared for, I kept making house calls, raised funds, and shared what I had witnessed with anyone who would listen. I spoke publicly about the urgent need to treat farmworker housing as a public health issue and reminded audiences that our food system rests on the labor of undocumented workers whose contributions are essential yet ignored. I met with local politicians, joined a farmworker housing advocacy group, and served on the board of a regional nonprofit working toward sustainable economies. I was featured as a physician expert in a documentary with Martin Sheen on farmworker housing. Yet my influence felt small, hyperlocal, compared to the enormity of a system built on undervaluing immigrant labor.

At times, it seemed there was nothing I could do to ensure that the babies I delivered had the support they needed to grow healthy and thrive in this country or elsewhere. I prescribed physical therapy, enrolled them in Head Start programs, and stayed committed to the families I cared for. I kept delivering babies, making sure my patients' needs were heard by the nursing staff and that their care was excellent. These were small, daily acts—repeated over and over.

Tens of thousands of others do the same every day: doctors, nurses, teachers, social workers, psychologists, therapists, and community health workers carrying out quiet acts of care and resistance. In the years since, I have fought alongside my patients in many more battles. If they are fighting for their lives, then so am I—and so must we all. None of us is free in a society that devalues human beings. Inhumane farmworker housing persists, even as our food system continues to depend on the sweat, sacrifice, and suffering of those who came here seeking a better life for their children. Now, people who work the land to feed Americans are being deported by a government that views them as criminals. This is not new. America has long relied on the labor of immigrants while simultaneously criminalizing their existence. It makes me cry, rage, feel sick, and it makes me want to fight. But what are we to do with this anger, this grief, this urge to fight?

I vividly remember listening to Bryan Stevenson at a Family Action Network talk in 2018, shortly after reading his book *Just Mercy*. Stevenson, founder of the Equal Justice Initiative (EJI), spoke to the same truths I felt so deeply when he urged us to get "proximate" to those who are suffering. He described how lawyers, clergy, and community members in Alabama rallied to stop unjust executions and expose the machinery of racial violence.[1] Their courage was not a matter of individual heroism, but of people choosing to bear one another's burdens and say something. Stevenson has long reminded us that proximity changes the narrative. His work at EJI has not only defended those on death row but also created the National Memorial for Peace and Justice, honoring the thousands of Black men, women, and children who were lynched in this country. In his words and in his work, he models a kind of radical empathy and truth-telling that insists justice and healing are inseparable, and that we are all called to be part of that work.

Another powerful voice for justice, lawyer and activist Valarie Kaur, in her book *See No Stranger*, reminds us that justice begins with how we choose to see one another. Her call to "see no stranger" is an invitation to recognize every person as kin, someone's child, someone's beloved, worthy of dignity and care. "Revolutionary love is the choice to enter into labor—for others, for our opponents, and for ourselves. Love is sweet labor. Fierce. Bloody. Imperfect. Life-giving. A choice we make over and over again."[2] In this way, love becomes not only an ethic of care but also a force for justice.

I often think that what's missing in how we speak about justice, and even how we work for it, is that we forget to stand for what we really love. We know how to fight, and we know how to resist, but to hold in our minds and hearts a vision of what is beautiful, necessary, and worthy of our utter devotion—that, somehow, is more difficult. Responsibility begins with proximity, with choosing to get close to what we care about, to witness it with our full attention, and to truly take in what is happening. From there, it grows into the shared work of fighting for and creating systems of justice. Collective responsibility means we do not look away. It means crying and raging, yes, and also standing in solidarity at protests even when you're not the one at risk. It means showing up at court hearings, delivering food or supplies through mutual-aid networks, alerting vulnerable people about threats to their safety, and raising the next generation to recognize the dignity in every human life.

Recognize that every small act of justice—taking care of your ailing parent, feeding someone in your community, voting with integrity, protecting a sacred grove, listening to a neighbor's grief—is a contribution to the collective immune system of our society. When we nurture this immune system with love, and accountability, healing becomes not just possible—it becomes inevitable. The moral arc only bends when ordinary people pull on it together.

Liberation Is the Goal

Gustavo Gutiérrez, Peruvian theologian and father of liberation theology, radically redefined what it means to love in a world structured by inequality. I first encountered his work through the writings of the late Dr. Paul Farmer, one of my heroes in global health equity and the visionary founder of Partners In Health.[3] Gutiérrez inspired Dr. Farmer profoundly. For Gutiérrez, love is not simply a feeling of charity or personal kindness—it is an ethical demand to transform the systems that perpetuate poverty, marginalization, and suffering. In his groundbreaking work *A Theology of Liberation*, he writes: "To love the poor is not enough. We must reject the conditions that make them poor."[4]

His work centers on Christian faith but could well expand and encompass any spiritual tradition. Gutiérrez insists that genuine Christian love must be historical, concrete, and structural. It is not enough to feel compassion for the poor while tolerating the economic and political forces that exploit them. To love the poor is to stand alongside them, to share in their struggles, and to confront the systems—colonial, capitalist, or patriarchal—that strip away life and dignity and keep people poor. This, he reminds us, is at the heart of Christian teaching, and indeed central to most world religions: to love one another.

In liberation theology, love cannot be separated from justice. Justice is not a separate domain from faith or spirituality. Rather, it is the very expression of love in a broken world. To claim love without working for justice is, in Gutiérrez's view, a contradiction. He reminds readers that the biblical God's preferential option for the poor is not a theological metaphor—it is a call to action. It demands that we shift our social, economic, and political arrangements so that the most vulnerable are centered, not discarded. This vision of love insists on proximity. It is not distant or abstract. It emerges in the fertile soil of community organizing, in the refusal to normalize hunger, in the courage to speak truth to power, and in the fierce, collective will to create a future where everyone can thrive. It is a love that takes sides, not in hatred of others, but in fidelity to those whose lives are being crushed.

Liberation means freedom from systems of domination. Healing, in this theology, is both personal and collective. It is the restoration of life—political, economic, and spiritual life—for all people, and especially for those whom history has silenced. In this framework, love is revolutionary because it does not settle for alleviating symptoms. It aims at transformation. The soup kitchen is sacred service, and so is the fight to ensure no one needs a soup kitchen. This is the kind of love that belongs at the heart of medicine. A love that listens. A love that organizes. A love that heals not just the body, but the body politic. As Gutiérrez teaches us, to love is to act. And to act in the name of justice is the most faithful expression of love.

Staying Energized for Collective Liberation

People engaged in social justice movements, activism, and advocacy face emotional and mental stress because the work is demanding, high stakes, and deeply charged. There is a historical precedent of self-sacrifice and dedication to a cause at any cost that may discourage individuals from prioritizing self-care. In some social justice circles, self-care is critiqued as promoting individualism over collectivism. However, I ardently believe it's important to reframe the inner work of self-care as a form of collective care, and as a necessary component of being an effective activist. How else can we sustain our activism and continue to advocate for social change? As the great poet, professor, feminist, and activist Audre Lorde said, "Caring for myself is not self-indulgence, it is self-preservation and that is an act of political warfare."[5]

To be clear, the medicines we've uplifted in this book are not to "keep your motor running." You're not meant to be "on" all the time, especially not at the high speeds modern life tries to force on you. These medicines in your pouch are in fact the soul and heart of our collective liberation. They are the essence of our humanness and our humanity. By leaning into the medicines of the earth, of connection, and of the spirit, we can build a new kind of medicine—for everyone. It's a medicine of love and justice, as we move away from a system built on endless industrial growth toward one that actually supports and sustains life. What these medicines can do is turn despair and disconnection into courage and creative action in the face of social and ecological breakdown. Because systems do not actually fall over all at once; they lose coherence over time.

The late, legendary eco-philosopher Joanna Macy coined the term "the great turning" to describe a profound shift in human consciousness and the social system, a transition from a society of industrial growth that prioritizes profit and extraction to a life-sustaining civilization rooted in ecology, justice, and interconnection. "The great turning is not instead of collapse, but what guides us through it. . . . You organize around new values and norms and become part of more capacity and sensitivity and greater reach."[6] Macy defines three dimensions of this global transformation. The first is "Holding Actions," efforts to slow the damage being done, such as protests, lawsuits, and policy reforms. These actions aim to protect what remains of our ecosystems, communities, and democratic structures. The second is "Structural Change," which creates new systems that support ecological and social well-being, such as regenerative agriculture, renewable energy, circular economies, and cooperative governance. The third is a "Shift in Consciousness," a deep awakening to our interdependence with all life. This includes practices that cultivate gratitude, connection, and purpose, such as mindfulness, Indigenous wisdom, and Earth-based spiritual traditions.

When we turn to the medicines meant for all people, we grow into the strength and clarity needed for this great turning. With them, we can imagine and bring forth a transformation in human consciousness—a shift toward a world that is sustainable, just, and whole. These are the same medicines that nourished our ancestral lineages, and they remain with us now, steadying us in resistance and fueling our movements. At the heart of this is the right of every person to care for themselves and their well-being, and to challenge the systems that exploit and devalue human labor.

We can reclaim our agency and autonomy over our own lives. In the face of systemic injustices that can make individuals feel powerless, these medicines for all people remind us that we have control over our own health and happiness and can acknowledge our worth while resisting the dehumanization perpetuated by oppressive systems. Healing is not just what happens in clinics—it is what happens when we return to land, to language, to rhythm and season. With the medicines we do have—those already within reach—we can cultivate spiritual strength and ignite hope.

In *Active Hope*, Joanna Macy and British resilience specialist Chris Johnstone define "active hope" as different from being hopeful. It is a way of engaging with the world that shapes our choices and actions and helps us move toward the future we hope for. And it helps us to overcome feelings of powerlessness or overwhelm, which can block us from action.[7] They describe what many of us are feeling: a mismatch between the scale of the problems we face and the strength of our response—and a deep longing to nourish and fortify our ability to act so we can truly make a difference. Active Hope training is available online for free, and it focuses on using many of the medicines described in this book (such as gratitude) as a way to center ourselves in how we show up to the world.

"Liberty and Justice for All"

We repeated these words every morning, hand on our hearts, facing the flag and never questioning them. But did we understand what we were pledging—or whether our country lived up to it? Do we inhabit a society that fulfills the promise of its own allegiance?

I believe that justice is both a moral ideal and a practical framework, a way of organizing life so that dignity, equity, and accountability are upheld for all people. At its core, justice is about giving each person what they are due. Yet what we believe people are "due" is shaped by our values, cultures, and systems. Philosophers frame justice as fairness; in law, it is the upholding of rules. But the medicines for all people align most closely with social justice—justice that seeks to dismantle structural inequities and to build systems where everyone has access to safety, opportunity, and well-being. They also resonate with restorative justice, which understands justice not as punishment but as healing: the work of repair, of acknowledging harm, and of restoring trust within communities.

When we activate the medicines for all people—bringing nature, nourishing food, healing plants, trust and community, selfless service, joyful dance, gratitude, and playful lightness into our lives—we can meet our needs and fuel the work we are meant to do. This is revolutionary. It is the way that epic revolutions have succeeded, time and again, across the centuries.

It's time for health care professionals, too, to speak the truth to those in power, to partner with our communities, advocate for healing on a personal, societal, and planetary level, and to offer our wisdom and knowledge to a deeper, co-created vision of health and well-being. We can commit to a daily practice of reconnecting ourselves to the sacred circle of life, while also doing the work of serving our families, workplaces, communities with that reconnected energy.

Justice Is Love Made Public

In Martin Luther King Jr.'s 1967 speech at Stanford University, he said, "Social progress never rolls in on the wheels of inevitability. It comes through the tireless efforts and persistent work of dedicated individuals."

In her book *Making Space for Justice*, Michele Moody-Adams argues that most successful social movements spark moral inquiry that deepens our understanding of justice through a clearer grasp of injustice.[8] One of the deepest truths to emerge from moral inquiry is our duty not to look away from injustice. Even when it is painful, we can face it, with love, and with the resolve to act.

Social movements have long taught us that resistance is not only marches and sit-ins, but also the power of story, the shaping of language, and the transformation of symbols. From the slave narratives of abolition to naming sexual harassment to removing monuments that dehumanize, love has carried each act of courage forward, widening the path toward justice. In our times, the Black Lives Matter movement and the youth-led climate action Sunrise Movement have been strongly driven by visual art, writing, music, and joyful community building.

Justice is not simply the mechanical application of fairness or the impartial distribution of rights. It is the embodiment of love in public, the architecture of compassion rendered into systems and structures. Justice is love made visible in policy, practice, and presence. It is how love shows up when we have the courage to organize it. It invites us to imagine justice not as retribution, but as restoration, a communal commitment to dignity, care, and accountability. Justice, in this view, is not born from punishment, but from a deep recognition of our shared humanity. It is the refusal to abandon anyone. bell hooks, in her writing on love as a transformative force, reminds us that love is an active ethic, an intentional commitment to nurturing one's own and another's spiritual growth, and she challenges us to reimagine justice as inherently relational. "Love," hooks writes, "is not a passive feeling but a choice to extend respect, care, responsibility, and knowledge."[9] Thus, when people and systems enact harm, erasure, or control, they betray the core conditions of love. Real justice, then, becomes the labor of rehumanizing those people and systems so that they can reflect a more loving and life-affirming world. This framing shifts our understanding of justice from abstraction to relationship.

This vision is not new. In many Indigenous communities around the globe, justice is guided by the principle of *right relationship*—with self, with others, with land, and with spirit. It is not about isolating and punishing the "offender," but about restoring wholeness to the community. In these traditions, justice flows from love—not as sentiment, but as interdependence, as responsibility to one another and to the Earth.

Justice, at its core, *is* love. Not in a soft way. On the contrary, this love is ferocious. It does not flinch in the face of oppression. It refuses the anesthetizing comfort of neutrality. It calls us to interrogate systems that devalue certain bodies and silence certain voices. It is a love that holds institutions accountable, that mourns publicly, and that organizes tirelessly. This kind of justice is radical because it roots itself in care. It asks not only what is legal, but what is right; not only what is efficient, but what is humane; not only what is profitable, but what is sacred. In a time when the language of justice is often diluted, we must remember its true origin. Justice, in its deepest form, is love that refuses to leave anyone behind—love with memory and structure, reaching into the wounds of history to heal them at the root.

These medicines for all people are fueled by love for life, for oneself, for each other. As we have seen together, they are mostly free, radically so, accessible to all and biologically wired into the cellular strands of our being. They remind us that we are strong and resilient, made to love and survive. And in this place of love, we can find liberation. Love is the deep, ancestral recognition that we belong to one another—and that no one is free until we all are. When we root our justice work in love, we shift from saving or fixing others to walking with them, listening, co-creating, and healing in relationship. Love turns transactional care into transformative care. It makes room for tenderness even in struggle. Here with the medicines we have carried together, we reveal a growing landscape of possibility in the midst of all that feels broken, where we recover ancient wisdom and embrace fresh perspectives, so that we might cultivate cultures of joy, safety, and mutual thriving.

After all these years, reflecting on the many thousands of patients I have been privileged to walk with in clinics and hospitals in Chicago, Ventura, Oxnard, Standing Rock, St. Lucia, Cuba, India, and Brazil, I have come to understand that taking care of each other is always a form of love. The stories I've shared with you are those of everyday people, families looking for something better, who came to me for help, and who, in turn, helped me grow. I feel so much love and gratitude for the people I care for, who share their lives with me and allow me to share in their pain, their joy, and everything in between.

Together, you and I have journeyed through science and spirit, through land and lineage, through nourishment and story and research. We have remembered what the body knows, what the ancestors whisper, what the science supports, and what the Earth still teaches us every day as the sun rises and sets. Your medicine pouch is filling. Justice and love are not the final chapter; they are the beginning of collective repair. Justice is a daily practice, as are all these medicines that move us toward an ecosystem of health, healing, and restoration. It is love made public, made policy, made possible. It is what happens when we hold each other sacred and refuse to accept systems that treat us as anything less.

If medicine is to be for all people, it must reach beyond the pharmacy and into the soil, the schools, the kitchens, the courtrooms, the streets.

The work ahead asks for tenderness.

It also demands fierceness.

It always has.

And we will not work alone.

Together we carry the gathered wisdom of generations—leaves and roots, foods and dances, loving care and mycelial connections, rest and rhythms, care and gratitude, trust and playfulness—a great bundle of medicines for all people, for all of us, no matter where we come from or what we hold.

Let this be the place where we nourish what was forgotten.

In this moment, when the weight of systemic inequity is felt in our bodies, our breath, our communities, and our Earth, the call to remember justice as medicine is louder than ever. Justice is what allows healing to move beyond the individual body and into the body of the people. This is what moves us out of the illusion of perfectionist individualism to the reality that we are all mutually responsible for each other.

May these medicines for all people be a source of strength for you, living cords that tie you to the great lineage that you come from and nourish the parts of you that crave healing.

My friend, the medicines you have been waiting for are already here, all around you.

Now go and reclaim them.

ROOTS, RELATIONS, AND THANKS

I dreamt of this book long before I wrote it, much as I dreamt of my children long before I carried them. After years of visioning and inquiry, and a gestation interrupted by the global pandemic, the book was born through the support of many midwives—beloveds and believers whose care made it possible. It is my privilege and honor to express my gratitude to them.

First, I thank my parents, Sushila and Vijay Maker, who immigrated to the unknown sixty years ago, leaving behind everything they loved. Your courage taught me how to live expansively and follow my dreams boldly. I am blessed to have your love and proud to carry your generosity forward. To my mother, your medicines of food and loving attention sustain me in ways both seen and unseen. To my father—the original Dr. Maker—you taught me early on that there is no greater privilege than being trusted to care for another human being's body and heart.

To my husband, Todd, who says "yes" and "why not?" to all my wild ideas and believes that I can do anything. I believe that now, too, because of you. I could not do life—or have written this book—without you. To our children—Sahaara, Sachin, and Devika—your love, your hugs, and the joy of our shared laughter sustain me. Thank you for allowing your stories to be woven into this work and for your sweet support. Being your mother expands my whole heart every day. Devika, your drawing of our sacred plant, Tulsi, opens each Remembrance, and it fills me with pride and gratitude that your art enhances this book.

I thank my ancestors—known and unknown.

The Castanea Fellowship nurtured the early seeds of this work, and my cohort of fierce, visionary activists helped me find my writing voice. In 2021, thanks to Anna Lappé and Michael Pollan, the Mesa Refuge offered a quiet cottage overlooking Tomales Bay, where this book first took shape, held by the legacy of many of my literary heroes who had written there before. The Center for Humans and Nature also provided and protected time away from patient care and family responsibilities—space to breathe, dance outdoors, and write. So much came through me in the few days of sacred quiet these places provided me.

Wise and generous teachers offered the guidance and intellectual rigor that shaped this book. I am deeply grateful to Dr. Andrew Weil, Dr. Tieraona Low Dog, Dr. Victoria Maizes, Dr. Audrey Stillerman, Dr. Quentin Young (rest in power), Dr. Vasant Lad, Midwife Karni Seymour-Brown, Paul Stamets, Betty McKune Karrer (rest in power), and Daphne Singingtree for illuminating many inspiring paths toward embodying health and healing for me. Dr. Myles Spar, Dr. Bernard Ewigman, Dr. Sonia Oyola, and Dr. Leslie Mendoza Temple make my work as an integrative physician exponentially better with their loving examples. Each of you has spoken my name kindly in rooms I was not in, and for that, I am profoundly grateful.

This book would not exist without the help of remarkable women. Rachel Lehmann-Haupt helped bring the proposal to life, preparing me for the opportunity that followed when my agent, Leslie Meredith, heard me on NPR. I am deeply grateful to Leslie for her clarity, steadiness, and belief in this work. And to Anna Bliss at Chelsea Green, thank you for your faith, your patience with me as a first-time author, and your compassion during the final stages of writing, when my city was under siege by ICE.

I am deeply grateful for the friends and family who fill my life with love and encourage my passions—even when I insist I'm doing too much and then joyfully decide to do more, like write a book. Arti Chandra, your love, loyalty, presence and devotion to our sisterhood are a true North Star. Hemalayaa Behl, your soulful, joyful spirit and our shared work together live everywhere in these pages. Emily Grayson, thank you for your honesty, your powerful and tender guidance, and your constant spiritual encouragement. Rachel Webster, you clarified my thoughts, strengthened my language and heart, and ensured this book could speak across disciplines without losing its ethical center. Sharmila Lodhia, your integration of rigorous scholarship and compassionate activism has been a model for my own work. Florencia Ramirez, Katie Metzger, and Vashti O'Keefe—years ago, you ensured our gatherings with our little ones fit my demanding work schedule, and so much of that shared love shaped my heart and my mothering and this book. Thank you to my brother and sister-in-law, Ajay and Manvi Maker, for your unconditional love and support. So much love and inspiration came from Vanessa Filley, Regina Sant'Anna, Anu Dewan, Rahul Sharma, Debi Buzil, Angira Patel, the Mycelium Collective, and my loving in-laws, Neil and Pat Clark. And to the queens of Ayodele Drum and Dance, Imania

Detry and T. Ayo Alston, thank you for trusting me with the dances of the ancestors, and for the opportunity to feel the unbridled joy of dancing with and for our great city. Without dancing, I could not do anything that I do nearly as well.

Thanks to Nicole DeBarber for working with me to create the beautiful illustrations that grace these pages. They bring magic to the book. To Maria Luiso, for your help with the research and endnotes, even while you were applying to medical school. The patients and healers around the globe that I have worked with, who shared their stories and lived expertise, expanded the boundaries of what counts as knowledge. Their insights challenged dominant hierarchies of evidence and demanded a broader epistemology of medicine from me. Deep gratitude.

This book draws from traditions that long predate modern health institutions and acknowledges that inheritance with humility. Everyone I mentioned in it helped me to reimagine medicine as a practice of solidarity and liberation. To all the people who imagine a more beautiful and just world, this book is for you. Take that medicine pouch and keep going.

APPENDIX A

Culinary Medicine Recipes from Around the World

These recipes are drawn from my years of teaching integrative medicine and community-based food as medicine classes. Many were developed for my Food Is Power and Culinary Medicine programs, designed around the idea that food can nourish the body while teaching and empowering communities. Each recipe highlights affordable, accessible, whole ingredients and reflects global culinary traditions that connect health to culture and land. They are the dishes most loved by students and families—simple to prepare, rooted in everyday wellness, and meant to remind us that food is medicine. Serving sizes are for four large portions but can be stretched to five or six, depending on your appetite. I hope you will use these recipes as launchpads to your own culinary explorations.

Lentil and Spinach Stew with Turmeric and Lemon (Indian subcontinent)

Serves 4 to 6

This nourishing and warming stew is packed with plant-based protein, fiber, and anti-inflammatory ingredients like turmeric and lemon.

1 tablespoon olive oil
1 onion, chopped
2 garlic cloves, minced
1 teaspoon ground turmeric
1 teaspoon cumin
1 cup red lentils, rinsed
4 cups vegetable broth
2 cups fresh spinach
Juice of 1 lemon
Salt and pepper to taste
Fresh parsley for garnish

1. Heat the olive oil in a large pot over medium heat. Sauté the onion and garlic until soft.
2. Add the turmeric and cumin, stirring for 1 minute.
3. Add the lentils and vegetable broth. Simmer for 20 minutes, until the lentils are soft.
4. Stir in the spinach and lemon juice. Cook for 5 more minutes. Season with salt and pepper.
5. Garnish with parsley and serve warm.

Black Bean and Sweet Potato Tacos (Mexico/Latin America)

Makes 4 large tacos

Here is a healthy take on tacos, using sweet potatoes and black beans, both rich in fiber, vitamins, and minerals.

2 medium sweet potatoes, diced
2 tablespoons olive oil
1 teaspoon chili powder
1 teaspoon cumin
1 15-oz can black beans, drained and rinsed
1 avocado, sliced
¼ cup fresh chopped cilantro
Whole-wheat or corn tortillas
Salsa (optional)

1. Preheat oven to 400°F (200°C). Toss the sweet potatoes in 1 tablespoon of olive oil, chili powder, and cumin. Roast for 20–25 minutes, until tender.
2. In a pan, heat the black beans in another tablespoon of olive oil over medium heat until warm.
3. Assemble tacos by placing roasted sweet potatoes and black beans on warmed tortillas. Top with avocado slices and fresh cilantro. Add salsa if desired.

Chickpea and Spinach Curry (Middle East/India)

Serves 4

This simple curry uses chickpeas and spinach, offering a great balance of protein, fiber, and antioxidants.

1 tablespoon olive oil
1 onion, chopped
1 teaspoon turmeric
1 teaspoon cumin
1 teaspoon garam masala
1 15-oz can chickpeas, drained and rinsed
1 can diced tomatoes
1 can coconut milk
2 cups fresh spinach leaves
Salt and pepper to taste

1. Heat the olive oil in a pan and sauté the onion until soft.
2. Add turmeric, cumin, and garam masala, stirring for 1 minute.
3. Add the chickpeas, tomatoes, and coconut milk. Simmer for 15 minutes.
4. Stir in spinach leaves and cook for 5 more minutes until they are wilted. Season with salt and pepper. Serve with brown rice or whole-wheat flatbread if desired.

Miso Soup with Tofu and Seaweed (Japan)

Serves 4

Here is a light, nutrient-rich soup. The fermented miso supports gut health, while tofu offers plant-based protein.

4 cups water
3 tablespoons miso paste
½ block firm tofu, cubed
¼ cup wakame seaweed (rehydrated for ten minutes in cold water, if dried)
1 tablespoon tamari or low-sodium soy sauce
1 green onion, sliced (for garnish)

1. Heat the water in a pot until it just starts to simmer (not boil).

2. Dissolve the miso paste in the warm water and stir well.
3. Add the tofu and the wakame seaweed. Simmer for 5 to 7 minutes.
4. Stir in the tamari and garnish with the green onion before serving.

Jollof Quinoa with Vegetables (West Africa)

Serves 4

This is a healthy twist on the traditional Jollof rice, using quinoa for added protein and fiber, combined with nutrient-packed vegetables.

1 tablespoon olive oil
1 bell pepper, diced
1 onion, chopped
2 cloves garlic, minced
1 teaspoon paprika
1 teaspoon cayenne pepper (optional)
1 cup quinoa, rinsed
1 14.5-oz can diced tomatoes, or 2 cups fresh diced tomatoes
2 cups vegetable broth
Salt and pepper to taste
Fresh parsley, chopped (for garnish)

1. Heat the olive oil in a large pan on medium heat. Sauté the onion, garlic, and bell pepper until softened.
2. Stir in the paprika and cayenne pepper if desired, followed by the quinoa.
3. Add the tomatoes and vegetable broth. Simmer for 15 to 20 minutes until the quinoa is cooked.
4. Season with salt and pepper, garnish with parsley, and serve warm.

Thai Coconut Curry with Tofu and Vegetables (Thai/Southeast Asia)

Serves 4

This is a simple, nourishing curry filled with plant-based protein, anti-inflammatory spices, and healthy fats from coconut milk.

1 tablespoon olive oil
2 tablespoons Thai red curry paste
1 13.5-oz can coconut milk

2 cups mixed vegetables (such as carrots, bell peppers, and broccoli)
1 block firm tofu, cubed into bite-sized pieces
1 tablespoon lime juice
Salt and pepper to taste
Fresh basil or cilantro, chopped (to garnish)

1. Heat the olive oil in a large pan. Add the tofu and sauté until golden brown. Remove from the pan.
2. In the same pan, add the curry paste and cook for 1 to 2 minutes while stirring.
3. Add the coconut milk and vegetables, simmering until the veggies are tender.
4. Stir in the tofu, lime juice, and season with salt and pepper.
5. Garnish with fresh basil or cilantro and serve with brown rice.

Zucchini Noodles with Pesto (Mediterranean)

Serves 4

Here is a low-carb, nutrient-dense meal featuring spiralized zucchini noodles with a healthy homemade pesto sauce. If you don't have a spiralizer, you can use a julienne peeler or regular peeler instead to shape the zucchini into pasta-like strands.

4 medium zucchini, spiralized into noodles
2 cups fresh basil leaves
¼ cup walnuts or pine nuts
1 clove garlic
¼ cup olive oil
1 tablespoon lemon juice
Salt and pepper to taste
Cherry tomatoes, halved (optional)

1. Blend the basil, nuts, garlic, olive oil, lemon juice, salt, and pepper to create the pesto sauce.
2. Lightly sauté the zucchini noodles in a pan for 2 to 3 minutes until tender.
3. Toss the zucchini noodles with the pesto sauce and cherry tomatoes if desired. Serve immediately.

Sweet Potato "Fries" with Yogurt Dip

Serves 4

This healthy take on fries is crispy and flavorful, and especially delicious when paired with a cool, protein-rich yogurt dip.

4 medium sweet potatoes, cut into thin fries
2 tablespoons olive oil
½ teaspoon paprika (optional)
½ teaspoon salt
½ cup plain Greek yogurt
1 tablespoon lemon juice
½ teaspoon garlic powder
Fresh parsley, chopped (for garnish)

1. Preheat the oven to 400°F (200°C).
2. Toss the sweet potato fries in the olive oil, paprika (optional), and salt.
3. Arrange the fries in a single layer on a baking sheet and bake for 20 to 25 minutes, flipping halfway through.
4. Meanwhile, mix the Greek yogurt, lemon juice, and garlic powder in a bowl to make the dip.
5. Sprinkle the parsley on top of the fries and serve with the yogurt dip.

Mini Veggie Pizzas on Whole-Wheat Pita

Serves 2

This is a fun, customizable pizza recipe that lets kids get creative with healthy toppings. In our Food Is Power classes, we provide a variety of toppings for them to choose from, including pineapple!

4 small whole-wheat pita breads
¼ cup tomato sauce (low-sodium preferred). *To make sauce from scratch with fresh tomatoes, see recipe below.*
¼ cup shredded mozzarella cheese
¼ cup sliced mushrooms (shiitake, maitake, or baby bellas)
¼ cup chopped spinach
¼ cup diced bell peppers
¼ cup cherry tomatoes, halved
Italian seasoning (optional)

1. Preheat the oven to 375°F (190°C).

2. Place the pita breads on a baking sheet and spread a thin layer of tomato sauce on each.
3. Sprinkle shredded mozzarella on top, then add the veggies (mushrooms, spinach, bell peppers, tomatoes).
4. Sprinkle with Italian seasoning if desired.
5. Bake for 10 to 12 minutes, until the cheese is melted and bubbly.
6. Let cool slightly and serve.

Tomato Sauce from Scratch

1 pound fresh tomatoes (3 to 4 medium, quartered)
1 six-ounce can tomato paste
2 tablespoons olive oil
2 teaspoons dried oregano
2 medium cloves garlic
½ teaspoon kosher salt (plus more to taste)
⅛ teaspoon freshly ground black pepper (plus more to taste)
2 to 3 tablespoons chopped fresh basil (optional)

1. Place all ingredients in a blender, and blend until completely pureed. Add additional salt and pepper to taste.
2. Spread on pizza crust or bread. Add toppings and bake as desired. (If you don't have a blender, chop the fresh tomatoes and finely mince the garlic, then add them along with the other ingredients to a bowl. Stir until combined, taste, and add additional salt and pepper if desired.)

Rainbow Veggie Wraps

1 wrap

This colorful and easy-to-make wrap encourages kids to eat a variety of veggies in a fun, hands-on way.

1 whole-wheat tortilla
¼ cup hummus (any flavor)
¼ cup grated carrots
¼ cup chopped cucumbers
¼ cup sliced bell peppers (red, yellow, and/or green)
¼ cup spinach or mixed greens
1 tablespoon sunflower seeds (optional)

1. Lay the whole-wheat tortilla flat and spread a thin layer of hummus on top.
2. Layer the vegetables in the center of the tortilla, creating a "rainbow" of colors.
3. Sprinkle sunflower seeds for added crunch if desired.
4. Roll up the tortilla tightly and slice it into smaller pieces for easy bites.

Healing Herbal Teas

These herbal, noncaffeinated teas are gentle and supportive medicines that you can easily lean on every day, or just when needed. These recipes will make a few cups and are good for sharing!

CCF Tea for Digestive Support (Cumin, Coriander, Fennel)

4–5 cups water
½ teaspoon cumin seeds
½ teaspoon coriander seeds
½ teaspoon fennel seeds

Bring the water to a boil in a stainless-steel pot. Add the seeds and let simmer for 5 to 10 minutes, depending on how strong you like your tea. Strain, pour into a thermos, and sip throughout the day while it's still warm.

To make CCF Tea a daily habit, make a big batch mix: Combine ½ cup each of cumin, coriander, and fennel in a glass jar. Each morning, scoop out 1½ teaspoons of the blend for your tea. This tea works best when sipped hot. It is wonderfully warming, soothing, and deeply supportive of digestion.

Tulsi Ginger Tea for Stress Regulation

If you are growing your own tulsi, you can easily make your own home-grown tea. Harvest in the early morning, after the dew has dried but before the sun is too strong. This is when tulsi's powerful essential oils and aroma are at their peak.

Select tender stems. Snip the top ⅓ of the plant, just above a node (where leaves branch off). This encourages the plant to grow back fuller and bushier.

Gather leaves and flowers, as both are medicinal. Use sharp scissors and avoid tearing the plant. Treat her gently.

To dry, spread the leaves and flowers in a single layer on a clean cloth or mesh tray in a shaded, well-ventilated area. Avoid direct sunlight, which can reduce potency. They're ready when crisp and fragrant—usually in 3 to 5 days.

To store, lightly crumble the dried leaves and store them in an airtight glass jar away from heat and light. Properly stored tulsi can retain its aroma and healing qualities for up to a year. Tulsi tea is also available in tea bags at most health food stores.

2 cups hot water
1 tablespoon dried tulsi (or 1½ teaspoons fresh)
1 teaspoon freshly grated ginger
½ teaspoon cinnamon
1 teaspoon raw honey (optional)
1 wedge lemon (optional)

In hot water, steep the tulsi, ginger, and cinnamon for ten minutes. Strain and sweeten with honey and lemon if desired.

Ginger Turmeric Tea for Clarity and Lightness of Energy

This tea is best for relieving lethargy, congestion, and sluggish digestion.

2 cups water
1 teaspoon grated fresh ginger
¼ teaspoon black pepper
½ teaspoon turmeric (freshly grated turmeric root or turmeric powder)
Juice of half a lemon

Bring water to simmer in a small pot. Stir in the ginger, black pepper, and turmeric and let steep at a simmer for ten minutes. Strain, stir in the lemon, and drink hot. It has a kick to it!

APPENDIX B

Oldways Food Pyramids

Oldways is a nonprofit organization that preserves and promotes traditional diets from around the world as tools for health, cultural pride, and chronic disease prevention. Their work centers food as a connector—between people, land, ancestry, and community—and counters the dominance of Eurocentric, industrialized nutrition advice.

Oldways offers five cultural food pyramids, each designed with nutrition experts, historians, and elders from within the cultures they represent:

African Heritage Diet Pyramid: Uplifts traditional African, African American, and Caribbean foods—rooted in lots of leafy greens, beans, okra, millet, yams, and spices.

Mediterranean Diet Pyramid: Based on the traditional diets of South Europe, Greece, Southern Italy, and North Africa , emphasizing olive oil, herbs, whole grains, beans, legumes, seafood, and seasonal vegetables.

Latin American Diet Pyramid: Centers maize (corn), beans, squash, peppers, tropical fruits, tubers, rice and the food wisdom of Indigenous and mestizo communities.

Asian Heritage Diet Pyramid: Highlights traditional East, Southeast, and South Asian foods, including rice, noodles, sea vegetables, seafood, fermented soy, herbs, and teas.

Vegetarian Diet Pyramid: A plant-centered approach to wellness rooted in diverse global traditions of meatless meals, including legumes, grains, nuts, and dairy.

These pyramids honor cultural knowledge, resist erasure, and reconnect people with foods their ancestors recognized. Each is designed to support heart health, diabetes prevention, and longevity, using whole, accessible ingredients. Oldways offers a wide range of free resources—including toolkits for families, clinicians, and community groups. I encourage you to explore their site for culturally grounded food pyramids, recipes, cooking demos, videos with leading ethnic chefs, and their culinary travel programs. It's an invaluable place to learn how to weave ancestral nutrition into your own life and into any programs you create. See oldwayspt.org for more.

APPENDIX C

The Farm Bill

Countries around the world use economic policy tools such as subsidies, tariffs, and quotas to stabilize their food systems. In the United States, these policies shape not only what gets grown, but also what becomes cheap and widely available. This is why some of the most inexpensive foods are also the least nutritious. To see how this has happened in the United States, we have to understand the Farm Bill.

Components of the US Farm Bill

The Farm Bill is a massive piece of legislation—renewed roughly every five years—that shapes what gets grown in America, how much it costs, and who can afford to eat. It has a huge impact on your everyday life and thus deserves your attention. Here are some core components and why they matter to you.

Commodity Programs: These programs provide financial support for farmers who grow corn, soybeans, wheat, cotton, and rice. The subsidies keep certain foods cheap, but since they favor processed food ingredients (like corn syrup, soybean oil, and animal feed), this *drives down the cost of processed foods, meat, and dairy*. Funding and grants for produce growers are historically a tiny slice of the Farm Bill. This is why a can of soda (filled with high fructose corn syrup) is cheaper than an apple. The USDA recommends filling 50 percent of your plate with fruits and vegetables, but less than 5 percent of federal farm subsidies support their production.

Nutrition Programs: The largest part of the Farm Bill—more than 75 percent of its budget—funds nutrition programs like SNAP (Supplemental Nutrition Assistance Program), school meals, and food banks. These programs determine who gets help buying food, how much assistance they receive, and how hunger is addressed nationwide. Recent massive cuts in SNAP funding are impacting millions of families.

Supporting Large-Scale Agriculture: The policies in the Farm Bill tend to favor large-scale, industrial farming operations that focus on high yields and efficiency. These farms can produce food at lower costs due to economies of scale, which keeps food prices low for consumers. Small farmers typically receive less support, while larger operations benefit from more subsidies and crop insurance from drought, floods, and climate change. Big Ag's massive output and efficiency (spreading fixed costs over more units) means lower average production costs, translating to cheaper groceries for consumers. However, this "cheap food" often comes with lower nutritional value, fewer quality ingredients, and suppressed wages for farmworkers.

Conservation Programs: These programs pay farmers to adopt sustainable and environmentally friendly practices, to protect soil, water, wetlands, and wildlife.

Trade and International Food Aid: The Farm Bill includes provisions for international trade and food aid programs that support US farmers by creating demand for US agricultural products abroad. Increased exports create a larger market for US farmers, helping stabilize prices domestically and keep food costs lower for consumers.

Rural Development: These programs focus on improving infrastructure in rural areas, where much of the nation's food is grown. Investments in transportation, broadband, utilities, health care, housing, and infrastructure help support the rural farming economy.

Research and Extension Programs: The Farm Bill funds agricultural research and development, land grant universities, and innovations in crop production, pest control, and food safety.

What Can *You* Do?

Whether you're acting as an individual citizen, a community member, or as part of a larger movement, there are a few concrete and effective ways that you can influence the Farm Bill. In fact, the Farm Bill *depends* on citizen involvement. Industry lobbyists are already at the table. Public voices ensure community health, hunger, and environmental justice are not ignored.

Contact Your Members of Congress

Reaching out to your representatives truly works. The Farm Bill is federal law, so your senators and house representatives vote on it in Congress. Your voice matters because Farm Bill negotiations are heavily shaped by constituent pressure, and staffers log every call and email. Even ten to twenty calls on a topic can shift a legislator's priorities.

What to do:

- Call your Congressional office and leave a message, following this basic script: "I'm a constituent concerned about _________ in the Farm Bill. Please support . . ."
- Email or use the representative's online form.
- Attend a town hall and ask a Farm Bill question on the record.

Join Food-Justice and Farming Organizations

These groups influence legislators directly and provide action steps.

- National Sustainable Agriculture Coalition (NSAC): sustainable agriculture.net
- Food & Water Watch: www.foodandwaterwatch.org
- National Family Farm Coalition: nffc.net
- HEAL Food Alliance: healfoodalliance.org
- Union of Concerned Scientists: www.ucs.org
- Environmental Working Group (EWG): www.ewg.org
- Farm Aid: www.farmaid.org

All of these organizations send alerts when key Farm Bill amendments need citizen pressure.

Support Local Farmers

Your dollars influence policy. Buy from farmers markets, CSAs, BIPOC-led farms, and regenerative farms. This builds the demand for sustainable agriculture that the Farm Bill either funds or ignores. Sustained consumer demand strengthens political arguments for shifting subsidy priorities.

Vote in Local, State, and Federal Elections

Food policy is shaped not only in Congress but also by agriculture commissioners, governors, state legislators, and county boards. Many local leaders pressure Congress or implement Farm Bill programs, such as SNAP, conservation funds, and water protections. Voting is one of the strongest levers citizens hold.

Support Youth and Community Food Advocacy

Youth voices—especially from communities impacted by food apartheid—often get national attention and are influential in Farm Bill debates. Support these programs:

- National Young Farmers Coalition: youngfarmers.org
- FoodCorps: foodcorps.org
- 4-H: 4-h.org

Educate Others

Most people have no idea that the Farm Bill shapes food prices, SNAP benefits, school meals farming livelihoods, and soil and water quality. Sharing infographics, articles, social media explainers, and book club discussions helps to build public awareness, which increases political pressure for change.

APPENDIX D

Additional Resources

Community Partners Working for Change

These are just a few of the many organizations creating meaningful change. I chose them because they reflect the values at the heart of this book—the true medicines. They span the United States and the globe, with several rooted in my home city of Chicago. Though many of the organizations are local in origin, their models, resources, and advocacy have far-reaching relevance. My hope is that they inspire you to support their work, join their efforts, or even build something of your own within the community you serve.

Active Hope Training: A free online course teaching practices for building resilience, courage, and community in the face of global challenges like climate change, social injustice, and ecological crises.
Website: activehope.training

Apna Ghar (Chicago): A human rights organization working to end gender violence using an evidence-based model. Apna Ghar provides critical, comprehensive, culturally competent services and conducts outreach and advocacy to empower survivors, engage communities, and elevate gender and racial justice.
Website: https://apnaghar.org

Arpana Trust (India): A nonprofit organization that integrates medical care, women's empowerment, and community development in rural Indian villages, using participatory approaches.
Website: arpana.org

Becoming a Man (Chicago): A program that supports young men through school-based group counseling and mentorship that fosters social-emotional skills, decision-making, and positive life outcomes.
Website: www.youth-guidance.org/bam-becoming-a-man

The Black Mesa Water Coalition (Arizona): A Diné and Hopi-led coalition working at the intersection of climate justice, land restoration,

and youth empowerment. They support traditional dryland farming, seed sharing, and community education to rebuild relationships with land while resisting extractive industries.
Website: nativevoicesrising.org/portfolio/black-mesa-water-coalition-bmwc

ChiFresh Kitchen (Chicago): A project of the Chicago Food Policy Action Council, ChiFresh is a Black-owned commercial food service contractor, structured as a worker cooperative. Their business development model centers around food justice and sovereignty, where marginalized workers are the primary decision-makers. The five formerly incarcerated co-owners of ChiFresh Kitchen served their first meals as a new business in May of 2020. During the pandemic, ChiFresh prepared fifty thousand fresh, hot, healthy meals for food-insecure residents of Chicago.
Website: www.chifreshkitchen.com

The Community Fridge Movement: Demonstrating collective liberation in action, this movement is a grassroots response to food insecurity that operates on the principles of mutual aid, dignity, and abundance. These fridges, often tucked onto sidewalks, porches, or storefronts, are publicly accessible and communally stocked refrigerators where anyone can take what they need or leave what they can. No forms. No proof. No shame. At their core, community fridges reject the narrative of scarcity that has been embedded in our food systems and policies. They affirm a deeper truth: We already have enough—it's the systems that hoard, gatekeep, and create hunger. By redistributing food directly, neighbor to neighbor, these fridges subvert bureaucratic models of charity and replace them with care that is immediate, intimate, and relational.
Find community fridges near you using this website: www.fridgefinder.app

Community Voices Heard (CVH) (New York State): A Black- and Brown-led organization focused on policy advocacy around public housing, welfare reform, immigrant justice, and participatory budgeting. CVH develops leaders from within directly impacted communities to lead campaigns and shape legislation.
Website: www.cvhaction.org

The Edible Schoolyard Project (California): A nonprofit organization founded by Chef Alice Waters in 1995, dedicated to the transformation of public education by using organic school gardens, kitchens, and cafeterias to teach academic subjects as well as the values of nourishment, stewardship, and community. Edible education provides hands-on experiences that connect students to food, nature, and each other; and it systematically

addresses the crises of climate change, public health, and social inequality. At its heart, it's a dynamic and joyful learning experience for every child.
Website: edibleschoolyard.org

Equiticity (Chicago): In Chicago's North Lawndale neighborhood, Equiticity organizes joy-based community rides and walks that double as civic engagement and healing communion. They center transportation justice as racial justice, and shift who gets to be seen as a planner, a healer, or a public space user.
Website: www.equiticity.org

Friends of the Children: A national nonprofit organization that provides long-term, professional mentoring, with mentors skilled in forming enduring, supportive relationships with youth who have faced substantial adversity. The mentors stay with their mentees from early childhood through high school graduation. Their model is grounded in research showing that the most important factor in helping children overcome adversity is a long-term, trusting relationship with a consistent, caring adult.
Website: friendsofthechildren.org

Health & Medicine Policy Research Group (Chicago): An independent nonprofit organization focused on advancing health equity and improving public health systems. HMPRG conducts rigorous policy analysis, leads coalitions across the state, and develops evidence-based recommendations on issues such as public health infrastructure, health workforce development, eldercare, behavioral health, and health system transformation. The organization is deeply rooted in the belief that health is a human right and that systems should be designed to support the well-being of all people, especially those most marginalized.
Website: www.hmprg.org

Hopi Tutskwa Permaculture (Arizona): An Indigenous community-led nonprofit on the Hopi Reservation run by my dear friend Lillian Hill. Their mission is to create community-based solutions in order to pass knowledge to future generations and rebuild culturally sustainable and healthy communities. They initiate learning projects that engage, train, and inspire Hopi youth and the community to revitalize Hopi culture, knowledge, and traditions, developing leadership skills to strengthen local food systems and to implement sustainable ecological projects within the Hopi community.
Website: www.hopitutskwa.org

Kāko'o 'Ōiwi (O'ahu, Hawai'i): A Native Hawaiian nonprofit restoring ancient taro (*kalo*) farming systems and fishponds in He'eia. A place where land restoration becomes cultural revival, and where food, water, and healing are braided into everyday life.
Website: kakoooiwi.org

La Via Campesina: An international movement uniting millions of peasants, small- and medium-scale farmers, landless workers, women farmers, Indigenous communities, migrants, and agricultural laborers worldwide. It champions small-scale, sustainable agriculture as a pathway to social justice and human dignity. Representing about two hundred million farmers, it is an autonomous, pluralist, and multicultural movement, independent from any political, economic, or other type of affiliation.
Website: viacampesina.org/en

Little Free Library: A nonprofit organization and movement that cultivates micro-ecosystems of collective liberation by removing barriers to literacy and learning. Little Free Libraries are multilingual, diverse, and inclusive by nature. They often become centers of care, as they are sometimes filled with not only books but also seed packets, menstrual products, snacks, travel-size toiletries . . . whatever a community needs most. The Little Free Library movement challenges the idea that expertise, authorship, and access should be centralized or commercialized.
Website: littlefreelibrary.org

Medact (UK): An organization of health workers that works at the intersection of health, peace, and social justice, addressing issues like migrant health, climate justice, and disarmament.
Website: www.medact.org

My Block, My Hood, My City (Chicago): A Chicago-based nonprofit that empowers youth by providing opportunities for exploration, mentorship, and community engagement to broaden their perspectives and build stronger, more connected neighborhoods.
Website: www.formyblock.org

One Fair Wage (California): led by Saru Jayaraman and Fekkak Mamdouh, OFW works to advance policy, drive industry change, and shift the narrative to ensure that all workers in America are paid at least the full minimum wage from their employers. They organize service workers, employers, and consumers to advance local, state, and federal policy requiring One Fair Wage—a full, fair minimum wage with tips on top for all workers.
Website: https://www.onefairwage.org

Playworks: A national nonprofit with a mission to improve the health and well-being of children by increasing opportunities for physical activity and safe, meaningful play. They help schools and districts make the most of recess through on-site staffing, consultative support, professional development, free resources, and more.
Website: www.playworks.org

Sierra Seeds (California): An Indigenous-led organization that seeks to reseed imaginations through seed stewardship. It uplifts and mentors emerging mentors, changemakers, visionaries, creative humans who are making nourishing contributions at the intersections of the landscape of food, seed sovereignty, and cultural revitalization, who are cultivating foodways that grow from a foundation of belonging, connection, and culture. Read this beautiful article, written by Rowen White, which describes the work of seed rematriation:
Website: sierraseeds.org/seed-rematriation

Sikh Coalition (New York City, California, Washington, D.C., Chicago): A national, nonprofit, nonpartisan community-based organization, the Sikh Coalition advances its mission through community engagement, litigation, education, and policy advocacy. Grounded in the Sikh values of truth (*sach*), service (*seva*), and perseverance in struggle (*sangarsh*), the organization works toward a country where Sikhs and other religious minorities can freely practice their faith without bias or discrimination.
Website: www.sikhcoalition.org

Sogorea Te' Land Trust (California): A Shoshone-led model of urban land rematriation. Through land return, ceremony, medicinal gardening, and solidarity economies, they center the sacred relationship between people and land in an urban context.
Website: sogoreate-landtrust.org

Soul Fire Farm (Upstate New York): An Afro-Indigenous farm dedicated to ending racism in the food system through regenerative farming, community education, and land justice. Leah Penniman and her team reclaim what was nearly stolen: the deep, dignified relationship between Black people and the land. New generations of Black and Brown farmers are growing not only food but also power, healing, and economic resilience.
Website: https://www.soulfirefarm.org

Urban Growers Collective (Chicago): Under the leadership of Erika Allen, UGC was created with community partners to build local, community-run food systems that strengthen a neighborhood's ability to grow, prepare, and distribute its own food. UGC operates eight urban farms on Chicago's South Side, a thirty-acre peri-urban farm in Chicago Heights, and is a strategic partner in the nine-acre Green Era Campus in Auburn Gresham. Together, these farms produce more than 23,000 pounds of food each year for farmers markets, a collective supported agriculture program, and Fresh Moves Mobile Market buses.

Ubuntu Village (New Orleans): A Black-led multiracial organization that supports and empowers those most impacted by systemic racism, violence, and mass incarceration. Instead of replicating systems of oppression, Ubuntu Village offers alternatives to prosecution and incarceration, and directly supports families in the legal system, in ways that are rooted in Indigenous African principles of interdependence and care.
Website: ubuntuvillagenola.org

White Earth Land Recovery Project (Minnesota): Founded by Winona LaDuke, this Anishinaabe-led initiative focuses on restoring Indigenous stewardship of ancestral lands, growing traditional foods (like wild rice), and reviving spiritual and ecological practices that link health with sovereignty.
Website: www.welrp.org

World Central Kitchen: A global humanitarian organization, founded by chef José Andrés, that uses the power of food to respond to crises and strengthen communities. WCK provides fresh, nourishing meals to people affected by natural disasters, conflict, and humanitarian emergencies, often mobilizing within hours of an event.
Website: wck.org

Connecting to Nature and Plants

Audubon Native Plants Database: Easy-to-use, science-backed tool designed to help people choose plants that support local ecosystems, especially birds. By entering a ZIP code, users receive tailored recommendations for native trees, shrubs, flowers, and grasses that provide essential food and habitat for the bird species in their region.
Website: www.audubon.org/native-plants

Peterson Field Guides: A series of nature books designed to help readers identify and learn about plants, animals, insects, rocks, and other natural phenomena. They use precise, scientifically accurate paintings and are known for being reliable, expertly researched, and comprehensive.

Plant ID Apps: Make it easy to recognize the plants you encounter and deepen your understanding of local ecosystems using apps like LeafSnap, iNaturalist, or PictureThis.

Lady Bird Johnson Wildflower Center (University of Texas at Austin): An extensive plant database that offers regional planting guides and design inspiration.
Website: www.wildflower.org

Regional Native Plant Societies: Most states and provinces have their own native plant societies offering plant lists, workshops, and plant sales.
Find your local group via: www.nanps.org/native-plant-societies

USDA PLANTS Database: Detailed scientific information and distribution maps for native plants in the United States.
Website: plants.sc.egov.usda.gov

Garden Growing

American Meadows: Native seeds and planting guides.
Website: www.americanmeadows.com

Pollinator Partnership: Region-specific planting guides for creating pollinator habitats.
Website: www.pollinator.org/guides

Prairie Moon Nursery: Excellent seed and plant source with detailed germination instructions.
Website: www.prairiemoon.com

Rodale Institute: A leading nonprofit in agricultural research and education, committed to advancing regenerative organic agriculture through rigorous scientific studies, farmer training, and community education.
Website: rodaleinstitute.org

Wild Ones: National nonprofit dedicated to promoting native landscapes. Chapters often have seed swaps, demonstration gardens, and mentoring.
Website: wildones.org

Dance Communities

Alvin Ailey American Dance Theater (New York): A premier modern dance company renowned for its powerful performances that celebrate the African American cultural experience.
Website: ailey.org

Ayodele Drum and Dance (Chicago): A performing arts collective that fosters community from a feminine perspective through the study and performance of diasporic African music and dance.
Website: ayodeledrumanddance.com

Daybreaker: A dance community that hosts morning dance parties, blending yoga, fitness, and immersive music experiences to foster joy, connection, and belonging.
Website: www.daybreaker.com

Funkadesi (Chicago): For thirty years, this electrifying dance band has blended Indian bhangra, Bollywood, and folk traditions with reggae, funk, and Afro-Caribbean grooves—creating a sound that radiates belonging and collective joy. Their guiding belief: "One family, many children . . . insisting we all belong."
Website: https://funkadesi.com

RECOMMENDED READING

Introduction

Boggs, Grace Lee, and Scott Kurashige. *The Next American Revolution: Sustainable Activism for the Twenty-First Century*. University of California Press, 2012.

Geronimus, Arline T. *Weathering: The Extraordinary Stress of Ordinary Life in an Unjust Society*. Little, Brown Spark, 2023.

Whyte, David. *Consolations: The Solace, Nourishment and Underlying Meaning of Everyday Words*. Many Rivers Press, 2021.

Whyte, David. *David Whyte: Essentials*. Many Rivers Press, 2019.

Nature

Jain, Shamini, PhD. *Healing Ourselves: Biofield Science and the Future of Health*. St. Martin's Essentials/Sounds True, 2021.

Li, Dr. Qing. *Forest Bathing: How Trees Can Help You Find Health and Happiness*. Penguin Life, 2018.

Miyazaki, Yoshifumi. *Shinrin-Yoku: The Japanese Art of Forest Bathing*. Timber Press, 2018.

Ober, Clinton, Dr. Stephen T. Sinatra, and Martin Zucker. *Earthing: The Most Important Health Discovery Ever!* Second Edition. Basic Health Publications, Inc., 2014.

Panda, Satchin, PhD. *The Circadian Diabetes Code: Discover the Right Time to Eat, Sleep, and Exercise to Prevent and Reverse Prediabetes and Diabetes*. Rodale Books, 2025.

Tiwari, Maya. *The Path of Practice: A Woman's Book of Healing with Food, Breath, and Sound*. Ballantine Books, 2000.

Food

Abramson, John, MD, MSc. *Sickening: How Big Pharma Broke American Health Care and How We Can Repair It*. Mariner Books, 2022.

Anderson, Stuart, ed. *Making Medicines: A Brief History of Pharmacy and Pharmaceuticals*. Pharmaceutical Press, 2013.

Dungy, Camille T. *Soil: The Story of a Black Mother's Garden*. Simon & Schuster, 2023.

La Puma, John, and Rebecca Powell Marx. *ChefMD's Big Book of Culinary Medicine: A Food Lover's Road Map to Losing Weight, Preventing Disease, and Getting Really Healthy*. Three Rivers Press, 2009.

Nestle, Marion. *Food Politics: How the Food Industry Influences Nutrition and Health*. University of California Press, 2013.

Patel, Raj. *Stuffed and Starved: The Hidden Battle for the World Food System*. Melville House, 2012.

Pollan, Michael. *The Omnivore's Dilemma: A Natural History of Four Meals*. Penguin Press, 2006.

Salmón, Enrique. *Eating the Landscape: American Indian Stories of Food, Identity, and Resilience*. University of Arizona Press, 2012.

Scrinis, Gyorgy. *Nutritionism: The Science and Politics of Dietary Advice*. Columbia University Press, 2013.

Shiva, Vandana. *Stolen Harvest: The Hijacking of the Global Food Supply*. University Press of Kentucky, 2016.

Plants

Arvigo, Rosita and Nadia Epstein. *Rainforest Home Remedies: The Maya Way to Heal Your Body and Replenish Your Soul—Botanical Solutions and Spiritual Practices from Your Garden and Spice Rack*. HarperOne, 2001.

Crawford, Amanda McQuade. *Herbal Remedies for Women: Discover Nature's Wonderful Secrets Just for Women*. Harmony, Rodale, and Convergent Books, 1997.

Darke, Rick, and Douglas Tallamy. *The Living Landscape: Designing for Beauty and Biodiversity in the Home Garden*. Timber Press, 2014.

Hernandez, Jessica, PhD. *Fresh Banana Leaves: Healing Indigenous Landscapes Through Indigenous Science*. North Atlantic Books, 2022.

Kimmerer, Robin Wall. *Braiding Sweetgrass: Indigenous Wisdom, Scientific Knowledge, and the Teachings of Plants*. Milkweed Editions, 2013.

Joseph, Leigh. *Held by the Land: A Guide to Indigenous Plants for Wellness*. Wellfleet Press, 2023.

Lad, Vasant. *The Complete Book of Ayurvedic Home Remedies: Based on the Timeless Wisdom of India's 5,000-Year-Old Medical System*. Harmony, 1999.

Lad, Vasant, and Usha Lad. *Ayurvedic Cooking for Self-Healing*. Ayurvedic Press, 2016.

Low Dog, Tieraona. *Life Is Your Best Medicine: A Woman's Guide to Health, Healing, and Wholeness at Every Age*. National Geographic Society, 2012.

Maier, Kat. *Energetic Herbalism: A Guide to Sacred Plant Traditions Integrating Elements of Vitalism, Ayurveda, and Chinese Medicine*. Chelsea Green Publishing, 2021.

Penniman, Leah, and Karen Washington. *Farming While Black: Soul Fire Farm's Practical Guide to Liberation on the Land*. Chelsea Green Publishing, 2018.

Rainer, Thomas, and Claudia West. *Planting in a Post-Wild World: Designing Plant Communities for Resilient Landscapes*. Timber Press, 2015.

Romm, Aviva, MD. *Botanical Medicine for Women*. Churchill Livingstone, 2017.

Rose, Karen M. *The Art & Practice of Spiritual Herbalism: Transform, Heal, and Remember with the Power of Plants and Ancestral Medicine*. Fair Winds Press, 2022.

Salmón, Enrique. *Iwígara: American Indian Ethnobotanical Traditions and Science*. Timber Press, 2020.

Singingtree, Daphne. *Eagletree Herbs Guide to Medicine Making*. Eagletree Press, 2024.

Tallamy, Douglas. *Bringing Nature Home: How You Can Sustain Wildlife with Native Plants*. Timber Press, 2009.

Community

Buettner, Dan. *The Blue Zones, Second Edition: 9 Lessons for Living Longer from the People Who've Lived the Longest*. National Geographic, 2012.

Estes, Nick, and Jaskiran Dhillon, eds. *Standing with Standing Rock: Voices from the #NoDAPL Movement*. University of Minnesota Press, 2019.

Estes, Nick. *Our History Is the Future: Standing Rock Versus the Dakota Access Pipeline, and the Long Tradition of Indigenous Resistance*. Verso, 2019.

Galea, Sandro. *Well: What We Need to Talk About When We Talk About Health*. Oxford University Press, 2019.

Gilio-Whitaker, Dina. *As Long as Grass Grows: The Indigenous Fight for Environmental Justice, from Colonization to Standing Rock*. Beacon Press, 2019.

Murthy, Vivek H., MD. *Together: The Healing Power of Human Connection in a Sometimes Lonely World*. HarperCollins, 2020.

Simard, Suzanne. *Finding the Mother Tree: Discovering the Wisdom of the Forest*. Vintage, 2022.

Stamets, Paul. *Mycelium Running: How Mushrooms Can Help Save the World*. Ten Speed Press, 2005.

Turner, Toko-pa. *Belonging: Remembering Ourselves Home*. Her Own Room Press, 2017.

Seva

Muñoz Ramírez, Gloria. *The Fire and the Word: A History of the Zapatista Movement*. City Lights Publishers, 2008.

Cope, Suzanne. *Power Hungry: Women of the Black Panther Party and Freedom Summer and Their Fight to Feed a Movement*. Lawrence Hill Books, 2021.

Spade, Dean. *Mutual Aid: Building Solidarity During This Crisis*. Verso, 2020.

Andrés, José. *Change the Recipe: Because You Can't Build a Better World Without Breaking Some Eggs*. Ecco, 2025.

Van Ness, Daniel W., Karen Heetderks Strong, Jonathan Derby, and L. Lynette Parker. *Restoring Justice: An Introduction to Restorative Justice*. Routledge, Taylor & Francis Group, 2022.

Trust

Brown, Brené. *Dare to Lead: Brave Work. Tough Conversations. Whole Hearts*. New York: Random House, 2018.

Brooks, David. *How to Know a Person: The Art of Seeing Others Deeply and Being Deeply Seen*. Random House, 2023.

Dance

Christensen, Julia F., and Dong-Seon Chang. *Dancing Is the Best Medicine: The Science of How Moving to a Beat Is Good for Body, Brain, and Soul*. Greystone Books, 2021.

DeFrantz, Thomas F. *Dancing Revelations: Alvin Ailey's Embodiment of African American Culture*. Oxford University Press, 2006.

Lovatt, Peter. *The Dance Cure: The Surprising Science to Being Smarter, Stronger, Happier*. HarperOne, 2021.

Roth, Gabrielle. *Sweat Your Prayers: The Five Rhythms of the Soul—Movement as Spiritual Practice*. New York: Tarcher/Putnam, 1998.

Gratitude

Emmons, Robert A. *Thanks! How the New Science of Gratitude Can Make You Happier*. Houghton Mifflin, 2007.

Kimmerer, Robin Wall, and John Burgoyne, illustrator. *The Serviceberry: Abundance and Reciprocity in the Natural World.* Scribner, 2024.

Porges, Stephen W. *The Polyvagal Theory: Neurophysiological Foundations of Emotions, Attachment, Communication, and Self-Regulation*. W. W. Norton, 2011.

Maté, Gabor, MD, with Daniel Maté. *The Myth of Normal: Trauma, Illness, and Healing in a Toxic Culture*. Avery, 2022.

Play

Brown, Stuart, MD, with Christopher Vaughan. *Play: How It Shapes the Brain, Opens the Imagination, and Invigorates the Soul.* Avery, 2009.

Frost, Joe L. *A History of Childhood Play and Play Environments: Toward a Contemporary Child-Saving Movement*. Routledge, 2010.

Panksepp, Jaak. *Affective Neuroscience: The Foundations of Human and Animal Emotions*. Oxford University Press, 2004.

Rogers, Fred. *You Are Special: Neighborly Words of Wisdom from Mister Rogers*. Penguin, 1995.

Justice & Love

Farmer, Paul. *Pathologies of Power: Health, Human Rights, and the New War on the Poor*. Berkeley: University of California Press, 2003.

Gutiérrez, Gustavo. *A Theology of Liberation: History, Politics, and Salvation*. 50th Anniversary Edition. Orbis Books, 2023.

hooks, bell. *All About Love: New Visions*. William Morrow, 2000.

Kaur, Valarie. *See No Stranger: A Memoir and Manifesto of Revolutionary Love*. One World, 2020.

Lorde, Audre. *A Burst of Light: And Other Essays*. Lushena Books, 2023.

Macy, Joanna, and Chris Johnstone. *Active Hope: How to Face the Mess We're in with Unexpected Resilience and Creative Power*. Revised Edition. New World Library, 2022.

Stevenson, Bryan. *Just Mercy: A Story of Justice and Redemption*. Spiegel & Grau, 2014.

NOTES

Prologue

1. West Health, "112 Million Americans Struggle to Afford Health care," *West Health Institute*, last modified October 18, 2022, https://westhealth.org/news/112-million-americans-struggle-to-afford-health care/.
2. US Department of Agriculture, Economic Research Service, "Food Prices and Spending," *Ag and Food Statistics: Charting the Essentials*, updated August 29, 2024, https://www.ers.usda.gov/data-products/ag-and-food-statistics-charting-the-essentials/food-prices-and-spending.
3. Akshay Sood, "Indoor Fuel Exposure and the Lung in Both Developing and Developed Countries: An Update," *Clinics in Chest Medicine* 33, no. 4 (December 2012): 649–65, https://doi.org/10.1016/j.ccm.2012.08.003.
4. American Medical Association, "Practice Transformation Measure," *AMA*, accessed September 26, 2025, https://www.ama-assn.org/practice-management/sustainability/practice-transformation-measure.
5. Sarah Rappaport, "The Global Wellness Industry Is Now Worth $6.3 Trillion," Bloomberg, November 5, 2024, https://www.bloomberg.com/news/articles/2024-11-05/global-wellness-industry-is-now-worth-6-3-trillion?embedded-checkout=true.

Introduction

1. Ariane Hegewisch and Yuko Hara, "Maternity, Paternity, and Adoption Leave in the United States," *Institute for Women's Policy Research*, May 9, 2013, https://iwpr.org/maternity-paternity-and-adoption-leave-in-the-united-states/.
2. "Asilomar 2025 Offsite Registration," David Whyte, accessed September 26, 2025, https://poetdavidwhyte.regfox.com/asilomar-2025-offsite-registration.

Nature

1. Patrick Barkham, "Britain Ranks Bottom in Europe for Nature Connectedness," *The Guardian*, June 23, 2022, https://www.theguardian.com/environment/2022/jun/23/britain-ranks-bottom-in-europe-for-nature-connectiveness.
2. D. F. Shanahan et al., "Health Benefits from Nature Experiences Depend on Dose," *Scientific Reports* 6 (2016): 28551, https://doi.org/10.1038/srep28551.
3. Caoimhe Twohig-Bennett and Andy Jones, "The Health Benefits of the Great Outdoors: A Systematic Review and Meta-Analysis of Greenspace Exposure and Health Outcomes," *Environmental Research* 166 (2018): 628–37, https://doi.org/10.1016/j.envres.2018.06.030; Richard Mitchell and Frank Popham, "Effect

of Exposure to Natural Environment on Health Inequalities: An Observational Population Study," *The Lancet* 372, no. 9650 (2008): 1655–60, https://doi.org/10.1016/S0140-6736(08)61689-X.

4. Yoshifumi Miyazaki, *Shinrin-Yoku: The Japanese Art of Forest Bathing* (Portland, OR: Timber Press, 2018); Qing Li, *Forest Bathing: How Trees Can Help You Find Health and Happiness* (New York: Viking, 2019).
5. Zhiyong Zhang and Bing Ye, "Forest Therapy in Germany, Japan, and China: Proposal, Development Status, and Future Prospects," *Forests* 13, no. 8 (2022): 1289, https://doi.org/10.3390/f13081289.
6. Bum Jin Park et al., "The Physiological Effects of Shinrin-Yoku: Evidence from Field Experiments in 24 Forests across Japan," *Environmental Health and Preventive Medicine* 15, no. 1 (2010): 18–26, https://doi.org/10.1007/s12199-009-0086-9; Q. Li et al., "Visiting a Forest, but Not a City, Increases Human Natural Killer Activity and Expression of Anti-Cancer Proteins," *International Journal of Immunopathology and Pharmacology* 21, no. 1 (2008): 117–27, https://doi.org/10.1177/039463200802100113; Qing Li, "Effect of Forest Bathing Trips on Human Immune Function," *Environmental Health and Preventive Medicine* 15, no. 1 (2010): 9–17; Marc M. Hansen, Reo Jones, and Kirsten Tocchini, "Shinrin-yoku (Forest Bathing) and Nature Therapy: A State-of-the-Art Review," *International Journal of Environmental Research and Public Health* 14, no. 8 (2017): 851, https://doi.org/10.3390/ijerph14080851.
7. Miyazaki, *Shinrin-Yoku*.
8. US Environmental Protection Agency, "Indoor Air Quality (IAQ)," accessed September 26, 2025, https://www.epa.gov/indoor-air-quality-iaq; World Health Organization, *WHO Guidelines for Indoor Air Quality: Selected Pollutants* (Geneva: WHO, 2010), https://www.who.int/publications/i/item/9789289002134.
9. Enrique Salmón, "Kincentric Ecology: Indigenous Perceptions of the Human–Nature Relationship." *Ecological Applications* 10, no. 5 (2000): 1327–1332, https://doi.org/10.1890/1051-0761(2000)010[1327:KEIPOT]2.0.CO;2.
10. Robin Wall Kimmerer, *Braiding Sweetgrass: Indigenous Wisdom, Scientific Knowledge, and the Teachings of Plants* (Minneapolis: Milkweed Editions, 2013).
11. National Alliance on Mental Illness (NAMI). "Mental Health by the Numbers." Accessed September 28, 2025, https://www.nami.org/about-mental-illness/mental-health-by-the-numbers/; Council of the European Union, "Mental Health," accessed September 28, 2025. https://www.consilium.europa.eu/en/policies/mental-health/.
12. Haley M. Lane et al., "Historical Redlining Is Associated with Present-Day Air Pollution Disparities in U.S. Cities," *Environmental Science & Technology Letters* 9, no. 4 (2022): 345–50, https://doi.org/10.1021/acs.estlett.1c01012.
13. Robert D. Bullard, "The Threat of Environmental Racism," *Natural Resources & Environment* 7, no. 3 (1993): 23–56, http://www.jstor.org/stable/40923229.
14. Patrick H. Ryan et al., "The Legacy of Redlining: Increasing Childhood Asthma Disparities through Neighborhood Poverty," *American Journal of Respiratory and Critical Care Medicine* 210, no. 10 (November 15, 2024): 1201–9, https://doi.org/10.1164/rccm.202309-1702OC.
15. Geeta Maker-Clark, email interview with David Victorson, July 2025.

16. Antonio Carrillo-Vico et al., "Melatonin: Buffering the Immune System," *International Journal of Molecular Sciences* 14, no. 4 (April 22, 2013): 8638–83, https://doi.org/10.3390/ijms14048638; Somayeh Ahmadi et al., "Gut Microbiota in Neurological Diseases: Melatonin Plays an Important Regulatory Role," *Biomedicine & Pharmacotherapy* 174 (May 2024): 116487, https://doi.org/10.1016/j.biopha.2024.116487; Gail A. Greendale et al., "Melatonin Patterns and Levels during the Human Menstrual Cycle and after Menopause," *Journal of the Endocrine Society* 4, no. 11 (August 27, 2020), https://doi.org/10.1210/jendso/bvaa115.
17. Michael A. Grandner et al., "Sleep Duration, Mortality, and Cardiometabolic Risk," *PLOS ONE* 11, no. 12 (2016): e0168651, https://journals.plos.org/plosone/article?id=10.1371/journal.pone.0168651.
18. Zoltan Ungvari et al., "Imbalanced Sleep Increases Mortality Risk by 14–34%: A Meta-Analysis," *GeroScience* 47, no. 3 (March 12, 2025): 4545–66, https://doi.org/10.1007/s11357-025-01592-y.
19. Kyriaki Papantoniou et al., "Rotating Night Shift Work, Sleep, and Thyroid Cancer Risk in the Nurses' Health Study 2," *Cancers* 15, no. 23 (November 30, 2023): 5673, https://doi.org/10.3390/cancers15235673; Ahmed Arafa et al., "Night Work, Rotating Shift Work, and the Risk of Cancer in Japanese Men and Women: The JACC Study," *Journal of Epidemiology* 31, no. 12 (December 5, 2021): 585–92, https://doi.org/10.2188/jea.JE20200208.
20. Kurt Straif et al., "Carcinogenicity of Shift-Work, Painting, and Fire-Fighting," *The Lancet Oncology* 8, no. 12 (December 2007): 1065–66, https://doi.org/10.1016/S1470-2045(07)70373-X.
21. Anne-Marie Chang et al., "Evening Use of Light-Emitting eReaders Negatively Affects Sleep, Circadian Timing, and Next-Morning Alertness," *Proceedings of the National Academy of Sciences* 112, no. 4 (2015): 1232–37, https://doi.org/10.1073/pnas.1418490112.
22. María-Paz Jiménez et al., "Associations between Nature Exposure and Health," *International Journal of Environmental Research and Public Health* 18, no. 4 (2021): 2046.
23. Gaétan Chevalier et al., "Earthing: Health Implications of Reconnecting the Human Body to the Earth's Surface Electrons," *Journal of Environmental and Public Health* 2012 (2012): 291541, https://doi.org/10.1155/2012/291541.
24. Maurice Ghaly and Dale Teplitz, "The Biologic Effects of Grounding the Human Body during Sleep as Measured by Cortisol Levels and Subjective Reporting of Sleep, Pain, and Stress," *The Journal of Alternative and Complementary Medicine* 10, no. 5 (October 1, 2004): 767–76, https://doi.org/10.1089/1075553042476696; Gaétan Chevalier et al., "Earthing"; Gaétan Chevalier et al., "One-Hour Contact with the Earth's Surface (Grounding) Improves Inflammation and Blood Flow: A Randomized, Double-Blind, Pilot Study," *Journal of Inflammation Research* 8 (2015): 83–96, https://doi.org/10.4236/health.2015.78119.
25. Namni Goel and Girardin R. Etwaroo, "Bright Light, Negative Air Ions and Auditory Stimuli Produce Rapid Mood Changes in a Student Population: A Placebo-Controlled Study," *Psychological Medicine* 36, no. 9 (2006): 1253–63, https://doi.org/10.1017/S0033291706008002; Vanessa Perez,

Dominik D. Alexander, William H. Bailey, "Air Ions and Mood Outcomes: A Review and Meta-Analysis," *BMC Psychiatry* 13 (2013): 29, https://doi.org/10.1186/1471-244X-13-29.

26. H. Iwama, "Negative Air Ions Created by Water Shearing Improve Erythrocyte Deformability and Aerobic Metabolism," *Indoor Air* 14, no. 4 (2004): 297–301, https://doi.org/10.1111/j.1600-0668.2004.00254.x.

Food

1. Jacob Bor et al., "Excess US Deaths Before, During, and After the COVID-19 Pandemic," *JAMA Health Forum* 6, no. 5 (2025): e251118, https://doi.org/10.1001/jamahealthforum.2025.1118.
2. Bradley Sawyer and Gary Claxton, "How Does Health Spending in the U.S. Compare to Other Countries?," *Peterson-KFF Health System Tracker*, February 14, 2019.
3. Rabah Kamal et al., *Health System Tracker* analyses (various reports), Peterson-KFF Health System Tracker.
4. John Abramson, *Sickening: How Big Pharma Broke American Health Care and How We Can Repair It* (Boston: Mariner Books, 2022).
5. Ali Mokdad et al., "The State of US Health, 1990-2016: Burden of Diseases, Injuries, and Risk Factors Among US States." *JAMA* 319, no. 14 (2018): 1444–72. https://doi.org/10.1001/jama.2018.0158.
6. Melissa M. Lane et al., "Ultra-Processed Food Exposure and Adverse Health Outcomes: Umbrella Review of Epidemiological Meta-Analyses," *BMJ* (February 28, 2024), https://doi.org/10.1136/bmj-2023-077310.
7. Dan Buettner and Sam Skemp, "Blue Zones: Lessons from the World's Longest Lived," *American Journal of Lifestyle Medicine* 10, no. 5 (July 7, 2016): 318–21, https://doi.org/10.1177/1559827616637066.
8. Alysha S. Thompson et al., "Association of Healthful Plant-Based Diet Adherence with Risk of Mortality and Major Chronic Diseases Among Adults in the UK," *JAMA Network Open* 6, no. 3 (2023): e234714, https://doi.org/10.1001/jamanetworkopen.2023.4714.
9. Alice H. Lichtenstein et al., "2021 Dietary Guidance to Improve Cardiovascular Health: A Scientific Statement From the American Heart Association," *Circulation* 144, no. 23 (2021): e472–e487.
10. Anahad O'Connor, "Do You Really Need More Protein?" *The New York Times*, April 9, 2025, https://www.nytimes.com/2025/04/09/well/eat/protein-fact-check.html.
11. Wayne W. Campbell et al., "Nutritional Interventions: Dietary Protein Needs and Influences on Skeletal Muscle of Older Adults," *The Journals of Gerontology: Series A* 78, suppl. 1 (June 1, 2023): 67–72, https://doi.org/10.1093/gerona/glad038.
12. OECD/FAO, *Agricultural Outlook 2025–2034* (Paris: OECD Publishing, 2025), chapter 5, "Meat," https://www.oecd.org/en/publications/2025/07/oecd-fao-agricultural-outlook-2025-2034_3eb15914/full-report/meat_5462e384.
13. Zoltan Ungvari et al., "Association between Red and Processed Meat Consumption and Colorectal Cancer Risk: A Comprehensive Meta-Analysis of Prospective Studies," *GeroScience* 47, no. 3 (2025): 5123–40, https://doi.org/10.1007/s11357

-025-01646-1; Wenming Shi et al., "Red Meat Consumption, Cardiovascular Diseases, and Diabetes: A Systematic Review and Meta-Analysis," *European Heart Journal* 44, no. 28 (2023): 2626–35, https://doi.org/10.1093/eurheartj/ehad336.
14. Plant Based Foods Institute, "Industrial Animal Agriculture's Large Footprint on Global Land," accessed September 26, 2025, https://pbfinstitute.org/blog/industrial-animal-agricultures-large-footprint-on-global-land.
15. P. W. Gerbens-Leenes, M. M. Mekonnen, and A. Y. Hoekstra, "The Water Footprint of Poultry, Pork and Beef: A Comparative Study in Different Countries and Production Systems," *Water Resources and Industry* 1–2 (March 2013): 25–36, https://doi.org/10.1016/j.wri.2013.03.001.
16. Hannah Ritchie, "How Much of the World's Land Would We Need in Order to Feed the Global Population with the Average Diet of a Given Country?," *Our World in Data*, October 3, 2017, https://ourworldindata.org/agricultural-land-by-global-diets.
17. Dariush Mozaffarian et al., "Evaluation of the Quality of Evidence of the Association of Foods and Nutrients with Cardiovascular Disease and Diabetes: A Systematic Review." *JAMA Network Open* 5, no. 1 (January 31, 2022): e2141231.
18. Youngyo Kim, Youjin Je, and Edward L. Giovannucci, "Association between Dietary Fat Intake and Mortality from All Causes, Cardiovascular Disease, and Cancer: A Systematic Review and Meta-analysis of Prospective Cohort Studies," Clinical Nutrition 40, no. 3 (March 2021): 1060–70, https://doi.org/10.1016/j.clnu.2020.07.007.
19. Ramón Estruch et al., "Primary Prevention of Cardiovascular Disease with a Mediterranean Diet," *New England Journal of Medicine* 368, no. 14 (2013): 1279–90, https://doi.org/10.1056/NEJMoa1200303.
20. Penny Kris-Etherton et al., "Lyon Diet Heart Study," *Circulation* 103, no. 13 (April 3, 2001): 1823–25, https://doi.org/10.1161/01.cir.103.13.1823; Dariush Mozaffarian et al., "Changes in Diet and Lifestyle and Long-Term Weight Gain in Women and Men," *New England Journal of Medicine* 364, no. 25 (2011): 2392–2404, https://pubmed.ncbi.nlm.nih.gov/21696306; M. Dinu et al., "Mediterranean Diet and Multiple Health Outcomes: An Umbrella Review of Meta-Analyses of Observational Studies and Randomised Trials," *European Journal of Clinical Nutrition* 72, no. 1 (January 2018): 30–43, https://doi.org/10.1038/ejcn.2017.58; Christopher Gardner et al., "Mind the Gap and the Guidelines: Whole Food Plant-Based Diets, Processed Foods, and Health," Nutrients 13, no. 10 (2021): 3580, https://pmc.ncbi.nlm.nih.gov/articles/PMC8540388/.
21. Camille T. Dungy, "From Dirt," *Emergence Magazine*, June 16, 2018, https://emergencemagazine.org/essay/from-dirt/.
22. "Explore Heritage Diets," Oldways, accessed September 21, 2025, https://oldwayspt.org/explore-heritage-diets/.
23. "Federal Farm Subsidies: What the Data Says," USAFacts, June 23, 2025, https://usafacts.org/articles/federal-farm-subsidies-what-data-says/.
24. "Corn and Other Feed Grains—Feed Grains Sector at a Glance," Economic Research Service, USDA, April 17, 2025, https://www.ers.usda.gov/topics/crops/corn-and-other-feed-grains/feed-grains-sector-at-a-glance.

25. Pekka Puska and Paresh Jaini, "The North Karelia Project: Prevention of Cardiovascular Disease in Finland through Population-Based Lifestyle Interventions," *American Journal of Lifestyle Medicine* 14, no. 5 (March 19, 2020): 495–99, https://doi.org/10.1177/1559827620910981.
26. "Our Programs," Wholesome Wave, accessed September 21, 2025, https://www.wholesomewave.org/what-we-do-1.
27. Kurt Hager et al., "Impact of Produce Prescriptions on Diet, Food Security, and Cardiometabolic Health Outcomes: A Multisite Evaluation of 9 Produce Prescription Programs in the United States," *Circulation: Cardiovascular Quality and Outcomes 16*, no. 9 (2023): e009520, https://doi.org/10.1161/CIRCOUTCOMES.122.009520; Dariush Mozaffarian et al., "Evaluation of the Quality of Evidence of the Association of Foods and Nutrients with Cardiovascular Disease and Diabetes: A Systematic Review." *JAMA Network Open* 5, no. 1 (January 31, 2022): e2141231.

Plants

1. Michael Heinrich and Hooi Lee Teoh, "Galanthamine from Snowdrop—The Development of a Modern Drug against Alzheimer's Disease from Local Caucasian Knowledge," *Journal of Ethnopharmacology* 92, nos. 2–3 (June 2004): 147–62, https://doi.org/10.1016/j.jep.2004.02.012.
2. Negar Jamshidi and Marc M. Cohen. "The Clinical Efficacy and Safety of Tulsi in Humans: A Systematic Review of the Literature." *Evidence-Based Complementary and Alternative Medicine*, vol. 2017 (2017): 9217567, https://doi.org/10.1155/2017/9217567.
3. Rakesh Arya et al., "Harnessing the Antibacterial, Anti-Diabetic and Anti-Carcinogenic Properties of *Ocimum sanctum* Linn (Tulsi)," *Plants* 13, no. 24 (2024), https://doi.org/10.3390/plants13243516.
4. Kate Clifford Larson, *Bound for the Promised Land: Harriet Tubman, Portrait of an American Hero* (New York: Random House, 2004).
5. Leah Penniman with Karen Washington, *Farming While Black: Soul Fire Farm's Practical Guide to Liberation on the Land* (White River Junction, VT: Chelsea Green, 2018).
6. Loris Pinto et al., "Antibacterial Activity of Oregano (*Origanum vulgare* L.) Essential Oil Vapors against Microbial Contaminants of Food-Contact Surfaces," *Antibiotics* 13, no. 4 (2024): 371, https://doi.org/10.3390/antibiotics13040371.

Community

1. Vivek H. Murthy, *Together: The Healing Power of Human Connection in a Sometimes Lonely World* (New York: Harper Wave, 2020).
2. Paul Stamets, *Mycelium Running: How Mushrooms Can Help Save the World* (Berkeley, CA: Ten Speed Press, 2005).
3. Susanne Shultz, Christopher Opie, and Quentin D. Atkinson, "Stepwise Evolution of Stable Sociality in Primates," *Nature* 479 (2011): 219–222, https://doi.org/10.1038/nature10601.
4. Muhammad Chutiyami et al., "Community-Engaged Mental Health and Wellbeing Initiatives in Under-Resourced Settings: A Scoping Review of Primary Studies,"

Journal of Primary Care and Community Health 16 (2025): https://doi.org/10.1177/21501319251332723.

Seva

1. Beth Nichol et al., "Exploring the Effects of Volunteering on the Social, Mental, and Physical Health and Well-Being of Volunteers: An Umbrella Review," *Voluntas* 35 (2023): 97–128, https://doi.org/10.1007/s11266-023-00573-z.
2. Seoyoun Kim et al., "Does Volunteering Reduce Epigenetic Age Acceleration among Retired and Working Older Adults? Results from the Health and Retirement Study," *Social Science & Medicine* 364 (2025): 117501, https://doi.org/10.1016/j.socscimed.2024.117501.
3. World Health Organization, *The Impact of COVID-19 on Health and Care Workers: A Closer Look at Deaths*, https://iris.who.int/handle/10665/345300.
4. Ned Rozell, "Formation Flying Makes Migration Less of a Drag," Geophysical Institute, University of Alaska Fairbanks, last modified August 17, 1995, https://www.gi.alaska.edu/alaska-science-forum/formation-flying-makes-migration-less-drag.
5. Nancy Fraser, *Cannibal Capitalism: How Our System Is Devouring Democracy, Care, and the Planet—and What We Can Do about It* (London: Verso Books, 2022)
6. Nils Carstensen, Mandeep Mudhar, and Freja Schurmann Munksgaard, "'Let Communities Do Their Work': The Role of Mutual Aid and Self-Help Groups in the COVID-19 Pandemic Response," *International Journal of Disaster Risk Reduction* 61 (2021): 102375, https://doi.org/10.1111/disa.12515.
7. Patrick Sharkey, Gerard Torrats-Espinosa, and Delaram Takyara, "The Causal Effect of Local Nonprofits on Violent Crime," *American Sociological Review* 82, no. 6 (2017): 1214–40, https://doi.org/10.1177/0003122417736289.

Trust

1. Darcell P. Scharff et al., "More than Tuskegee: Understanding Mistrust about Research Participation," *Journal of Health Care for the Poor and Underserved* 21, no. 3 (2010): 879–97, https://doi.org/10.1353/hpu.0.0323.
2. Nicolás C. Zanetta-Colombo et al., "Impact of Mining on the Metal Content of Dust in Indigenous Communities of Northern Chile," *Environment International* 169 (2022): 107490, https://doi.org/10.1016/j.envint.2022.107490; Rosie Worthen, "Guatemala: Communities Displaced, Water Contaminated," Indian Law Resource Center, accessed September 26, 2025, http://indianlaw.org/en/enews/issue3/Rosie_guatemala.
3. Renee Hsia and Yu-Chu Shen, "Possible Geographical Barriers to Trauma Center Access in the United States," *JAMA Surgery* 146, no. 2 (2011): 172–78.
4. Katrina Armstrong et al., "Distrust of the Health Care System and Self-Reported Health in the United States," *Journal of General Internal Medicine* 21, no. 4 (2006): 292–97, https://doi.org/10.1111/j.1525-1497.2006.00396.x.
5. Carrington Moore et al., "'It's Important to Work with People That Look like Me': Black Patients' Preferences for Patient-Provider Race Concordance," *Journal of Racial and Ethnic Health Disparities* 10 (2023): 2552–64, https://doi.org/10.1007/s40615-022-01435-y.

6. Sue Dunlevy, "Hospitals' Culture of Fear Exposed as Doctors Flee Public Health System," *The Australian*, accessed September 26, 2025, https://www.theaustralian.com.au/health/medical/hospitals-culture-of-fear-exposed-as-doctors-flee-public-health-system/news-story/6d19096e79020716abdba9a657e7f102.
7. Tait D. Shanafelt et al., "Changes in Burnout and Satisfaction with Work–Life Integration in Physicians and the General U.S. Working Population between 2011 and 2023," *Mayo Clinic Proceedings* 100, no. 7 (2025): 1142–58.
8. "Health care.gov Insurers Denied Nearly 1 in 5 In-Network Claims in 2023, but Information about Reasons Is Limited in Public Data," KFF, accessed September 26, 2025, https://www.kff.org/affordable-care-act/press-release/health care-gov-insurers-denied-nearly-1-in-5-in-network-claims-in-2023-but-information-about-reasons-is-limited-in-public-data/.
9. Richard Edelman, "Trust: A Key Determinant of Health," Edelman, accessed September 26, 2025, https://www.edelman.com/trust-key-determinant-health.
10. Ning He et al., "Understanding Medical Distrust among African American/Black and Latino Persons Living with HIV with Sub-Optimal Engagement along the HIV Care Continuum: A Machine Learning Approach," *SAGE Open* 11, no. 4 (2021): https://doi.org/10.1177/21582440211061314.
11. Brené Brown, *Dare to Lead: Brave Work. Tough Conversations. Whole Hearts.* (New York: Random House, 2018).
12. Julie M. Feinsilver, *Healing the Masses: Cuban Health Politics at Home and Abroad* (Berkeley: University of California Press, 1993).
13. David Brooks, "America Is Having a Moral Convulsion," *The Atlantic*, October 5, 2020, https://www.theatlantic.com/ideas/archive/2020/10/collapsing-levels-trust-are-devastating-america/616581/.
14. Nazgol Ghandnoosh, "One in Five: Disparities in Crime and Policing," The Sentencing Project, November 2, 2023, https://www.sentencingproject.org/reports/one-in-five-disparities-in-crime-and-policing.
15. "Case Study: CAHOOTS," Vera Institute of Justice, November 2020, https://www.vera.org/behavioral-health-crisis-alternatives/cahoots.
16. "What Happened When Camden Started Rethinking Policing to Build Trust," PBS News, June 30, 2017, https://www.pbs.org/newshour/show/happened-camden-started-rethinking-policing-build-trust.

Dance

1. Sebastian Ruiz-Blais, Michele Orini, and Elaine Chew, "Heart Rate Variability Synchronizes When Non-Experts Sing in a Choir," *Frontiers in Physiology* 11 (2020): 557950, https://doi.org/10.3389/fphys.2020.00762. Aniruddh D. Patel, "Beat-Based Dancing to Music Has Evolutionary Foundations in Advanced Vocal Learning," *BMC Neuroscience* 25 (2024): 65, https://doi.org/10.1186/s12868-024-00843-6.
2. Marcel Zentner and Tuomas Eerola, "Rhythmic Engagement with Music in Infancy," *Proceedings of the National Academy of Sciences* 107, no. 13 (March 30, 2010): 5768–73, https://doi.org/10.1073/pnas.1000121107.
3. Scott S. Wiltermuth and Chip Heath, "Synchrony and Cooperation," *Psychological Science* 20, no. 1 (2009): 1–5, https://doi.org/10.1111/j.1467-9280.2008.02253.x;

Bronwyn Tarr, Jacques Launay, and Robin I. M. Dunbar, "Silent Disco: Dancing in Synchrony Leads to Elevated Pain Thresholds and Social Closeness," *Evolution and Human Behavior* 37, no. 5 (2016): 343–49, https://doi.org/10.1016/j.evol humbehav.2016.02.004.

4. Kathrin Rehfeld, Angie Lüders, Anita Hökelmann, et al., "Dance Training Is Superior to Repetitive Physical Exercise in Inducing Brain Plasticity in the Elderly," *PLoS One* 13, no. 7 (July 11, 2018): e0196636, https://doi.org/10.1371/journal.pone.0196636.
5. Lavinia Teixeira-Machado, Ricardo Mario Arida, and Jair de Jesus Mari, "Dance for Neuroplasticity: A Descriptive Systematic Review," *Neuroscience & Biobehavioral Reviews* 96 (January 2019): 232–40, https://doi.org/10.1016/j.neubiorev.2018.12.010.
6. Hubbard Street Dance Chicago, "Parkinson's Project," accessed September 30, 2025, https://www.hubbardstreetdance.com/education-community/parkinsons-project/.
7. Joe Verghese et al., "Leisure Activities and the Risk of Dementia in the Elderly," *The New England Journal of Medicine* 348, no. 25 (June 19, 2003): 2508–16, https://doi.org/10.1056/NEJMoa022252.
8. Daybreaker, "Daybreaker," accessed September 30, 2025, https://www.daybreaker.com/.
9. Anodea Judith, *The Chakra System: A Complete Course in Self-Diagnosis and Healing* (Wheaton, IL: Theosophical Publishing House, 1987); Harish Johari, *Chakras: Energy Centers of Transformation* (Rochester, VT: Destiny Books, 2000).

Gratitude

1. Zinzi D. Bailey et al., "Structural Racism and Health Inequities in the USA: Evidence and Interventions," *The Lancet* 389, no. 10077 (2017): 1453–63, https://doi.org/10.1016/S0140-6736(17)30569-X; Andreea A. Creanga et al., "Race, Ethnicity, and Nativity Differentials in Pregnancy-Related Mortality in the United States: 1993–2006," *Obstetrics & Gynecology* 120, no. 2 (2012): 261–68, https://doi.org/10.1097/AOG.0b013e31825cb87a
2. Robert Emmons, "The Power of Gratitude," Grateful Living, accessed September 26, 2025, https://grateful.org/resource/the-power-of-gratitude/.
3. Robert A. Emmons and Michael E. McCullough, "Counting Blessings versus Burdens: An Experimental Investigation of Gratitude and Subjective Well-Being in Daily Life," *Journal of Personality and Social Psychology* 84, no. 2 (2003): 377–89, https://doi.org/10.1037/0022-3514.84.2.377.
4. Anna Powers, "The Science of Gratitude: How It Affects Your Brain and How You Can Use It to Create a Better Life," *Forbes*, November 29, 2019, https://www.forbes.com/sites/annapowers/2019/11/29/the-science-of-gratitude-how-it-affects-your-brain-and-how-you-can-use-to-create-a-better-life/.
5. Robin Wall Kimmerer, *The Serviceberry: Abundance and Reciprocity in the Natural World* (New York: Scribner, 2024).
6. Rollin McCraty et al., "The Coherent Heart: Heart–Brain Interactions, Psychophysiological Coherence, and the Emergence of System-Wide Order," *Integral Review* 5, no. 2 (2009): 10–115, https://www.integral-review.org/issues/vol_5_no_2_mccraty_et_al_the_coherent_heart.pdf.

7. Julian F. Thayer et al., "A Meta-Analysis of Heart Rate Variability and Neuroimaging Studies: Implications for Heart Rate Variability as a Marker of Stress and Health," *Neuroscience & Biobehavioral Reviews* 36, no. 2 (2012): 747–56.
8. Laura Redwine et al., "A Randomized Controlled Trial of a Daily Gratitude Intervention on Heart Rate Variability and Inflammatory Biomarkers in Patients with Stage B Heart Failure," *Psychosomatic Medicine* 78, no. 6 (2016): 667–76.
9. Masanori Tani et al., "Association between Gratitude, the Brain, and Cognitive Function in Older Adults: Results from the NEIGE Study," *Scientific Reports* 12 (2022): 1199.
10. Stephen W. Porges, *The Polyvagal Theory: Neurophysiological Foundations of Emotions, Attachment, Communication, and Self-Regulation* (New York: W. W. Norton, 2011).
11. Gabor Maté with Daniel Maté, *The Myth of Normal: Trauma, Illness, and Healing in a Toxic Culture* (New York: Avery, 2022).

Play

1. Fred Rogers, *You Are Special: Neighborly Words of Wisdom from Mister Rogers* (New York: Penguin, 1995).
2. United Nations, *Convention on the Rights of the Child*, https://www.ohchr.org/en/instruments-mechanisms/instruments/convention-rights-child.
3. Anna A. Eyler et al., "Children's Physical Activity and Screen Time during COVID-19," *International Journal of Environmental Research and Public Health* 18, no. 1 (2021): 1–13.
4. Jaak Panksepp, "The Joy of Being: Affective Neuroscience Perspectives on Play," in *Play and Exploration in Children and Animals* by Thomas G. Power, ed. Anthony D. Pellegrini (Mahwah, NJ: Lawrence Erlbaum Associates, 2005), 1–12.
5. Jaak Panksepp, "The Science of Emotions," filmed November 2013 at TEDxRainier, video, 17:39, posted January 13, 2014, YouTube, https://tedxseattle.com/talks/the-science-of-emotions-jaak-panksepp-at-tedxrainier/.
6. Joe L. Frost, *A History of Childhood Play and Play Environments: Toward a Contemporary Child-Saving Movement* (New York: Routledge, 2010).
7. Stuart Brown with Christopher Vaughan, *Play: How It Shapes the Brain, Opens the Imagination, and Invigorates the Soul* (New York: Avery, 2009).
8. Bob De Schutter, "Never Too Old to Play: The Appeal of Digital Games to an Older Audience," *Games and Culture* 6, no. 2 (2011): 155–70, https://doi.org/10.1177/1555412010364978; Young Yim Oh and Carolyn Ellis, "Playful Connectedness: Online Gaming for Older Adults," *Gerontology & Geriatrics Education* 39, no. 4 (2018): 423–40.
9. Elizabeth Johnson, Laura Lorusso, and John Miller, "Digital Gaming and Inclusion: Examining the Social Benefits for People with Disabilities," *Disability & Society* 36, no. 4 (2021): 567–84.
10. Jean M. Twenge and W. Keith Campbell, "Associations between Screen Time and Lower Psychological Well-Being among U.S. Adolescents: Evidence from Three Nationally Representative Datasets," *Preventive Medicine* 104 (2018): 1–10.
11. Andrew K. Przybylski and Netta Weinstein, "Digital Screen Time Limits and Young Children's Psychological Well-Being: Evidence from a Population-Based Study," *Child Development* 90, no. 1 (2019): e56–e65, https://doi.org/10.1111/cdev.13007.

Epilogue

1. Bryan Stevenson, *Just Mercy: A Story of Justice and Redemption* (New York: Spiegel & Grau, 2014).
2. Valarie Kaur, *See No Stranger: A Memoir and Manifesto of Revolutionary Love* (New York: One World, 2020).
3. Paul Farmer, *Pathologies of Power: Health, Human Rights, and the New War on the Poor* (Berkeley: University of California Press, 2003).
4. Gustavo Gutiérrez, *A Theology of Liberation: History, Politics, and Salvation*, rev. ed., trans. Sister Caridad Inda and ed. John Eagleson (Maryknoll, NY: Orbis Books, 1988).
5. Audre Lorde, *A Burst of Light: and Other Essays* (Ithaca, NY: Firebrand Books, 1988).
6. Chris Landry, "Joanna Macy and the Great Turning," *Films for the Planet*, 2014, video, https://filmsfortheplanet.com/joanna-macy-and-the-great-turning/.
7. Joanna Macy and Chris Johnstone, *Active Hope: How to Face the Mess We're in with Unexpected Resilience and Creative Power* (Novato, CA: New World Library, 2012).
8. Michele Moody-Adams, *Making Space for Justice: Social Movements, Collective Imagination, and Political Hope* (New York: Columbia University Press, 2022).
9. bell hooks, *All About Love: New Visions* (New York: William Morrow, 2000).

INDEX

G

H

ABOUT THE AUTHOR

Jessie Hearn

Geeta Maker-Clark, MD, is a physician, educator, and systems-level thinker who has spent more than twenty-five years reshaping how medicine approaches healing. She is a clinical assistant professor at the Pritzker School of Medicine at the University of Chicago and codirector of one of the nation's first Culinary Medicine programs, where she helps to redefine medical education at the intersection of nutrition, culture, and health equity. Dr. Maker-Clark also serves as the Director of Integrative Nutrition and Advocacy at Endeavor Health. Grounded in her training in family medicine, integrative medicine, and maternal child health, and in her dedication to rigorous clinical science, Dr. Maker-Clark's work bridges modern medicine with spiritual traditions to advance a whole-person, justice-centered model of care.

Dr. Maker-Clark received her bachelor's degree in English literature from Northwestern University and her MD from Rush Medical College before completing a family medicine residency, Maternal Child Health fellowship, and Integrative Medicine fellowship at the University of Arizona. Her multidisciplinary work in food justice, dance neuroscience, integrative medicine, and personalized patient care has been featured in *National Geographic*, *Women's Health*, *Chicago Tribune*, and NPR.

An internationally recognized speaker and award-winning thought leader, Dr. Maker-Clark teaches regularly at medical conferences, universities, retreat centers, and in communities. She is the founder of multiple social justice initiatives, including Food Is Power in Chicago Public Schools—a pioneering program that brings decolonized nutrition education and food justice into middle-school classrooms. She is also a leading voice in the emerging field of dance as medicine, advancing its role in neurodegenerative disease prevention, embodied intelligence, and collective vitality. Drawing on decades of direct patient care, global training in ancient medical systems, and community-based leadership,

Dr. Maker-Clark challenges conventional hierarchies of knowledge and invites a radical reimagining of medicine that includes joy and connection. Her vision is one that is relational rather than extractive, accessible rather than elite, and alive to the many forms of medicine already present in our bodies, cultures, and communities.

Dr. Maker-Clark lives in Evanston, Illinois, with her husband, Todd. They have three children, Sahaara, Sachin, and Devika.